QUEERE MODERNE 1900 BIS 1950

~

QUEER MODERNISM 1900 TO 1950

Gefördert durch ~ *Supported by*

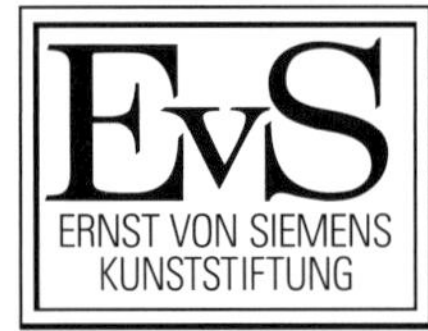

Medienpartner der Ausstellung ~
Media Partner of the Exhibition

WELTKUNST

Medienpartner ~ *Media Partner*

Frankfurter Allgemeine

Gefördert durch ~ *Supported by*

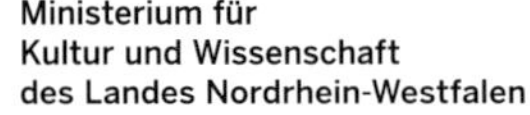

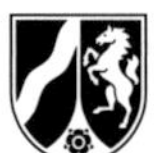

QUEERE MODERNE 1900 BIS 1950

QUEER MODERNISM 1900 TO 1950

HERAUSGEGEBEN VON

EDITED BY

SUSANNE GAENSHEIMER

ISABELLE MALZ

ANKE KEMPKES

Kunstsammlung Nordrhein-Westfalen

HIRMER

INHALT ~ CONTENTS

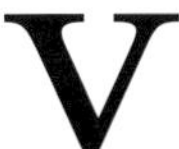

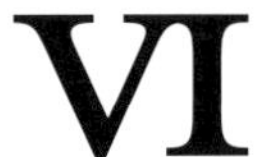

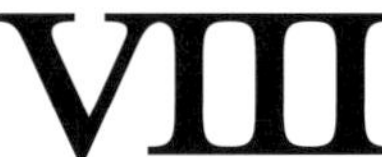

S. ~ PP. 29, 32, 33

RICHMOND BARTHÉ

(1901 in Bay St. Louis, USA–1989 in Pasadena, USA)

S. ~ PP. 23, 27

ROSA BONHEUR

(1822 in Bordeaux, Frankreich ~ *France*–1899 in By-Thomery, Frankreich ~ *France*)

S. ~ PP. 61, 64–65, 67, 89

ROMAINE BROOKS

(1874 in Rom, Italien ~ *Rome, Italy*–1970 in Nizza, Frankreich ~ *Nice, France*)

S. ~ PP. 129, 219, 240

TIL BRUGMAN

(1888 in Amsterdam, Niederlande ~ *Netherlands*–1958 in Gouda, Niederlande ~ *Netherlands*)

S. ~ P. 181

PAUL CADMUS

(1904 in New York City, USA–1999 in Weston, USA)

S. ~ PP. 222–224, 228–235

CLAUDE CAHUN

(1894 in Nantes, Frankreich ~ *France*–1954 in Saint Helier, Jersey)

S. ~ PP. 195–197

JEAN COCTEAU

(1889 in Maisons-Laffitte, Frankreich ~ *France*–1963 in Milly-la-Forêt, Frankreich ~ *France*)

S. ~ PP. 97, 100, 102, 118, 120

ITHELL COLQUHOUN

(1906 in Shillong, Indien ~ *India*–1988 in Lamorna, UK)

S. ~ PP. 186–187

NILS DARDEL

(1888 in Bettna, Schweden ~ *Sweden*–1943 in New York City, USA)

S. ~ PP. 177, 182

BEAUFORD DELANEY

(1901 in Knoxville, USA–1979 in Paris, Frankreich ~ *France*)

S. ~ PP. 101, 103–104, 123, 125

LEONOR FINI

(1907 in Buenos Aires, Argentinien ~ *Argentina*–1996 in Paris, Frankreich ~ *France*)

S. ~ P. 137

LOÏE FULLER

(1862 in Fullersburg, USA–1928 in Paris, Frankreich ~ *France*)

S. ~ PP. 66, 68–71, 83

GLUCK

(1895 in London, UK–1978 in Steyning, UK)

S. ~ PP. 177, 183

DUNCAN GRANT

(1885 in Rothiemurchus, UK–1978 in Aldermaston, UK)

S. ~ PP. 129, 134–135, 161

JACOBA VAN HEEMSKERCK

(1876 in Den Haag, Niederlande ~ *The Hague, Netherlands*–1923 in Domburg, Niederlande ~ *Netherlands*)

S. ~ PP. 219, 236–237, 239, 241, 263, 267

HANNAH HÖCH

(1889 in Gotha ~ *Gotha, Germany*–1978 in Berlin ~ *Berlin, Germany*)

S. ~ P. 36

LUDWIG VON HOFMANN

(1861 in Darmstadt ~ *Darmstadt, Germany*–1945 in Pillnitz bei Dresden ~ *Pillnitz near Dresden, Germany*)

S. ~ PP. 188–190

ROBIN IRONSIDE

(1912 in London, UK–1965 in London, UK)

S. ~ PP. 132–133, 162

LOUISE JANIN

(1893 in Durham, USA–1997 in Meudon, Frankreich ~ *France*)

S. ~ PP. 40–41

LOTTE LASERSTEIN

(1898 in Preußisch-Holland, heute: Pasłęk, Polen ~ *today Pasłęk, Poland*–1993 in Kalmar, Schweden ~ *Sweden*)

S. ~ PP. 37, 72–75

MARIE LAURENCIN

(1883 in Paris, Frankreich ~ *France*–1956 in Paris, Frankreich ~ *France*)

S. ~ PP. 219, 242–246

JEANNE MAMMEN

(1890 in Berlin ~ *Berlin, Germany*–1976 in Berlin ~ *Berlin, Germany*)

S. ~ PP. 224–227, 232–234

MARCEL MOORE

(1892 in Nantes, Frankreich ~ *France*–1972 auf Jersey ~ *on Jersey*)

S. ~ PP. 129, 136, 138–139, 141, 174

MARLOW MOSS

(1889 in London, UK–1958 in Penzance, UK)

S. ~ PP. 97, 105–107

MILENA PAVLOVIĆ-BARILI

(1909 in Požarevac, Serbien ~ *Serbia*–1945 in New York City, USA)

S. ~ PP. 34–35

GLYN WARREN PHILPOT

(1884 in London, UK–1937 in London, UK)

S. ~ PP. 192–193

GEORGE PLATT LYNES

(1907 in East Orange, USA–1955 in New York City, USA)

S. ~ PP. 129, 142–149

ANTON PRINNER

(1902 in Budapest, Ungarn ~ *Hungary*–1983 in Paris, Frankreich ~ *France*)

S. ~ PP. 273, 277

SONJA SEKULA

(1918 in Luzern, Schweiz ~ *Lucerne, Switzerland*–1963 in Zürich, Schweiz ~ *Switzerland*)

S. ~ PP. 150–151, 153, 177, 191, 201

PAVEL TCHELITCHEW

(1898 in Dubrowka, Russland ~ *Dubrovka, Russia*–1957 in Grottaferrata, Italien ~ *Italy*)

S. ~ PP. 219, 247–249, 251

TOYEN

(1902 in Prag, Tschechoslowakei ~ *Prague, Czechoslovakia*–1980 in Paris, Frankreich ~ *France*)

S. ~ P. 185

HENRY SCOTT TUKE

(1858 in York, UK–1929 in Falmouth, UK)

S. ~ PP. 38–39

DAME ETHEL WALKER

(1861 in Edinburgh, UK–1951 in London, UK)

S. ~ PP. 108–109, 111–113

GERDA WEGENER

(1886 in Hammelev, Dänemark ~ *Denmark*–1940 in Frederiksberg, Dänemark ~ *Denmark*)

Anmerkung der Redaktion zum Sprachgebrauch

Wir nutzen in dieser Publikation eine gendergerechte und diversitätssensible Sprache und verwenden im Deutschen das Gendersternchen (*), um alle Menschen gleichwertig einzubeziehen und sichtbar zu machen. In dieser Publikation wird das Gendersternchen als Teil des typografischen Konzepts in das Wort eingebunden.

Im Kontext aktueller Diskussionen über den sprachlichen Umgang mit genderqueeren Protagonist*innen der Kunstgeschichte des 20. Jahrhunderts und insbesondere im Hinblick auf die Revision geschlechtlicher Zuschreibungen durch Pronomengebrauch folgen wir hier weitestgehend den aktuellen Argumentationen von Wissenschaftler*innen, die sich umfassend mit den Werken und dem Leben von Künstler*innen in der Ausstellung befasst haben, die nicht binäre Pseudonyme und Selbstdarstellungen bevorzugt haben. Basierend auf historischen Dokumenten und zeitgenössischen Zeug*innenaussagen zum eigenen Sprachgebrauch und zur gewählten genderqueeren Selbstrepräsentation der in der Ausstellung gezeigten Künstler*innen Gluck, Toyen und Marlow Moss haben wir uns entschieden, für diese Protagonist*innen geschlechtsneutrale (oder gar keine) Pronomen zu verwenden, was heute angemessener sein kann – auch wenn ein entsprechender Sprachgebrauch zu Lebzeiten der Künstler*innen in der Regel nicht angewandt wurde. Diese revisionistische Praxis wird breit und offen diskutiert. Tatsächlich berichten Zeitzeug*innen, dass Toyen in den 1930er-Jahren in Prag männliche Pronomen verwendete. Gluck lehnte in der öffentlichen Ansprache geschlechtsspezifische Präfixe und Titel ausdrücklich ab, was ein von Gluck selbst verfasstes Schreiben in der Ausstellung dokumentiert. Dennoch entschieden sich Gluck-Expert*innen in aktuellen wissenschaftlichen Publikationen, wie im Ausstellungskatalog *Gluck: Art and Identity* (Brighton Museum & Art Gallery, 2017), mehrheitlich für die Verwendung des weiblichen Pronomens – unter Rückgriff auf den historischen Sprachgebrauch. Expert*innen zu Marlow Moss' Werk benutzen mit Verweis auf Moss' eigenen Sprachgebrauch und dem ihrer*seiner Lebenspartnerin zumeist das weibliche Pronomen. In jüngster Zeit wird Moss jedoch auch als transmännlich betrachtet. Einige Institutionen verwenden daher das Pronomen they/them oder verzichten ganz auf den Gebrauch eines Pronomens.

Die amerikanische Kritikerin Laura Cottingham betrachtet derweil die nonbinären performativen Selbstdarstellungen von Claude Cahun und Marcel Moore als Ausdruck moderner lesbischer Identität.

In dieser Publikation entschieden die eingeladenen Autor*innen selbst über die Verwendung von Pronomen – basierend auf ihrer jeweiligen Forschung und ihrem Verständnis des historischen Kontextes.

In Fällen, in denen Künstler*innen ihren Namen geändert haben, verzichten wir bewusst auf sogenanntes Deadnaming, indem wir den Geburtsnamen nicht erneut aufführen. So etwa bei Anton Prinner, einem sich als transmännlich definierenden Bildhauer und Druckgrafiker, der sich mit seiner Ankunft in Paris 1928 konsequent in einer Art Drag innerhalb der männlich-dominierten Pariser Künstlerboheme darzustellen begann. Wo hiervon abgewichen wird, finden sich entsprechende Hinweise der jeweiligen Autor*innen.

Historische Selbstbezeichnungen werden dort verwendet, wo sie sich durch Quellen nachweisen lassen, jedoch abwertende Begriffe, falls möglich, nicht reproduziert.

Editorial Note on Language Usage

We have used inclusive and diversity-sensitive language in this publication.

In light of ongoing discussions surrounding the linguistic treatment of genderqueer figures in twentieth-century art history, especially concerning revisions to the historical use of gendered pronouns, we have largely followed prevailing scholarly arguments based on in-depth study of the lives and works of those artists in this exhibition who favored nonbinary pseudonyms and forms of self-identification. Based on historical documents and contemporary accounts of how the artists spoke about themselves and expressed their gender-queer identities, we have made an editorial decision to use gender-neutral (or no) pronouns for Gluck, Toyen, and Marlow Moss, all artists featured in this exhibition. Such language is fitting from today's perspective, though it would not have been generally used during the artists' lifetimes. The revisionist nature of this practice is currently the subject of broad and open debate. Indeed, according to firsthand testimony, Toyen used masculine pronouns in 1930s Prague. Gluck explicitly rejected gendered prefixes and titles when publicly addressed, as documented by a letter written by Gluck included in this exhibition. However, scholars specializing in Gluck have predominantly opted to use feminine pronouns in recent academic publications—such as the exhibition catalogue Gluck: Art and Identity *(Brighton Museum & Art Gallery, 2017)—drawing on historical linguistic practices. Referencing both Marlow Moss's own language use and that of Moss's life partner, experts have generally used feminine pronouns. More recently, however, Moss has also been considered through a transmasculine lens. As a result, some institutions now use the gender-neutral pronouns they/them or choose to avoid pronouns altogether.*

Meanwhile, American critic Laura Cottingham interprets the nonbinary, performative self-representation of Claude Cahun and Marcel Moore as the expression of a modern lesbian identity. In this publication, the invited authors have made independent decisions regarding pronoun usage based on their respective research and understanding of the historical context.

In cases where artists changed their names, we deliberately avoid deadnaming by not referencing their birth names. This is the case, for example, with Anton Prinner, a sculptor and printmaker who identified as transmasculine and, upon arriving in Paris in 1928, began consistently presenting in a form of drag situated within the male-dominated Parisian artistic bohemia. Where exceptions occur, the authors provide contextual notes.

Historical forms of self-identification are used when supported by sources; however, derogatory terms are avoided wherever possible.

VORWORT UND DANK

~

PREFACE AND ACKNOWLEDGMENTS

SUSANNE GAENSHEIMER

Die Kunstsammlung Nordrhein-Westfalen zeigt mit *Queere Moderne. 1900 bis 1950* die erste umfassende Ausstellung in Europa, die den bahnbrechenden Beitrag queerer Künstler*innen zur Moderne vorstellt. Mit über 100 Werken – darunter Gemälde, Zeichnungen, Fotografien, Skulpturen, Filme, Literatur und Archivalien – von 34 internationalen Künstler*innen fokussiert das Ausstellungsprojekt die erste Hälfte des 20. Jahrhunderts. Es zeichnet eine alternative Geschichte der Moderne, in der der Einfluss und die Perspektive von queeren Künstler*innen auf die Stile, Bewegungen und Programme der modernen Kunst im Zentrum stehen. Wenn man der These von Jonathan D. Katz in diesem Katalog folgt, dann haben die künstlerische Moderne und die Homosexualität als „zweieiige Zwillinge" vieles gemeinsam. Und trotz ihrer Gemeinsamkeiten und der engen Verflochtenheit queerer Positionen mit den Entwicklungen der Avantgarden wurden diese von den Hüter*innen des kunsthistorischen Kanons – wie etwa den Formalismus verteidigende Kunstkritiker*innen und dominierende Kunstschaffende der Moderne selbst – marginalisiert und oft als antimodern betrachtet. Viele Formfindungen, in denen die hier gezeigten Künstler*innen spezifische Ansätze alternativer Repräsentationen und Inhalte entwickelten, gerieten später in Vergessenheit, obwohl diese Protagonist*innen in ihrer Zeit zentral im kosmopolitischen Kunstgeschehen situiert und vernetzt waren. Es ist dies das „Vergessen der westlich-normativen Moderne" – jenes *modern oblivion*, von dem Angela Miller im Hinblick auf das heute kaum mehr bekannte, hybride Werk des transnationalen Malers und Bühnenbildners Pavel Tchelitchew spricht.[1] Nachdem die Kunstsammlung Nordrhein-Westfalen mit dem umfassenden Recherche- und Ausstellungsprojekt *museum global. Mikrogeschichten einer ex-zentrischen Moderne* und den beiden internationalen Symposien *Rethinking the Museum I* und *II* stetig daran arbeitet, die eigene Sammlung und etablierte kunstgeschichtliche Narrative zu hinterfragen und zu erweitern, stellt *Queere Moderne* einen weiteren Schritt dieser Neubetrachtung der kanonisierten Kunstgeschichte der Moderne dar. Das Projekt unterstreicht zugleich unser Bestreben, fortwährend neue und visionäre Perspektiven mit den eigenen Sammlungspräsentationen und Ausstellungsprojekten zu verbinden. Die von einem Prolog und Epilog gerahmte und in weitere sechs thematische Kapitel unterteilte Ausstellung zeigt ein künstlerisch fruchtbares und dichtes internationales Netzwerk von queeren Künstler*innen, das sich Anfang des letzten Jahrhunderts in verschiedenen Metropolen in Europa und den USA auszubilden begann. Queere Künstler*innen wie Richmond Barthé, Claude Cahun, Marlow Moss oder Pavel Tchelitchew schufen Alternativen zu vorherrschenden Lebensentwürfen und rückten Begehren, Gender und Sexualität sowie die Politik der Selbstdarstellung in den Mittelpunkt ihres Kunstschaffens. Aufgrund oft fehlender Aussagen und Berichte über sexuelle Orientierungen und Lebensweisen ist das Erforschen queerer Geschichte der Moderne vor dem schwul-lesbischen Aktivismus der Stonewall Riots 1969 in New York und der damit einhergehenden positiven Umdeutung des zuvor als Schimpfwort verwendeten Begriffs „queer" eine Herausforderung und ein Arbeiten mit einer in vielen Fällen uneindeutigen und fragmentierten Quellenlage. Diese betrifft in besonderem Maße marginalisierte Gruppen wie Frauen, Künstler*innen aus nicht privilegierten sozialen Klassen oder aus dem „Globalen Süden" – zu einer

1 Angela Miller, „‚Vibrant Matter': The Countermodern World of Pavel Tchelitchew", in: *The Art Bulletin* 102, Nr. 2 (Juni 2000), S. 121–145, hier: S. 121.

With *Queer Modernism. 1900 to 1950*, the Kunstsammlung Nordrhein-Westfalen presents the first comprehensive exhibition in Europe dedicated to the pioneering contributions of queer artists to modernism. Featuring over one hundred works by thirty-four international artists—ranging from paintings, drawings, photographs, sculptures, and films to literature and archival materials—the exhibition focuses on the first half of the twentieth century. It traces an alternative history of modernism, concentrating on the perspectives and influences of queer artists on the styles, movements, and agendas of modern art. If one accepts the thesis advanced by Jonathan D. Katz in this publication, then the "fraternal twins" modernism and homosexuality share much in common. Yet despite these affinities and the close interconnection of queer perspectives with the evolution of the avant-garde, they have been marginalized and often deemed anti-modern by the guardians of the art-historical canon, such as those art critics who championed formalism and even some of modernism's most prominent artists themselves.

Many formal inventions, in which the artists presented here developed distinct approaches to alternative modes of representation and content, subsequently fell into obscurity, despite the fact that these key figures were well-connected protagonists situated at the center of cosmopolitan art production of their time. This is the "amnesia of Western-normative modernism," that "modern oblivion" coined by Angela Miller[1] in regard to the hybrid work of the transnational painter and stage designer Pavel Tchelitchew, who is largely forgotten today. The Kunstsammlung Nordrhein-Westfalen previously questioned its own collection, as well as expanded established art-historical narratives, through the extensive research and exhibition project *museum global. Microhistories of an Ex-centric Modernism* and the two-part symposium *Rethinking the Museum I* and *II*. Now, with *Queer Modernism*, the Kunstsammlung Nordrhein-Westfalen has taken a further step in (re)examining the art-historical canon of modernism. This project underscores both our ongoing efforts to fuse new and visionary perspectives with the presentation of our own collection and exhibition projects.

The exhibition is bookended by a prologue and epilogue and divided into six additional thematic chapters. It reveals an artistically fertile and tightly connected international network of queer artists who began their training at the start of the previous century across various cities in Europe and the United States. Queer artists such as Richmond Barthé, Claude Cahun, Marlow Moss, and Pavel Tchelitchew created alternatives to prevailing life models, placing desire, gender, and sexuality, as well as the politics of self-representation, at the center of their artistic practice.

The frequent lack of statements and reports on sexual orientation and ways of life makes research into the queer history of modernism a challenge—especially prior to the gay and lesbian activism sparked by the 1969 Stonewall riots in New York and the subsequent positive reclaiming of the formerly pejorative term "queer"—and requires investigation of sources that in many cases are ambiguous and fragmentary. This is especially true when dealing

1 Angela Miller, "'Vibrant Matter': The Countermodern World of Pavel Tchelitchew," *The Art Bulletin* 102, no. 2 (June 2000): pp. 121–145, here p. 121.

SUSANNE
GAENSHEIMER

Zeit, in der der Kolonialismus noch seinen Höhepunkt erlebte und das westliche Verständnis kultureller Hegemonie weitgehend unhinterfragt blieb. Gleichzeitig entwickelten sich Metropolen wie Paris, London und New York zunehmend zu „kosmopolitischen Kontaktzonen"[2] zwischen den etablierten Avantgarden und den Vertreter*innen dekolonialer künstlerischer und aktivistischer Bewegungen. Viele Protagonist*innen der Moderne und Vormoderne, denen wir auch in dieser Ausstellung begegnen, haben ihre sexuelle Orientierung nicht offen ausgelebt. Sie lebten nach außen oft einen heteronormativen Lebensstil, gingen vielfach eine sogenannte Marriage of Convenience ein und hatten eine Familie, Verhältnisse, die die Geschichtsschreibung vorrangig und normalisierend festgehalten hat. Was die Quellen verbergen, ist daher manchmal sogar wichtiger als das, was sie offenbaren. Bereits im 19. Jahrhundert brachen Künstler*innen mit traditionellen Genderrollen und lebten in nicht konformen und gleichgeschlechtlichen Lebensgemeinschaften. Der Prolog der Ausstellung stellt stellvertretend für viele weitere Positionen die aus einer liberalen verarmten Künstlerfamilie stammende französische Malerin Rosa Bonheur vor, die für ihre außergewöhnlichen Tierdarstellungen bekannt ist. Als emanzipierte Frau lebte sie 40 Jahre in einer Lebenspartnerschaft mit der Erfinderin Nathalie Micas wie auch mit einer Menagerie von Tieren als eine Art alternativem Familienzusammenhang. Für einen besseren Zugang zu ihrem Arbeitsfeld, wie etwa Besuche bei Schlachthäusern, um die Tieranatomie studieren zu können, beantragte sie 1857 bei der zuständigen Präfektur die *Permission de travestissement*, die Erlaubnis des Staates, Männerkleidung tragen zu dürfen. Wir zeigen das großformatige „Doppelporträt" von Rosa Bonheur mit einem Stier von Édouard Dubufe aus dem Jahr 1857, wo die Malerin – unzufrieden mit dem Ergebnis eines in ihren Augen zu traditionellen Künstler*innenporträts – selbstbewusst den Stier ihrem Porträt zur Seite gestellt hat. Das Kapitel „Modernes Arkadien" zeigt, wie sich Künstler*innen wie Glyn Warren Philpot, Dame Ethel Walker, Lotte Laserstein oder Ludwig von Hofmann mythologischer, fantastischer oder intimer Bilder bedienten, um unkonventionelle Repräsentationen zu schaffen, in denen homoerotisches Begehren zum Ausdruck kommt. Der Schwarze US-amerikanische Künstler Richmond Barthé schuf im Umfeld der Harlem Renaissance – eine literarische und künstlerische Bewegung Schwarzer Schriftsteller*innen und Künstler*innen in New York – Skulpturen, die den Schwarzen männlichen Körper zu einem Verhandlungsort seiner Homosexualität werden ließ. Das Kapitel „Sapphische Moderne" fokussiert auf von lesbischen Frauen geführte Salons und transkulturell aktive Netzwerke in Paris. Während in den modernen Metropolen queere Subkulturen blühten, prägte eine Gruppe intellektueller Amerikaner*innen wie Romaine Brooks, Natalie Barney, Gertrude Stein oder Sylvia Beach die Szene in Paris. Das Kapitel „Surreale Welten" vereint Positionen im Stilmilieu des Surrealismus, die sich mit Konzepten der Androgynie und des Hermaphroditismus (heute als „Intergeschlechtlichkeit" bezeichnet) auseinandersetzten, was von dem Berliner Sexualwissenschaftler Magnus Hirschfeld in der Weimarer Ära auch als sogenanntes drittes Geschlecht proklamiert wurde. Zahlreiche Künstler*innen der Zwischenkriegsmoderne schufen Mensch-Maschinen-Hybride und entwarfen damit in Technologie gebannte, aufbrechende Geschlechterverhältnisse. Einige Werke in der Kunstsammlung Nordrhein-

2 Kobena Marcer, „Cosmopolitan Contact Zones", in: *Afro Modern: Journeys Through the Black Atlantic*, hrsg. von Tanja Barson und Peter Gorschlüter, Ausst.-Kat. Tate Liverpool, London 2010, S. 40–47.

with marginalized groups such as women, artists from less privileged social classes, or those from the "Global South"—at a time when colonialism was at its peak and the Western understanding of cultural hegemony remained largely unquestioned. At the same time, however, cities such as Paris, London, and New York increasingly developed into "cosmopolitan contact zones"[2] between established avant-gardes and the proponents of decolonial artistic and activist movements. Many of the figures of modernism and pre-modernism featured in this exhibition did not openly express their sexual orientation. Instead, they often outwardly adhered to a heteronormative lifestyle, frequently entering into so-called marriages of convenience and establishing families, relationships that historiography has predominantly recorded in a normalizing manner. Consequently, what the sources conceal is sometimes more significant than what they reveal. Already in the nineteenth century, artists were rejecting traditional gender roles and living in nonconformist and same-sex partnerships. The exhibition's prologue presents—as representative of many such perspectives—the French painter Rosa Bonheur, who came from a liberal, though impoverished, family of artists and was renowned for her pictures of animals. She lived for forty years as an emancipated woman in a long-term relationship with the inventor Nathalie Micas and maintained a menagerie of animals as a sort of alternative family. In order to better pursue her line of work, such as visits to slaughterhouses to study the anatomy of animals, she applied in 1857 to the local prefecture for a *permission de travestissement*, that is, a state-sanctioned permit to wear men's clothing publicly. We display the large-format "double portrait" of Rosa Bonheur with a bull by Édouard Dubufe, in which Bonheur, dissatisfied with what she considered an overly traditional artist's portrait, confidently positioned the bovine at her own side. The chapter "Modern Arcadia" illustrates how artists such as Glyn Warren Philpot, Dame Ethel Walker, Lotte Laserstein, and Ludwig von Hofmann made use of mythological motifs, fantastical scenes, and intimate images to create unconventional representations in which homoerotic desire found expression. The Black American artist Richmond Barthé—working within the context of the Harlem Renaissance, a literary and artistic movement of African American writers and visual artists in New York—created sculptures in which the Black male body became a site for negotiating his homosexuality. The chapter titled "Sapphic Modernism" focuses on the salons hosted by lesbian women and their transcultural networks in Paris. While autochthonous queer subcultures flourished in many modern cities, a group of American intellectual women, such as Romaine Brooks, Natalie Barney, Gertrude Stein, and Sylvia Beach, came to define the scene in Paris. The chapter "Surreal Worlds" brings together perspectives within the stylistic milieu of Surrealism, which engaged with the concepts of androgyny and "hermaphroditism" (a term now largely replaced by intersexuality) proclaimed during the Weimar Republic by Berlin sexologist Magnus Hirschfeld as the so-called "third sex." Numerous artists working during the interwar period of modernism created

2 Kobena Mercer, "Cosmopolitan Contact Zones," in *Afro Modern: Journeys Through the Black Atlantic*, ed. Tanja Barson and Peter Gorschlüter (London: Tate, 2010), pp. 40–47.

SUSANNE GAENSHEIMER

Westfalen, die wir in dieses Kapitel integriert haben, zeugen von diesem neuen Ausdrucksrepertoire. In einer Zeit wachsender Destabilisierung von Gendernormen neigten jedoch vor allem die Surrealisten dazu, gewaltvolle Darstellungen eines modernen Geschlechterkampfs zu schaffen, wie etwa in René Magrittes bedrohlichem Gemälde *Les jours gigantesques* von 1928 (Abb. 1) oder in Max Ernsts *La carmagnole de l'amour* von 1926 (Abb. 2).

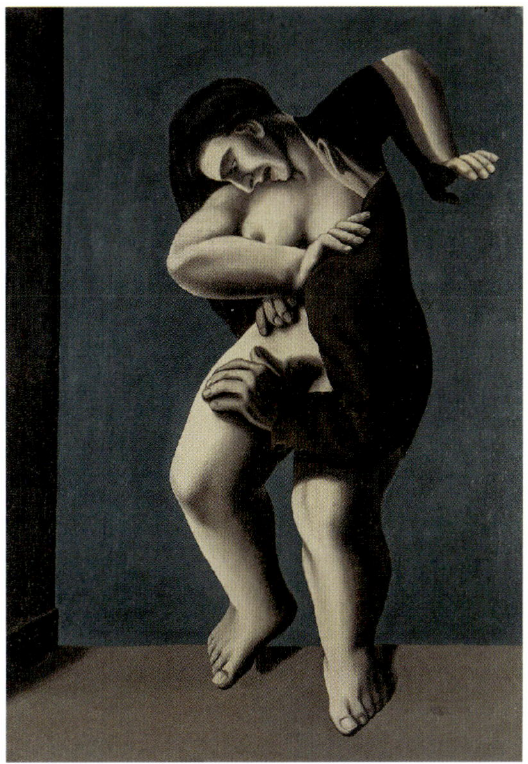

ABB. ~ FIG. 1

René Magritte, *Les jours gigantesques*, 1928
Die gigantischen Tage ~ *The Titanic Days*

Öl auf Leinwand ~ *Oil on canvas*, 116 × 80,8 × 2,8 cm
Kunstsammlung Nordrhein-Westfalen, Düsseldorf

In den heteronormativen Avantgardebewegungen wurde Androgynie als ultramodernes Konzept betrachtet, jedoch zumeist realisiert in einer idealisierten Entgeschlechtlichung und entsexualisierten Darstellung der menschlichen Form. Künstler*innen wie Toyen, Leonor Fini, Ithell Colquhoun, Marie Laurencin, Gerda Wegener oder Milena Pavlović-Barili hingegen bildeten mit ihren Werken Visionen queerer Identitäten und Szenarien aus, in denen Konventionen herausgefordert und transzendiert werden konnten. Vor dem Hintergrund queerer Diskurse, wie denen von David J. Getsy, will das Kapitel „Queere Lesarten von Abstraktion" die vermeintlichen Grenzen zwischen Abstraktion und Figuration in der Moderne aufbrechen und neu denken. Zugleich stellt sich angesichts der konstruktivistischen sowie biomorphen Kompositionen von Künstler*innen wie Marlow Moss, Anton Prinner, Jacoba van Heemskerck oder Louise Janin die Frage nach einer unfigürlichen genderqueeren Ästhetik. Können auch in abstrakten Formen sinnliche Verkörperung sowie soziale Beziehungen symbolisch zum Ausdruck kommen? Das Kapitel „Queere Avantgarden und intime Netzwerke" stellt im Gegensatz zu den vorhergehenden Kapiteln, in denen der Fokus hauptsächlich auf lesbischen und

human-machine hybrids that inscribed destabilizing gender relations into technological form. Some of the works from the Kunstsammlung Nordrhein-Westfalen collection that we have integrated in this chapter bear witness to this new repertoire of expression. In an age of growing destabilization of gender norms, however, it was above all male Surrealists who tended to create violent representations of a modern battle of the sexes, such as in René Magritte's threatening 1928 painting *Les jours gigantesques* (fig. 1) or Max Ernst's 1926 *La carmagnole de l'amour* (fig. 2). Androgyny was regarded by the heteronormative avant-garde movements as an ultra-modern concept, but was principally realized in an idealized, degendered, and desexualized representation of the human form. By contrast, artists such as Toyen, Leonor Fini, Ithell Colquhoun, Marie Laurencin, Gerda Wegener, and Milena Pavlović-Barili developed visions of queer identities and scenarios in their works, in which conventions could be challenged and transcended. Against a background of queer theoretical discourses, such as that of David J. Getsy, the chapter "Queer Readings of Abstraction" seeks to dissolve and rethink the boundaries between abstraction and figuration in modernism. At the same time, the Constructivist as well as biomorphic compositions by artists such as Marlow Moss, Anton Prinner, Jacoba van Heemskerck, and Louise Janin raise the question of a nonfigurative, genderqueer aesthetics. Can sensual embodiment and social relationships also be symbolically expressed through abstract forms? The chapter "Queer Avant-Gardes and Intimate Networks," in contrast to earlier chapters that focus primarily on lesbian and nonbinary artists, presents male homosexuality and perspectives through artists such as Pavel Tchelitchew, George Platt Lynes, Beauford Delaney, and Nils Dardel, who engaged with the international avant-garde in New York and Paris. The chapter "Queer Resistance since 1933" unites perspectives such as those of Toyen and Jeanne Mammen, along with queer artist couples Claude Cahun and Marcel Moore, as well as Hannah Höch and Til Brugman, who each pursued distinct forms of anti-fascist resistance. Following three decades of fragile gains in new freedoms and the emergence of a flourishing queer artistic culture, many hopes were brutally crushed under the heel of European fascism. The epilogue shows that even in the conservative 1950s, when many émigré artists shaped developments in the American postwar avant-garde movements, artists like Sonja Sekula and John Cage faced the homophobic cultural politics of the restrictive McCarthy era. In their works—Sekula in a 1951 painting dedicated to Cage titled *Silence*, and Cage in his legendary, entirely silent 1952 composition *4'33"*—they responded to these repressive policies with a form of conceptual and subversive silence.[3]

This exhibition demonstrates on many levels just how topical, as well as socially and politically relevant, the themes raised in the works and lives of these artists remain today. At a time when queer people once again live in danger—as Tirza True Latimer emphatically warns in this publication—and when, moreover, "the word 'difference,' too, often prompts hostility rather than enthusiasm or curiosity," it is all the more important for public

3 See Jonathan D. Katz, "John Cage's Queer Silence; Or, How to Avoid Making Matters Worse," *Journal of Lesbian and Gay Studies* 5, no. 2 (April 1999): pp. 231–252.

SUSANNE
GAENSHEIMER

nonbinären Künstler*innen lag, männliche Homosexualität und Positionen vor, die wie Pavel Tchelitchew, George Platt Lynes, Beauford Delaney und Nils Dardel in New York und Paris auf die dortigen internationalen Avantgarden stießen.

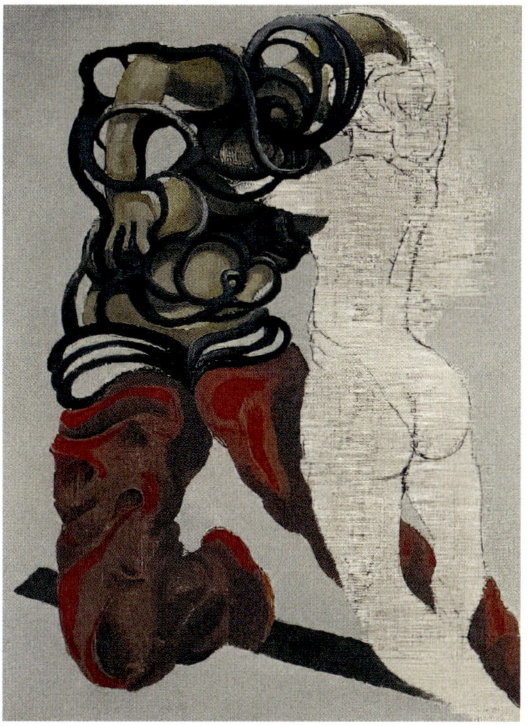

ABB. ~ FIG. 2

Max Ernst, *La carmagnole de l'amour*, 1926
Die Carmagnole der Liebe ~ *The Carmagnole of Love*

Öl und Zeichnung auf Leinwand ~
Oil and drawing on canvas, 101 × 73,5 cm
Kunstsammlung Nordrhein-Westfalen, Düsseldorf.
Erworben 1999 durch die Freunde der Kunstsammlung Nordrhein-Westfalen ~ *Acquired by the Friends of the Kunstsammlung Nordrhein-Westfalen*

Das Kapitel „Queerer Widerstand seit 1933" vereint Positionen wie von Toyen, von Jeanne Mammen und die von queeren Künstler*innenpaaren wie Claude Cahun und Marcel Moore oder Hannah Höch und Til Brugman, die ganz unterschiedliche Formen des antifaschistischen Widerstands entwickelt haben. Nach drei Jahrzehnten der fragilen Errungenschaften neuer Freiheiten und eines reichhaltigen queeren künstlerischen Schaffens wurden viele Hoffnungen unter dem Schatten des europäischen Faschismus brutal zerschlagen. Der Epilog zeigt, dass noch in den konservativen 1950er-Jahren, als viele Künstler*innen im Exil die Entwicklung der US-amerikanischen Nachkriegsavantgarden prägten, Künstler*innen wie Sonja Sekula oder John Cage mit einer homophoben Kulturpolitik der restriktiven McCarthy-Ära konfrontiert wurden. In ihren Werken – Sekula in einem Cage gewidmeten Gemälde mit dem Titel *Silence* von 1951 und Cage in seiner legendären, völlig stillen Komposition *4'33"* von 1952 – konterten sie diese repressive Politik mit einer Form des konzeptuellen und „subversiven Schweigens".[3]

Die Ausstellung zeigt auf vielen Ebenen, wie aktuell und gesellschaftspolitisch relevant die in den Werken aufgeworfenen Themen und die Lebensläufe der Künstler*innen sind. In einer Zeit, in der queere Menschen

3 Jonathan D. Katz, „John Cage's Queer Silence; Or, How to Avoid Making Matters Worse", in: *Journal of Lesbian and Gay Studies*, Bd. 5, Heft 2, 01.04.1999, Durham 1999, S. 231–252.

institutions to take a stand, understanding diversity as a unifying social force, against every form of exclusion and discrimination.

We would like to thank all the lenders who made their key works available for this important exhibition. They have enabled us to present these extraordinary artistic perspectives, which—lying outside the established canon—have only gradually been recognized by the art world. In those cases where the loan of a desired work was not possible—for various reasons, including, unfortunately, explicit reservations about a queer reading of modernism—the curators have bridged these crucial gaps with informative and illustrated wall texts offering context. I am grateful to the curatorial team at the Kunstsammlung Nordrhein-Westfalen, Isabelle Malz and Isabelle Tondre, as well as guest curator Anke Kempkes, for carrying out such a complex and significant research and exhibition project, which they have developed and prepared together over the past three years.

Queer scholars, artists, and experts from a range of disciplines supported the project with their expertise. A queer advisory committee provided critical input on the exhibition, developed formats for public engagement, and contributed suggestions for the accompanying program. The fruitful exchange of ideas—critical of all forms of discrimination—took place during several workshops and was extremely valuable for us; we are sincerely grateful for the expertise, insights, and suggestions they shared.

I would like to thank the authors for their enriching contributions, which engage with these artistic perspectives against the backdrop of socially and politically urgent themes and discourses: Jonathan D. Katz, Anke Kempkes, Tirza True Latimer, Isabelle Malz, Diana Souhami, and Isabelle Tondre. My gratitude also goes to Marie Artaker, Alexandra Möllner, and Hannah Sakai, who have found a captivating and visually refined language for the catalogue and exhibition design. My thanks to the translators Claudia Kotte, David Sánchez Cano, and Alexandra Titze-Grabec, as well as to the copy editors Iris Seemann and José Enrique Macián for their meticulous work. I am grateful to Cordula Frevel at the Kunstsammlung Nordrhein-Westfalen and the team at Hirmer Publishers under the leadership of Kerstin Ludolph with Karen Angne, Verena Hüttner, and Susanne Röhrig for guiding the production of this exhibition catalogue.

This exhibition project would not have been possible without the outstanding team at the Kunstsammlung Nordrhein-Westfalen. I would like to express my sincere thanks to all staff involved in this project for their professionalism and extraordinary dedication, without whom such an exhibition could never have been realized: to the Head of Education, Annika Schank, along with Sebastian Bartel, Jacqueline Est, and Annika Plank, who, together with Critical Friends, created an educational space in the exhibition whose program reflects on and expands the exhibition from a contemporary perspective; to Christine Breitschopf, Head of the Library, who, together with Michelle Borrey, researched a wide range of scholarly literature for the exhibition; to Giulia D'Allotta of Exhibition Management; to Katharina Nettekoven, Head of

wieder in Gefahr leben – worauf Tirza True Latimer in diesem Katalog eindringlich hinweist – und „das Wort ‚Unterschied' zudem oftmals eher für Feindseligkeit anstatt für Begeisterung oder Neugier" stehe, ist es als öffentliche Institution umso wichtiger, sich im Sinne von Diversität gesellschaftsverbindend gegen jegliche Formen von Ausgrenzung und Diskriminierung zu positionieren.

Wir danken all jenen Leihgeber*innen, die uns ihre zentralen Werke für diese wichtige Ausstellung zur Verfügung gestellt haben. Mit ihnen können wir großartige künstlerische Positionen vorstellen, die abseits des etablierten Kanons nur langsam vom Kunstbetrieb wahrgenommen werden. In jenen Fällen, in denen aus unterschiedlichen Gründen eine Ausleihe der gewünschten Werke nicht möglich war – darunter leider auch ausdrückliche Vorbehalte gegenüber einer queeren Lesart der Moderne –, haben die Kurator*innen wichtige Leerstellen in Form einer Kontextualisierung über einführende und bebilderte Wandtexte aufgefangen. Ich danke dem kuratorischen Team der Kunstsammlung Nordrhein-Westfalen mit Isabelle Malz und Isabelle Tondre sowie der Gastkuratorin Anke Kempkes für dieses so wichtige und komplexe Recherche- und Ausstellungsvorhaben, das sie in den letzten drei Jahren gemeinsam entwickelt und vorbereitet haben.

Queere Wissenschaftler*innen, Künstler*innen und Expert*innen aus verschiedenen Bereichen unterstützten das Projekt mit ihrer Expertise. Ein queerer Beirat hat die Ausstellung kritisch beraten, Vermittlungssituationen konzipiert und Vorschläge zum Rahmenprogramm beigetragen. Der fruchtbare und diskriminierungskritische Austausch im Rahmen mehrerer Workshops war für uns sehr wertvoll und wir danken ihnen herzlich für ihre Expertise, ihre wichtigen Impulse und Ideen, die sie mit uns geteilt haben. Den Autor*innen des Katalogs danke ich für ihre bereichernden und die künstlerischen Positionen auch vor dem Hintergrund gesellschaftspolitisch virulenter Themen und ihre die Diskurse reflektierenden Beiträge: Jonathan D. Katz, Anke Kempkes, Tirza True Latimer, Isabelle Malz, Diana Souhami und Isabelle Tondre. Mein Dank gilt zudem Marie Artaker, Alexandra Möllner und Hannah Sakai, die für den Ausstellungskatalog und die Ausstellungsgrafik eine eindrucksvolle und visuell sensible Sprache gefunden haben. Den Übersetzer*innen Claudia Kotte, David Sánchez Cano, Alexandra Titze-Grabec sowie den Lektor*innen Iris Seemann und José Enrique Macián sei für ihre professionelle Arbeit gedankt. Cordula Frevel von der Kunstsammlung Nordrhein-Westfalen und dem Team des Hirmer Verlags unter der Leitung von Kerstin Ludolph mit Karen Angne, Verena Hüttner und Susanne Röhrig danke ich für die Produktionsbegleitung des Ausstellungskatalogs.

Ohne das fantastische Team der Kunstsammlung Nordrhein-Westfalen wäre die Realisierung dieses Ausstellungsprojekts nicht möglich gewesen. Für ihre Professionalität und ihr außerordentliches Engagement möchte ich mich bei allen Mitarbeiter*innen, die in das Projekt eingebunden waren, sehr bedanken: bei der Leiterin der Abteilung Bildung Annika Schank mit Sebastian Bartel, Jacqueline Est und Annika Plank, die zusammen mit den Critical Friends einen Vermittlungsraum in der Ausstellung konzipiert haben, der mit seinem Programm die Ausstellung aus einer heutigen Perspektive reflektierend erweitert, bei der Leiterin der Bibliothek Christine Breitschopf, die mit Michelle Borrey ein breites Literaturangebot für die Ausstellung recherchiert hat, bei Giulia D'Allotta aus dem

the Registrar's Office, with Jennifer Buchholz and Lea März; to Susanne Fernandes Silva, Head of Communications, with Johanna Chromik, Susanne Hafner, Sophie Krause, Jule Laerz-Haase, Linda Inconi, and Meike Lotz-Kowal; to Nina Quabeck, Head of Conservation, with Juan Garcia, Bianca Grüger, Sven Kamp, Anne Skaliks, Naja Staats, Lea Vieler, and Jessica Völkert-Lunk; to the Head of the Technical Department, Bernd Schliephake, with both media technicians Jens Meller and Oswin Schmidt; to carpenter Bernd Strauchmann; to building inspectors Sascha Lemmer and Frank Mankell; to the Head of Administration, Christina Rock, and her team working behind the scenes. My special thanks also go to the Head of the Curatorial Department, Karen Archey, and last but not least to my colleague on the Kunstsammlung Executive Board, Commercial Manager Julia Niggemann.

Such an extensive exhibition would not have been possible without the support of generous sponsors. I am very grateful to the Ernst von Siemens Art Foundation for its financial contribution to this exhibition catalogue. As always, I am deeply indebted to the Ministry of Culture and Science of the State of North Rhine-Westphalia for its ongoing and steadfast commitment.

Susanne Gaensheimer
Director, Kunstsammlung Nordrhein-Westfalen

Ausstellungsmanagement, bei der Leiterin der Abteilung Registrar Katharina Nettekoven mit Jennifer Buchholz und Lea März, bei der Leiterin der Abteilung Kommunikation Susanne Fernandes Silva mit Johanna Chromik, Susanne Hafner, Sophie Krause, Jule Laerz-Haase, Linda Inconi, Meike Lotz-Kowal, bei der Leiterin der Abteilung Restaurierung Nina Quabeck mit Juan Garcia, Bianca Grüger, Sven Kamp, Anne Skaliks, Naja Staats, Lea Vieler und Jessica Völkert-Lunk, bei dem technischen Leiter Bernd Schliephake mit den beiden Medientechnikern Jens Meller und Oswin Schmidt, bei dem Schreiner Bernd Strauchmann, bei den Hausinspektoren Sascha Lemmer und Frank Mankel, bei der Leitung Verwaltung Christina Rock und ihrem Team im Hintergrund, ohne das eine solche Ausstellung nicht zu realisieren wäre. Mein besonderer Dank gilt darüber hinaus der Leiterin der kuratorischen Abteilung Karen Archey und nicht zuletzt meiner Kollegin im Vorstand der Kunstsammlung und kaufmännischen Leiterin Julia Niggemann.

Eine so umfangreiche Ausstellung wäre ohne die Unterstützung großzügiger Förderer nicht möglich. Ich danke der Ernst von Siemens Kunststiftung sehr für die finanzielle Unterstützung des Ausstellungskatalogs. Dem Ministerium für Kultur und Wissenschaft des Landes Nordrhein-Westfalen bin ich wie immer für ihre dauerhafte und zuverlässige Förderung sehr dankbar.

Susanne Gaensheimer
Direktorin, Kunstsammlung Nordrhein-Westfalen

WERKE

~

WORKS

I PROLOG

PROLOGUE

1

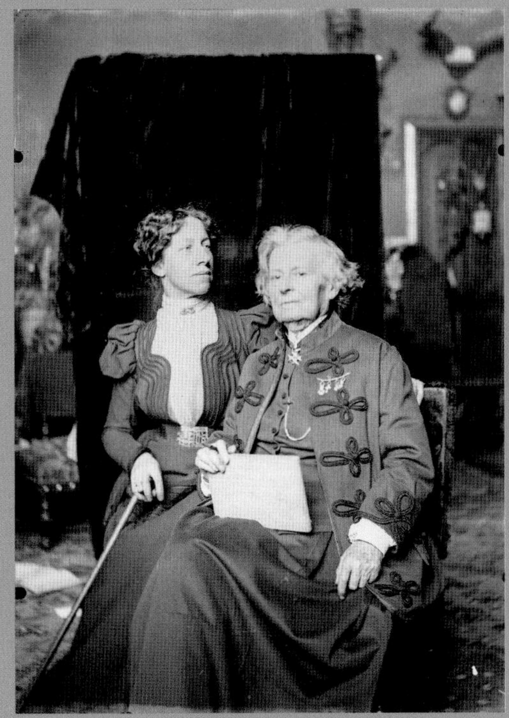

2

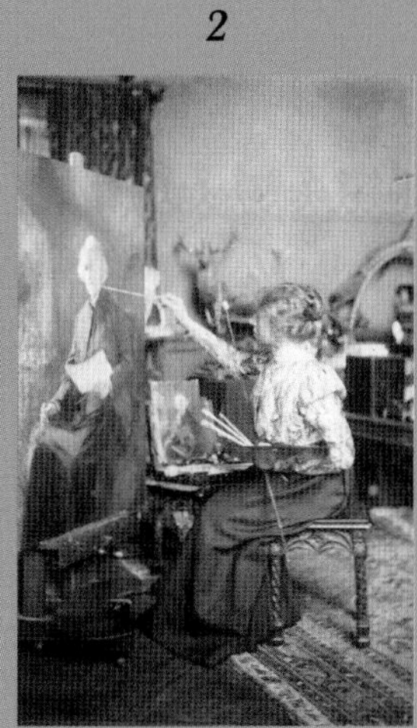

3

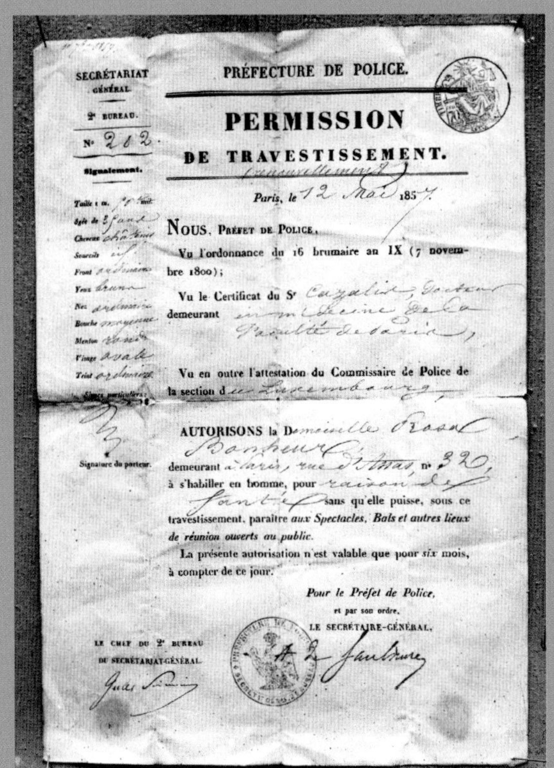

SECRÉTARIAT GÉNÉRAL.

2e BUREAU.

No 212.

Signalement.

Taille 1 m.
Âgé de
Cheveux châtains
Sourcils
Front ordinaire
Yeux bruns
Nez ordinaire
Bouche moyenne
Menton
Visage ovale
Teint ordinaire
Signes particuliers:

Signature du porteur.

PRÉFECTURE DE POLICE.

PERMISSION

DE TRAVESTISSEMENT.

(renouvellement)

Paris, le 12 Mai 1857.

NOUS, PRÉFET DE POLICE,

Vu l'ordonnance du 16 brumaire an IX (7 novembre 1800);

Vu le Certificat du Sr Cazalis, Docteur en médecine de la demeurant Faculté de Paris,

Vu en outre l'attestation du Commissaire de Police de la section du Luxembourg,

AUTORISONS la Demoiselle Rosa Bonheur demeurant à Paris, rue d'Assas, no 32, à s'habiller en homme, pour raison de santé sans qu'elle puisse, sous ce travestissement, paraître *aux Spectacles, Bals et autres lieux de réunion ouverts au public.*

La présente autorisation n'est valable que pour *six* mois, à compter de ce jour.

Pour le Préfet de Police,
et par son ordre,
LE SECRÉTAIRE-GÉNÉRAL.

LE CHEF DU 2e BUREAU
DU SECRÉTARIAT-GÉNÉRAL.

4

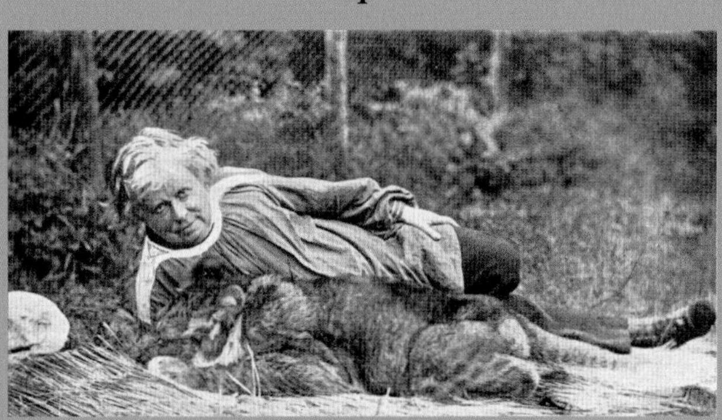

5

„Wäre ich ein Mann gewesen, hätte ich sie geheiratet, und niemand hätte sich all diese dummen Geschichten ausdenken können“, sagte Rosa Bonheur über ihre Langzeitgefährtin, Nathalie Micas.

~

“Had I been a man, I would have married her, and nobody could have dreamed up all those silly stories,” Rosa Bonheur said of her longtime companion, Nathalie Micas.

1

Anna Klumpke und Rosa Bonheur, Château de By, By-Thomery, um 1898

Bonheur stammte ursprünglich aus einer verarmten liberalen Künstlerfamilie. Sie lebte mit Nathalie Micas, einer Erfinderin, bis zu deren Tod zusammen. Es folgte die Beziehung zu der jungen amerikanischen Malerin Anna Klumpke, laut Bonheur „eine göttliche Ehe von zwei Seelen".

~

Anna Klumpke and Rosa Bonheur, Château de By, By-Thomery, ca. 1898

Bonheur was born into a liberal but impoverished artist family. She lived with her partner, the inventor Nathalie Micas, until Micas's death. Later, she began a relationship with the young American painter Anna Klumpke, "a divine marriage of two souls," as Bonheur later put it.

2

Anna Klumpke malt Rosa Bonheurs Porträt 1898, im Atelier, das Bonheur für sie errichtet hat (im Château de By, By-Thomery).

~

Anna Klumpke painting Rosa Bonheur's portrait in 1898 in the studio that Bonheur had built for her at the Château de By, By-Thomery.

3

An Rosa Bonheur ausgestellte Erlaubnis, Männerkleidung zu tragen, Paris, 12. Mai 1857

Bonheur wurde international bekannt für ihre modernen realistischen Tierdarstellungen. Um etwa in Schlachthäusern Tieranatomie studieren zu können, beantragte sie die *Permission de travestissement*.

~

Permit issued to Rosa Bonheur to wear men's clothing while working, Paris, May 12, 1857

Bonheur gained international recognition for her realistically modern depictions of animals. To study animal anatomy in places like slaughterhouses, she applied for a permission de travestissement.

4

Rosa Bonheur und ihre Löwin Fathma, um 1889

~

Rosa Bonheur and her lioness Fathma, ca. 1889

5

Testament von Rosa Bonheur, in: Anna Klumpke, *Rosa Bonheur: Sa vie, son œuvre*, Paris 1908, S. 435–436

~

Rosa Bonheur's will, in Anna Klumpke, Rosa Bonheur: Sa vie, son œuvre *(Paris: Ernst Flammarion, 1908), pp. 435–436*

Wenn Sie nur wüßten, wie wenig ich mir aus Ihrem ganzen Geschlecht mache [...]. In Wirklichkeit interessiere ich mich, was männliche Wesen anbelangt, nur für die Stiere, die ich male.

~

If you only knew how little I care for your sex
[...]. The fact is, in the way of males,
I like only the bulls I paint.

Anna Elizabeth Klumpke, *Rosa Bonheur: Sa vie, son œuvre*, Bd. 2, Paris 1908, S. 150.

~

Anna Elizabeth Klumpke, Rosa Bonheur: Sa vie, son œuvre, *vol. 2 (Paris: Ernst Flammarion, 1908), p. 150.*

I

PROLOG
~
PROLOGUE

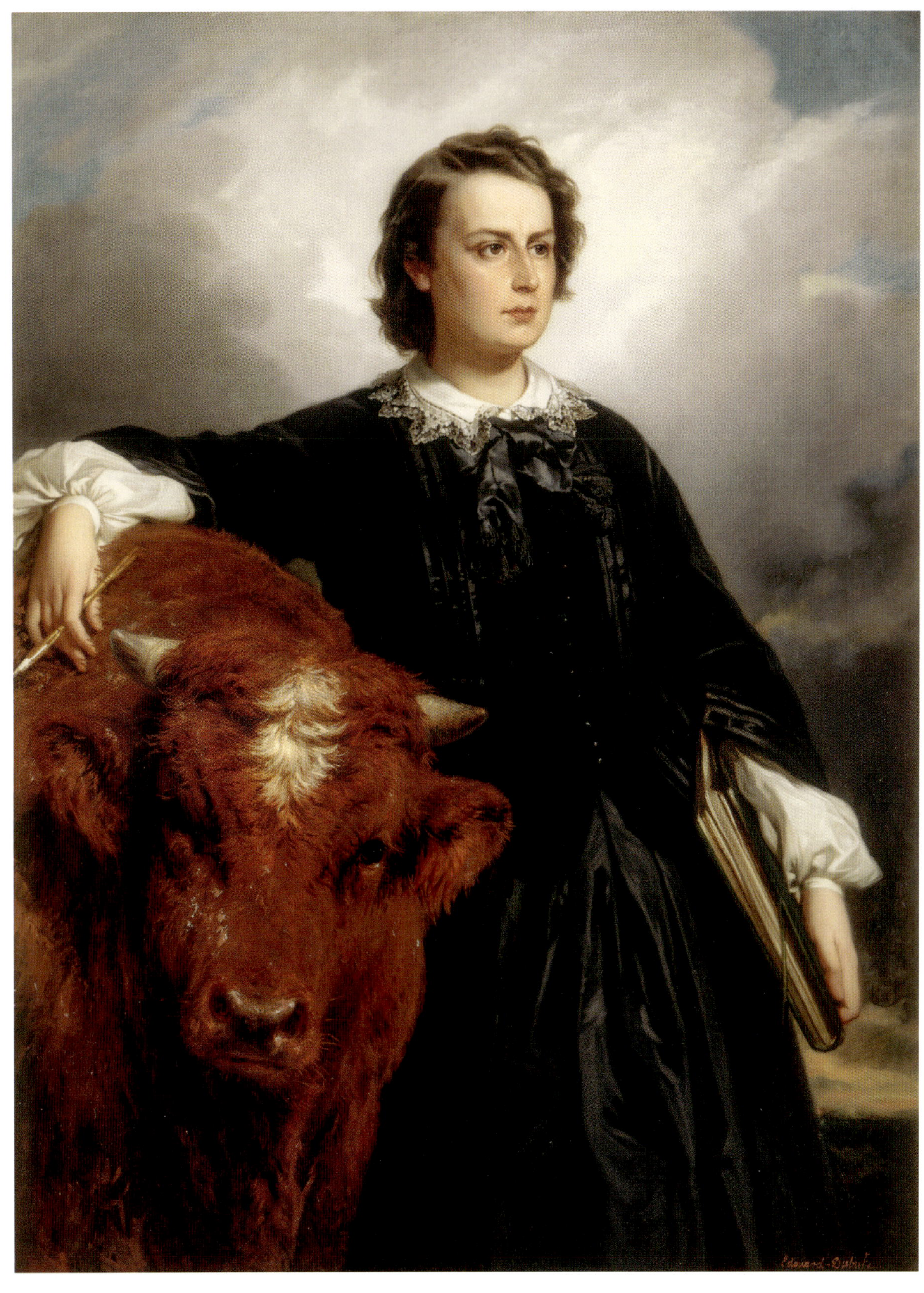

Édouard Dubufe
Portraît du peintre Rosa Bonheur aux côtés d'un bovidé, 1857
Porträt der Malerin Rosa Bonheur mit einem Stier ~
Portrait of the Painter Rosa Bonheur with a Bull

II MODERNES ARKADIEN

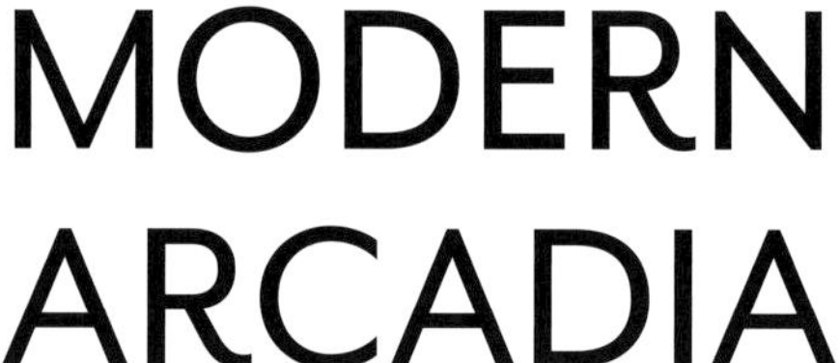

MODERN ARCADIA

1

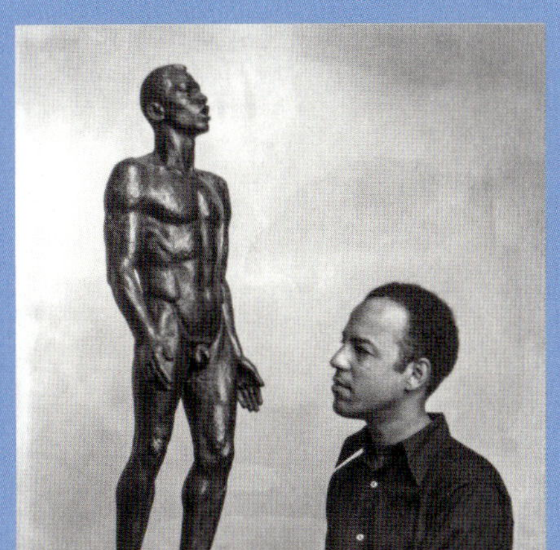

2

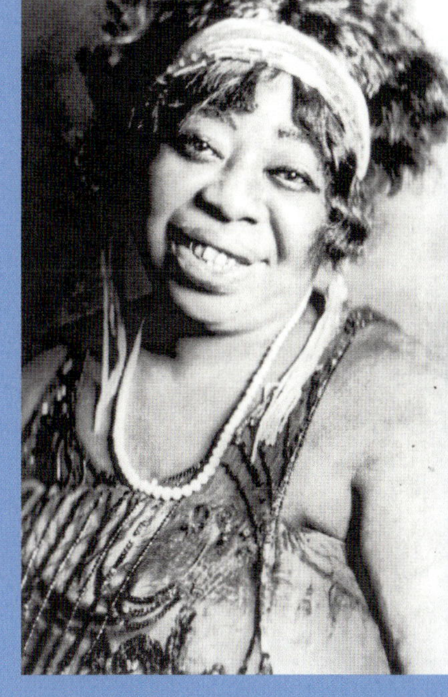

3

Gladys Bentley

5

GAY REBEL OF THE HARLEM RENAISSANCE

Selections from the Work of Richard Bruce Nugent

RICHARD BRUCE NUGENT

Edited and with an Introduction by Thomas H. Wirth

4

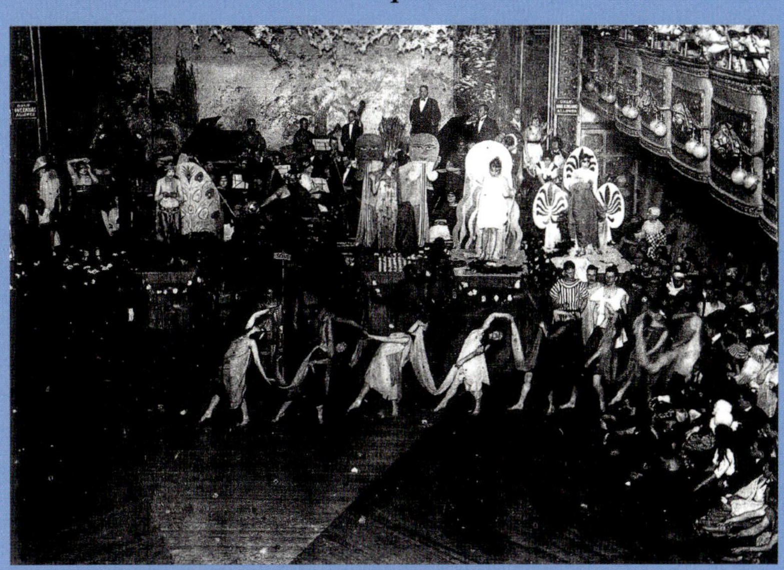

1

Richmond Barthé, undatiert

Der Schwarze US-amerikanische Künstler schuf im Umfeld der literarischen und künstlerischen Bewegung der Harlem Renaissance Skulpturen, die den Schwarzen männlichen Körper zu einem Verhandlungsort seiner Homosexualität werden ließen.

~

Richmond Barthé, undated

The African American artist Richmond Barthé was part of the Black literary and artistic movement known as the Harlem Renaissance, creating sculptures in which the Black male body became a site for negotiating his own homosexuality.

2

Gertrude „Ma" Rainey, um 1923

Ma Rainey war eine der einflussreichsten Schwarzen US-amerikanischen Bluessänger*innen. Sie wurde 1925 von der Polizei in Chicago wegen einer sogenannten Lesbenparty verhaftet und reagierte mit ihrem Song *Prove It on Me Blues* (1928) auf Gerüchte über ihre Sexualität.

~

Gertrude "Ma" Rainey, ca. 1923

Ma Rainey was among the most influential African American blues singers. She was arrested in 1925 by Chicago police for hosting what was alleged to be a lesbian party. She responded to rumors about her sexuality with the song Prove It on Me Blues *(1928).*

3

Gladys Bentley, zwischen 1946 und 1949

Die Schwarze US-amerikanische Bluessänger*in und Drag-Entertainer*in trat im Umfeld der Harlem Renaissance in den 1920er-Jahren in verschiedenen homosexuellen Clubs in New York auf und war bekannt für ihre provokanten Songtexte und ihre offen gelebte lesbische Sexualität.

~

Gladys Bentley, between 1946 and 1949

The African American blues singer and drag entertainer Gladys Bentley performed in several New York queer clubs during the Harlem Renaissance of the 1920s. She was famous for her provocative lyrics and openly expressing her lesbian sexuality.

4

Webster Hall war neben der Hamilton Lodge ein für die queere Community historisch bedeutender Veranstaltungsort in Greenwich Village in New York, in dem in den 1910er- und 1920er-Jahren die ersten Drag Balls stattfanden. Diese gehörten zu den wenigen Ereignissen, bei denen sich Drags offen zeigen durften.

~

Webster Hall, alongside Hamilton Lodge, was one of the leading venues for the queer community of Greenwich Village in New York, where the first drag balls were celebrated in the 1910s and 1920s. These were among the few events where people could openly appear in drag.

5

Der Schwarze US-amerikanische Künstler, Schriftsteller und Schauspieler Richard Bruce Nugent war als „schwuler Rebell" eine der prägenden Figuren der Harlem Renaissance. Homoerotische Freundschaften verbanden ihn mit Künstler*innen, Literat*innen und Philosoph*innen wie zum Beispiel Richmond Barthé, Langston Hughes oder Alain Locke.

~

The African American artist, writer, and performer Richard Bruce Nugent, a "gay rebel," was one of the key figures of the Harlem Renaissance. He maintained homoerotic friendships with artists, writers, and philosophers such as Richmond Barthé, Langston Hughes, and Alain Locke.

Richard Bruce Nugent

Schatten

Ein Umriss
Auf dem Mondgesicht
Bin ich.
Ein dunkler Schatten im Licht.
Ein Umriss bin ich
Auf dem Mondgesicht
Ohne Farbe
Und Leuchtkraft
Doch umso klarer
In meinem
Dunkel,
Schwarz auf dem Mondgesicht.
Ein Schatten bin ich,
Wachsend im Licht,
Nicht leicht zu verstehen
Wie der Tag
Doch leichter zu sehen
Denn ich
Bin ein Schatten im Licht.

~

Shadow

Silhouette
On the face of the moon
Am I.
A dark shadow in the light.
A silhouette am I
On the face of the moon
Lacking color
Or vivid brightness
But defined all the clearer
Because
I am dark,
Black on the face of the moon.
A shadow am I
Growing in the light,
Not understood
As is the day,
But more easily seen
Because
I am a shadow in the light.

Richard Bruce Nugents Gedicht von 1925 wurde auf Initiative von Langston Hughes zuerst in der Zeitschrift *Opportunity* veröffentlicht.

~

Richard Bruce Nugent's 1925 poem was first published in the journal Opportunity *at the urging of Langston Hughes.*

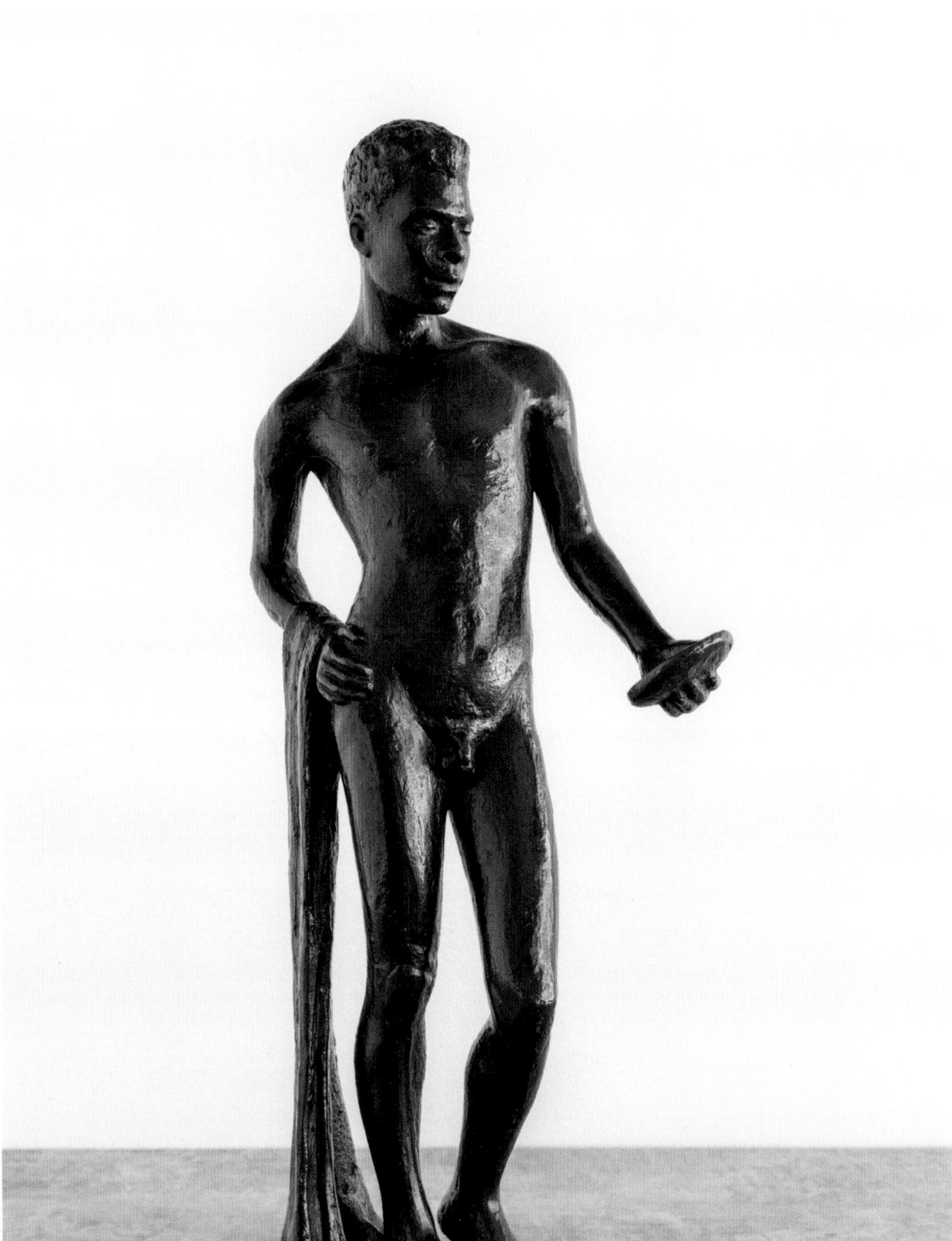

Richmond Barthé
Black Narcissus, 1929
Schwarzer Narziss

Richmond Barthé
Faun, 1942

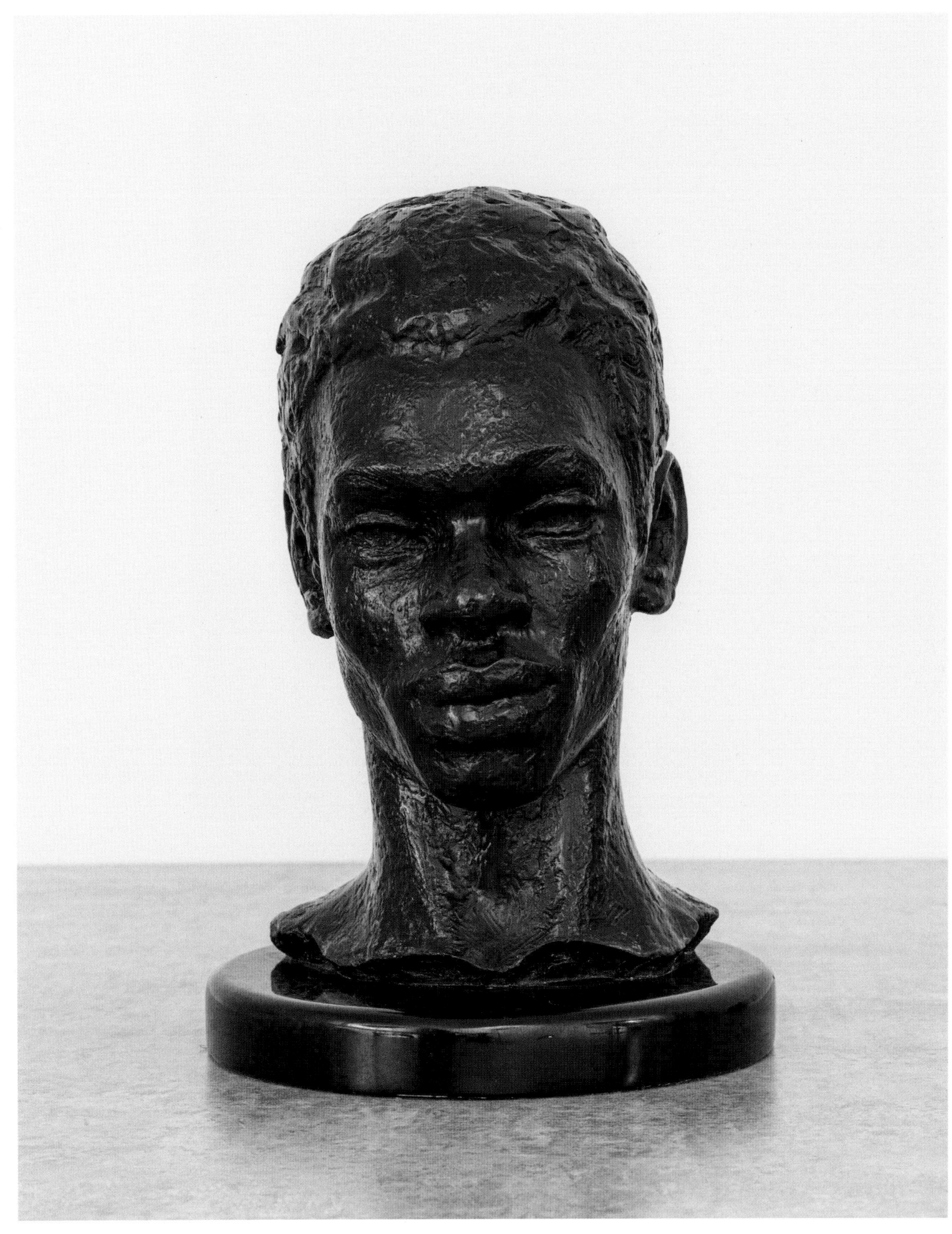

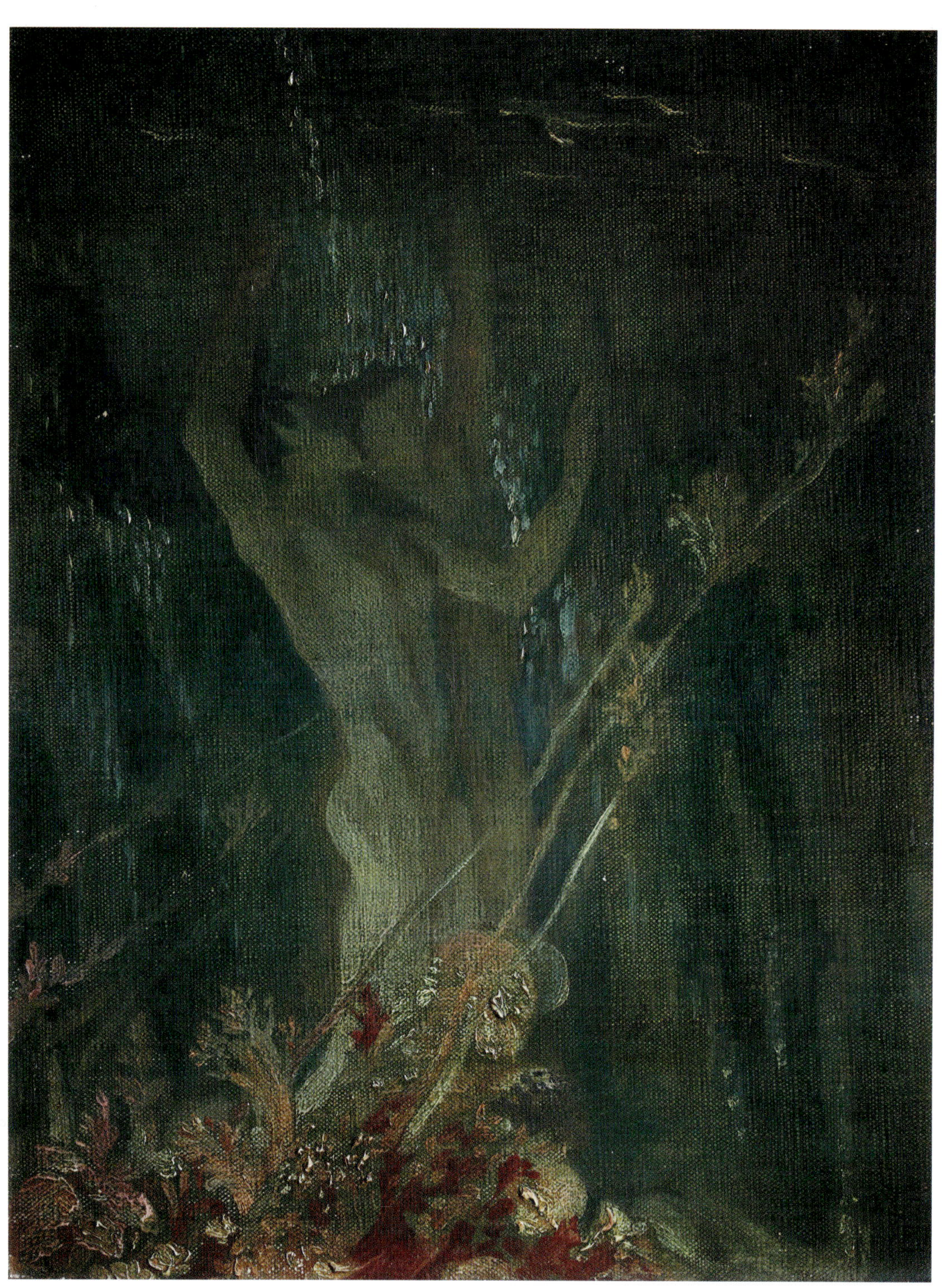

Glyn Warren Philpot
Two Figures under the Sea, 1914–1918
Zwei Figuren unter dem Meer

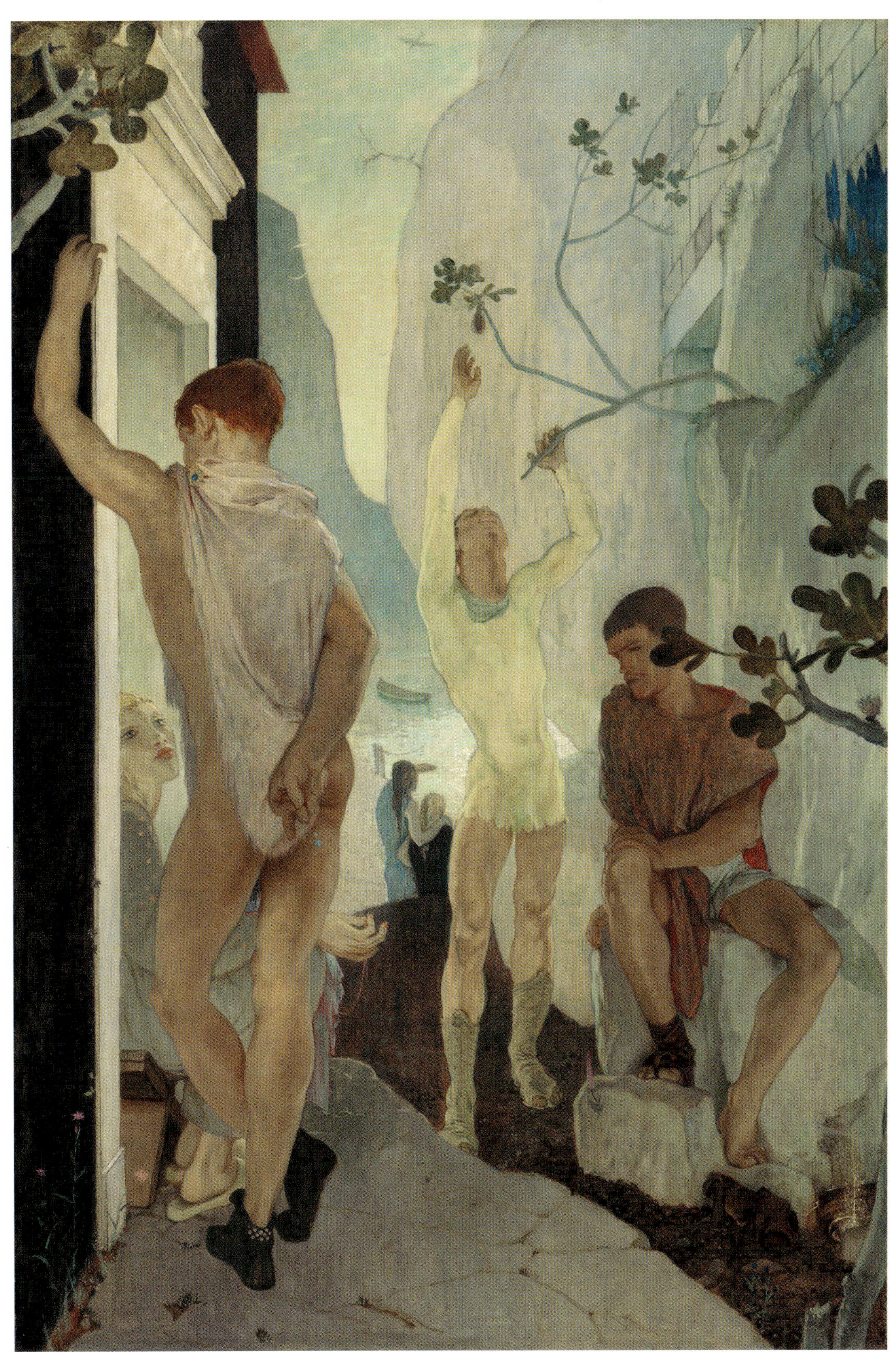

Glyn Warren Philpot
Penelope, 1923

Ludwig von Hofmann
Die Quelle, 1913
The Source

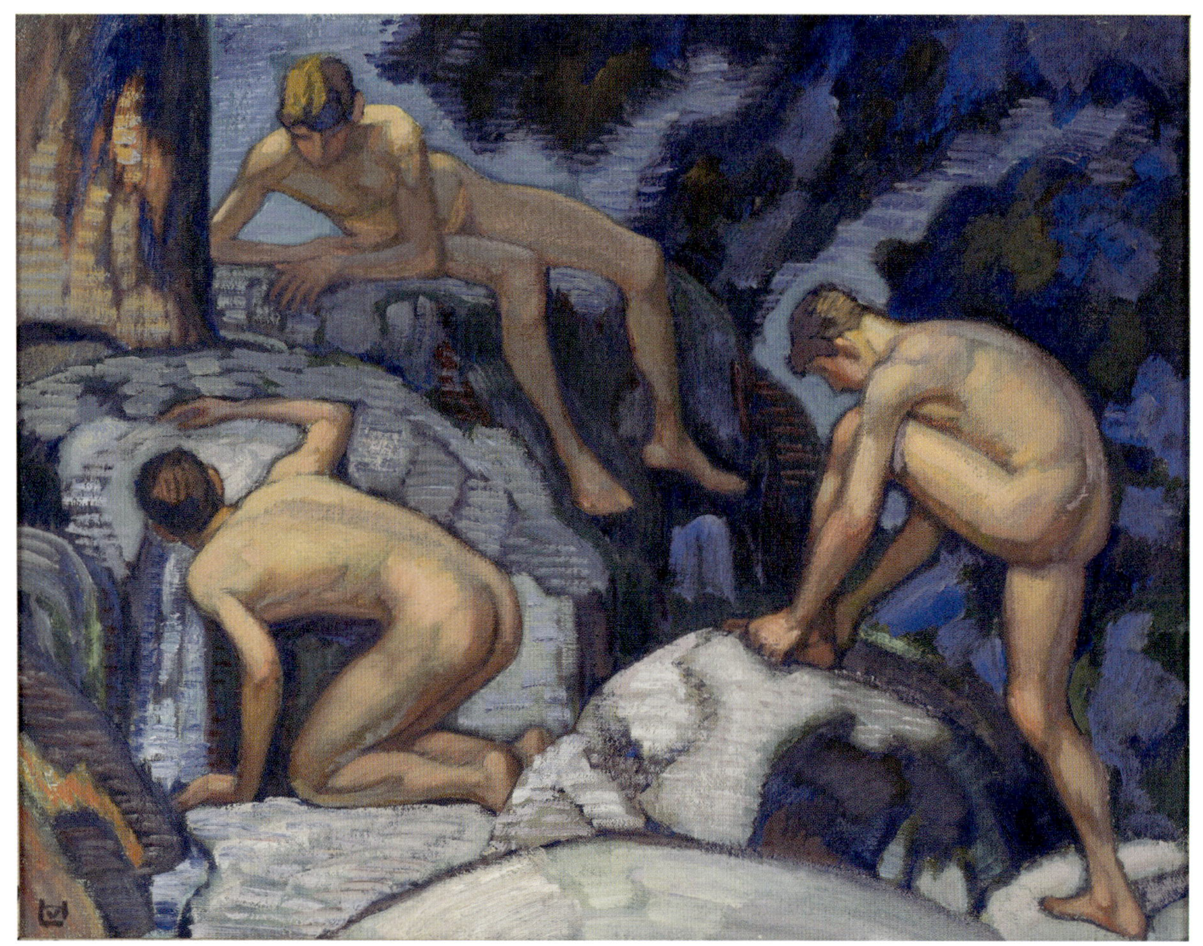

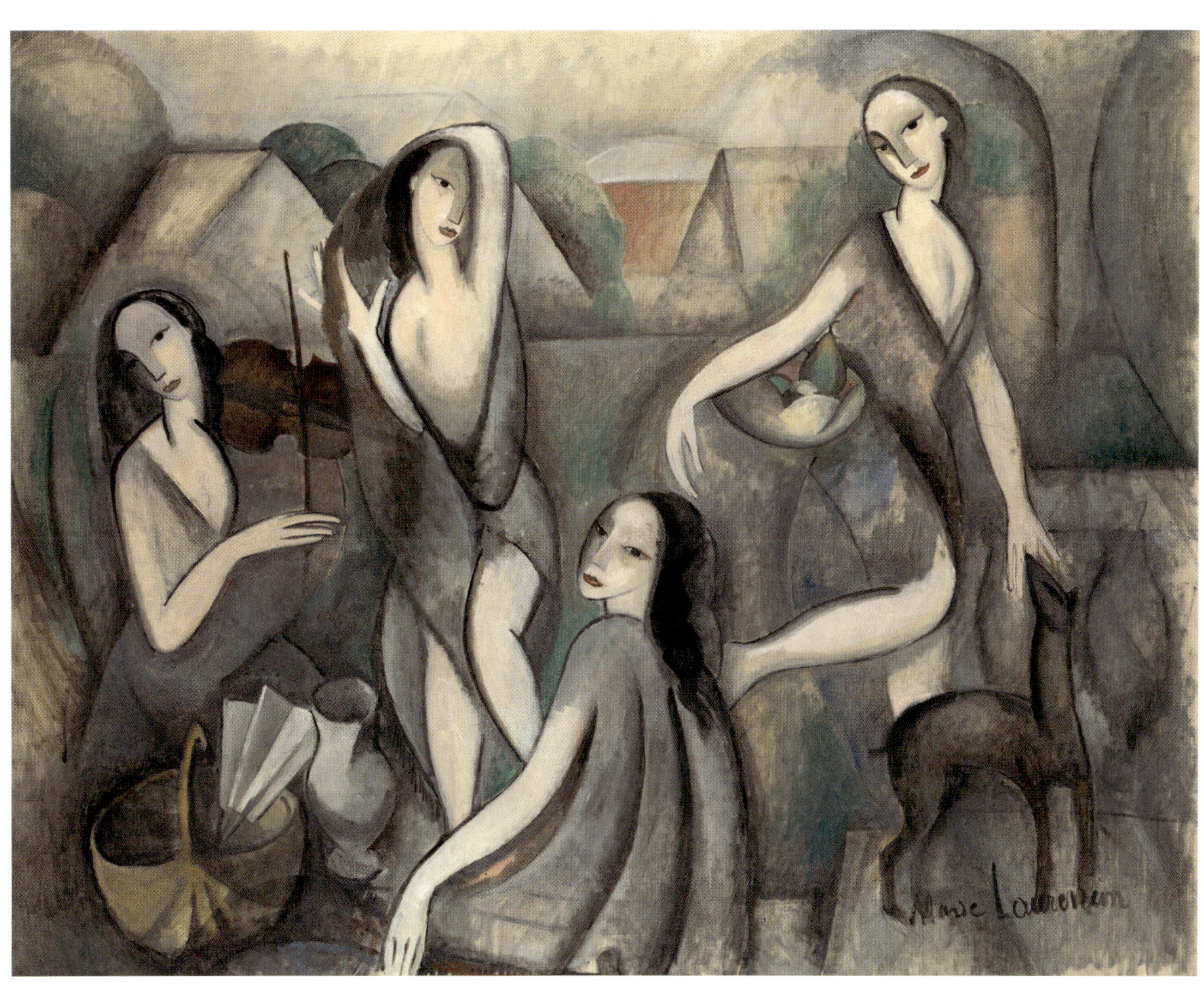

Marie Laurencin

Jeunes femmes, 1910
Junge Frauen ~ *Young Women*

Dame Ethel Walker

Two Models Resting, 1939

Zwei Modelle beim Ausruhen

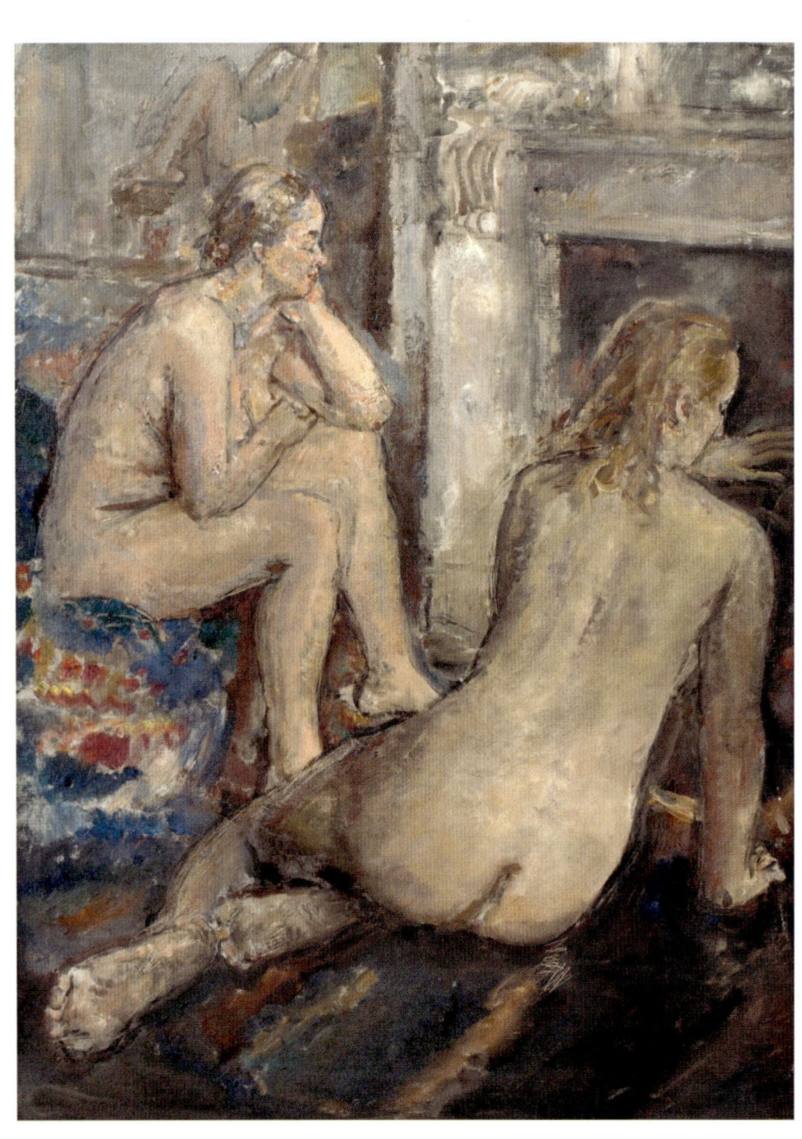

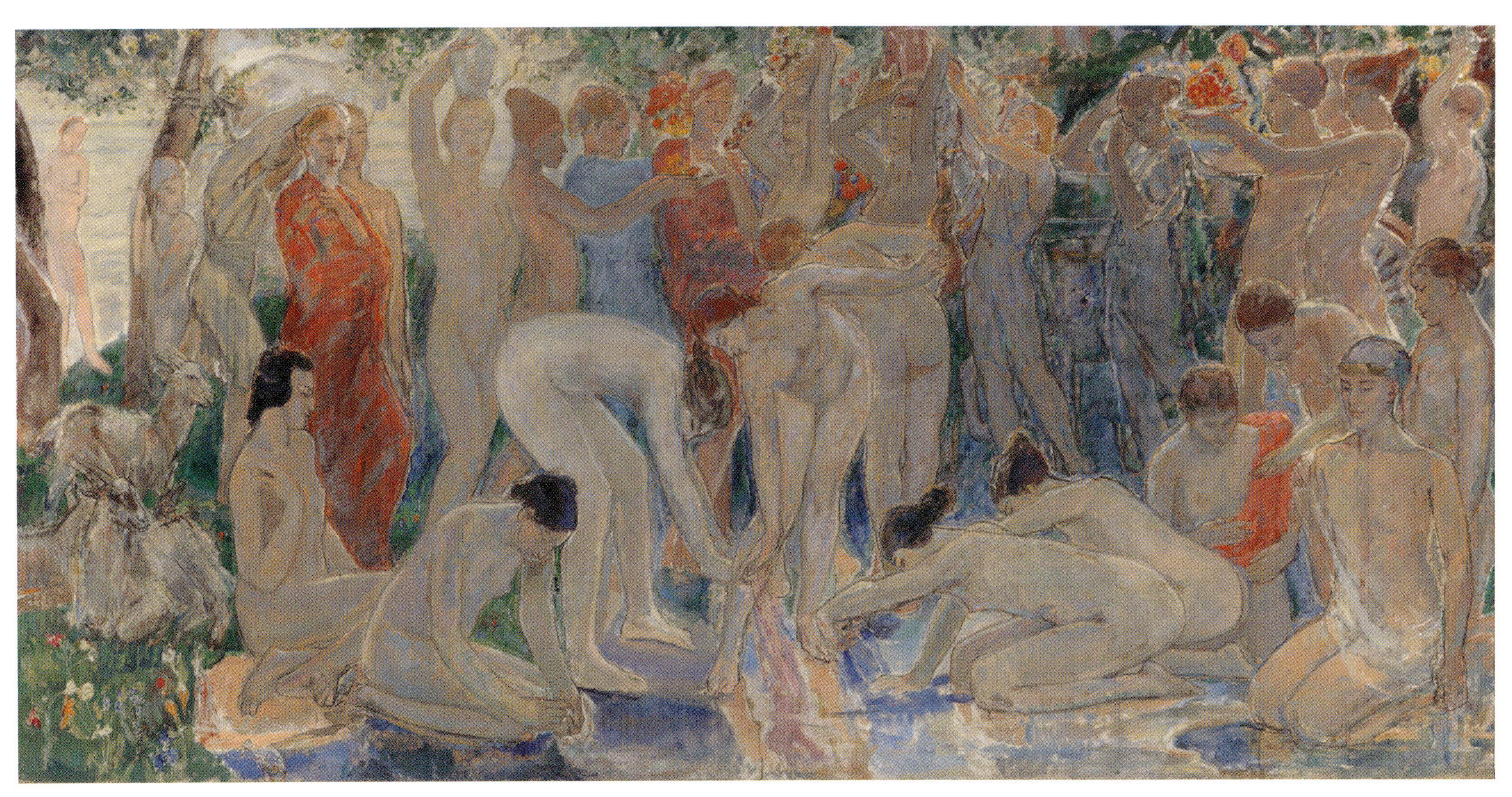

Dame Ethel Walker
Decoration: The Excursion of Nausicaa, 1920
Dekoration: Der Ausflug der Nausicaa

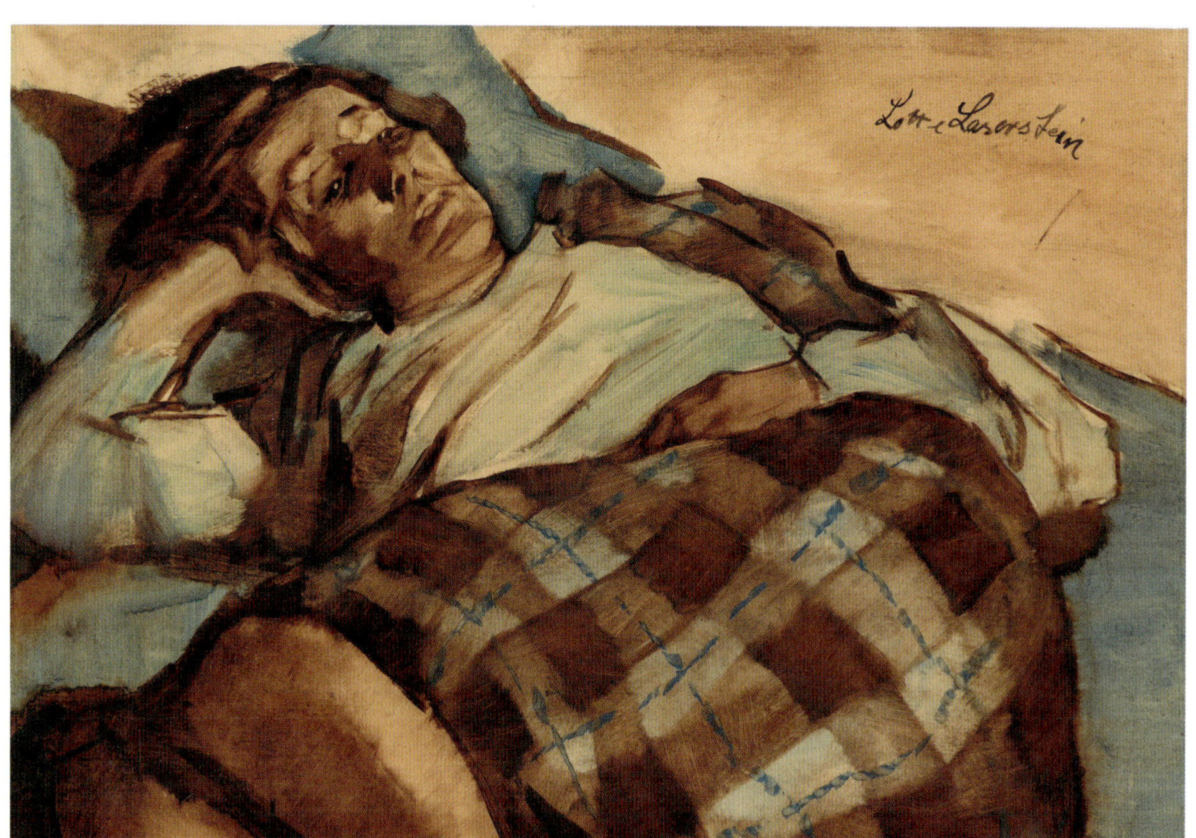

Lotte Laserstein
Das Karo-Kostüm, um ~ *ca.* 1931
The Plaid Suit

Lotte Laserstein

Ich und mein Modell, 1929/30
I and My Model

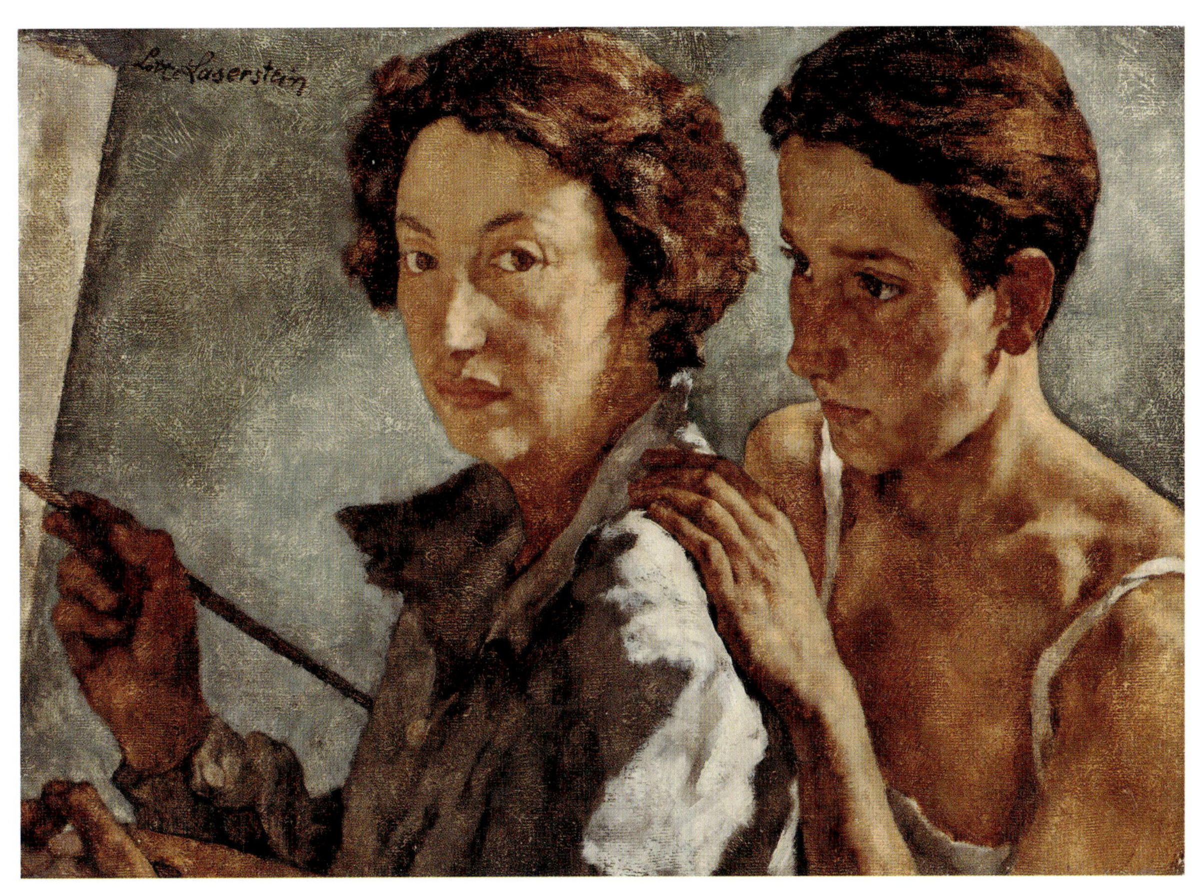

DIE VERDRÄNGTE ÄHNLICHKEIT

~e

THE REPRESSED RESEMBLANCE

JONATHAN D. KATZ

Die künstlerische Moderne und Homosexualität sind wie zweieiige Zwillinge. Sie gleichen einander kein bisschen, sind jedoch zur selben Zeit entstanden – Mitte der 1850er-Jahre – und haben sich im selben, weitgehend europäischen Kontext entwickelt. Abgesehen von dieser chronologischen Gemeinsamkeit haben sie aber auch in Teilen dieselbe DNA, wie wir sehen werden. Beide stehen für die bewusste Abkehr von der Tradition, für die selbstgewählte Zugehörigkeit zu einer Subkultur und für eine elitäre Ästhetik. Die herrschende Kultur galt ihnen aufgrund dessen als minderwertig, und sie glaubten zugleich, als überlegene stilprägende Instanz deren Mängel beheben zu können. Noch entscheidender: Beide wurden zutiefst missverstanden, ja verachtet, waren aber dennoch der festen Überzeugung, dass die Geschichte auf ihrer Seite sein würde. Und schließlich kommunizierten beide mit ihren jeweiligen Mitgliedern in einer verschlüsselten Sprache, die schwer, wenn überhaupt, zu dechiffrieren war, sofern man nicht zum Club gehörte oder zumindest mit dessen Codes vertraut war. Die diskursiven und visuellen Zeichen von Zugehörigkeit und Inklusion wirkten also wie eine Mauer, die jene fernhielt, die die Codes nicht kannten. Als Gemeinschaften selbstgewählter eingeweihter Personen rechneten sowohl Homosexuelle als auch Modernist*innen mit breiter Ablehnung, bis ihre Zeit kommen würde. Beide gründeten auf hochgradig instrumentalisierten Binaritäten und wurden ebenso sehr über das definiert, was sie nicht waren, wie über das, wofür sie eintraten. Tatsächlich nahmen beide so völlig unterschiedliche Formen an, dass ihre ursprüngliche definitorische Kohärenz nur in der Gegenüberstellung mit den vertrauten, vorherrschenden Praktiken erkennbar wurde, die sie ablehnten. Ihre Verbundenheit ist kein Zufall: Die Moderne wurde bei aller stilistischen, thematischen und formalen Vielfalt zum bevorzugten Format, um sexuelle Differenz zu kommunizieren. Daher waren viele namhafte Modernist*innen selbst homosexuell oder repräsentierten Homosexualität, auch wenn sie selbst nicht homosexuell waren. Diese Tatsache verweist auf ein letztes, entscheidendes Korrelat beider: Sie waren zukunftsorientiert und richteten den Blick stets nach vorn, auch wenn sie, was häufig der Fall war, auf die Vergangenheit verwiesen.

Umso verwunderlicher daher, dass ihre Beziehung so wenig beachtet wird. Vermutlich liegt es daran, dass sie oberflächlich betrachtet so grundverschieden erscheinen: die eine der ästhetischen, die andere der sozialen Form verpflichtet.[1] Beide eint jedoch der feste Glaube an eine bessere, andere Zukunft, in der ästhetische wie persönliche Freiheit herrschen und Unterdrückung nur noch als Erinnerung existiert. Die queere Moderne erweitert diesen politischen Anspruch noch einmal erheblich, indem sie eine neue Gesellschaft entwirft, die sich selbst als offen und experimentell versteht und Werke schafft, die Impuls oder Verführung zu einer alternativen Lebensweise sein können. Hierin liegt eine weitere Gemeinsamkeit der neuen ästhetischen und sexuellen Definitionen und Kategorien: Beide fungieren als Zukunftslaboratorien und stehen für eine offene, experimentelle Ästhetik, die wirklich daran glaubt, dass man etwas nicht abstrakt erfassen kann, sondern es ausprobieren muss, wenn es überzeugen soll. Aber wie sollte diese neue queere, moderne Gesellschaft aussehen? Es fällt erstaunlich schwer, unsere Identität ohne Sexualität zu denken – nicht ohne Sex, das ist etwas anderes –, ohne eine Vorstellung von Begehren entsprechend

1 Die bemerkenswerteste Ausnahme ist Chris Reeds *Art and Homosexuality: A History of Ideas*, Oxford 2011.

Modernism in the arts and homosexuality are fraternal twins. They do not at all look alike, but both were born in the mid-1850s and grew up together in the same largely European context. But they share more than mere chronology, for as we will see, much of their DNA is also shared. After all, modernism and homosexuality both entailed a self-conscious declaration of dissidence from tradition, self-selected membership in a subculture, and an elitist aesthetic perspective that caused them to decry dominant culture while believing they could rectify its shortcomings in their role as superior tastemakers. Even more significantly, both were profoundly misunderstood, even despised, but remained convinced history was on their side. Finally, and most importantly, both addressed their respective membership communities in an encoded language that was difficult, if not impossible to decipher if one were not a member of their club, or at least deeply educated in its ways. Thus, for both, the discursive and visual signs of membership and inclusion were also at the same time a solid barrier that guaranteed exclusion to those ignorant of the codes. As societies of self-selected initiates, both homosexuals and modernists anticipated and expected widespread rejection before their day would come. Both were founded in highly instrumentalized binaries, defined as much against what they were not, as for what they endorsed. Indeed, both entailed such widely different forms that they achieved their most pristine definitional coherence only when viewed against the more familiar, dominant practices that they opposed. And their fellowship is no mere coincidence: modernism became the privileged format for communicating sexual difference, though this modernism varied considerably, whether we are discussing format, style, subject matter, or all three. That is why so many of the leading modernists were themselves homosexual or represented homosexuality even if they were not. This fact points to one final, and very important correlate for both, they were both future oriented, always facing forward, even when they, as they often did, pointed back.

Strange, then, that their rapport is so little noted; I assume it is because they appear superficially so radically different, one dedicated to aesthetic, and the other to social, form.[1] But the abiding faith for both is a better, different future, one where aesthetic and personal freedoms rule, and repression is but a memory. Queer modernism doubles up on that political charge, attempting to imagine a new society that understands itself as open and experimental, producing works that can function as prods or seductions to another way of living. This is yet a further quality shared by new aesthetic and new sexual definitions and categories; both constitute laboratories for possible futures, an open, experimental aesthetic that really believes that one cannot know something in the abstract—it must be attempted if it is to compel conviction.

But what would this new queer modernist society look like? It is surprisingly difficult to imagine our identity without sexuality—not without sex, which is a very different thing—but rather absent a conception of desire categorized according to our now familiar homo/hetero binary. Yet before the middle

1 The most notable exception to this is Chris Reed's *Art and Homosexuality: A History of Ideas* (Oxford: Oxford University Press, 2011).

der vertrauten Homo/Hetero-Binarität. Bis zur Mitte des 19. Jahrhunderts wurde Sex als erlaubt oder verboten, legal oder illegal, tugend- oder sündhaft bewertet. Sex war jedoch nicht starr an eine dauerhafte Kategorie gebunden, die auf dem Geschlecht der beteiligten Person(en) beruhte. Noch entscheidender ist: Sex wurde noch nicht als Auslöser für eine ganze Reihe von Charakterzügen, Verhaltensweisen und psychischen Konstrukten angesehen, die scheinbar nichts mit dem Akt selbst zu tun haben. Oder anders gesagt: Sex musste eine Sexualität erst hervorbringen. Auch vor 1850 gab es selbstverständlich schon die allfälligen Assoziationen mit Weiblichkeit bei Männern oder Männlichkeit bei Frauen, doch galten diese Eigenschaften als unabhängig vom Geschlechtsakt selbst. So wird Captain Whiffle, eine markante Figur in Tobias Smolletts Roman *The Adventures of Roderick Random* (1748; dt. *Die Abenteuer des Roderick Random*), in Aussehen, Kleidung und Verhalten zweifellos als *Queen* beschrieben.[2] Doch dass bestimmte Typen mit nicht normativem Geschlecht oder gar mit gleichgeschlechtlicher Erotik assoziiert wurden, bedeutete nicht, dass jeder gleichgeschlechtliche Sexualakt automatisch in die Kategorie eingeordnet wurde, die wir heute mit Sexualität bezeichnen.

2
Vgl. Tobias Smollett, *The Adventures of Roderick Random*, London 1748, Kap. 34 und 35.

3
Martin Duberman, „'Writhing Bedfellows' in Antebellum South Carolina: Historical Interpretation and the Politics of Evidence", in: *Hidden from History: Reclaiming the Gay and Lesbian Past*, hrsg. von Martin Duberman, Martha Vicinius und George Chauncey, New York 1989, S. 153–168; der Briefwechsel zwischen James H. Hammond und Thomas J. Withers aus dem Jahr 1826 ist abgedruckt auf den S. 155 bis 157.

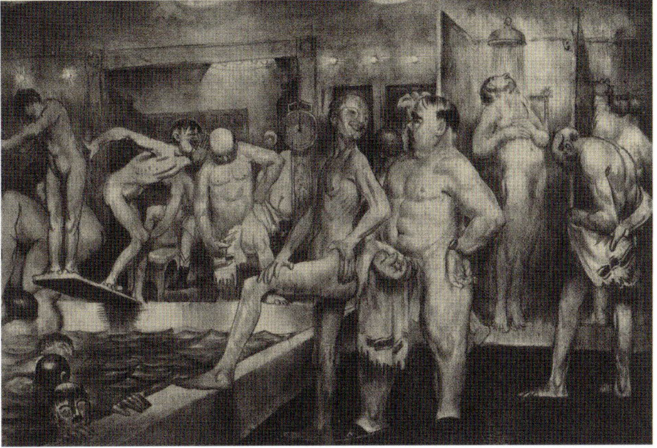

ABB. ~ FIG. 1

George Bellows, *Shower Bath*, first state, 1917
Brausebad, Erster Zustand

Lithografie auf elfenbeinfarbenem Velinpapier
~ *Lithograph on ivory wove paper*, 53 × 67 cm

Vielmehr belegen zahlreiche historische Quellen, dass gleichgeschlechtlicher Sex oft so normativ und selbstverständlich war, dass er keiner weiteren Erwähnung bedurfte. Ja, man legte sich dadurch weder auf einen bestimmten erotischen Weg fest noch auf künftige sexuelle Handlungen. Ein amerikanischer Briefwechsel aus dem 18. Jahrhundert schildert in anschaulicher Drastik eine gleichgeschlechtliche Sexualität der zwei jugendlichen Brieffreunde. Doch mit zunehmendem Alter schreiben sie ebenso selbstverständlich über Freundinnen, Ehefrauen und Kinder.[3] Da die Autoren *weiße* Architekten der Sklaverei aus den Südstaaten waren, verfolgten sie eindeutig keine progressive soziale Agenda. Sex war noch nicht untrennbar mit einer bestimmten Sexualität verknüpft, sodass es Menschen freistand, gleichgeschlechtliche Beziehungen auszuprobieren. Sogar die Definition gleichgeschlechtlicher Sexualität war oft willkürlich und austauschbar. So galten noch in den 1920er-Jahren in den USA nur jene Personen als (im damaligen Sprachgebrauch) „queer", die sich nicht geschlechtskonform

of the nineteenth century, sex was adjudged licit or illicit, legal or illegal, moral or sinful, but it was not locked into a permanent category according to the gender of the other(s) involved. More importantly, sex was not yet taken to catalyze a whole series of character traits, manners, and psychic constructs seemingly far removed from the sex act itself. In other words, sex had yet to yield a sexuality. Before the middle of the nineteenth century, there were, of course, plenty of familiar associations to male effeminacy or female masculinity. But these traits were deemed separate from the sex act itself. Captain Whiffle, for example, a memorable character in the English writer Tobias Smollett's 1748 novel *The Adventures of Roderick Random* is described in appearance, dress, and manners as a *queen*, no doubt.[2] But the fact that there were certain types associated with non-normative gender and even same-sex erotics was different from suggesting that every act of same-sex sexuality fell under a binary categorization we would term sexuality.

Indeed, ample historical sources testify to the fact that same-sex sex was often so normative and familiar that it did not merit much address, and more significantly still, did not lock one onto a particular erotic path nor predict future sexual acts. One eighteenth-century American exchange of letters is shockingly graphic in its description of same-sex sexuality between its teenage correspondents, but as they age, the letters in turn seamlessly address girlfriends, wives, and children.[3] As the correspondents were white Southern architects of slavery, there is clearly no progressive social agenda at stake. Because sex did not yet equal a sexuality, people were free to dip in and out of same-sex relations. Moreover, the very definition of same-sex sexuality was often quite fungible. For example, we know that as late as the 1920s in America, only the sexual partner who was understood as acting in opposition to their gender was deemed a queer (in the parlance of the time), but his or her chosen partner, through acting in accordance with the norms of their gender, was not, and remained entirely unmarked by their choice of sexual partner. In George Bellows's *Shower Bath*, from 1917 (fig. 1), only one figure in the male couple front and center is a queer. And he is composed of every available stereotype of homosexuality from his leering grin to his hand on his hip, with his buttocks thrust back. His sexual partner, the stockier man, is coded as normatively male, for he is doing what men do, as his curiously starched towel underscores. In short, what mattered according to this frame of reference was not the sex of one's partner, but one's own putative sex in the sex act. Significantly all these definitional issues and conundrums were meaningful largely in a Euro-American cultural context. Throughout most of the rest of the world, same-sex desire was an accepted, even celebrated aspect of human sexuality. Islamic art and poetry, for example, until the middle of the eighteenth century almost invariably featured a man addressing the beloved beauty, who was a boy.[4] And this tradition continues in the Muslim former Soviet satellite states ranging from Afghanistan to Azerbaijan, Turkmenistan, and Kazakhstan. In these regions, there is the tradition of wealthy men choosing a *bacha*

2 See Tobias Smollett, *The Adventures of Roderick Random* (1748), chapters 34 and 35.

3 Martin Duberman, "'Writhing Bedfellows' in Antebellum South Carolina: Historical Interpretation and the Politics of Evidence," in *Hidden from History: Reclaiming the Gay and Lesbian Past*, ed. Martin Duberman, Martha Vicinius and George Chauncey, Jr. (New York: Meridian, 1989), pp. 153–168; the letters between James H. Hammond and Thomas J. Withersfrom from 1826 are reprinted, pp. 155–157.

4 See Thadeus Dowad, "A Mosaic with Missing Parts: Art & 'Homosexuality' in the Modern Middle East & North Africa," in *The First Homosexuals: The Birth of a New Identity, 1869–1939*, by Jonathan D. Katz, exh. cat. Wrightwood 659, Chicago (New York: Monacelli of Phaidon, 2025), pp. 306–314.

verhielten. Der oder die Partner*in, dessen*deren Verhalten den Normen ihres biologischen Geschlechts entsprach, blieb – unabhängig von den Sexualpartner*innen – unmarkiert. In George Bellows' *Shower Bath* von 1917 (Abb. 1) ist nur der eine Part des männlichen Paars in der Mitte queer. Er verkörpert alle gängigen Stereotypen von Homosexualität – vom anzüglichen Grinsen über die Hand in der Hüfte bis hin zum ausgestreckten Gesäß. Sein Partner, der kräftigere Mann, ist hingegen normativ männlich kodiert, denn er tut, was Männer tun, wie sein seltsam starres Handtuch unterstreicht. Kurzum, entscheidend war in diesem Zusammenhang nicht das Geschlecht des Partners, sondern das eigene vermeintliche bzw. angenommene Geschlecht im sexuellen Akt.

Bezeichnenderweise waren all diese Definitionsfragen und -probleme vor allem im europäischen und US-amerikanischen kulturellen Kontext von Bedeutung. In vielen anderen Teilen der Welt war gleichgeschlechtliches Begehren ein akzeptierter, oft sogar gefeierter Teil der menschlichen Sexualität. So wandte sich in der islamischen Kunst und Poesie bis ins 18. Jahrhundert fast ausnahmslos ein Mann an die geliebte Schönheit – einen Jungen.[4] Diese Tradition lebt in den muslimischen, ehemals sowjetischen Satellitenstaaten von Afghanistan bis Aserbaidschan, Turkmenistan und Kasachstan fort. Wohlhabende Männer wählen einen *bacha bazi* aus, einen Jungen, der in den „weiblichen" Künsten des Singens, Tanzens und Verführens von Männern geschult ist. Vermittler kaufen diese Jungen häufig von armen Familien, bilden sie aus und verkaufen sie dann an reiche Landbesitzer. In der Kunst dieser Region existiert eine reiche Tradition der Darstellung von *bacha bazi* (siehe Abb. 2). Obwohl diese Männer Sex mit männlichen Jugendlichen haben, gelten die Jungen nicht als maskulin, da sie in der „weiblichen" Rolle geschult werden. Nach lokaler Definition handelt es sich daher nicht um gleichgeschlechtliche Sexualität.

4
Vgl. Thadeus Dowad, „A Mosaic with Missing Parts: Art & ‚Homosexuality' in the Modern Middle East & North Africa", in: *The First Homosexuals: The Birth of a New Identity, 1869–1939*, hrsg. von Jonathan D. Katz, Ausst.-Kat. Wrightwood 659, Chicago, New York 2025, S. 306–314.

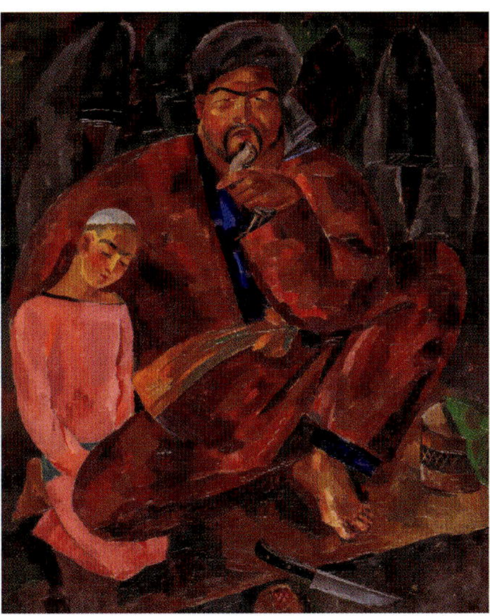

ABB. ~ FIG. 2

Usto Mumin, „*Bai*", 1932
Großgrundbesitzer ~ *Rich Landowner*

Tempera und Öl auf Sperrholz ~
Tempera and oil on plywood, 49 × 39,5 cm
State Museum of Oriental Art, Moscow

bazi, which is essentially a boy trained in the "female" arts of singing, dancing, and seducing men. Often sold by poor families to brokers who train the boys and then sell them on to affluent landowners, there is a rich tradition of representing the *bacha bazi* in the arts of this region, as depicted here (fig. 2). But though these men are having sex with male youths, since the latter are trained in the "female" role, they are not seen as male and thus this is not, by local definition, same-sex sexuality. All these baroque shifts and definitional conundrums have, of course, profound consequences for an exhibition addressing queer modernism, as the first order of business is to determine what is meant by "queer." If this signifies a self-conscious adoption of a homosexual identity, then it must necessarily postdate the 1850s, when the original definition of sexual difference, the first stirrings of an inborn sexuality, were put forward by the German lawyer Karl Heinrich Ulrichs. His early taxonomy of sexuality was entirely gender-based, and he thought of queers as a literal third sex, one in whom a soul of one gender was trapped in a body of the opposite gender. Arguably the world's earliest queer rights advocate, the courageous Ulrichs wrote what was likely the first ever coming out letter to his family and, even more impressively, spoke to a conference of jurists attempting to win legal reform, knowing that he would surely be shouted down, as indeed he was. While his third sex nomenclature, "uranian" (*Urning* in German), earned a sizeable number of adherents, its highbrow etymology proved a problem. This problem of terminology was then solved by another early queer rights advocate, Karl Maria Kertbeny, an Austro-Hungarian writer, who in disputing the inborn essentialism of Ulrichs's biologized sexuality, instead argued in a 1868 letter to Ulrichs that it was far better to sue for rights on the basis of a universal acceptance of all kinds of erotic desire rather than pin your hopes on minority status, since minority status has obviously hardly helped most minorities.[5] In the end, history harvested what it wanted from each advocate: from Ulrichs came the notion of an essentialized, inborn erotic difference (even if we no longer characterized it as a third sex) and from Kertbeny, the far more self-evident terminology of "homosexual," even if that adoption proved hostile to his argument for the universality of homosexual desire. With that, our modern binary division of sexuality into homosexual and heterosexual was born. We can watch the page turn from a pre- to a post-binary sexuality by attending to the reception of John Singer Sargent's portrait *W. Graham Robertson* from 1894.[6] At the time the work was being completed, sexuality was not yet a significant public issue, though it would become so a year later with the start of the Oscar Wilde trials. There is nothing in the painting per se that telegraphs a homosexual identity for painter or subject. But in 1931, W. Graham Robertson published a memoir that recalled his sessions posing for Sargent in terms so self-evidently queer and campy as to make immediately clear the not-so-secret secret that informs the work. The very picture of Aestheticist style, Robertson was

5
See Karl Heinrich Ulrichs, "Four Letters to His Kinsfolk," in *Sodomites and Urnings: Homosexual Representations in Classic German Journals*, ed. and trans. Michael Lombardi-Nash (Binghamton, NY: Harrington Park, 2006), pp. 1–20.

6
John Singer Sargent, *W. Graham Robertson*, 1894, oil on canvas, 230.5 × 118.7 cm, Tate, London.

All diese barocken Verschiebungen und definitorischen Dilemmata wirken sich selbstverständlich tiefgreifend auf eine Ausstellung aus, die sich mit der queeren Moderne befasst. Denn zunächst muss geklärt werden, was unter „queer" zu verstehen ist. Wenn damit das bewusste Bekenntnis zu einer homosexuellen Identität gemeint ist, dann wird der Begriff in der Bedeutung nach den 1850er-Jahren verwendet, als der deutsche Jurist Karl Heinrich Ulrichs die erste Definition sexueller Differenz vorlegte und von einer angeborenen Sexualität sprach. Seine frühe Einteilung der Sexualität war strikt geschlechtsspezifisch: Für ihn bildeten Queers tatsächlich ein „drittes Geschlecht", bei dem die Seele des einen Geschlechts im Körper des anderen gefangen war. Ulrichs, ein mutiger Pionier, war wohl der erste Verfechter queerer Rechte und schrieb vermutlich den ersten Coming-out-Brief an seine Familie. Noch beeindruckender war, dass er sich bei einer juristischen Konferenz für eine Gesetzesreform einsetzte, obwohl er wusste, dass man ihn niederbrüllen würde – und genau das geschah. Der Begriff „Urning", den er für sein „drittes Geschlecht" prägte, fand zwar viele Anhänger*innen, seine anspruchsvolle Etymologie erwies sich jedoch als problematisch. Dieses terminologische Problem löste ein anderer früher Verfechter queerer Rechte, der österreichisch-ungarische Schriftsteller Karl Maria Kertbeny, der Ulrichs Vorstellung von angeborener, biologisch begründeter Sexualität widersprach. 1868 schrieb er Ulrichs, es sei besser, Rechte auf Grundlage einer allgemeinen Akzeptanz aller Formen erotischen Begehrens zu fordern, statt auf den Minderheitenstatus zu setzen, da dieser den Minderheiten ja erwiesenermaßen auch zuvor kaum geholfen habe.[5]

Die Geschichte nahm sich am Ende von beiden das, was sie wollte: Ulrichs lieferte die Vorstellung angeborener, wesenhafter erotischer Differenz (auch wenn wir diese heute nicht mehr als das „drittes Geschlecht" bezeichnen). Von Kertbeny kam der viel selbstverständlichere Begriff „Homosexuelle*r", obwohl dieser letztlich seiner Überzeugung zuwiderlief, homosexuelles Begehren sei eine menschliche Konstante. Damit war die heutige binäre Einteilung der Sexualität in homosexuell und heterosexuell geboren.

An der Rezeption von John Singer Sargents Porträt *W. Graham Robertson* (1894)[6] lässt sich der Wandel von der Zeit vor dieser binären Einteilung zu der Zeit danach gut nachvollziehen. Als Sargent das Gemälde fertigstellte, war Sexualität noch kein wichtiges Thema in der Öffentlichkeit – was sich ein Jahr später mit den Prozessen gegen Oscar Wilde ändern sollte. Nichts im Bild selbst signalisiert eine homosexuelle Identität des Malers oder des Porträtierten. 1931 veröffentlichte W. Graham Robertson jedoch seine Erinnerungen an die Sitzungen bei Sargent. Sein Ton ist so unverkennbar queer und camp, dass er sofort das gar nicht so geheime Geheimnis hinter dem Werk offenbart. Robertson, Verkörperung des Ästhetizismus, war wohlhabend, gutaussehend, blond und schlank. Manche vermuten in ihm das Vorbild für Dorian Gray in Oscar Wildes *Das Bildnis des Dorian Gray*. In seinem Bericht über die Begegnungen beschreibt er den Künstler als Inbegriff unterdrückter Sexualität und äußeren Anstands. Robertson war 28 Jahre alt, als Sargent ihn bat, ihm Modell zu stehen. Kennengelernt hatten sie sich, als Robertson seine Mutter zu ihren Sitzungen für eines der Gesellschaftsporträts begleitet hatte, mit denen Sargent seinen Lebensunterhalt verdiente.[7] Robertson, selbst Maler und ein talentierter Erzähler, gibt sich in seinen

5
Vgl. Karl Heinrich Ulrichs, „Four Letters to His Kinsfolk", in: *Sodomites and Urnings: Homosexual Representations in Classic German Journals*, hrsg. und übers. von Michael Lombardi-Nash, Binghamton 2006, S. 1–20.

6
John Singer Sargent, *W. Graham Robertson*, 1894, Öl auf Leinwand, 230,5 × 118,7 cm, Tate, London.

7
John Singer Sargent, *Mrs. Graham Moore Robertson (Marion Greatorex Robertson)*, 1880, Öl auf Leinwand, 159 × 102,5 cm, Watts Gallery – Artists' Village, Compton, Surrey.

wealthy, good looking, blond, and thin. Indeed, there is speculation that he may have served as the living model for Dorian Gray in Wilde's *The Picture of Dorian Gray*. In Robertson's account of what it was like sitting for the artist, Sargent is a model of repression and decorum. Robertson was twenty-eight years of age when he was asked to pose, having met the artist when he accompanied his mother during her own sittings, for one of Sargent's bread-and-butter society portraits.[7] Robertson was himself a painter and a gifted raconteur, and in his narrative of the making of the portrait, published almost four decades later, he does his best to drop as many hints as he possibly can about Sargent's sexuality without ever having to name it. Robertson tells us that when he arrived at the studio at the duly appointed hour, Sargent decided to pose him dressed in a heavy winter coat in the midst of a hot summer. With a disingenuousness air, Robertson wonders, "Why a very thin boy (I then looked no more) in a very tight coat should have struck him as a subject worthy of treatment I never discovered."[8] Robertson then goes on to narrate how he became faint in the midst of posing, and his tale is so littered with raised eyebrows and campy allusions to homosexuality as to make it comic: "I had been standing for over an hour and saw no reason why I should not go on for another hour, when I became aware of what seemed a cold wind blowing in my face accompanied by a curious 'going' at the knees. I tried to ask for a rest, but found that my lips were frozen stiff and refused to move. Hundreds of years passed—I suppose about twenty seconds. Sargent glanced at me. 'What a horrid light there is just now,' he remarked. 'A sort of green—' He looked more steadily. 'Why, it's *you*!' he cried, and seizing me by the collar, rushed me into the street, where he propped me up against the door-post. It was a pity that Oscar Wilde opposite was not looking out of the window: the 'wonderful possibilities of Tite Street' were yet unexhausted." Tite Street was famously the street in Chelsea where Oscar Wilde lived, and the image of the artist holding the "boy" up by his fur collar against the doorpost opposite Wilde's home was the visualization of exactly that which Robertson refused to name but still expected to communicate. Such, I want to argue is the chief strength of art as an historical archive of sexual difference. By showing, but not saying, it devolves interpretive responsibility onto the viewer, allowing that which is not said to nonetheless be understood. And of course, not saying, but merely showing, offered the artist a significant political advantage, since any attempt to label the work as homosexual could be met with an incriminating, "well, maybe to your eye, but..." This is the distinction between Édouard Dubufe's *Portrait du peintre Rosa Bonheur aux côtés d'un bovidé* (1857, cat. p. 27) before the word homosexuality was coined, and Lotte Laserstein's *Ich und mein Modell,* which was completed after. In the Dubufe canvas, Bonheur's famously butch persona is merely intimated in her ability to enlist a dangerous bull, that traditional masculinist symbol, as her personal attribute. But in every other respect, such as dress, comportment, etc., she in no way breaks with Victorian constructs around femininity. By contrast,

7 John Singer Sargent, *Mrs. Graham Moore Robertson (Marion Greatorex Robertson)*, 1880, oil on canvas, 159 × 102.5 cm, Watts Gallery – Artists' Village, Compton, Surrey.

8 See W. Graham Robertson, *Life Was Worth Living: The Reminiscences of W. Graham Robertson* (New York: Harper & Brothers, 1931), pp. 233–244, for a full description of the incident; here and the following quotation, pp. 237–238, 236.

fast 40 Jahre später veröffentlichten Memoiren alle Mühe, so oft wie möglich auf Sargents Sexualität anzuspielen, ohne sie je direkt zu benennen.

Robertson erschien pünktlich im Atelier, und Sargent beschloss mitten im heißen Sommer, ihn in einem dicken Wintermantel posieren zu lassen. Nicht ganz ehrlich fragt sich Robertson: „Warum ein sehr dünner Junge (damals sah ich nicht nach mehr aus) in einem sehr engen Mantel ihm als würdiges Motiv erschien, habe ich nie herausgefunden."[8] Er berichtet weiter, wie ihn beim Posieren eine Ohnmacht überkam. Seine Schilderung ist so voller Ironie und Anspielungen auf Homosexualität, dass sie schon komisch wirkt: „Ich hatte bereits über eine Stunde gestanden und sah keinen Grund, weshalb ich dies nicht noch eine weitere Stunde tun sollte, als ich einen kalten Luftzug im Gesicht spürte und merkte, wie meine Knie seltsam ‚weich' wurden. Ich wollte um eine Pause bitten, aber meine Lippen waren steif vor Kälte und bewegten sich nicht. Hunderte von Jahren vergingen – ich schätze etwa zwanzig Sekunden. Sargent betrachtete mich ‚Was für ein abscheuliches Licht', sagte er. ‚Irgendwie grünlich …' Er blickte mich unverwandt an. ‚Ach, das sind Sie!', rief er, packte mich am Kragen und schleifte mich auf die Straße, wo er mich gegen einen Türpfosten lehnte. Schade, dass Oscar Wilde von gegenüber nicht aus dem Fenster blickte: Die ‚wunderbaren Möglichkeiten der Tite Street' waren noch nicht ausgeschöpft." Die Tite Street war bekannt als die Straße in Chelsea, in der Oscar Wilde lebte. Das Bild des Künstlers, der den „Jungen" am Pelzkragen gegen den Türpfosten gegenüber von Wildes Haus drückt, war die genaue Visualisierung dessen, was Robertson selbst nicht benennen wollte, aber dennoch zu vermitteln hoffte. Darin, so behaupte ich, liegt die größte Stärke der Kunst als historisches Archiv sexueller Differenz. Indem sie zeigt, ohne zu benennen, überträgt sie die Verantwortung für die Deutung auf die Betrachter*innen und erlaubt es, dass das Ungesagte dennoch verstanden wird. Zugleich verschaffte das bloße Zeigen, aber nicht Benennen dem Künstler einen wichtigen politischen Vorteil: Jeder Versuch, das Werk als homosexuell zu etikettieren, ließ sich in eine entlastende Verdächtigung umkehren: „Na ja, vielleicht in deinen Augen, aber …"

Das unterscheidet Édouard Dubufes *Portrait du peintre Rosa Bonheur aux côtés d'un bovidé* (1857, Kat., S. 27), entstanden vor der Prägung des Begriffs „Homosexualität", von dem späteren Bild Lotte Lasersteins *Ich und mein Modell* (1929/30, Kat., S. 41). Dubufe deutet die Persönlichkeit der als Butch bekannten Bonheur lediglich an, indem er ihr einen gefährlichen Stier, das traditionell maskulinistische Symbol, als Attribut beigibt. In Kleidung, Haltung und allen übrigen Aspekten bleibt die Dargestellte jedoch den viktorianischen Konstrukten von Weiblichkeit verpflichtet. Lasersteins *Ich und mein Modell* hingegen zeigt eine intime, körperliche Nähe zwischen der Künstlerin und ihrem bevorzugten Modell, ihrer mutmaßlichen Geliebten Traute Rose. 1929/30 ist es Laserstein möglich, nicht nur eine lesbische Identität zu leben, sondern sie auch sichtbar zu machen. Durch ein Konzept kollektiver Identität und getragen von einer größeren Gemeinschaft weiß sie, dass ihre Selbstverortung in einer Minderheit ein Publikum findet, zumindest eines, das sich in ihrer Darstellung zusammen mit ihrer Geliebten wiedererkennt. Ungewöhnlich ist jedoch die Unmittelbarkeit, mit der Laserstein ihre Sexualität darstellt. Die meisten queeren Künstler*innen wählten eher einen produktiven Mittelweg und schufen Werke, die innerhalb einer entsprechend sensibilisierten Subkultur

8
Vgl. W. Graham Robertson, *Life Was Worth Living: The Reminiscences of W. Graham Robertson*, New York 1931; eine vollständige Beschreibung des Vorfalls findet sich auf S. 233 bis 244; dieses und das folgende Zitat stammen von S. 237 bis 238, 236.

Ich und mein Modell (1929/30, cat. p. 41) by Laserstein figures an intimate, physical connection between the artist and her favored model, and presumed lover, Traute Rose. By 1929/30, Laserstein not only has the ability to inhabit an extant lesbian identification, but to literally picture it. Enabled by a concept of collective identity and buoyed by a larger community, Laserstein knows she has an audience for her minoritizing self-identification, at minimum an audience that will see itself in her painting with her lover.

But the directness with which Laserstein figures her sexuality is unusual, and most queer artists instead sought out a productive middle ground, crafting images that read as demonstrably queer to a subculture so inclined to view that way, but at the same time, capable of passing muster even within the policed confines of a municipal art museum. In Henry Scott Tuke's *The Critics* (1927, cat. p. 185) painted but two years before the Laserstein, the two youths at the shore greeting a friend in the water can be interpreted as either boyish innocence or knowing eroticism, depending on the perspective of the viewer. Tuke's mainstream success testifies to the fact that his pictorial undecidability enabled his broad success.

By contrast, for American lesbians in Paris, distance from home and family offered a reassuring insulation from provincial expectations, one that enabled a frank depiction of queer identity. In Berenice Abbott's portrait of *Janet Flanner*,[9] we see the artist striving to invent a new iconography for an open lesbian identity. Flanner was a well-known journalist in the United States, working as the Paris correspondent of *The New Yorker*, a key source of information about what was happening in the art world's capital city at the time. But in Abbott's hands, she literally enacts a demasked identification, while dressed mannishly, proffering a very unfeminine, direct gaze. The photograph is declarative to an audience that knows the utility of masks and how mannish clothing might signify.

Another American expatriate, Romaine Brooks, is experimental only in her choice of subject matter, not in terms of style or form. Fantastically wealthy, and thus insulated from the art market and the necessity to sell her work, Brooks instead painted what she wanted as she wanted. Her portrait of her lover, Natalie Barney, often dubbed "L'Amazone,"[10] at once harks back to Édouard Manet's portrait of the same name, but also forward, to the "New Woman" of the 1920s, who was independent, self-sufficient, and capable of challenging men on their own turf, in this instance on horseback. But its style is notably conservative, even if the subject was not. In this regard, we can glimpse an alternative firing of queerness and modernism, for both Brooks and Barney were stridently anti-communist, fearing that their substantial inheritances would be lost if the Bolshevik Revolution were generalized across Europe. This ultimately led them to support fascism and indeed, although American and not Nazis per se, they both elected to remain in Fascist Italy throughout the war, praising the government of Mussolini. For them, what might seem like a paradox, painting a radical lifestyle of lesbian erotic independence in a traditional realist style, made personal sense, looking ahead

9
Berenice Abbott, *Janet Flanner*, 1927, gelatin silver print, 22.6 × 17.2 cm, Prints and Photographs Division, Library of Congress, Washington, DC.

10
Romaine Brooks, *Miss Natalie Barney, "L'Amazone,"* 1920, oil on canvas, 86.5 × 65.5, Musée Carnavalet – Histoire de Paris.

klar als queer lesbar waren, gleichzeitig aber auch innerhalb der streng bewachten Grenzen kommunaler Kunstmuseen bestehen konnten. In Henry Scott Tukes *The Critics* (1927, Kat., S. 185), entstanden nur zwei Jahre vor Lasersteins Bild, unterhalten sich zwei Jugendliche am Ufer mit einem Freund im Wasser. Je nach Blickwinkel der Betrachter*innen können sie entweder als Inbild jugendlicher Unschuld oder als Ausdruck von Erotik unter Eingeweihten interpretiert werden. Tukes breiter Erfolg zeigt, dass gerade diese malerische Uneindeutigkeit den Reiz seiner Bilder ausmachte. Für amerikanische Lesben in Paris hingegen bot die räumliche Distanz zu Heimat und Familie eine beruhigende Isolation von provinziellen Vorstellungen – eine Entfernung, die die offene Darstellung queerer Identität möglich machte. In *Janet Flanner*[9] von 1927 versucht Berenice Abbott, eine neue Bildsprache für eine offen lesbische Identität zu schaffen. Die prominente US-amerikanische Journalist*in Flanner arbeitete als Korrespondent*in für *The New Yorker* in Paris und war eine wichtige Quelle für Berichte aus der damaligen Kunstmetropole der Welt. Auf Abbotts Fotografie trägt sie männliche Kleidung und blickt – sehr unfeminin – direkt in die Kamera, sie inszeniert förmlich eine Demaskierung der Identifikation. Das Foto ist somit eine Deklaration gegenüber Betrachter*innen, die die Nützlichkeit von Masken kennen und die Symbolik männlicher Kleidung verstehen. Eine andere im Ausland lebende Amerikanerin, Romaine Brooks, zeigte sich zwar in der Wahl ihrer Themen experimentierfreudig, nicht aber in Stil und Form. Als ungeheuer vermögende Frau war sie unabhängig vom Kunstmarkt und dem Verkauf ihrer Werke. Sie malte daher, was und wie sie wollte. Das Porträt ihrer Geliebten Natalie Barney, oft als „L'Amazone"[10] bezeichnet, verweist einerseits auf das gleichnamige Bild von Édouard Manet, deutet andererseits aber auch auf die „Neue Frau" der 1920er-Jahre voraus: unabhängig, selbstbestimmt und bereit, Männern auf deren eigenem Terrain, in diesem Fall dem Pferderücken, die Stirn zu bieten. Im Unterschied zur Motivwahl bleibt Brooks im Stil jedoch bemerkenswert konservativ. Hier lässt sich erahnen, wie sich Queerness und Moderne auf andere Weise befeuerten. Brooks und Barney waren überzeugte Antikommunistinnen und fürchteten den Verlust ihres beträchtlichen Erbes, sollte die bolschewistische Revolution auf Europa übergreifen. Aus dieser Angst heraus unterstützten sie den Faschismus. Obwohl sie Amerikanerinnen und per se keine Nazis waren, blieben sie während des gesamten Zweiten Weltkriegs bewusst im faschistischen Italien und priesen die Regierung Mussolinis. Was paradox erscheinen mag – einen radikalen Lebensstil lesbischer erotischer Unabhängigkeit in einem traditionell realistischen Stil zu malen –, ergab für sie persönlich durchaus Sinn: Sie blickten in eine Zukunft lesbischer Freiheit und Unabhängigkeit, griffen dabei aber auf eine Malweise zurück, die Europas ungebrochene Verbindung zur Vergangenheit symbolisierte. Diese Vergangenheit war eine, in der Frauen wie sie an der Spitze der gesellschaftlichen Hierarchie standen – oder zumindest so weit oben, wie es Frauen damals möglich war. Doch als sich Europa dem Zweiten Weltkrieg näherte, wehte ein zutiefst konservativer, antimodernistischer Wind über den Kontinent. Dieses faschistische Klima versprach den queer- und modernefeindlichen Achsenmächten Schutz vor den sozialen Umwälzungen des Kommunismus, allerdings zum scheinbar akzeptablen Preis einer immer aggressiveren polizeilichen Überwachung und Verfolgung sexueller

9
Berenice Abbott, *Janet Flanner*, 1927, Silbergelatineabzug, 22,6 × 17,2 cm, Prints and Photographs Division, Library of Congress, Washington D. C.

10
Romaine Brooks, *Miss Natalie Barney, „L'Amazone"*, 1920, Öl auf Leinwand, 86,5 × 65,5, Musée Carnavalet – Histoire de Paris.

to lesbian freedom and independence even as they looked backwards to a form of traditional painting that signified Europe's unbroken continuity with the past. Moreover, this was a past that put women like them at the top of the social hierarchy—or at least as high as women could get at the time. But as Europe moved closer to the Second World War, profoundly conservative, anti-modernist winds blew across the continent. For the Axis powers, hostile to both queers and modernists, these Fascist winds, promised shelter from Communist social revolutions, but at the apparently acceptable cost of an increasingly aggressive policing and persecution of both sexual and aesthetic revolutionaries, along with Jews, Roma, the disabled, and other vulnerable populations. Presciently, Hannah Höch caricatures the rise of this new fascism in her 1931 satirical collage *Flucht* (cat. p. 239). But in America, amidst economic depression and record unemployment, a queer modernism flourished. Led by the impresario A. Everett ("Chick") Austin, the handsome and charismatic young director of the Wadsworth Atheneum—the country's first public art museum established in the insurance capital of Hartford, Connecticut—queer modernism in America had a home base. Austin was not officially out, but neither did he expend much energy hiding his sexuality. Although married to the daughter of the Chair of his Board of Directors, he repeatedly dropped hints as to his sexuality. For example, for an article in the local newspaper about the curious new house he designed for himself, a house that was extremely wide, but only one room deep, he remarked, "The house is just like me—all façade."[11] His tenure as director not only saw, for example, America's first Picasso exhibition, first Surrealist exhibition, first Bauhaus interiors (designed by Austin himself), but also what is arguably queer modernism's most successful enterprise, the modern opera *Four Saints in Three Acts*, with a libretto by Gertrude Stein and music by Virgil Thomson. Everyone involved in creating the opera was queer, including the choreographer Frederick Ashton (George Platt Lynes, the gay photographer, even took photos of Ashton getting intimate with some of his dancers), set and costume designer Florine Stettheimer (who, though sexually inclined toward men, ran with an all-queer crowd), and of course, Stein and Thomson. Though the Stein libretto makes little conventional sense—and its narrative, if there is one, is impossible to parse—*Four Saints in Three Acts* was an enormous popular success when it premiered in 1934. So much so that the New York railroad ran a special train that left New York City in time for curtain up and returned after the opera was finished. *Four Saints* even toured the country to sold-out audiences everywhere. The most striking aspect of this production in the virulently racist America of the period was its all-Black cast. It was unknown whether American audiences would come out for a modern opera with a Black cast, a book that made little conventional sense, sets fashioned of wrapped cellophane (then newly invented), and an essentially abstract storyline. They need not have worried, as *Four Saint in Three Acts* became a runaway hit, uniformly praised, despite refusing most every norm of the genre.

11 Quoted in Alfred H. Barr, Jr., "Modern Architecture," *The Hound & Horn*, April–June 1930, p. 431.

und ästhetischer Revolutionär*innen sowie von Jüdinnen und Juden, Rom*nja, Menschen mit Behinderung und anderen marginalisierten Gruppen. In ihrer satirischen Collage *Flucht* (1931, Kat., S. 239) karikierte Hannah Höch diesen aufziehenden Faschismus auf geradezu prophetische Weise. Zur gleichen Zeit erlebte die queere Moderne trotz Wirtschaftskrise und Rekordarbeitslosigkeit in den USA eine Blüte. Angeführt vom Impresario Arthur Everett („Chick") Austin, dem jungen, gutaussehenden und charismatischen Direktor des Wadsworth Atheneum Museum of Art – des ersten öffentlichen Kunstmuseums der USA, gegründet in Hartford, Connecticut, der Hauptstadt der Versicherungen –, fand die queere Moderne in Amerika eine Heimstatt. Austin lebte zwar nicht offen schwul, unternahm aber auch keine großen Anstrengungen, seine sexuelle Identität zu verbergen. Obwohl er mit der Tochter des Vorstandsvorsitzenden verheiratet war, ließ er seine Sexualität immer wieder durchblicken. So wurde er in einem Artikel der Lokalzeitung über sein kurioses, selbst entworfenes Haus – ein extrem breites, aber nur ein Zimmer tiefes Gebäude – zitiert mit der Bemerkung: „Das Haus ist genau wie ich – alles Fassade."[11] In seine Amtszeit als Direktor des Wadsworth Atheneum fielen die ersten Ausstellungen zu Picasso und zu den Surrealist*innen sowie die ersten Raumausstattungen im Bauhaus-Stil in den USA (von Austin selbst entworfen). Außerdem realisierte er das womöglich erfolgreichste Projekt der queeren Moderne, die Oper *Four Saints in Three Acts* mit einem Libretto von Gertrude Stein und Musik von Virgil Thomson. Alle an der Entstehung Beteiligten waren queer, darunter der Choreograf Frederick Ashton, der von dem schwulen Fotografen George Platt Lynes sogar in intimen Momenten mit einigen seiner Tänzer fotografiert wurde; die Bühnen- und Kostümbildnerin Florine Stettheimer, die sich trotz ihrer Vorliebe für Männer mit einer rein queeren Clique umgab; und natürlich Stein und Thomson. Obwohl Steins Libretto nach konventionellem Verständnis kaum Sinn ergibt und sich die Handlung, sofern überhaupt vorhanden, nicht erschließt, wurde *Four Saints in Three Acts* nach der Uraufführung 1934 ein großer Publikumserfolg. So groß war der Andrang, dass die New Yorker Eisenbahn einen Sonderzug einsetzte, der die Besucher*innen rechtzeitig zur Vorstellung brachte und sie im Anschluss wieder nach New York zurückfuhr. *Four Saints* tourte durch das ganze Land und war stets ausverkauft. Besonders bemerkenswert im Kontext des damals massiv rassistischen Amerika war die rein Schwarze Besetzung. Es war ungewiss, ob das US-amerikanische Publikum eine moderne Oper mit dieser Besetzung, einem schwer zugänglichen Libretto, einem Bühnenbild aus Zellophan (einer damals neuen Erfindung) und einer im Wesentlichen abstrakten Handlung akzeptieren würde. Doch die Sorge erwies sich als unbegründet. *Four Saints in Three Acts* wurde ein durchschlagender Erfolg und erhielt einhelliges Lob, obwohl die Oper gegen fast alle Konventionen des Genres verstieß.

Während Romaine Brooks' realistischer Stil als modern gelten kann, weil sie selbstbewusste Lesben (und einige Schwule) porträtierte, entwickelte der aus Russland emigrierte Pavel Tchelitchew einen hybriden Stil, in dem sich zahlreiche Einflüsse verbanden, vor allem Surrealismus, Picasso und Elemente der Populärkultur. 1936 wurde Tchelitchew von Chick Austin beauftragt, die jährliche Spendenaktion des Wadsworth Museums zu koordinieren, einen Höhepunkt im Kalender der regionalen High Society. Tchelitchew verwandelte das Museum in ein riesiges Zirkuszelt aus

11 Zit. nach: Alfred H. Barr, „Modern Architecture", in: *The Hound & Horn*, April–Juni 1930, S. 431.

While Romaine Brooks's realist style was modern by virtue of its subject matter of assertive lesbians (and a few gay men), the Russian émigré artist, Pavel Tchelitchew invented a hybrid style, mingling numerous influences, chiefly Surrealism, Picasso, and aspects of popular culture. Tchelitchew was tapped by Chick Austin to direct the annual museum fundraiser for the Wadsworth in 1936, one of the singular high society events in the region's social calendar. He turned the interior of the museum into an enormous circus tent using papier-mâché (so costs would be minimal during the Depression) and also designed costumes out of paper, many also devised by the artist Alexander Calder, who animated paintings shown in the museum as costumes—such as a walking Picasso *Three Musicians*. Tchelitchew also invited his partner, the celebrated New York poet and editor (and beauty) Charles Henri Ford, who brought along several other queer New York poets. Together, these gay men styled themselves the NY Poets and scandalized the local high society by wearing make-up. But that scandal paled in comparison with another one later in the evening, when, drunk, the "Poets" began to push one another into the museum's Late Renaissance central fountain. The combination of paper costumes and water was at best infelicitous, and by evening's end, drunken, nude gay men smeared with make-up were terrifying the conservative, monied crowd. Chick Austin, despite his genius, lost the trust of the Board that night and began his long, slow departure from the museum he loved.

This seamless melding of the queer and the modern to public acclaim began to erode immediately after the Second Word War with the start of the Cold War. Cynically manipulated by right-wing demagogues such as Senator Joseph McCarthy, aided and abetted by the closeted homosexual lawyer Roy Cohn, queers became the face of an internal, domestic threat, easily blackmailed, weak of constitution and conviction, ready to sell the country to the highest bidder. In response, a series of increasingly strict directives were signed by President Dwight D. Eisenhower that essentially prevented anyone who was queer from working in any capacity in government. Soon, witch hunts started, and capable, life-long government employees were hounded out of their jobs, outing many people, and spurring a rash of suicides. Arguably the most homophobic decade ever in American history, this so-called "Lavender Scare" of the 1950s also saw a remarkable efflorescence of queer art making, as a generation of all heterosexual artists, the Abstract Expressionists, who worked very hard to put the macho back into working with one's wrist, gave way to an all queer, intellectual generation of artists, including such defining figures as Robert Rauschenberg, John Cage, Jasper Johns, Agnes Martin, Ellsworth Kelly, Robert Indiana, Louise Nevelson, Leon Polk Smith, and Cy Twombly. Centrally, each of these artists turned their back on the wild expressionism of the previous generation, for self-expression for queers promised not success but censure. Instead, many of these artists, and especially Rauschenberg and his partners Twombly and Johns, and his good friend John Cage, all sought to ask in their work how meaning was

Pappmaché (um die Kosten während der Wirtschaftskrise niedrig zu halten) und entwarf gemeinsam mit dem Künstler Alexander Calder Papierkostüme, die die Gemälde aus der Sammlung in lebende Bilder verwandelten, etwa Picassos *Drei Musikanten*. Tchelitchew lud auch seinen Partner, den berühmten (und attraktiven) New Yorker Dichter und Verleger Charles Henri Ford ein. Dieser brachte einige queere Dichter aus New York mit, die sich als NY Poets bezeichneten, und zusammen schockierten sie die Gesellschaft in Hartford mit ihrem Make-up. Doch dieser Skandal verblasste gegenüber den Ereignissen später am Abend: Betrunken stießen sich die „Poets" in den zentralen Spätrenaissance-Brunnen des Museums. Die Kombination aus Papierkostümen und Wasser war denkbar unglücklich und am Ende des Abends jagten betrunkene, nackte und geschminkte Männer dem betuchten konservativen Publikum einen gehörigen Schrecken ein. Trotz seiner genialen Idee verlor Chick Austin an diesem Abend das Vertrauen des Vorstands. Der Vorfall leitete seinen langsamen Abschied von dem Museum ein, das er so liebte.

Unmittelbar nach dem Zweiten Weltkrieg und mit Beginn des Kalten Kriegs begann die zuvor öffentlich gefeierte Verschmelzung von Queerness und Moderne sich aufzulösen. Zynisch manipuliert von rechten Demagogen wie Senator Joseph McCarthy und unterstützt von dem nicht geouteten homosexuellen Anwalt Roy Cohn, galten queere Menschen nun als Inbegriff einer nationalen Bedrohung von innen: leicht erpressbar, schwach und prinzipienlos, bereit, das Land an den Meistbietenden zu verkaufen. Präsident Dwight D. Eisenhower reagierte mit einer Reihe immer schärferer Richtlinien, die queeren Menschen eine berufliche Tätigkeit für die Regierung faktisch unmöglich machten. Bald begannen Hexenjagden. Qualifizierte Angestellte, die ihr Leben lang in Regierungsbehörden gearbeitet hatten, wurden zwangsgeoutet und aus ihren Ämtern gejagt, was zu einer Suizidwelle führte. Die sogenannte Lavender Scare der 1950er-Jahre, dem wohl homophobsten Jahrzehnt der amerikanischen Geschichte, brachte zugleich eine bemerkenswerte Blüte queerer Kunst hervor. Während die vorangegangene Generation ausschließlich heterosexueller Künstler – die Abstrakten Expressionisten – versucht hatte, mit dem Gestus des Machos aus dem Handgelenk zu arbeiten, formierte sich nun eine ganz und gar queere, intellektuelle Künstler*innengeneration. Zu ihr gehörten Persönlichkeiten wie Robert Rauschenberg, John Cage, Jasper Johns, Agnes Martin, Ellsworth Kelly, Robert Indiana, Louise Nevelson, Leon Polk Smith und Cy Twombly. Sie alle wandten sich von der wüsten Expressivität der älteren Maler ab, denn Selbstausdruck lief für queere Künstler*innen nicht auf Erfolg hinaus, sondern auf Zensur. Stattdessen stellten viele von ihnen, vor allem Rauschenberg und seine Partner Twombly und Johns sowie sein enger Freund Cage, in ihren Werken die Frage, wie Bedeutung vermittelt und untergraben werden kann.

Tatsächlich ließ sich Cage bei seiner legendären Komposition der Stille *4'33"* (1952) von Robert Rauschenbergs *White Paintings* (1951) inspirieren, einer Serie großformatiger Leinwände im Stil der Abstrakten Expressionisten, die jedoch radikal bildlos blieben; Rauschenberg verfügte sogar, dass die *White Paintings*, sollten sie im Laufe der Zeit vergilben, von Dritten mit Fassadenfarbe und Rolle genau so übermalt werden sollten, wie er sie ursprünglich geschaffen hatte. Der zentrale Gedanke dabei war natürlich, dass sie keinerlei expressiven Inhalt haben sollten außer dem, was Betrachter*innen in sie hineinprojizierten. Damit stellten sie das genaue

conveyed and how it might be subverted. In fact, Cage modeled his infamous *4'33"* of silence composition of 1952 on Robert Rauschenberg's 1951 *White Paintings*, a series of canvases of the scale of a typical Abstract Expressionist painting, but resolutely without any image; Rauschenberg even decreed that when the *White Paintings* yellowed in time, they were to be repainted by others using house paint and roller—just as he had painted them originally. The point, of course, was that there was nothing expressive in them, nothing to see save what you, the viewer projected. As a result, they were the very obverse of the self-expressive, emotively hot images common to Abstract Expressionist artists such as Jackson Pollock. When Cage borrowed the idea for *4'33"*, he was interested in Rauschenberg's notion of meaning as a projection of the audience, but in creating music that was literally silent, he added a further metaphorical resonance. A piece of silent music announces not so much silence per se, as a silencing, the active state of being unable to express. Informed by his experience of queerness under the Lavender Scare, *4'33"* moreover works to erase any hierarchical distinctions, such as those between composer and orchestra, orchestra and audience, silence and noise, listening and creating, and so on. And of course, this leveling of hierarchies is itself an act of queer liberation, given the degree to which queers were marginalized and oppressed under most all cultural definitions of the time.

Johns's infamous 1954/55 *Flag* painting may not resemble anything queer, but like so many other of his works of the period, it interrogates the conditions of meaning-making.[12] What made it extraordinary was that it took what was arguably the most sacred symbol of the United States during the height of Cold War patriotic fervor and converted it into a question mark. After all, a flag does not exist in nature. It is a symbol given significance by a collective social construct. Johns managed to meet all the usual conditions of flagness—a particular design in red, white, and blue on fabric—but then posed the question of whether his work was literally a flag or merely a painting of a flag. In denaturalizing this sacred symbol, in interrogating the conditions of its identity, Johns showed that all meanings, even the most authoritative ones, are subject to pressure. No surprise then that a closeted homosexual artist in the 1950s like Johns would seek to put pressure on the automatic attribution of meaning. If something as closely guarded as the American flag could be made to questions its identity, then the association of homosexuality with crime, weakness, perversion, and so forth, were similarly subject to pressure. This, then is the final turn of the screw: from a struggle to depict homosexuality to a struggle to explode it, queer modernism has done much more than expand the canons of representation. It has instead asked the deepest, most profound questions about representation itself, underscoring how the attribution of significance is always already rooted in the social, and not in God, nature, biology, or some other transcendental abstraction. To ask the question of how meanings adhere to things and people is the first step in opening up the process of meaning-making; as such, it is at once the precondition of true liberation and the final evidence of the fecund cross-pollination of queerness with modernism.

12
Jasper Johns, *Flag*, 1954/55 (dated on reverse 1954), encaustic, oil, and collage on fabric mounted on plywood, three panels, 107.3 × 153.8 cm, Museum of Modern Art (MoMA), New York.

Gegenteil der ausdrucksstarken, emotional aufgeladenen Bilder von Vertretern des Abstrakten Expressionismus wie Jackson Pollock dar.

Cage lieh die Idee für *4'33"* von Rauschenberg, weil er sich für dessen Auffassung von Bedeutung als Projektion des Publikums interessierte. Indem er jedoch ein Musikstück schuf, das buchstäblich stumm blieb, erweiterte er sie um einen weiteren metaphorischen Resonanzraum. Ein tonloses Stück kündet nicht so sehr von der Stille an sich als vielmehr vom Verstummen, dem aktiven Zustand des Sich-nicht-Ausdrücken-Könnens. Geprägt von seinen Erfahrungen als queerer Künstler während der „Lavender Scare" löst Cage in *4'33"* zudem die Hierarchien auf: zwischen Komponist und Orchester, Orchester und Publikum, Stille und Geräusch, Zuhören und Schaffen und so fort. Diese Nivellierung ist zugleich ein Akt queerer Befreiung, betrachtet man das Ausmaß an Marginalisierung und Unterdrückung, die queere Menschen in einem Großteil der Kultur jener Zeit erfuhren.

Johns' legendäres Werk *Flag* (1954/55) mag auf den ersten Blick nichts Queeres an sich haben, doch wie viele seiner Werke aus dieser Phase hinterfragt es die Bedingungen der Bedeutungszuschreibung.[12] Das Besondere daran ist, dass es das wohl heiligste Symbol der USA auf dem Höhepunkt des patriotischen Eifers im Kalten Krieg in ein Fragezeichen verwandelt. Schließlich ist eine Flagge nicht naturgegeben. Sie ist ein Symbol, das nur durch ein kollektives soziales Konstrukt Bedeutung erhält. Johns erfüllte alle üblichen Voraussetzungen einer Flagge – ein bestimmtes Muster aus Rot, Weiß und Blau auf Stoff –, stellte dann aber die Frage, ob sein Werk tatsächlich eine Flagge oder nur ein Gemälde von einer Flagge sei. Durch die Verfremdung dieses heiligen Symbols und die Befragung der Bedingungen seiner Identität zeigte Johns, dass jede Bedeutung, selbst die verbindlichste, unter Druck geraten kann. Es überrascht daher nicht, dass ein nicht geouteter homosexueller Künstler der 1950er-Jahre wie Johns die automatische Zuweisung von Bedeutung infrage stellt. Wenn etwas so streng Bewachtes wie die amerikanische Flagge dazu gebracht werden konnte, die eigene Identität zu hinterfragen, dann konnte auch die Assoziation von Homosexualität mit Verbrechen, Schwäche, Perversion und so weiter infrage gestellt werden. Dies ist also die letzte Stufe: Die queere Moderne hat sich nicht nur vom Ringen um die Darstellung von Homosexualität zu einem Kampf um ihre Zersprengung entwickelt, sondern die Darstellungskanons weit mehr als erweitert. Sie hat die weitreichendsten und tiefgründigsten Fragen zur Repräsentation selbst aufgeworfen und gezeigt, dass Bedeutungszuschreibungen stets im Sozialen wurzeln – und nicht in Gott, der Natur, der Biologie oder anderen transzendenten Konzepten. Um den Prozess der Bedeutungszuschreibung zu öffnen, ist der erste Schritt, zu fragen, wie sich Bedeutungen an Dinge und Menschen heften; dies ist gleichzeitig die Voraussetzung für wahre Befreiung und der endgültige Beweis der gegenseitigen Befruchtung von Queerness und Moderne.

12
Jasper Johns, *Flag*, 1954/55 (rückseitig datiert 1954), Enkaustik, Öl und Collage, auf Stoff auf Sperrholz montiert, drei Tafeln, 107,3 × 153,8 cm, Museum of Modern Art (MoMA), New York

III SAPPHISCHE MODERNE

SAPPHIC MODERNISM

1

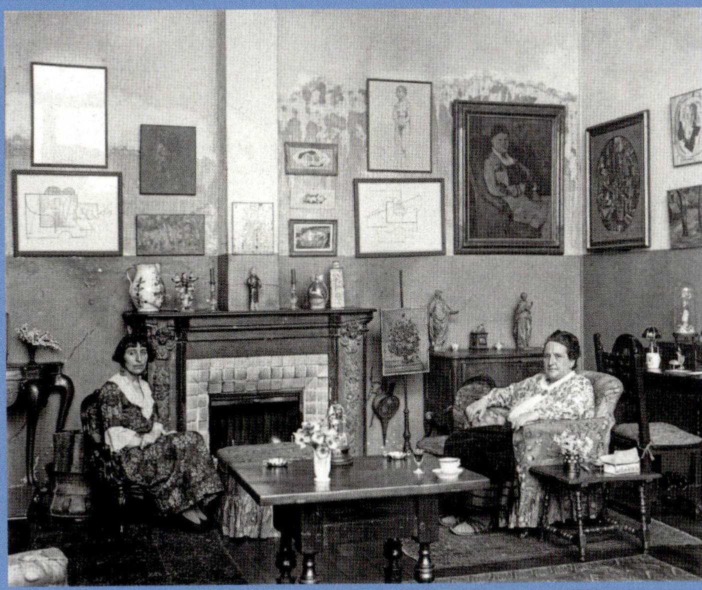

2

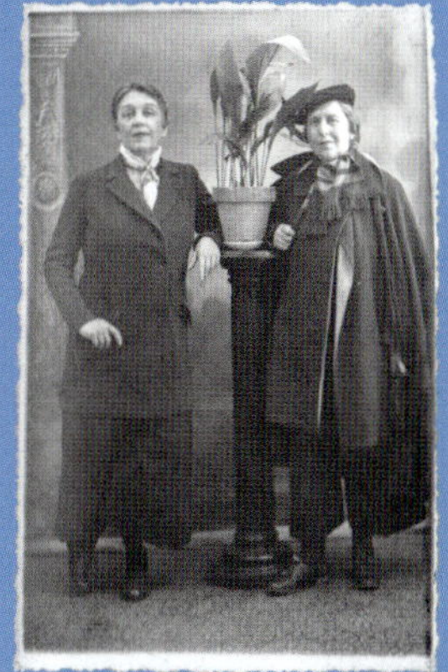

3

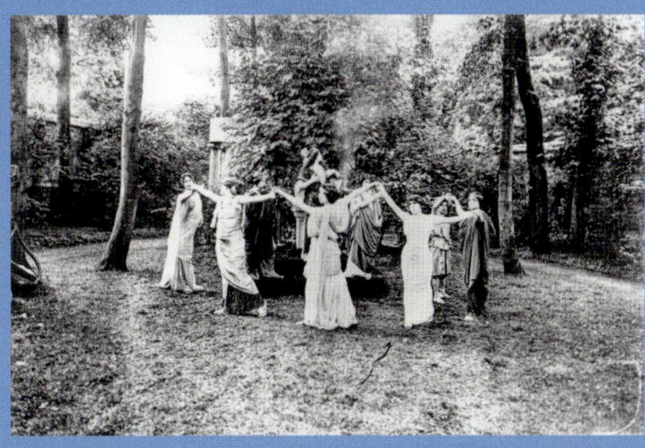

5

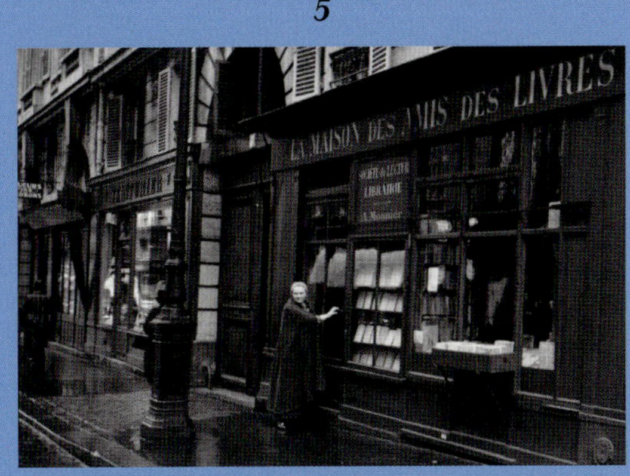

4

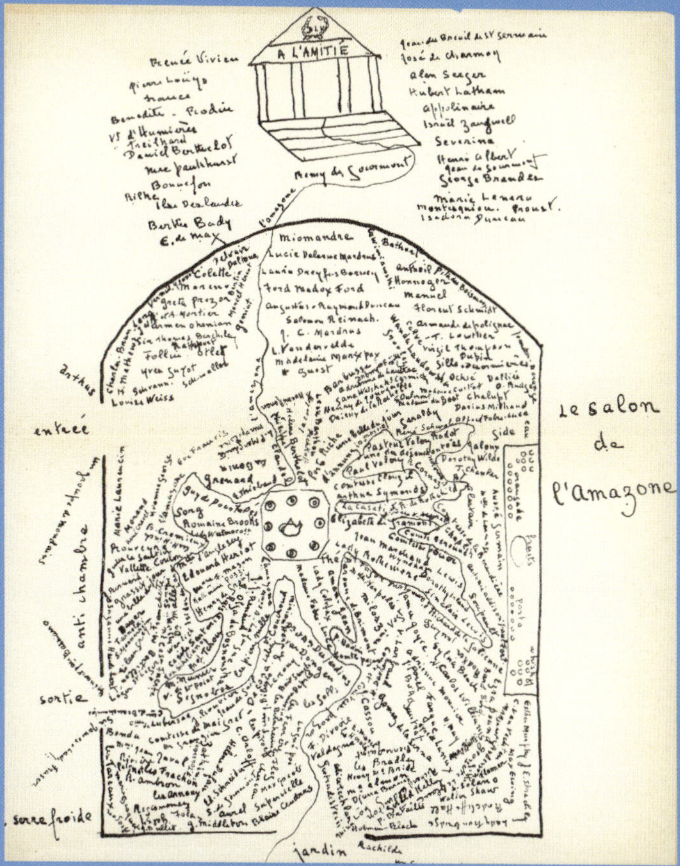

A L'AMITIÉ

entrée

anti chambre

sortie

serre froide

jardin

Le salon de l'Amazone

6

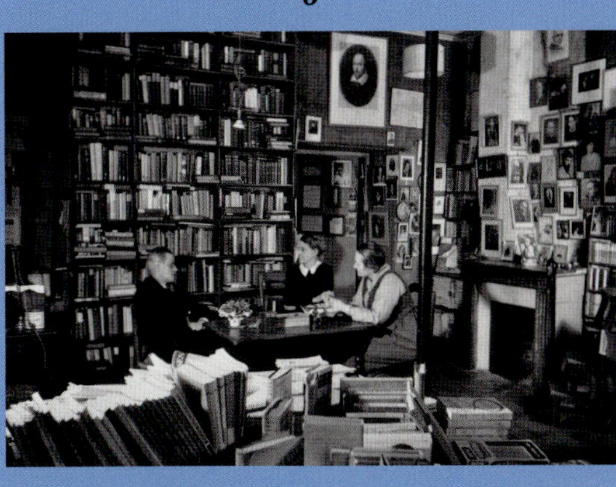

1

Das Foto von Man Ray aus dem Jahr 1922 zeigt die US-amerikanische Literatin, Kunstsammlerin und Mäzenin Gertrude Stein und ihre Lebensgefährtin, die Autorin Alice B. Toklas, deren Salon in der Rue de Fleurus 27 in Paris einer der einflussreichsten Treffpunkte der künstlerischen und literarischen Avantgarde war.

This photograph by Man Ray from 1922 shows Gertrude Stein, the American writer, art collector, and patron of the arts, and her partner, the author Alice B. Toklas. Their salon at 27 rue de Fleurus in Paris was one of the most influential gathering places for the literary and artistic avant-garde.

2

Die US-amerikanische Malerin Romaine Brooks, die für die moderne lesbische Kunstgeschichte ikonische Porträts ihrer Liebhaber*innen geschaffen hat, und Natalie Barney lernten sich 1915 kennen und blieben fast fünfzig Jahre als Paar zusammen. Das Foto zeigt beide im Jahr 1935 in Paris.

The American painter Romaine Brooks created portraits of her female lovers that have become iconic in the history of modern lesbian art. She met her partner, Natalie Barney, in 1915, and they remained together for nearly fifty years. This photograph shows them both in Paris in 1935.

3

Natalie Barney veranstaltete in ihrem Garten mit ihrem „Tempel für die Freundschaft" bacchantische Rituale und Theatervorstellungen. Als Vorbild lesbischer Liebe galt ihr die antike Dichterin Sappho und deren kulturelles Zentrum auf der griechischen Insel Lesbos.

Natalie Barney organized bacchanalian rituals and theater performances in her garden, with its "Temple to Friendship." Her model of lesbian love was the ancient poet Sappho and her cultural center on the Greek island of Lesbos.

4

Die von Natalie Barney 1929 gezeichnete Karte zeigt die Begegnungen und Freundschaften, die zwischen 1910 und 1930 in ihrem „Salon de l'Amazone" in der Rue Jacob 20 in Paris stattfanden. Er war einer der Zentren der lesbischen Subkultur und Gemeinschaften von Künstler*innen, Literat*innen und Tänzer*innen.

The map drawn by Natalie Barney in 1929 traces the encounters and friendships that took place between 1910 and 1930 at her "Salon de l'Amazone" at 20 rue Jacob in Paris. The salon was a central gathering place for the lesbian subculture and a thriving community of women artists, writers, and dancers.

5

Die Buchhändlerin und Verlegerin Adrienne Monnier auf einem Foto von Gisèle Freund aus dem Jahr 1937 vor ihrer Buchhandlung La Maison des Amis des Livres, die sie 1915 in der Rue de l'Odéon in Paris eröffnete und die in der Zwischenkriegszeit ein wichtiger Treffpunkt der „sapphischen Moderne" war.

The bookseller and publisher Adrienne Monnier seen in a 1937 photograph by Gisèle Freund, standing in front of her bookshop, La Maison des Amis des Livres, which she had opened in 1915 on the rue de l'Odéon in Paris. The shop became a key meeting place for the community of "Sapphic Modernism" during the interwar years.

6

Die US-amerikanische Verlegerin Sylvia Beach, langjährige Lebensgefährtin von Adrienne Monnier, eröffnete 1919 in Paris die englischsprachige Leihbücherei und Buchhandlung Shakespeare & Company, einen bedeutenden Treffpunkt der Avantgarde. Sie veröffentlichte als Erste James Joyces Roman *Ulysses*.

The American publisher Sylvia Beach, longtime partner of Adrienne Monnier, opened the English-language lending library and bookshop Shakespeare & Company in Paris in 1919, a prominent gathering place for the avant-garde. She was the first to publish James Joyce's novel Ulysses.

Meine *Queerness* ist kein Laster, sie ist nicht vorsätzlich und schadet niemandem. [...] Die Leute nennen es unnatürlich, ich kann nur sagen, für mich war es immer natürlich.

My queerness is not a vice, is not deliberate, and harms no one. [...] people call it unnatural, all I can say is it's always come naturally to me.

Natalie Barney

Lettres à une connue (1899)
Letters to a Woman I Have Known (1899)

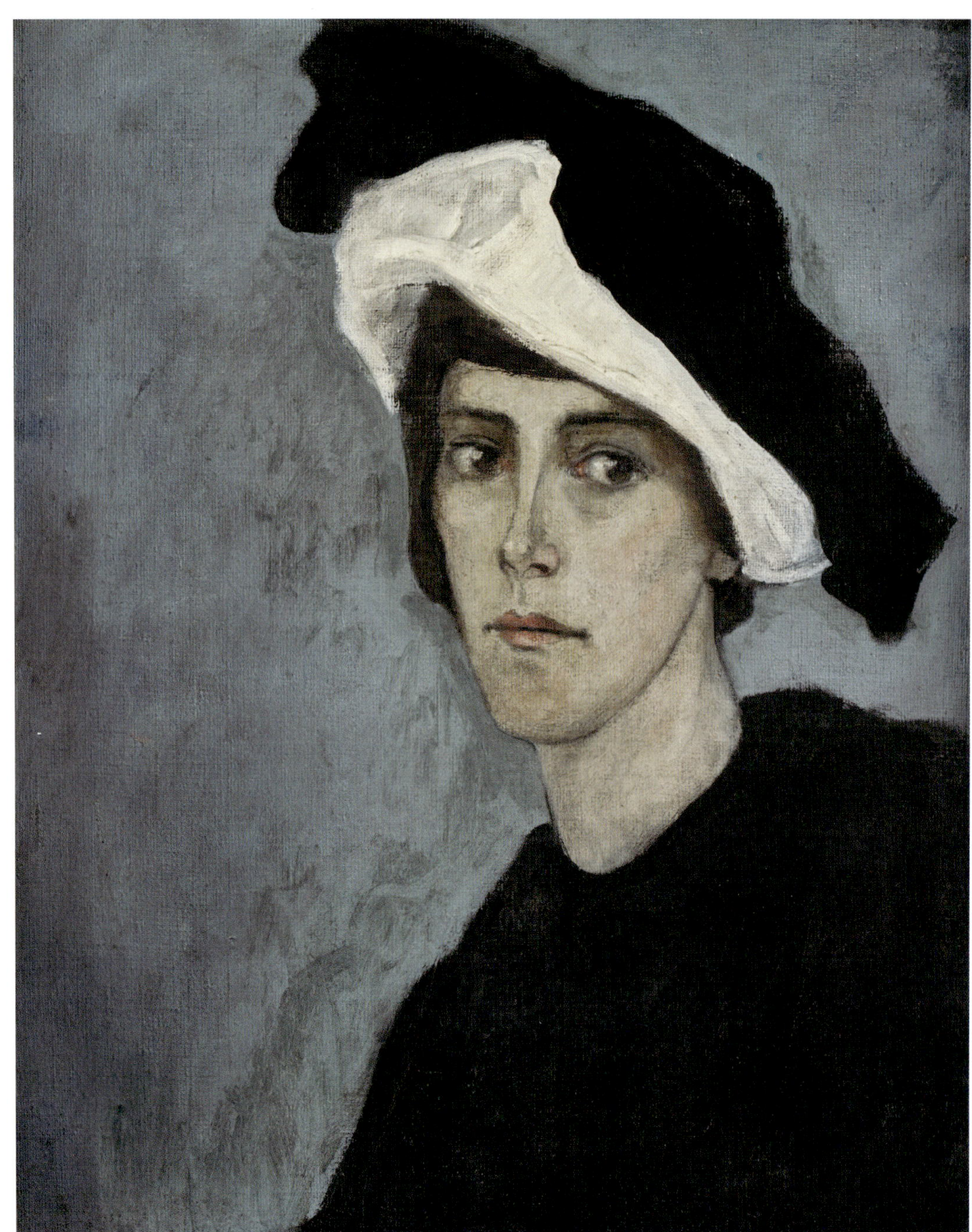

Romaine Brooks
Self-Portraît, um ~ *ca.* 1912
Selbstporträt

Romaine Brooks

Portraît of the Marchesa Casati, um ~ *ca.* 1920
Porträt der Markgräfin Casati

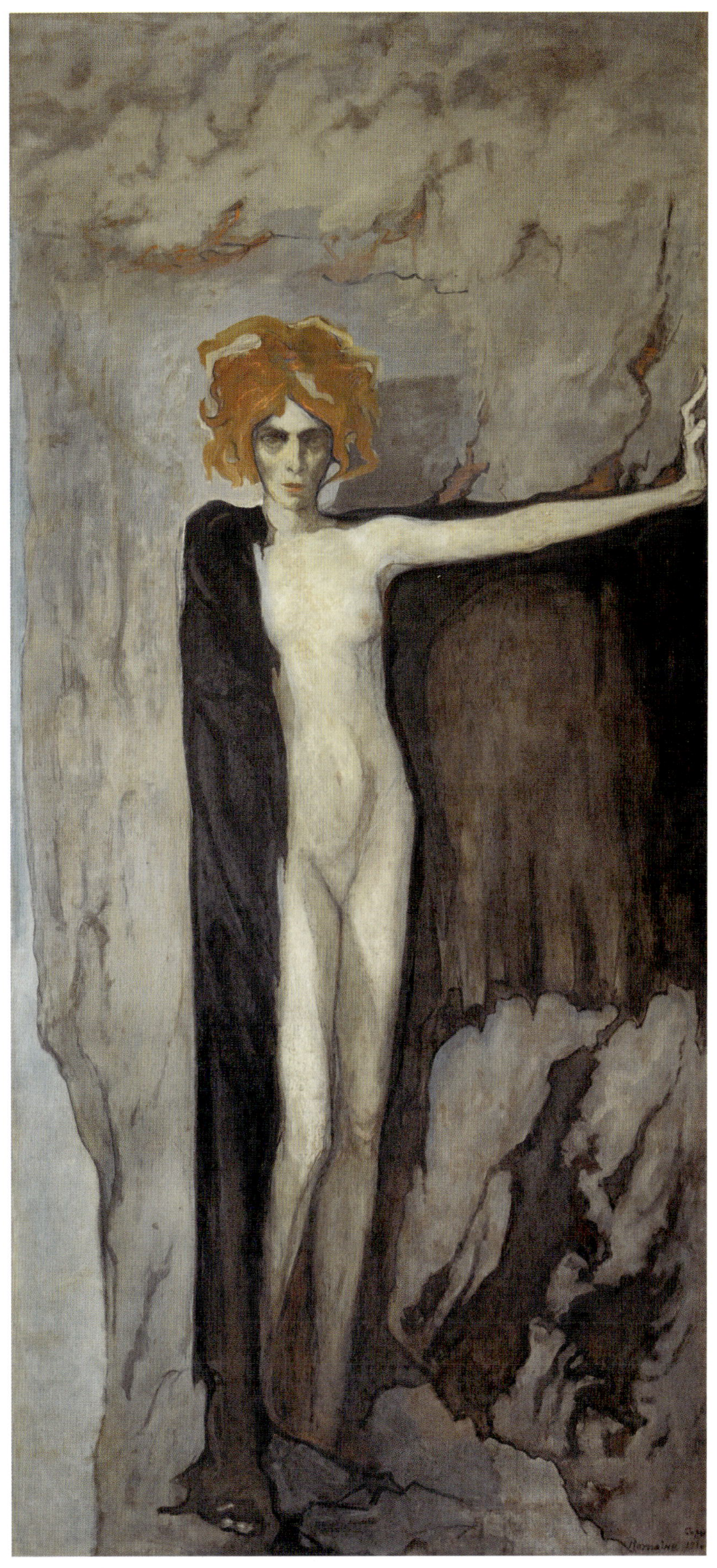

Gluck
The Punt, um ~ *ca.* 1937
Der Kahn

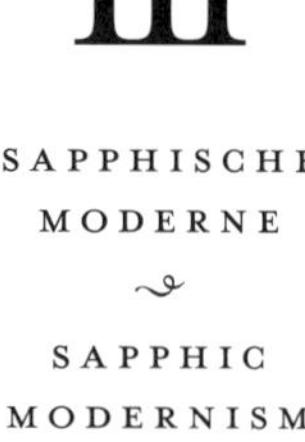

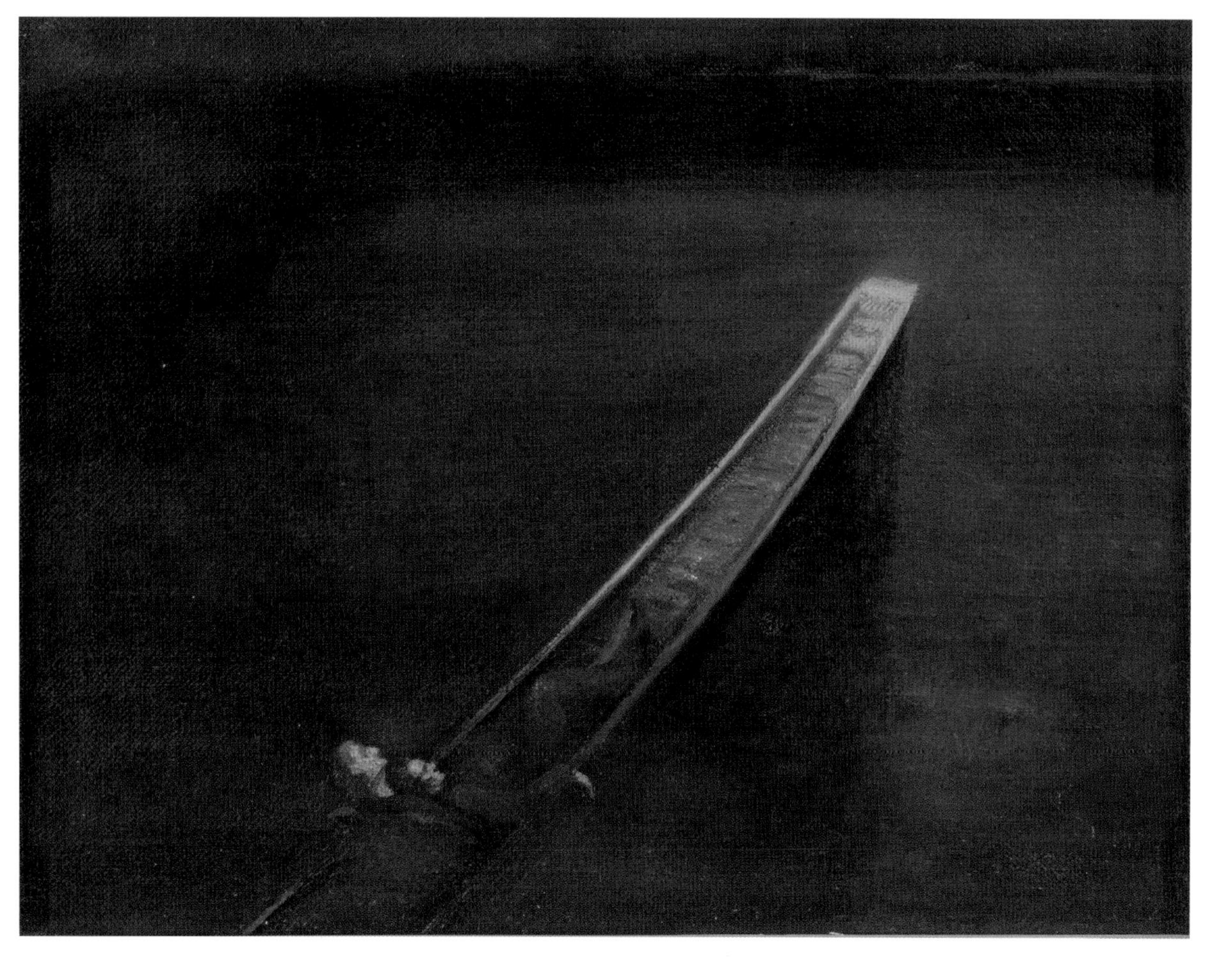

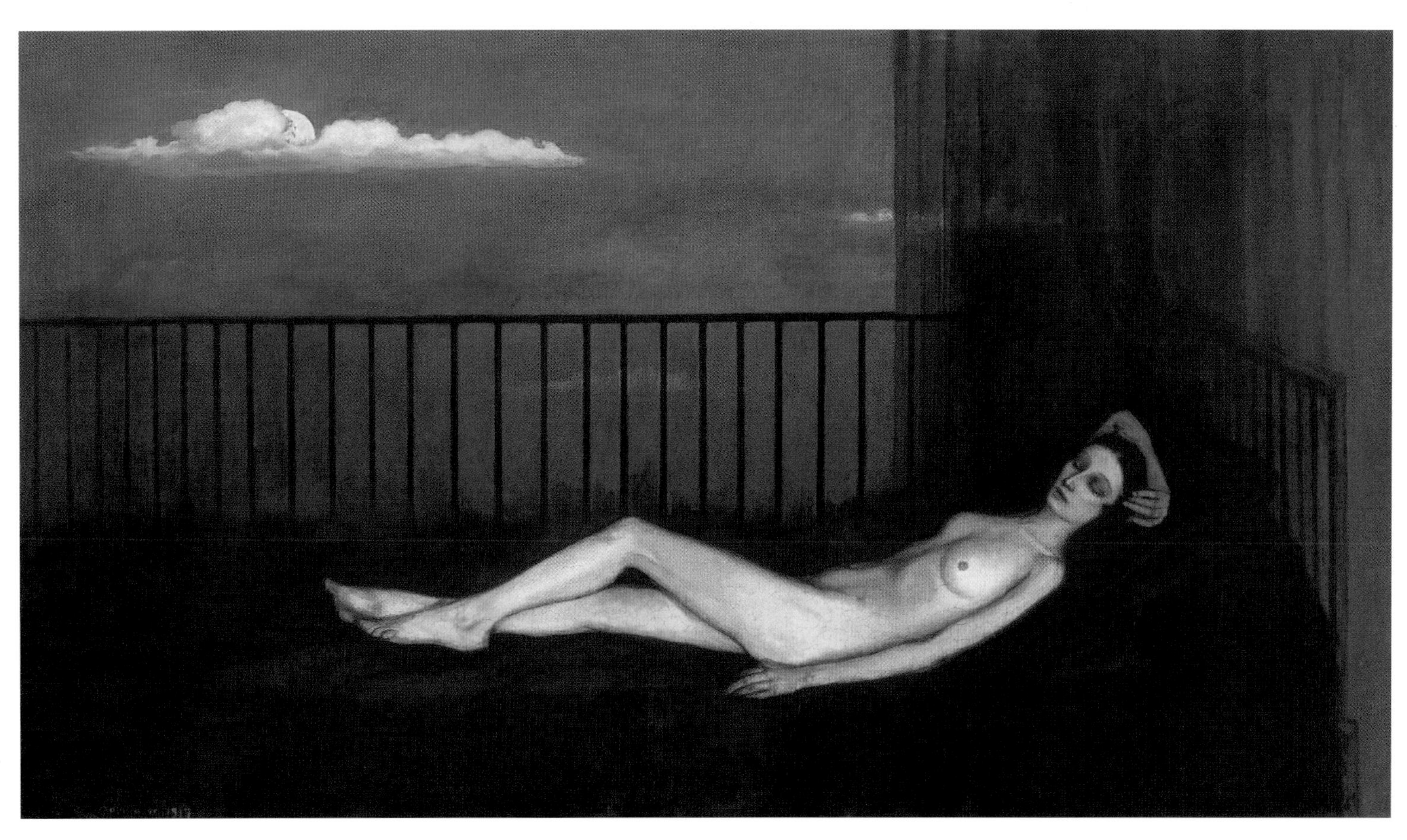

Romaine Brooks

La Vénus triste, 1917
Die traurige Venus ~ *The Weeping Venus*

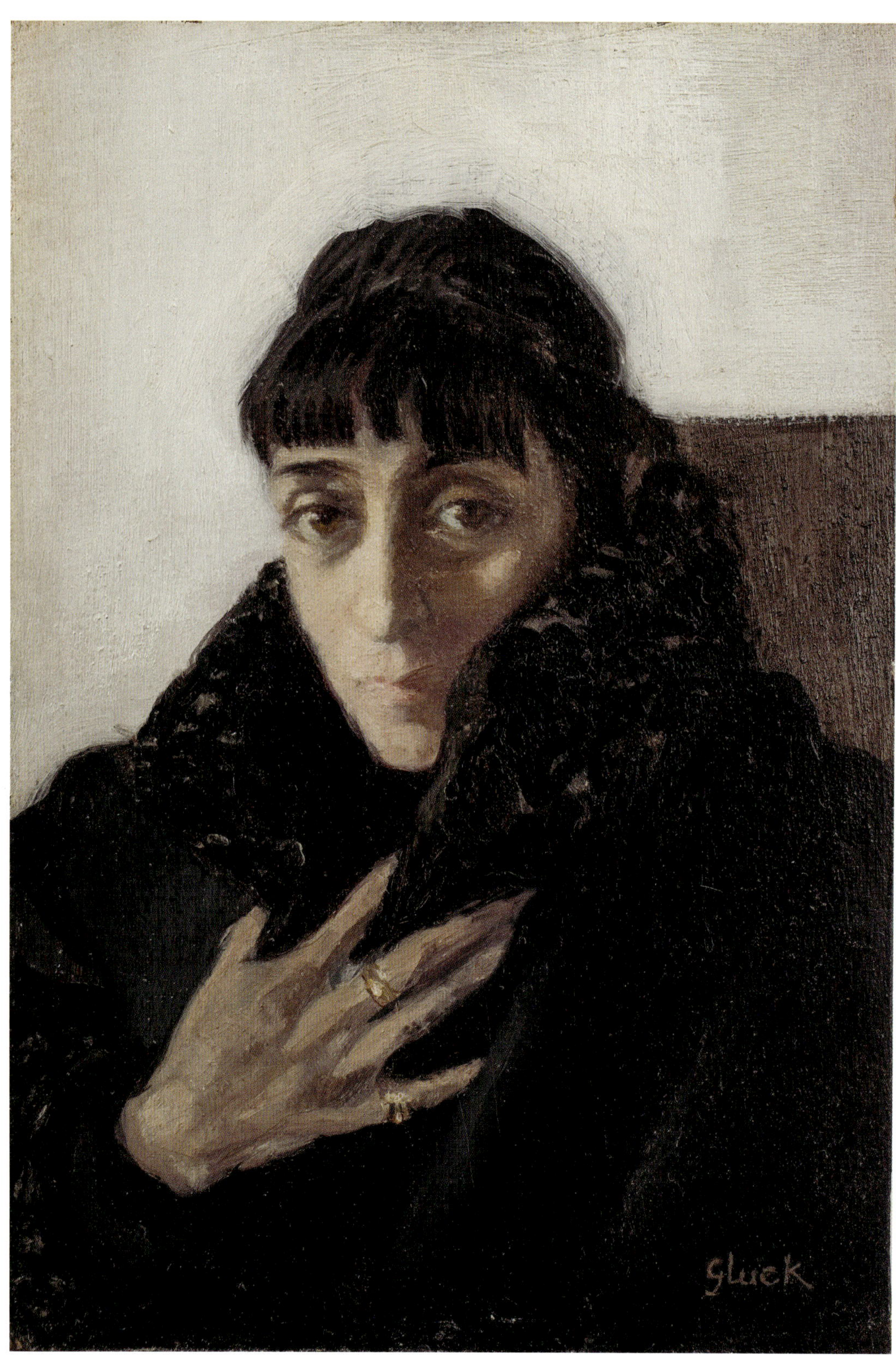

Gluck
Portrait of Miss E. M. *Craig*, 1920
Porträt von Miss E. M. Craig

Gluck

Lords and Ladies, um ~ *ca.* 1936

Herren und Damen

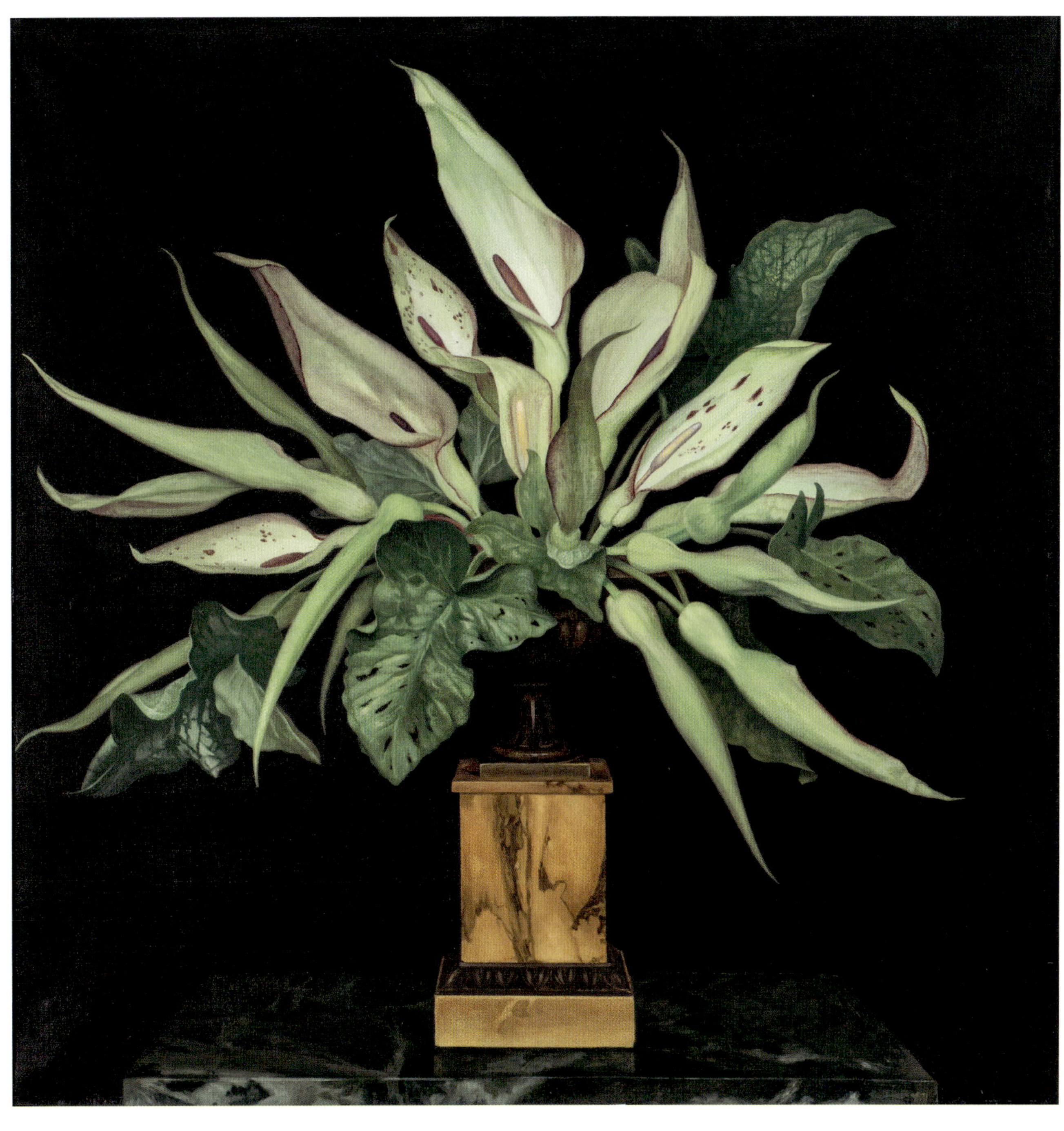

Gluck
Bank Holiday Monday, um ~ *ca.* 1937
Feiertagsmontag

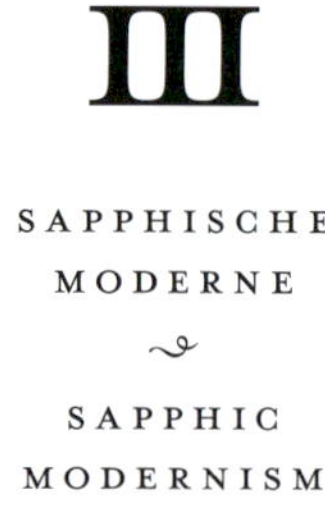

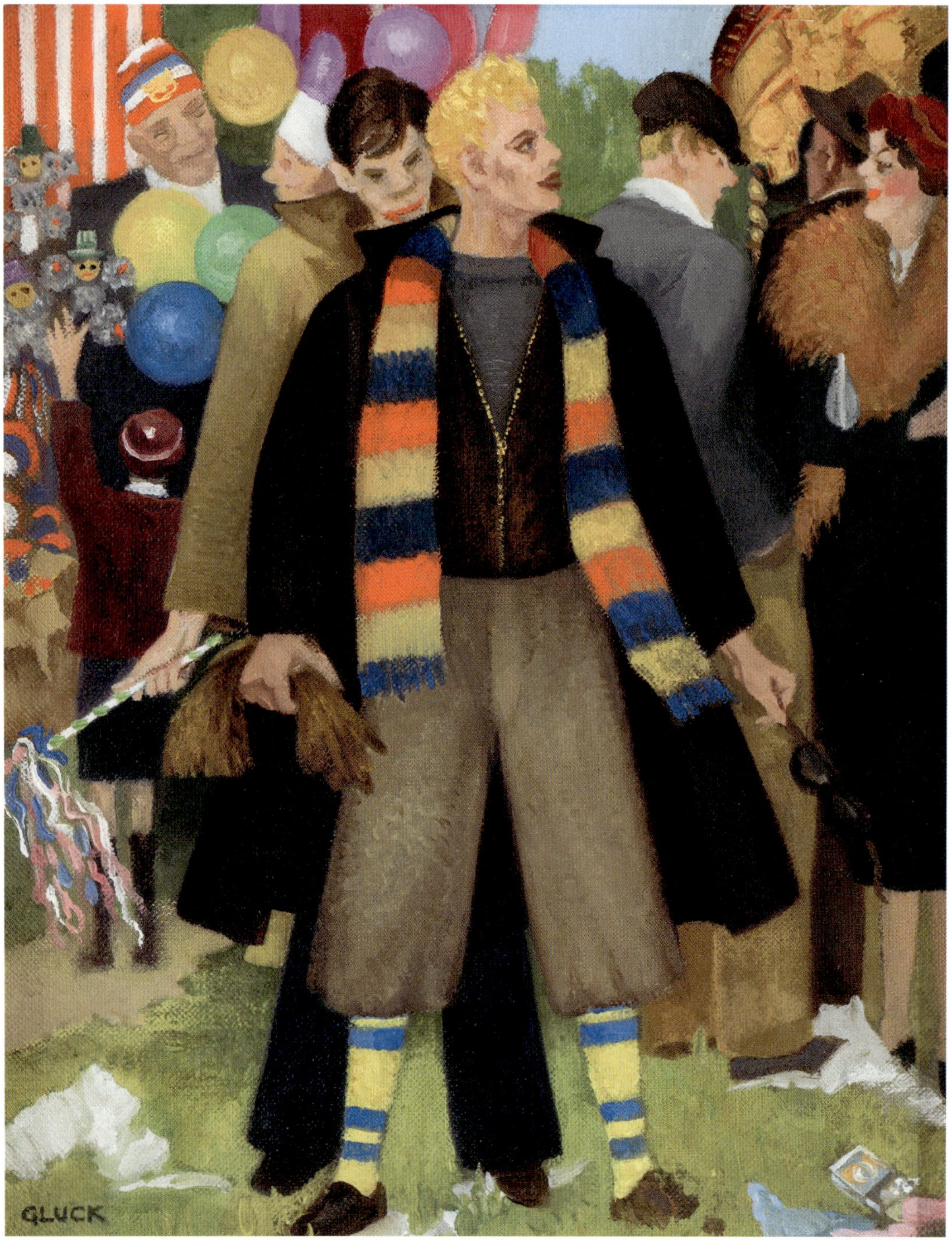

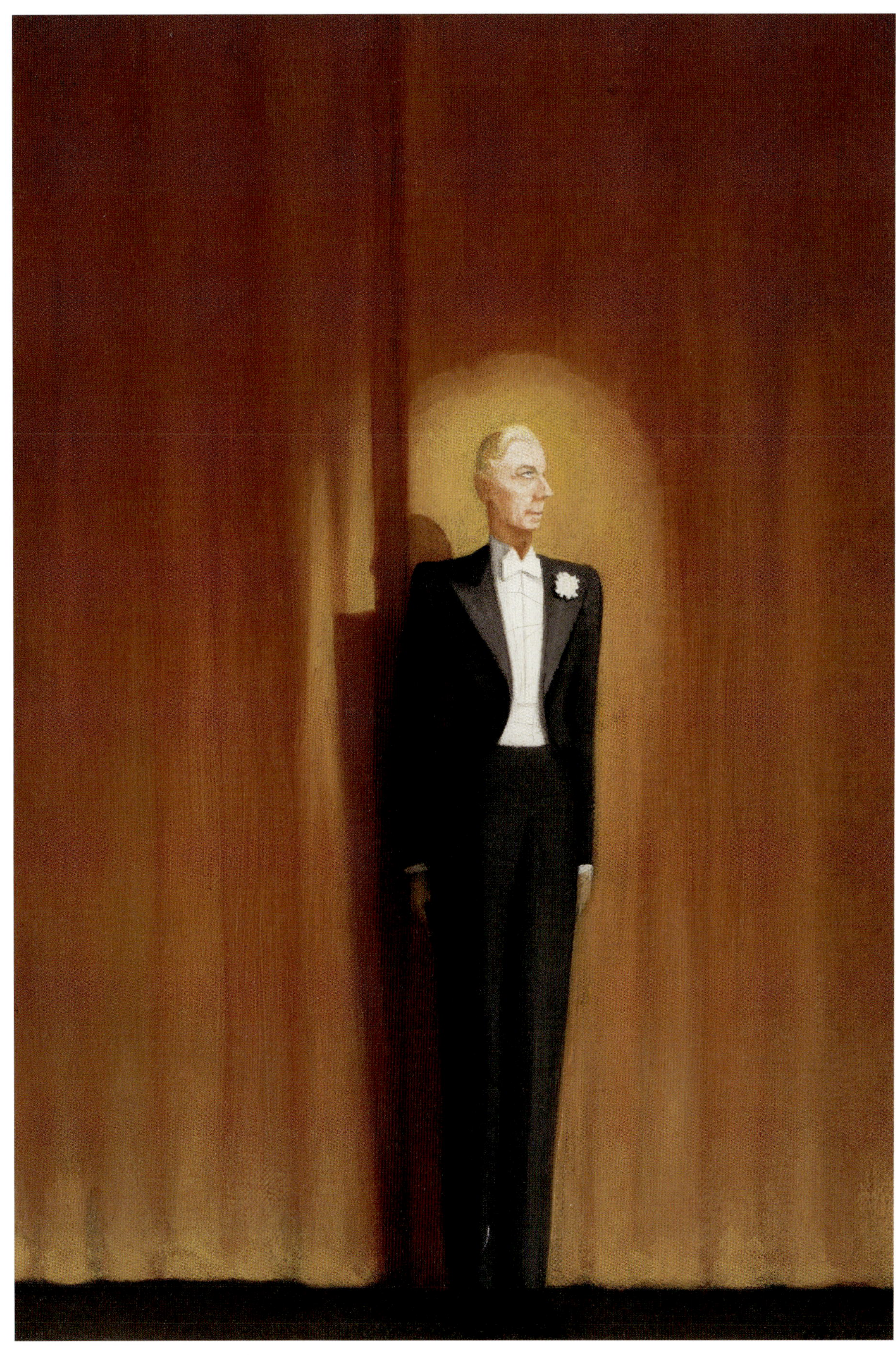

Gluck
Ernest Thesiger, 1925/26

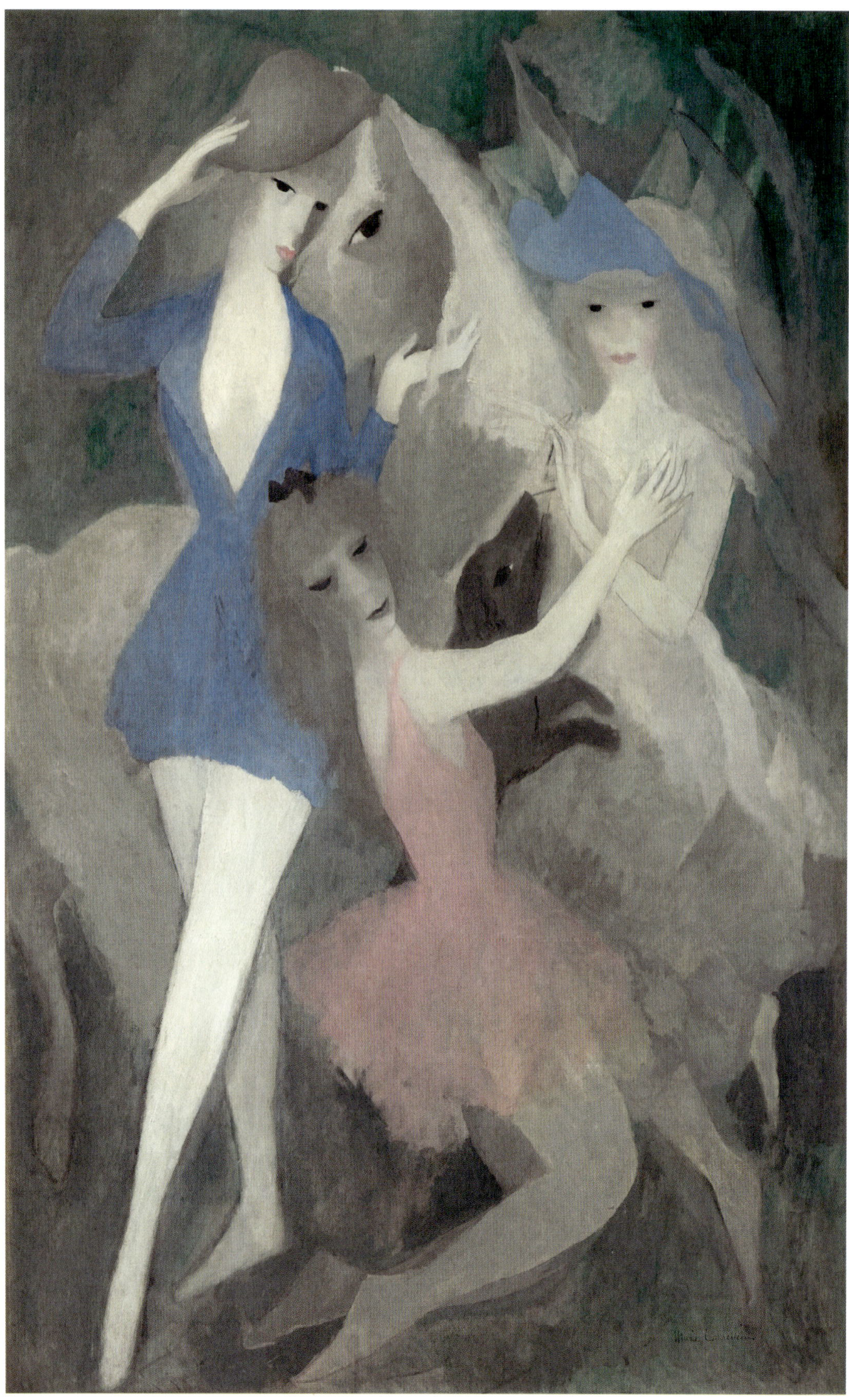

Marie Laurencin

Danseuses espagnoles, 1920/21
Spanische Tänzerinnen ~
Spanish Dancers

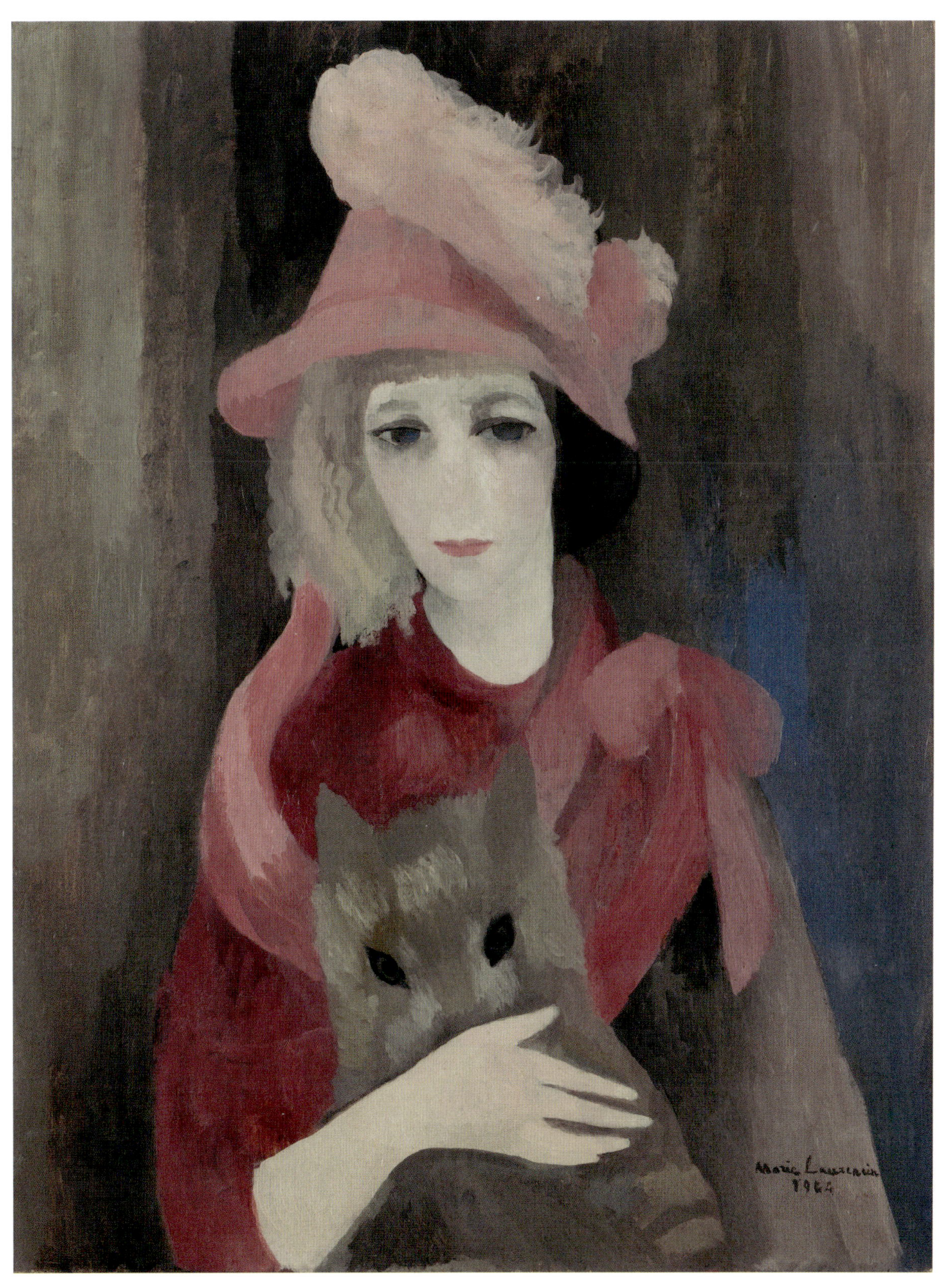

Marie Laurencin

La Femme au chien (portrait), 1924
Frau mit einem Hund (Porträt)
Woman with a Dog (Portrait)

Marie Laurencin

Théâtre Serge de Diaghilew, Les Biches, 1924
Théâtre Serge de Diaghilew, Die Hindinnen ~
Théâtre Serge de Diaghilew, The Hinds

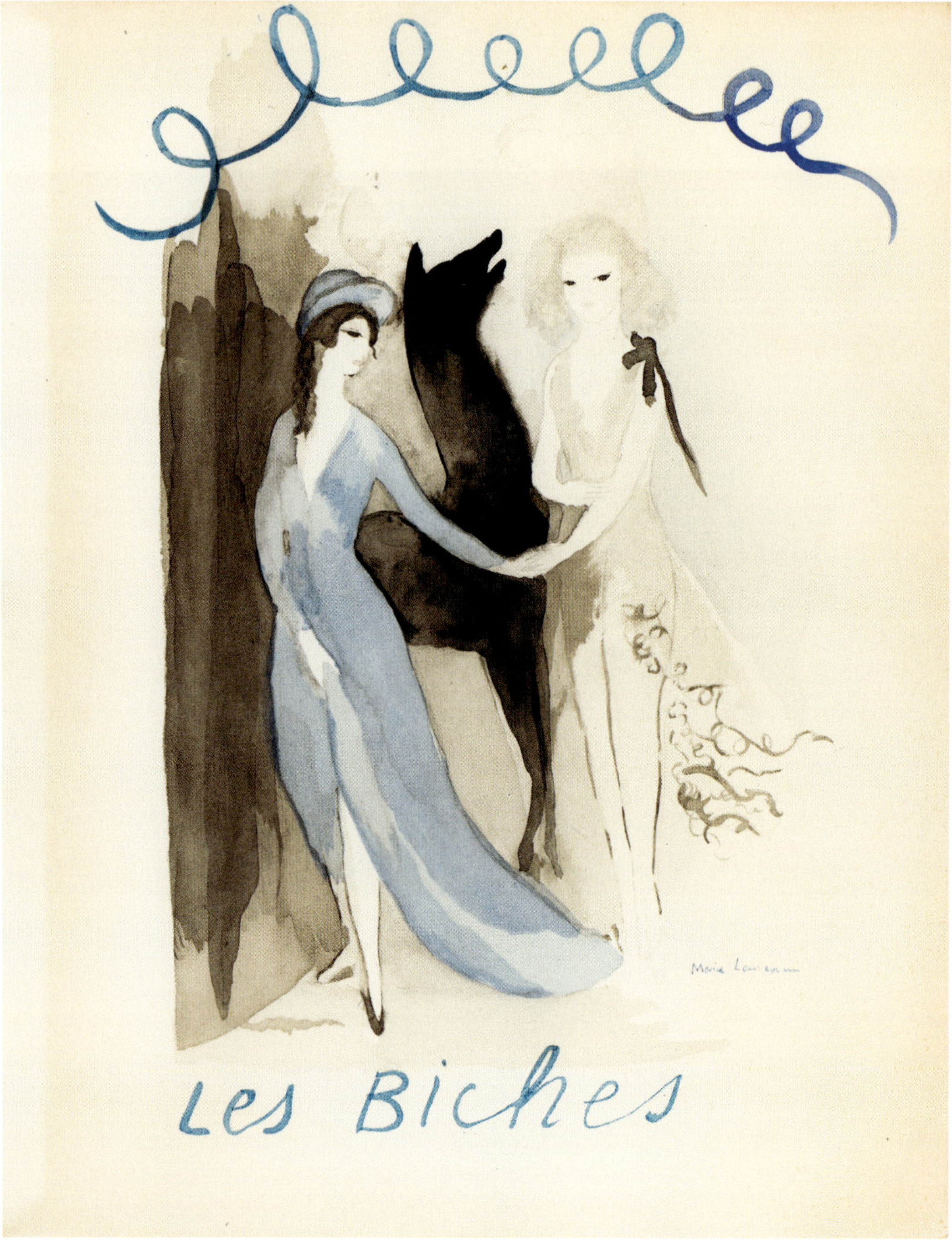

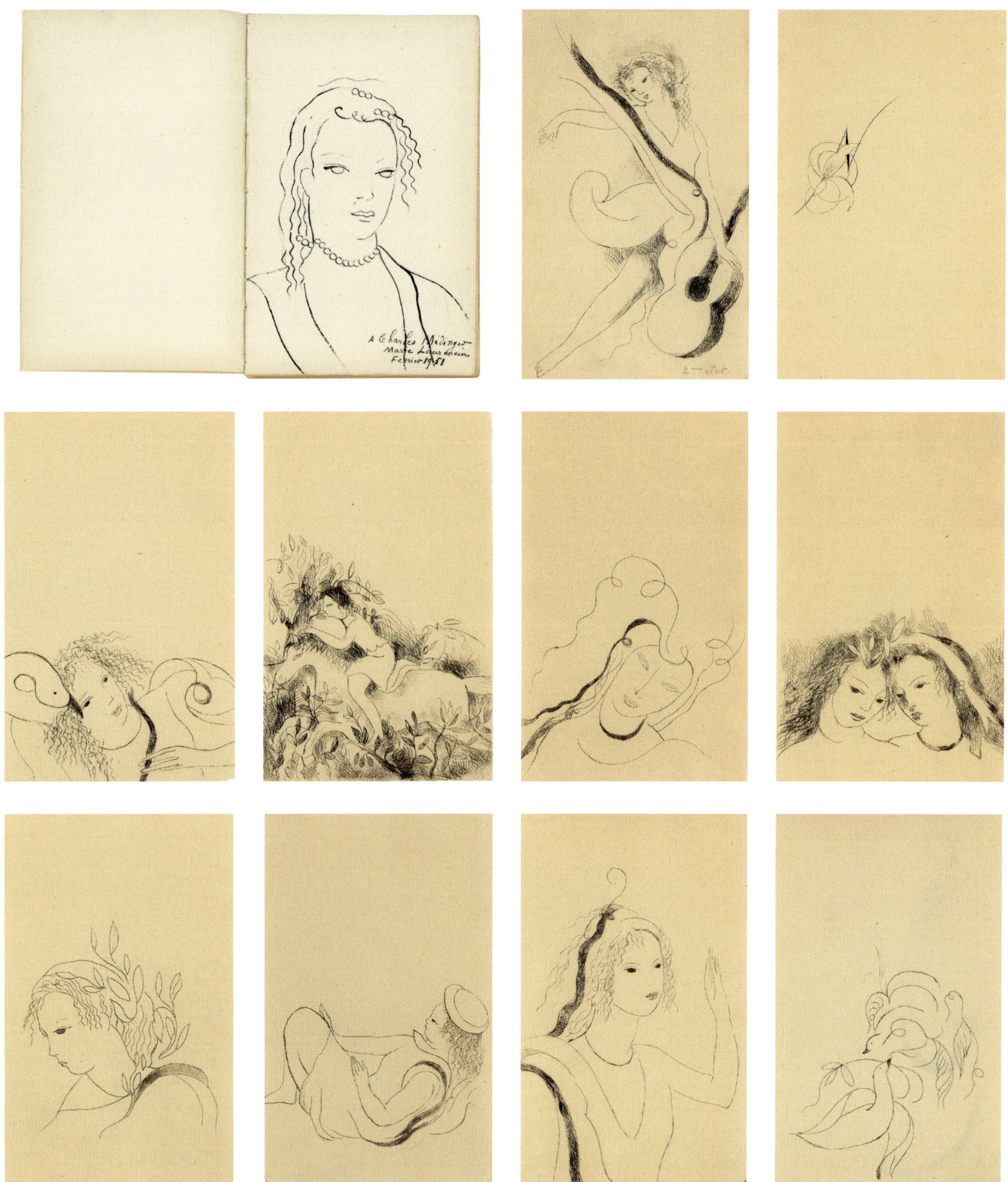

Marie Laurencin

Poèmes de Sappho, 1950
Gedichte von Sappho ~
Poems by Sappho

LESBEN UND MODERNE

~

LESBIANS AND MODERNISM

DIANA SOUHAMI

Alle in diesem Essay vorgestellten Frauen haben einen künstlerischen Beitrag zur Bewegung der Moderne geleistet, dem Bruch mit den Konventionen des 19. Jahrhunderts. In meinem 2020 erschienenen Buch *No Modernism Without Lesbians*[1] untersuche ich, wie tief und weitreichend der kollektive Einfluss von Lesben und genderqueeren Frauen war und welch zentrale Rolle diese als Innovator*innen und Wegbereiter*innen gespielt haben.

„Paris [war], wo das 20. Jahrhundert war", schrieb Gertrude Stein, „der Ort, der denjenigen von uns entsprach die die Kunst und Literatur des zwanzigsten Jahrhunderts schaffen sollten".[2] In den Jahrzehnten vor dem Zweiten Weltkrieg zogen viele lesbische und genderqueere Künstler*innen und Schriftsteller*innen aus Städten wie Washington oder London nach Paris. Wie Stein sagte, lag der Reiz von Paris nicht nur in dem, was die Stadt ihnen bot, sondern auch in dem, was sie ihnen nicht nahm.[3]

In Amerika und Großbritannien wurden Kunstwerke und Schriften, die als unsittlich oder obszön galten, streng zensiert: Der Prozess gegen Oscar Wilde 1895, der seinen Ruin besiegelte, lag noch als Warnung für männliche Homosexuelle in der Luft; Frauen hatten kaum Rechte, Lesben keine Stimme. Wer seine Persönlichkeit entfalten wollte, brauchte Freiheit. Natalie Barney, Romaine Brooks, Mariette Lydis, Sylvia Beach, Bryher, Janet Flanner, Djuna Barnes, Thelma Wood, Claude Cahun, Marcel Moore, Marlow Moss, Gisèle Freund und so weiter – die Liste der Neuankömmlinge in Paris, die Konventionen brachen, sich von den vorgegebenen Frauenrollen lösten, offen Liebhaber*innen hatten, lebten, wie sie wollten, innovative Werke schufen und im Mikrokosmos ihre eigene Gesellschaft mit eigenen Beziehungen und Bezügen bildeten, ist lang. Es war eine Graswurzelbewegung, inspiriert von Sappho, der Dichterin aus dem 6. Jahrhundert vor Christus, und ihrer Gemeinschaft von Frauen auf der griechischen Insel Lesbos, die die Selbstbestimmung und das Ideal eines kreativen Lebens wählten und sich männlicher Herrschaft entzogen.

Der Modernismus in der Kunst brach mit etablierten Formen und Inhalten, suchte andere Perspektiven und schockierte mit Neuem. Alte Regeln für Form und Inhalt wurden revidiert oder verworfen. Die Modernist*innen lösten sich von linearen Narrativen in der Literatur und abbildhaften Darstellungen in der Kunst und setzten stattdessen auf individuelle Ausdrucksformen in Stil und Inhalt. Für genderqueere Frauen bedeutete dieser Bruch nicht nur künstlerische, sondern auch persönliche Freiheit: Sie wählten neue Lebensstile, um ihrer Identität Ausdruck zu verleihen, zeigten offen ihre Sexualität, brachen mit den Rollenbildern des 19. Jahrhunderts und warfen Vorstellungen von Scham und Fehlverhalten über Bord. Natalie Barney, die den Zwängen der Washingtoner Gesellschaft entfloh, erklärte, sie wolle Paris zum sapphischen Zentrum der westlichen Welt machen. „Meine *Queerness* ist kein Laster, sie ist nicht vorsätzlich und schadet niemandem"[4], schrieb sie. Ein weiteres Epigramm lautete: „Die Leute nennen es unnatürlich, ich kann nur sagen, für mich war es immer natürlich."[5] Und ein drittes: „Liebe war immer die Hauptsache in meinem Leben."[6]

In Paris waren Mieten und Lebensmittel zu der Zeit erschwinglich. Sapphische Künstler*innen und Schriftsteller*innen bildeten ein Netzwerk. Ihr Leben und Schaffen markierte einen kollektiven Umbruch, der weitgehend unbeachtet blieb. Viele lehnten ihren Geburtsnamen ab, änderten oder verfremdeten ihn, um die Kontrolle über ihr eigenes Leben zu erlangen

1 Diana Souhami, *No Modernism Without Lesbians*, London 2020.

2 Gertrude Stein, *Paris Frankreich*, Übers. aus dem Amerik. von Marie-Anne Stiebel, Frankfurt am Main 1975, S. 16, 18. [Anmerkung der Redaktion: Wir haben die etwas eigenwillige Rechtschreibung von Gertrude Stein wie in der Originalübersetzung belassen.]

3 Gertrude Stein, „An American and France" (1936), in: *What Are Masterpieces*, 1940; New York 1970, S. 70.

4 Natalie Barney, *Lettres à une connue* (1899), zit. nach: Diana Souhami, *Wild Girls: Paris, Sappho and Art; The Lives & Loves of Natalie Barney and Romaine Brooks*, London 2004, S. 57.

5 Ebd., S. 150.

6 Natalie Barney, *Éparpillements*, Paris 1910, zit. nach: Souhami 2020 (wie Anm. 1), S. 215.

The women who feature in this essay each made an artistic contribution to the breakaway movement of modernism, the fracture from nineteenth-century orthodoxies. In my recent book, *No Modernism Without Lesbians*,[1] I focus on how deep and far reaching the collective impact was of lesbians and genderqueer women, and how central their roles were as innovators and enablers.

"Paris was where the twentieth century was," Gertrude Stein wrote, "the place that suited those of us that were to create the twentieth century art and literature."[2] In the decades of the twentieth century before the Second World War, many lesbians and genderqueer women artists and writers left their hometowns, like Washington or London, and gravitated to Paris. It was not, Gertrude Stein said, only what Paris gave, it was all it did not take away.[3] In America and Britain, there was strict censorship of art and writing deemed immoral or obscene: the 1895 trials and ruin of Oscar Wilde hung in the air as a warning to male homosexuals; women had few rights; lesbians had no voice. For those intent on self-expression, freedom was key. Natalie Barney, Romaine Brooks, Mariette Lydis, Sylvia Beach, Bryher, Janet Flanner, Djuna Barnes, Thelma Wood, Claude Cahun, Marcel Moore, Marlow Moss, Gisèle Freund... the list was long of Paris incomers who defied convention, sloughed off prescribed views of a woman's place, openly had same-sex lovers, lived as they chose, created innovative works of art, and formed in microcosm their own society with its own connections and references. It was a grass roots revolution with classical reference to Sappho, the sixth century BC poet and her community of women on the Greek island of Lesbos, who chose self-determination, the ideal of a creative life, and eschewed male rule. Modernism in art involved departure from orthodoxies of form and content, new ways of seeing, and the shock of the new. Old rules of form and content were revised or broken. Modernists moved from linear narrative in writing and from representation in art to individual manifestations of style and content. For genderqueer women, breaking the mold extended to lifestyle and personal expression of identity, openness about sexuality, departure from nineteenth-century ideas of a woman's place, and shucking off ideas of shame or wrongdoing. Natalie Barney who fled the constraints of Washington society, said she aspired to make Paris the Sapphic Center of the Western world. "My queerness is not a vice, is not deliberate, and harms no one,"[4] was one of her epigrams. Another was "people call it unnatural, all I can say is it's always come naturally to me,"[5] and yet a third was, "Love has always been the main business of my life."[6]

In Paris, rent and food were cheap. Sapphic artists and writers formed a network. They and their work marked a collective sea change, the significance of which went largely undocumented. Many rejected, amended, or bowdlerized their birth names to reflect control over their own lives and refute patriarchal assumptions. The poet Renée Vivien, lover of Natalie Barney and briefly of Colette, left London, dropped her given name Pauline Mary Tarn and chose Renée Vivien to signify that in Paris she was "born again to life." Colette was born Sidonie-Gabrielle Colette. The artists Claude

1 Diana Souhami, *No Modernism Without Lesbians* (London: Head of Zeus, 2020).

2 Gertrude Stein, *Paris France* (New York: Charles Scribner's Sons, 1940), pp. 11, 12.

3 Gertrude Stein, "An American and France" (1936), in *What Are Masterpieces* (1940; New York: Pitman, 1970), p. 70.

4 "[...] mon étrangeté n'est pas un vice, n'est pas 'voulue' et ne nuit à personne": Natalie Clifford Barney, *Lettres à une connue* [Letters to a Woman I Have Known] (1899), quoted in English in Diana Souhami, *Wild Girls: Paris, Sappho and Art; The Lives & Loves of Natalie Barney and Romaine Brooks* (London: Weidenfeld & Nicolson, 2004), p. 57.

5 Ibid., quoted in English in Souhami, *Wild Girls*, p. 150.

6 Natalie Clifford Barney, *Éparpillements* [Scatterings] (Paris: Sansot, 1910), quoted in English in Souhami, *No Modernism Without Lesbians*, p. 215.

und patriarchalische Annahmen zu widerlegen. Die Dichterin Renée Vivien, Geliebte von Barney und zeitweise auch von Colette, verließ London, legte ihren Geburtsnamen Pauline Mary Tarn ab und wählte Renée Vivien, um ihre „Wiedergeburt“ in Paris zu signalisieren. Colette kam als Sidonie-Gabrielle Colette zur Welt. Die Künstler*innen Lucy Schwob, Suzanne Malherbe und Marjorie Jewel Moss nahmen die Namen Claude Cahun, Marcel Moore und Marlow Moss an. Janet Flanner, die für das Magazin *The New Yorker* alle zwei Wochen einen „Letter from Paris“ (Brief aus Paris) über Kultur und Leben in der Stadt schrieb, nannte sich Genêt – was wie eine französische Version von Janet klang. Ihre Lebensgefährtin, die Schriftstellerin Solita Solano, wurde als Sarah Wilkinson im Bundesstaat New York geboren. Die englische Künstler*in Gluck wählte ihren einsilbigen Namen so, dass er sich auf Englisch auf „duck“ reimte, und weigerte sich, mit ihrem Geburtsnamen Hannah Gluckstein oder mit dem Pronomen „she“ angesprochen zu werden.[7]

Gertrude Stein, eine unerschrockene Vorkämpferin für Innovationen, zog 1903 mit 29 Jahren aus Amerika nach Paris, fest entschlossen, Schriftstellerin zu werden. Sie lebte mit ihrem Bruder Leo in dessen Mietwohnung in der Rue de Fleurus 27 im sechsten Arrondissement. Gemeinsam frönten sie ihrer Leidenschaft für zeitgenössische Kunst und kauften Bilder, vor allem bei dem Händler Ambroise Vollard in der Rue Laffitte, um sie in ihrer Wohnung aufzuhängen. Mit einem Budget von 300 Francs pro Bild konnten sie nur Werke junger, relativ unbekannter Künstler erwerben, darunter Henri Matisse, Pablo Picasso, Paul Cézanne und andere Wegbereiter der Moderne und weitere. Für Gertrude spiegelten deren provokante Werke und ihr Bruch mit traditionellen Ausdrucksformen ihr eigenes Denken wider und beeinflussten ihr Schreiben. Die Künstler wurden ihre Freunde und ihr Mäzenatentum förderte deren Karrieren. Zusammen mit ihrem Bruder trug sie eine außergewöhnliche Sammlung zusammen.[8] Jedes neue Bild eröffnete ihnen eine neue Art des Sehens.

Weil Besucher*innen die innovativen Gemälde zu jeder Tageszeit sehen wollten, richtete Gertrude Stein Samstagabendsalons ein: „Matisse brachte Bekannte mit, jeder brachte jemanden mit sie kamen zu jeder beliebigen Zeit, und es begann unerträglich zu werden“, schrieb sie.[9] Menschen aller Art kamen vorbei. Gertrude beobachtete ihre Charaktere, um sie für ihr modernistisches Hauptwerk, *The Making of Americans*, in ein „charakteriologisches System“ einzuordnen. Dieses tausendseitige, kapitellose Buch sollte von allen handeln, die je gelebt hatten, fand jedoch bei den Verlagen wenig Anklang.[10]

Einer dieser innovativen Kunstschaffenden war Picasso, der zu Gertrudes engsten Freunden zählte. Im Winter 1906 bat er sie, ihm Modell zu sitzen. Drei Monate lang verbrachte sie fast jeden Nachmittag in seinem Atelier im Bateau-Lavoir im 18. Arrondissement. Sie redeten so viel, dass er etwa 90 Sitzungen für das Porträt brauchte. Im Frühjahr 1907 vollendete Picasso ihren Kopf und klagte, er habe sie so lange betrachtet, dass er sie nicht mehr sehen könne. Später im Jahr malte er ihr Gesicht aus dem Gedächtnis, so als wäre es eine Maske.

Gertrude gefiel das Porträt. Sie hatte das Gefühl, dass sie beide wie Chronist*innen des 20. Jahrhunderts die Wirklichkeit auf verschiedene Weise rekonstruierten. „[F]ür mich, bin ich es, und es ist das einzige Abbild von mir das immer ich ist, für mich“, sagte sie über das Porträt.[11] Rund 20 Jahre später ging die genderqueere Künstler*in Claude Cahun mit ihren Masken und der schwer fassbaren

7
Sowohl im Kollektiv als auch individuell legten genderqueere Kreative jegliche Patronyme, Pronomen und Vorannahmen ab, die ihnen eine falsche Identität auferlegten.

8
Vgl. *The Steins Collect: Matisse, Picasso, and the Parisian Avant-Garde*, hrsg. von Janet Bishop, Cécile Debray und Rebecca Rabinow, Ausst.-Kat. San Francisco Museum of Modern Art/Réunion des Musées Nationaux-Grand Palais, Paris/The Metropolitan Museum of Art, New York, New Haven 2011.

9
Gertrude Stein, *Autobiographie von Alice B. Toklas*, Übers. aus dem Amerik. von Elisabeth Schnack, Hamburg 1993, S. 49/50.

10
Vgl. Diana Souhami, *Gertrude und Alice. Gertrude Stein und Alice B. Toklas. Zwei Leben – eine Biographie*, Übers. aus dem Engl. von Ulrike Budde, München 1994, S. 88–90.

11
Gertrude Stein, „Picasso 1938“, in: *Picasso. Sämtliche Texte 1909–1938*, Übers. aus dem Amerik. von Roseli und Saskia Bontjes van Beek, Zürich/Hamburg 1958, S. 35.

Cahun, Marcel Moore, and Marlow Moss changed their names from Lucy Schwob, Suzanne Malherbe, and Marjorie Jewel Moss. Janet Flanner, who wrote a fortnightly letter from Paris for *The New Yorker* magazine about the city's culture and life, used the byline Genêt, which maybe sounded like a French version of Janet. Her partner, the writer Solita Solano, was born Sarah Wilkinson in New York State. The English artist Gluck pronounced her chosen monosyllabic name to rhyme with "duck" and balked if called by her birth name, Hannah Gluckstein, or if assigned the pronoun "she."[7]

Gertrude Stein, a fearless champion of innovation, arrived in Paris from America in 1903, aged twenty-nine, ambitious to be a writer. She joined her brother Leo in the apartment he rented at 27 rue de Fleurus in the sixth arrondissement. To indulge their passion for contemporary art, they together bought paintings, mainly from the dealer Ambroise Vollard on rue Laffitte, to hang on the apartment walls. They set a limit of three hundred francs a picture and could only afford work by young, relatively unknown artists. These happened to be Henri Matisse, Pablo Picasso, Paul Cézanne, and others at the cutting edge of modernism... For Gertrude, their startling work and departure from received forms of expression, echoed her own thinking and influenced her writing. They became her friends, and her patronage furthered their careers. She and Leo assembled an extraordinary collection.[8] With each picture they bought, they looked for a new way of seeing.

Gertrude Stein said their weekly evening salons began because, at all hours of the day, people wanted to see these innovative paintings: "Matisse brought people, everybody brought somebody, and they came at any time and it began to be a nuisance."[9] She and Leo formalized the visiting to Saturday evenings. All kinds of people turned up. Gertrude studied their characters so as to fix them into a "characterological system" for her modernist magnum opus, *The Making of Americans*, which was to be about everyone who had ever lived, was a thousand pages long, had no chapters, and which no publisher was in a hurry to take on.[10]

Picasso was Gertrude's particular friend among these innovative artists. In the winter of 1906, he asked to paint her. For three months, most afternoons, she sat for him in his studio at the Bateau-Lavoir in the eighteenth arrondissement. They talked so much the portrait took about ninety sittings. In the spring of 1907, Picasso painted out her head, complaining he had looked so long at her he could not see her anymore. Later that year, from memory, he painted her face as if it were an imposed mask.

Gertrude liked the portrait and felt they were both on the same path as twentieth-century chroniclers who reconstructed reality in different ways. "For me, it is I, and it is the only reproduction of me which is always I, for me,"[11] she said of the portrait. Some twenty years later, the genderqueer artist Claude Cahun took the idea of the mask and elusive identity even further: in her self-portraits, she assumed a range of personas: weightlifter, aviator, doll, man. "Under this mask, another mask," she wrote, "I will never finish removing all these faces."[12]

Marie Laurencin also had a studio in the Bateau-Lavoir. She was the only woman

7
Collectively and individually, genderqueer creatives sloughed off patronymics, pronouns, and assumptions that imposed false identity on them.

8
See Janet Bishop, Cécile Debray, and Rebecca Rabinow (eds.), *The Steins Collect: Matisse, Picasso, and the Parisian Avant-Garde*, exh. cat. San Francisco Museum of Modern Art; Réunion des Musées Nationaux–Grand Palais, Paris; The Metropolitan Museum of Art, New York (New Haven, CT: Yale University Press, 2011).

9
Gertrude Stein, *The Autobiography of Alice B. Toklas* (New York: The Literary Guild, 1933), p. 50.

10
See Diana Souhami, *Gertrude and Alice* (London: Pandora, 1991), pp. 72–73.

11
Gertrude Stein, "Picasso" (1938), in *Gertrude Stein on Picasso*, ed. Edward Burns (New York: Liveright, 1970), p. 14.

12
Claude Cahun, *Disavowals; or, Cancelled Confessions*, trans. Susan de Muth (London: Tate, 2007), p. 183; the quotation is written in French on the photomontage *I.O.U.* (1930): "Sous ce masque un autre masque. Je n'en finirai pas de soulever tous ces visages."

Identität dahinter noch einen Schritt weiter. In ihren Selbstporträts schlüpfte sie in verschiedene Rollen: Gewichtheber*in, Flieger*in, Puppe, Mann. „Unter dieser Maske eine andere Maske“, schrieb sie, „Ich werde nie aufhören, diese Gesichter zu lüften.“[12] Marie Laurencin hatte ebenfalls ein Atelier im Bateau-Lavoir, als einzige Frau unter 20 Künstlern. Sie war mit Guillaume Apollinaire liiert. Picasso hatte sie dem Dichter 1907 als „die perfekte Verlobte“ vorgestellt.[13] Laurencin nahm an den Salons der Steins teil und stellte ihre Werke neben denen ihrer Kollegen aus. Dennoch fühlte sie sich als „Künstlerin“ und Muse Apollinaires oft ausgegrenzt und herabgesetzt. Gertrude Stein kaufte ihr Gemälde *Group of Artists* (1908), das Laurencin mit Apollinaire sowie Picasso mit seinem Hund Frika und seiner Geliebten Fernande Olivier zeigt. Erst als Laurencin den Dichter verließ und sich von ihrem späteren Ehemann, dem deutschen Künstler Otto von Wätjen, scheiden ließ, befreite sie sich vom ständigen Vergleich mit ihren männlichen Zeitgenossen und gewann Selbstvertrauen als Künstlerin. „Doch während mich das Genie der Männer einschüchtert“, schrieb sie, „fühle ich mich mit allem Weiblichen vollkommen wohl.“[14] Ab 1920 arbeitete sie als Malerin, Grafikerin, Buchillustratorin sowie als Kostüm- und Bühnenbildnerin für Sergei Djagilew und die Comédie-Française. Sie hatte offen Affären mit Frauen, darunter eine lange Beziehung mit ihrer Haushälterin Suzanne Moreau, die sie adoptierte, um deren Erbansprüche zu sichern. Laurencin malte Frauen und Tiere in arkadischer Heiterkeit. *Basket II* ist ein sentimentales Ölgemälde des zweiten französischen Pudels von Gertrude Stein, einem Hund namens Basket. Es gab drei aufeinanderfolgende Baskets und jeder spielte im Haushalt der Steins eine entscheidende Rolle. Starb einer, erhielt der nächste denselben Namen – nach dem Motto: „Der König ist tot, es lebe der König.“

Alice B. Toklas kam am 7. September 1907 aus San Francisco nach Paris. Hinter ihr lagen die Schrecken des Erdbebens von 1906, das 3 000 Menschen das Leben gekostet hatte, und die anstrengende Pflege ihres verwitweten Vaters, ihres Großvaters und ihres Bruders. Am Tag nach ihrer Ankunft lernten sie und Gertrude Stein sich bei einem Spaziergang durch den Jardin du Luxembourg kennen und waren von da an unzertrennlich. Sie sahen sich als Ehepaar. Alice war Gertrudes Geliebte, Freundin, Haushälterin, Sekretärin, Köchin, Ehefrau, alles in einer Person. Oft nannte sie Gertrude „er“ oder „ihren Mann“. Gertrude wiederum unterschrieb Briefe gelegentlich mit „Gertrude und Alice Stein“ und feierte in ihren Liebesgedichten die Freuden des Ehelebens. „Die kleine Alice B. ist meine Ehefrau“, schrieb sie.[15] Ihr tiefster Konsens und der Kern ihres gemeinsamen Lebens lag darin, dass Gertrude ein Genie war – und dass sie und ihr Genie bedient werden mussten. Alice zog als Impresario im Hintergrund die Fäden. Mit ihrem Organisationstalent begründete sie Gertrudes Ruhm: Sie tippte die Manuskripte, verhandelte mit Agent*innen, überprüfte die Besucher*innen und führte den Haushalt. Cecil Beatons Fotografien fingen die Unzertrennlichkeit des Paares ein. Auch Claude Cahun und Marcel Moore waren in Kunst und Leben untrennbar miteinander verbunden. Sie lernten sich als Teenager*innen in Nantes in der Bretagne kennen und wurden Stiefschwestern, als Cahuns Vater Moores Mutter heiratete. Gemeinsam schufen sie montierte Selbstporträts: „Porträt des einen oder des anderen, unsere beiden Narzissmen ertrinken darin“, schrieb Cahun in *Aveux non avenus*.[16] „Das hängt vom Einzelfall

12 Claude Cahun, *Aveux non avenus*, in: François Leperlier (Hrsg.), *Écrits. Claude Cahun*, Paris 2002, S. 405; das Zitat erscheint auf Französisch auf der Fotomontage *I.O.U.* (1930): „Sous ce masque un autre masque. Je n'en finirai pas de soulever tous ces visages.“

13 Zit. nach: Roger Shattuck, *The Banquet Years*, New York 1961, S. 265.

14 Marie Laurencin, *Le Carnet des Nuits*, Genf 1956, S. 16.

15 Gertrude Stein, „The Song of Alice B.“, Teil von „A Sonatina Followed by Another“, in *Bee Time Vine and Other Pieces, 1913–1927*, New Haven 1953, S. 12.

16 Claude Cahun 2002 (wie Anm. 12), S. 191.

among the twenty artists there. She and the poet Guillaume Apollinaire were lovers. Picasso had introduced her to Apollinaire in 1907 and told him she would be the "perfect fiancée."[13] She went to the Stein salon meetings and exhibited her work alongside her male contemporaries but felt sidelined and diminished as a "woman artist" and Apollinaire's muse. Gertrude bought her painting *Group of Artists* (1908). It shows Marie Laurencin with Apollinaire, and Picasso with his dog Frika and his lover Fernande Olivier. Only when Marie Laurencin left Apollinaire and divorced her subsequent husband, the German artist Otto von Waetjen, did she feel free from comparison to and scrutiny by her male contemporaries and find her confidence as an artist. "But if the genius of men intimidates me," she wrote, "I feel perfectly at ease with everything that is feminine."[14] From 1920 on, she was prolific as a painter, printmaker, book illustrator, and as a costume and set designer for Sergei Diaghilev and the Comédie-Française. She had open affairs with women, including a long relationship with her housekeeper, Suzanne Moreau, whom she adopted to safeguard inheritance rights for her. She painted women and animals in arcadian tranquility. *Basket II* was a sentimental oil painting of the second of Gertrude Stein's large French poodles. There were three consecutive Baskets and each in turn was essential to the Stein ménage. When one died the next was also called Basket on the understanding "The King is dead, long live the King."

Alice B. Toklas arrived in Paris from San Francisco on September 7, 1907. She had left the destruction caused by the 1906 earthquake, which killed three thousand people, and the drudgery of caring for her widowed father, her grandfather, and brother. The day after her arrival she and Gertrude Stein met and walked together in the Luxembourg Garden. From then on, they were inseparable. They regarded themselves as married. Alice was Gertrude's lover, friend, housekeeper, amanuensis, cook, wife, everything. She often called Gertrude "he," or "her husband," and Gertrude on occasion signed letters from them both, "Gertrude and Alice Stein," and in her love poems referenced the joys of their conjugal life. "Little Alice B. is the wife for me," she wrote.[15] Their deepest point of agreement and the focus of much of their shared life was that Gertrude was a genius and that she and her genius needed to be served. Alice was the power behind the throne, the impresario; her managerial talent created Gertrude's fame: she typed her manuscripts, negotiated with agents, vetted all visitors, and saw to all household affairs. Cecil Beaton's photographs captured their inseparability. Claude Cahun and Marcel Moore were also joined in every aspect of their art and lives. They met as teenagers in Nantes, in Brittany, and became stepsisters when Cahun's father married Moore's mother. They worked collaboratively on merged self-portraits: "Portrait of one or the other, our two narcissisms drowning there," Cahun wrote in *Aveux non avenus* (*Disavowals; or, Cancelled Confessions*),[16] "Masculine? Feminine? It depends on the situation. Neuter is the only gender that always suits me."[17] The most striking and iconic image of lesbian merging, of becoming one

13
Quoted in Roger Shattuck, *The Banquet Years* (1955; New York: Anchor, 1961), p. 265.

14
Marie Laurencin, *Le Carnet des Nuits* (1942; Geneva: Pierre Cailler, 1956), p. 16.

15
Gertrude Stein, "The Song of Alice B.," part of "A Sonatina Followed by Another," in *Bee Time Vine and Other Pieces, 1913–1927* (New Haven, CT: Yale University Press, 1953), p. 12.

16
Claude Cahun, *Disavowals*, p. 12.

17
Ibid., p. 151.

ab. Neutrum ist das einzige Geschlecht, das mir immer entspricht.“[17] Das eindrucksvollste und ikonischste Bild lesbischer Verschmelzung, des Einswerdens durch gleichgeschlechtliche Liebe, stammt von der englischen Künstler*in Gluck. Sie malte mehrere Selbstporträts, die feste Geschlechtsidentitäten infrage stellten: Auf einem von 1925 trägt sie Baskenmütze und Krawatte und raucht eine Zigarette. Ein anderes von 1942, nach der Trennung von ihrer Geliebten, zeigt sie männlich und kämpferisch. Doch ihr kühnstes und aufsehenerregendstes Werk sind die verschmolzenen Profile von ihr und ihrer großen Liebe Nesta Obermer, einer Frau der High Society. Gluck nannte das Bild *Medallion* oder „YouWe“-Porträt: *Medallion* (Abb. 1) in Anlehnung an die römischen Porträts hochrangiger Würdenträger; „YouWe“, weil sie das Gefühl hatte, Nesta und sie seien in ihrer Liebe ein Leib und eine Seele. Es war ein trotziges Bekenntnis zur gleichgeschlechtlichen Liebe, ein frecher Seitenhieb auf die Sicht des Establishments. Der Stolz in den Gesichtern der beiden Frauen strahlt die Kraft revolutionärer Kunst aus. Gluck begann das Werk im Juni 1936, nachdem sie mit Nesta Mozarts Oper *Don Giovanni* in Glyndebourne in East Sussex gesehen hatten. Die Intensität der Musik spiegelte ihre Leidenschaft wider und ließ sie eins werden. Als das Bild fertig war, schrieb sie an Nesta: „Jetzt ist es draußen […] und dem Rest des Universums rufe ich zu: Obacht! Obacht! Mit uns ist nicht zu spaßen.“[18] Mit ihrem Mäzenatentum prägte Gertrude Stein zwar die modernistische Revolution und förderte den freien Ausdruck, ihre sapphischen Schwestern unterstützte sie jedoch nicht übermäßig. Djuna Barnes, die 1921 aus New York nach Paris kam, empfand sie als chauvinistisch: „Ich konnte sie nicht ausstehen. Sie musste immer im Mittelpunkt stehen. Ein monströses Ego“, erinnerte sie sich: „Weißt du, was sie über mich sagte? Sie meinte, ich hätte schöne Beine! Was soll so eine Bemerkung?“[19]

17
Ebd., S. 366.

18
Gluck an Nesta Obermer, undatiert 1937, zit. nach: Diana Souhami, *Gluck, 1895–1978: Her Biography*, überarb. Fassung, London 2000, S. 130.

19
Zit. nach: Andrew Field, *Djuna: The Formidable Miss Barnes* (1983), Austin 1985, S. 104.

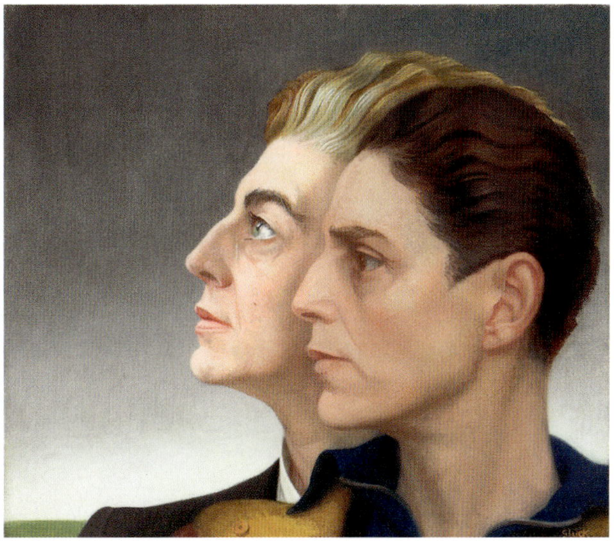

ABB. ~ FIG. 1

Gluck, *Medallion (YouWe)*, 1936

Öl auf Leinwand ~ *Oil on canvas*,
30,5 × 35,6 cm
Privatsammlung ~ *Private Collection*

through same-sex love, was by the English artist Gluck. She did several gender-questioning self-portraits, one in 1925 wearing a beret and tie and smoking a cigarette, one in 1942 when love had failed, looking mannish and combative; but her most innovative and startling work was of the merged profiles of her and the love of her life, the socialite Nesta Obermer.

Gluck called the painting *Medallion* or the "YouWe" portrait: *Medallion* (fig. 1) in allegiance to the Roman casting of portraits of high-ranking dignitaries; "YouWe" because she felt she and Nesta merged body and soul in love. It was a defiant declaration of same-sex love, a brazen snook at the establishment view. The pride in both the women's faces has something of the feel of revolutionary art. Gluck began it in June 1936 after she and Nesta went to Mozart's opera *Don Giovanni* at Glyndebourne in East Sussex. She felt the intensity of the music matched their passion and merged them into one. When the painting was finished, she wrote to Nesta, "Now it is out [...] and to the rest of the Universe I call Beware! Beware! We are not to be trifled with."[18]

Though Gertrude Stein's patronage influenced the modernist revolution and encouraged candor, she was not particularly supportive of her Sapphic sisters. Djuna Barnes, who arrived in Paris from New York in 1921, viewed her as chauvinistic: "I couldn't stand her. She had to be the centre of everything. A monstrous ego." She recalled, "D'you know what she said of me? Said I had beautiful legs! Now what does that have to do with anything?"[19]

In her classic modernist novel *Nightwood*, published in 1936, Djuna Barnes abandoned rules of form and sentence structure. She described the book as "a soul talking to itself in the heart of the night."[20] Into it she channeled the torment of her tempestuous eight-year relationship with the American silverpoint artist Thelma Wood. After the relationship ended, Djuna wrote, "I have *had* my great love, there will never be another."[21] She did though have a brief affair with Natalie Barney and was a visitor to her Friday afternoon salons at 20 rue Jacob. Natalie moved permanently from Washington to Paris in 1909. She acquired the soubriquet *l'Amazone* (the Amazon), for the way she rode bareback in the Bois de Boulogne most mornings. Her salons, dubbed "the hazardous Fridays,"[22] were both a showcase of artistic innovation and a lesbian club. Sylvia Beach, who owned the English-language bookshop Shakespeare and Company at 12 rue de l'Odéon, wrote, "At Miss Barney's one met the ladies with high collars and monocles, though Miss Barney herself was so feminine."[23]

Natalie aspired to make Paris the Sapphic center of the Western world. She categorized her lovers into relationships, affairs, and adventures. The adventures were too numerous to tally. Alice B. Toklas said she picked up some of them in the toilets of Paris department stores. "I didn't create a salon. A salon was created around me,"[24] Natalie wrote. In 1918, Apollinaire had published a book of poems, *Calligrammes*, meaning "beautiful lines" in Greek. The poems related to the First World War and the typography of each formed a drawing. As the frontispiece to her *Aventures de l'esprit* (Adventures of the Mind), published in 1929, Natalie doodled her

18
Gluck to Nesta Obermer, undated 1937, quoted in Diana Souhami, *Gluck, 1895–1978: Her Biography*, rev. ed. (1988; London: Phoenix, 2000), p. 130.

19
Quoted in Andrew Field, *Djuna: The Formidable Miss Barnes* (1983; Austin: University of Texas Press, 1985), p. 104.

20
A reference to a comment by Peter Neagoe, Djuna Barnes to Emily Coleman, June 26, 1935.

21
Phillip Herring, *The Life and Work of Djuna Barnes* (New York: Viking, 1995), p. 166.

22
See George Wickes, "A Natalie Barney Garland," *The Paris Review*, no. 61 (Spring 1975): pp. 115–116.

23
Sylvia Beach, *Shakespeare and Company* (1956; London: Faber and Faber, 1960), p. 123.

24
See Souhami, *Wild Girls*, p. 62. Jean Chalon remembers Natalie Barney using this phrasing with him many times: personal correspondence with Chalon, April 10, 2025. A similar sentiment is found in Jean Chalon, *Portrait of a Seductress: The World of Natalie Barney*, trans. Carol Barko (1976, New York: Crown, 1979), p. 159.

In ihrem klassischen modernistischen Roman *Nachtgewächs* (1936) bricht Barnes bewusst mit den Regeln von Form und Syntax. Sie beschreibt das Buch als „eine Seele, die im Herzen der Nacht mit sich selbst spricht,“[20] und verarbeitet darin die Qualen ihrer achtjährigen stürmischen Beziehung zur amerikanischen Silberstiftkünstlerin Thelma Wood. Nach dem Ende dieser Beziehung schrieb Djuna: „Ich habe meine große Liebe *gehabt*, es wird nie eine andere geben.“[21] Sie hatte jedoch eine kurze Affäre mit Natalie Barney und besuchte freitagnachmittags deren Salon in der Rue Jacob 20. 1909 zog Natalie endgültig von Washington nach Paris. Man nannte sie „l'Amazone“, weil sie morgens oft ohne Sattel durch den Bois de Boulogne ritt. Ihre Salons, die sie die „gefährlichen Freitage“[22] nannte, waren nicht nur ein Schaufenster künstlerischer Innovation, sondern auch ein Treffpunkt für Lesben. Sylvia Beach, die die englischsprachige Buchhandlung Shakespeare and Company in der Rue de l'Odéon 12 führte, schrieb: „Man traf bei Miss Barney Damen mit hohen Krägen und Monokel, obwohl Miss Barney selbst so weiblich war.“[23] Natalie wollte Paris zum sapphischen Zentrum der westlichen Welt machen. Ihre Liebhaber*innen unterteilte sie in Beziehungen, Affären und Abenteuer. Die Abenteuer waren zu zahlreich, um sie alle zu zählen. Einige hatte sie laut Alice B. Toklas auf den Toiletten der Pariser Kaufhäuser getroffen. „Ich habe keinen Salon geschaffen. Um mich herum ist ein Salon entstanden“[24], schrieb Natalie. 1918 veröffentlichte Apollinaire den Gedichtband *Calligrammes*, wörtlich übersetzt „schöne Zeilen“. Die Gedichte thematisierten den Ersten Weltkrieg, wobei die Typografie jeweils eine Zeichnung bildete. Für den Umschlag ihres 1929 erschienenen Buchs *Aventures de l'esprit* (dt. *Abenteuer des Geistes*) entwarf Natalie ihr eigenes Kalligramm, „Le Salon de l'amazone“ (Abb. 4, S. 61). Es zeigt das Wohnzimmer ihres Hauses und den kleinen Pavillon aus dem 18. Jahrhundert im Garten, den „Temple à l'Amitié“ (Tempel für die Freundschaft), in den die Namen der vielen Besucher*innen eingeflochten sind, die zu ihren freitäglichen Treffen kamen. Jeder Name steht für eine Person und einen Beitrag zur Moderne. In der Mitte steht ein Tisch mit Tee und Erdbeertörtchen. Ein weiterer Anreiz für die Gäste bestand darin, Gleichgesinnte oder Liebhaber*innen zu treffen und über die neuesten Entwicklungen in der Kunst zu diskutieren. Nach 1927 konzentrierten sich die Freitagstreffen auf die Arbeit von Frauen. Natalie nannte sie „Académie des Femmes“ (Frauenakademie) – als rebellische Antwort auf die rein männliche Académie Française. Auf Anregung von Natalie schrieb Djuna Barnes 1928 den *Ladies Almanack*, eine freche Satire auf Natalie und ihren Kreis, voller Anspielungen auf sexuelle Techniken und wildes Verhalten. Das Werk, gestaltet wie ein mittelalterliches Brevier mit monatlichen Einträgen und Tierkreiszeichen, spiegelt Aspekte lesbischen Begehrens wider – den „sich windenden Schenkel“, den „suchenden Arm“ – und diente als Handbuch für Lesben, die „Staubwedel, Kinder und Ehepartner ablegen“ wollten.[25] Die Sprache war eine Mischung aus blumigem elisabethanischem Englisch und Umgangssprache, gespickt mit Großbuchstaben, kryptischen Anspielungen und schmutzigen Witzen. Natalie war Dame Evangeline Musset, eine lesbische Päpstin mit unendlichen Gelüsten und einem Bett, das nie leer war. Ihre Liebhaber*innen und Freund*innen waren unverkennbar. Finanziert wurde die Veröffentlichung des *Ladies Almanack* von Bryher, die viele innovative queere Projekte in

20 Eine Anspielung auf einen Kommentar von Peter Neagoe, Djuna Barnes an Emily Coleman, 26. Juni 1935.

21 Phillip Herring, Djuna: *The Life and Work of Djuna Barnes*, New York 1995, S. 166.

22 Vgl. George Wickes, „A Natalie Barney Garland“, in: *The Paris Review*, Nr. 61, Frühjahr 1975, S. 115–116.

23 Sylvia Beach, *Shakespeare and Company. Ein Buchladen in Paris*, Übers. aus dem Amerik. von Lilly von Sauter, Frankfurt am Main 1982, S. 131.

24 Vgl. Souhami 2004 (wie Anm. 4), S. 62. Jean Chalon erinnert sich, dass Natalie Barney diese Formulierung ihm gegenüber oft benutzte (persönliche Korrespondenz mit Chalon, 10. April 2025). Eine ähnliche Haltung schildert er in seinem Buch *Portrait of a Seductress: The World of Natalie Barney*, übers. von Carol Barko (1976), New York 1979, S. 159.

25 Djuna Barnes, *Ladies Almanack* (1928), Normal 1992, S. 52, 7.

own calligram, “Le Salon de l'amazone” (p. 61, fig. 4). It depicts the front room of her house and the small eighteenth-century pavilion in the garden, the Temple à l'Amitié, the Temple to Friendship, and weaving in and out are the names of the multitude of visitors who came to her Friday gatherings. Each name speaks of an individual and a contribution to modernism. At the center is a table with tea and strawberry tarts. Other incentives for guests were to meet like minds or lovers and discuss the cutting edge of art. After 1927, the Friday gatherings focused on the work of women. Natalie styled these meetings the Académie des Femmes (Women's Academy) as a defiant response to the all-male Académie Française.

At Natalie's suggestion, Djuna Barnes, in 1928, wrote *Ladies Almanack*. It was an outrageous satire on Natalie and her circle, full of reference to sexual technique and wild behavior. Constructed like a medieval breviary, with monthly entries and zodiac signs that corresponded to some aspect of lesbian desire—the “twining thigh,” the “seeking arm”—it was a manual for lesbians who “discard Duster, Offspring and Spouse.”[25] The language was a mix of ornate Elizabethan and colloquial English with many capital letters, cryptic allusions, and dirty jokes. Natalie was Dame Evangeline Musset, a lesbian pope, whose desires were infinite and her bed never empty. Her lovers and friends were recognizable. Publication of *Ladies Almanack* was financed by Bryher, benefactor to many cutting-edge queer projects in art, film, and writing. Bryher (her chosen name was one of the Scilly Isles she loved) was born Winifred Ellerman in 1894, daughter of the richest man in England. To pacify her parents and secure her inheritance, she married a queer penniless American writer, Robert McAlmon. She set him up in Paris as the publisher of Contact Editions, then lived and travelled freely in Europe with her partner, the American modernist poet H.D.—Hilda Doolittle. With Bryher's money, Contact published, often for the first time, the work of Gertrude Stein, Djuna Barnes, H.D., Ernest Hemingway, Ezra Pound… Sappho and her circle of creative women inspired Natalie's salon creation. In ancient Greece, no other woman poet achieved Sappho's recognition. Natalie hoped to emulate her life and ideals and create a utopia, free from patriarchal rule, of women who supported and loved each other. In 1900, in Paris she published a collection of poems to and about her lovers, *Quelques portraits-sonnets de femmes* (Some Portrait-Sonnets of Women). She wrote of hearts pounding like the sea, her lovers' orgasmic cries. (Her father bought up and destroyed the printer's plates and all unsold copies.) With two of her lovers, the artist Eva Palmer, then the poet Renée Vivien, Natalie learned Greek to understand Sappho's verses and wrote poems in her honor. Eva Palmer left for Greece when her relationship with Natalie ended. Natalie and Renée Vivien made a journey together to Lesbos in homage to Sappho. The Sapphic ideal was a recurring theme for lesbian modernists. Dame Ethel Walker's huge painting, *Decoration: The Excursion of Nausicaa* (1920, cat. p. 39), suggests Sappho and her followers. She took the description in Homer's *Odyssey* where Nausicaa, a Phaeacian princess, and her handmaidens,

25 Djuna Barnes, *Ladies Almanack* (1928, Normal, IL: Dalkey Archive, 1992), pp. 52, 7.

Kunst, Film und Literatur unterstützte. Bryher (sie wählte ihren Namen in Anlehnung an die Scilly-Inseln, die sie liebte) wurde 1894 als Winifred Ellerman, Tochter des reichsten Mannes Englands, geboren. Um ihre Eltern zu besänftigen und ihr Erbe zu sichern, heiratete sie den mittellosen, queeren amerikanischen Schriftsteller Robert McAlmon. Mit ihm gründete sie in Paris den Verlag Contact Editions und reiste mit ihrer Partnerin, der amerikanischen modernistischen Dichterin H. D. – Hilda Doolittle – frei durch Europa. Dank Bryhers Unterstützung veröffentlichte Contact Editions erstmals Werke von Gertrude Stein, Djuna Barnes, H. D., Ernest Hemingway, Ezra Pound und anderen.

Sappho und ihr Kreis kreativer Frauen inspirierten Natalie bei der Gestaltung ihres Salons. Keine Dichterin der griechischen Antike genoss so viel Ruhm wie Sappho. Natalie wollte ihrem Vorbild folgen, ihre Ideale leben und eine Utopie frei von patriarchalischer Herrschaft schaffen, in der Frauen sich gegenseitig unterstützten und liebten. Im Jahr 1900 veröffentlichte sie in Paris eine Sammlung von Gedichten an und über ihre Geliebten, *Quelques portraits-sonnets de femmes* (Einige Porträt-Sonette von Frauen). Darin schrieb sie von Herzen, die wie das Meer pochen, und von den ekstatischen Schreien ihrer Liebhaber*innen. (Ihr Vater ließ die Druckplatten und alle nicht verkauften Exemplare vernichten.) Gemeinsam mit zwei Geliebten, der Künstlerin Eva Palmer und der Dichterin Renée Vivien, lernte Natalie Griechisch, um Sapphos Verse zu verstehen, und widmete der griechischen Dichterin eigene Gedichte. Als die Beziehung zu Natalie zerbrach, zog Eva Palmer nach Griechenland. Natalie und Renée Vivien reisten gemeinsam nach Lesbos, um Sappho zu huldigen.

Das sapphische Ideal faszinierte lesbische Künstler*innen der Moderne immer wieder. Dame Ethel Walkers großes Gemälde *Decoration: The Excursion of Nausicaa* (1920, Kat., S. 39) erinnert an Sappho und ihre Gefährtinnen. Walker greift Homers *Odyssee* auf, in der die phäakische Prinzessin Nausikaa mit ihren Mägden zum Fluss geht, um Kleider in der Mittagssonne zu waschen und zu trocknen. Das Bild zeigt eine utopische, rein weibliche Gemeinschaft, in der nackte Frauen in verschiedenen Posen ein harmonisches Ganzes bilden und vor männlichen Blicken geschützt sind. In Homers Erzählung entdeckt Odysseus sie beim Waschen, und Nausikaa begleitet ihn auf seiner Heimreise nach Ithaka nach dem Trojanischen Krieg. In Walkers Darstellung bleibt Odysseus eine Randfigur, kaum wahrnehmbar.

Die Liebe zum weiblichen Körper war eine erklärte Konstante in Walkers Werk. In den 1880er-Jahren lebte sie mit der Künstlerin Clara Christian in London. Auf einem androgynen Selbstporträt von 1925 trägt sie ein Herrenjackett, Hemd und Krawatte. Wie viele andere wollte sie nicht als „Künstlerin" gelten. „Künstlerinnen gibt es nicht", sagte sie, „es gibt nur zwei Arten von Künstlern – schlechte und gute. Nennen Sie mich einen guten Künstler, wenn Sie wollen."[26]

Die sapphischen Modernist*innen befreiten sich von der destruktiven Vorstellung, Frauenkunst sei zwangsläufig minderwertig. Diese bequeme Haltung der Männer rechtfertigte es, sie aus Galerien auszuschließen und ihre Werke zu ignorieren. Die französische Künstlerin Rosa Bonheur soll sich geschmeichelt gefühlt haben, als man ihr sagte, sie male wie ein Mann. Wie ihr eindrucksvolles Gemälde *The Horse Fair* (1852–1855) vom Pariser Pferdemarkt zeigt, zogen sich Frauen keineswegs ins Boudoir zurück. Für ihre Studien auf Pferdemärkten musste Bonheur eine polizeiliche Erlaubnis zum Tragen von Hosen

26 Zit. nach: *Modern Scottish Women: Painters and Sculptors, 1885–1965*, hrsg. von Alice Strang, Edinburgh 2015, S. 104.

go to the river to wash and dry their clothes in the noonday sun. The composition is a utopian vision of an all-female community, the nude women, in a variety of poses, are in harmony and safe from the male gaze. In Homer's version, as they do their washing, they are discovered by Odysseus, whom Nausicaa then guides through the next stage of his journey home to Ithaca after the Trojan War. Dame Ethel Walker's Odysseus seems like an irrelevant afterthought in the picture and is hard to find. Love of the female body was a declared constant in Dame Ethel's work. In the 1880s, she lived in London with the artist Clara Christian, and in an androgynous self-portrait in 1925, she wears a mannish jacket, shirt, and tie. Like many, she did not want to be viewed as a "woman artist." "There is no such thing as a woman artist," she is recorded as saying, "There are only two kinds of artist—bad and good. You can call me a good artist if you like."[26] The Sapphic modernists freed themselves from the annihilating assumption that art by women was necessarily inferior. It was a convenient male stance to justify omitting them from the galleries and for ignoring their work. The French artist Rosa Bonheur is supposed to have felt flattered when told she painted like a man. Her undoubtedly great painting *The Horse Fair* (1852–1855), depicting the Paris horse market, has no hint of the ladies' boudoir. She had to get *permission de travestissement*—police permission to wear trousers—when researching her subject at horse sales. She lived with her partner, the painter Nathalie Micas, was inspired by her love and knowledge of animals, had short hair, smoked, and to improve her anatomical accuracy, visited slaughterhouses and dissected animals. "The fact is, in the way of males, I like only the bulls I paint," was her rebuke.[27]

Romaine Brooks was Natalie Barney's lover and lifelong friend. She painted portraits of many in their circle. She fitted Natalie's superior category of "relationship." The writer Truman Capote visited her Paris studio after the Second World War and saw the array of her large paintings of genderqueer women. He said, "It was the all-time ultimate gallery of all the famous dykes from 1880 to 1935 or thereabouts. [...] and it was like an international daisy chain":[28] "You know how you know when you're not going to forget something? I wasn't going to forget this moment, this room, this array of butch-babes."[29] One of Romaine's portraits was of Gluck, painted in 1926, ten years before Gluck met Nesta Obermer. They intended to paint reciprocal portraits of each other. Romaine, twenty years older than Gluck, called hers *Peter, a Young English Girl* (1923/24, fig. 2). Gluck's large portrait of Romaine was never finished. She satirically called it *Mrs. Romaine Brooks* in reference to Romaine's cover-up marriage to John Ellingham Brooks, pianist, classical scholar, and lover of Somerset Maugham. She and Romaine quarreled during the sitting, Romaine stormed out and Gluck eventually used the canvas for something else. Gluck's cast of mind was rebellious and challenging, but her painting technique showed allegiance to the skills of the Old Masters. To establish her own identity, she disassociated herself from her wealthy patriarchal Jewish family, the Glucksteins, who founded the J. Lyons & Company catering empire and owned most of London's leading hotels, and

26 Quoted in Alice Strang, ed., *Modern Scottish Women: Painters and Sculptors, 1885–1965* (Edinburgh: National Galleries of Scotland, 2015), p. 104.

27 Dore Ashton, *Rosa Bonheur: A Life and a Legend* (New York: Viking, 1981), p. 59.

28 Truman Capote, quoted in Wickes, "A Natalie Barney Garland": p. 121.

29 Truman Capote, "Unspoiled Monsters," in *Answered Prayers: The Unfinished Novel* (New York: Random House, 1987), p. 40.

(*Permission de travestissement*) einholen. Sie lebte mit ihrer Lebensgefährtin, der Malerin Nathalie Micas, zusammen, ließ sich von ihrer Tierliebe und ihrem Wissen über Tiere inspirieren, trug kurzes Haar, rauchte, besuchte Schlachthöfe und sezierte Tiere, um ihren anatomischen Blick zu schärfen. „Was männliche Wesen betrifft, interessieren mich nur die Stiere, die ich male", sagte sie.[27] Romaine Brooks war die Geliebte und lebenslange Freundin von Natalie Barney. Sie porträtierte viele Menschen aus ihrem Umfeld. In Natalies Taxonomie passte sie in die übergeordnete Kategorie der „Beziehung". Als der Schriftsteller Truman Capote nach dem Zweiten Weltkrieg ihr Pariser Atelier betrat und ihre großformatigen Porträts genderqueerer Frauen betrachtete, sagte er: „Es war die ultimative Galerie aller berühmten Lesben von 1880 bis 1935 oder so. [...] es war wie ein internationaler Reigen von Menschen, die miteinander Affären hatten."[28] Und weiter: „Kennen Sie das, wenn Sie wissen, *das* werden Sie nicht vergessen? Mir jedenfalls ist das unvergesslich geblieben, dieser Augenblick, dieser Raum, diese Phalanx von kessen Vätern".[29]

1926 malte Romaine ein Porträt von Gluck, zehn Jahre, bevor diese Nesta Obermer kennenlernte. Beide wollten sich gegenseitig porträtieren. Romaine, 20 Jahre älter als Gluck, nannte ihr Porträt *Peter (A Young English Girl)* (1923/24, Abb. 2). Glucks großes Porträt von Romaine blieb unvollendet. Sie gab ihm den satirischen Titel *Mrs. Romaine Brooks*, eine Anspielung auf Romaines Scheinehe mit John Ellingham Brooks, einem Pianisten, Altphilologen und Liebhaber von Somerset Maugham. Während der Porträtsitzung stritten sich Gluck und Romaine, worauf Romaine hinausstürmte. Gluck nutzte die Leinwand später für ein anderes Werk.

27 Dore Ashton, *Rosa Bonheur: A Life and a Legend*, New York 1981, S. 59.

28 Truman Capote, zit. nach: Wickes 1975 (wie Anm. 22), S. 121.

29 Truman Capote, „Unverdorbene Ungeheuer", in: *Erhörte Gebete*, Übers. aus dem Amerik. von Heidi Zerning, München 2010, S. 9–123, hier: S. 55.

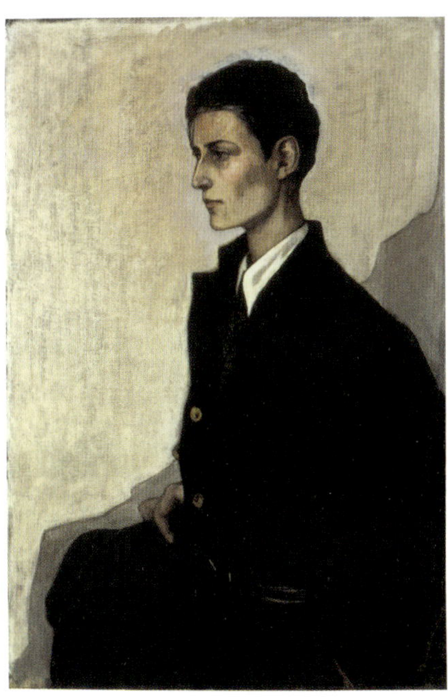

ABB. ~ FIG. 2

Romaine Brooks,
Peter (A Young English Girl), 1923/24
Peter (Ein junges englisches Mädchen)

Öl auf Leinwand ~ *Oil on canvas*, 91,9 × 62,3 cm
Smithsonian American Art Museum (SAAM), Washington D.C. Collection Pascal ALCAN LEGRAND, Paris

among whom women were wives, mothers, and daughters without careers. Gluck's American mother had trained as a singer, but ambition ended when she married. "I could not allow my wife to work for her living," her husband Joseph Gluckstein said.[30] He accepted his daughter studying at the amateurish St. John's Wood Art School, but when she had her hair barbered, bought her shirts in London's Jermyn Street, wore men's jackets and ties, blew her nose on large handkerchiefs monogrammed with a G and ran off to Cornwall to paint with the Newlyn school, he wrote of an unhappiness "too strong for philosophy." Her mother referred to "a kink in the brain."[31] Gluck braved her way despite family discouragement. Her work was successful and her exhibitions at The Fine Art Society in London highly praised. On the backs of photographic prints of her work, sent out for publicity purposes, she always wrote, "Please return in good condition to Gluck, no prefix, suffix, or quotes."[32] Her paintings were autobiographical: landscapes of Cornwall, the London revues of the 1920s, her absorption into Nesta Obermer's life in the 1930s. Many were portraits of her lovers or aspects of their lives. When in a relationship with Constance Spry, flower arranger to royalty and the English aristocracy, Gluck painted abundant arrangements of white flowers at a time when the all-white interior characterized modernist design.

Gluck lived and worked in England, resisted identifying with any group or movement and referred scornfully to Romaine Brooks's Paris social circle as the "lesbian haute-monde."[33] She did though record frequent meetings in a Paris hotel with the Viennese artist Mariette Lydis and painted a portrait of her, which she destroyed when she met Nesta Obermer and wanted no reminders of past lovers. Born in Vienna in 1887, Mariette Lydis arrived in Paris in 1926 with two marriages behind her. She intended to make the city her home and described it as "the only place where it is possible to forget the brutality of men."[34] That year she published *Lesbiennes*, seventy-one copies of twenty-five etched and hand-colored signed plates of sex between women.[35] It was one of the most fearless books of that decade. Much of her work was for book illustration linked to censored literature of the time. She was a friend of James Joyce, and in 1925, when his banned modernist novel *Ulysses* (1922) was available only in pirated form, she did the first portrait of its hero Leopold Bloom for *900*, a radical Italian literary review Joyce edited. In 1928, her lithographs illustrated a publication of Charles Baudelaire's *Les Fleurs du mal* (*The Flowers of Evil*). Baudelaire was prosecuted when *Les Fleurs du mal* was first published in 1857 because of the lesbian and erotic themes of some of the poems. Lithographs by Mariette Lydis were exhibited at the 1928 Salon d'Automne in Paris, and in 1933, she published *Sappho*, forty copies of sixteen etchings with translations from Greek to French by Renée Vivien of the extant fragments of Sappho's poems. Punitive censorship laws in Britain and America governed what could or could not be viewed or published. These laws prevented lesbians from disseminating work about their sexual orientation. As subject matter, it was deemed

30 Joseph Gluckstein, letter to Mr. and Mrs. Louis Hallé, August 8, 1894, quoted in Souhami, *Gluck*, p. 29.

31 Quoted in Ibid., pp. 39, 10.

32 Ibid., p. 9.

33 Ibid., p. 63.

34 Quoted in Justin Croft and Cult Jones, *Mariette Lydis: Dreams and Destiny* (London: Justin Croft, Antiquarian Books, 2023), p. 3.

35 Mariette Lydis, *Lesbiennes* (Paris, 1926), see Croft and Jones, *Mariette Lydis*, lot 6, pp. 10–15.

Gluck war rebellisch und provozierend, doch ihre Maltechnik war den Alten Meistern verpflichtet. Um sich selbst zu finden, brach sie mit ihrer wohlhabenden, patriarchalischen jüdischen Familie, den Glucksteins, die das Catering-Imperium J. Lyons & Company gegründet hatten und viele der führenden Hotels Londons besaßen. In ihrer Welt waren Frauen Gattinnen, Mütter und Töchter – Karrieren blieben ihnen verwehrt. Glucks amerikanische Mutter hatte Gesang studiert, doch mit der Heirat endeten ihre Träume. „Ich konnte meiner Frau nicht erlauben, für ihren Lebensunterhalt zu arbeiten", erklärte ihr Mann Joseph Gluckstein.[30]

Er duldete zwar, dass seine Tochter an der amateurhaften St. John's Wood Art School studierte. Doch als sie sich den Kopf kahl rasierte, Hemden aus der Londoner Jermyn Street trug, Herrenjacken und Krawatten wählte, die Nase in großen Taschentüchern mit einem monogrammierten G schnäuzte und nach Cornwall zog, um in der Künstler*innenkolonie Newlyn School zu malen, schrieb er von einer Traurigkeit, „die zu stark für die Philosophie" war. Glucks Mutter sprach von einem „Tick im Gehirn".[31]

Trotz der Warnungen ihrer Familie ging Gluck unbeirrt ihren Weg. Ihre Arbeiten fanden Anerkennung und ihre Ausstellungen in der Fine Art Society in London wurden hochgelobt. Auf die Rückseite der Fotos ihrer Gemälde, die sie zu Werbezwecken verschickte, schrieb sie stets: „Bitte in gutem Zustand an Gluck zurücksenden, ohne Präfix, Suffix oder Anführungszeichen".[32] Ihre Bilder waren autobiografisch grundiert: Landschaften aus Cornwall, die Londoner Revuen der 1920er-Jahre, ihr Eintauchen in das Leben von Nesta Obermer in den 1930er-Jahren. Viele waren Porträts ihrer Liebhaber*innen oder zeigten Szenen aus deren Leben. Während ihrer Beziehung zu Constance Spry, der Blumenarrangeurin des Königshauses und der englischen Aristokratie, malte Gluck zahlreiche weiße Blumenarrangements – passend zu den in Weiß gehaltenen Interieurs, die den modernistischen Stil jener Zeit prägten.

Gluck lebte und arbeitete in England, hielt sich von allen Gruppen und Bewegungen fern und verspottete die Pariser Gesellschaft um Romaine Brooks als „lesbische Haute-Monde".[33] Dennoch berichtete sie von häufigen Treffen mit der Wiener Künstlerin Mariette Lydis in einem Pariser Hotel und malte ein Porträt von ihr. Dieses zerstörte sie später, als sie Nesta Obermer kennenlernte und alle Erinnerungen an frühere Liebhaber*innen tilgen wollte.

Mariette Lydis, 1887 in Wien geboren, zog nach zwei Ehen 1926 nach Paris. Sie wollte die Stadt zu ihrem Zuhause machen und nannte sie „den einzigen Ort, an dem man die Brutalität der Männer vergessen kann".[34] Im selben Jahr veröffentlichte sie *Lesbiennes*, 25 handkolorierte und signierte Radierungen, die Sex zwischen Frauen zeigen und in einer Auflage von 71 Exemplaren erschienen.[35] Es galt als eines der gewagtesten Bücher des Jahrzehnts.

Einen Großteil ihrer Arbeit widmete sie der Illustration von Büchern, die mit der zensierten Literatur jener Zeit verbunden waren. Sie war mit James Joyce befreundet und zeichnete 1925, als sein verbotener modernistischer Roman *Ulysses* (1922) nur als Raubdruck kursierte, das erste Porträt seines Helden Leopold Bloom. Es erschien in *900*, einer radikalen italienischen Literaturzeitschrift, die von Joyce herausgegeben wurde. 1928 schmückten ihre Lithografien eine Ausgabe von Charles Baudelaires *Les Fleurs du mal* (dt. *Die Blumen des Bösen*). Bei der Erstveröffentlichung 1857 war Baudelaire wegen der lesbischen und erotischen Themen einiger Gedichte strafrechtlich

30 Joseph Gluckstein, Brief an Mr. und Mrs. Louis Hallé, 8. August 1894, zit. nach: Souhami 2000 (wie Anm. 18), S. 29.

31 Zit. nach: ebd., S. 39, 10.

32 Ebd., S. 9.

33 Ebd., S. 63.

34 Zit. nach: Justin Croft and Cult Jones, *Mariette Lydis: Dreams and Destiny*, London 2023, S. 3.

35 Mariette Lydis, *Lesbiennes*, Paris 1926, vgl. Croft und Jones 2023 (wie Anm. 34), lot 6, S. 10–15.

obscene. Sex between consenting men was a criminal act. Sex between women was not illegal because it was not countenanced by society. Silence and threat of censorship were weapons for its repression. Government agents were assiduous in tracking down offenders. In New York, Eva Kotchever, known also as Eve Adams, wrote *Lesbian Love* as a series of vignettes in 1925 and ran Eve's Hangout, an openly lesbian literary salon. She was apprehended by an undercover policewoman, jailed for obscenity, and deported to Poland in 1927. In 1928, in London there was the startling trial and censorship of Radclyffe Hall's anodyne lesbian novel *The Well of Loneliness*. The subject matter was deemed untenable even though the only sexy bits in it are "she kissed her full on the lips" and "that night they were not divided."[36] The editor of the *Sunday Express*, James Douglas, wrote in an editorial "I would rather give a healthy boy or a healthy girl a phial of prussic acid than this novel." The Chairman of the Court that passed sentence, Sir Robert Wallace, said the book was "more subtle, demoralising, corrosive and corruptive than anything ever written."[37]

The book was indicted under the Criminal Law Amendment Act of 1885 against obscene libel, which criminalized male homosexuality. It was "burned in the King's furnace." Radclyffe Hall left England for Paris with her partner Una Troubridge and never lived in Britain again. Janet Flanner said *The Well* should have paved the way for better books on the same subject. Banning this sorry novel caused a cloak of shame to hang over same-sex love. In Britain, fearing prosecution, no publisher risked reprinting it until 1949 when Falcon Press brought out an edition without legal challenge. Since then, it has been in print continuously and widely translated. In 1974, the BBC serialized it as Radio 4's *A Book at Bedtime*.
The Paris lesbians escaped the repression of censors and male authority. Financed by benefactors, like Bryher, they created what they chose, defined their own terms, and shaped their own lives. Sylvia Beach sold pirated copies of *The Well* from her English language bookshop, Shakespeare and Company, on rue l'Odéon. She founded the shop in 1919 with the help of her partner Adrienne Monnier who had a French-language bookshop opposite. Shakespeare and Company became as much a hub for modernist innovation as the salons of Gertrude Stein and Natalie Barney. When no commercial publisher would touch James Joyce's ground-breaking novel *Ulysses*, because of the certainty of prosecution and censorship, Sylvia Beach single handedly privately published and distributed it. She called this her "missionary endeavor." She thought *Ulysses* a work of genius. "My loves were Adrienne Monnier, James Joyce and Shakespeare and Company,"[38] she wrote in her memoir. She and Adrienne Monnier shared an apartment until 1936. She moved out when the photographer Gisèle Freund arrived and became Adrienne's lover. Gisèle fled Germany when Hitler became chancellor and leader of the German government. She strapped her negatives documenting social unrest to her body to get past the border guards and reach the lesbian network in Paris. She created a portfolio of portraits of queer and straight artists and

36 Radclyffe Hall, *The Well of Loneliness* (1928; London: BCA, 1998), pp. 164, 351.

37 Quoted in Diana Souhami, *The Trials of Radclyffe Hall* (London: Weidenfeld & Nicolson, 1998), pp. 178, 217.

38 Quoted in Noël Riley Fitch, *Sylvia Beach and the Lost Generation: A History of Literary Paris in the Twenties and Thirties* (New York: W. W. Norton, 1983), p. 11.

verfolgt worden. Mariette Lydis' Lithografien wurden 1928 im Pariser Salon d'Automne gezeigt. 1933 veröffentlichte sie *Sappho*, eine Sammlung von 16 Radierungen, die in einer Auflage von 40 Exemplaren erschienen. Die Gedichtfragmente der antiken Dichterin hatte Renée Vivien aus dem Griechischen ins Französische übertragen. In Großbritannien und Amerika regelten strenge Zensurgesetze, was ausgestellt oder veröffentlicht werden durfte. Sie verhinderten, dass Lesben Werke über ihre sexuelle Orientierung verbreiteten, denn das Thema galt als obszön. Einvernehmlicher Sex zwischen Männern war strafbar. Sex zwischen Frauen war zwar nicht illegal, wurde jedoch von der Gesellschaft nicht geduldet. Schweigen und Zensurandrohung dienten als Mittel der Unterdrückung.

Staatliche Aufsichtsbehörden verfolgten eifrig jeden möglichen Verstoß. In New York schrieb Eva Kotchever, auch bekannt als Eve Adams, 1925 *Lesbian Love* in Vignettenform und betrieb Eve's Hangout, einen offen lesbischen Literatursalon. Sie wurde von einer verdeckten Ermittlerin verhaftet, wegen Obszönität inhaftiert und 1927 nach Polen abgeschoben. 1928 sorgte der Prozess um Radclyffe Halls seichten Lesbenroman *The Well of Loneliness* (dt. *Quell der Einsamkeit*) in London für Aufsehen und Zensur. Das Thema galt als inakzeptabel, obwohl die einzigen erotischen Passagen „sie küsste sie voll auf die Lippen" und „in dieser Nacht trennten sie sich nicht" lauteten.[36] „Ich würde einem gesunden Jungen oder Mädchen eher eine Ampulle Blausäure geben als diesen Roman", schrieb James Douglas, Herausgeber des *Sunday Express*, in einem Leitartikel. Der vorsitzende Richter, Sir Robert Wallace, bezeichnete das Buch als „heimtückischer, demoralisierender, zersetzender und korrumpierender als alles, was je geschrieben wurde".[37] Der Roman wurde nach dem Strafrechtsänderungsgesetz von 1885, das männliche Homosexualität unter Strafe stellte, mit einer Klage wegen Obszönität belegt und „im Ofen des Königs verbrannt". Radclyffe Hall zog daraufhin mit ihrer Lebensgefährtin Una Troubridge nach Paris und kehrte nie wieder nach England zurück. Janet Flanner meinte, *The Well of Loneliness* hätte den Weg für bessere Bücher zum gleichen Thema bereiten sollen. Das Verbot des Romans warf jedoch einen Schatten der Schande auf die gleichgeschlechtliche Liebe. Aus Angst vor Strafverfolgung wagte es kein britischer Verlag, das Buch nachzudrucken, bis die Falcon Press 1949 eine rechtlich unbedenkliche Ausgabe herausbrachte. Seitdem wurde es immer wieder neu aufgelegt und in viele Sprachen übersetzt. 1974 sendete BBC Radio 4 das Werk als Hörspiel in der Reihe *Book at Bedtime*.

Die Pariser Lesben entkamen den Repressionen von Zensur und männlicher Autorität. Finanziert von Wohltäter*innen wie Bryher schufen sie frei, was sie wollten, definierten ihre eigenen Bedingungen und gestalteten ihr Leben selbst. In ihrer englischsprachigen Buchhandlung Shakespeare and Company in der Rue l'Odéon verkaufte Sylvia Beach Raubkopien von *The Well of Loneliness*. Das Geschäft hatte sie 1919 mithilfe ihrer Partnerin Adrienne Monnier gegründet, die gleich gegenüber eine französischsprachige Buchhandlung betrieb. Shakespeare and Company wurde ein ebenso bedeutendes Innovationszentrum der Moderne wie die Salons von Gertrude Stein und Natalie Barney. Als kein kommerzieller Verlag aus Angst vor Strafverfolgung und Zensur James Joyces bahnbrechenden Roman *Ulysses* veröffentlichen wollte, nahm Sylvia Beach die Sache selbst in die Hand und verlegte und vertrieb das Werk im Alleingang – ihr „missionarisches Unterfangen", wie sie sagte. *Ulysses* hielt sie für

36
Radclyffe Hall, *The Well of Loneliness* (1928), London 1998, S. 164, 351.

37
Zit. nach: Diana Souhami, *The Trials of Radclyffe Hall*, London 1998, S. 178, 217.

writers: André Gide, Paul Valéry, Jean Cocteau, Jean-Paul Sartre, Henri Matisse, Colette, James Joyce, Virginia Woolf, T. S. Eliot, Bryher, Vita Sackville-West ... Freedom from constraint of expression was essential to this network of genderqueer women who were innovators. In 1940, they were silenced by brute force. The German army marched into Paris on June 14. They closed Shakespeare and Company and arrested Sylvia Beach. She was American and lesbian, she befriended Jews, published *Ulysses*, traded in "Noxious and Unwanted Literature," and opposed and derided fascist occupation. She was sent to an internment camp at Vittel. Her Jewish assistant, Françoise Bernheim was transported to Auschwitz and murdered. Gisèle Freund and Mariettte Lydis, who were also Jewish, fled to Argentina. Marcel Moore and Claude Cahun moved to the Island of Jersey, resisted German occupation, were imprisoned, and had much of their art destroyed.

Gertrude Stein regarded war as a plunge back into medievalism.[39] Virginia Woolf called war "this preposterous masculine fiction."[40] The preposterous masculine fact of war broke up the international daisy chain, the all-time ultimate gallery of famous dykes, and diminished the world.

39 Gertrude Stein, *Wars I Have Seen* (London: B. T. Batsford, 1945), for example, pp. 36, 55, 93, 96, 160.

40 Virginia Woolf, letter to Margaret Llewelyn Davies, January 23, 1916, in *The Letters of Virginia Woolf*, ed. Nigel Nicolson, vol. 2, *1912–1922* (London: Hogarth, 1976), p. 76.

ein Meisterwerk. „Meine Leidenschaften waren Adrienne Monnier, James Joyce und Shakespeare and Company“[38], schrieb sie in ihren Memoiren. Mit Adrienne Monnier lebte sie bis 1936 zusammen, als die Fotografin Gisèle Freund in ihr Leben trat und Adriennes Geliebte wurde. Gisèle war aus Deutschland geflohen, als Hitler Reichskanzler wurde. Um die Grenze zu überqueren, schnallte sie sich ihre Negative der Fotos von sozialen Unruhen um den Leib und schloss sich dann dem lesbischen Netzwerk in Paris an. Später erstellte sie eine Mappe mit den Porträts queerer und heterosexueller Künstler*innen und Schriftsteller*innen: André Gide, Paul Valéry, Jean Cocteau, Jean-Paul Sartre, Henri Matisse, Colette, James Joyce, Virginia Woolf, T. S. Eliot, Bryher, Vita Sackville-West und so weiter.

Meinungsfreiheit war für dieses Netzwerk innovativer genderqueerer Frauen von zentraler Bedeutung. 1940 wurden sie mit brutaler Gewalt zum Schweigen gebracht. Am 14. Juni marschierte die deutsche Wehrmacht in Paris ein, schloss Shakespeare and Company und verhaftete Sylvia Beach. Sie war Amerikanerin, Lesbe, verkehrte mit Juden, veröffentlichte den *Ulysses*, handelte mit „schädlicher und unerwünschter Literatur“, lehnte die faschistische Besatzung ab und verspottete sie. Man brachte sie in ein Internierungslager in Vittel. Ihre jüdische Mitarbeiterin Françoise Bernheim wurde nach Auschwitz deportiert und ermordet. Gisèle Freund und Mariette Lydis, ebenfalls Jüdinnen, flohen nach Argentinien. Marcel Moore und Claude Cahun zogen auf die Insel Jersey, widersetzten sich der deutschen Besatzung und wurden inhaftiert. Viele ihrer Kunstwerke wurden zerstört. Gertrude Stein sah im Krieg einen Rückfall ins Mittelalter.[39] Virginia Woolf bezeichnete ihn als „groteske männliche Fiktion“.[40] Die groteske männliche Realität des Kriegs zerriss den internationalen Reigen queerer Kontakte, die ultimative Galerie berühmter Lesben und ließ die Welt kleiner werden.

38 Zit. nach: Noël Riley Fitch, *Sylvia Beach. Eine Biographie im literarischen Paris. 1920–1940*, Frankfurt am Main 1989, S. 7.

39 Gertrude Stein, *Wars I Have Seen*, London 1945, z.B. S. 36, 55, 93, 96, 160.

40 Virginia Woolf, Brief an Margaret Llewelyn Davies, 23. Januar 1916, in: *The Letters of Virginia Woolf*, hrsg. von Nigel Nicolson, Bd. 2, *1912–1922*, London 1976, S. 76.

IV SURREALE WELTEN

SURREAL WORLDS

2

LILI ELBE

EIN MENSCH WECHSELT
SEIN GESCHLECHT

EINE LEBENSBEICHTE

AUS HINTERLASSENEN PAPIEREN
HERAUSGEGEBEN VON
NIELS HOYER

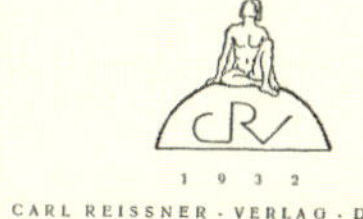

1 9 3 2

CARL REISSNER · VERLAG · DRESDEN

1

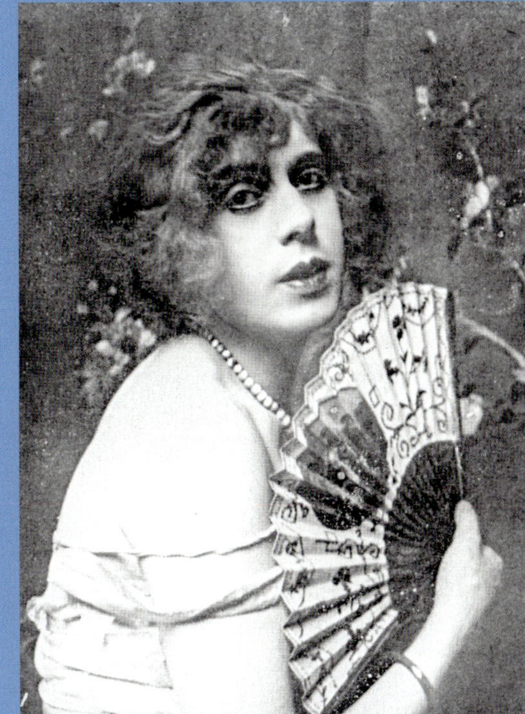

3

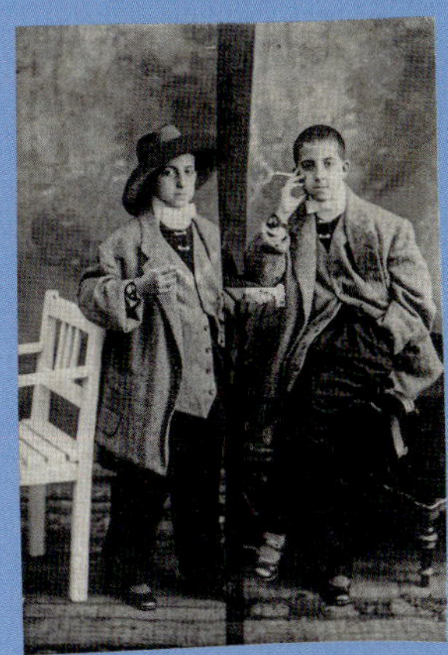

4

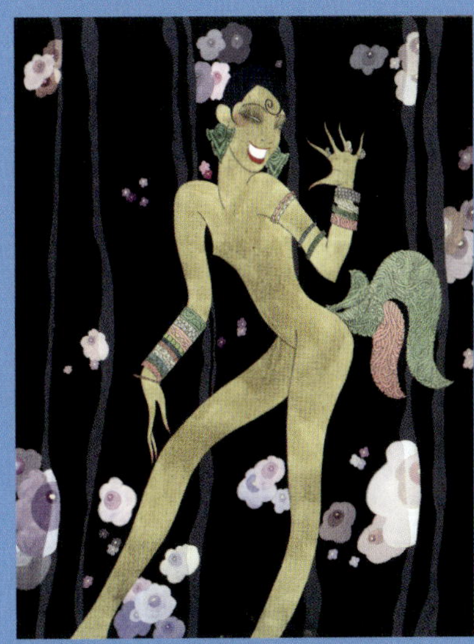

6

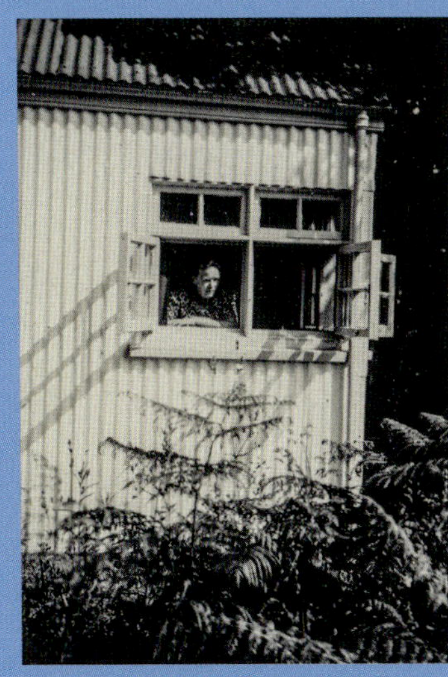

5

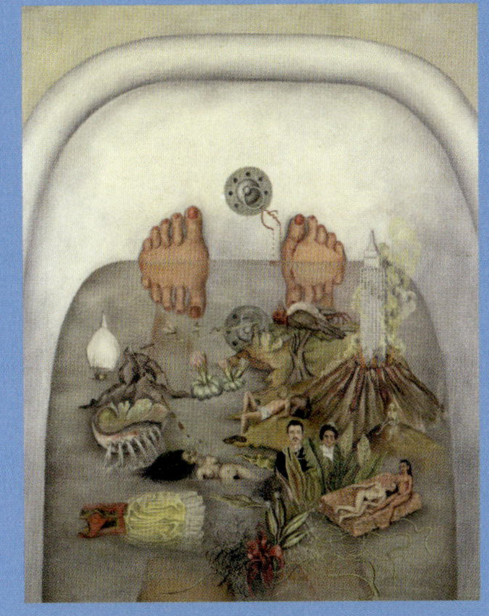

1

Die dänische Malerin Lili Elbe war einer der ersten Menschen, die sich geschlechtsangleichenden Operationen unterzogen, die 1930 in Magnus Hirschfelds Institut für Sexualwissenschaft in Berlin und in der Städtischen Frauenklinik in Dresden durchgeführt wurden. Sie lebte offen als Frau in Paris und stand ihrer Ehefrau, der Malerin Gerda Wegener, Modell.

The Danish painter Lili Elbe was one of the first people to undergo gender-affirming surgeries, which took place in 1930 at Magnus Hirschfeld's Institute for Sexual Science in Berlin and at the Municipal Women's Clinic in Dresden. She lived openly as a woman in Paris and modeled for her wife, the painter Gerda Wegener.

2

Lili Elbes Lebensgeschichte, *Ein Mensch wechselt sein Geschlecht*, wurde 1932 in einer deutschen Version und 1931 auf Dänisch unter dem Titel *Fra Mand til Kvinde* veröffentlicht. Dieses Werk der Moderne erzählt von Elbes Transition und bietet einen seltenen (auto-)biografischen Bericht zu moderner sexueller Identität.

The German edition of Lili Elbe's life story, Ein Mensch wechselt sein Geschlecht *(1932) or "A Person Changes Gender," was first published in Danish in 1931 under the title* Fra Mand til Kvinde (Man into Woman, *1933). This modernist work narrates Elbe's transition and offers a rare (auto)biographical record of modern sexual identity.*

3

Die serbische Künstler*in, Dichter*in und Modeillustrator*in Milena Pavlović-Barili stellte in Belgrad nicht nur gesellschaftliche Konventionen infrage, sondern prägte auch eine moderne Sichtweise von Weiblichkeit, während sie gleichzeitig ihre facettenreiche Identität erforschte. Durch ihre Kunst und Selbstdarstellung griff sie den androgynen Stil der Pariser „neuen Frau" auf.

Challenging social conventions in Belgrade, the Serbian artist, poet, and fashion illustrator Milena Pavlović-Barili shaped a modern vision of femininity while exploring her multifaceted identity. Through her art and self-performance, she embraced the androgynous styles of the Parisian "new woman."

4

Milena Pavlović-Barili bezog ihre Inspiration aus zeitgenössischen Zeitschriften und der florierenden Art-déco-Ästhetik während ihres Kunststudiums in Belgrad und München. 1928 schuf sie eine Zeichnung der einzigartigen Schwarzen Ikone Josephine Baker, die mit ihren gewagten Auftritten Geschlechts- und Kulturnormen in ganz Europa infrage stellte.

Milena Pavlović-Barili drew inspiration from contemporary periodicals and the flourishing Art Deco style during her art studies in Belgrade and Munich. In 1928, she created a drawing of the sensational Black icon Josephine Baker, whose daring performances challenged gender and cultural norms across Europe.

5

Frida Kahlos *Lo que el agua me dio* (dt. *Was das Wasser mir gab*, 1938) ist eine im Wasser gespiegelte visuelle Erinnerung. Ein brennender Wolkenkratzer und zwei weibliche Liebende verweisen auf Kahlos politische Ansichten und ihre sexuelle Fluidität. Zu ihren intimen Bekanntschaften mit Frauen gehörte 1939 in Paris möglicherweise auch Josephine Baker.

Frida Kahlo's Lo que el agua mc dio (What the Water Gave Me, *1938) is a visual memoir reflected in water. A burning skyscraper and two female lovers suggest Kahlo's political views and fluid sexuality. Among her intimate relationships with women was, possibly, Josephine Baker in Paris in 1939.*

6

In den 1930er-Jahren traf Ithell Colquhoun im Mittelmeerraum die Griechin Andromache Kazou – eine leidenschaftliche Begegnung, die sie in ihrem Manuskript „Lesbian Shore" festhielt. 1949 mietete sie das Atelier „Vow Cave" in Lamorna in Cornwall und freundete sich mit den genderqueeren Künstler*innen Gluck und Marlow Moss an.

In the 1930s, Ithell Colquhoun met the Greek woman Andromache Kazou along the Mediterranean—a passionate encounter she recounted in her manuscript "Lesbian Shore." In 1949, she rented the studio "Vow Cave" in Lamorna, Cornwall, where she befriended the genderqueer artists Gluck and Marlow Moss.

Ich kämpfe gegen die Voreingenommenheit des Spießbürgers, der in mir ein Phänomen, eine Abnormität sucht. Wie ich jetzt bin, so bin ich eine ganz gewöhnliche Frau.

I am fighting against the prepossession of the Philistine who looks upon me as a phenomenon, as an abnormality. As I am now, I am a perfectly ordinary woman among other women.

Lili Elbe in einem Brief vom 15. Juni 1931 an ihren deutschen Freund, in: Lili Elbe, *Ein Mensch wechselt sein Geschlecht. Eine Lebensbeichte*, aus hinterlassenen Papieren hrsg. von Niels Hoyer, Dresden 1932.

Lili Elbe in a letter from June 15, 1931, to her German friend in Lili Elbe, Man into Woman: An Authentic Record of a Change of Sex *(London: Jarrolds, 1933), p. 277.*

Ithell Colquhoun
Nativity, 1929
Geburt Christi

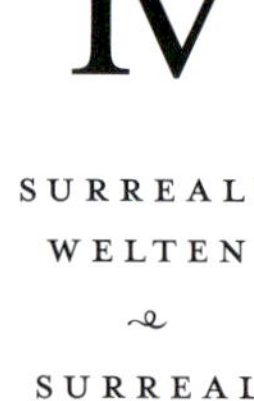

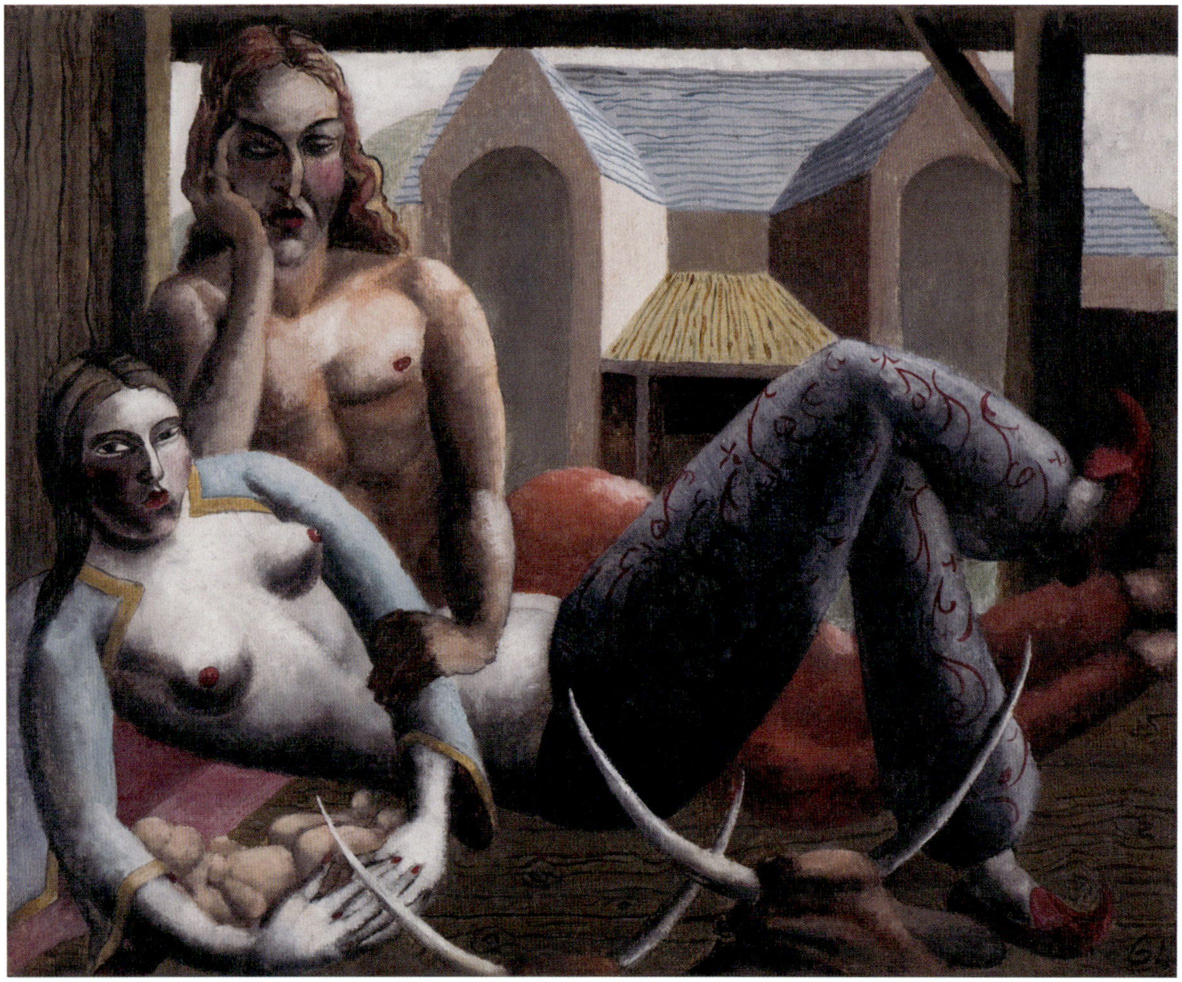

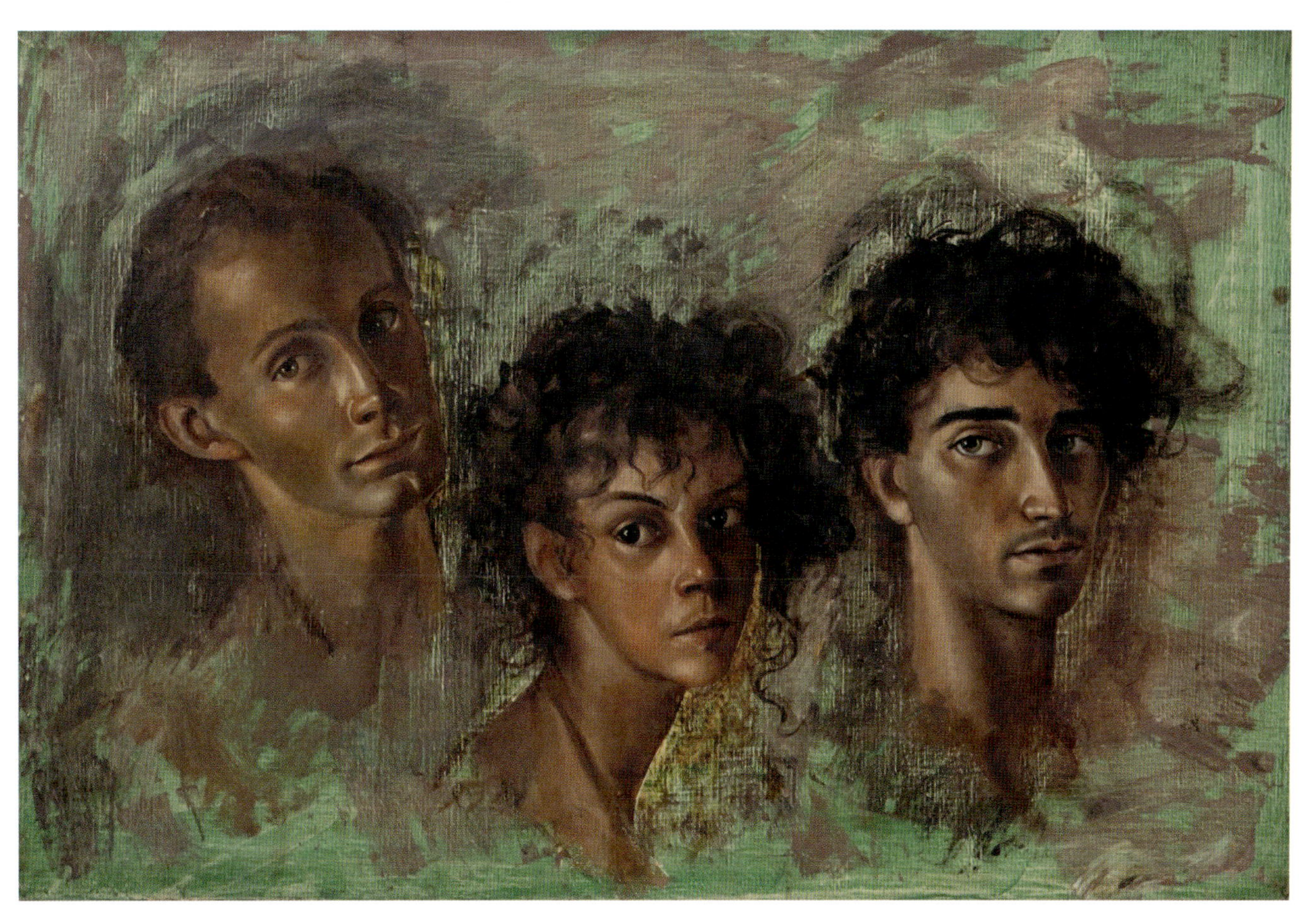

Leonor Fini

Autoportrait avec Kot et Sergio (Kot Jelenski et Sergio Gajardo), 1952

Selbstporträt mit Kot und Sergio (Kot Jelenski und Sergio Gajardo) ~

Self-Portrait with Kot and Sergio (Kot Jelenski and Sergio Gajardo)

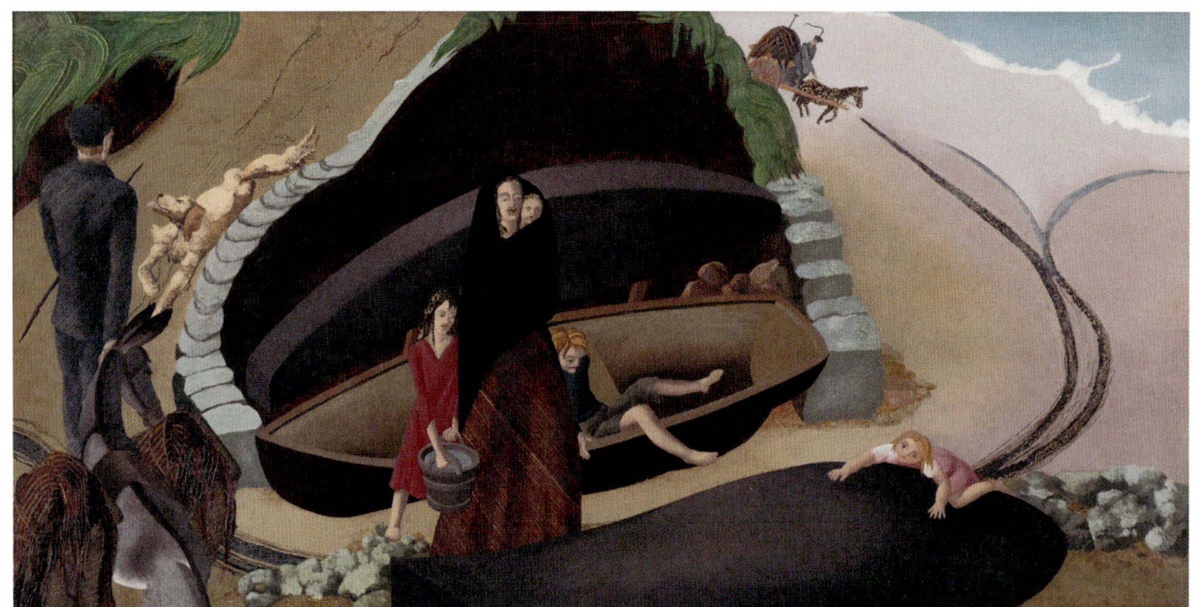

IV

SURREALE
WELTEN

SURREAL
WORLDS

Ithell Colquhoun
Kelp Gathering, 1949
Seetang sammeln

Leonor Fini

Les Étrangères, 1968
Die Fremden ~ *The Strangers*

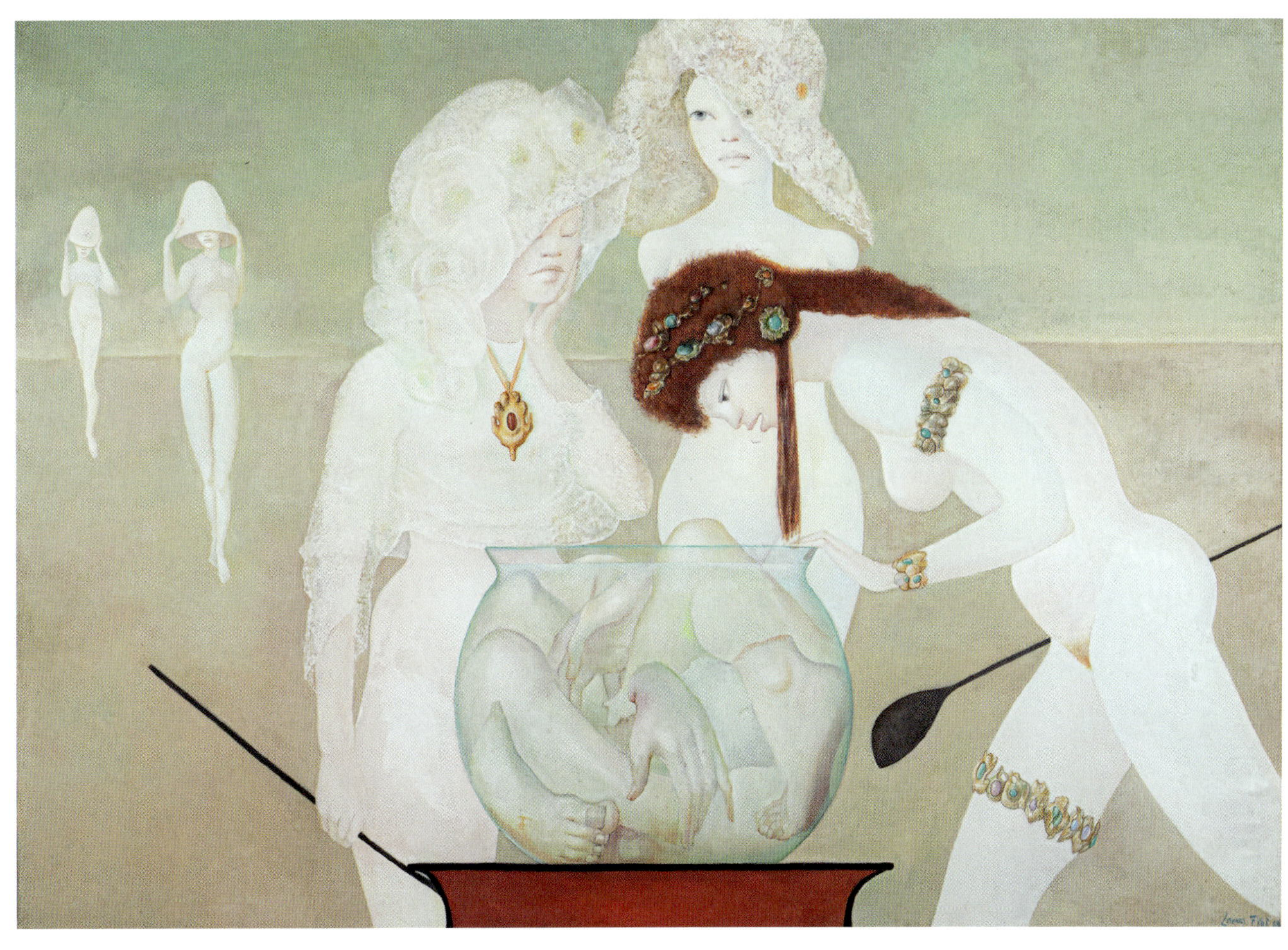

Leonor Fini

Portrait féminin n. 9 / Ritratto di signora seduta, 1936
Weibliches Porträt Nr. 9 / Porträt einer sitzenden Dame ~
Female Portrait No. 9 / Portrait of a Seated Lady

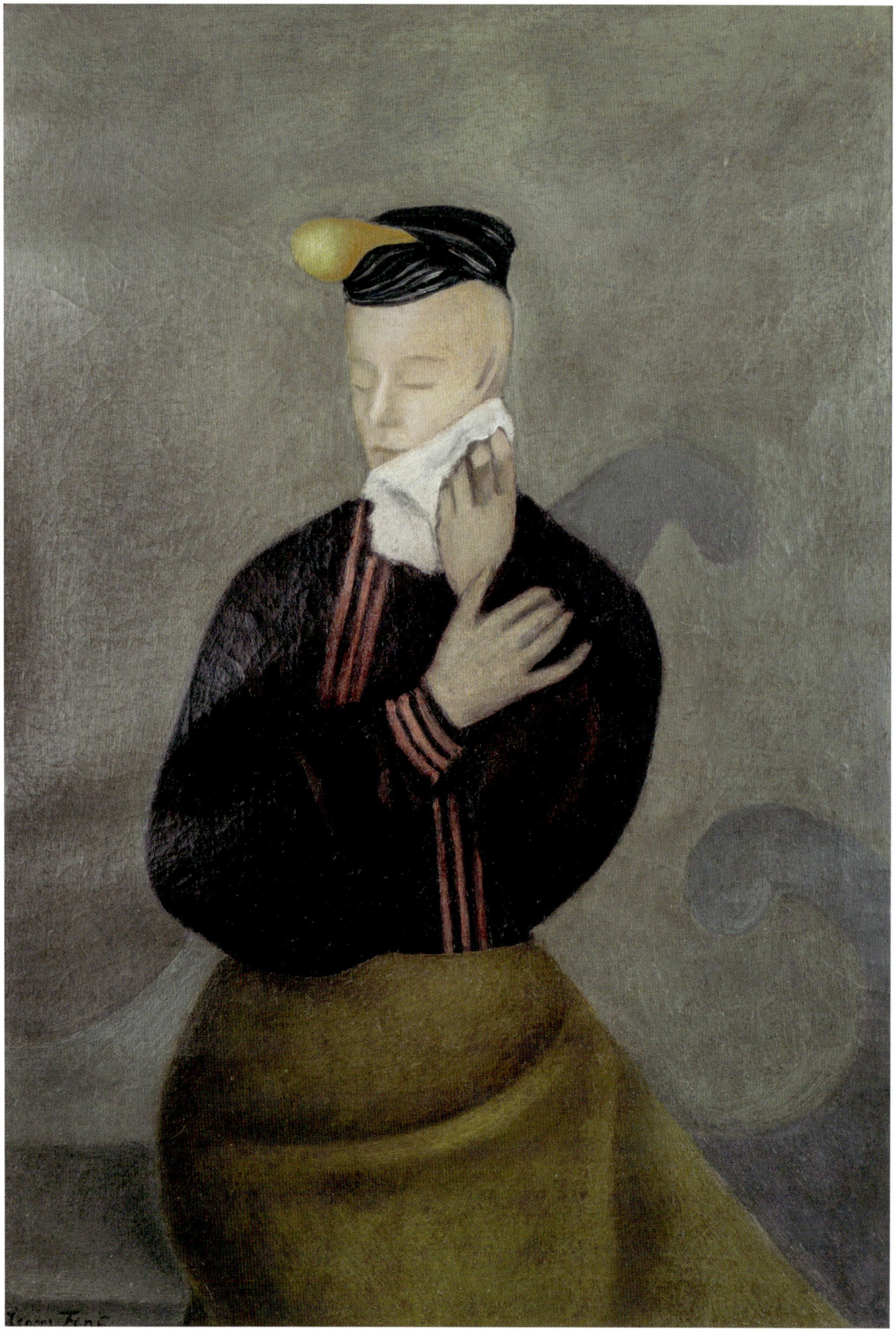

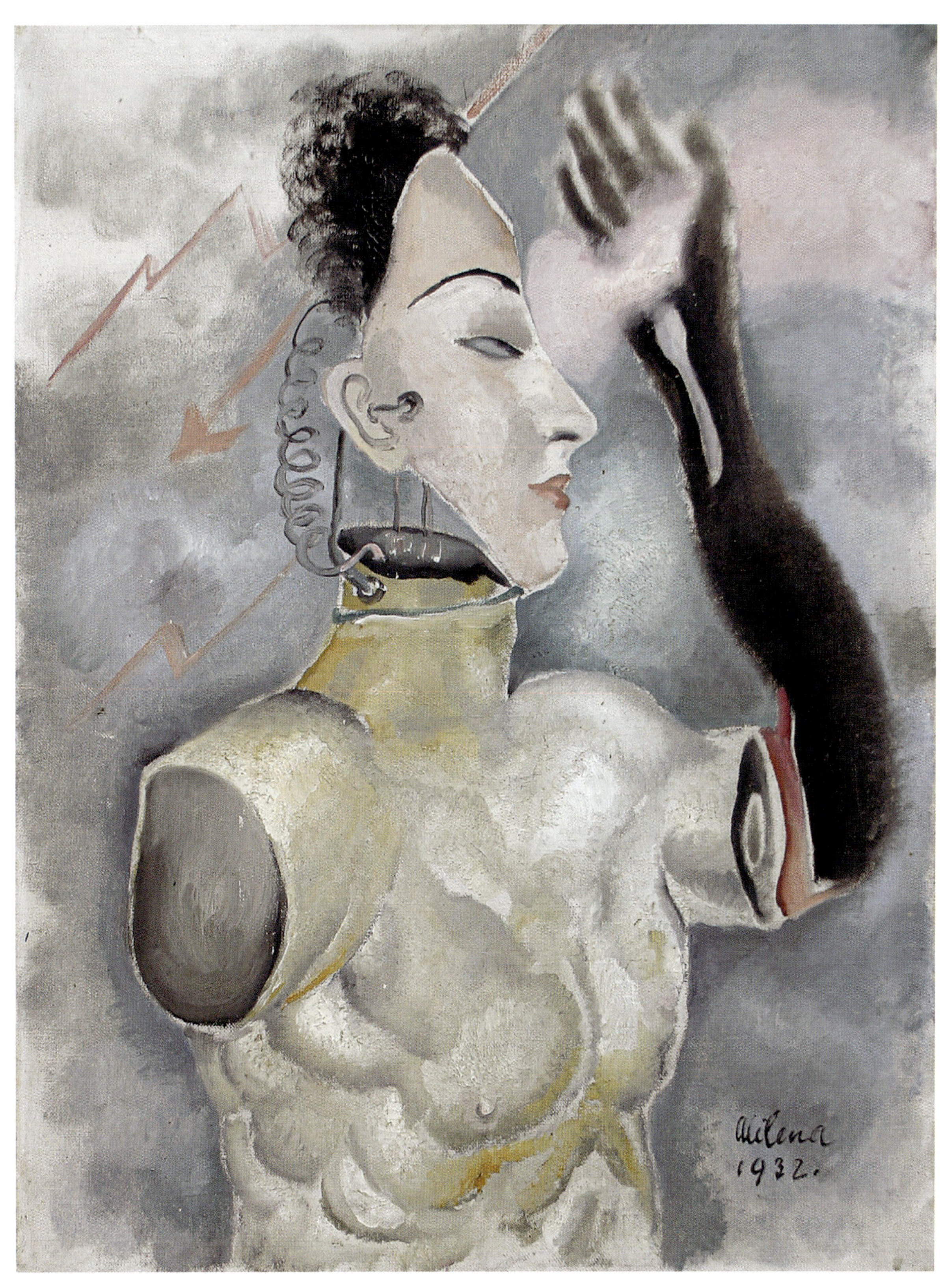

Milena Pavlović-Barili

Enigmatska kompozicija sa crnom rukom, 1932

Torso mit schwarzem Arm

Torso with Black Arm

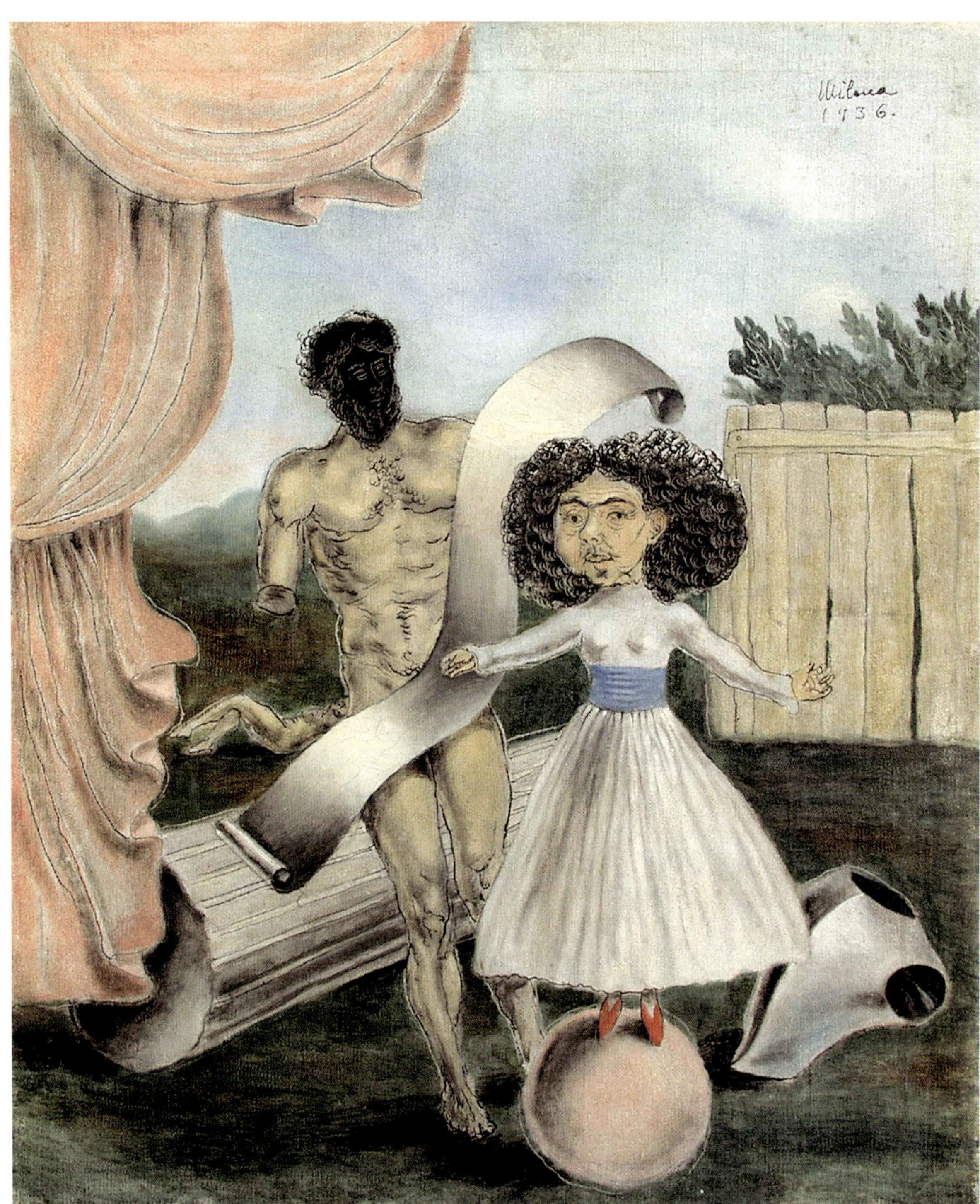

Milena Pavlović-Barili
Lutka, 1936
Puppe ~ *Doll*

Milena Pavlović-Barili

Fantastična kompozicija sa ženskim aktom I zmajem, 1936
Fantastische Komposition mit einer Frau und einem Drachen ~
Fantastic Composition with a Female and a Dragon

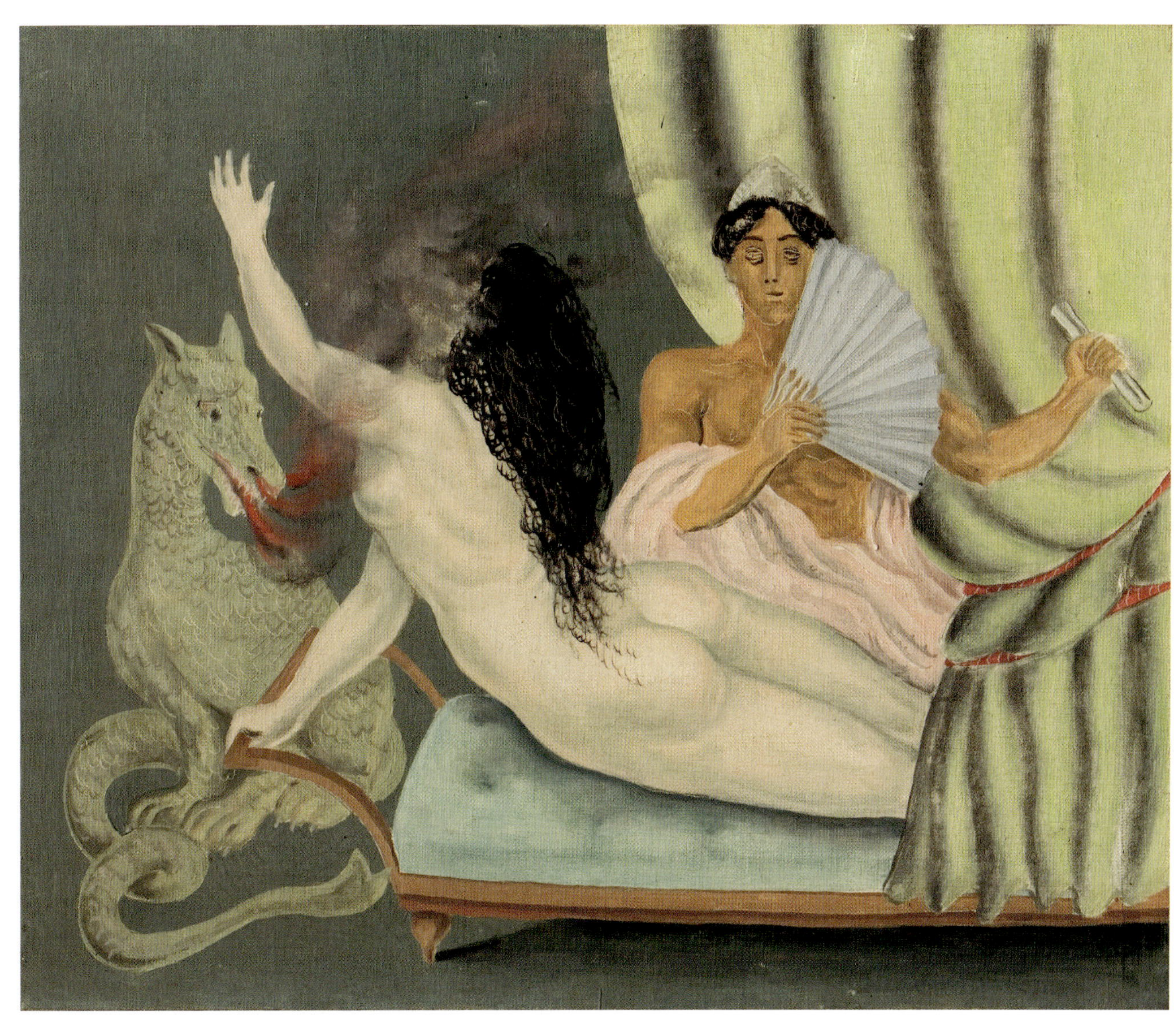

Gerda Wegener
Lili with a Feather Fan, 1920
Lili mit einem Federfächer

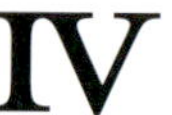

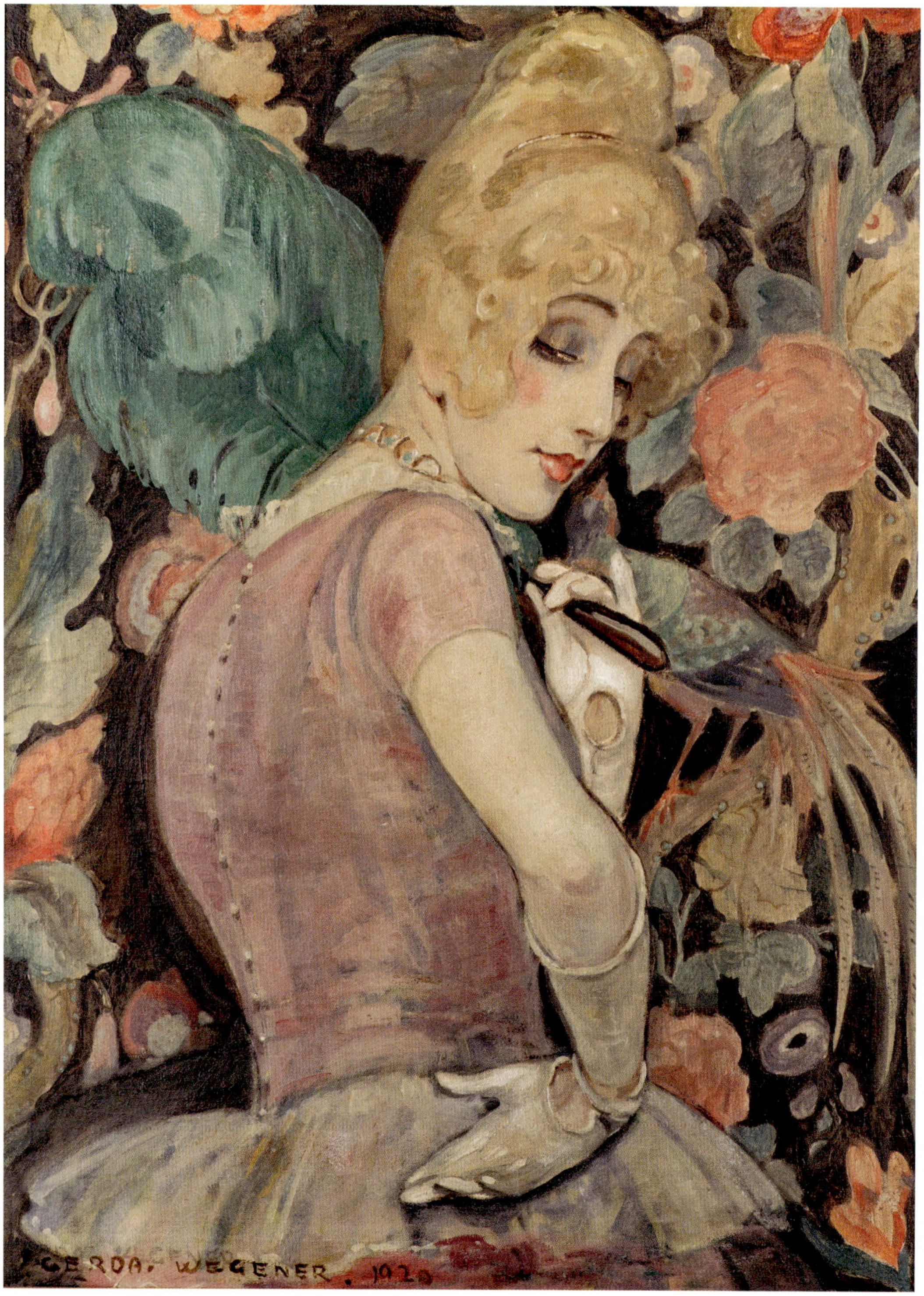

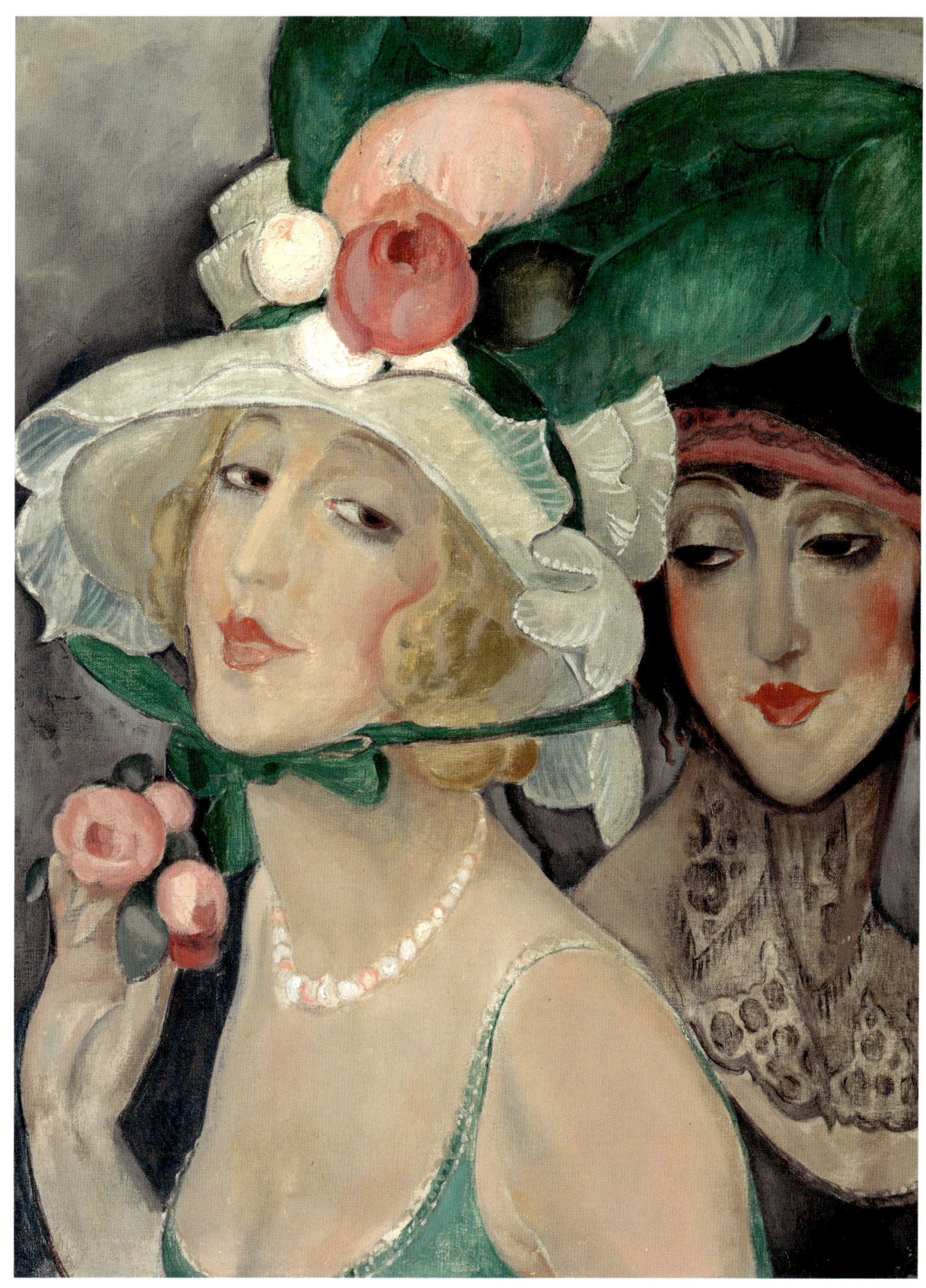

Gerda Wegener
Two Coquettes with Hats – Lili with Friend, um ~ *ca.* 1920
Zwei Koketten mit Hüten – Lili mit Freundin

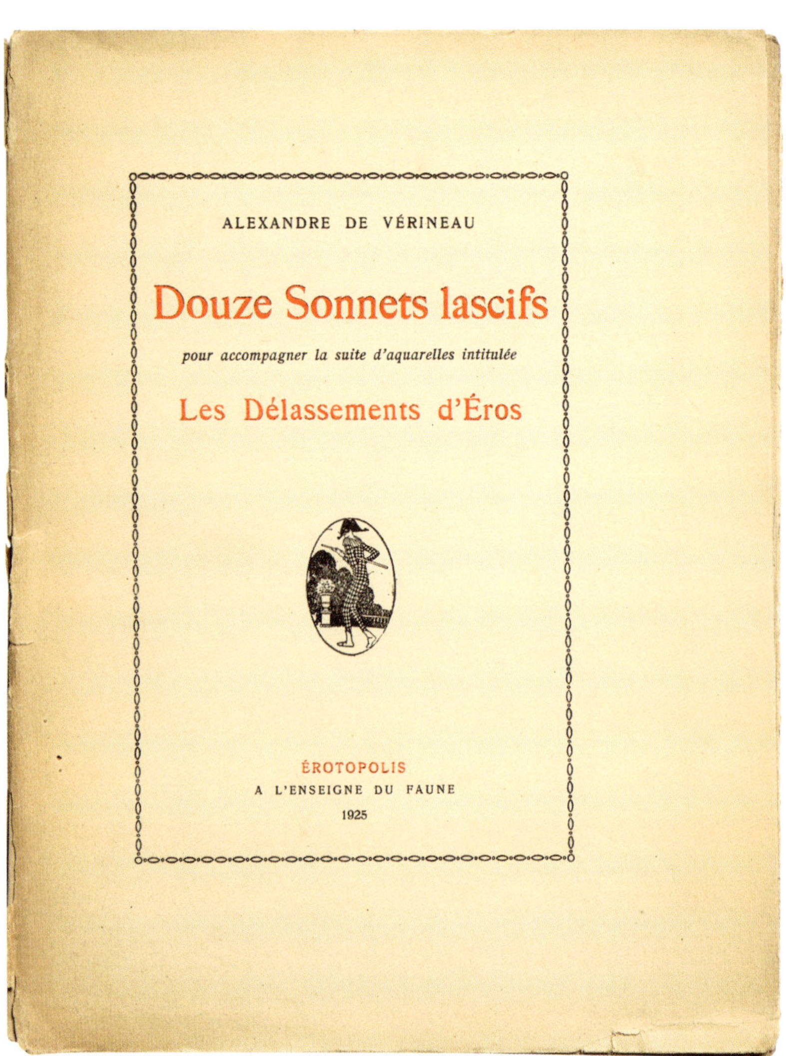

Alexandre de Vérineau (Louis Perceau)
Douze Sonnets lascifs pour accompagner la suite d'aquarelles intitulée.
Les Délassements d'Éros, ÉROTOPOLIS, À l'Enseigne du faune, 1925
Zwölf laszive Sonette zur Begleitung der Aquarellsuite mit dem Titel
Les Délassements d'Éros, ÉROTOPOLIS, À l'Enseigne du faune ~
Twelve Lascivious Sonnets to Accompany a Suite of Watercolors Entitled
Les Délassements d'Éros, ÉROTOPOLIS, À l'Enseigne du faune

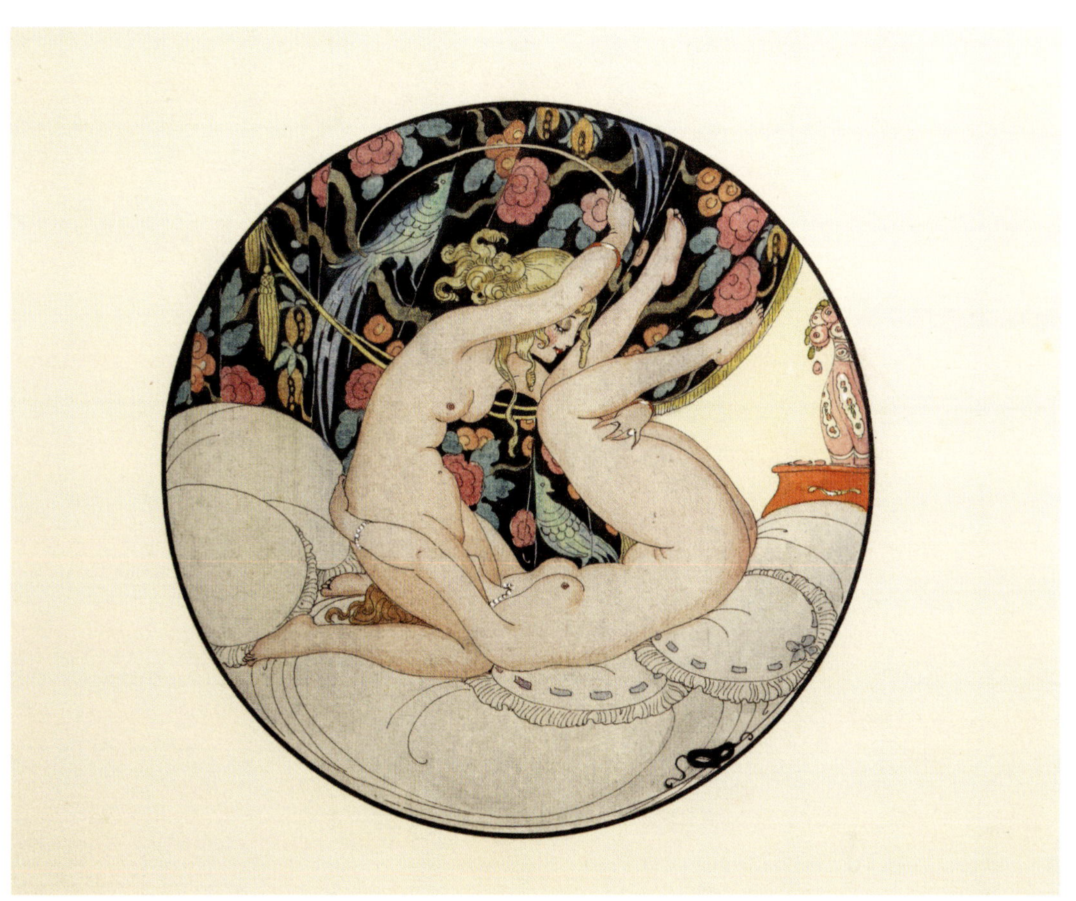

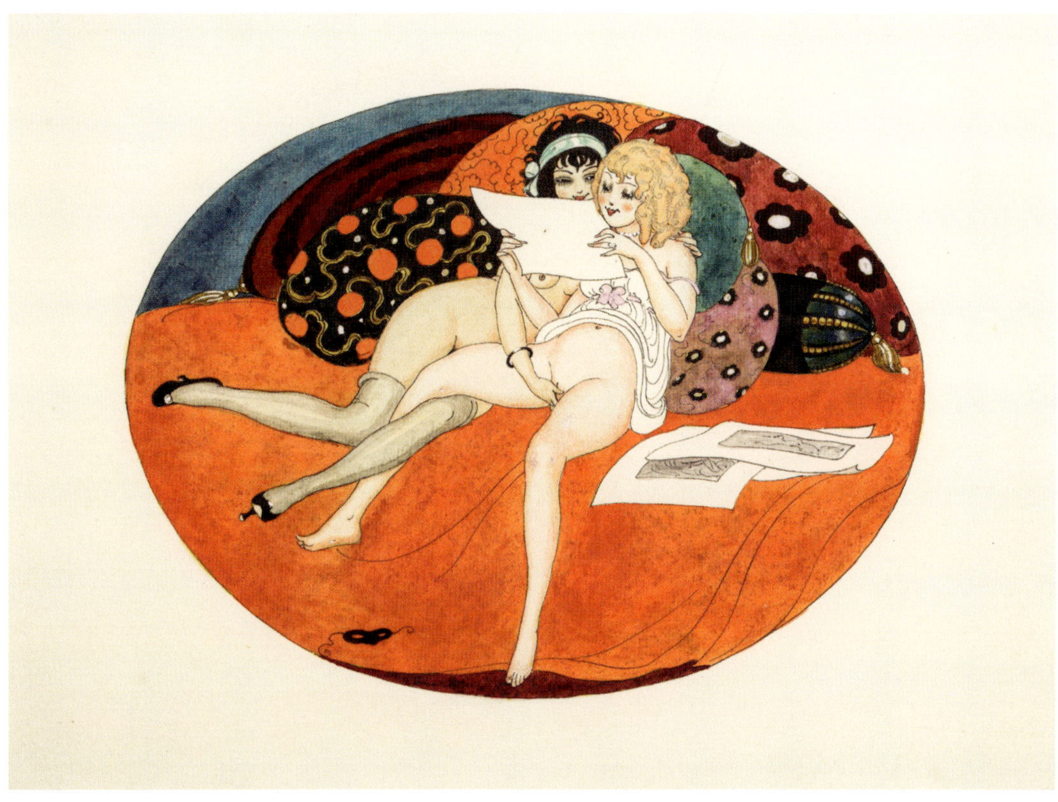

Gerda Wegener
Les Délassements d'Éros, 1925
Die Freuden des Eros ~ *The Diversions of Eros*

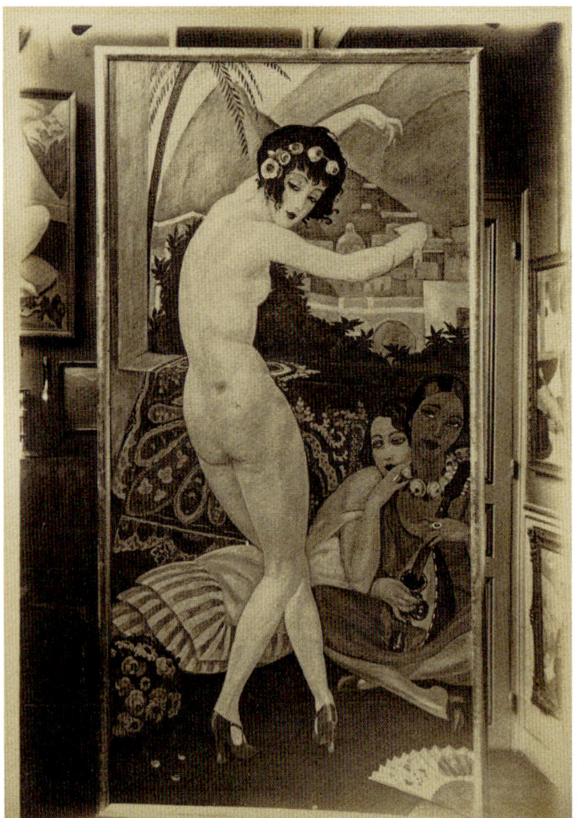

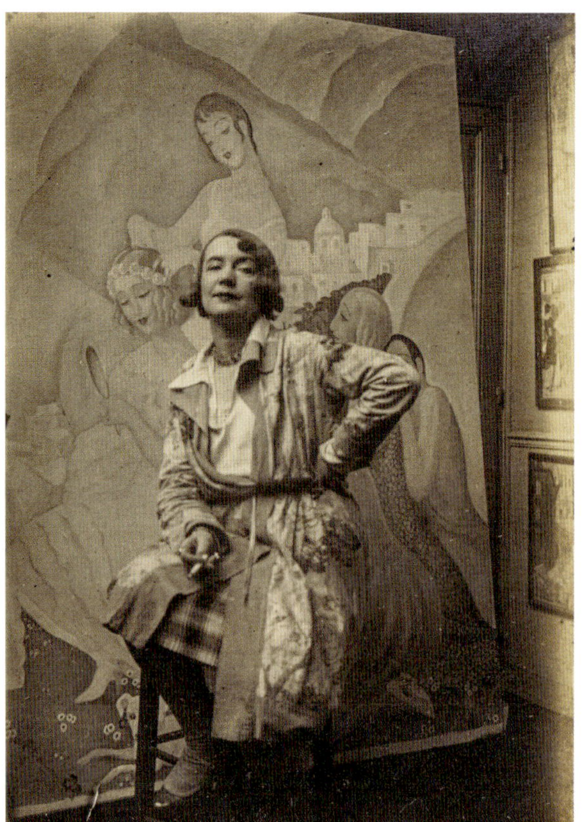

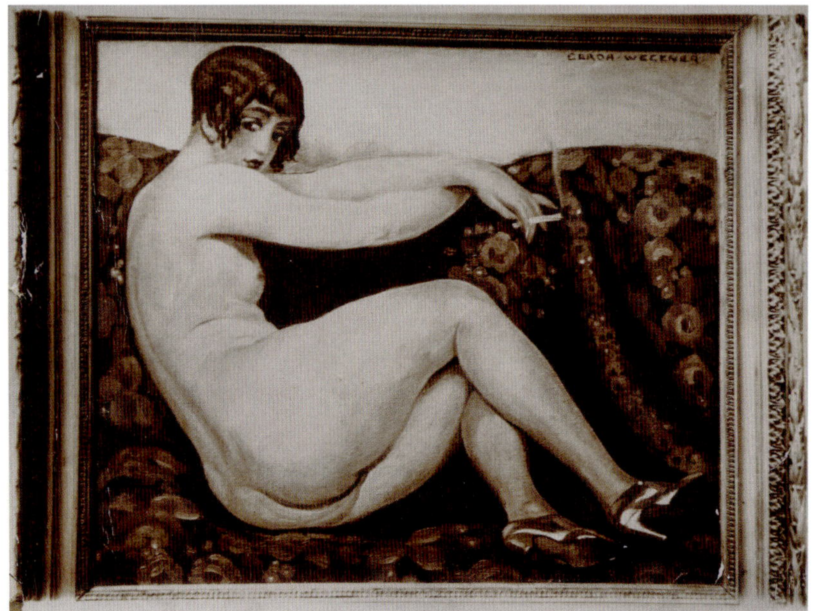

Gerda Wegener
Fotoalbum ~ *Photo Album*,
wahrscheinlich ~ *probably* 1925–1935

Gerda Wegener

Fotoalbum ~ *Photo Album*, wahrscheinlich ~ *probably* 1925–1935

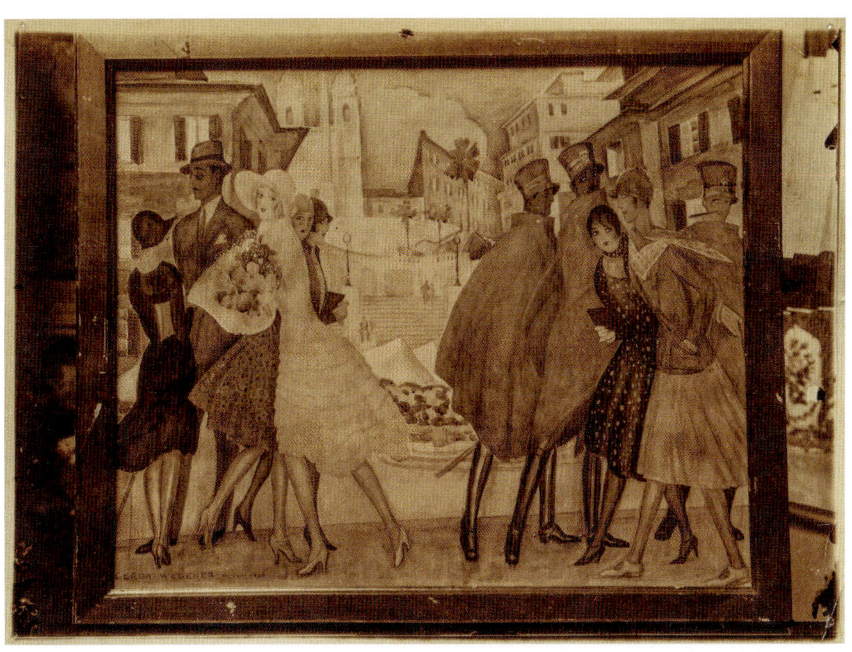

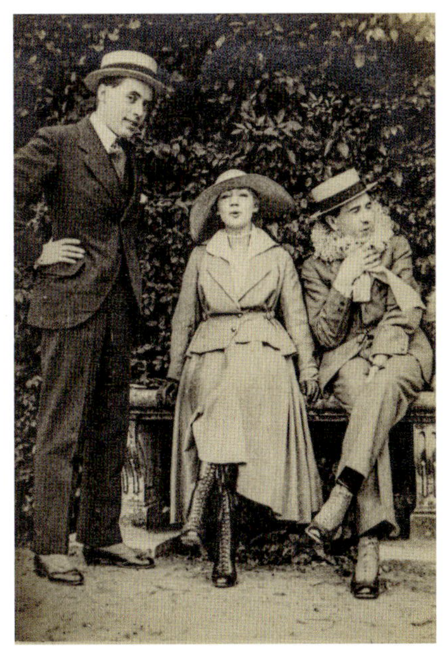

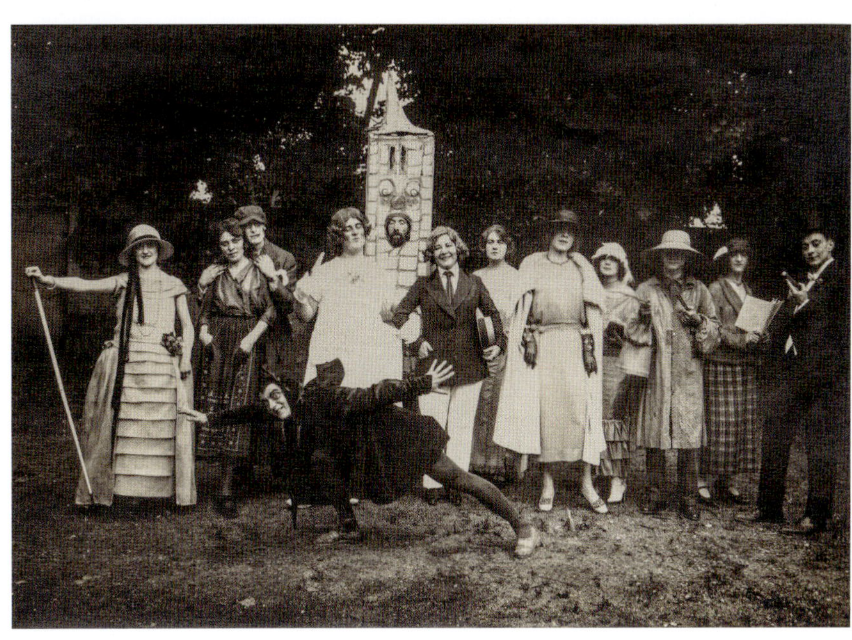

DER ANDROGYNE TRAUM

~

THE ANDROGYNOUS DREAM

ISABELLE TONDRE

Dieser Essay setzt sich mit der surrealistischen Welt und den utopischen Visionen von Ithell Colquhoun, Leonor Fini und Milena Pavlović-Barili auseinander und offenbart deren innovative Ausdrucksformen von queerem Begehren, Freundschaft und Weiblichkeit. Zwei Figuren in einem Stall, zwei Ochsen und ein neugeborenes Kind: Wie so viele von Colquhouns jugendlichen Frühwerken zeigt das kleinformatige Gemälde *Nativity* (1929, Kat., S. 100) ein typisches Motiv der christlichen Ikonografie. Das Bild verrät nicht nur die akademische Ausbildung der Künstlerin und ihre religiösen Wurzeln im Südwesten Englands, es enthüllt auch die anfänglichen Zeichen eines freien und Grenzen überschreitenden Geistes. In Colquhouns Komposition nehmen die beiden erwachsenen Figuren – vermutlich die Jungfrau Maria und der heilige Josef – das Zentrum ein, während das Jesuskind in die untere Ecke des Bilds verbannt und nur mit einigen schnellen Pinselstrichen ausgeführt wurde. Das in tiefe Rot- und pudrige Rosa- und Blautöne getauchte heilige Paar posiert mit nacktem Oberkörper und verströmt eine für die Zeit beeindruckende androgyne Anziehungskraft. Ungewöhnlicherweise wendet Maria den Blick vom Kind ab, ihr Blick ist vielmehr auf die Betrachtenden gerichtet. Colquhoun, die 1906 in Assam während der britischen Herrschaft in Indien geboren wurde, wuchs in einer britischen Familie mit traditionellen Werten und einer langen Geschichte von Diensten im Militär der Krone auf. Nachdem sie in recht jungen Jahren nach England zog, wo sie immer wieder auch längere Zeit ohne ihre Eltern lebte, entwickelte Colquhoun ihre eigene ideologische und kreative Unabhängigkeit. „Ich kannte meinen eigenen Verstand bereits", schrieb sie in ihren autobiografischen Notizen. Dabei bezog sie sich auf ihr zehnjähriges Ich und ihre Entschlossenheit, Künstlerin und Schriftstellerin zu werden.[1] Ihre Ausbildung fand in einer Zeit statt, die von strengen Geschlechterbeschränkungen, aber auch von bahnbrechenden Entwicklungen im gesellschaftlichen Leben von Frauen im Vereinigten Königreich von Großbritannien geprägt war. 1918 erhielt ein Teil der Frauen das Wahlrecht, und der Sex Disqualification (Removal) Act von 1919 beseitigte gesetzliche Hindernisse für die Anstellung und Hochschulbildung von Frauen, was ihnen den Zugang zum Rechtswesen, zum Staatsdienst und zur akademischen Welt ermöglichte. Im gleichen Jahr schrieb sich Colquhoun am Cheltenham Ladies' College ein, einer wegweisenden Schule, die Mädchen und jungen Frauen eine ernstzunehmende akademische Ausbildung bot, die ansonsten Jungen vorbehalten war.[2] 1925 begann Colquhoun ihr Studium an der Cheltenham Art School und setzte ihre Ausbildung dann an der Londoner Slade School of Fine Art fort. 1931 reiste sie nach Paris, wo sie in die französische Avantgarde eintauchte. In einer kürzlich erfolgten Neubewertung des Surrealismus wurde Colquhouns radikale Position herausgearbeitet, die von der Kunstgeschichte lange übersehen wurde. Erst seit den 1980er-Jahren erfährt sie für ihre eindringliche Erkundung von Sexualität, Natur, Spiritualität und dem Unbewussten wieder Aufmerksamkeit. Obwohl ihre Verbindung zum Surrealismus durch ihre Arbeiten deutlich wird – vom Einsatz von Doppelbildern in ihren botanischen Miniaturen bis hin zu ambivalenten, biomorphen Landschaften –, beschritt sie auch jenseits der Bewegung autonome Pfade.[3] Genau dieser Sinn für künstlerische Komplexität führte 1940 zu ihrem formellen Ausschluss aus der Gruppe britischer Surrealist*innen, gerade als ihre Karriere in Gang kam. *Nativity*, das während Colquhouns Zeit an der Slade

1 Ithell Colquhoun, zit. nach: Amy Hale, *Ithell Colquhoun: Genius of the Fern Loved Gully*, London 2020, S. 25, siehe auch S. 25–29; Ithell Colquhoun, „Until Twelve", unveröffentl. Manuskript, 1940er-Jahre, TGA 929/2/1/68/1, Tate Gallery Archive, London; Richard Shillitoe, *Ithell Colquhoun: Magician Born of Nature*, 2. überarb. Auflage (veröffentl. durch den Verfasser, 2010), S. 1.

2 Hale 2020 (wie Anm. 1), S. 29.

3 Siehe ebd., S. 43.

This essay explores the Surrealist worlds and utopian visions of Ithell Colquhoun, Leonor Fini, and Milena Pavlović-Barili, unfolding their innovative expressions of queer desire, friendship, and femininity. Two figures in a stable, two oxen, and a newborn child: like many of Ithell Colquhoun's youthful early works, the small-format canvas, *Nativity* (1929, cat. p. 100), presents an emblematic motif of Christian iconography. While it speaks of the artist's academic training and religious roots in South West England, it also reveals nascent signs of a free and transgressive mind. In Colquhoun's composition, the two adult figures—presumably the Virgin Mary and St. Joseph—take center stage, while the infant Jesus is relegated to the lower corner of the picture, rendered with just a few rough brushstrokes. Bathed in deep reds and powdered pinks and blues, the holy couple poses bare-chested, radiating a strikingly androgynous allure for the time. Unconventionally, Mary looks away from the Christ child. Her gaze is fixed on the viewer.

Born in Assam in the British Raj in 1906, Colquhoun grew up in a British family with traditionalist values and a long history of service in the Crown's military. Having moved to England at a young age, where she lived for extended periods without her parents, Colquhoun developed her own ideological and creative independence. "I already knew my own mind," she wrote in her autobiographical notes, referring to her ten-year-old self and her determination to become an artist and writer.[1] Her formation took place during a period marked by severe gender restrictions but also groundbreaking advancements in women's social life in Britain: in 1918, a fraction of women gained the right to vote, and the Sex Disqualification (Removal) Act of 1919 lifted legal barriers to employment and higher education for women, allowing them to enter fields such as law, the civil service, and academia. It was in that same year that Colquhoun was enrolled at Cheltenham Ladies' College, a pioneering school for girls and young women offering serious academic education normally reserved for boys.[2] In 1925, Colquhoun began her studies at Cheltenham Art School, followed by enrollment at London's Slade School of Fine Art. In 1931, she departed for Paris, where she immersed herself in the French avant-garde. Recent feminist reevaluations of Surrealism have situated Ithell Colquhoun as a radical position long overlooked by art history, gaining renewed attention since the 1980s for her powerful explorations of sexuality, nature, spirituality, and the unconscious. While her connection to Surrealism is evident throughout her work—from the infusions of double images in her botanical miniatures to ambivalent, biomorphic landscapes—she also charted autonomous paths beyond the movement.[3] It is precisely this sense of artistic complexity that led to her formal expulsion from the British Surrealist group in 1940, just as her career was gaining momentum. *Nativity*, painted during Colquhoun's time at the Slade, marks an early expression of her enduring interest in gender roles and alternative visions of femininity, portraying Mary wearing ornately patterned slacks and Joseph adopting a glamorously effeminate pose, challenging traditional depictions and offering a liberatory,

1 Ithell Colquhoun, quoted in Amy Hale, *Ithell Colquhoun: Genius of the Fern Loved Gully* (London: Strange Attractor, 2020), p. 25, see also pp. 25–29; Ithell Colquhoun, "Until Twelve," unpublished manuscript, ca. 1940s, TGA 929/2/1/68/1, Tate Gallery Archive, London; Richard Shillitoe, *Ithell Colquhoun: Magician Born of Nature*, 2nd rev. ed. (pub. by author, 2010), p. 1.

2 Hale, *Ithell Colquhoun*, p. 29.

3 See ibid., p. 43.

entstand, markiert einen frühen Ausdruck ihres anhaltenden Interesses an Geschlechterrollen und alternativen Formen von Weiblichkeit. Sie zeigt Maria mit langen ornamental gemusterten Hosen und Josef in einer glamourös verweiblichten Pose, die traditionelle Darstellungen infrage stellt und einen befreienden, queer-inspirierten Blick auf Geburt als heiligen Akt der Selbstverwirklichung bietet.[4] Obwohl eine solche Bildsprache als blasphemisch interpretiert werden könnte, formte Colquhouns tiefe Verehrung für Religion und das androgyne Göttliche – verwurzelt in ihrer Auseinandersetzung mit Okkultismus, Alchemie und kabbalistischem Denken – eine Vision, in der spirituelle Androgynie die totale Verwirklichung der menschlichen Gestalt symbolisierte, wobei sie mit ihrer Kunst nicht politische Konfrontation anstrebte, sondern, wie Amy Hale bemerkt, „die Bedingungen für Erleuchtung, aufrichtige Freiheit und Frieden".[5] In ihren Denkmodellen ließ sich Colquhoun von radikalen esoterischen Theosoph*innen, insbesondere Helena Blavatsky und ihrer östlich orientierten magisch-okkultistischen Philosophie, inspirieren, um die alchemistische Wiedervereinigung von männlich und weiblich zu erkunden und moderne Weltsichten von Identität und Geschlechtertrennung infrage zu stellen.

„Welt verändern" und „das Leben ändern" waren zentrale Schlagworte des surrealistischen Projekts, wie André Breton 1935 in seiner „Rede auf dem Schriftstellerkongress" erklärte.[6] Als revolutionäre Bewegung, die tief in jene Politik eingebunden war, die die 1920er- und 1930er-Jahre prägte, stellte der Surrealismus Kritik und Zersetzung etablierter sozialer Werte ins Zentrum der Bewegung. Bewusstseinsverändernde Darstellungen von Körpern, Gegenständen und Landschaften – sowohl in der Kunst als auch in der Literatur – sollten durch die Nutzbarmachung unterbewusster Register von Begehren und Träumen die Wahrnehmung der Wirklichkeit erweitern. Obwohl die Bewegung erheblich mehr Künstlerinnen und Schriftstellerinnen umfasste als jede andere zeitgenössische Gruppe, fanden viele der Debatten zu sexuellem Begehren und Identität trotzdem innerhalb des begrenzten Kreises der Männer statt.[7] Eingehende Diskussionen aus dem Januar 1928, die kurz danach in der elften Ausgabe von *La Révolution surréaliste* erschienen, boten unter anderem Einblicke in die Auseinandersetzungen der Surrealisten mit weiblicher Sexualität und gleichgeschlechtlichem Verlangen. Spekulationen zu Moral und Ethik, körperliche Anziehung, sexuelle Vorlieben und Fantasien wurden darin aufgeworfen – ganz ohne die Anwesenheit von Frauen.[8] Während das Thema des homosexuellen Begehrens zwischen Männern von Breton und den gleichrangigen Mitgliedern Benjamin Péret und Pierre Unik ausführlich erörtert und vehement verdammt wurde, nimmt die Frage von „Liebe zwischen Frauen" im neunseitigen Bericht kaum ein paar Zeilen ein. „Körperliche Liebe?", fragt Breton. Ein anderes Mitglied antwortet, ehe es weiter zum nächsten Thema geht: „Ich glaube, eine Frau spielt die Rolle des Mannes und die andere die der Frau."[9] Der Widerspruch zwischen der gelebten Realität von Frauen und ihrer idealisierten Darstellung in der surrealistischen Kunst wurde im Laufe der Zeit sowohl von Surrealistinnen als auch später von feministischen Wissenschaftler*innen thematisiert.[10] Colquhoun war sich dieses Widerspruchs bewusst und bemerkte in einem Brief von 1981, dass – obwohl Breton verkündet habe, Frauen sollten „frei und verehrt" werden – die meisten seiner Anhänger zutiefst chauvinistisch blieben und Frauen „gestattet, aber nicht notwendig" waren.[11]

4 Colquhoun äußerte sich in ihren Texten unverblümt zu den Zwängen von Frauenbekleidung. Siehe Ithell Colquhoun, „My Ideas about Clothes", unveröffentl. Manuskript, um 1961, TGA 929/1/225; Amy Hale, „The Magical Life of Ithell Colquhoun", in: Nevill Drury (Hrsg.), *Pathways in Modern Western Magic*, Richmond 2012, S. 313.

5 Hale 2020 (wie Anm. 1), S. 187–188. Siehe Shillitoe 2010 (wie Anm. 1), S. 107–108. Etwa um die Zeit, als sie an *Nativity* arbeitete, verfasste Ithell Colquhoun auch einen Essay für die Search Society, deren Mitglied sie war, und befasste sich darin u. a. mit dem Potenzial der Blasphemie, „das Göttliche und das Menschliche in Kontakt miteinander zu bringen". Amy Hales umfassende Recherchen zu Colquhoun beleuchten das frühe Interesse der Künstlerin an „den Möglichkeiten des Sakrilegischen, zu verändern und zu erheben". Siehe Hale 2020 (wie Anm. 1), S. 179–180; Ithell Colquhoun, „The Connection between Mysticism and Blasphemy", unveröffentlichtes Manuskript, um 1928/29, TGA 929/2/3/2.

6 „‚Welt verändern' hat Marx gesagt, ‚das Leben ändern' sagte Rimbaud, uns verschmelzen beide Aussprüche zu einem." André Breton, in: *Paris 1935. Erster Internationaler Schriftstellerkongreß zur Verteidigung der Kultur. Reden und Dokumente*, hrsg. von der Akademie der Wissenschaften der DDR, Einleitung und Anhang von Wolfgang Klein, Berlin 1982, S. 309.

7 Whitney Chadwick, *Women Artists and the Surrealist Movement*, London 1985, S. 7, 11–13; Dawn Ades, „Notes on Two Women Surrealist Painters: Eileen Agar and Ithell Colquhoun", in: *Oxford Art Journal* 3, Nr. 1, April 1980, S. 36–42, hier: S. 41–42; siehe auch Dawn Ades, „Surrealism: Male-Female", in: Jennifer Mundy, Dawn Ades und Vincent Gille (Hrsg.), *Surrealism: Desire Unbound*, Ausst.-Kat. Tate

queer-inflected take on birth as a sacred act of self-realization.[4] Though such imagery could have been read as blasphemous, Colquhoun's deep reverence for religion and the androgynous divine—rooted in her engagement with occultism, alchemy, and kabbalistic thought—shaped a vision in which spiritual androgyny symbolized the full realization of the human form, with her art seeking not political confrontation but, as Amy Hale notes, "the conditions for enlightenment, genuine liberty and freedom."[5] In her thought patterns, Colquhoun drew from radical, esoteric Theosophists, particularly Helena Blavatsky's Eastern-oriented, magical, and occultist philosophy, to explore the alchemical reunion of male and female, challenging modern worldviews of identity and sexual division.

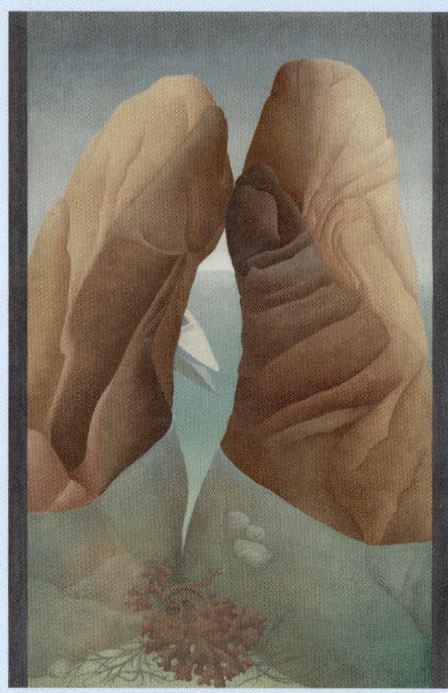

ABB. ~ FIG. 1

Ithell Colquhoun, *Scylla*, 1938

Öl auf Holz ~ *Oil on board*,
91,4 × 61 cm
Tate, Purchased 1977

"Transform the world" and "change life" were central mottos of the Surrealist project, as declared by André Breton in his 1935 "Speech to the Congress of Writers."[6] As a revolutionary movement deeply invested in the politics that shaped the 1920s and 1930s, Surrealism placed critique and subversion of established social values at the movement's core. Mind-bending representations of bodies, objects, and landscapes—both in art and literature—sought to expand the perceptions of reality by tapping into the subconscious registers of desire and dreams. Although the movement included significantly more women artists and writers than any other contemporary group, many of the debates on sexual desire and identity occurred within the restricted circle of men.[7] In-depth discussions from January 1928 and published shortly after in the eleventh issue of *La Révolution surréaliste* provide insight into the Surrealists' concerns

4
Colquhoun was outspoken in her writing about the constraints of women's clothing: see Ithell Colquhoun, "My Ideas about Clothes," unpublished manuscript, ca. 1961, TGA 929/1/225; Amy Hale, "The Magical Life of Ithell Colquhoun," in *Pathways in Modern Western Magic*, ed. Nevill Drury (Richmond, CA: Concrescent Scholars, 2012), p. 313.

5
Hale, *Ithell Colquhoun*, pp. 187–188. See Shillitoe, *Ithell Colquhoun*, pp. 107–108. Around the time she was working on *Nativity*, Colquhoun also wrote an essay for the Search Society, of which she was a member, reflecting in part on the potential of blasphemy to bring "the divine and the human into contact." Amy Hale's extensive research on Colquhoun highlights the artist's early interest in "the possibilities of the sacrilegious to transform and uplift." See Hale, *Ithell Colquhoun*, pp. 179–180; Ithell Colquhoun, "The Connection between Mysticism and Blasphemy," unpublished manuscript, ca. 1928/29, TGA 929/2/3/2.

6
"'Transform the world,' Marx said; 'change life,' Rimbaud said. These two watchwords are one for us." André Breton, "Speech to the Congress of Writers" (1935), in *Manifestoes of Surrealism*, trans. Richard Seaver and Helen R. Lane (Ann Arbor: University of Michigan Press, 1969), p. 241.

7
Whitney Chadwick, *Women Artists and the Surrealist Movement* (London: Thames & Hudson, 1985), pp. 7, 11–13; Dawn Ades, "Notes on Two Women Surrealist Painters: Eileen Agar and Ithell Colquhoun," in *Women in Art*, *Oxford Art Journal* 3, no. 1 (April 1980): pp. 41–42; see also Dawn Ades, "Surrealism: Male-Female," in *Surrealism: Desire Unbound*, ed. Jennifer Mundy, Dawn Ades, and Vincent Gille (Princeton: Princeton University Press, 2001), pp. 171–174.

In Anbetracht dieser Spannungen ist es verführerisch, sich einige von Colquhouns Arbeiten als eine direkte Zersetzung des männlichen Blicks der Bewegung vorzustellen. Stillleben aus dem Ende der 1930er- und Anfang der 1940er-Jahre wie *Pitcher-Plant* oder *Untitled work (Sardine and Eggs)* sind Doppelbilder, die an schlaffe Phalli erinnern und Themen wie männliche Impotenz und Kastration beschwören.[12] *Scylla* (1938, Abb. 1) lässt sich als auffälliger Verstoß gegen sexuelle Konventionen in der Naturlandschaft betrachten. Zwei gigantische Felsformationen erheben sich aus einem ruhigen Meer und erinnern entweder an die untergetauchten Beine und die Vulva einer Frau oder aber an zwei erigierte männliche Geschlechtsorgane, die sich berühren.[13] Dawn Ades wagte einmal die Vermutung, dass Colquhouns sexuell aufgeladene Darstellungen von Pflanzen und Landschaften, „eine so explizite Herausforderung" des unerschöpflichen Einsatzes des weiblichen Körpers im Surrealismus seien, „dass es an Parodie grenzt".[14] Die Künstlerin, zur Zeit von Ades' Essay etwa Mitte siebzig, zögerte nicht, sie zu korrigieren: „All meine Arbeiten, egal welchen Datums, sind völlig ernsthaft, was die Intention anbelangt", und fügte hinzu, sie empfände jede Form von Parodie als „abstoßend".[15] Colquhouns Entwicklung war von bewusstem Widerstand gegen auferlegte Definitionen geprägt. Ihr Bruch mit den britischen Surrealist*innen, als Folge der Weigerung, sich den strikten Vorgaben der Gruppe zu unterwerfen und ihre Verbindung zu okkultistischen Kreisen aufzulösen, hielt sie nicht davon ab, ein Jahrzehnt später mit „The Mantic Stain" den ersten umfassenden englischen Text zum Thema Automatismus zu verfassen.[16] Auch ihre Kritik an den sexistischen Tendenzen der Bewegung führte nicht dazu, dass sie die Arbeiten der Surrealisten zum Begehren generell ablehnte. Doch sie spricht – in Übereinstimmung mit Ades' Bemerkung – für eine tiefgreifende Auseinandersetzung mit surrealistischer Sprache, die den Horizont der Bewegung sowie ihre eigene und spirituelle Welt erweiterte. Es ist auch dieser inhärente Sinn für Freiheit, verbunden mit der finanziellen Sicherheit ihres Hintergrunds, der es Colquhoun erlaubte, weitgehend außerhalb der Zwänge der Ehe zu leben. In ihren Texten spürt sie einer Reihe von Beziehungen nach, darunter ihrer Liebe zu einer griechischen Frau, Andromache Kazou, die in ihrem unveröffentlichten Manuskript „Lesbian Shore" leidenschaftlich beschworen wurde: „Ihre Schönheit muss mondgleich sein", schreibt sie, „ihr morbider Charme entspringt der bleich gewobenen Zauberei der Hekate."[17] Colquhoun pflegte Freundschaften mit lesbischen und genderqueeren Künstler*innen und Intellektuellen wie Gluck und Marlow Moss, besonders nach dem Zweiten Weltkrieg, als sie sich in der Künstler*innenkolonie in Lamorna in Cornwall niederließ.

Im Fall der Künstlerin, Schriftstellerin und Designerin Leonor Fini ging es hingegen um explizite Rebellion. Die 1907 in Buenos Aires als Tochter von Eltern mit italienischen und mitteleuropäischen Wurzeln geborene Fini kam Anfang der 1930er-Jahre nach Paris, nachdem sie den Großteil ihrer Kindheit in Triest verbracht hatte. Ihr frühes Auftreten in der französischen Avantgardeszene hatte Reaktionen zur Folge, die von Ehrfurcht bis hin zu Verwirrung reichten. Fini war eine autodidaktische Künstlerin, deren Blick durch Triests vielschichtige Zwischenkriegsidentität an der Grenze sowohl von italienischen, österreichisch-ungarischen als auch nahöstlichen Einflüssen geprägt war. Damals war sie bereits vertraut mit den Arbeiten von Franz Kafka und Sigmund Freud – zum Erstaunen

Modern, London/The Metropolitan Museum of Art, New York, Princeton 2001, S. 171–174.

8 „Der Eindruck sexueller Freiheit, der durch die Tatsache entsteht, dass es überhaupt solche Diskussionen gab, wird durch mangelnde Offenheit in zwei Bereichen Lügen gestraft – weibliche Sexualität und Homosexualität." Ades 1980 (wie Anm. 7), S. 41–42; siehe auch Chadwick 1985 (wie Anm. 7) S. 103.

9 André Breton u.a., „Recherches sur la sexualité: Part d'objectivité, déterminations individuelles, degré de conscience", in: *La Révolution surréaliste*, Nr. 11, 15.03.1928, S. 33; veröffentl. auf Englisch in: José Pierre (Hrsg.), *Investigating Sex: Surrealist Discussions*, übers. von Malcolm Imrie, London 2011, S. 5. Siehe Ades 1980 (wie Anm. 7), S. 41–42; Chadwick 1985 (wie Anm. 7), S. 103–105.

10 Siehe Chadwick 1985 (wie Anm. 7), S. 13, 105; Ades 1980 (wie Anm. 7), S. 171, 174.

11 Ithell Colquhoun, „Women in Art", Brief an die Herausgeber, in: *Oxford Art Journal* 4, Nr. 1, Juli 1981, S. 65.

12 Eine vertiefte Auseinandersetzung mit den Themen Kastration und männliche Fragilität in Colquhouns Schaffen findet sich in Hale 2020 (wie Anm. 1), S. 60–64. Siehe auch Shillitoe 2010 (wie Anm. 1), S. 102–106.

13 Colquhoun beschrieb ihr Gemälde *Scylla* als „in erster Linie weibliches Symbol", fügte jedoch als Reaktion auf Ades' eigene Interpretation der Arbeit hinzu, „aber ich nehme an, man könnte es auch als phallisch betrachten. Colquhoun 1981 (wie Anm. 11), S. 65; Ades 1980 (wie Anm. 7), S. 40.

with female sexuality and same-sex desire, among other topics. Speculations on morals and ethics, physical attraction, sexual preferences, and fantasies were raised—without women present.[8] While the subject of homosexual desire between men was disputed at length and firmly condemned by Breton, along with peer members Benjamin Péret and Pierre Unik, the question of "love between women" occupies barely a few short lines in the nine-page report. "Physical love?" Breton asks. Another member replies before moving on to the next topic: "I imagine that one woman plays the part of the man and the other that of the woman."[9] The contradiction between women's lived realities and their idealized portrayal in Surrealist art has been addressed over time by both Surrealist women and later feminist scholars.[10] Colquhoun was aware of this disparity, noting in a 1981 letter that although Breton claimed women should be "free and adored," most of his followers remained deeply chauvinistic, with women "permitted not required."[11] It is tempting, in light of these tensions, to look at some of Colquhoun's work as a direct subversion of the movement's male-driven gaze. Still lifes from the late 1930s and early 1940s such as *Pitcher Plant* or *Sardine and Eggs* are double images resembling drooping phalluses, evoking themes of male impotence and castration.[12] *Scylla* (1938, fig. 1) may be thought of as a conspicuous transgression of sexual conventions in natural landscape. Two giant rock formations rise from a quiet sea, suggesting the immersed legs and vulva of a woman; alternatively, they may just as well be read as two erect male organs teasing each other.[13] Dawn Ades once ventured to suggest that Colquhoun's sexually infused depictions of plants and landscapes pose "a challenge, so explicit as to verge on parody," to Surrealism's inexhaustible use of the female body.[14] The artist, in her mid-seventies at the time of Ades's essay, did not hesitate to correct her: "All my work of whatever date is completely serious in intention," adding that she found any form of parody "repugnant."[15] Colquhoun's trajectory was one of deliberate resistance to imposed definitions. Her break with the British Surrealists, following her refusal to adhere to the group's strict criteria and to sever ties with occultist circles, did not keep her from authoring a decade later the first major English text on automatism, "The Mantic Stain."[16] Nor does her critique of the movement's sexist bias reduce her to a merely reactionary stance toward the Surrealists' work on desire. But it does—aligning with Ades's thought—speak to a profound engagement with Surrealist language that expanded the movement's horizons and her own psychic and spiritual world. It is also this inherent sense of freedom, coupled with the financial stability of her background, that enabled Colquhoun to live largely outside the constraints of marriage. Her writings trace a series of relationships, including her love for a Greek woman, Andromache Kazou, passionately evoked in her unpublished 1933 manuscript "Lesbian Shore": "Her beauty must be lunar," she writes, "her morbid charm derives from the pallid spell weaving of Hecate."[17] Colquhoun cultivated friendships with lesbian and genderqueer artists and intellectuals such as Gluck and Marlow Moss, especially after

8 "The impression of sexual liberation that is given by the very fact of having such open discussion is belied by the lack of openness in two areas—women's sexuality and homosexuality." Ades, "Notes on Two Women Surrealist Painters," pp. 41–42; see also Chadwick, *Women Artists*, p. 103.

9 André Breton, et al., "Recherches sur la sexualité: Part d'objectivité, déterminations individuelles, degré de conscience," *La Révolution surréaliste*, no. 11 (March 15, 1928): p. 33; published in English in *Investigating Sex: Surrealist Discussions*, ed. José Pierre, trans. Malcolm Imrie (London: Verso, 2011), p. 5. See Ades, "Notes on Two Women Surrealist Painters," pp. 41–42; Chadwick, *Women Artists*, pp. 103–105.

10 See Chadwick, pp. 13, 105; Ades, "Surrealism," pp. 171, 174.

11 Ithell Colquhoun, "Women in Art," letter to the editor, *Tradition*, *Oxford Art Journal* 4, no. 1 (July 1981): p. 65.

12 An in-depth reading of the themes of castration and male fragility in Colquhoun's oeuvre can be found in Hale, *Ithell Colquhoun*, pp. 60–64; see also Shillitoe, *Ithell Colquhoun*, pp. 102–106.

13 Colquhoun described her painting *Scylla* in terms of "primarily a feminine symbol," adding, in response to Ades's own interpretation of the work, "but I suppose one could see it as phallic as well." Colquhoun, "Women in Art," p. 65; Ades, "Notes on Two Women Surrealist Painters," p. 40.

14 Ades, "Notes on Two Women Surrealist Painters," p. 40.

15 Colquhoun, "Women in Art," p. 65.

16 See Chadwick, *Women Artists*, p. 154.

der Surrealist*innen, für die diese Art der Literatur in Paris relativ neu war.[18] Häufig besuchte Fini Zusammenkünfte und Bälle in auffallenden Kostümen in einer Mischung von hyperfemininer Belle-Époque-Mode mit gotischen, sogar monströsen Elementen. Schrecken und Schönheit standen im Mittelpunkt ihrer Selbstdarstellung, die in der Kunst der Zeit in gewisser Weise wie ein trojanisches Pferd innerhalb der vorherrschenden Frauen-Archetypen – göttlich, kindlich, erotisch oder gefährlich – funktionierte.[19]

Fini weigerte sich, sich selbst als Surrealistin zu bezeichnen. Obwohl ihre Gemälde stark in das Innenleben von Träumen eingebettet waren, distanzierte sie sich von Bretons Befürwortung des „Denk-Diktats ohne jede Kontrolle der Vernunft, jenseits jeder ästhetischen oder ethischen Überlegung".[20] Stattdessen war sie bestrebt, akribisch genaue Bilder zu erschaffen, die, mit ihren Worten, „die Mechanismen des Traumes enthalten".[21] Sie war auch kritisch, was die diskriminierenden Ansichten der Bewegung betraf: „Mir missfiel die Unterwürfigkeit, mit der alle Breton begegneten. Ich hasste seine anti-homosexuelle Einstellung und auch seine Misogynie [...] Ich lehnte das Etikett Surrealistin ab [und] agierte lieber alleine."[22] Finis Sinn für Unabhängigkeit spiegelte sich in den sich stets verändernden, machtvollen, geschlechtsneutralen Charakteren wider, die sie sowohl in ihrem Leben als auch in ihrer Kunst verkörperte. Ihre Leidenschaft für Verkleidungen und die Erforschung ihrer eigenen Vielfalt – „ma multiplicité", wie sie es nannte – wird oft auf ihre Kindheit zurückgeführt.[23] Nach der turbulenten Trennung ihrer Eltern kleidete die Mutter, Malvina Fini, ihre fünfjährige Tochter oftmals wie einen Jungen, um sie vor den aggressiven Versuchen des Vaters, sie in sein Gewahrsam zu bringen, zu schützen.[24] In ihren Arbeiten wurden intime Schauplätze und raffinierte Kleidung zum Terrain transformativer Erfahrungen, in denen Identität in beständigem Fluss ist: Das Gemälde *Portrait féminin n. 9* (1936, Kat., S. 104) spiegelt zum Beispiel die fortwährende Hinwendung der Künstlerin zu androgynen Porträts wider.

Whitney Chadwicks Interpretation von *L'Alcôve* (1940, Abb. 2) verortet Finis Auflösung von Geschlecht und sexueller Dualität durch Kostümierung und die Übertragung des häuslichen Raums vor dem Hintergrund des Zweiten Weltkriegs.[25] Inmitten des Aufstiegs des Nationalsozialismus in Deutschland und der zunehmenden Spannungen in ganz Europa zeigt *L'Alcôve* die Szene einer weiblichen Gemeinschaft mit einem großen androgynen Ritter, der ein Bett bewacht, auf dem zwei Frauen verweilen, die einander an den Händen halten. Bewacherin dieses intimen Raums ist ihre enge Freundin, die Künstlerin Leonora Carrington, die sich zum damaligen Zeitpunkt in einer Beziehung mit Max Ernst befand, einem ehemaligen Liebhaber Finis. Fini floh bei Ausbruch des Kriegs mit dem Gemälde von Paris nach Saint-Martin-d'Ardèche, im Südosten von Frankreich, wo sie den Sommer mit dem Paar und anderen Freund*innen und Liebhaber*innen im Exil verbrachte. Fotografien dieser Periode zeigen die Fluidität ihrer Beziehung und ihr kollektives Durchhaltevermögen in politisch schwierigen Zeiten durch die Entfaltung von Traumwelten (Abb. 3). Performative Kleidung, kulinarische Experimente und die bildhauerische Gestaltung mythischer Figuren bildeten das, was Chadwick als „einen Fantasiehintergrund für eine Welt, in der Unsicherheiten an der Tagesordnung waren und Grenzen mit der Geschwindigkeit eines Pinselstriches, des Falls eines Stemmeisens [...] oder des Lesens einer Kurz-

14 Ades 1980 (wie Anm. 7), S. 40.

15 Colquhoun 1981 (wie Anm. 11), S. 65.

16 Siehe Chadwick 1985 (wie Anm. 7), S. 154.

17 Zit. nach: Hale 2020 (wie Anm. 1), S. 34–35.

18 Peter Webb, *Sphinx: The Life and Art of Leonor Fini*, New York 2009, S. 6; Alyce Mahon, „La Féminité triomphante: Surrealism, Leonor Fini, and the Sphinx", in: *Dada/Surrealism* 19, Nr. 1, 2013, S. 6.

19 Andrea Kollnitz, „Terrifying Beauty: Theatrical Self-Performance in Leonor Fini's Art and Life", in: Royce Mahawatte und Jacki Willson, *Dangerous Bodies: New Global Perspectives on Fashion and Transgression*, London 2023, S. 191 im E-Book; für eine ausführliche Analyse der Beziehung zwischen den Konzepten von Schrecken und Schönheit in Finis Arbeiten, siehe S. 200–202.

20 André Breton, *Die Manifeste des Surrealismus*, übers. von Ruth Henry, Reinbek bei Hamburg 1968, S. 26.

21 Zit. nach: Webb 2009 (wie Anm. 18), S. 72. Siehe Chadwick 1985 (wie Anm. 7), S. 86–87.

22 Interview zwischen Fini und Webb, 09.02.1994, Paris, zit. nach: Webb 2009 (wie Anm. 18), S. 69–72. Siehe auch Rachel Grew, „Leonor Fini and Dressing Up: An Act of Creativity", in: *Woman's Art Journal* 40, Nr. 1, Frühling/Sommer 2019, S. 13–14.

23 Leonor Fini und José Alvarez, *Le Livre de Leonor Fini*, Lausanne und Paris 1975, S. 32. Siehe auch Grew 2019 (wie Anm. 22), S. 14.

the Second World War, when she settled in the artists' colony in Lamorna, Cornwall. The case of artist, writer, and designer Leonor Fini, by contrast, was one of explicit rebellion. Born in Buenos Aires in 1907 to a family with mixed Italo–Central European roots, Fini arrived in Paris in the early 1930s after spending most of her childhood in Trieste. Her early appearances on the French avant-garde scene elicited reactions ranging from awe to confusion: Fini was a self-taught artist whose vision was shaped by Trieste's layered interwar identity, at the crossroads of Italian, Austro-Hungarian, and Near Eastern influences. By then, she was already well-versed in the works of Franz Kafka and Sigmund Freud—to the astonishment of the Surrealists, for whom such literature was still relatively new in Paris.[18] Fini frequently attended gatherings and balls in striking costumes, creating a hybrid of hyper-feminine, belle-époque fashion fused with gothic and even monstrous elements. Terror and beauty were equally central to her self-performance, which functioned, in a sense, as a Trojan horse within the dominant archetypes of woman—divine, childlike, erotic, or dangerous—in the art of the period.[19] Fini refused to call herself a Surrealist. Though her paintings were deeply invested in the inner life of dreams, she distanced herself from Breton's advocacy of the "absence of any control exercised by reason, exempt from any aesthetic or moral preoccupations."[20] Rather, she sought to create meticulous images which, in her words, "*contain the mechanism* of the dream."[21] She was also critical of the movement's discriminatory views: "I disliked the deference with which everyone treated Breton. I hated his anti-homosexual attitudes and also his misogyny [...] I refused the label surrealist [... and] preferred to walk alone."[22]

Fini's sense of independence was mirrored in the ever-changing, powerful, and gender-bending characters she embodied both in her life and her art. Her passion for dressing up and exploring her own multiplicity—"ma multiplicité," as she called it—is often traced back to her childhood.[23] As a protective gesture following the turbulent separation of her parents, her mother, Malvina Fini, would dress her five-year-old daughter as a boy to shield her from her father's aggressive attempts to seize custody.[24] In her work, intimate settings and sophisticated outfits become the terrain of transformative experience in which identity is in constant flux: the painting *Portrait féminin n. 9* (1936, cat. p. 104), for instance, reflects the artist's ongoing attachment to androgynous portraiture. Whitney Chadwick's interpretation of *L'Alcôve* (1940, fig. 2) further situates Fini's dissolution of gender and sexual binaries through costuming and the negotiation of domestic space against the backdrop of the Second World War.[25] Amid the rise of Nazism in Germany and mounting tensions across Europe, *L'Alcôve* depicts a scene of female companionship with a tall, androgynous knight guarding a bed on which two women, holding hands, linger. The guardian of this intimate space is her close friend, the artist Leonora Carrington, who at the time was in a relationship with Max Ernst, a former lover of Fini. Fini fled with the painting from Paris to Saint-Martin-d'Ardèche, in southeastern

17
Quoted in Hale, *Ithell Colquhoun*, pp. 34–35.

18
Peter Webb, *Sphinx: The Life and Art of Leonor Fini* (New York: Vendome, 2009), p. 6; Alyce Mahon, "La Féminité triomphante: Surrealism, Leonor Fini, and the Sphinx," *Dada/Surrealism* 19, no. 1 (2013), p. 6.

19
Andrea Kollnitz, "Terrifying Beauty: Theatrical Self-Performance in Leonor Fini's Art and Life," in *Dangerous Bodies: New Global Perspectives on Fashion and Transgression*, ed. Royce Mahawatte and Jacki Willson, Palgrave Studies in Fashion and the Body (London: Palgrave Macmillan, 2023), p. 191, ebook; for an extended analysis of the relation between the concepts of terror and beauty in Fini's work see pp. 200–202.

20
André Breton, "Manifesto of Surrealism" (1924), in *Manifestoes of Surrealism*, p. 26.

21
Quoted in Webb, *Sphinx*, p. 72, emphasis added. See Chadwick, *Women Artists*, pp. 86–87.

22
Interview between Fini and Webb (February 9, 1994, Paris) quoted in Webb, *Sphinx*, pp. 69–72. See also Rachel Grew, "Leonor Fini and Dressing Up," *Woman's Art Journal* 40, no. 1 (Spring/Summer 2019), pp. 13–14.

23
Leonor Fini and José Alvarez, *Le Livre de Leonor Fini* (Lausanne: La Guilde du Livre and Les Éditions Clairefontaine; Paris: Vilo, 1975), p. 32. See also Grew, "Leonor Fini," p. 14.

24
See Grew, p. 14; Webb, *Sphinx*, p. 8.

25
Also titled *The Black Room*. Whitney Chadwick, *Farewell to the Muse: Love, War and the Women of Surrealism* (London: Thames & Hudson, 2017), pp. 68–70.

geschichte fielen", beschrieb.[26] Finis Kunst unterlief festgeschriebene soziale und sexuelle Definitionen durch das Prisma ihrer eigenen Beziehungen, zog sie doch polyamouröse Freundschaften und Gemeinschaften ehelichen Konventionen vor. Das Gemälde *Autoportrait avec Kot et Sergio* (1952, Kat., S. 101) zeigt Fini Jahre später in einem leidenschaftlichen Dreiergespann mit zwei queeren Bewunderern. Links der polnische Intellektuelle und Emigrant Konstanty („Kot") Jelénski, mit dem Fini jahrzehntelang zusammenlebte, gemeinsam mit ihrem anderen Langzeitpartner, dem italienischen Maler und ehemaligen Diplomaten Stanislao Lepri (nicht abgebildet). Die drei, die sich nach dem Krieg zusammen in Paris niedergelassen hatten, reisten 1952 in die Küstenstadt Anzio in Italien, wo Fini den zwanzig Jahre alten Sergio Gajardo kennenlernte – rechts abgebildet – einen queeren chilenischen Mann, von dem nur wenig überliefert ist. Ein nebulöses Grün umgibt das fein ausgeführte Dreifachporträt, das womöglich einen Versuch darstellt, die Spannungen einzufangen, die mutmaßlich zwischen Finis beiden Verehrern auftraten. Die genauen Umstände ihrer Freundschaft bleiben im Dunklen – wie so viele der Verbindungen in Finis Umlaufbahn, die an ihrem Streben nach einem unsteten Lebenswandel jenseits aller Etiketten festhielt.[27]

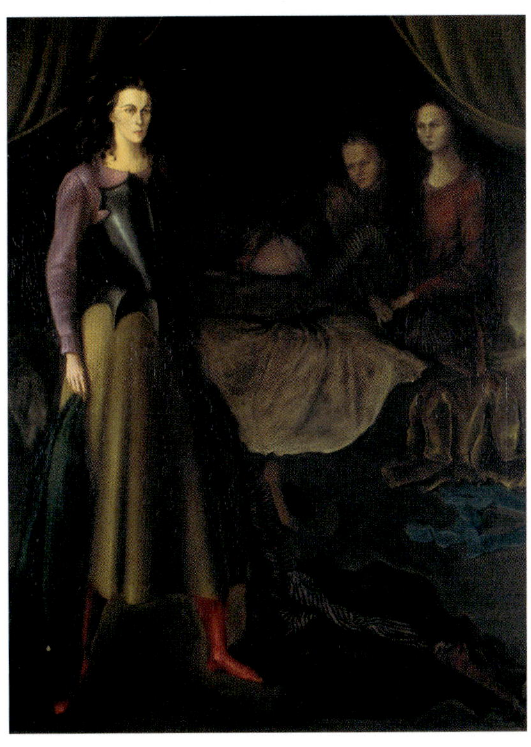

ABB. ~ FIG. 2

Leonor Fini, *L'Alcôve*, 1940
Der Alkoven ~ *The Alcove*

Öl auf Leinwand ~ *Oil on canvas*, 101 × 73 cm
Privatsammlung ~ *Private Collection*

24 Grew 2019 (wie Anm. 22), S. 14; Webb 2009 (wie Anm. 18), S. 8.

25 Whitney Chadwick, *Farewell to the Muse: Love, War and the Women of Surrealism*, London 2017, S. 68–70.

26 Ebd., S. 70.

27 Siehe Webb 2009 (wie Anm. 18), S. 171–173. Eine eingehende Betrachtung von Leben und Sexualität Konstanty Jelénskis, aber auch der Art seiner Beziehung zu Fini, findet sich in Piotr Sobolczyk, *Polish Queer Modernism*, Polish Studies: Transdisciplinary Perspectives 14, hrsg. von Krzysztof Zajas und Jarosław Fazan, Frankfurt am Main 2015, S. 165–167.

France, at the outbreak of the war and spent the summer in exile with the couple and other friends and lovers. Photographs of this period capture the fluidity of their relationship and their collective endurance of politically troubled times through the elaboration of dream worlds (fig. 3). Performative dressing, culinary experiments, and the sculpting of mythical creatures formed what Chadwick describes as "an imagined backdrop for a world in which uncertainties reigned and boundaries fell with the stroke of a paintbrush, the fall of a chisel [...] or the reading of a short story."[26] Fini's art subverted fixed social and sexual definitions through the prism of her own affinities, as the artist prioritized polyamorous friendships and community over marital conventions. The painting *Autoportrait avec Kot et Sergio* (1952, cat. p. 101) captures Fini years later in a passionate triangle with two queer admirers: to the left, the Polish intellectual and émigré Konstanty ("Kot") Jeleński, who shared Fini's life for decades together with her other long-term partner, the Italian painter and former diplomat Stanislao Lepri (not depicted). The three, who had settled together in Paris after the war, traveled in 1952 to the coastal town of Anzio in Italy, where Fini encountered the enchanting twenty-year-old Sergio Gajardo—depicted on the right—a queer Chilean man of whom little record remains. A nebulous green surrounds the finely executed triple-portrait, in what may have been an attempt to capture the tensions that allegedly arose between Fini's two worshippers. The exact conditions of their friendship remain opaque—as did many of the ties within Fini's orbit, who held fast to her aspiration toward an unsettled lifestyle beyond labels.[27] The Surrealist movement was an international project that resonated beyond Western European cultural hubs. In Eastern European circles, women and genderqueer artists who lived outside social expectations embraced Surrealism as part of their programs in distinct and deeply personal ways.[28] The pioneering Serbian artist Milena Pavlović-Barili—whose paintings, fashion illustrations, and poetry received only slight recognition in her homeland during her lifetime—has been increasingly recognized since the 1990s as a major influence on post-Surrealist art.[29] Born in Požarevac, in the Kingdom of Serbia, in 1909, she was of aristocratic descent on her mother's side, Danica Pavlović; her father, Bruno Barilli,[30] was a prominent Italian composer and music critic. Though her career was short-lived—Pavlović-Barili died in New York at the age of thirty-five—the artist left behind a dense body of work that carved a modern perspective on questions of gender and sexual identity through masterful associations of old and new. Pavlović-Barili's oeuvre opens up a world of visual metaphors inspired by motifs from Italian Renaissance and Neoclassical architecture combined with an air of the carnivalesque and burlesque. A profound engagement with avant-garde, particularly metaphysical and surrealist languages can be felt in the melancholic settings of her paintings, frequently referencing Giorgio de Chirico's enigmatic cityscapes. Early on, her works manifested a sensibility for androgynous femininity through intense aesthetic reflections on the status of the female model, both in art

26
Ibid., p. 70.

27
See Webb, *Sphinx*, pp. 171–173. An in-depth reflection on the life and sexuality of Konstanty Jeleński, as well as the nature of his relationship with Fini can be found in Piotr Sobolczyk, *Polish Queer Modernism*, Polish Studies: Transdisciplinary Perspectives 14, ed. Krzysztof Zajas and Jarosław Fazan (Frankfurt am Main: Peter Lang, 2015), pp. 165–167.

28
See Anke Kempkes, "I Saw the Other Side of the Sun with You: Female Surrealists from Eastern Europe," exh. brochure (Cromwell Place, London, April 12–30, 2023), pp. 2–5; Sanja Bahun-Radunovic, "When the Margin Cries: Surrealism in Yugoslavia," *RiLUnE*, no. 3 (2005): pp. 41–43.

29
The public reception of Pavlović-Barili's art in Serbia both during her lifetime and afterward is discussed in Magdalena Koch, "A Quest for Milena Pavlović Barilli in Serbian Literature," in *Milena Pavlović Barilli. EX POST*, ed. Lidija Merenik, Aleksandar Petrović, *and Magdalena Koch* (Belgrade: Hesperia, 2009), pp. 114–128. See also Stefan Žarić, *Maison Barilli: Belgrade/New York; One Study of High Fashion and High Art*, exh. cat. (Požarevac: Fondacija Milenin dom—Galerija Milene Pavlović Barilli, 2017), p. 15.

30
The orthographic variations in the artist's surname—Pavlović-Barili versus Pavlović-Barilli, sometimes hyphenated and sometimes not—correspond to the diverse linguistic and cultural contexts she inhabited.

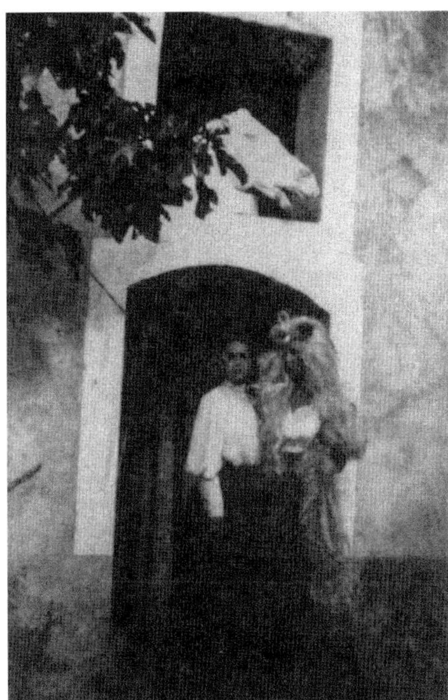

ABB. ~ FIG. 3

Leonor Fini und Leonora Carrington als Pferde in Saint-Martin-d'Ardèche ~ *Leonor Fini and Leonora Carrington as Horses at Saint-Martin-d'Ardèche*, 1939

Die surrealistische Bewegung war ein internationales Projekt, das auch jenseits westlich-europäischer Kulturknotenpunkte Widerhall fand. In osteuropäischen Kreisen griffen Frauen und genderqueere Künstler*innen den Surrealismus als Teil ihres Programms auf eigenständige und zutiefst persönliche Art und Weise auf.[28] Die wegweisende serbische Künstler*in Milena Pavlović-Barili – deren Gemälde, Modeillustrationen und Poesie in ihrem Heimatland zu ihren Lebzeiten nur wenig Anerkennung fanden – erfährt seit den 1990er-Jahren zunehmend Beachtung als wesentlicher Einflussfaktor auf die postsurrealistische Kunst.[29] Die 1909 in Požarevac im Königreich Serbien geborene Künstler*in war vonseiten ihrer Mutter, Danica Pavlović, adeliger Abstammung. Ihr Vater, Bruno Barilli,[30] war ein bekannter italienischer Komponist und Musikkritiker. Obwohl ihre Karriere nur kurz währte – sie starb mit fünfunddreißig Jahren in New York –, hinterließ Pavlović-Barili ein dichtes Werk, das durch meisterhafte Assoziationen von alt und neu eine moderne Perspektive zu Fragen von Geschlecht und sexueller Identität bot.

Pavlović-Barilis Œuvre eröffnet eine Welt visueller Metaphern, inspiriert von italienischer Renaissance und neoklassizistischer Architektur, verbunden mit einer Atmosphäre des Karnevalesken und Burlesken. Eine umfassende Auseinandersetzung mit der Avantgarde, besonders mit metaphysischer und surrealistischer Sprache, wird in den melancholischen Kulissen ihrer Gemälde deutlich, die sich häufig auf Giorgio de Chiricos rätselhafte Stadtlandschaften beziehen. Schon sehr früh ließen ihre Arbeiten ein Gespür für androgyne Weiblichkeit erkennen, das in intensiven ästhetischen Spiegelungen zum Status des weiblichen Modells, sowohl in der Kunstgeschichte als auch in der Mode- und Schönheitsbranche, zum Ausdruck kommt. Zahlreiche Modeillustrationen aus der Zwischenkriegszeit, als sie noch Student*in an der Königlichen Kunstschule in Belgrad und später an der Akademie der

28 Siehe Anke Kempkes, „I Saw the Other Side of the Sun with You: Female Surrealists from Eastern Europe", Ausst.-Brosch. Cromwell Place, London 2023, S. 2–5; Sanja Bahun-Radunovic, „When the Margin Cries: Surrealism in Yugoslavia", in: *RiLUnE*, Nr. 3, 2005, S. 37–52, hier: S. 41–43.

29 Die öffentliche Rezeption von Milena Pavlović-Barilis Kunst in Serbien, sowohl zu Lebzeiten als auch danach, wird erörtert in: Magdalena Koch, „A Quest for Milena Pavlović Barilli in Serbian Literature", in: Lidija Merenik, Aleksandar Petrović und Magdalena Koch (Hrsg.), *Milena Pavlović Barilli. EX POST*, Belgrad 2009, S. 114–128. Siehe auch Stefan Žarić, *Maison Barilli: Belgrade/New York; One Study of High Fashion and High Art*, Ausst.-Kat. Požarevac: Fondacija Milenin dom – Galerija Milene Pavlović Barilli, 2017, S. 15.

30 Die orthografischen Varianten im Nachnamen der Künstler*in – Pavlović-Barili oder Pavlović-Barilli sowie mal mit, mal ohne Bindestrich – entsprechen den verschiedenen linguistischen und kulturellen Kontexten, in denen sie sich bewegte.

history and the fashion and beauty industries. Numerous fashion illustrations from the interwar period, when she was still a student at the Royal School of Arts in Belgrade and later at the Academy of Fine Arts in Munich, bear traces of the ideological shifts occurring in popular culture across Europe. She incorporated new, trending visions of the "garçonne" and other hybrid models of womanhood in her works as well as her own appearance, thereby posing a challenge to the cultural dogmas of Serbian interwar society.[31] "I am not of any sex," Pavlović-Barili wrote in one of her *Spanish Poems* during her travels in 1930.[32] Her defiance of social etiquette materialized in fantastic paintings such as *Enigmatska kompozicija sa crnom rukom* (1932, cat. p. 105), in which Surrealist ideas of metamorphosis, illusion, and artificiality come together, suggesting a transgression of human anatomy and identity through the symbolism of the mannequin. Her nomadic career, leading her to various European cultural centers before she relocated to New York in 1939, was marked by success among the Surrealists and in the world of fashion—she became an illustrator for American beauty magazines such as *Harper's Bazaar*, *Vogue*, and *Glamour*—and by a deep longing for more visibility back in her home country.

31 See Stefan Žarić, *Maison Barilli*, pp. 18–23.

32 Quoted in ibid., p. 39; see Milena Pavlović Barili, "Poem 9" of her *Spanish Poems*, in Violeta Tornić, *Milena Pavlović Barili. Poezija* (Požarevac: Fondacija Milenin dom—Galerija Milene Pavlović Barilli, 2016), p. 105.

Bildenden Künste in München war, lassen den ideologischen Wandel erkennen, der sich in der Populärkultur in ganz Europa abzeichnete. Sie integrierte nicht nur neue, trendige Visionen der „garçonne" und anderer hybrider Modelle von Frausein in ihre Arbeiten, sondern auch ihr eigenes Erscheinungsbild, und stellte damit die kulturellen Dogmen der serbischen Zwischenkriegsgesellschaft infrage.[31] „Ich bin keinerlei Geschlechts", schrieb Pavlović-Barili 1930 auf Reisen in einem ihrer Gedichte.[32] Ihre Verweigerung sozialer Etikette fand in fantastischen Gemälden wie *Enigmatska kompozicija sa crnom rukom* (1932, Kat., S. 105) Ausdruck, in dem sich surrealistische Vorstellungen von Metamorphose, Illusion und Künstlichkeit verbinden und eine Überschreitung der menschlichen Anatomie und Identität durch den Symbolismus des Mannequins suggerieren. Ihre nomadische Karriere, die sie in zahlreiche europäische Kulturzentren führte, ehe sie sich 1939 in New York niederließ, war von Erfolgen unter den Surrealist*innen, aber auch in der Welt der Mode gekennzeichnet – sie war als Illustrator*in amerikanischer Modezeitschriften wie *Harper's Bazaar*, VOGUE und *Glamour* tätig – und von einer tiefen Sehnsucht nach größerer Sichtbarkeit in ihrem Heimatland.

31 Siehe Žarić 2017 (wie Anm. 29), S. 18–23.

32 Zitiert in ebd., S. 39. Siehe Milena Pavlović-Barili, „Poem 9" ihrer *Spanish Poems*, in: Violeta Tornić, *Milena Pavlović Barili. Poezija*, Požarevac: Fondacija Milenin dom – Galerija Milene Pavlović Barilli, 2016, S. 105.

V QUEERE LESARTEN VON ABSTRAKTION

QUEER READINGS OF ABSTRACTION

1

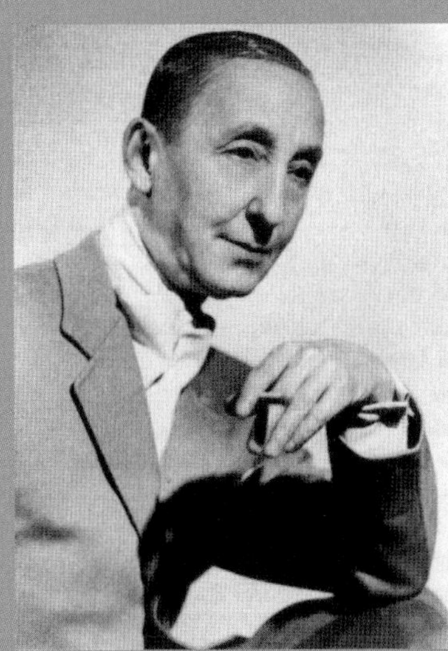

2

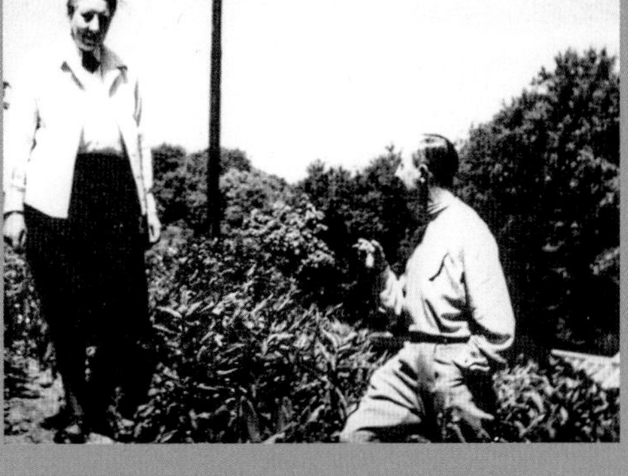

3

[...] das Geheimnis von Form liegt nicht in der Form selbst, sondern in der beständigen Veränderung und im Wandel von Formen [...].

~

[...] the secret of form lies not in form itself but in the continual changing and shifting of forms [...].

4

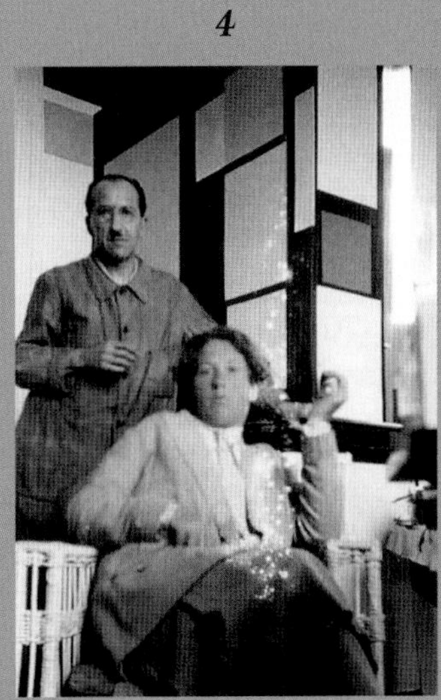

5

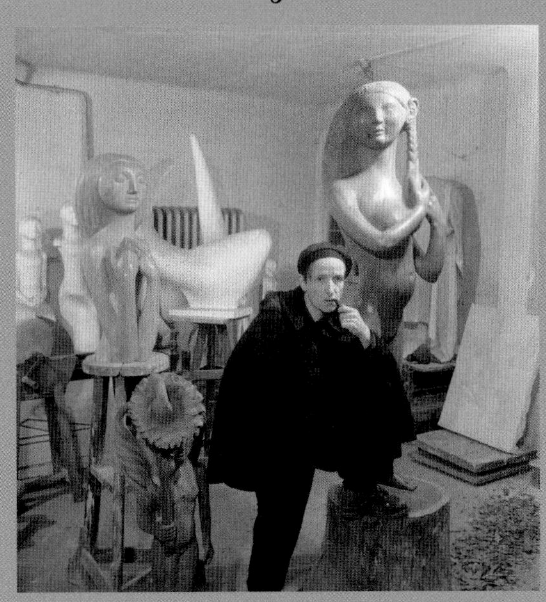

6

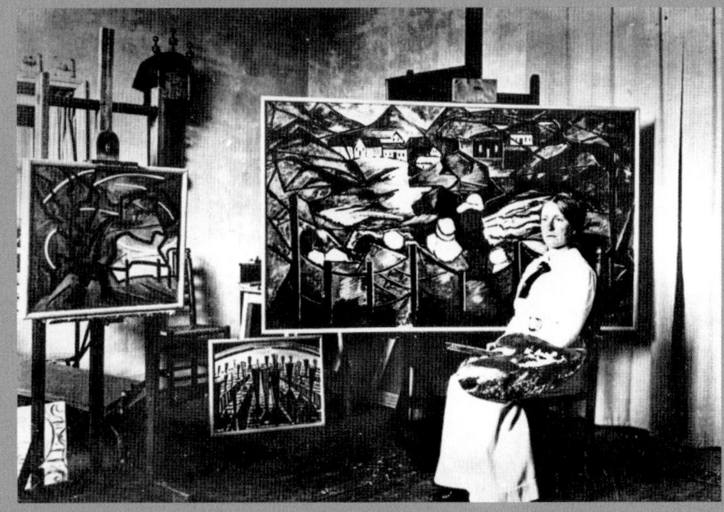

1

Marlow Moss (mit Krawatte und Zigarette), undatiert

1929 begegnete Moss in Paris ihrer*seiner Lebenspartnerin, der Dichterin A. H. Nijhoff, die Moss Mondrian und die De-Stijl-Bewegung vorstellte. Moss erweiterte fortan den Neoplastizismus mit formalen Elementen, die sich heute als queer definieren lassen.

~

Marlow Moss (with cravat and cigarette), undated

In 1929, Moss met their life partner in Paris, the poet A. H. Nijhoff, who introduced Moss to Mondrian and the De Stijl movement. From then on, Moss expanded Neo-Plasticism with formal elements that can today be read as queer.

2

A. H. Nijhoff und Marlow Moss in Lamorna in Cornwall, um 1950

~

A. H. Nijhoff and Marlow Moss in Lamorna, Cornwall, ca. 1950

3

Marlow Moss, in: Lucy Howarth, *Marlow Moss, Modern Women Artists*, Bd. 3, Bath 2019, S. 6.

~

Marlow Moss, quoted in Lucy Howarth, Marlow Moss, *vol. 3, Modern Women Artists (Bath: Eiderdown, 2019), p. 6.*

4

Til Brugman und Piet Mondrian im September 1927 in dessen Atelier in der Rue du Départ 26 in Paris

Die Avantgardedichterin Til Brugman war auch eine Spezialistin für die und Händlerin der Gruppe De Stijl. Seit 1926 war sie die Lebenspartnerin der Dada-Künstlerin Hannah Höch.

~

Til Brugman and Piet Mondrian in September 1927 in his studio at 26 rue du Départ in Paris

The avant-garde poet Til Brugman was also a specialist in and promoter of the De Stijl group. From 1926 onward, she was the partner of the Dada artist Hannah Höch.

5

Anton Prinner in seinem Atelier, 1947

Nach seiner Ankunft in Paris 1928 nahm der ungarische Künstler den Vornamen Anton und die Rolle eines Bohemiens an. Sein Atelier diente der Inszenierung multipler Identitäten. In einer Holzskulptur nistend empfing er dort Besucher*innen wie den befreundeten Picasso.

~

Anton Prinner in his studio, 1947

After arriving in Paris in 1928, the Hungarian artist adopted the name Anton and assumed the role of a Bohemian. His studio became a stage for the performance of multiple identities. Nesting inside a wooden sculpture, he received visitors such as his friend Picasso.

6

Jacoba van Heemskerck, um 1915

Van Heemskerck lebte mit ihrer Partnerin, der Kunstmäzenin Marie Tak van Poortvliet, in der Künstlerkolonie Domburg. Dort empfingen sie Piet Mondrian und entwickelten gemeinsam eine spiritualistisch geprägte abstrakte Kunst im Umfeld der Theosophie.

~

Jacoba van Heemskerck, ca. 1915

Van Heemskerck lived with her partner, patron of the arts Marie Tak van Poortvliet, in the artists' colony at Domburg. There, they hosted Piet Mondrian and together developed a spiritually influenced abstract art shaped by Theosophy.

Ich zerstörte meine alte Persönlichkeit und schuf eine neue.

~

I destroyed my old personality and created a new one.

Marlow Moss, in: *Marlow Moss*, Ausst.-Kat. Stedelijk Museum Amsterdam, Amsterdam 1962, o.S.

~

Marlow Moss, Marlow Moss, *exh. cat. (Amsterdam: Stedelijk Museum, 1962), n.p.*

V

QUEERE LESARTEN VON ABSTRAKTION

~

QUEER READINGS OF ABSTRACTION

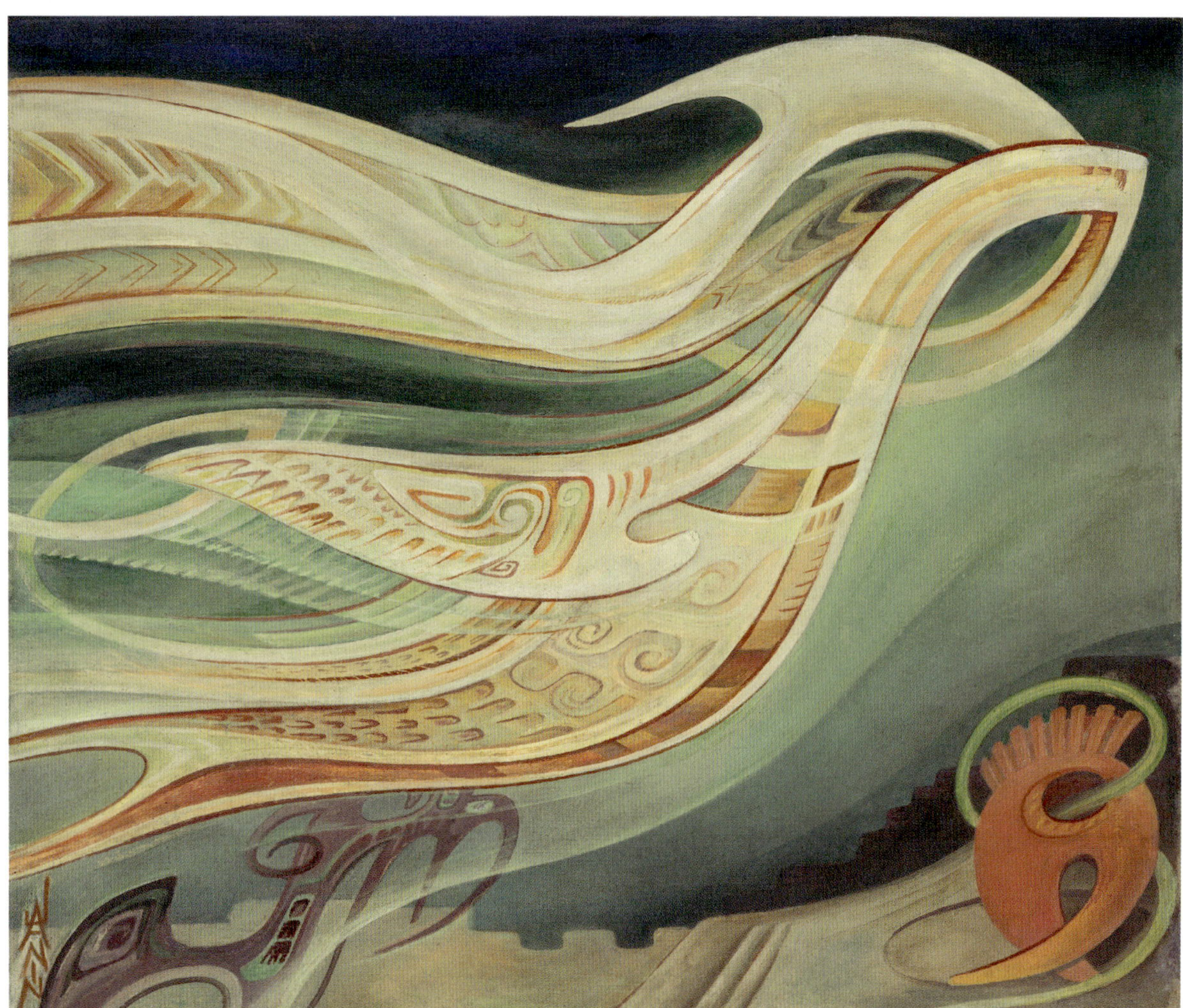

Louise Janin
Envol, 1955
Flug ~ *Flight*

Louise Janin

Les Plantes dressées, 1934
Aufstrebende Pflanzen ~
Erect Plants

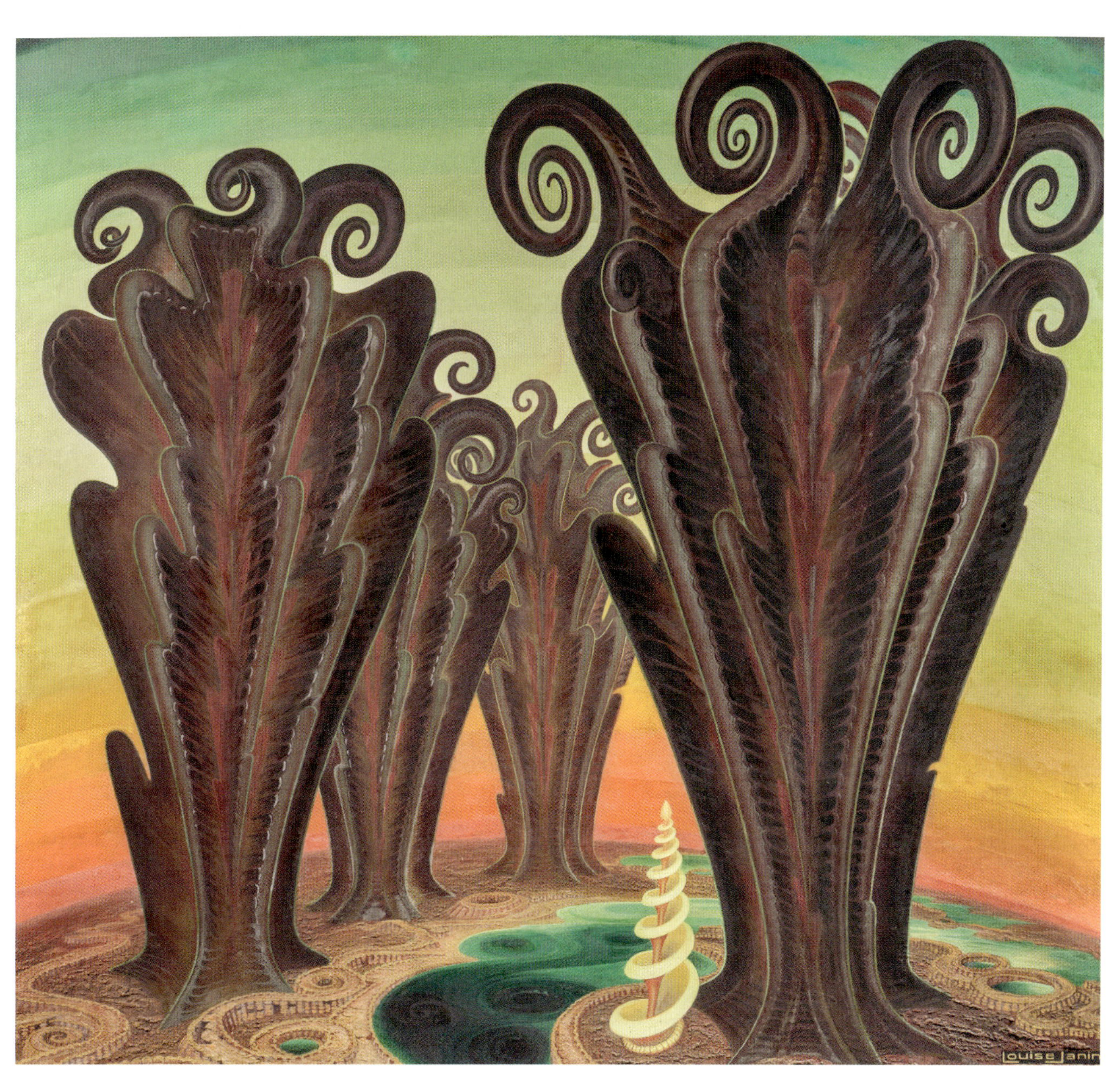

Jacoba van Heemskerck
Bild no. 105, 1915–1920
Bild Nr. 105 ~ *Composition No. 105*

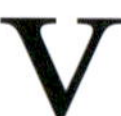

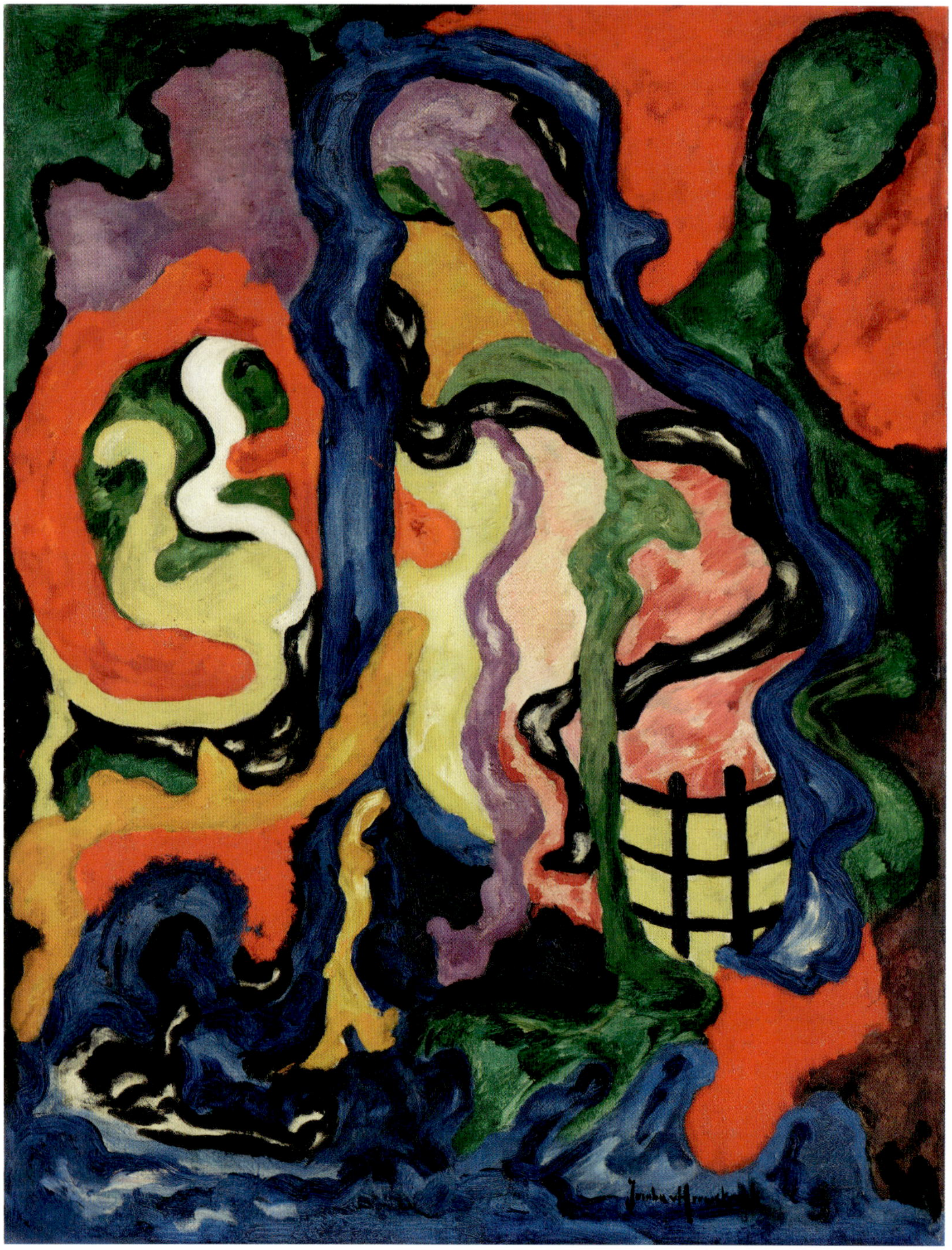

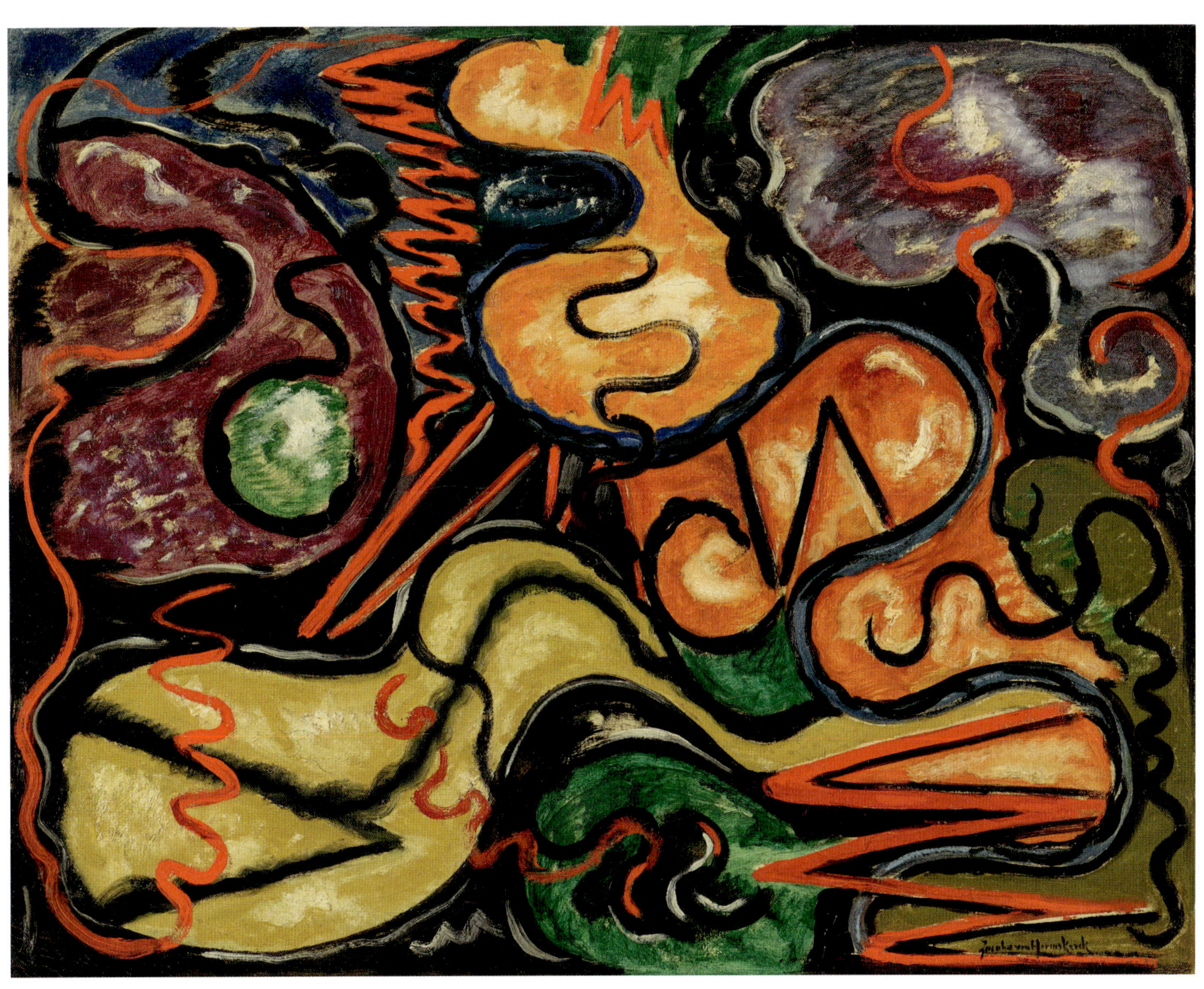

Jacoba van Heemskerck

Bild no. 90, 1918

Bild Nr. 90 ~ *Composition No. 90*

Marlow Moss

Spheres and Curved Line, 1945

Kugeln und gekrümmte Linie

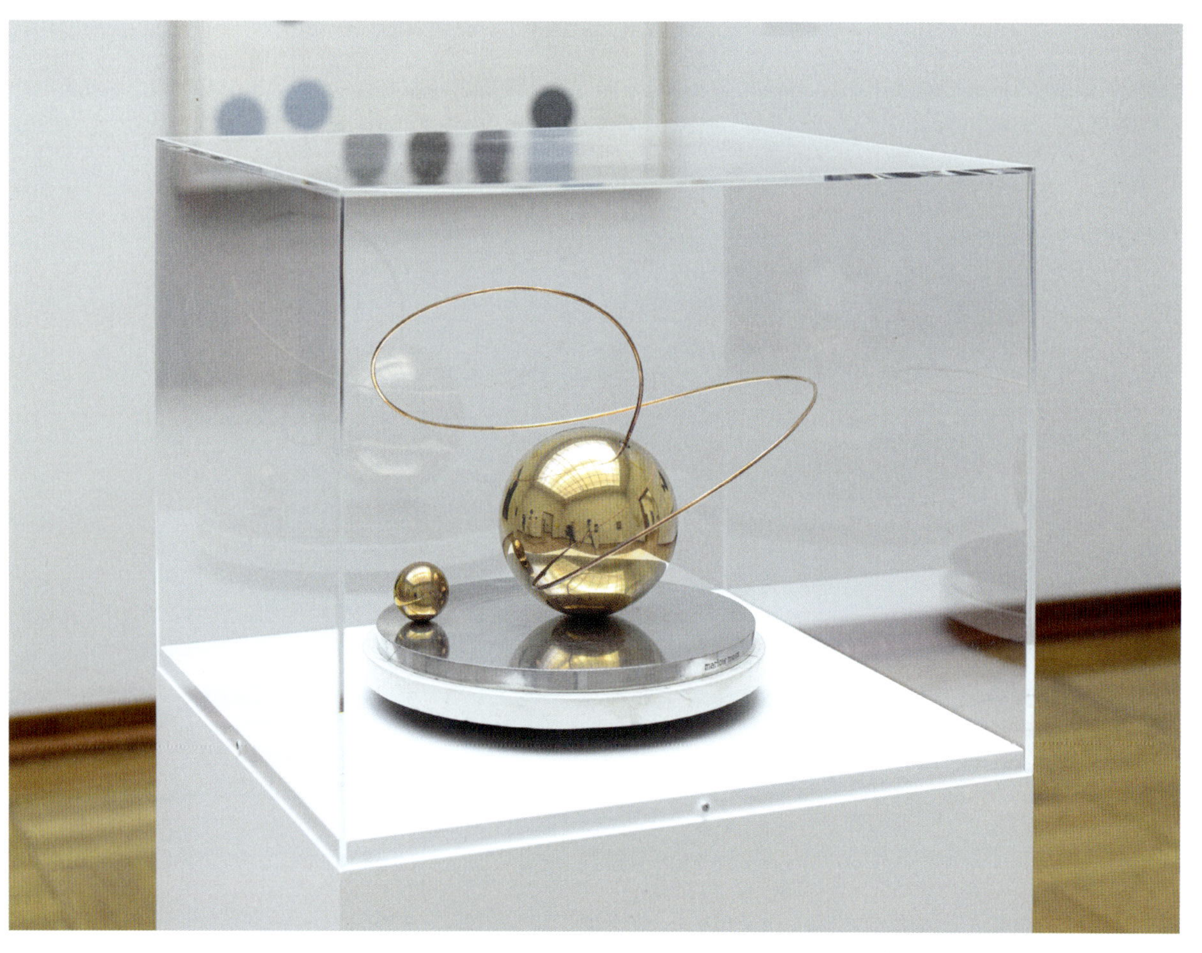

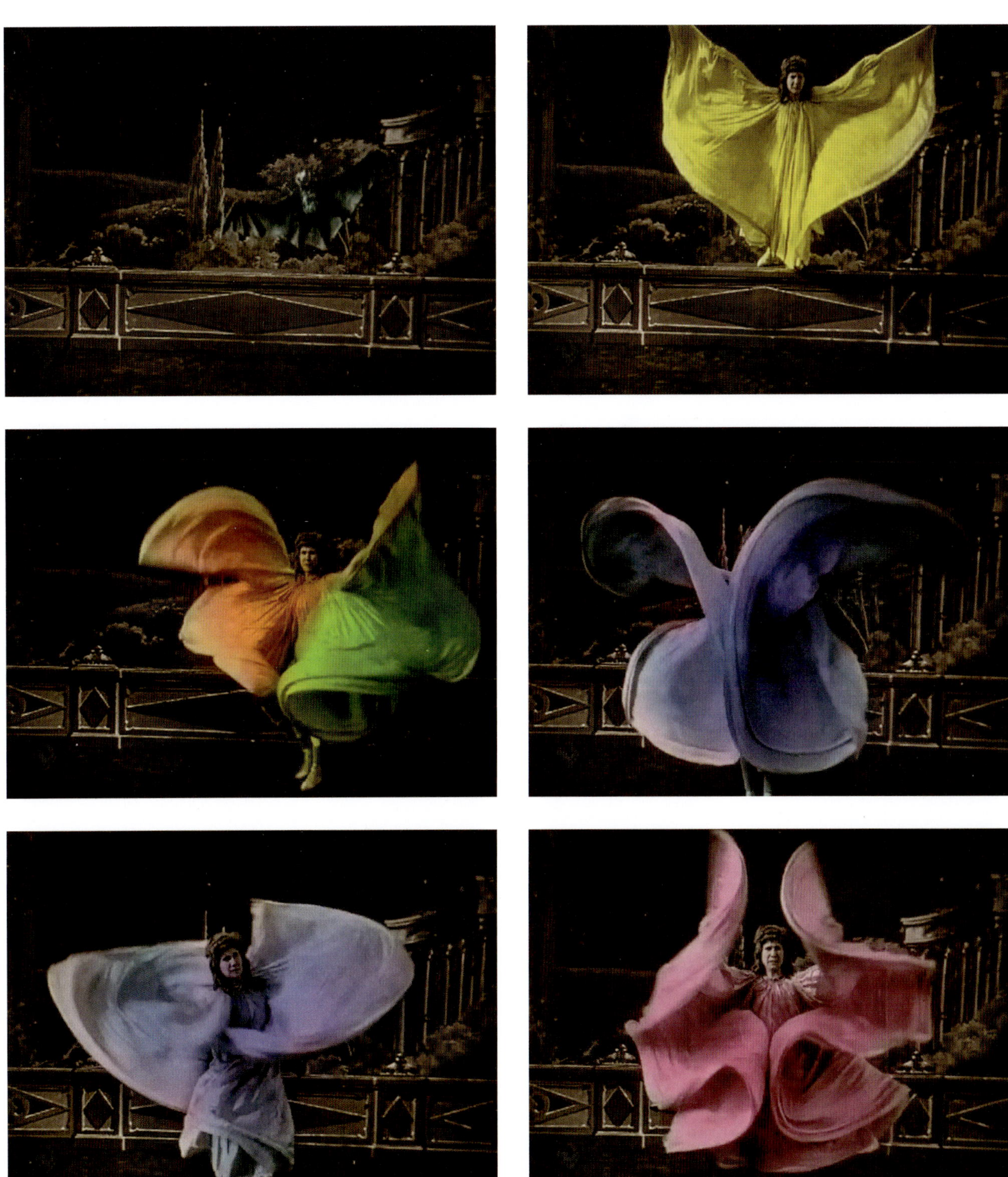

Loïe Fuller
La Danse Serpentine, 1905
Serpentinentanz ~ *The Serpentine Dance*

Marlow Moss
White with Bent Cord (Relief), 1936
Weiß mit gebogener Kordel (Relief)

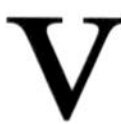

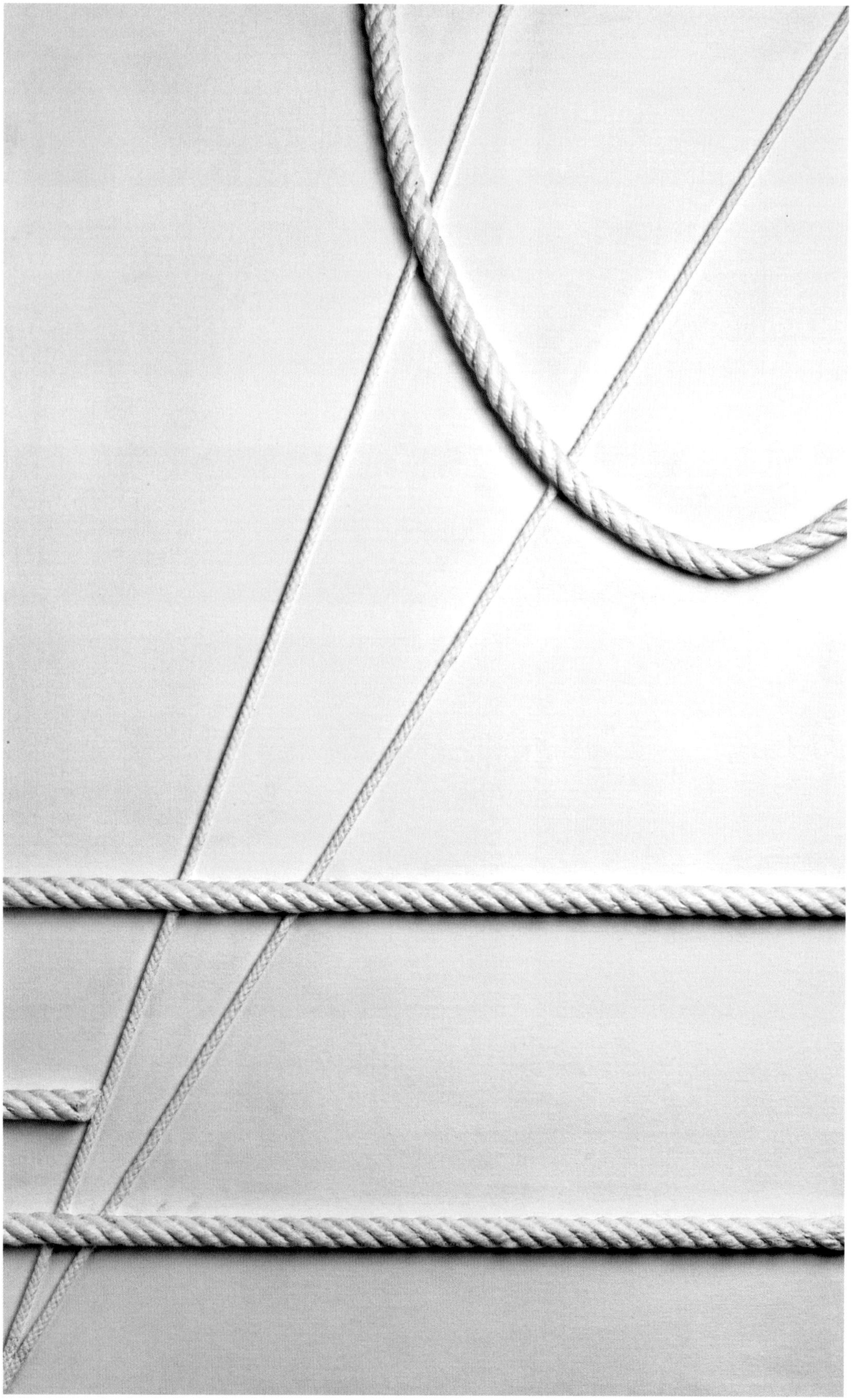

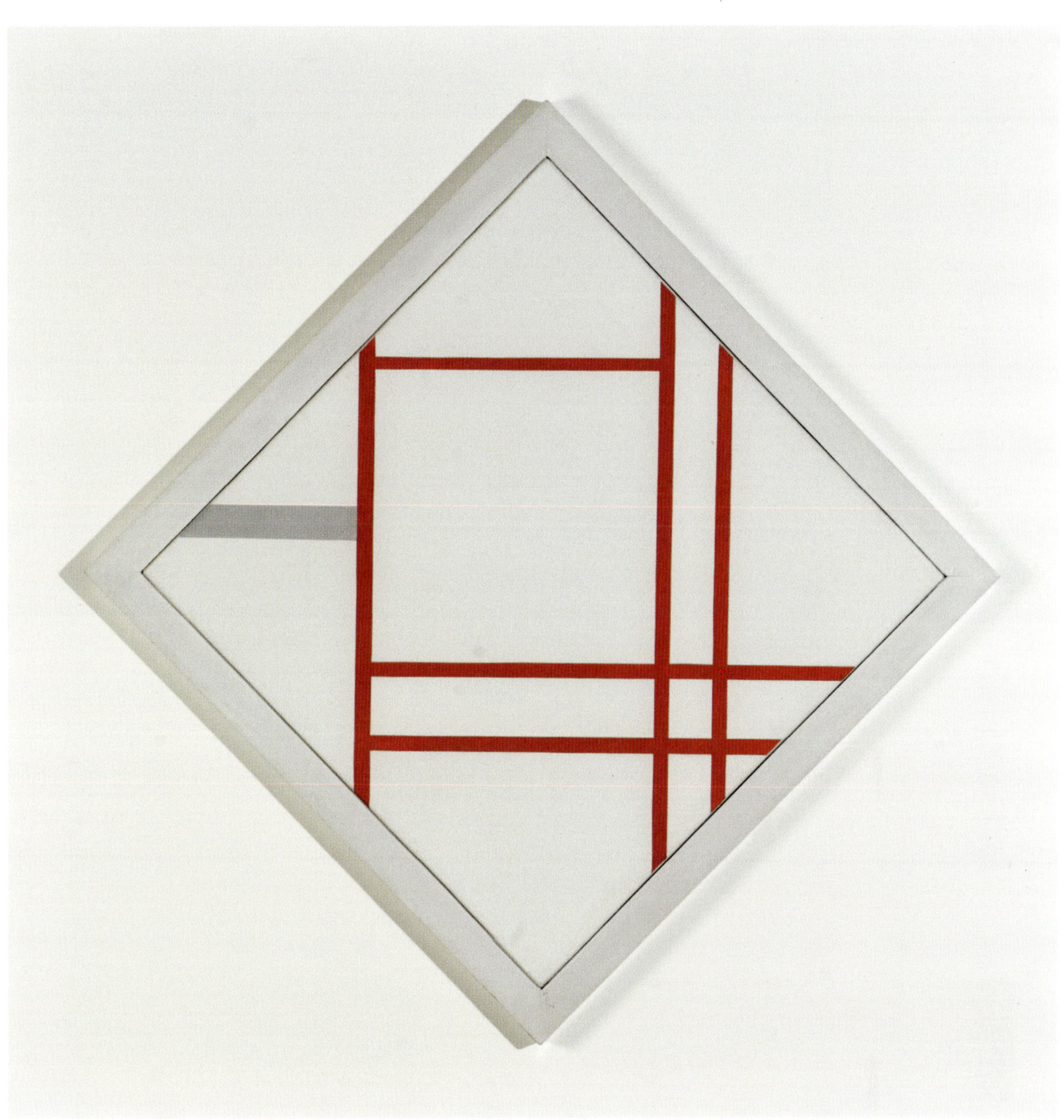

Marlow Moss
White, Red, and Grey, 1935
Weiß, Rot und Grau

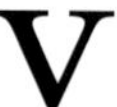

QUEERE LESARTEN VON ABSTRAKTION

~

QUEER READINGS OF ABSTRACTION

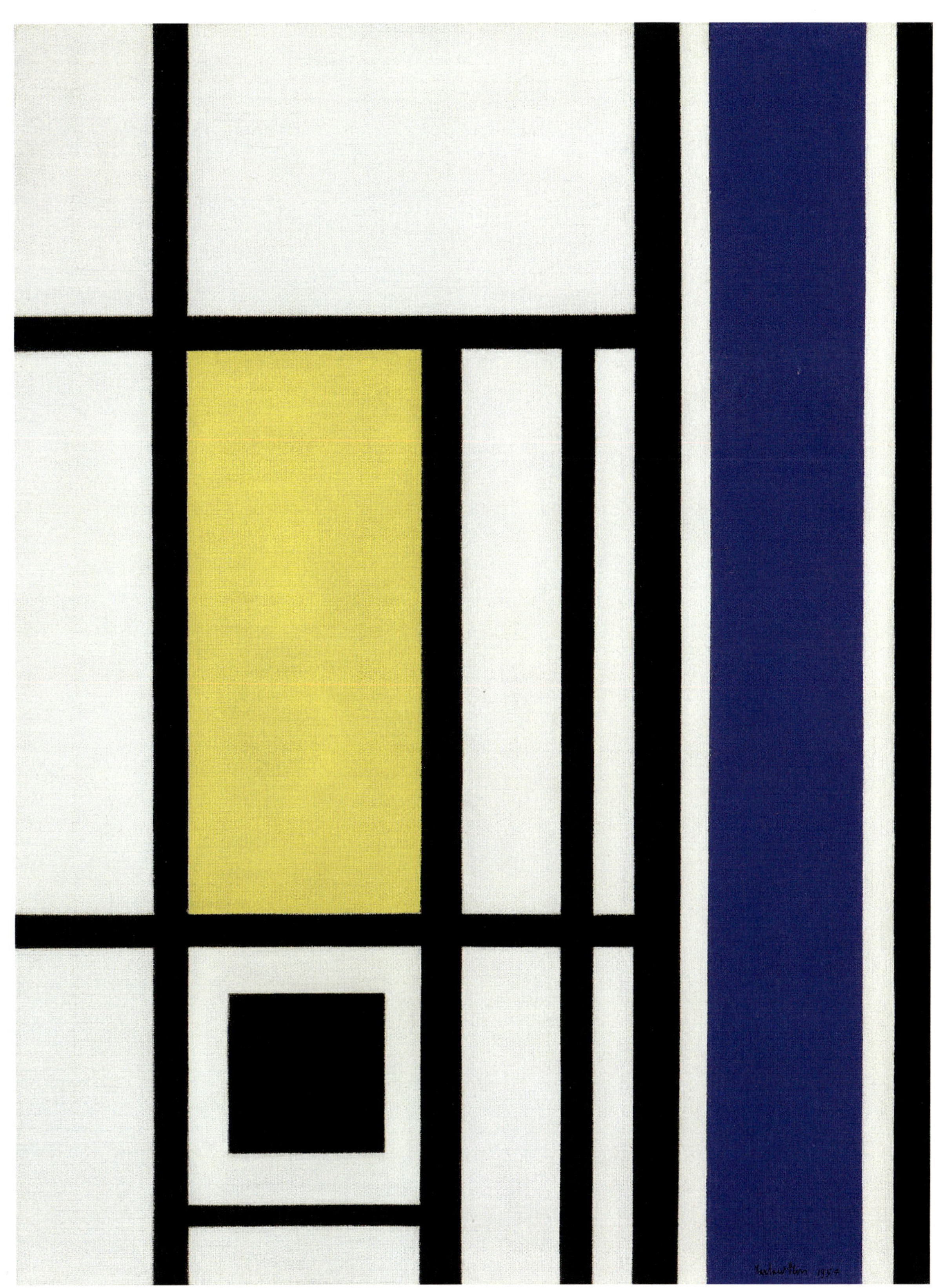

Marlow Moss
Untitled (White, Black, Blue, and Yellow), um ~ *ca.* 1954
Ohne Titel (Weiß, Schwarz, Blau und Gelb)

Anton Prinner
Untitled, 1933
Ohne Titel

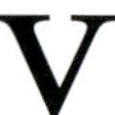

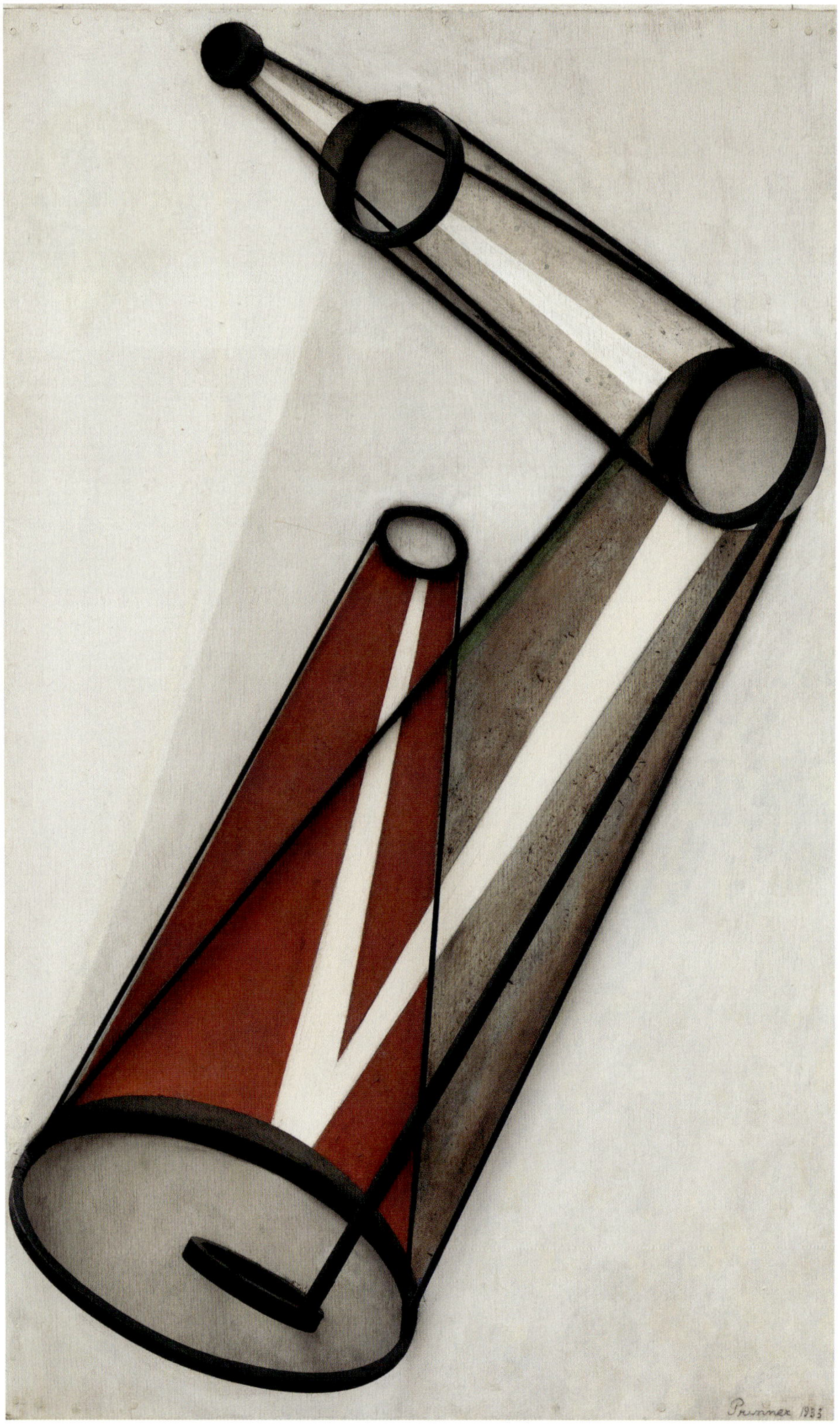

QUEERE LESARTEN VON ABSTRAKTION

~

QUEER READINGS OF ABSTRACTION

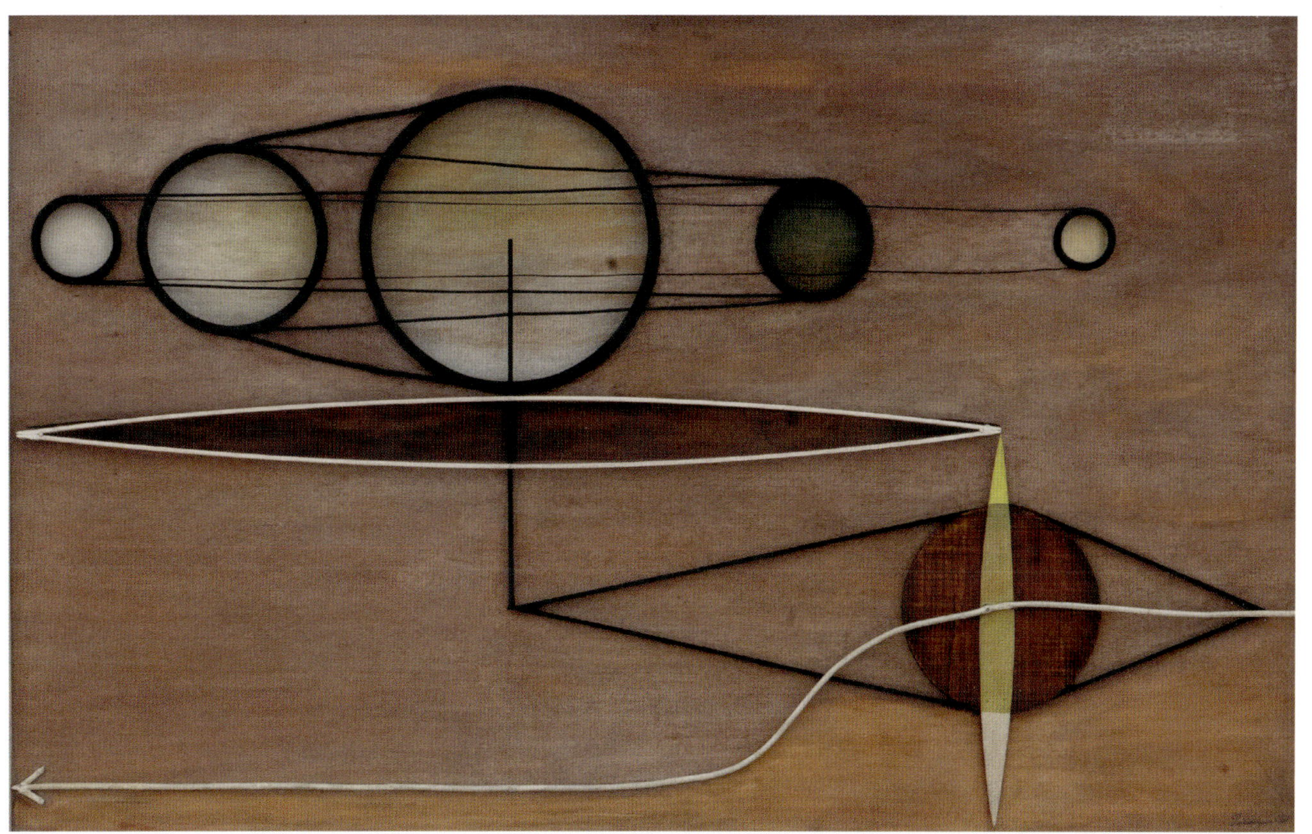

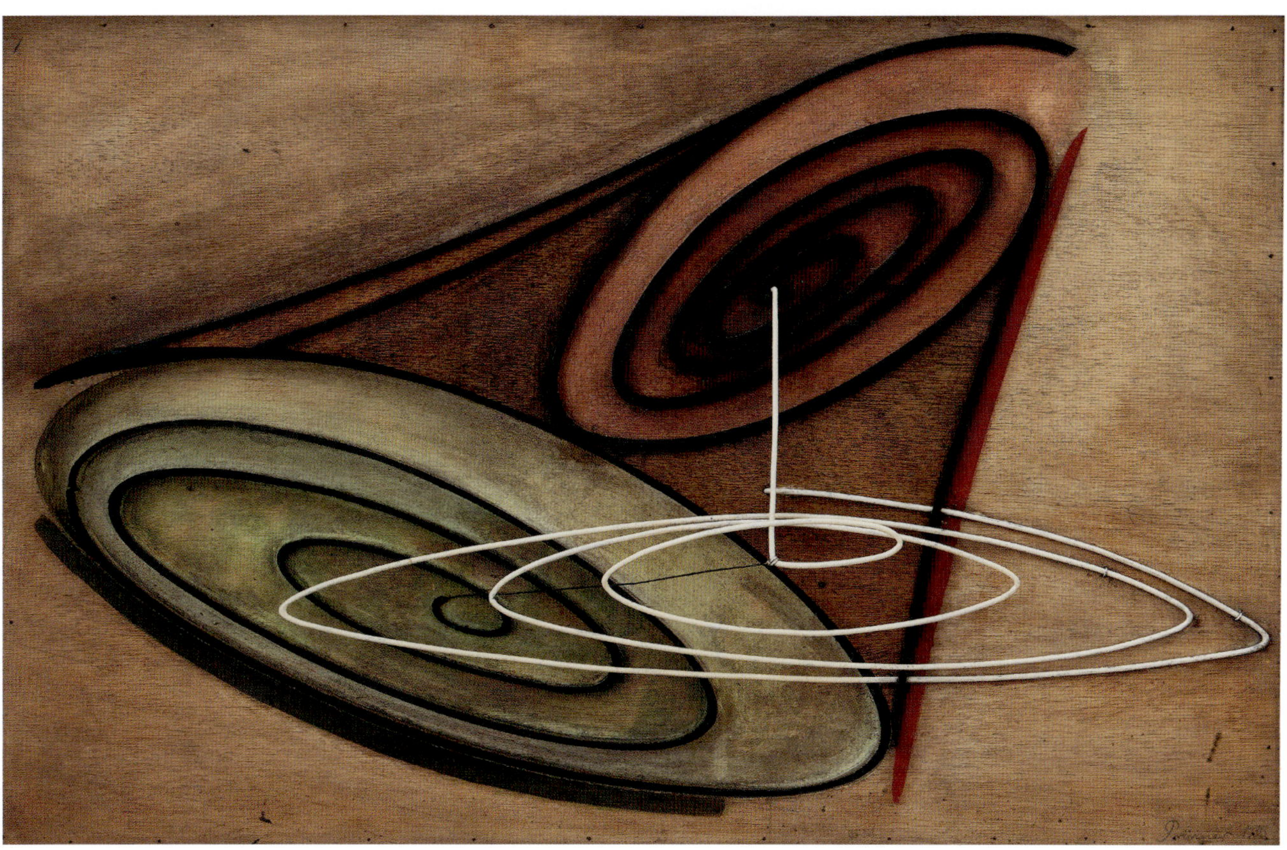

Anton Prinner

Untitled (Les Hublots), 1932
Ohne Titel (Die Bullaugen) ~
Untitled (The Portholes)

Anton Prinner

Spirales Plastiques, 1935
Plastische Spiralen ~
Plastic Spirales

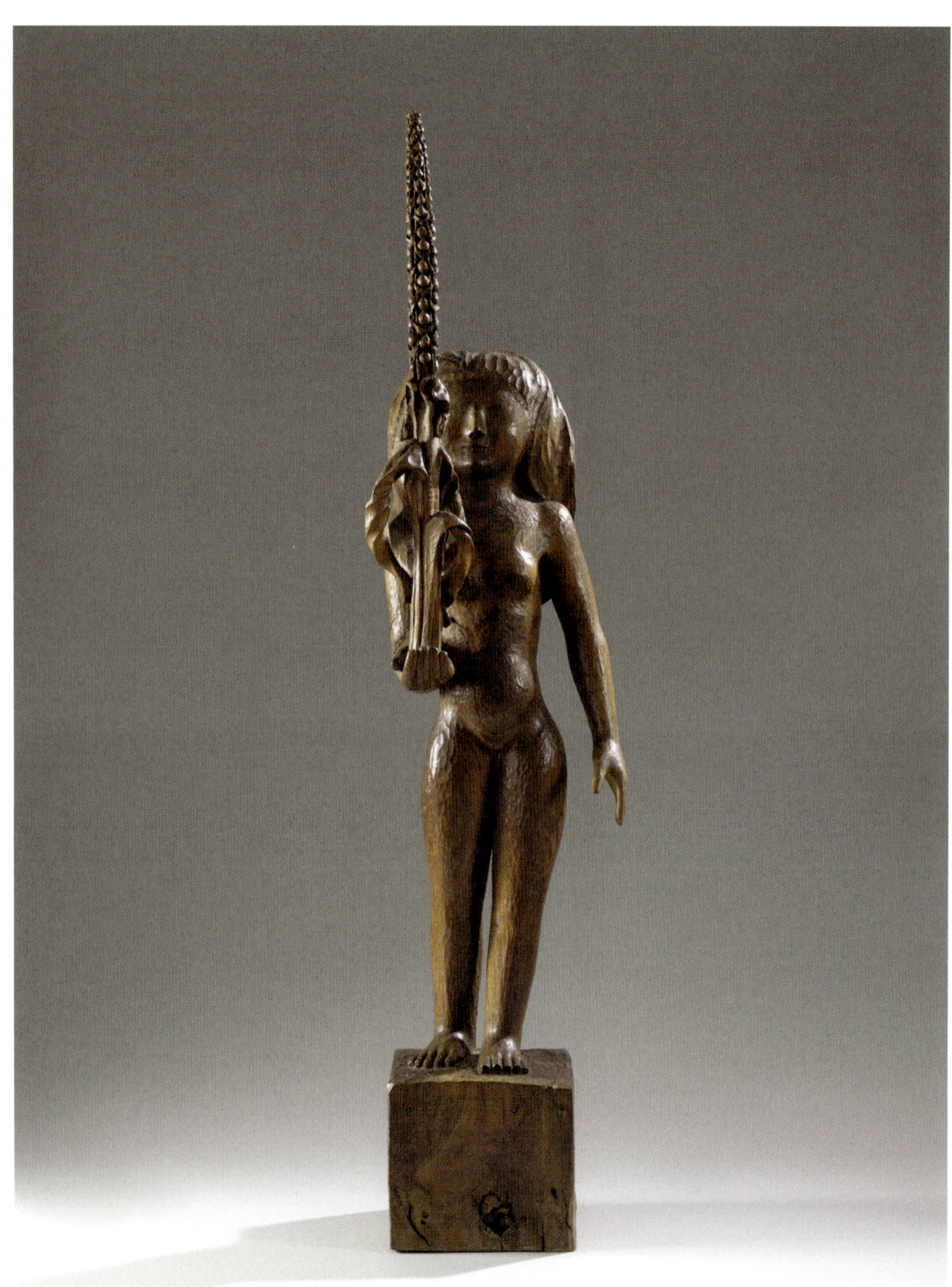

Anton Prinner
L'équilibriste, 1942
Die Balancierkünstlerin ~
The Balancing Act

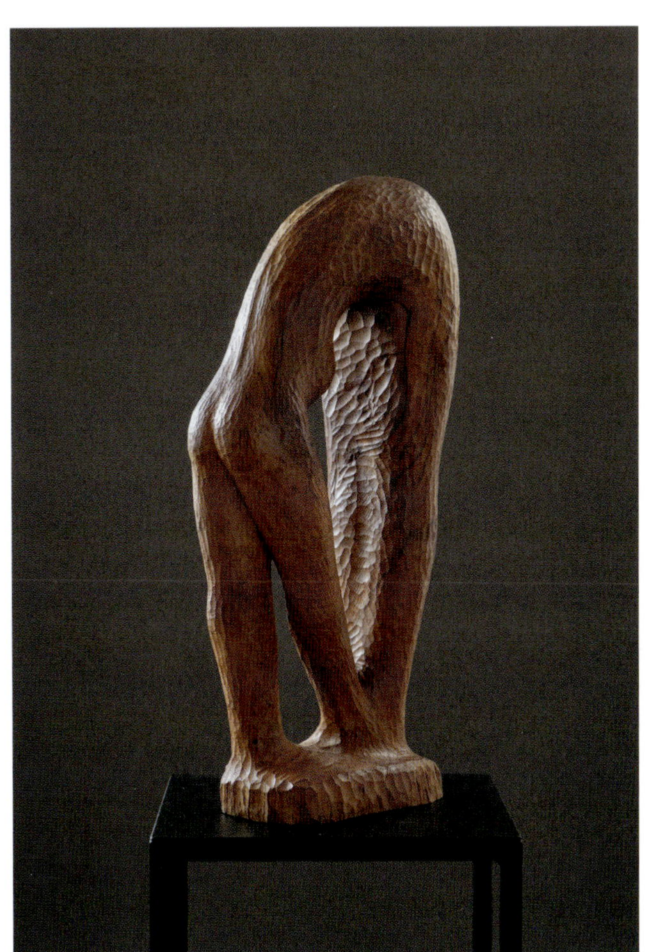

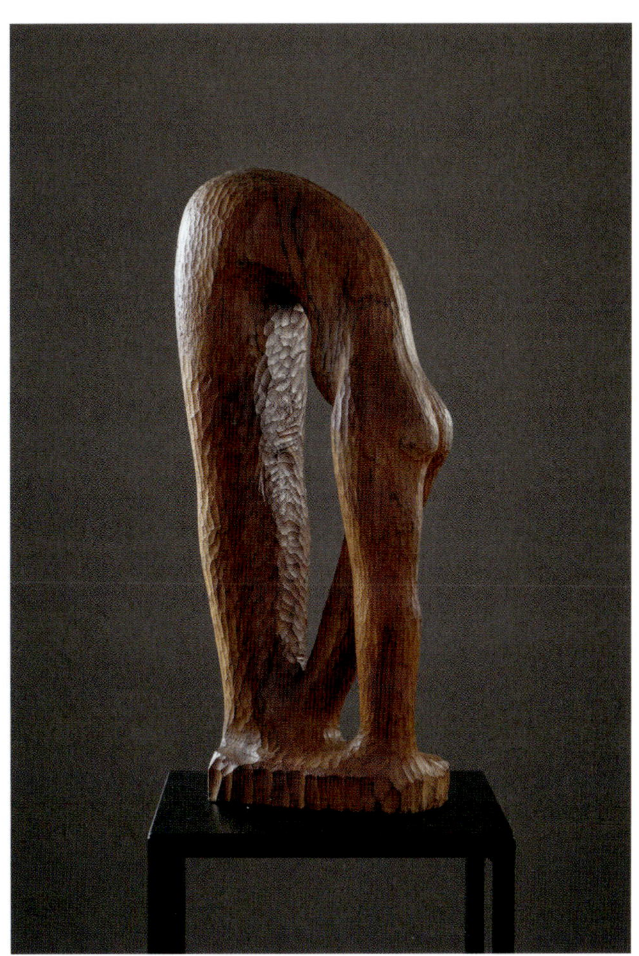

Anton Prinner

Double personnage (Personnage renversé), 1937
Doppelte Figur (Umgekehrte Figur) ~
Double Figure (Overturned Character)

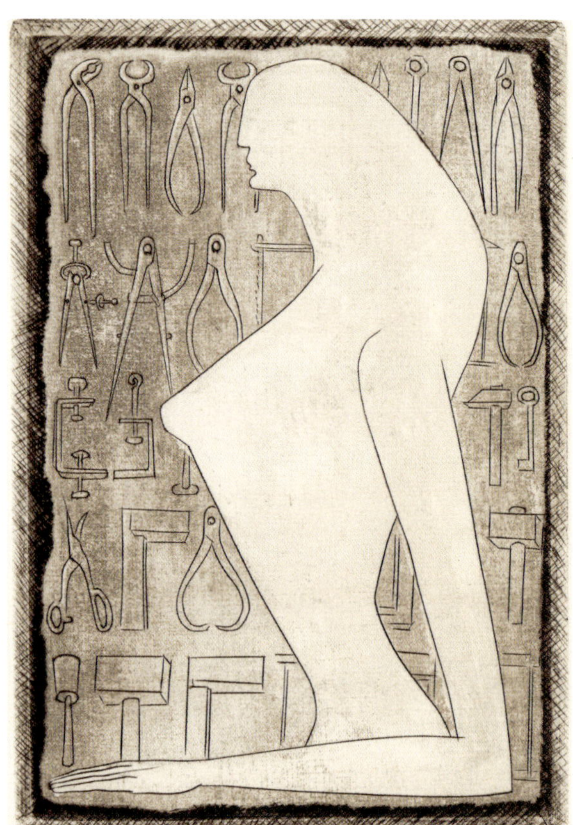

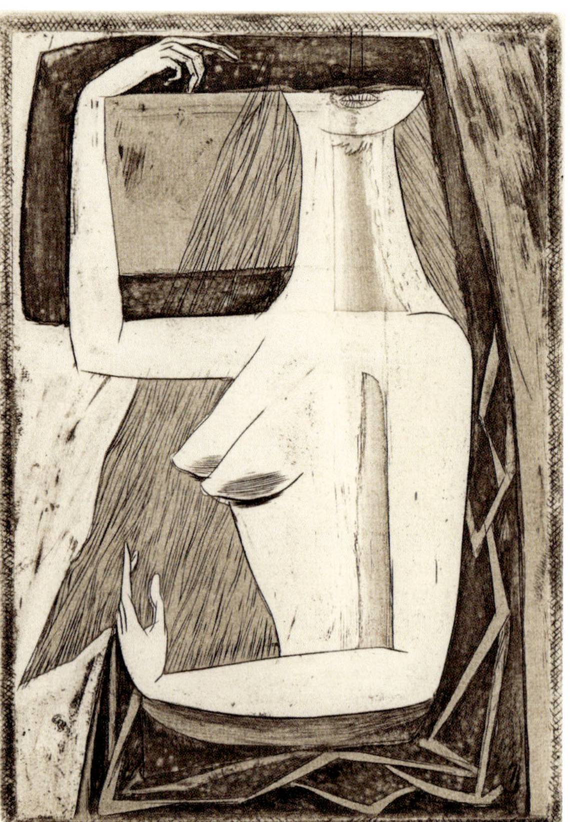

Anton Prinner

La femme tondue, 1946
Die geschorene Frau ~
The Shorn Woman

Anton Prinner
Woman with a Candle, um ~ *ca.* 1940
Frau mit Kerze

Anton Prinner
Woman with an Otter, um ~ *ca.* 1940
Frau mit einem Otter

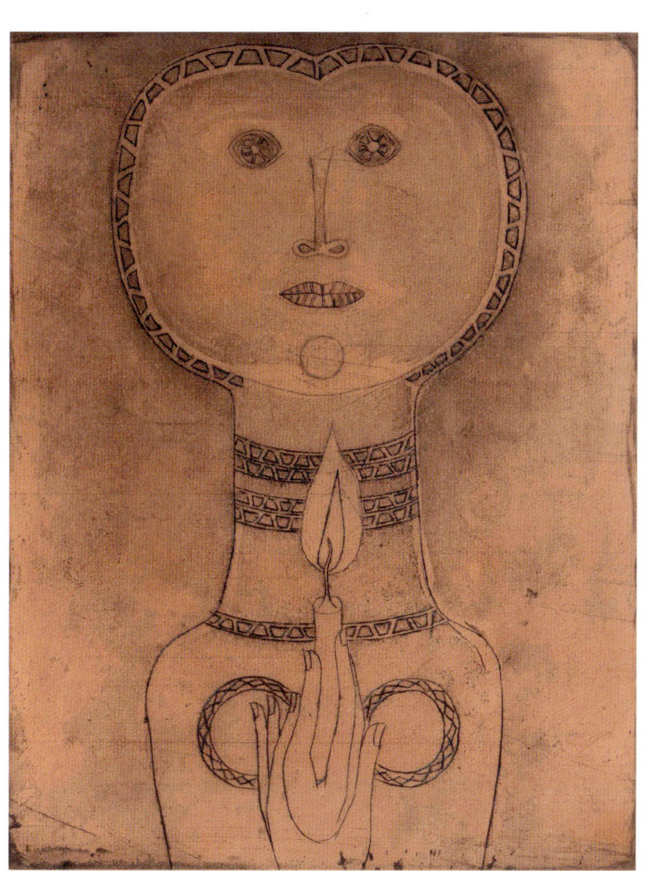

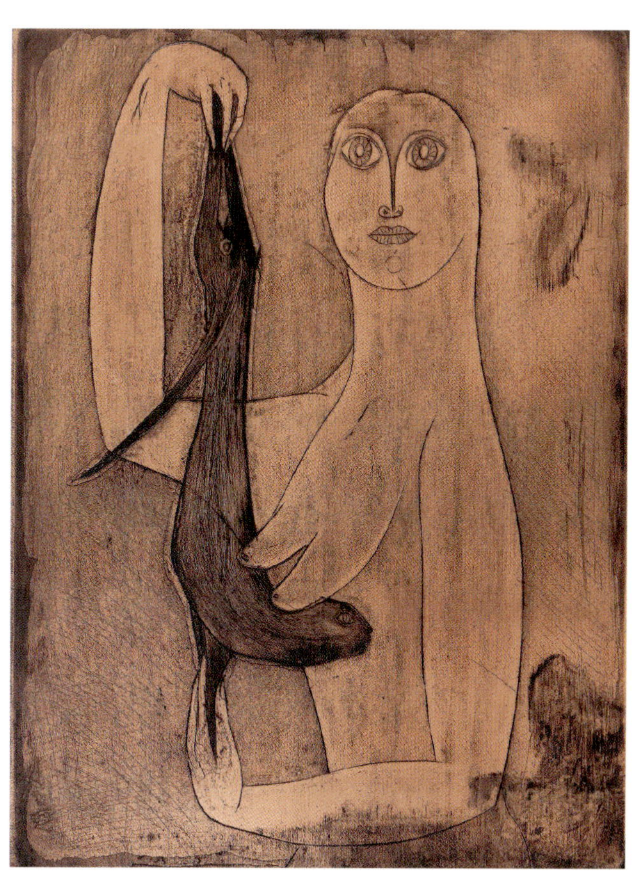

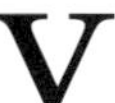

QUEERE LESARTEN VON ABSTRAKTION

~

QUEER READINGS OF ABSTRACTION

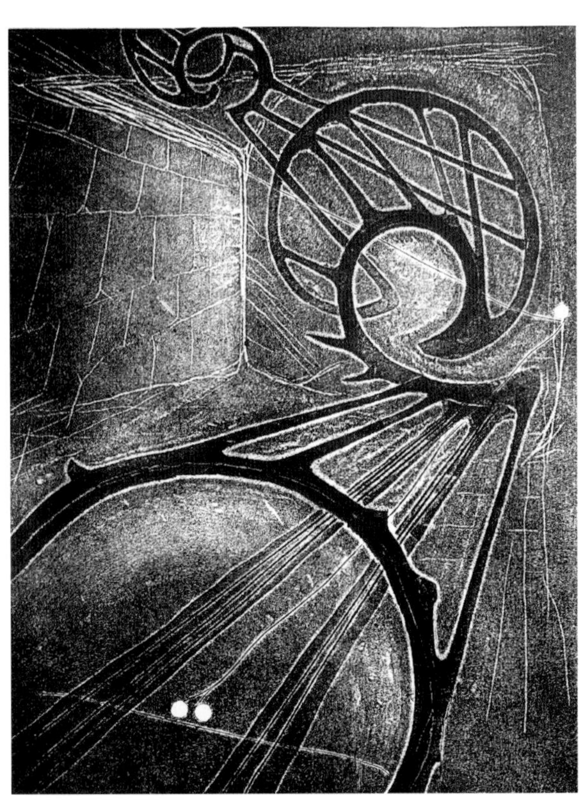

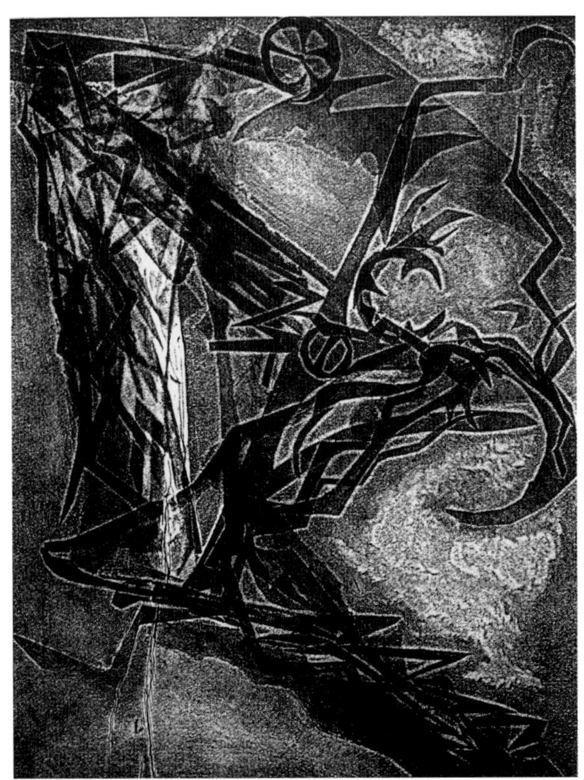

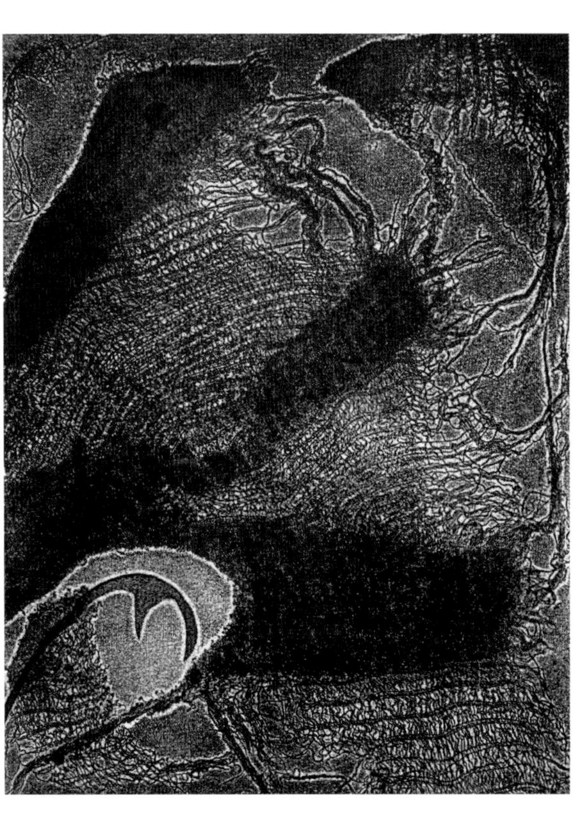

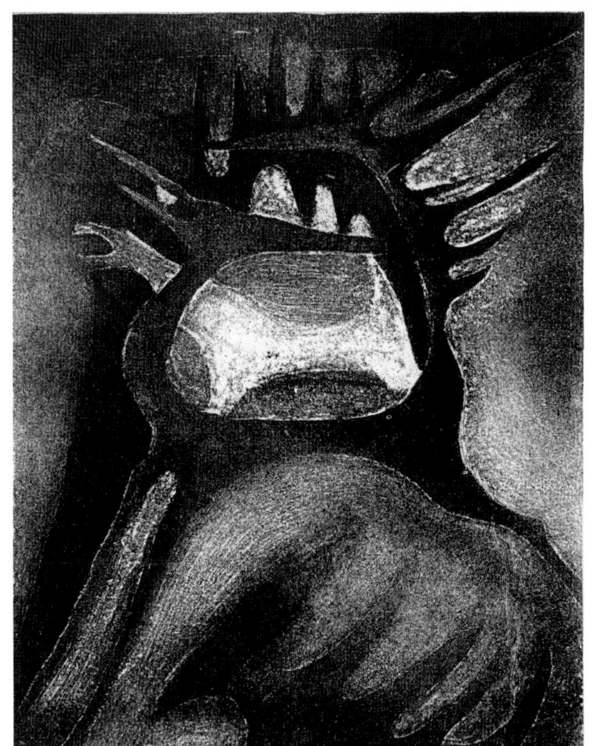
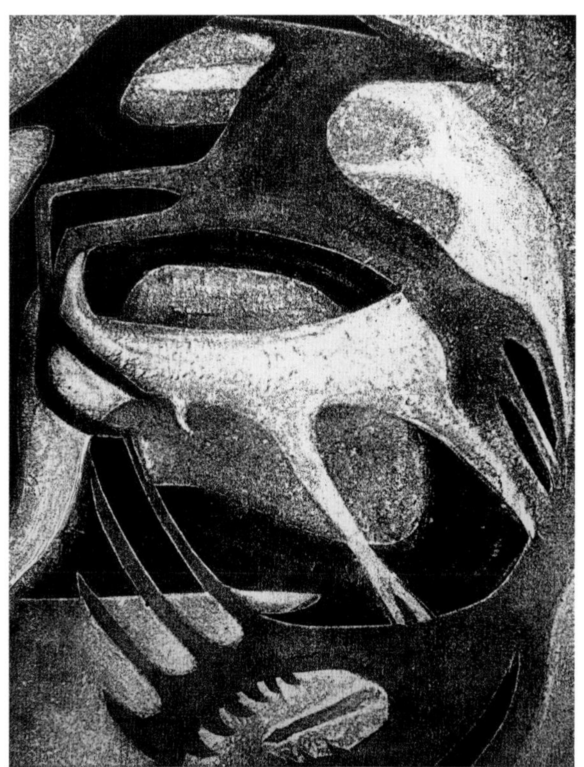

Anton Prinner

L'Apocalypse, 1948
Die Apokalypse ~
The Apocalypse

V

QUEERE LESARTEN VON ABSTRAKTION

~

QUEER READINGS OF ABSTRACTION

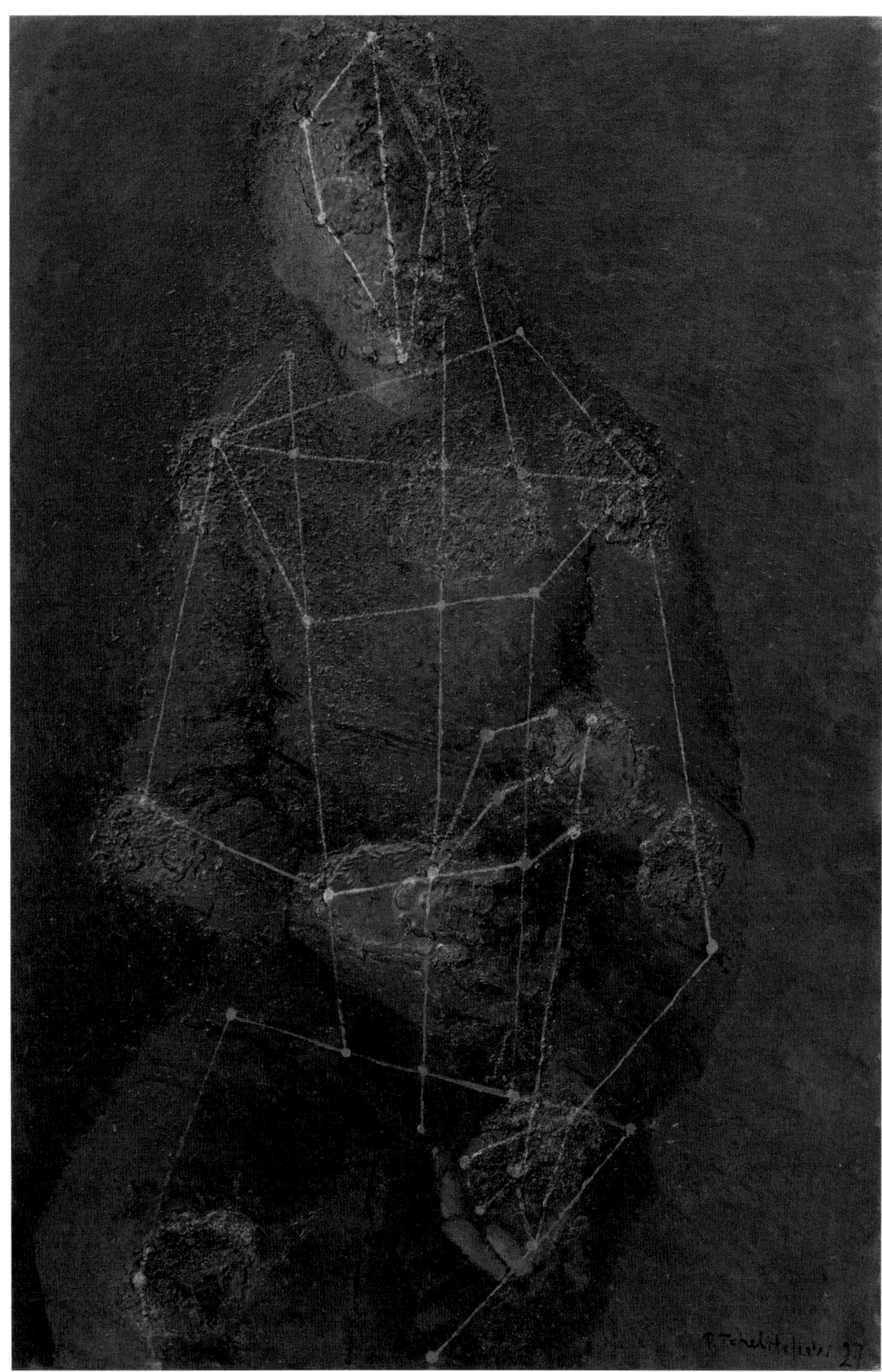

Pavel Tchelîtchew
Personage, 1927
Figur

Pavel Tchelitchew
Untitled (Seated Man, Multiple Images), 1927
Ohne Titel (Sitzender Mann, mehrere Bilder)

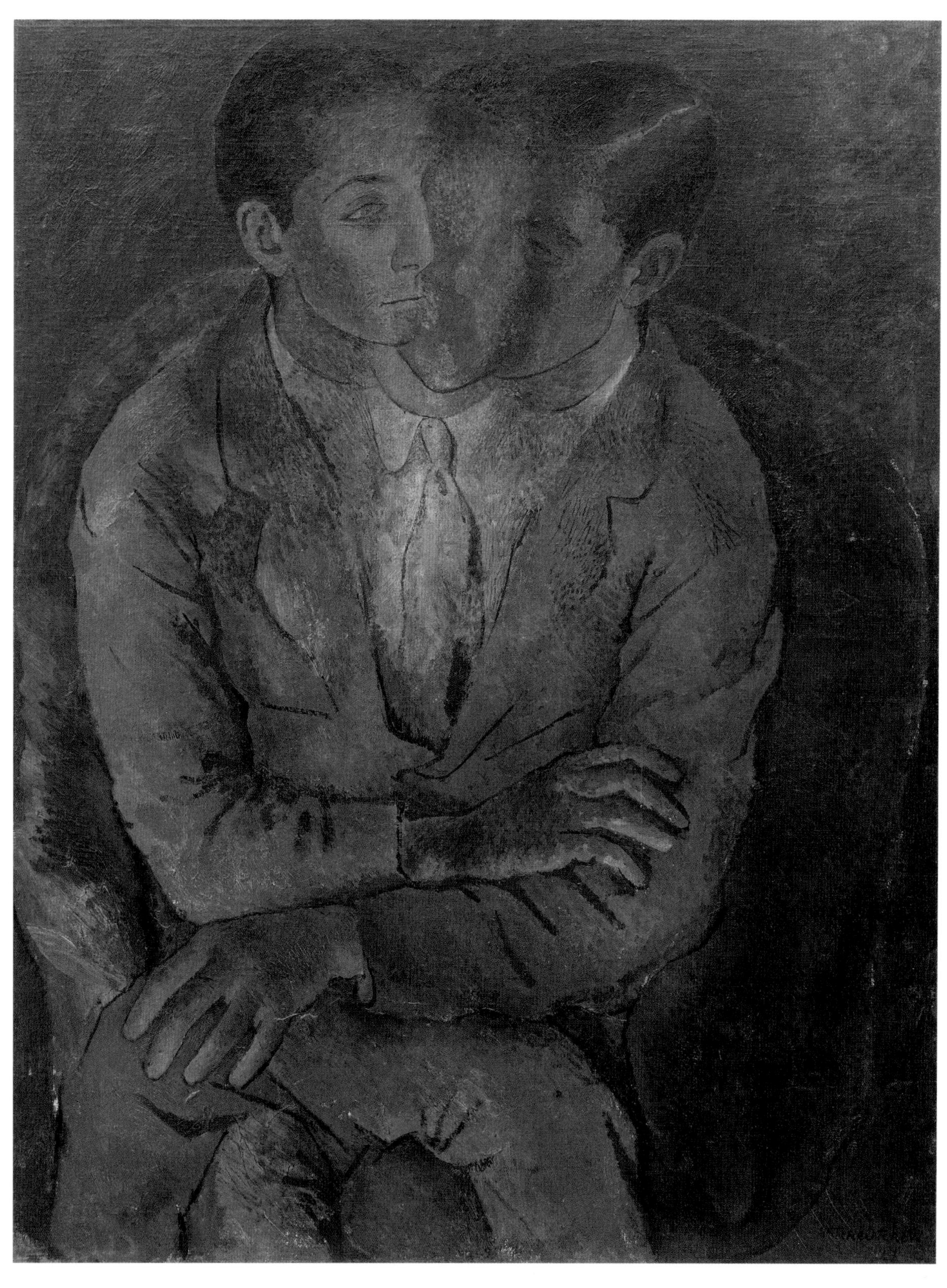

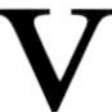

QUEERE LESARTEN VON ABSTRAKTION

~

QUEER READINGS OF ABSTRACTION

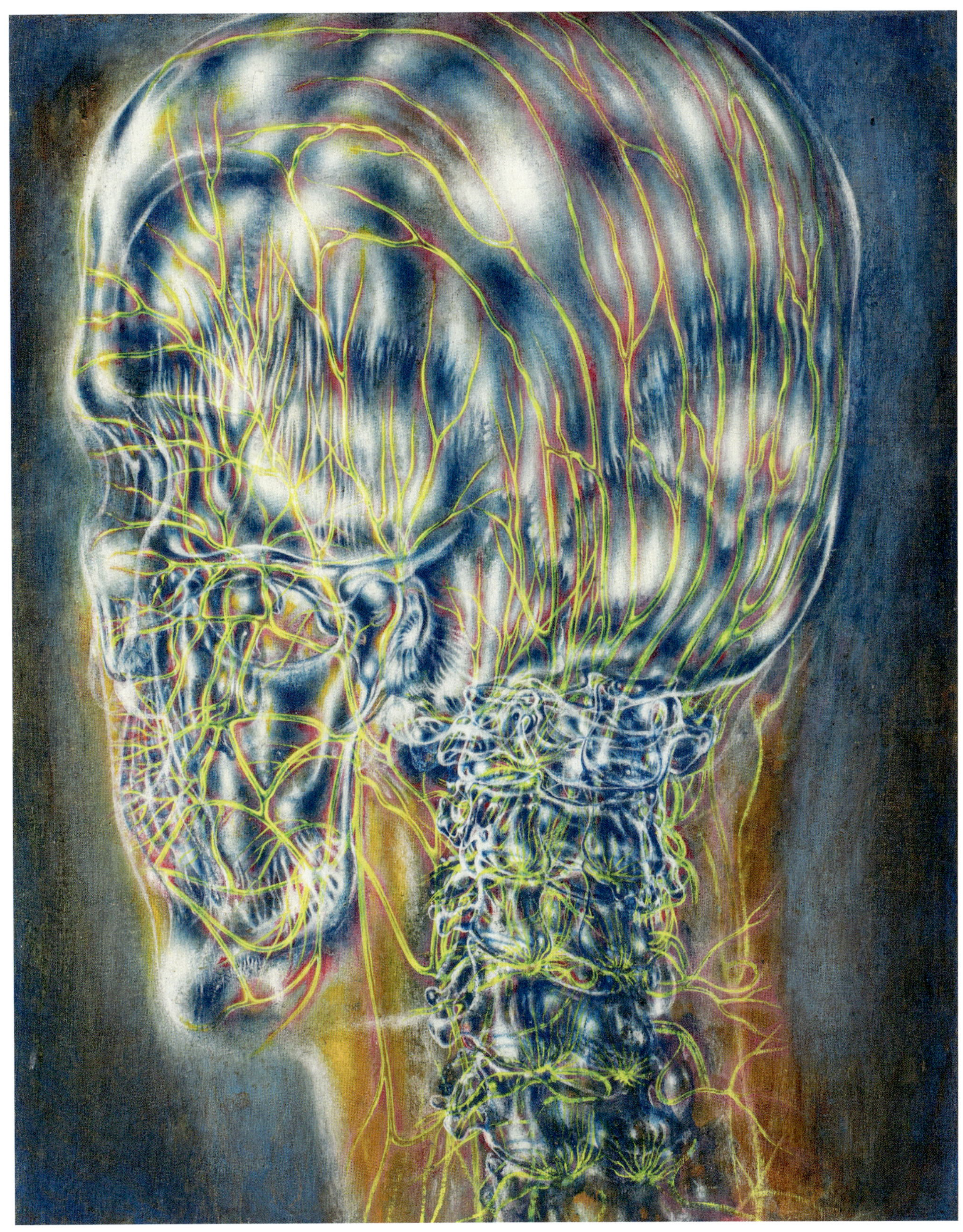

Pavel Tchelîtchew
Interior Landscape, um ~ *ca.* 1947
Innere Landschaft

QUEERE ABSTRAKTION
~
QUEER ABSTRACTION

ANKE KEMPKES

Neuere Entwicklungen in queeren und transgender Theorien bieten interessante Perspektiven für Revisionen des Kanons der modernen Kunst. Der amerikanische Autor Jack Halberstam schärft unser Bewusstsein dafür, dass in Zeiten einer repressiven Politik der Erkennung emanzipatorische Bedürfnisse nach Anerkennung alternativer, nicht normativer Körper und Sexualitäten gefährdet sind. Solche neuen Sichtbarkeiten können nicht nur zum Ziel disziplinierender Macht werden, sondern auch selbst neue Taxonomien und Repräsentationen verfestigen, wenn sie nicht als temporäre und fluide Kategorien gedacht werden.[1] Diese Ausstellung schlägt eine Kunstgeschichte des Modernismus vor, in der ein klassisches Verständnis von Figuration neu gedacht und erweitert wird. Dies umfasst auch eine kritische Auseinandersetzung mit den vermeintlich klaren Grenzen zwischen Abstraktion und Figuration in der modernen Kunst. Können abstrakte Formen einen variableren, fließenderen und nicht festgelegten Ausdruck von Verkörperung, sinnlicher Interaktion und sozialer Verbundenheit zum Ausdruck bringen? In den letzten Jahren hat der amerikanische Kunsthistoriker David J. Getsy den Fokus in seinen Studien von der „queeren Repräsentation" hin zur „queeren Abstraktion" verlagert. Er argumentiert, dass die menschliche Figur in ihrer Darstellung unweigerlich kulturell markiert ist und dass Abstraktion und deren „A-figuration" als eine Taktik dienen können, um „der kulturellen Markierung des menschlichen Körpers zu widerstehen".[2] Er spricht von einer „queeren Investition in die Abstraktion", durch die soziale Beziehungen über formale Kompositionselemente ausgedrückt und symbolisiert werden können. Getsy verweist darauf, dass solche Potenziale bereits in der historischen Abstraktion latent vorhanden waren. Etablierte Bildhauer der Avantgarde wie Hans (Jean) Arp, Alberto Giacometti und Constantin Brâncuși führten eine sexuell ambivalente, biomorphe Abstraktion ein, die von instabilen Geschlechterzuordnungen und, besonders in Giacomettis surrealen Objekten, von abjekten Vorstellungen von Körperlichkeit geprägt war – mit Formen, die als symbolische Abweichungen von Norm und Akzeptanz verstanden werden können. Ein einschlägiges Beispiel hierfür findet sich in Brâncușis genderambivalenten minimalistischen Skulpturen. *Male Torso* (1917, Abb. 1) zeigt trotz des explizit geschlechtsspezifischen Titels eine so radikal reduzierte Abstraktion der menschlichen Form, dass dessen Geschlecht ungelöst bleibt – eher ein visuelles Rätsel als eine anatomische Geltendmachung.[3] Es ist gut möglich, dass es diese offenen Genderkonzepte in Brâncușis Abstraktion waren, die queere Künstler*innen und Schriftsteller*innen in sein Atelier zogen, wie ein Foto aus der Zeit um 1921/22 belegt, das den Künstler in Gesellschaft von Berenice Abbott, Mina Loy, Jane Heap und Margaret Anderson zeigt – einige der zentralen Protagonist*innen des „sapphischen Paris" (Abb. 2). Im Gegensatz zur verbreiteten Auffassung wurde historische Abstraktion tatsächlich selten als geschlechtsneutral konzipiert oder wahrgenommen. Piet Mondrian zum Beispiel ordnete den formalen Elementen seiner neoplastizistischen Kunst und Theorie geschlechtsspezifische Bedeutungen zu. Mondrians Vision blieb jedoch fest in einer traditionellen und hierarchischen Geschlechterbinarität verankert. Seine rigide, idealisierende Ästhetik wurde von anderen Künstler*innen der Zeit herausgefordert, insbesondere von queeren Frauen, die alternative Modelle der Abstraktion vorschlugen. Nichtsdestotrotz zog Mondrians betonte Selbststilisierung – wie sein Leben in

1 In seinem Buch *Female Masculinity* (1998) schreibt Halberstam: „Ich bin mir der problematischen Geschichte von Taxonomien innerhalb der Geschichte der Sexualität durchaus bewusst. Aber ich denke, das Hauptproblem bei der Taxonomisierung war erstens, dass sie den Sexualwissenschaftlern überlassen wurde, und zweitens, dass wir es versäumt haben, immer genauere, farbenfrohere, elaboriertere, fantasievollere oder flamboyantere Taxonomien zu entwickeln." Jack Halberstam, *Female Masculinity*, Durham u.a. 1998, S. 47. Sofern nicht anders angegeben, stammen alle Übersetzungen von der Autorin.

2 David J. Getsy, „Ten Queer Theses on Abstraction", in: *Queer Abstraction*, hrsg. von Jared Ledesma, Ausst.-Kat. Des Moines Art Center, Des Moines 2019, S. 65–75, hier: S. 67, 66.

3 Brâncușis berüchtigte *Princess x* (1915/16) „führt das Auge dazu, sowohl eine weibliche Brust als auch einen großen goldenen Phallus wahrzunehmen, indem sie das Weibliche und das Männliche in einem alterierenden Muster figurativer Darstellung vermischt, wobei das Element der Überraschung und die Entdeckung dieser unerwarteten Zweideutigkeit eine weitere Komponente hinzufügt." Magali Le Mens, *Modernité hermaphrodite: art, histoire, culture*, Paris 2019, S. 23.

Recent developments in queer and transgender theory offer some of the most compelling perspectives for reimagining the canon of modern art. The American scholar Jack Halberstam heightens our awareness that in a political crisis of representation the emancipatory needs for recognition of alternative, non-normative bodies and sexualities are at risk. Such new visibilities can become not only a target of disciplinary power, but can also reiterate and foreclose new taxonomies and normative representations themselves.[1] This exhibition proposes an art history of modernism in which figuration is reconsidered and expanded. This also involves a critical reflection on the supposedly clear-cut boundaries between abstraction and figuration within modern art. Can abstract forms give expression to a more variable, fluid, and indeterminate understanding of embodiment, sensual interaction, and social connectivity? In recent years, American art historian David J. Getsy has shifted the focus of his own studies from "queer representation" to "queer abstraction," arguing that the human figure as represented is inevitably culturally marked, and that abstraction, and the non-representational, with its "afiguration," can serve as one tactic to "resist the cultural marking of the human body."[2] He speaks of a "queer investment in abstraction," through which social relations can be played out and symbolized through formal compositional elements. Getsy recognizes that such potentials were already latent within historical abstraction. Established sculptors of the avant-garde, such as Jean Arp, Alberto Giacometti, and Constantin Brâncuși, introduced a sexually ambivalent, biomorphic abstraction marked by unstable gender assignments and abject notions of embodiment—forms that may be seen as symbolic and formal deviants. A striking example is found in Brâncuși's gender-shifting minimalist sculptures. *Male Torso* (1917, fig. 1), despite its explicitly gendered title, presents such a radically reduced abstraction of the human form that its gender remains unresolved, more visual enigma than anatomical assertion.[3] It may well have been these open gender-concepts in Brâncuși's abstraction that drew queer women artists and writers to his studio, as evidenced by a photograph from around 1921/22, which shows the artist in the company of Berenice Abbott, Mina Loy, Jane Heap, and Margaret Anderson, some of the central protagonists of "Sapphic Paris" (fig. 2).

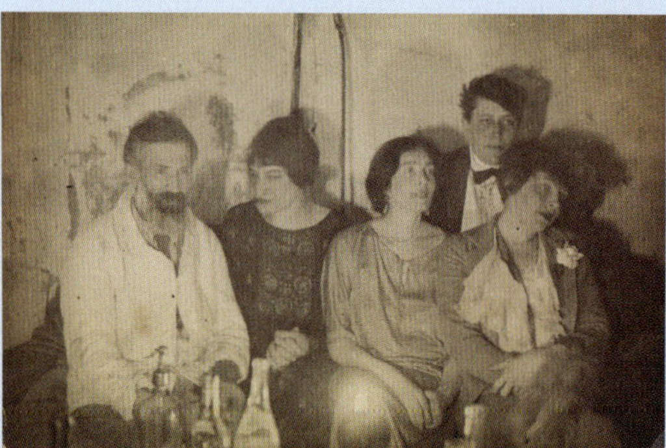

ABB. ~ FIG. 2

Constantin Brâncuși in seinem Studio mit Berenice Abbott, Mina Loy, Jane Heap und Margaret Anderson ~ *Constantin Brâncuși in his studio with Berenice Abbott, Mina Loy, Jane Heap, and Margaret Anderson*, um ~ *ca.* 1921/22.

1 Jack Halberstam writes in his book *Female Masculinity*, "I am well aware of the damaging history of taxonomies within the history of sexuality, but I think that the main problem with taxonomizing was first that it was left to sexologists, and second that we have not continued to produce ever more accurate or colorful or elaborate or imaginative or flamboyant taxonomies." Jack Halberstam (Durham: Duke University Press, 1998), p. 47.

2 David J. Getsy, "Ten Queer Theses on Abstraction," in *Queer Abstraction*, ed. Jared Ledesma, exh. cat. (Des Moines: Des Moines Art Center, 2019), pp. 65–75, here pp. 67, 66.

3 Brâncuși's notorious *Princess X* (1915/16) "leads the eye to perceive both a female bust and a large golden phallus, mixing the feminine and the masculine in an alternating pattern of figurative representation, with the element of surprise and the discovery of this unexpected duplicity adding a further component." Magali Le Mens, *Modernité hermaphrodite: Art, histoire, culture* (Paris: Éditions du Félin, 2019), p. 23. Unless otherwise stated, all translations are by the author.

einem monastischen abstrakten Innenraum seiner eigenen Gestaltung und seine dandyhafte Persona – Künstler*innen wie die*der britische Konstruktivist*in Marlow Moss und die deutsche Dadaistin Hannah Höch an. Beide wurden von ihren niederländischen Lebenspartnerinnen, den Schriftstellerinnen Antoinette Hendrika Nijhoff und Til Brugman, die bereits mit dem De-Stijl-Zirkel verbunden waren, in Mondrians Kreis eingeführt. Zeitgenössische Fotografien belegen ihre Atelierbesuche und anhaltende Verbindung.

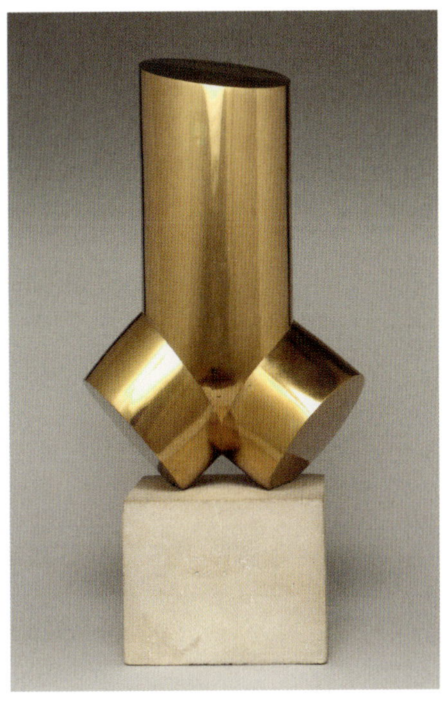

ABB. ~ FIG.1

Constantin Brâncuși, *Male Torso*, 1917
Männlicher Torso

Messing ~ *Brass*, mit Sockel ~ *with base*,
63,8 × 30,5 × 19,1 cm
The Cleveland Museum of Art, Hinman B. Hurlbut Collection 1937.3205

Spiritualistischer Modernismus: inklusive Glaubensvorstellungen und unabhängige Wege

Das Aufkommen alternativer religiöser und esoterischer Praktiken – wie die Theosophie, die 1875 in New York von Helena Blavatsky und Henry Steel Olcott gegründet wurde, sowie Rudolf Steiners spirituelle Wissenschaft der Anthroposophie – wurde eine wichtige Inspirationsquelle für viele frühe Modernist*innen, insbesondere für diejenigen, die abstrakt arbeiteten. Die Theosophie strebte danach, die Verbundenheit von Wissenschaft, Naturgesetz und Philosophie zu erforschen, und gründete ihre Weltanschauung auf pantheistischen Prinzipien, die hinduistischen und buddhistischen Lehren entnommen und mit Elementen des westlichen Okkultismus verwoben wurden: „Die Bewegung kam in der zweiten Hälfte des 19. Jahrhunderts in einer Zeit einschneidender sozialer, wirtschaftlicher, wissenschaftlicher und religiöser Veränderungen auf. Angespornt, eine Alternative zu den neuen materialistischen und rationalistischen Wertesystemen zu formieren, beförderte ihr stark individualistischer und egalitärer Ansatz die Verbreitung von libertären Ideen, insbesondere der Frauenrechte. Dies könnte

Contrary to common belief, historical abstraction was rarely conceived or perceived as gender neutral. Piet Mondrian, for example, assigned gendered meanings to the formal elements of his Neo-Plasticist art and theory. Yet Mondrian's vision remained firmly rooted in a traditional and hierarchical gender binary. His rigid, idealizing aesthetic was challenged by other artists of the period, particularly queer women, who proposed alternative models of abstraction. Nonetheless, Mondrian's deliberate self-stylization—living in a monastic cell-like abstract interior of his own design and cultivating a modern dandyism—attracted queer women artists such as British Constructivist Marlow Moss and German Dadaist Hannah Höch. Both were introduced to Mondrian by their Dutch partners, the writers Antoinette Hendrika Nijhoff and Til Brugman, respectively, who were already connected to the De Stijl circle. Period photographs attest to their studio visits and enduring connection.

Spiritualist Modernism: Inclusive Beliefs and Independent Paths

The emergence of alternative religious and esoteric practices—such as Theosophy, founded in New York in 1875 by Helena Blavatsky and Henry Steel Olcott, as well as Rudolf Steiner's pantheist spiritual science of Anthroposophy—became a major source of inspiration for many early modernists, particularly those working in abstraction. Theosophy sought to explore the interconnectedness of science, natural law, and philosophy, grounding its worldview in pantheistic principles drawn from Hindu and Buddhist teachings, interwoven with elements of Western occultism: "The movement arrived in the second half of the 19th century at a time of unprecedented social, economic, scientific, and religious change. Fueled by a reaction against materialist values and rationalist systems, its strong individualistic and egalitarian approach greatly facilitated the dissemination of libertarian ideas, in particular, women's rights. This might explain why so many Spiritualist artists were women, and why they propagated a sense of sisterhood and explored the concept of the Divine Feminine, elements of which would be reflected in their art."[4] In 1896, Swedish painter Hilma af Klint formed a group known as The Five with four other women, gathering regularly for spiritualist sessions. She wanted to create through her organic abstraction and spiritual geometry an alternative way of thinking: "flexible and lively, in order to breakdown destructive and rigid orders, such as the dualism of man and woman. She did not believe in gender boundaries."[5] Queer women artists such as af Klint, along with Dutch and American painters Jacoba van Heemskerck and Louise Janin, developed abstract visual languages deeply intertwined with their Spiritualist convictions and esoteric practices. After her return from Paris in 1904, Jacoba van Heemskerck was introduced to Marie Tak van Poortvliet, a patron of modern art and social reformer who became her life partner. The two women spent their summers in the artists' colony

4 Simon Grant, "Art, Spiritualism, and Theosophy," in *Women in Abstraction*, ed. Christine Macel and Karolina Ziebinska-Lewandowska, exh. cat. Centre Pompidou, Musée national d'Art moderne, Paris, 2021; Guggenheim Museum Bilbao, 2021/22 (London: Thames & Hudson, 2021), p. 46.

5 Julia Voss, "Hilma af Klint," in *Women in Abstraction*, ed. Macel and Ziebinska-Lewandowska, p. 52

erklären, warum so viele spiritistische Künstler*innen Frauen waren, die zudem ein Gefühl von Schwesternschaft propagierten und das Prinzip des ‚Göttlich Femininen' erforschten, Elemente, die sich in ihrer Kunst widerspiegeln würden."[4] 1896 gründete die schwedische Malerin Hilma af Klint mit vier weiteren Frauen die Gruppe The Five, die sich regelmäßig zu spiritistischen Sitzungen traf. Sie wollte durch ihre organische Abstraktion und spirituelle Geometrie eine alternative Denkweise schaffen: „Flexibel und lebendig, um destruktive und starre Ordnungen zu durchbrechen, wie den Dualismus von Mann und Frau. Sie glaubte nicht an Geschlechtergrenzen."[5] Queere Künstlerinnen wie af Klint entwickelten zusammen mit den niederländischen und amerikanischen Malerinnen Jacoba van Heemskerck und Louise Janin abstrakte visuelle Sprachen, die tief mit ihren spiritistischen Überzeugungen und esoterischen Praktiken verflochten waren. Nach ihrer Rückkehr aus Paris im Jahr 1904 lernte van Heemskerck die Förderin moderner Kunst und Sozialreformerin Marie Tak van Poortvliet kennen, die ihre Lebenspartnerin wurde. Die beiden Frauen verbrachten ihre Sommer in der Künstlerkolonie Domburg. Seit 1908 empfingen sie gelegentlich Piet Mondrian in ihrer Villa Loverendale. In enger Zusammenarbeit tauschten Mondrian und van Heemskerck Ideen über die aufkommenden Sprachen der modernen Kunst und ihre eigenen sich entwickelnden Ansätze zur Abstraktion aus. Beide wollten spirituelle und universelle Werte mit ihrer Kunst zum Ausdruck bringen, aber Mondrian entfernte sich zunehmend von Referenzen aus der Natur, während van Heemskerck versuchte, das Spirituelle mit dem Materiellen zu vereinen, indem sie sich auf das Elementare der sichtbaren Welt stützte – wie etwa den Baum, der seit jeher mit reicher symbolischer Bedeutung behaftet war. Beide, Mondrian 1909 und van Heemskerck 1910, traten schließlich der Theosophischen Gesellschaft bei und wurden Mitglieder der Blavatsky-Loge in Den Haag, zusammen mit Tak van Poortvliet. Durch die Rituale der Gesellschaft wurden sie in die transzendentale Kraft von Symbolen eingeweiht. Die Loge diente auch als lebendiges intellektuelles Zentrum, in dem eine Vielzahl von Gruppen, von der Suffragetten-Bewegung bis hin zu vegetarischen Gesellschaften, zusammenkamen, um Vorträge zu halten und neue Ideen auszutauschen. Tak van Poortvliet und van Heemskerck sollten später lebenslange Anhängerinnen von Steiners anthroposophischer Bewegung werden. In ihrer Weltanschauung und künstlerischen Praxis verkörperte van Heemskerck Steiners Vision einer Ära, in der männliche und weibliche Kräfte im Gleichgewicht existieren würden und das Geschlecht nicht länger das Schicksal eines Menschen bestimmen würde. Um 1913 wurde van Heemskerck mit *Der Sturm* in Verbindung gebracht, dem avantgardistischen Kunst- und Literaturmagazin sowie der gleichnamigen Galerie, die 1910 von Herwarth Walden in Berlin gegründet worden war. Während ihr Werk mit den zentralen Werten von *Der Sturm* übereinstimmte, insbesondere mit dessen Fokus auf expressive Formen und spirituelle Inhalte, wich es von den auf Umwälzung zielenden Energien der Bewegung und ihrer offen politischen Ausrichtung ab. Ihr Werk entwickelte sich zunehmend hin zu einer lebendigen organischen Abstraktion, wie in *Bild no. 90* (1918, Kat., S. 135) und *Bild no. 105* (1915–1920, Kat., S. 134) zu sehen ist. Sie interpretierte die Natur als eine spirituelle Welt, die sie in Linien, Farben und fließenden biomorphen Kompositionen ausdrückte, die oft

4 Simon Grant, „Art, Spiritualism, and Theosophy", in: *Women in Abstraction*, hrsg. von Christine Macel und Karolina Ziebinska-Lewandowska, Ausst.-Kat. Centre Pompidou, Paris/Musée national d'Art moderne, Paris/Guggenheim Museum Bilbao, London 2021, S. 46.

5 Julia Voss, „Hilma af Klint", in: Ausst.-Kat. 2021 (wie Anm. 4), S. 52.

of Domburg. Since 1908, they occasionally hosted Piet Mondrian at their Villa Loverendale. Collaborating closely, Mondrian and Van Heemskerck exchanged ideas about the emerging languages of modern art and their own evolving approaches to abstraction. While both pursued the expression of spiritual and universal values, Mondrian increasingly distanced himself from natural referents, whereas Van Heemskerck sought to unite the spiritual with the material by drawing on primordial elements of the visible world—such as the tree, rich in symbolic meaning. Both artists, eventually, became involved with Theosophy, joining the Blavatsky Lodge in The Hague—Mondrian in 1909 and Van Heemskerck in 1910—alongside Marie Tak van Poortvliet. Through the society's rituals, they were initiated into the transcendental power of symbols. The lodge also served as a vibrant intellectual hub, where a wide range of groups, from the women's suffrage movement to vegetarian societies, gathered to hold lectures and exchange new ideas. Tak van Poortvliet and Van Heemskerck would later become lifelong adherents of Rudolf Steiner's anthroposophic movement. In both her worldview and artistic practice, Van Heemskerck embodied Steiner's vision of an era in which masculine and feminine forces would exist in equilibrium and gender would no longer determine one's destiny. Around 1913, Van Heemskerck became associated with *Der Sturm*, the avant-garde art and literary magazine and gallery founded in 1910 by Herwarth Walden in Berlin. While her work aligned with *Der Sturm*'s core values, particularly its emphasis on expressive form and spiritual content, it diverged from the movement's more disruptive energies and overtly political thrust. Her work increasingly evolved toward a vibrant organic abstraction, as seen in *Bild no. 90* (1918, cat. p. 135) and *Bild no. 105* (1915–1920, cat. p. 134). She interpreted nature as a spiritual world composed of lines and colors, which she expressed through fluid biomorphic compositions that often appear voluptuous and are imbued with a subtle (homo)erotic charge. In *Bild no. 46 (Rog)* (1916, fig. 3), a floating, green, floral form is punctuated by two red spots that evoke the shape of breasts. Van Heemskerck's style exemplifies the subversive potential of biomorphism in contrast to the rigid formalism of the constructivist avant-gardes.[6]

Louise Janin's Pantheist Geometry

Louise Janin was a largely self-taught painter, who began her career in San Francisco and whose father had been a collector of Asian art. Situated on the Pacific Rim, California has long witnessed a strong presence of Asian migrants, whose cultural and religious traditions have shaped the region's identity. Janin herself embarked on extensive travels throughout Asia, immersing herself in Buddhist, Hindu, and Taoist mythologies—sources that profoundly influenced the Orientalist symbolism in her early work. Janin was drawn to Eastern spirituality as an alternative to Western materialism and artistic orthodoxies. She saw herself as an interpreter between worlds and believed that the true modern artist was not a follower of stylistic

6 Van Heemskerck anticipates in these works what Polish art historian Andrzej Turowski describes as the new biomorphic formalism or "neo-formalism" of the mid-1930s that "accepted that which was hidden and incomplete" in the Constructivist language of forms, and "referring to that which is personal and singular, to the body, instead of to that which is common and universal, [...] a transition from abstraction to a strategy of identity founded on the ruins of modernism, on the ruins of Logos." Andrzej Turowski, "Biomorphism as Avant-Garde Deconstruction," in *A Reader in East-Central-European Modernism, 1918–1956*, ed. Beáta Hock, Klara Kemp-Welch, and Jonathan Owen (London: Courtauld Institute of Art, 2019), pp. 157–171, here pp. 164, 168; in the second quotation, Turowski references Polish art historian Piotr Piotrowski on the subjective materiality of the body in art.

sinnlich erscheinen und von einer subtilen (homo)erotischen Spannung durchzogen sind. In *Bild no. 46 (Rog)* (1916, Abb. 3) ist eine schwebende, grüne, pflanzenartige Kreation markiert mit zwei roten Punkten, was die Form von Brüsten suggeriert. Van Heemskercks Stil veranschaulicht das subversive Ausdruckspotenzial des Biomorphismus im Gegensatz zum starren Formalismus der konstruktivistischen Avantgarden.[6]

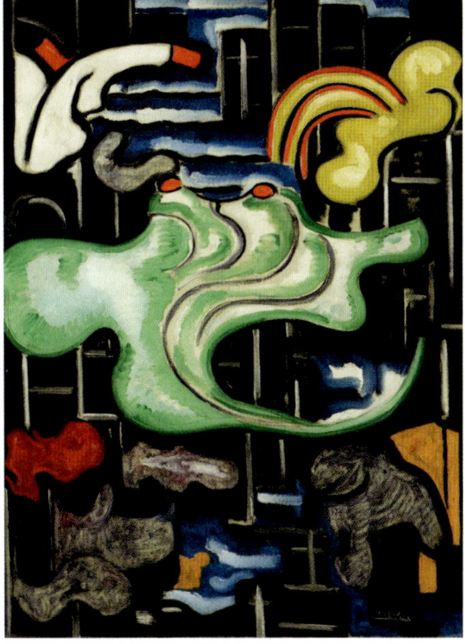

ABB. ~ FIG. 3

Jacoba van Heemskerck, *Bild no. 46 (Rog)*, 1916
Bild Nr. 46 (Rochen) ~ *Composition No. 46 (Ray)*

Öl auf Leinwand ~ *Oil on canvas*, 95,5 × 72,5 cm
Kunstmuseum Den Haag – bequest Marie Tak van Poortvliet

Louise Janins pantheistische Geometrie

Louise Janin war eine weitgehend autodidaktische Malerin, die ihre Karriere in San Francisco begann. Ihr Vater war ein Sammler asiatischer Kunst. Kalifornien, das im Pazifischen Ozean liegt, hatte eine lange asiatische Migrationsgeschichte, wodurch fernöstliche kulturelle und religiöse Traditionen die Identität der Region geprägt haben. Janin selbst unternahm umfangreiche Reisen durch Asien und tauchte tief in buddhistische, hinduistische und taoistische Mythologien ein – Quellen, die den „orientalischen Symbolismus" in ihrem frühen Werk maßgeblich beeinflussten. Sie fühlte sich von der fernöstlichen Spiritualität als Alternative zum westlichen Materialismus und den sich dort entwickelnden künstlerischen Orthodoxien angezogen. Janin sah sich selbst als eine Vermittlerin zwischen Welten und glaubte, dass wahre moderne Künstlerinnen nicht Anhänger*innen stilistischer Dogmen oder -ismen seien, sondern vielmehr Suchende und Experimentierende auf der Suche nach immer neuen kreativen Wegen. Obwohl sie sich ab den 1920er-Jahren zunehmend der Abstraktion zuwandte, die sie als „den einzigen authentischen Beitrag des 20. Jahrhunderts zu den bildenden Künsten" beschrieb, gab sie nie vollständig ihre Hinwendung zu einer stilisierten Figuration auf.[7]

6 Van Heemskerck antizipiert in diesen Arbeiten, was der polnische Kunsthistoriker Andrzej Turowski als den neuen biomorphen Formalismus oder „Neo-Formalismus" beschreibt, der Mitte der 1930er-Jahre auftritt und der „das [V]erborgene und [U]nvollständige" in der konstruktivistischen Formensprache „akzeptierte" und „sich auf das Persönliche und Einzigartige, d. h. auf den Körper bezog, statt auf das Gemeinsame und Universelle, […] ein Übergang von der Abstraktion zu einer Strategie der Identität, begründet auf den Trümmern des Modernismus, auf den Trümmern des Logos". Andrzej Turowski, „Biomorphism as Avant-Garde Deconstruction", in: *A Reader in East-Central-European Modernism, 1918–1956*, hrsg. von Beáta Hock, Klara Kemp-Welch und Jonathan Owen, London 2019, S. 157–171, hier: S. 164, 168; im zweiten Zitat verweist Turowski auf den polnischen Kunsthistoriker Piotr Piotrowski und dessen Aussagen zur subjektiven Materialität des Körpers in der Kunst.

7 Louise Janin, „Facts, Fads and Fallacies in Art", in: *Women's City Club Magazine* 2, Nr. 1, Februar 1929, S. 10, zit. nach: Marion Sergent, *Louise Janin: l'art de l'entre-deux*, Lyon 2022, S. 42.

dogma or -isms, but rather a seeker and experimenter in pursuit of ever new creative pathways. Although she increasingly embraced abstraction from the 1920s onward, which she described as "the only authentic contribution of the twentieth century to the visual arts," she never fully abandoned her stylized approach to figuration.[7]

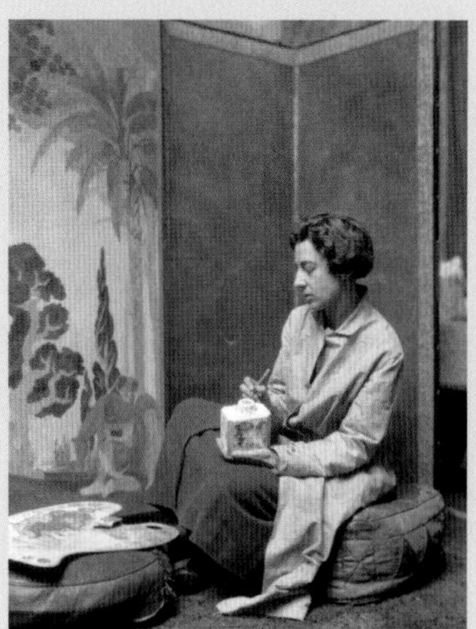

ABB. ~ FIG.4

Louise Janin, um ~ *ca.* 1925

In 1923, Janin painted an archaic tableau of intimate encounters between women, *La Dixième Muse à Mytilène* (*The Tenth Muse at Mytilene*). The title evokes the figure of Sappho, the ancient poet who lived in Mytilene on the island of Lesbos during the seventh and sixth centuries BC. French art historian Marion Sergent raises the question of whether "such a subject—resonating with Janin's own homosexuality—might stem from her association with the salon of Natalie Clifford Barney, a true gathering place for modernist circles. It is known that Barney, together with her lover Renée Vivien, dreamt of founding a school for female poets during their time in Mytilene."[8] One of Janin's first works to merge abstract motifs with figuration was *L'Après-midi d'un faune* (*The Afternoon of a Faun*, 1925), inspired by Claude Debussy's 1894 symphonic poem, later adapted into a short ballet by the legendary dancer Vaslav Nijinsky in 1912. Nijinsky's performance, with its non-traditional, angular movements and the faun's overtly erotic final gesture—interpreted by many as masturbatory frottage—provoked a scandal at the time. His self-absorbed, sensual choreography quickly became iconic in modern queer culture. The faun itself emerged as a recurring motif in queer iconography, appearing in the work of artists such as American sculptor Richmond Barthé and the British painters Gluck and Glyn Warren Philpot. With her move to Paris in 1923, Janin increasingly embraced a distinctive form of lyrical and pantheistic abstraction. She became acquainted with key figures of the international avant-garde, including Robert and Sonia Delaunay, František Kupka, Albert Gleizes, and Filippo Tommaso Marinetti. During this period, Janin's characteristic arabesques, spirals, and similarly sinuous lines began to assert themselves as increasingly autonomous visual elements. In dynamic and fluid abstract compositions such as *Les Plantes dressées* (1934, cat. p. 133) and

7 Louise Janin, "Facts, Fads and Fallacies in Art," *Women's City Club Magazine* 2, no. 1 (February 1929): p. 10, quoted in Marion Sergent, *Louise Janin: L'Art de l'entre-deux* (Lyon: FAGE éditions, 2022), p. 42.

8 Sergent, *Louise Janin*, p. 20.

1923 malte Janin ein archaisches Tableau, *La Dixième Muse à Mytilène*, das intime Begegnungen unter Frauen darstellt. Der Titel bezieht sich auf die Figur der Sappho, der antiken Dichterin, die im 7. und 6. Jahrhundert v. Chr. in Mytilene auf der Insel Lesbos lebte. Die französische Kunsthistorikerin Marion Sergent stellt die Frage, ob „ein solches Thema – das mit Janins eigener Homosexualität in Resonanz steht – aus ihrer Verbindung mit dem Salon von Natalie Barney stammen könnte, einem originären Treffpunkt für modernistische Kreise. Es ist bekannt, dass Barney gemeinsam mit ihrer Geliebten Renée Vivien während ihrer Zeit in Mytilene davon träumte, eine Schule für Dichter*innen zu gründen."[8] Eines von Janins ersten Werken, das abstrakte Motive mit Figuration verband, war *L'Après-midi d'un faune* (1925), inspiriert von Claude Debussys symphonischem Gedicht von 1894, das 1912 von dem legendären Tänzer Vaslav Nijinsky in einem kurzen Ballett adaptiert wurde. Nijinskys Aufführung mit den unkonventionellen, angewinkelten Bewegungen und der offen erotischen letzten Geste des Fauns – die von vielen als eine Szene des Masturbierens interpretiert wurde – provozierte damals einen Skandal. Seine selbstabsorbierte, sinnliche Choreografie wurde schnell ikonisch in der modernen queeren Kultur. Der Faun selbst trat als wiederkehrendes Motiv in einer frühen queeren Ikonografie auf und erschien in den Werken von Künstler*innen wie dem amerikanischen Bildhauer Richmond Barthé und den britischen Maler*innen Gluck und Glyn Warren Philpot.

Mit ihrem Umzug nach Paris im Jahr 1923 entwickelte Janin zunehmend eine eigenständige Form lyrischer und pantheistischer Abstraktion. Sie machte Bekanntschaft mit Schlüsselfiguren der internationalen Avantgarde, darunter Robert und Sonia Delaunay, František Kupka, Albert Gleizes und Filippo Tommaso Marinetti. In dieser Zeit begannen sich Janins charakteristische Arabesken, Spiralen und geschwungene Linien als zunehmend autonome visuelle Elemente zu etablieren. In dynamischen und fließenden abstrakten Kompositionen wie *Les Plantes dressées* (1934, Kat., S. 133) und *Envol* (1955, Kat., S. 132) entwickelte sich ihr Stil zu einer vollständig unabhängigen Form moderner Abstraktion. In dieser Bildsprache überwiegt die Kurve und jedes Element erhält symbolische Bedeutung – ähnlich wie im malerischen System von Mondrian –, jedoch hier von deutlich queer-femininen und sinnlichen stilistischen Impulsen geprägt. Für Janin signalisieren Spiralen moralische Konzentration, kosmische Energie oder spirituelle Evolution. Konzentrische Kreise repräsentieren das Absolute, die Perfektion und die Kontinuität. Die Orientierung der Linien fungiert als expressiver Parameter: Die horizontale Linie vermittelt Ruhe und Materialismus, während die vertikale Linie Erhebung und Idealismus evoziert. Janins geometrisierte Darstellungen ermöglichten dadurch eine neue abstrahierte Interpretation der Realität: „Der geometrische Geist manifestiert sich zwischen den Partikeln der Welt, um in sie zu intervenieren, sie zu fragmentieren und neu zu kombinieren."[9]

Janin verfolgte in ihrer „morpho-sentimentalen"[10] Abstraktion das Streben nach einer Neuerfindung der Welt und einer Abkehr von realistischer Repräsentation, ähnlich den Intentionen der britischen Konstruktivist*in Marlow Moss. Doch im Gegensatz zu vielen ihrer konstruktivistischen Zeitgenoss*innen hat Janin die Natur als göttlichen Bezugspunkt nie aufgegeben. Wie sie 1935 schrieb: „Zurück zur Natur. Natur gegen Abstraktion? Gibt es das wirklich – lassen Sie uns sehen. Die

8 Ebd., S. 20.

9 Louise Janin, „Les Éléments du style", in: *A.B.C. Magazine d'art*, Nr. 94, Oktober 1932, S. 265, zit. nach: Sergent 2022 (wie Anm. 7), S. 46.

10 Sergent 2022 (wie Anm. 7), S. 60.

Envol (1955, cat. p. 132), her style developed into a fully independent form of modern abstraction. In this language, the curve predominates, and each element takes on symbolic meaning—much as in Piet Mondrian's pictorial system—though reimagined here with a distinctly queer-feminine and voluptuous stylistic impulse. For Janin, spirals signal moral concentration, cosmic energy, or spiritual evolution; concentric circles represent the absolute, perfection, and continuity; the orientation of lines functions as an expressive parameter: the horizontal conveys calm and materialism, while the vertical evokes elevation and idealism. Janin's geometrized representations enabled a new interpretation of reality: "The geometric spirit insinuates itself between the particles of the world to disrupt it, fragment it, and recombine it."[9] Her drive toward an abstract reinvention of the world, and a disassociation from realist representation, aligns the intent of her "morpho-sentimental"[10] abstraction with that of the hard-edged Constructivism of the British artist Marlow Moss. Yet unlike many of her Constructivist contemporaries, Janin never abandoned nature as a divine referent. As she wrote in 1935, "Return to nature. Nature against abstraction? Does that really exist—let's see. Nature is a geometer. If she clothes her geometry, softens it, and shades it infinitely, is the artist to be forbidden from doing the same? For my part, I believe there is a close and steady relationship between the painter of abstractions and the spectacles of the everyday world. If the eye does not take its nourishment from the earth, the aesthetic faculty dies of starvation."[11]

Stylistic Promiscuities

This exhibition presents numerous examples of artists who countered and expanded the boundaries of avant-garde styles as a particular trait of queer modernist aesthetic. What we see, in fact, is the emergence of distinct stylistic developments that are non-conformist and, at times, strikingly anti-canonical. The Russian émigré and transnational artist Pavel Tchelitchew became associated with the interwar Neo-Romantic movements in Paris and New York. But more to the point, Tchelitchew galvanized diverse avant-garde currents—such as Cubism, Futurism, and Surrealism—into kaleidoscopic perspectives, driven not by formalism, but by desire, emotion, intimate relationships, memory, and trauma. In light of his radically hybrid aesthetic, Tchelitchew emerges as a central figure within the context of this exhibition. American scholar Angela Miller argues that the "modern oblivion" surrounding Tchelitchew's work may be a result of its *stylistic promiscuity* and of his "integrated vision that transcended the dualisms of reason/magic, matter/spirit, body/nature."[12] His painting *Untitled (Seated Man, Multiple Images)* (1927, cat. p. 151) portrays an anonymous figure whose face appears in three overlapping phases suggesting a fractured or multiple identity: a complex interplay of selfhood, perception, and psychological depth. The composition may equally be read as two identical figures locked in a passionate embrace—an image that evokes Freud's theorization of homosexuality as a form of narcissism.

9 Louise Janin, "Les Éléments du style," *A.B.C. Magazine d'art*, no. 94 (October 1932), p. 265, quoted in Sergent, *Louise Janin*, p. 46.

10 Sergent, *Louise Janin*, p. 60.

11 Louise Janin, "Peinture et Musique," *Sud Magazine*, no. 126 (April 15, 1935), p. 16, quoted in Sergent, *Louise Janin*, p. 60.

12 Angela Miller, "Vibrant Matter: The Countermodern World of Pavel Tchelitchew," *The Art Bulletin* 102, no. 2 (June 2020): pp. 121–145, here pp. 121, 123.

Natur ist ein Geometer. Wenn sie ihre Geometrie kleidet, sie abmildert und unendlich schattiert, soll der Künstler dann daran gehindert werden, das Gleiche zu tun? Was mich betrifft, so glaube ich, dass eine enge und stetige Beziehung zwischen dem Maler der Abstraktionen und den Schauplätzen der alltäglichen Welt besteht. Wenn das Auge seine Nahrung nicht von der Erde nimmt, stirbt das ästhetische Vermögen an Hungersnot."[11]

Stilistische Promiskuität

Diese Ausstellung zeigt zahlreiche Beispiele von Künstler*innen, die die Grenzen avantgardistischer Stile herausforderten und erweiterten – ein besonderes Merkmal der queeren modernistischen Ästhetik. Was wir hier sehen, ist tatsächlich das Aufkommen eigenständiger stilistischer Entwicklungen, die nonkonformistisch und bisweilen auffallend antikanonisch sind. Der russische Emigrant und transnationale Künstler Pavel Tchelitchew wurde mit der neoromantischen Bewegung der 1920er- und 1930er-Jahre in Paris und New York in Verbindung gebracht. Doch noch entscheidender ist, dass Tchelitchew verschiedene avantgardistische Strömungen – wie Kubismus, Futurismus und Surrealismus – in kaleidoskopischen Perspektiven aufbrach, die nicht vorrangig durch ein Bestreben nach formalistischer Sprache und stilistischen Abgrenzungen geprägt, sondern vielmehr von Verlangen, Emotionen, intimen Beziehungen, Erinnerung und Trauma durchzogen waren. Im Hinblick auf seine radikal hybride Ästhetik tritt Tchelitchew als eine zentrale Figur im Kontext dieser Ausstellung auf. Die amerikanische Kunsthistorikerin Angela Miller argumentiert, dass das „moderne Vergessen" rund um Tchelitchews Werk – dessen Marginalisierung im Kanon der Moderne – möglicherweise auf eine „disziplinäre Promiskuität" und eine „integrierte Vision zurückzuführen ist, die die Dualismen von Vernunft/Magie, Materie/Geist, Körper/Natur überwand".[12] Tchelitchews Gemälde *Untitled (Seated Man, Multiple Images)* (1927, Kat., S. 151) zeigt eine anonyme Figur, deren Gesicht in drei überlappenden Phasen erscheint, was eine fragmentierte oder multiple Identität andeutet: ein komplexes Zusammenspiel von Bewusstsein, Wahrnehmung und psychologischer Tiefe. Die Komposition kann ebenso als zwei identische Figuren gelesen werden, die in einer leidenschaftlichen Umarmung eingeschlossen sind – ein Bild, das Freuds Theorie von der Identifikation von Homosexualität mit der Konstellation des Narzissmus evoziert. Tchelitchew war zutiefst skeptisch gegenüber dem, was er als einen übermäßig analytischen und sterilen Modernismus ansah. In einem Brief an seinen Freund und Mäzen, den New Yorker Ballet-impresario Lincoln Kirstein, übte er eine scharfe Kritik am Kubismus und verurteilte diesen als eine nihilistische Ästhetik, einen „Haufen Fragmente [...], der es nicht schafft, einen lebenden Organismus zu erschaffen"[13]. Er argumentierte, dass der Kubismus es versäumte, „eine lebendige, atmende, tatsächliche Welt zu suggerieren", und stattdessen Objekte in „eine starre Struktur sperrte, die sie ‚vollständig außerhalb des Begehrens einer Person, von Liebe oder Körper' stellte."[14] In *Personage* (1927, Kat., S. 150) malte Tchelitchew den schemenhaften Körper einer sitzenden Figur in gedämpften, erdigen Tönen, überlagert von einem kosmischen Netz, das eine neue, visionäre Geometrie der menschlichen Form abbildet und sein Interesse an Astronomie und den neuen Wissenschaften der Zeit widerspiegelt. Die

11 Louise Janin, „Peinture et Musique", in: *Sud Magazine*, Nr. 126, 15. April 1935, S. 16, zit. nach: Sergent 2022 (wie Anm. 7), S. 60.

12 Angela Miller, „Vibrant Matter: The Countermodern World of Pavel Tchelitchew", in: *The Art Bulletin* 102, Nr. 2, Juni 2020, S. 121–145, hier: S. 121, 123.

13 Pavel Tchelitchew, zit. nach: ebd., S. 134.

14 Ebd.

Tchelitchew was deeply skeptical of what he saw as an overly analytic and sterile modernism. In a letter to his friend and patron, the New York ballet impresario Lincoln Kirstein, he launched a pointed critique of Cubism, denouncing it as a nihilistic aesthetic, a "heap of fragments [...] not succeeding in the creation of a living organism."[13] He argued that Cubism failed to "suggest a living breathing actual world," instead locking objects into "a rigid structure that placed them 'completely outside one's desire, love or body.'"[14] In *Personage* (1927, cat. p. 150), Tchelitchew painted the ghostly body of a seated figure in muted, earthy tones, layered with a cosmic web that maps a new, visionary geometry of the human form, reflecting his interest in astronomy and emerging sciences. German art historian Antje Krause-Wahl observes, "In the early twentieth century, quantum mechanics and the theories of relativity understood space and matter as energy levels. Tchelitchew, however, raises above all the question of the subject within this dynamic, new world order."[15] In *Personage*, the body is further treated with patches of coffee grounds applied to joints, hands, and face, meeting the nodal points of the overlaid cosmic grid. "In this abstract portrait," she continues, "Tchelitchew attempts to free the body from its fixation to the pictorial surface."[16] It can only be speculated if the artist experimented with the unorthodox material of coffee grounds in order to hint at a substance long used in popular culture for divination and fortune telling. Like Tchelitchew, the Hungarian artist Anton Prinner underwent radical stylistic shifts throughout his multifaceted and unconventional practice. In the early 1930s, he produced a series of "constructivist" works, followed by a phase of post-Cubist sculptures and an extensive body of prints for which he developed a new technique he called *papyrogravure*. Since the late 1940s, Prinner developed his modern pagan sculptures out of a deep interest in Egyptian mythology, the occult, and the concept of transmutation. In the early 1920s, Prinner studied at the Academy of Fine Arts in Budapest. In 1928, he moved to Paris, adopting the first name Anton and male pronouns along with the persona of a Parisian bohemian, complete with black beret and signature pipe.[17] In a series of dramatically lit studio photographs from the 1940s, the artist staged himself with striking effect amid his idiosyncratic universe of eerily emblematic, androgynous sculptures. The Hungarian scholar Júlia Cserba notes, "His male dress, pipe-smoking, and deliberate deep voice concealed much more than his actual sex. He only revealed his true face in his sculptures, easily recognisable for the attentive observer in the dignified *Beggar* (*Le Mendiant*[, 1950s]), in whose hands Pablo Picasso often discretely left money on his frequent visits to Prinner's studio, or in the *She-Bull* (*Femme-taureau*, 1937), combining male strength with gentle femininity, or in the mystical *Totem* (1946), yet he revealed something of himself in almost all his sculptures."[18]

In 1936, Prinner signed the *Dimensionist Manifesto*, and his early spatial constructions were planned for inclusion in the First International Dimensionist Exhibition that same year, alongside Sophie Taeuber-Arp, László Moholy-Nagy, Joan Miró,

13 Pavel Tchelitchew, quoted in Miller, "Vibrant Matter," p. 134.

14 Ibid.

15 Antje Krause-Wahl, "Cosmic Surfaces: Materiality and Portraiture in Queer Modernism," in *Materials, Practices, and Politics of Shine in Modern Art and Popular Culture*, ed. Antje Krause-Wahl, Petra Löffler, and Änne Söll (London: Bloomsbury, 2021), pp. 139–154, here pp. 142–143.

16 Ibid., 143.

17 "For a long time, it was perhaps only his closest friend, Árpád Szenes, who knew that 'Monsieur Prinner attended the Academy with two braids,'" recollected Endre Rozsda (in the mid-1990s), painter and mutual friend of Szenes and Prinner, quoted in Júlia Cserba, "The Hungarian Prinner", in *A Reader in East-Central-European Modernism*, pp. 217–225, here p. 219. Prinner described himself as possessing "a certain homosexual drive" and expressed an attraction to men: ibid., p. 218.

18 Ibid., p. 218.

deutsche Kunsthistorikerin Antje Krause-Wahl bemerkt: „Im frühen 20. Jahrhundert wurden in der Quantenmechanik und in der Relativitätstheorie Raum und Materie als Energieniveaus verstanden. Tchelitchew jedoch stellt vor allem die Frage nach dem Subjekt innerhalb dieser dynamischen, neuen Weltordnung."[15] In *Personage* wird der Körper zudem mit Kaffeepulver markiert, das auf Gelenke, Hände und Gesicht aufgetragen ist und die Knotenpunkte des überlagerten kosmischen Rasters berührt. „In diesem abstrakten Porträt", fährt Krause-Wahl fort, „versucht Tchelitchew, den Körper von seiner Fixierung auf die bildliche Oberfläche zu befreien."[16] Es kann nur spekuliert werden, ob der Künstler mit dem unorthodoxen Material von Kaffeepulver experimentierte, um auf eine Substanz hinzuweisen, die in der populären Kultur schon lange für Wahrsagerei und Orakelsprüche verwendet wurde. Ähnlich wie Tchelitchew durchlief der ungarische Künstler Anton Prinner starke stilistische Wandlungen während seiner vielschichtigen und unkonventionellen Praxis. In den frühen 1930er-Jahren schuf er eine Reihe von abstrakten Werken, die als konstruktivistisch betrachtet werden könnten, die er jedoch nicht als solche bezeichnete, gefolgt von einer Phase postkubistischer Skulpturen und einem umfangreichen Werk an Druckgrafik, für die er eine neue Technik auf Papyrus entwickelte, die er *„papyrogravure"* nannte. Ab den späten 1940er-Jahren kreierte Prinner moderne fantastische Skulpturen, deren emblematische bis exzentrische Figuration aus einem tiefen Interesse an ägyptischer Mythologie, am Okkulten und am Konzept der Transmutation genährt wurde. In den frühen 1920er-Jahren studierte Prinner an der Akademie der bildenden Künste in Budapest. 1928 zog er nach Paris und nahm den Vornamen Anton an. Im Zuge der Neuerfindung seiner Identität gestaltete sich Prinner fortan als Pariser Bohemien komplett mit schwarzem Barett und charakteristischer Pfeife.[17] In einer Reihe dramatisch beleuchteter Studioaufnahmen aus den 1940er-Jahren inszenierte sich der Künstler mit eindrucksvollem Effekt inmitten seines eigenwilligen Universums von enigmatischen und androgynen Skulpturen. Die ungarische Wissenschaftlerin Júlia Cserba stellt fest: „Seine männliche Kleidung, das Pfeifenrauchen und die absichtlich tiefe Stimme verbargen viel mehr als nur sein tatsächliches Geschlecht. Er zeigte sein wahres Gesicht nur in seinen Skulpturen, die für den aufmerksamen Betrachter leicht erkennbar waren, wie im würdevollen *Bettler* (*Le Mendiant*, 1950er-Jahre), in dessen Händen Pablo Picasso oft diskret Geld hinterließ, bei seinen häufigen Besuchen im Prinners Atelier, oder in der *Stierfrau* (*Femme-taureau*, 1937), die männliche Stärke mit sanfter Weiblichkeit vereint, oder im mystischen *Totem* (1946). Er offenbarte jedoch etwas von sich in fast allen seinen Skulpturen."[18] 1936 unterzeichnete Prinner das *Dimensionistische Manifest* und seine frühen räumlichen Konstruktionen waren für die Teilnahme an der ersten Internationalen Dimensionistischen Ausstellung im selben Jahr geplant, zusammen mit Sophie Taeuber-Arp, László Moholy-Nagy, Joan Miró, Alexander Calder, Francis Picabia, Marcel Duchamp und Max Ernst. Das Manifest rief Künstler*innen dazu auf, über traditionelle zweidimensionale Formen hinauszugehen und eine erweiterte Vision des Universums anzustreben – eine Vision, die von Einsteins Relativitätstheorie, nichteuklidischer Geometrie und den Entdeckungen der modernen Physik geprägt war – und letztlich auf eine kosmische Kunst hinzuzielen. Zu dieser Zeit hatte Prinner bereits begonnen, abstrakte

15 Antje Krause-Wahl, „Cosmic Surfaces: Materiality and Portraiture in Queer Modernism", in: *Materials, Practices, and Politics of Shine in Modern Art and Popular Culture*, hrsg. von Antje Krause-Wahl, Petra Löffler und Änne Söll, London 2021, S. 139–154, hier: S. 142–143.

16 Ebd., S. 143.

17 „Lange Zeit war es vielleicht nur sein engster Freund, Árpád Szenes, der wusste, dass ‚Monsieur Prinner die Akademie mit zwei Zöpfen besuchte'", erinnerte sich der Maler und gemeinsame Freund von Szenes und Prinner, Endre Rozsda, in den mittleren 1990er-Jahren, zit. nach: Júlia Cserba, „The Hungarian Prinner", in: Hock/Kemp-Welch/Owen 2019 (wie Anm. 6), S. 217–225, hier: S. 219. Prinner beschrieb sich selbst als jemanden mit „einem bestimmten homosexuellen Drang" und äußerte, sich von Männern angezogen zu fühlen. Ebd., S. 218.

18 Ebd., S. 218.

Alexander Calder, Francis Picabia, Marcel Duchamp, and Max Ernst. The manifesto called on artists to move beyond traditional two-dimensional forms and embrace an expanded vision of the universe—one shaped by Einstein's theory of relativity, non-Euclidean geometry, and the discoveries of modern physics—ultimately advancing toward a *Cosmic Art.* By that time, Prinner had already begun producing abstract works such as *Untitled (Les Hublots)* (1932, cat. p. 143) and *Spirales plastiques* (1935, cat. p. 143). In these constructions, space folds and spirals inward and outward into fantastical dimensions. In *Spirales plastiques*, a white cord extends from the center of the relief's surface into the viewer's space, simultaneously anchoring the work in the physical world and triggering the imagination like an optical game. The use of this string element reaches a fetishistic intensity, recalling the taut cords applied to the surfaces of white paintings by Constructivist Marlow Moss from the same period, such as *White with Bent Cord (Relief)* (1936, cat. p. 138). In his later print work—particularly in the postwar album *L'Apocalypse* (1948, cat. pp. 148/149)—the motif of the spiral takes on a far more dramatic and existential dimension. Prinner soon distanced himself from the movements of "constructivist art," against being "named, grouped, and categorized like a grocer names his cheese."[19] Instead, he invested his abstract compositions increasingly with esoteric beliefs: "Isolated in my room, I built my boards and drew my prints, which looked like 'signatures' of cosmic bodies. Phenomena captured in their evolution of crystallization. [...] Believing in the purity of an imaginary crystal that was to represent the universe, I constructed lines and shapes like a manic alchemist."[20] In 1937, he created his first figurative sculptures out of a desire to "change direction"—to free himself from predefined movements and formalist constraints—only to realize, as he later reflected, "that the only way is the way that has no direction."[21] It was the time when Prinner carved his *Double personnage (Personnage renversé)* (1937, cat. p. 145) out of a block of wood. The work's unusual, and in many ways programmatic, composition features one androgynous figure merging into another, the two forms growing into a single body. With *Double personnage*, Prinner advanced the development of Cubism from a gender-political perspective, effectively queering its visual language. With the enigmatic wood sculpture *L'équilibriste* (1942, cat. p. 144), Prinner reached the pinnacle of his idiosyncratic paganism. A statuesque, goddess-like figure balances a large erect floral stem delicately on her open palm. Her gaze turns inward; like a sphinx, she withholds her secrets. Given the central role that the concept of equilibrium—between oppositional forces, and particularly between masculine and feminine elements—played in early spiritual abstraction, especially in Mondrian's Neo-Plasticism, one might speculate whether Prinner's mysterious idol, with its bold sexual symbolism, represents a queered response to the purified, rationalist abstractions of his modernist predecessors.

19 Prinner quoted in *Prinner 1932–35*, exhibition booklet, Galerie Yvon Lambert, Paris (Paris: Nouvelles éditions Debresse, 1965), n.p.

20 Ibid.

21 Ibid.

Werke wie *Untitled (Les Hublots)* (1932, Kat., S. 143) und *Spirales Plastiques* (1935, Kat., S. 143) zu schaffen. In diesen Konstruktionen faltet sich der Raum nach innen und außen in fantastische Dimensionen. In *Spirales Plastiques* erstreckt sich eine weiße Schnur spiralförmig von der Mitte des Reliefs in den Raum der Betrachter*innen und manifestiert das Werk einerseits in der dritten Dimension, während es als optisches Spiel die Wahrnehmung auf weiteren Ebenen anregt. Der Einsatz dieses Schnur-Objekts erreicht eine fetischistische Intensität und erinnert an die linear gespannten sowie gebogenen Seil-Segmente, die von der*dem konstruktivistischen Künstler*in Marlow Moss in derselben Periode auf die Oberflächen weißer Gemälde appliziert wurden, wie etwa in *White with Bent Cord (Relief)* (1936, Kat., S. 138). In den späteren Druckwerken von Prinner – insbesondere im Nachkriegsalbum *L'Apocalypse* (1948, Kat., S. 148/149) – nimmt das Motiv der Spirale eine weitaus dramatischere und existenzialistische Dimension an. Prinner distanzierte sich bald von den Bewegungen der „konstruktivistischen Kunst", weil er dagegen war, „benannt, gruppiert und kategorisiert zu werden, wie ein Händler seinen Käse benennt"[19]. Stattdessen füllte er seine abstrakten Kompositionen zunehmend mit esoterischen Vorstellungen: „Isoliert in meinem Raum, baute ich meine Tafeln und zeichnete meine Drucke, die wie ‚Signaturen' kosmischer Körper aussahen. Phänomene, die in ihrer Evolution der Kristallisation eingefangen wurden. [...] Ich glaubte an die Reinheit eines imaginären Kristalls, der das Universum darstellen sollte, und konstruierte Linien und Formen wie ein manischer Alchemist."[20] 1937 schuf er seine ersten figurativen Skulpturen aus dem Wunsch heraus, „die Richtung zu ändern" – sich von vorgegebenen Bewegungen und formalistischen Einschränkungen zu befreien –, nur um später, wie er reflektierte, zu erkennen, „dass der einzige Weg der ist, der keine Richtung hat."[21] Es war die Zeit, als Prinner seine *Double personnage (Personnage renversé)* (1937, Kat., S. 145) aus einem Holzblock schnitzte. Diese ungewöhnliche und in vielerlei Hinsicht programmatische Komposition zeigt eine androgyne Figur, die fließend in eine andere übergeht, wobei die beiden Formen zu einem einzigen Körper verschmelzen. Mit *Double personnage* trieb Prinner die Entwicklung des Kubismus aus einer genderpolitischen Perspektive voran und queerte effektiv dessen visuelle Sprache.

Mit der rätselhaften Holzskulptur *L'équilibriste* (1942, Kat., S. 144) erreichte Prinner den Höhepunkt seines eigenwilligen Paganismus. Eine statueske, einer Naturgöttin ähnliche Figur balanciert einen großen aufrechten Pflanzenstängel auf ihrer offenen Handfläche. Ihr Gesicht ist schemenhaft, der Blick ist nach innen gerichtet; wie eine Sphinx behält sie ihre Geheimnisse für sich. Angesichts der zentralen Rolle, die das Konzept des Equilibriums – zwischen gegensätzlichen Kräften und insbesondere zwischen männlichen und weiblichen Elementen – in der frühen spirituellen Abstraktion spielte, insbesondere in Mondrians Neoplastizismus, könnte man spekulieren, ob Prinners mysteriöses Idol mit seiner unverfrorenen sexuellen Symbolik eine queer gewendete Antwort auf die rationalistischen Abstraktionen seiner modernistischen Vorgänger*innen darstellt.

19
Prinner, zit. nach: *Prinner 1932–35*, Ausst-Brosch. Galerie Yvon Lambert, Paris, Paris 1965, o.S.

20
Ebd.

21
Ebd.

Marlow Moss: A Queer Investment in Constructivism

A line or a square have no gender unless such categories are ascribed to them. As Tate curator Alex Pichler states, "the human social world continues to persuade us that people, clothes, colours and even works of art are either 'feminine,' 'masculine' or a blend of the two. Each choice we make about how we look or act, what we wear or create, is assigned a gendered reading under this polarising doctrine."[22] The discourse of abstraction has, indeed, been gendered from its programmatic beginnings. For Piet Mondrian the question of the sexes was fundamental to the principles that guided his path toward abstraction. He invented a symbolic system aimed at newly balancing sexual forces through aesthetic equilibrium. The early twentieth-century change of traditional gender roles and the heightened visibility—though also increased policing—of non-heteronormative sexualities, spurred by the impact of war, as well as by the new social sciences, played a central role in the formation of modern art, its concepts, styles, and agendas.[23] In 1917, Mondrian proclaimed that "The physical hermaphrodite is the unity of an *apparent* duality, while the spiritual hermaphrodite (the ideal of the ancient philosophers) is the unity of a *real* duality."[24] Mondrian developed his abstract vocabulary with rigid precision, reducing visual language to the minimal use of vertical and horizontal lines intersecting at right angles, with no more room for the curve, and limiting color to the primary hues. His pamphlet on "Neo-Plasticism in Painting" (1917/18) culminates in the "Conclusion: Nature and Spirit as Female and Male Elements" assigning to his formal principles, essentialist gender attributes—with his vertical and horizontal lines representing male and female elements. Mondrian ultimately sought a "female-male equilibrium" through universal abstraction potent enough to symbolize forces in society that, in his mind, had increasingly been steeped in disorder and destabilization. Regarding the past, he thought of traditional representational art as "predominantly female," tied to nature, beauty, and figuration, while the male element embodied spiritual and rational forces. Mondrian's thinking remained steeped in misogynistic notions, including the belief that abstraction was contrary to women's innermost nature. He asserted that "regression is female" and "progression is male," characterizing the feminine as "static, conservative, obstructive," and the masculine as "dynamic."[25] This system of gender attribution ultimately reinforced traditional stereotypes rather than challenging them. Nonetheless, many (queer) women artists were drawn to the Constructivist and Concrete Art movements, whose abstract aesthetics were perceived as gender-transcending, offering a means of liberation from the biases historically attached to women's artistic practice. The Constructivist Marlow Moss was rarely described as anything more than a "disciple" of the older Mondrian and a minor follower of his style. Their position as a queer British artist (from the periphery of the interwar European art centers)

22 Alex Pilcher, *A Queer Little History of Art* (London: Tate, 2017), p. 67.

23 These new developments—especially the perceived "feminization" of society—unleashed disruptive forces that unsettled the established hierarchical gender order, a dynamic that male avant-garde artists often sought to contain, even as their declarations of a radical break with the past fostered expectations of greater inclusivity. F. T. Marinetti openly provoked with his infamous call for "the scorn of woman" in his 1909 *Futurist Manifesto*: "Declaration of Futurism," *Poesia* 5, nos. 3–6 (April–July 1909), pp. 1–2. Marcel Duchamp experimented with gender deception through his Dada drag persona Rrose Sélavy (1921–1923), while Man Ray's and Francis Picabia's mechanomorphic sexual imagery often carried unmistakably misogynist undertones.

24 Piet Mondrian, "The New Plastic in Painting" (1917), in *The New Art—The New Life: The Collected Writings of Piet Mondrian*, ed. and trans. Harry Holtzman and Martin S. James (New York: Da Capo, 1993), pp. 27–74, here p. 67. Twentieth-century modernism was marked by the revival of a "hermaphroditic" culture and the celebration of androgynous or ambiguous gender representations, as reflected in numerous works featured in this exhibition. "Hermaphroditism" is a term now considered obsolete and has been replaced by "intersex." Swiss scholar Magali Le Mens notes that modern artists, in depicting hermaphrodites and androgynous figures, often reinforce "the trap of ambiguity caught within a heteronormative and binary mindset" and that "a system of two well-separated poles, can admit an in-between and an ambiguity." Instead, she draws on intersex activist Vincent Guillot's expanded concept of an "archipelago of gender," which departs from the Western canon of sexual binarity: Le Mens, *Modernité hermaphrodite*, p. 9.

Eine Linie oder ein Quadrat haben kein Geschlecht, es sei denn, solche Kategorien werden diesen formalen Elementen zugeschrieben. Wie der Tate-Kurator Alex Pichler bemerkt: „Die menschliche soziale Welt überzeugt uns weiterhin davon, dass Menschen, Kleidung, Farben und sogar Kunstwerke entweder ‚weiblich‘, ‚männlich‘ oder eine Mischung aus beidem sind. Jede Entscheidung, die wir treffen, wie wir aussehen oder handeln, was wir tragen oder schaffen, wird unter dieser polarisierten Doktrin einer geschlechtsspezifischen Lesart zugewiesen.“[22] Der Diskurs der Abstraktion war in der Tat von seinen programmatischen Anfängen an von Geschlechtszuschreibungen geprägt. Für Mondrian war die Frage der Geschlechter fundamental für die Prinzipien, die seinen Weg zur Abstraktion leiteten. Er erfand ein symbolisches System, das darauf abzielte, sexuelle Kräfte mittels eines ästhetischen Gleichgewichts neu in Einklang zu bringen. Die Veränderung der traditionellen Geschlechterrollen zu Beginn des 20. Jahrhunderts und die erhöhte Sichtbarkeit – aber auch verstärkte Verfolgung – nicht heteronormativer Sexualitäten, angestoßen durch die Auswirkungen des Kriegs sowie durch die neuen Sozial- wie Sexualwissenschaften, spielten eine zentrale Rolle bei der Entstehung der modernen Kunst, ihrer Konzepte, Stile und Agenden.[23] 1917 erklärte Mondrian, dass „der physische Hermaphrodit die Einheit einer ersichtlichen Dualität ist, während der spirituelle Hermaphrodit (das Ideal der antiken Philosophen) die Einheit einer realen Dualität darstellt“[24]. Mondrian entwickelte seine abstrakte Sprache mit strenger Präzision, indem er diese auf die minimale Verwendung von vertikalen und horizontalen Linien reduzierte, die im rechten Winkel aufeinandertreffen – ohne Platz für die Kurve – und sich auf die Primärfarben beschränkte. Sein Pamphlet über den „Neoplastizismus in der Malerei“ (1917/18) kulminiert in der „Schlussfolgerung: Natur und Geist als weibliche und männliche Elemente“, in der er seinen formalen Prinzipien essenzialistische Geschlechterattribute zuweist – wobei seine vertikalen und horizontalen Linien männliche und weibliche Elemente repräsentieren sollen. Mondrian strebte letztlich ein „weiblich-männliches Equilibrium“ durch universelle Abstraktion an, fähig, Kräfte in der Gesellschaft zu symbolisieren, die seiner Meinung nach zunehmend von Unordnung und Destabilisierung geprägt waren. Mit Hinblick auf die Vergangenheit betrachtete er die traditionelle repräsentative Kunst als „vorwiegend weiblich“, verbunden mit Natur, Schönheit und Figuration, während das männliche Element geistige und rationale Kräfte verkörperte. Mondrians Denken blieb von misogynen Vorstellungen durchzogen, einschließlich der Überzeugung, dass Abstraktion im Widerspruch zur innersten Natur der Frauen stand. Er behauptete, dass „Rückschritt weiblich“ und „Fortschritt männlich“ sei, wobei er das Weibliche als „statisch, konservativ, hemmend“ und das Männliche als „dynamisch“ charakterisierte.[25] Dieses System der Geschlechterzuschreibung verstärkte letztlich traditionelle Stereotype, anstatt sie herauszufordern. Nichtsdestotrotz fühlten sich viele (queere) Künstler*innen von den konstruktivistischen und konkreten Kunstbewegungen angezogen, deren abstrakte Ästhetik als geschlechtstranszendierend wahrgenommen wurde und ein Mittel zur Befreiung von den

22 Alex Pilcher, *A Queer Little History of Art*, London 2017, S. 67.

23 Diese neuen Entwicklungen – insbesondere die rezipierte „Feminisierung“ der Gesellschaft – setzten soziale Kräfte frei, die die etablierte hierarchische Geschlechterordnung ins Wanken brachten, eine Dynamik, die männliche Avantgardekünstler oft zu kontrollieren versuchten, auch wenn ihre Erklärungen eines radikalen Bruchs mit der Vergangenheit Erwartungen an eine größere Inklusivität schürten. F. T. Marinetti provozierte offen mit seinem berüchtigten Aufruf zur „Verachtung der Frau“ in seinem *Manifesto del Futurismo* von 1909, in: *LE FIGARO*, 20. Februar 1909. Marcel Duchamp experimentierte mit Geschlechtertäuschung in seiner Dada-Drag-Persona *Rrose Sélavy* (1921–1923), während Man Rays und Francis Picabias *mechanomorphe* sexuelle Bilder oft unverkennbar misogyne Untertöne trugen.

24 Piet Mondrian, „The New Plastic in Painting“ (1917), in: *The New Art – The New Life: The Collected Writings of Piet Mondrian*, hrsg. und übersetzt von Harry Holtzman und Martin S. James, New York 1993, S. 27–74, hier: S. 67. Der Modernismus des 20. Jahrhunderts war geprägt von der Wiederbelebung einer „hermaphroditischen“ Kultur und dem Zelebrieren androgyner oder ambivalenter Geschlechterdarstellungen, wie sie in zahlreichen Werken zu sehen sind, die in dieser Ausstellung präsentiert werden. „Hermaphroditismus“ ist ein Begriff, der heute als nicht mehr adäquat gilt und durch „Intergeschlechtlichkeit“ ersetzt wurde. Die Schweizer Wissenschaftlerin Magali Le Mens merkt an, dass moderne Künstler*innen, die Hermaphroditen und androgyne Figuren darstellen, oft „die Falle der Ambiguität verstärken, die in einer heteronormativen und binären Denkweise gefangen ist“, und dass „ein System von zwei gut getrennten Polen

limited an unbiased reading of their work by critics and peers alike.[26]

Moss's life partner, Antoinette Hendrika "Netty" Nijhoff, recalled the artist's declaration during their transformation in the early 1920s, when they changed their name from Marjorie to Marlow and embarked on a radically new artistic path: "I destroyed my old personality and created a new one."[27] It reflects the impetus Moss placed on the power of constructing one's own identity as much as one's art. The recent rediscovery of Marlow Moss has sparked renewed interest, particularly among a younger generation of scholars and curators. Their appearance, marked by a consistent choice to dress in the modernized style of an English country gent, has been variously described as "fairly masculine" or "completely androgynous." However, as American scholar Laura Cottingham argues, such characterizations often rely on conservative assumptions. The more compelling question, she contends, is what difference the lesbianism of artists like Moss or Claude Cahun brought to their processes of self-representation.[28] American scholar Jessica Schouela, meanwhile, asks to what extent Moss's "transgender identity is echoed in certain formal aspects of her abstract work."[29]

Moss's partner A. H. Nijhoff, a Dutch poet and novelist, published her debut novel *Twee meisjes en ik (Two Girls and I)* in 1930, a year after meeting Moss in Paris. Lived experience, as Moss emphasized, was always the source of inspiration for Nijhoff's writings—along with her emotional and intellectual partnership with the British artist, whose theories on abstraction she engaged with deeply. "Netty" Nijhoff introduced Moss to Piet Mondrian, Theo van Doesburg, and other members of the De Stijl circle. From that point on, Moss devoted themself to Neo-Plasticism and entered into close dialogue with Mondrian. Drawing on scientific, methodical analysis, they introduced the "double line" as a dynamic compositional element, an innovation that Mondrian would soon adopt without crediting his peer.[30] In recent scholarship, the double line in Moss's work has been interpreted as a queering of Constructivism, disrupting Mondrian's rigid orthogonal gender axis, in which horizontal and vertical lines were meant to symbolize "female" and "male" elements, respectively. Moss's double line introduces a notion of "sameness," further suggesting equality and mutual reinforcement. Its inherent rhythm, as Magali Le Mens emphasizes, serves to destabilize the pure and fixed expression of oppositional relationships.[31] In *Untitled (White, Black, Blue and Yellow)* (ca. 1954, cat. p. 141), Moss introduces a floating black square—detached from the surrounding composition—as a strikingly autonomous element. Instead of an intersection created by the crossing of opposing lines, Moss, by contrast, conceives in their composition an entirely independent point, unanchored by linear contact, serving as yet another disruptive gesture in their reimagining of Neo-Plasticism.

The now-lost, enigmatic twin sculpture *Egg-Shaped and Cylindrical Form on a Pentagonal Base* (1956/57, fig. 5) may well support the argument for Moss's queer investment in abstraction. The two in fact identical shapes can convey surprisingly opposing qualities. Depending on the angle from

25 Robert P. Welsh and J. M. Joosten, *Two Mondrian Sketchbooks, 1912–1914* (Amsterdam: Meulenhoff/Landshoff, 1987), pp. 14–16.

26 In a 1934 edition of the avant-garde magazine *Abstraction-Création*, Moss appealed to "the lay spectator [...] to look at my work without prejudice." *Abstraction-Création: Art Non-Figuratif*, no. 3 (Paris, 1934).

27 Marlow Moss, quoted from memory by A. H. Nijhoff, *Marlow Moss*, exh. cat. (Amsterdam: Stedelijk Museum, 1962), n.p.

28 Laura Cottingham, "Considering Claude Cahun," in *Seeing through the Seventies: Essays on Feminism and Art* (London: Routledge, 2000), p. 193.

29 Jessica Schouela, "Marlow Moss," *Woman's Art Journal* 39, no. 2 (Fall/Winter 2018): pp. 34–42, here p. 34.

30 Moss employed strictly mathematical methods to generate their compositions and never publicly commented on the symbolic meaning of their formal elements. It can be assumed, however, that they were well aware of Mondrian's gender-essentializing theories.

31 Le Mens, *Modernité hermaphrodite*, p. 690.

historischen Vorurteilen bot, die der künstlerischen Praxis von Frauen anhafteten. Die*Der konstruktivistische Künstler*in Marlow Moss wurde zumeist als „Schüler*in" des älteren Mondrian und untergeordnete Anhänger*in seines Stils beschrieben. Ihre*Seine Position als queere*r britische Künstler*in (damals noch als von der Peripherie der europäischen Kunstzentren aus betrachtet) schränkte eine unvoreingenommene Lesart ihres*seines Werks sowohl durch Kritiker*innen als auch durch Kolleg*innen ein.[26] Die Lebensgefährtin von Moss, Antoinette Hendrika „Netty" Nijhoff, eine niederländische Dichterin und Romanautorin, erinnerte sich an die Erklärung während ihrer*seiner Transformation in den frühen 1920er-Jahren, als sie*er ihren*seinen Namen in Marlow änderte und einen radikal neuen künstlerischen Weg einschlug: „Ich zerstörte meine alte Persönlichkeit und erschuf eine neue."[27] Dies spiegelt den starken Drang von Moss wieder, die eigene Identität ebenso wie die eigene Kunst neu zu konstruieren. Die jüngste kunsthistorische und museale Wiedereinführung des Werks von Moss als auch seine*ihre queere Selbstdarstellung hat ein erneutes Interesse geweckt, insbesondere bei einer jüngeren Generation von Wissenschaftler*innen und Kurator*innen. Ihr*Sein Auftreten, sich konsequent im modernisierten Stil eines englischen Landaristokraten zu kleiden, wurde als „ziemlich männlich" oder „völlig androgyn" beschrieben. Wie die amerikanische Wissenschaftlerin Laura Cottingham jedoch argumentiert, basieren solche Charakterisierungen oft auf konservativen Annahmen. Die überzeugendere Frage, so Cottingham, ist, welchen Einfluss die lesbische Identität von Künstler*innen wie Moss oder Claude Cahun auf Prozesse der Selbstrepräsentation hatte.[28] Die amerikanische Wissenschaftlerin Jessica Schouela fragt unterdessen, inwieweit Moss' „transgender Identität in bestimmten formalen Aspekten ihres abstrakten Werks widerhallt"[29]. Nijhoff veröffentlichte ihren Debütroman *Twee meisjes en ik (Zwei Mädchen und ich)* unter den genderneutralen Initialen A. H. Nijhoff im Jahr 1930, ein Jahr, nachdem sie Moss in Paris kennengelernt hatte. Gelebte Erfahrung war, wie Moss einmal hervorhob, immer die Inspirationsquelle für Nijhoffs Schriften, ebenso wie die emotionale und intellektuelle Partnerschaft mit der britischen Künstler*in, mit deren*dessen Theorien zur Abstraktion sie sich intensiv auseinandersetzte. Nijhoff führte Moss in den Kreis von Mondrian, Theo van Doesburg und anderen Mitgliedern des De-Stijl-Zirkels ein. Ab diesem Zeitpunkt widmete sich Moss dem Neoplastizismus und trat in einen engen Dialog mit Mondrian. Auf der Grundlage wissenschaftlicher, methodischer Analysen führte Moss die „doppelte Linie" als dynamisches kompositorisches Element ein, eine Innovation, die Mondrian bald ohne Anerkennung seiner Kolleg*in übernahm.[30]

In der jüngsten wissenschaftlichen Auseinandersetzung wurde die doppelte Linie in Moss' Werk als eine queere Wendung des Konstruktivismus verstanden, die Mondrians rigide Geschlechterachse aufbricht und bei der horizontale und vertikale Linien „weibliche" bzw. „männliche" Elemente symbolisieren sollten. Moss' doppelte Linie führt einen Begriff von „Gleichheit" ein, der des Weiteren Gleichwertigkeit und gegenseitige Verstärkung suggeriert. Der inhärente Rhythmus in Moss' Kompositionen, wie Magali Le Mens betont, destabilisiert einen fixierten Ausdruck oppositioneller Beziehungen.[31] In *Untitled (White, Black, Blue, and Yellow)* (um 1954, Kat., S. 141) führt Moss ein schwebendes schwarzes Quadrat

ein Dazwischen und eine Ambiguität zulassen kann". Stattdessen stützt sie sich auf das erweiterte Konzept des „Archipels der Geschlechter" des Intersex-Aktivisten Vincent Guillot, dass sich vom westlichen Kanon der sexuellen Binarität entfernt: Le Mens 2019 (wie Anm. 3), S. 9.

25 Robert P. Welsh and J. M. Joosten, *Two Mondrian Sketchbooks, 1912–1914*, Amsterdam 1987, S. 14–16.

26 In einer Ausgabe des avantgardistischen Magazins *abstraction création* von 1934 appellierte Moss an „den laienhaften Betrachter […], mein Werk ohne Vorurteile zu betrachten." *abstraction création: art non-figuratif*, Nr. 3, Paris 1934.

27 Marlow Moss, zit. aus dem Gedächtnis von Antoinette Hendrika Nijhoff, *Marlow Moss*, Ausst.-Kat. Stedelijk Museum Amsterdam, Amsterdam 1962), o. S.

28 Laura Cottingham, „Considering Claude Cahun", in: *Seeing through the Seventies: Essays on Feminism and Art*, London 2000, S. 193.

29 Jessica Schouela, „Marlow Moss", in: *Woman's Art Journal* 39, Nr. 2, Herbst/Winter 2018, S. 34–42, hier: S. 34.

30 Moss verwendete strikt mathematische Methoden für die Kompositionen und kommentierte nie öffentlich die symbolische Bedeutung der formalen Elemente. Es kann jedoch angenommen werden, dass sie*er sich der geschlechtsspezifischen Theorien von Mondrian sehr wohl bewusst war.

31 Le Mens 2019 (wie Anm. 3), S. 690.

which they are viewed, the forms appear either as a harmoniously connected pair or as locked in a confrontational relation.

Alex Pilcher finally observes, "Is it legitimate to wonder whether Moss consciously 'wore' hard-edged abstraction—much like the favored tailored jackets, cravats and jodhpurs—as a strategy to disrupt the gender first assigned to the artist?"[32]

32 Pilcher, *A Queer Little History of Art*, p. 67.

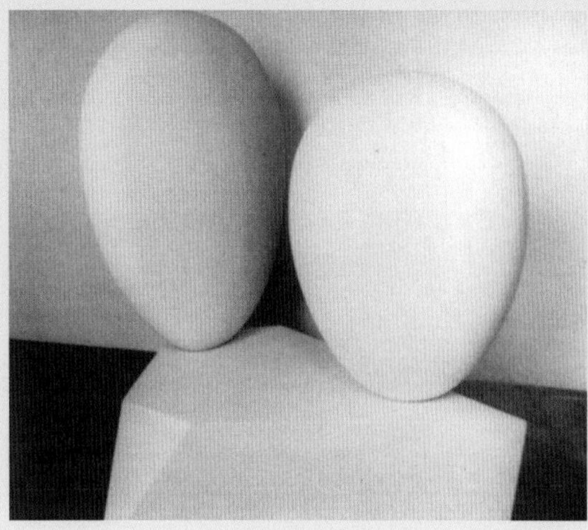

ABB. ~ FIG. 5

Marlow Moss, *Egg-Shaped and Cylindrical Form on a Pentagonal Base*, 1956/57
Ei-runde und zylindrische Form auf fünfeckigem Sockel

Verbleib unbekannt ~ *whereabout unknown*

ein – losgelöst von der umgebenden Konstruktion – als auffallend autonomes Element. Statt einer durch die Überkreuzung von sich entgegenstehenden Linien erzeugten Schnittstelle konzipiert Moss in dieser Komposition einen völlig unabhängigen Punkt, der nicht durch linearen Kontakt verankert ist, und damit ein weiteres radikal neues Element in ihrer Neuinterpretation des Neoplastizismus. Die mittlerweile verlorene, enigmatische Zwillingsskulptur *Egg-Shaped and Cylindrical Form on a Pentagonal Base* (1956/57, Abb. 5) könnte das Argument für Moss' queere Investition in die Abstraktion stützen. Die beiden tatsächlich identischen Formen können überraschend gegensätzliche Qualitäten vermitteln. Je nach Blickwinkel erscheinen die Formen entweder als harmonisch verbundenes Paar oder als in einer konfrontativen Beziehung zueinander stehend. Alex Pilcher stellt schließlich fest: „Ist es legitim zu fragen, ob Moss bewusst die harte Abstraktion ‚trug' – ähnlich wie die bevorzugten maßgeschneiderten Jacken, Krawatten und Jodhpurhosen – als eine Strategie, um in das Geschlecht zu intervenieren, das der*dem Künstler*in ursprünglich zugewiesen wurde?"[32]

32 Pilcher 2017 (wie Anm. 22), S. 67.

VI QUEERE AVANTGARDEN UND INTIME NETZWERKE

QUEER AVANT-GARDES AND INTIMATE NETWORKS

2

1

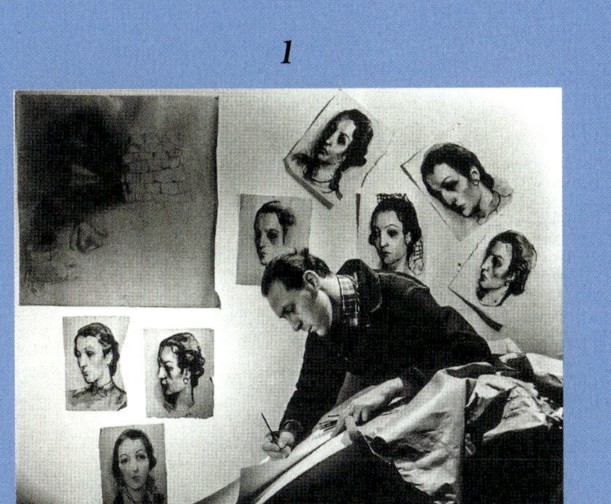

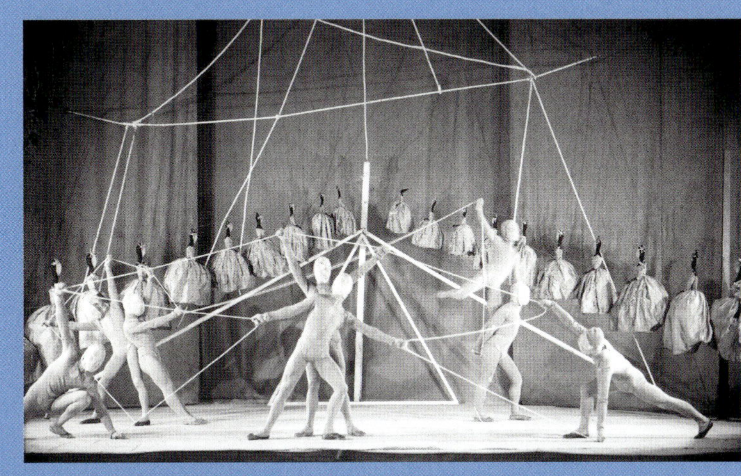

4

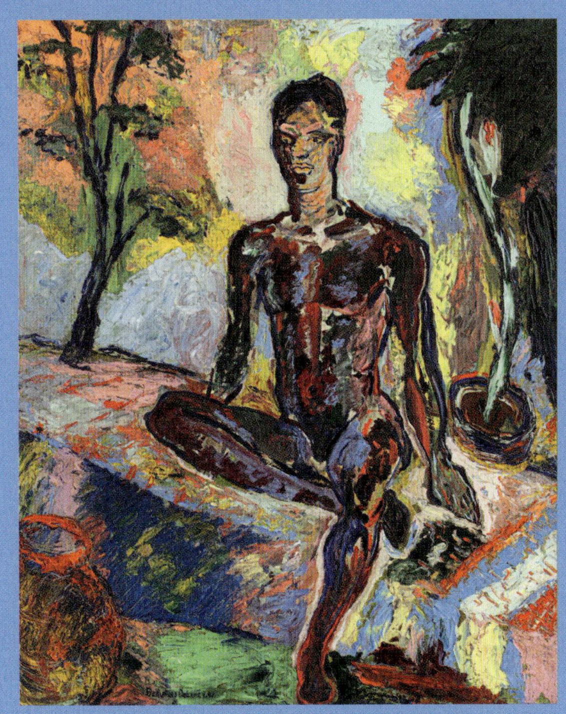

6

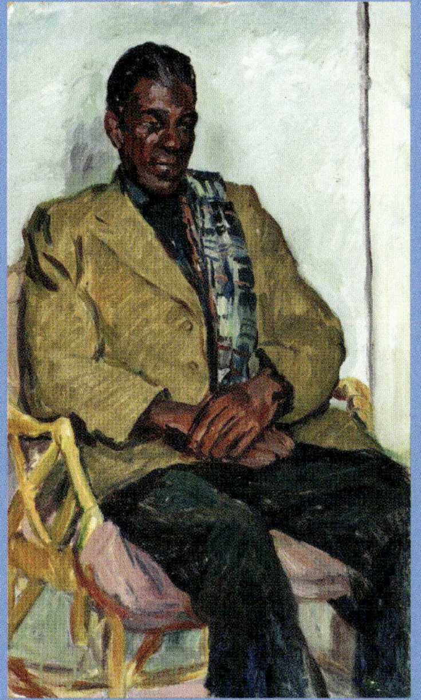

3

View
december 75c
series iii, no. 4

5

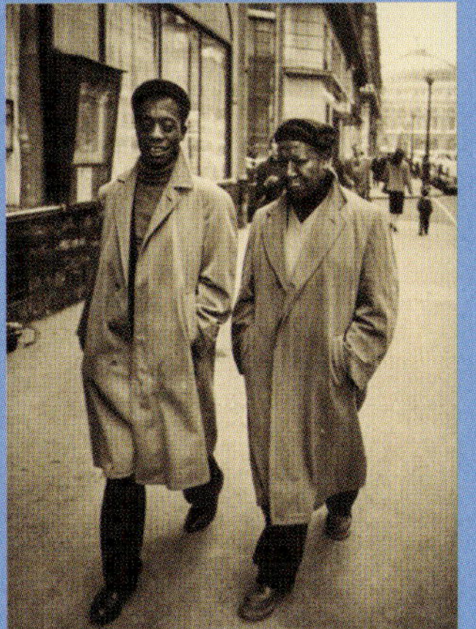

1

Pavel Tchelitchew, Foto von Cecil Beaton, 1936

~

Pavel Tchelitchew, photograph by Cecil Beaton, 1936

2

Ode, Ballets Russes de Diaghilev, Paris 1928, Bühnendesign: Pavel Tchelitchew

Der russische Exilkünstler vernetzte in Léonide Massines Ballet die Körper der Tänzer*innen zu einer Geometrie, die auf Sternenkonstellationen beruhte. Zuvor hatte er die Figuren in seinen Gemälden mit kosmischen Netzen überzogen.

~

Ode, *Ballets Russes de Diaghilev, Paris, 1928, stage design: Pavel Tchelitchew*

For Léonide Massine's ballet choreography, the Russian émigré artist linked the dancers' bodies into a geometry inspired by star constellations. This echoed his earlier paintings, in which he overlaid figures with cosmic nets.

3

Die Avantgardezeitschrift *View* (New York, 1940–1947), herausgegeben von Charles Henri Ford und Tyler Parker. Titelbild: Pavel Tchelitchew

~

The avant-garde magazine View *(New York, 1940–1947), edited by Charles Henri Ford and Tyler Parker. Cover illustration: Pavel Tchelitchew*

4

Beauford Delaney, *Dark Rapture (James Baldwin)*, 1941, Collection of halley k harrisburg and Michael Rosenfeld, New York

Delaneys Aktporträt seines Freundes Baldwin verweist „auf die *racial distinction* in einer bejahenden und begehrenden Weise, während ‚rapture' ein emotionales Gefühl intensiver spiritueller Freude andeutet." (James Smalls, „Queer Harlem: Gay Sociability and Transatlantic Modernism", in: *The Harlem Renaissance and Transatlantic Modernism*, hrsg. von Denise Murrell, Ausst.-Kat. The Metropolitan Museum of Art, New York, New York 2024. S. 93)

~

Beauford Delaney, Dark Rapture (James Baldwin), *1941, Collection of halley k harrisburg and Michael Rosenfeld, New York*

Delaney's nude portrait of his friend James Baldwin signals "racial distinction in an affirming and desirous way, whereas 'rapture' connotes an emotional feeling of intense spiritual pleasure." (James Smalls, "Queer Harlem: Gay Sociability and Transatlantic Modernism," in The Harlem Renaissance and Transatlantic Modernism, *ed. Denise Murrell, exh. cat. [New York: Metropolitan Museum of Art, 2024], p. 93)*

5

James Baldwin und Beauford Delaney, Paris, um 1960

~

James Baldwin and Beauford Delaney, Paris, ca. 1960

6

Duncan Grant, *Portrait of Pat Nelson*, 1960–1963

Der britische Maler Duncan Grant widmete dem jamaikanischen Jurastudenten Patrick Nelson dieses Respekt zollende Porträt aus den späten 1960er-Jahren. Nelson war Grants Liebhaber sowie vor dem Zweiten Weltkrieg ein häufiger Gast der Londoner Bloomsbury Group.

~

Duncan Grant, Portrait of Pat Nelson, *1960–1963*

The British painter Duncan Grant respectfully dedicated this portrait from the early 1960s to the former Jamaican law student Patrick Nelson. Nelson had been Grant's lover and a frequent guest of the London-based Bloomsbury Group in the late 1930s until the outbreak of war.

Ich habe von Beauford Delaney etwas über Licht gelernt, über das Licht, das in allem steckt, in jeder Oberfläche, in jedem Gesicht.

I learned about light from Beauford Delaney, the light contained in everything, in every surface, in every face.

James Baldwin, „Introduction to Exhibition of Beauford Delaney Opening December 4, 1964 at the Gallery Lambert", in: *Beauford Delaney: A Retrospective*, Ausst.-Kat. New York: Studio Museum in Harlem, New York 1978, S. 20–22.

James Baldwin, "Introduction to Exhibition of Beauford Delaney Opening December 4, 1964 at the Gallery Lambert," in Beauford Delaney: A Retrospective, *exh. cat. (New York: Studio Museum in Harlem, 1978), pp. 20–22.*

VI

QUEERE AVANTGARDEN UND INTIME NETZWERKE

~

QUEER AVANT-GARDES AND INTIMATE NETWORKS

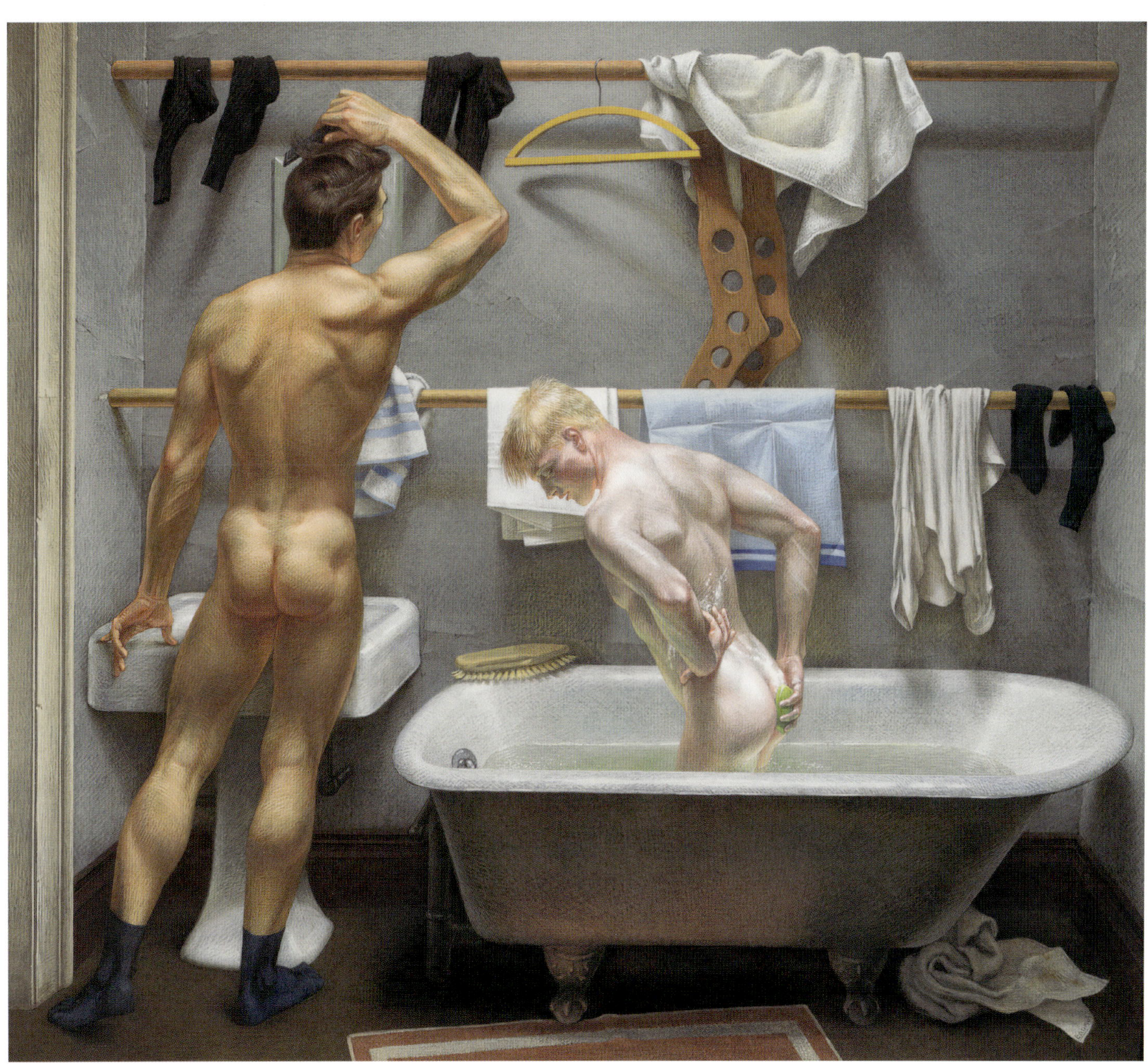

Paul Cadmus
The Bath, 1951
Das Bad

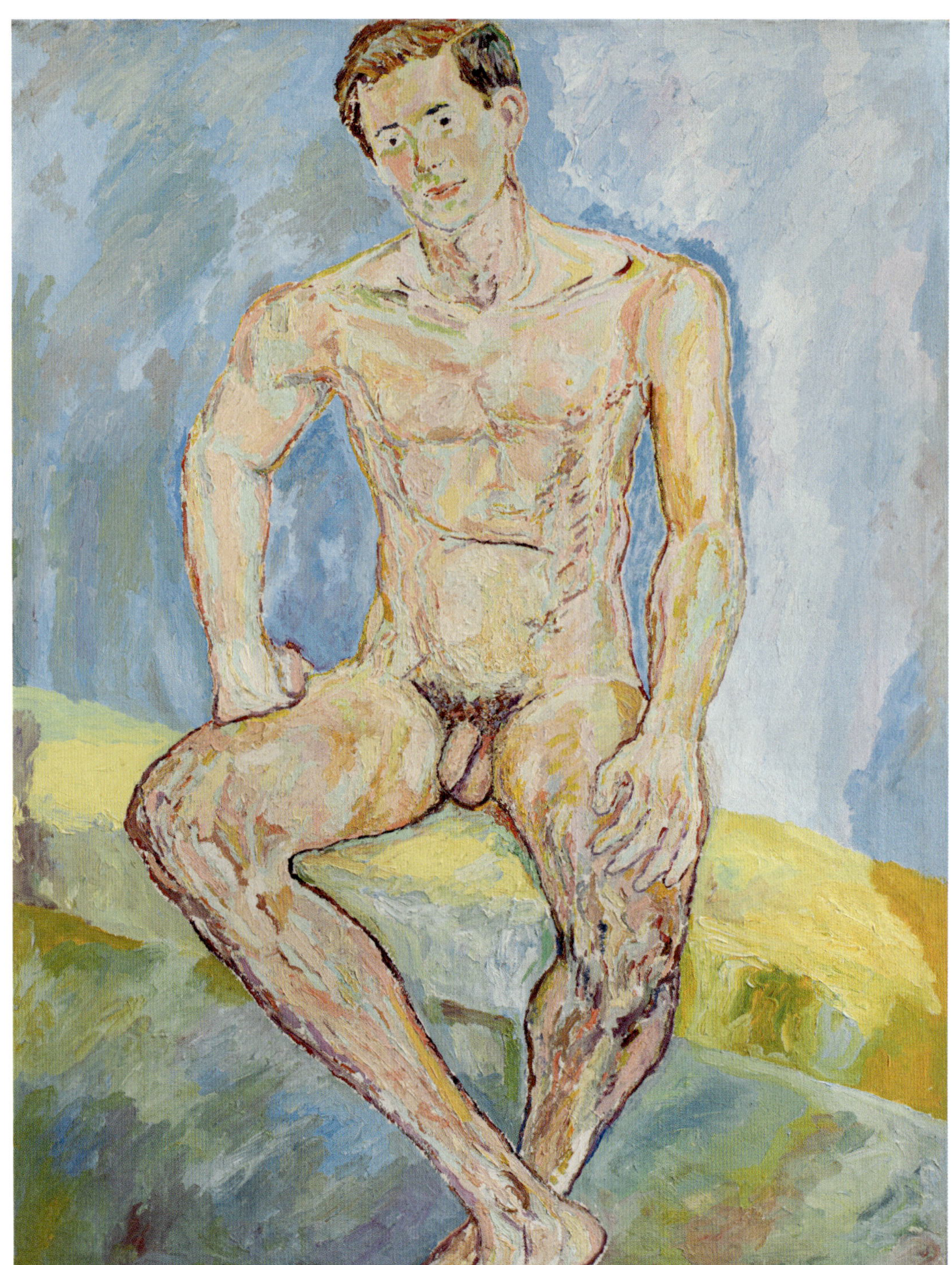

VI

QUEERE AVANTGARDEN UND INTIME NETZWERKE

QUEER AVANT-GARDES AND INTIMATE NETWORKS

Beauford Delaney
Untitled, um ~ *ca.* 1940
Ohne Titel

Duncan Grant
Male Nude (Pat Nelson), 1930
Männlicher Akt (Pat Nelson)

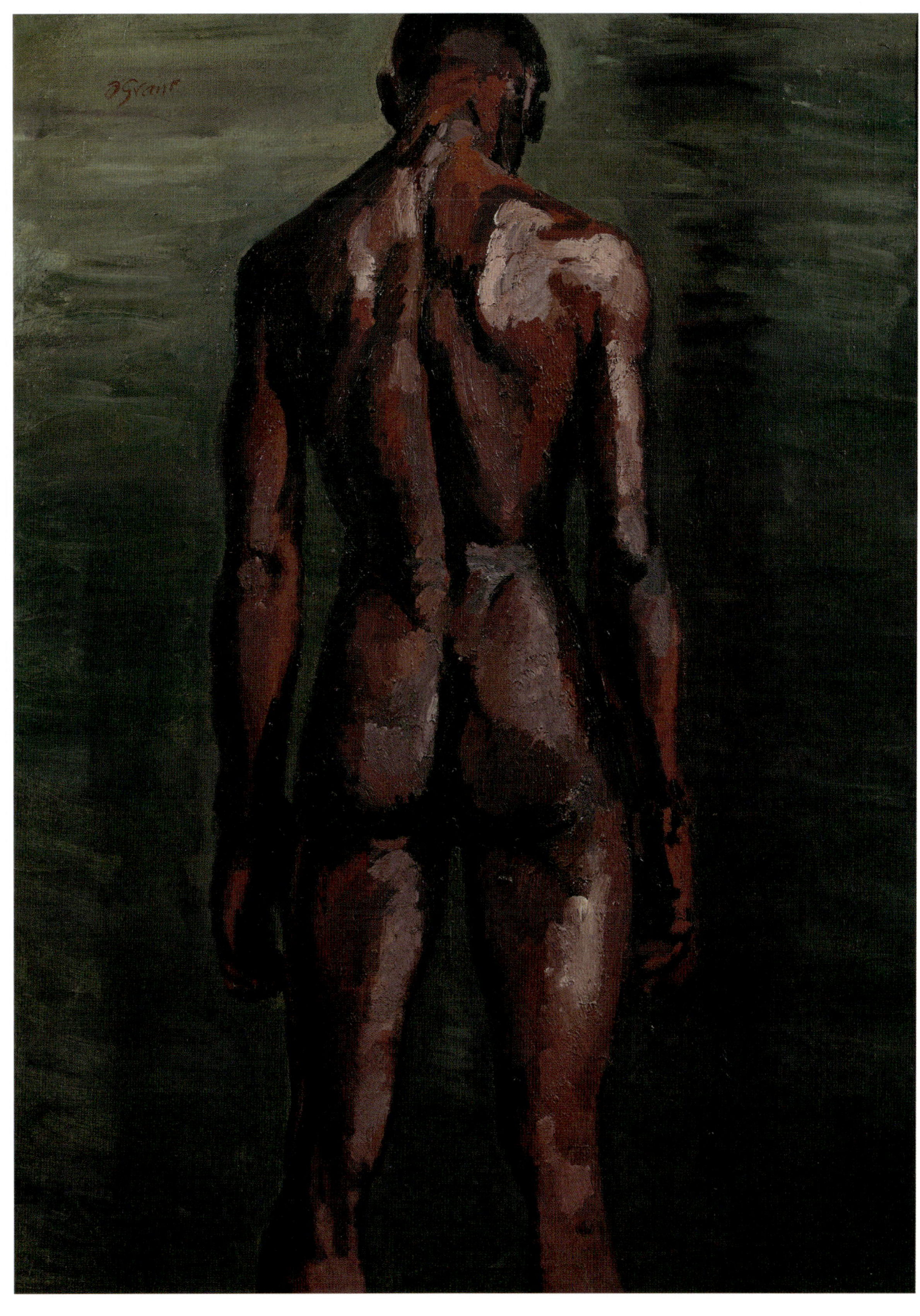

VI

QUEERE AVANTGARDEN UND INTIME NETZWERKE

~

QUEER AVANT-GARDES AND INTIMATE NETWORKS

Henry Scott Tuke
The Critics, 1927
Die Kritiker

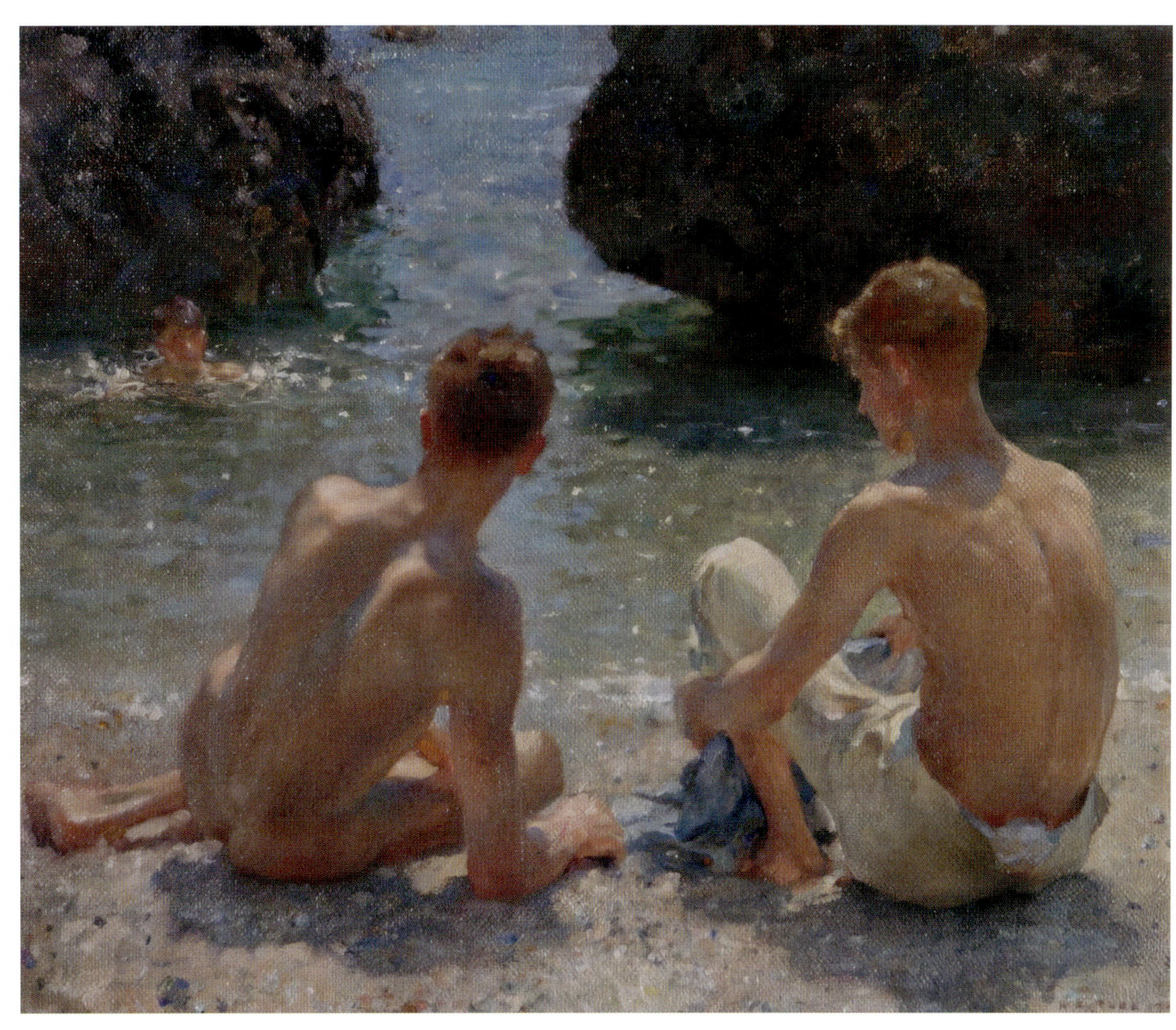

Nils Dardel

Visit hos excentrisk dam, 1921
Besuch bei einer exzentrischen Dame ~
Visit to an Eccentric Lady

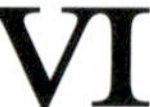

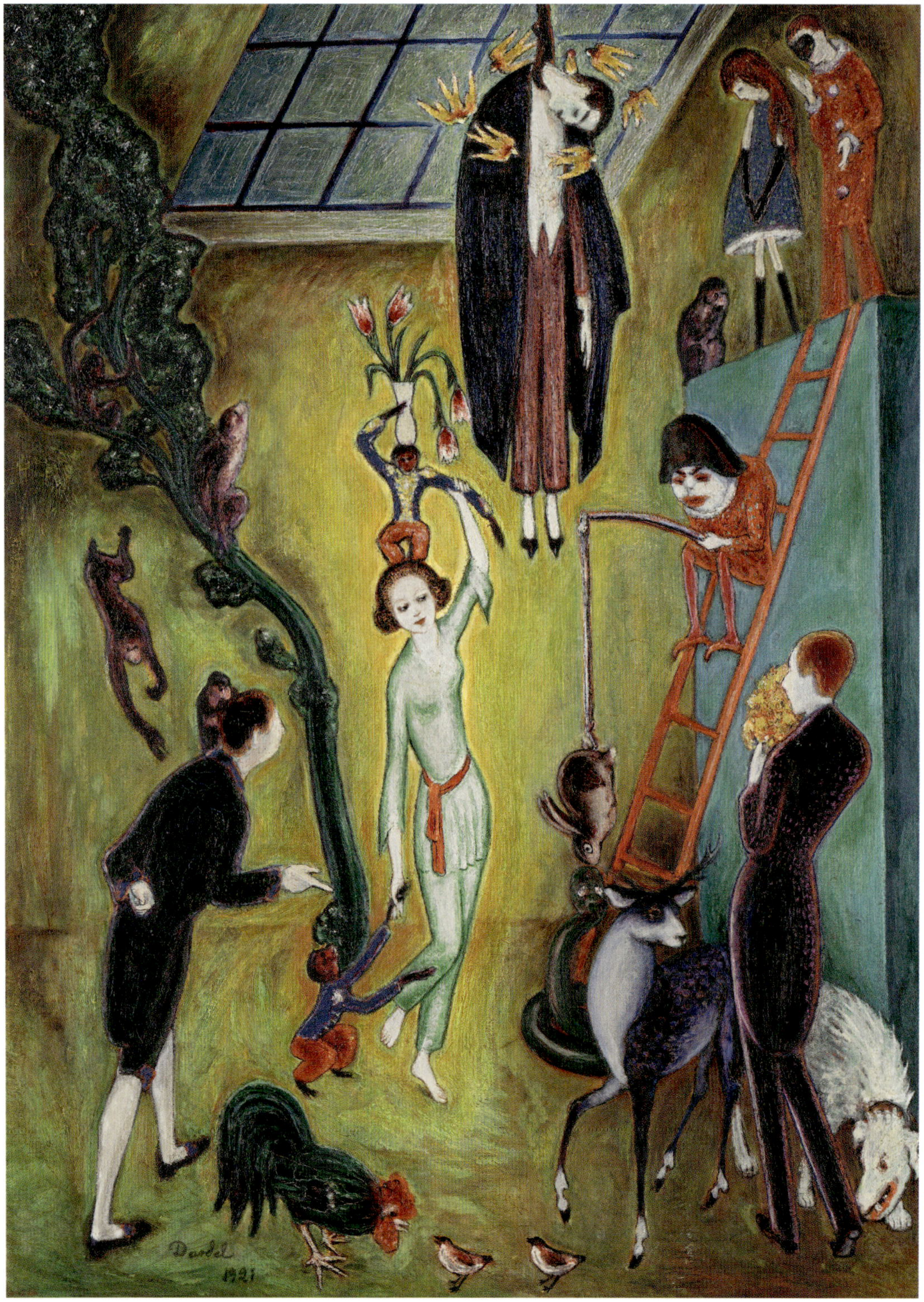

VI

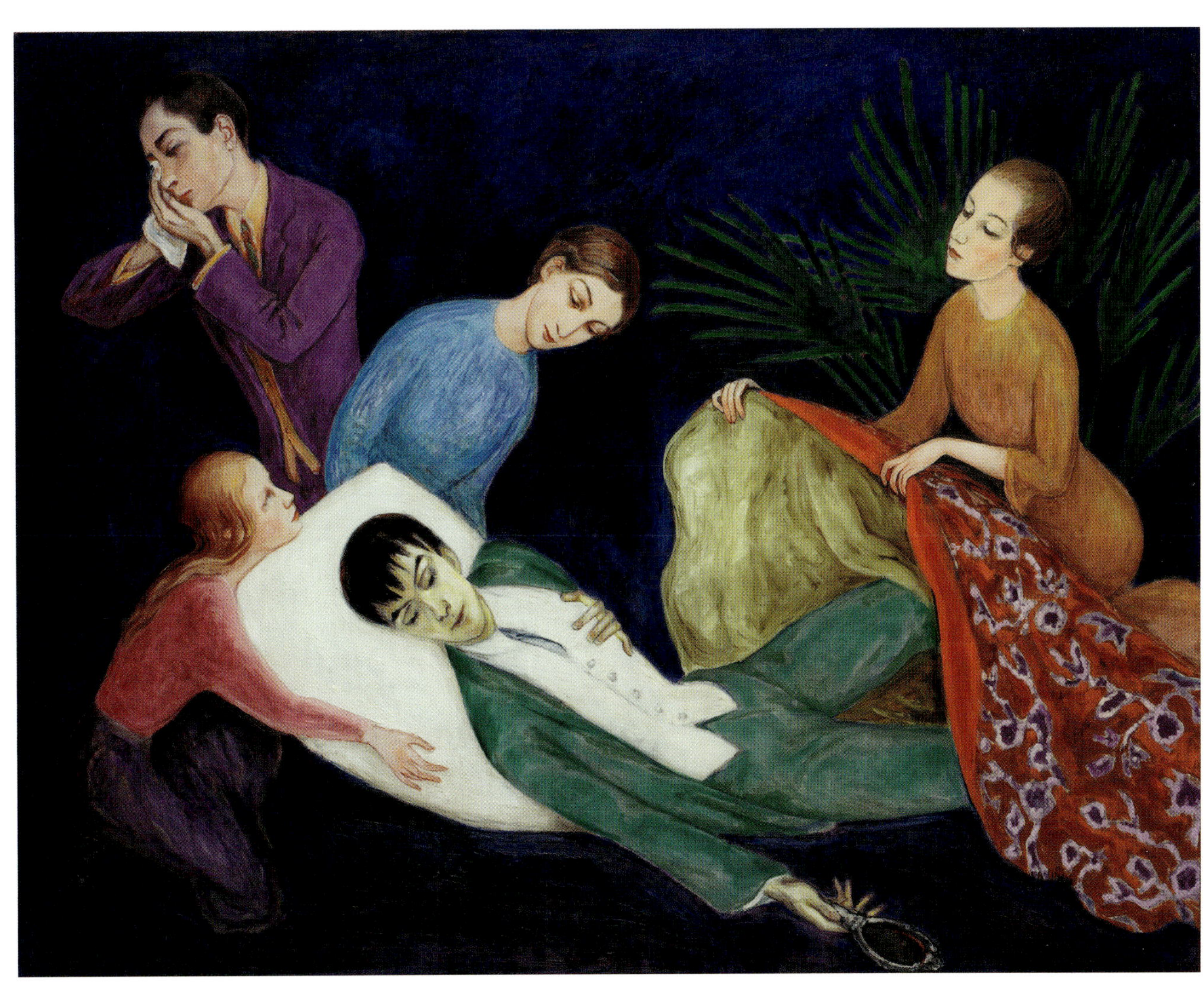

Nils Dardel
Den döende dandyn, 1918
Der sterbende Dandy ~
The Dying Dandy

VI

QUEERE AVANTGARDEN UND INTIME NETZWERKE

QUEER AVANT-GARDES AND INTIMATE NETWORKS

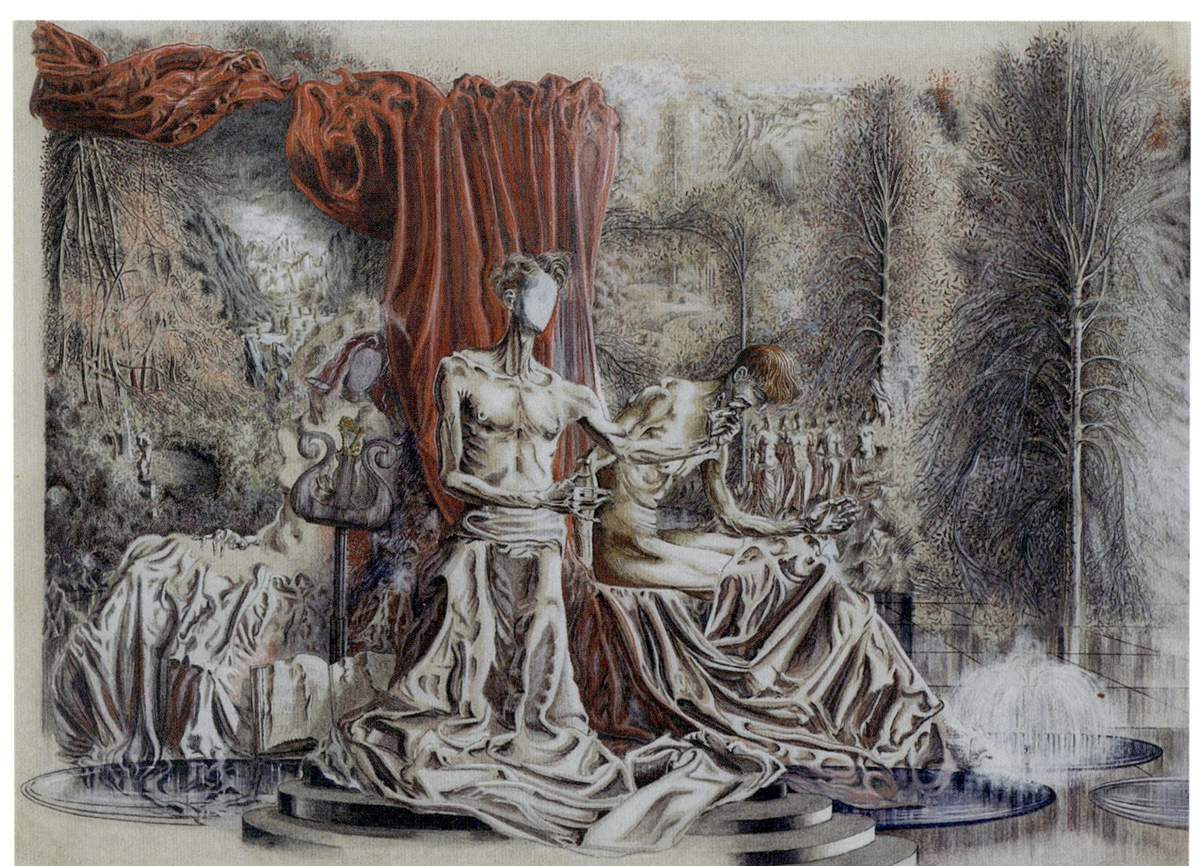

Robin Ironside
Rossetti's Willowwood, um ~ *ca.* 1944
Rossettis Weidenwald

Robin Ironside

Death Bed, 1949/50

Totenbett

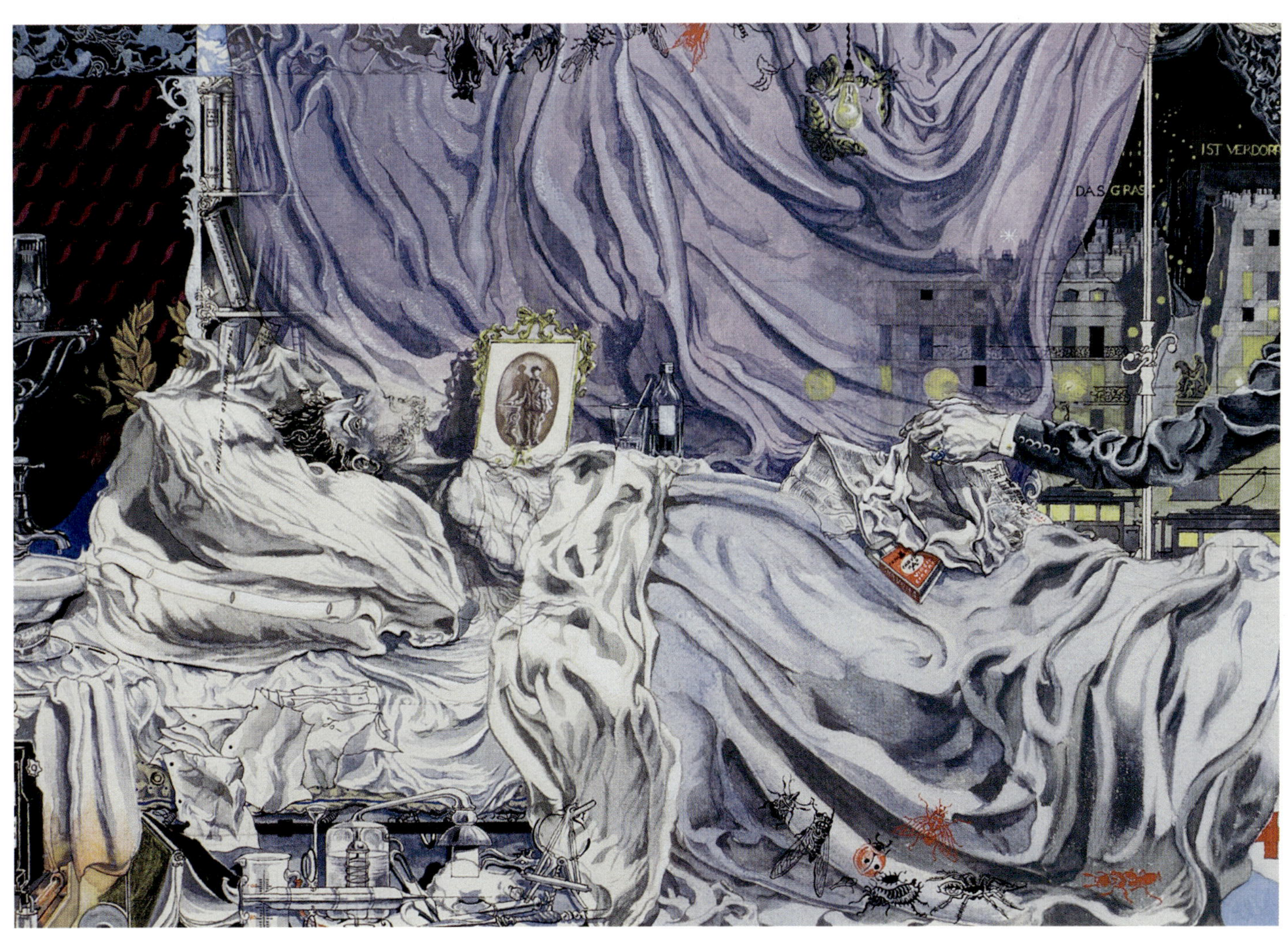

Robin Ironside

Escaping from the Hospital, um ~ *ca.* 1951
Flucht aus dem Krankenhaus

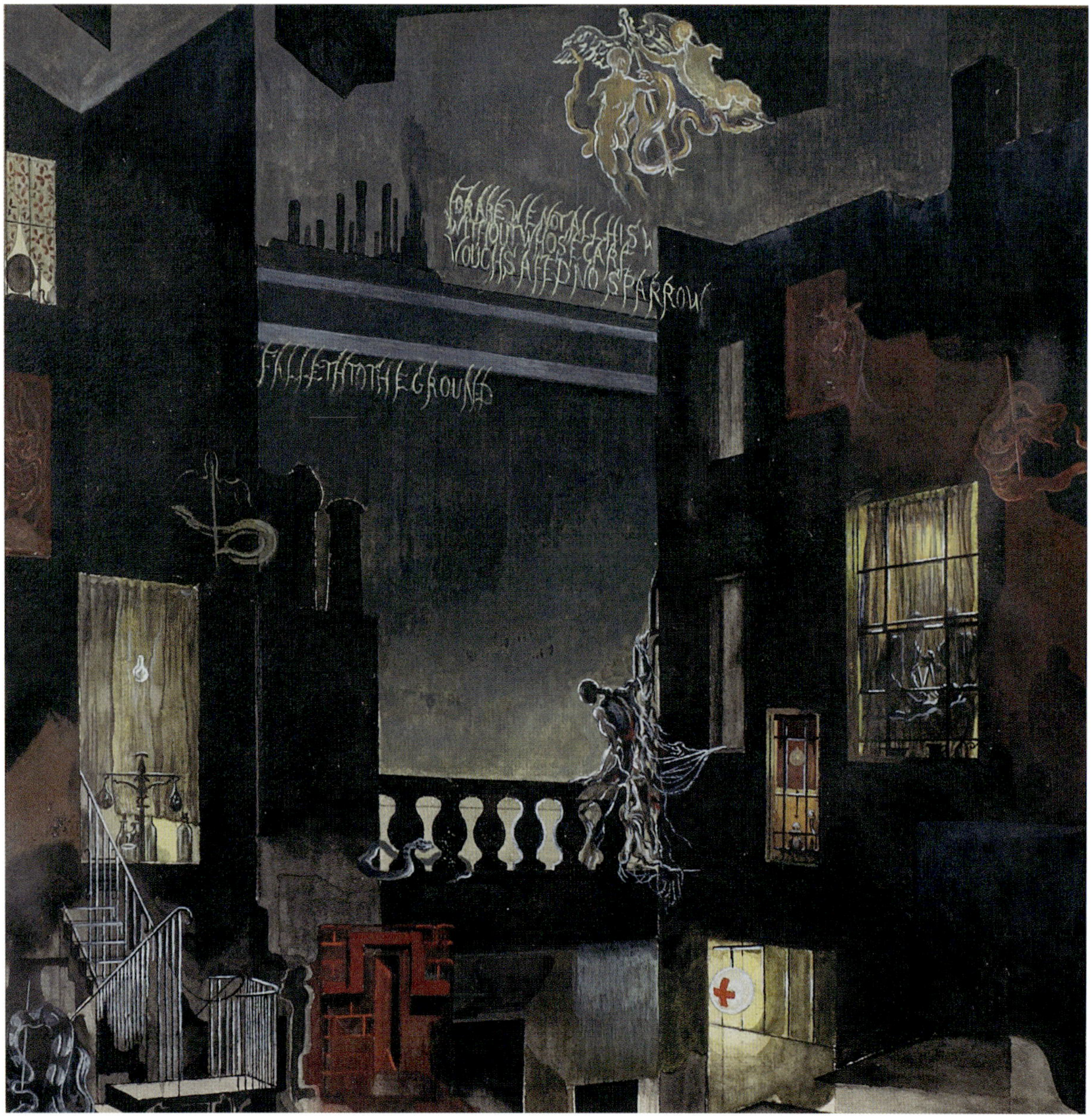

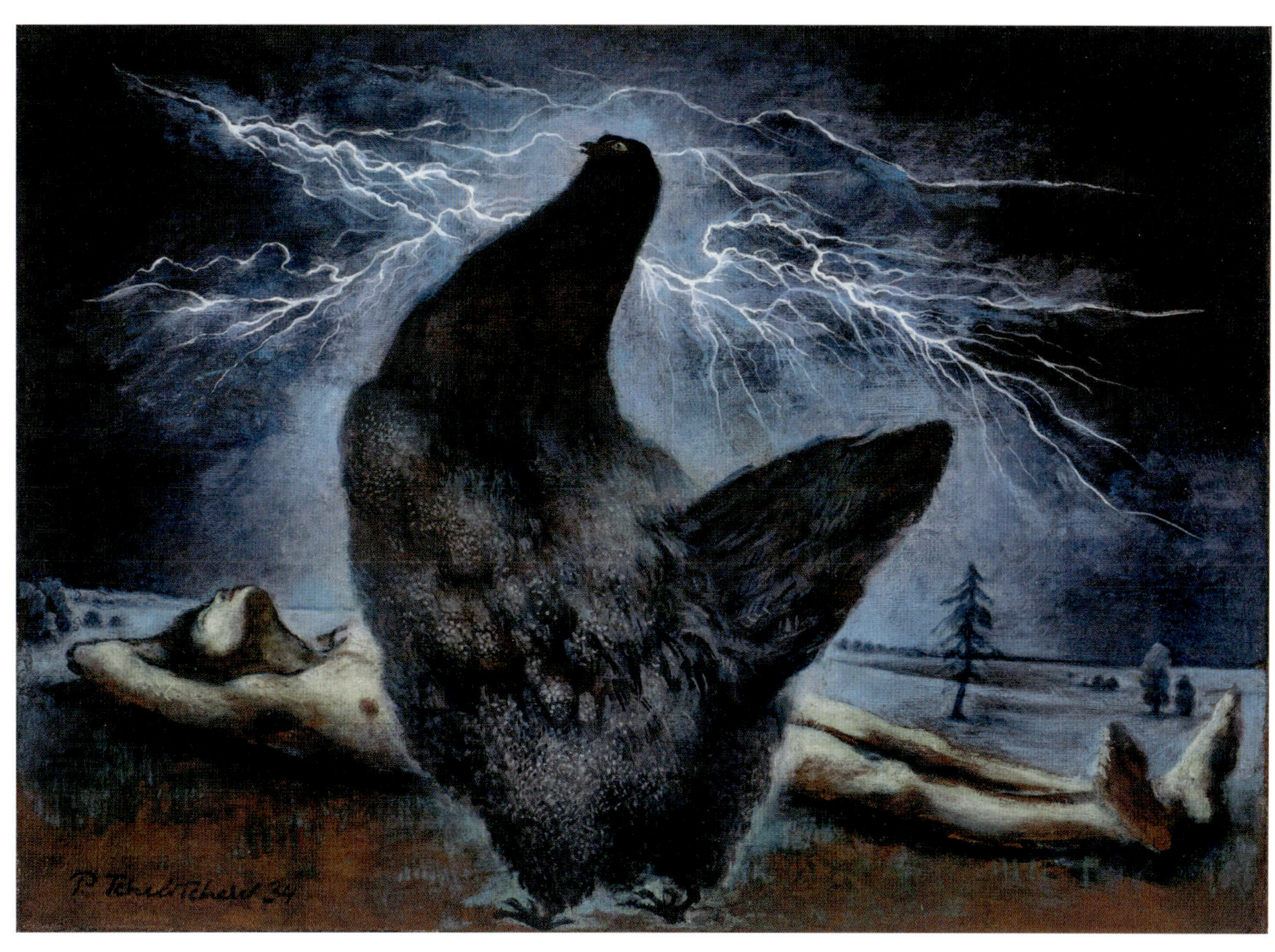

Pavel Tchelîtchew

The Hen and the Man, 1934

Die Henne und der Mann

VI

QUEERE AVANTGARDEN UND INTIME NETZWERKE

QUEER AVANT-GARDES AND INTIMATE NETWORKS

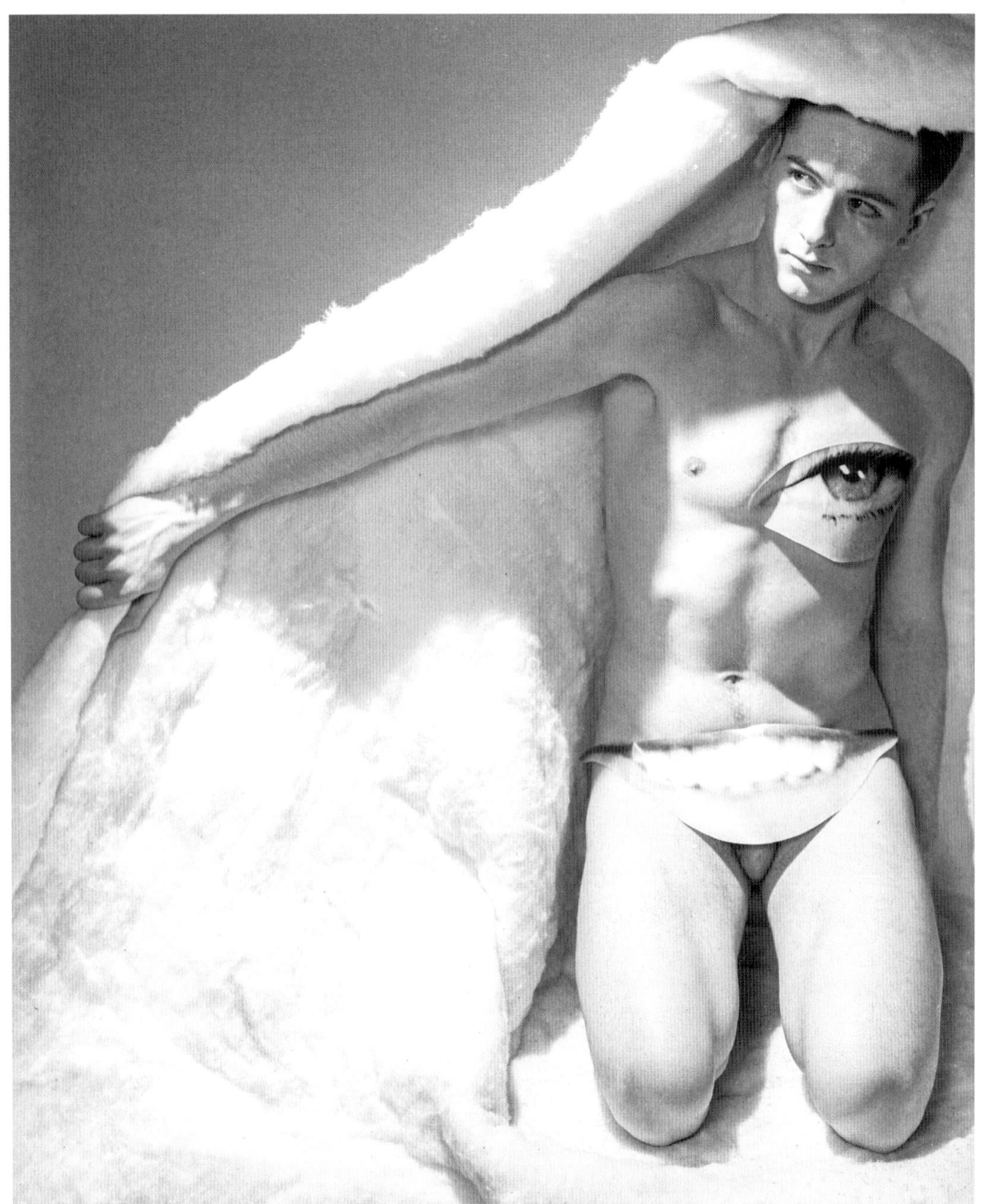

George Platt Lynes
The Dancer Fred Danieli, 1937
Der Tänzer (Fred Danieli)

George Platt Lynes
Tex Smutney, 1941

George Platt Lynes
Ralph McWilliams, 1952

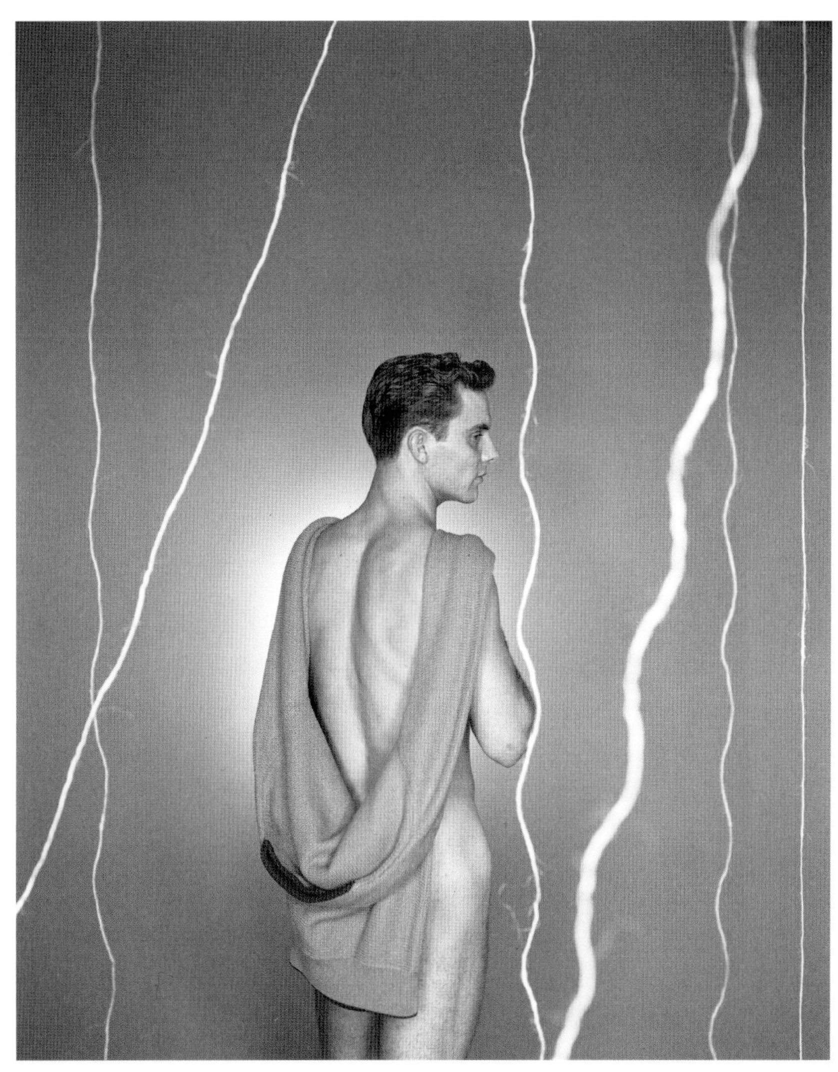

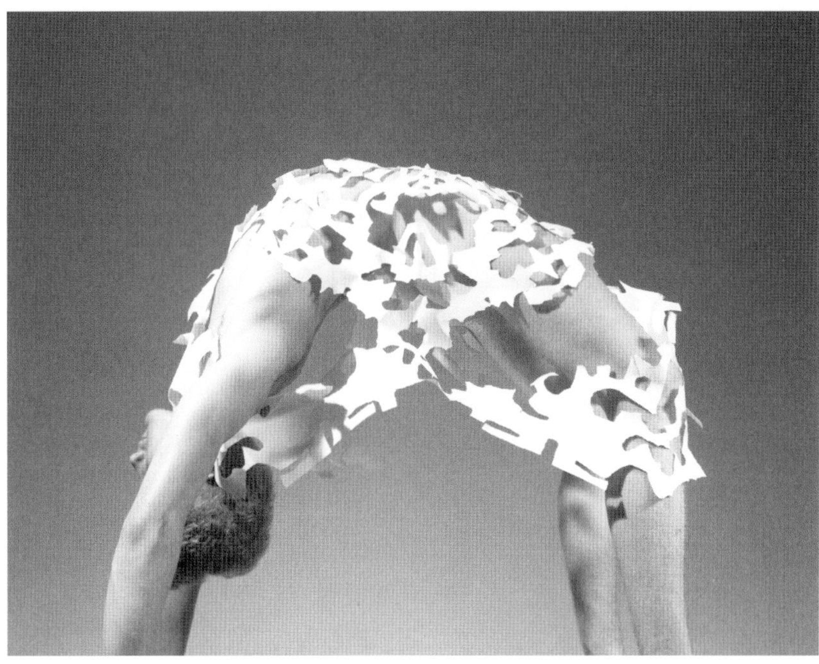

VI

QUEERE
AVANTGARDEN
UND INTIME
NETZWERKE

~

QUEER
AVANT-GARDES
AND INTIMATE
NETWORKS

Jean Cocteau
Le Sang d'un poète, 1930
Das Blut eines Dichters ~
The Blood of a Poet

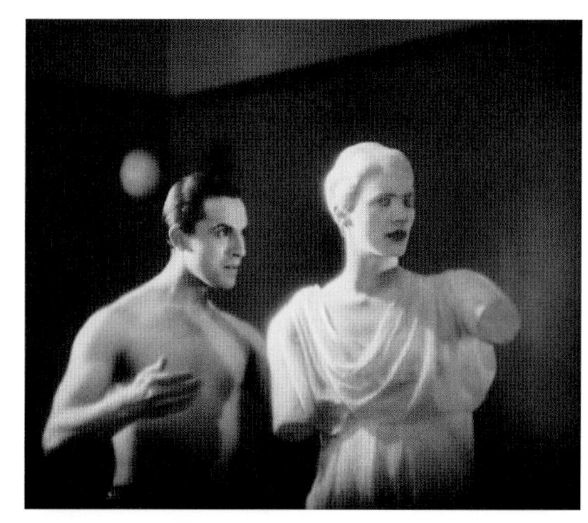

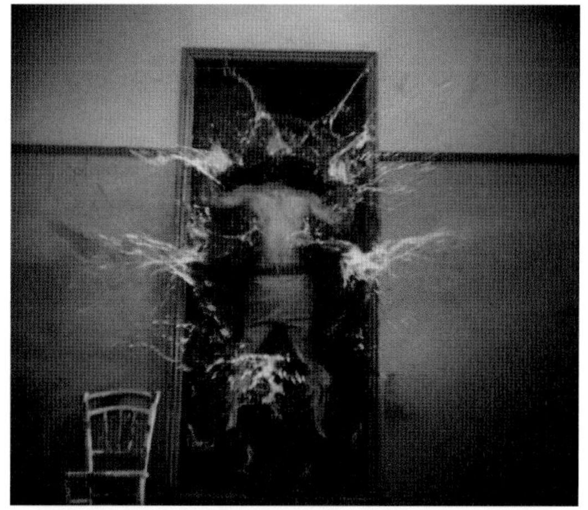

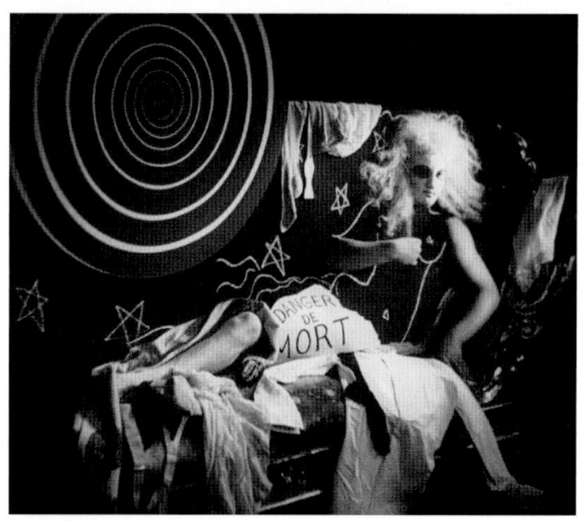
DANGER
DE
MORT

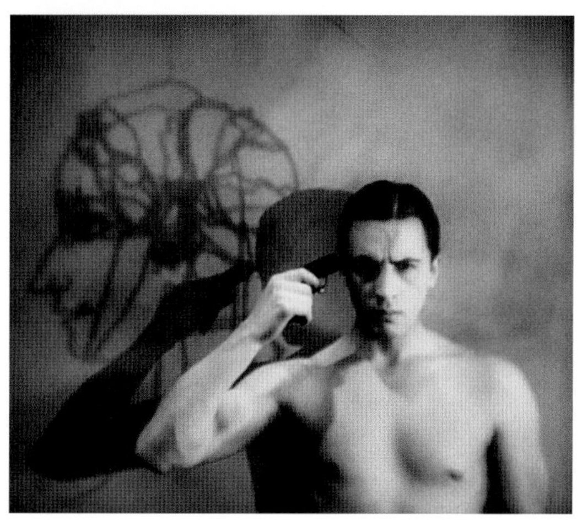

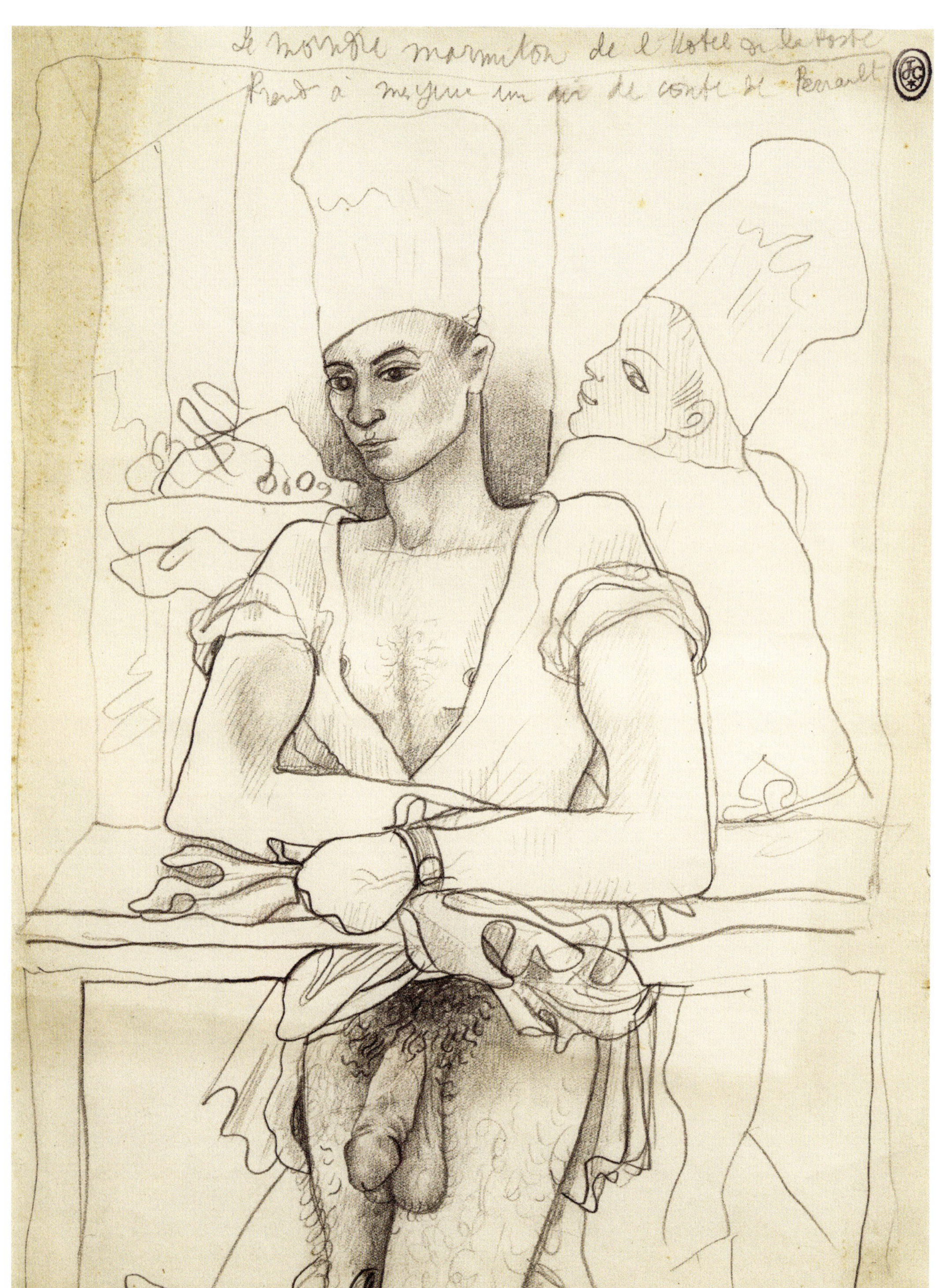

Jean Cocteau
Le Moindre marmiton de l'Hôtel de la Poste prend à mes yeux un air de conte de Perrault, 1930
Der kleinste Küchenjunge im Hotel de la Poste erscheint mir wie aus einem Märchen von Perrault
The Lowliest Scullion at l'Hôtel de la Poste Appears to Me like Something out of a Fairy Tale by Perrault

Jean Cocteau

Édouard Dermît (nu), 1948

Édouard Dermît (Akt) ~

Édouard Dermît (Nude)

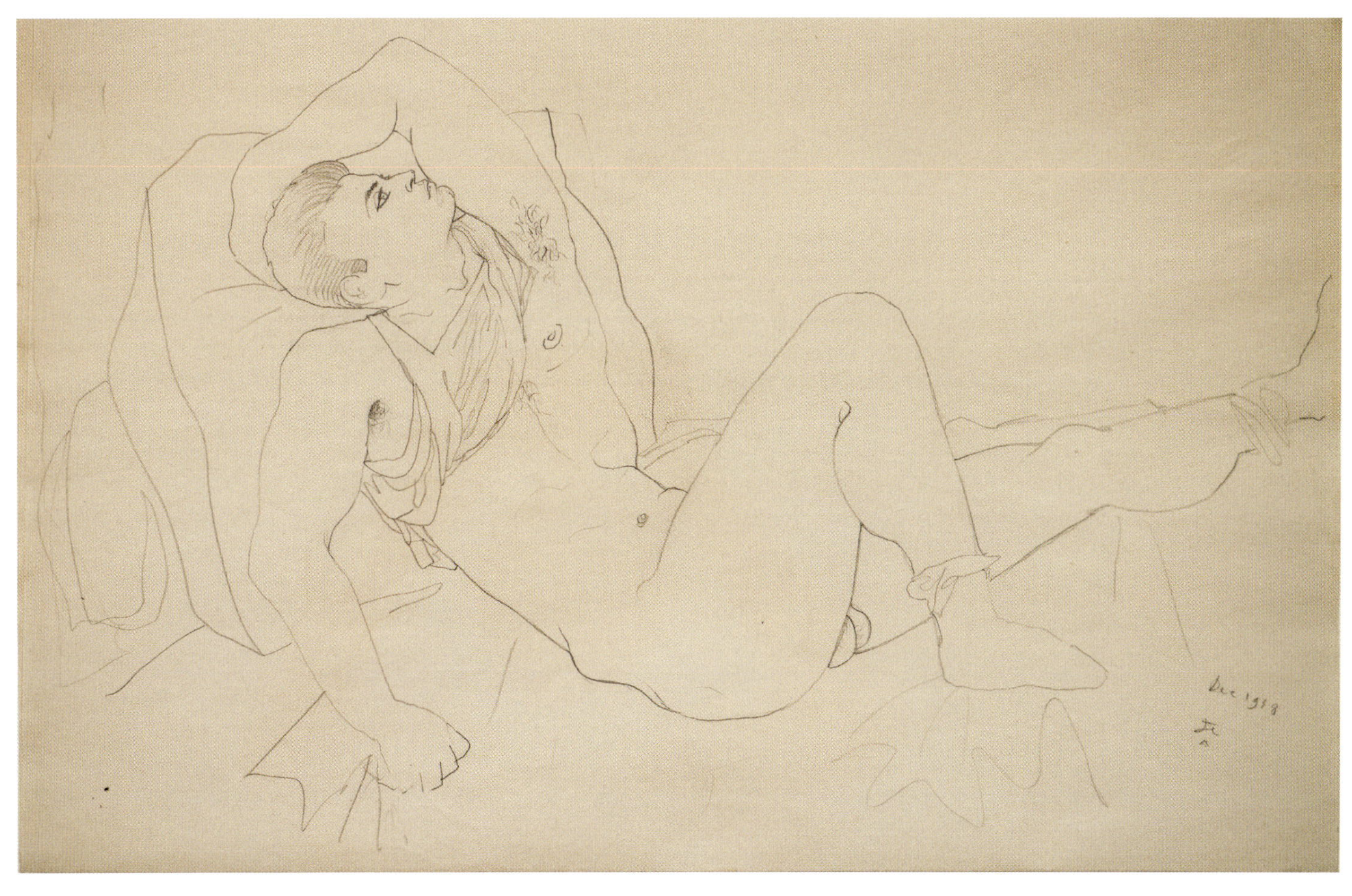

EXZENTRISCHE STUDIEN

ECCENTRIC STUDIES

TIRZA TRUE LATIMER

„Exzentrisch", also die Eigenschaft, von der Norm abzuweichen oder nicht im Zentrum zu stehen, wurde oftmals synonym mit dem Begriff „queer" verwendet. Es beschreibt Subjekte, die typischerweise dem historischen Nichtbeachten anheimfallen (einem Zustand, in dem diese in Vergessenheit geraten, unbekannt sind, ausgelöscht werden). Aus dem Blickwinkel der in Vergessenheit geratenen queeren Moderne verweist auch der Begriff „exzentrisch" auf künstlerische Praktiken und Menschen, die nicht in konventionelle historische oder kulturelle Schablonen passen.

Die herkömmlichen kunsthistorischen Herangehensweisen an Modernität und Modernismus in der Kunst bevorzugen üblicherweise bahnbrechende Innovationen einzelner Schöpfer*innen. „Modernität" und „Modernismus" mit Worten wie „exzentrisch" oder „queer" zu beschreiben, verleiht uns dagegen die Freiheit, von individualistischen Diskursen abzuweichen und diese Geschichte(n) als leidenschaftliche soziale Transaktionen zu betrachten – und somit als oftmals kollaborative und kollektive Unternehmungen, anstatt nur als einzelne Durchbrüche.[1] Wenn wir im Rahmen des Begriffs „exzentrisch" denken, können wir den kulturellen Einfluss von Menschen in Betracht zu ziehen, deren Sichtbarkeit und Einfluss vor dem 20. Jahrhundert zwar vernachlässigbar war, sich jedoch im Einklang mit der Moderne entwickelte. Zu diesen Menschen gehörten „moderne Frauen", Lesben, Kosmopolit*innen und Mitwirkende an der „New Negro Renaissance" (oder Harlem Renaissance, wie die Bewegung später genannt wurde). Zu diesen Menschen gehörten – gleichbedeutend – auch sexuell Andersdenkende. Diese Gruppen, die oftmals getrennt voneinander untersucht wurden, überschnitten einander, interagierten miteinander und bildeten bestärkende (wenn auch oft unbeständige) Allianzen. Als eines von vielen möglichen Beispielen verdeutlicht der Kreis homosexueller männlicher Künstler, der sich in Paris um die ausgewanderte amerikanische Schriftstellerin Gertrude Stein gebildet hatte, den Nutzen von Exzentrizität als Kategorie historischer Analyse. Steins homosexueller Zirkel, den sie als „zweite Familie" betrachtete, trug zur Entwicklung von Kunst und Kultur der Avantgarde in Europa und auf der anderen Seite des Atlantiks bei. Die Mitglieder des Zirkels formten weder eine Bewegung noch eine Schule, und Kritiker*innen, die über ihre Arbeiten schrieben, erfanden Kategorien wie „neo-romantisch", „super-realistisch" und „magisch-realistisch",[2] mit denen ihnen eine Stellung abseits der Innovationen der Moderne zugeschrieben wurde.

„Familie" ist der Begriff, der hier am besten passt. Während es für queere Menschen heute ganz normal ist, eine „Wahlfamilie" zu haben, bedeutete es zu Steins Zeit einen radikalen Schritt, eine „zweite" (nicht biologische) Familie zu benennen. Die Mitglieder der Wahlfamilie der Schriftstellerin woben ein genealogisches Netz, in deren Zentrum sie Stein und ihre „Ehefrau" Alice B. Toklas stellten; und sie rechtfertigten ihre Verwandtschaftsbeziehungen mithilfe von Porträts.[3] Diese als „Exzentriker*innen" wahrgenommenen Freigeister standen nicht nur in sozialer, sondern auch in künstlerischer Hinsicht in Beziehung zueinander. Exzentrizität – ein toleriertes, geradezu erwartetes Attribut künstlerischer Berufung – verlieh den Mitgliedern dieser queeren Familie ein gewisses Maß an Freiheit gegenüber vorherrschenden Normen in Bezug auf soziales und sexuelles Verhalten.

Ihr künstlerischer Austausch – gemeinschaftlich produzierte Arbeiten, von Kunstpublikationen über Performances bis hin zur Herstellung

1 Für eine umfassendere Erörterung dieser Methodologie siehe Tirza True Latimer, *Eccentric Modernisms: Making Differences in the History of American Art*, Oakland 2017.

2 Der in Polen geborene französische Kritiker Waldemar George prägte den Begriff „neo-romantisch", als er im Februar 1926 die erste Gruppenausstellung in der Pariser Galerie Druet von Künstlern rezensierte, die später in *Dix Portraits* auftauchten. Siehe Waldemar George, „Christian Bérard", in: *Formes: Revue internationale des arts plastique*, Nr. 1, Dezember 1929, S. 6–9, und „Eugène Bermann[sic!]", in: ebd., Nr. 3, März 1930, S. 5–12. Der Begriff „super-realistisch" wurde erstmals verwendet, um Arbeiten zu beschreiben, die später als „surrealistisch" bekannt werden sollten. Arthur Everett („Chick") Austin benutzte den Begriff im Titel seiner Ausstellung im Wadsworth Atheneum in Hartford in Connecticut, *Newer Super-Realism*, die im November 1931 eröffnet wurde. Der Begriff „magisch-realistisch" wurde vom New Yorker Galeristen Julien Levy geprägt, der dazu beitrug, die New Yorker Karrieren der Neo-Romantiker*innen, Surrealist*innen und der mexikanischen Malerin Frida Kahlo voranzutreiben, die er als „magische Realistin" bezeichnete.

3 Porträtkunst diente lesbischen Frauen auch dazu, Beziehungen zu sanktionieren, Zugehörigkeit und eine künstlerische Herkunft zu bezeichnen; noch wichtiger, sie bot ein Mittel, um neue Formen kultureller und sozialer Subjektivität selbst zu erfinden und selbst zu besiegeln. Drei Fallstudien zur Funktionsweise von lesbischer Kultur Anfang des 20. Jahrhunderts finden sich in: Tirza True Latimer, *Women Together/Women Apart: Portraits of Lesbian Paris*, New Brunswick 2005.

"Eccentric," meaning the quality of deviating from the norm or not being situated in the center, has often been used synonymously with the word "queer." It describes subjects typically consigned to historical oblivion (a state of being forgotten, unknown, erased). Seen from the oblivion into which queer modernism has receded, the term "eccentric" points toward practices and people that do not fit conventional historical or cultural templates. Traditional approaches to the study of modernity, including the study of modernism in the arts, typically privilege game-changing innovations conceived by singular creators. Qualifying "modernity" and "modernism" with words like "eccentric" or "queer" frees us to deviate from individualist discourses and reframe these histories as passionate social transactions—thus, often collaborative and collective enterprises, rather than singular breakthroughs.[1] Thinking in terms of the "eccentric" enables us to consider the cultural impact of people whose visibility and influence, although negligible before the twentieth century, emerged in step with modernity. These people include "modern women," lesbians, cosmopolitans, and participants in the "New Negro Renaissance" (or Harlem Renaissance, as the movement was later dubbed). These people also—and, of equal importance—included sexual dissidents. Often studied in isolation from one another, these communities overlapped, interacted, and formed empowering (if sometimes fleeting) alliances. Focusing on one of many possible examples, the circle of gay male artists that formed in Paris around the expatriate American author Gertrude Stein, demonstrates the usefulness of eccentricity as a category of historical analysis. Stein's gay coterie, which she embraced as a "second family," contributed to the development of avant-garde art and culture in Europe and across the Atlantic. They did not form a movement or school, and critics writing about their work invented categories like "neo-romantic," "super-realist," and "magic realist" that position them off the charts of modernist innovation.[2] "Family" is the word that best suits them. While, for queers, embracing a "chosen family" is now commonplace, in Stein's day, identifying a "second" (non-biological) family was a radical move. The author's second family members wove a genealogical web, placing Stein and her "wife" Alice B. Toklas at the center; they sanctified their kinship affiliations through portraiture.[3] Perceived as "eccentrics," these free spirits interrelated for social, as well as artistic, purposes. Eccentricity—a tolerated, indeed expected, attribute of artistic vocation—afforded the members of this queer family a degree of liberty in relation to prevailing norms of social and sexual behavior. Their artistic exchanges—collaboratively produced work, from art publications to performances, as well as portrait transactions—illuminate dimensions of modernism long consigned to the shadows. I argue that these initiatives contributed to the development of alternative languages, as well as alternative systems of value, within modernism. An eccentric modernism, in short. Let us begin with *Dix Portraits* (Ten Portraits), an illustrated volume, published in France in 1930, featuring Gertrude Stein and several members of her entourage.[4] The book opens with

1
For a more in-depth discussion of this methodology, see Tirza True Latimer, *Eccentric Modernisms: Making Differences in the History of American Art* (Oakland: University of California Press, 2017).

2
The Polish-born, French critic Waldemar George coined the term "neo-romantic" in February 1926, when he reviewed the first group show in Paris, at Galerie Druet, of artists who later appeared in *Dix Portraits*. See Waldemar George, "Call of the Occident, Christian Bérard," *Formes: An International Review of Plastic Art*, no. 1 (December 1929): pp. 6–9, and "The Call of Italy, Eugène Berman," *Formes*, no. 3 (March 1930): pp. 5–12. The term "super-realist" was first used to describe work later known as "surrealist." Arthur Everett ("Chick") Austin used the term in the title of his exhibition at the Wadsworth Atheneum in Hartford, Connecticut, *Newer Super-Realism*, which opened in November 1931. The term "magic realist" was popularized by the New York Gallerist Julien Levy, who helped to launch the New York careers of the neo-romantics, surrealists, and the Mexican painter Frida Kahlo, whom he described as a "magic realist."

3
Portraiture served lesbians, similarly, to sanctify relationships, mark affiliation, and establish lineage; importantly, it also provided a means to self-invent and self-ratify new forms of cultural and social subjectivity. For three case studies illuminating the ways portraiture functioned in lesbian culture of the early twentieth century, see Tirza True Latimer, *Women Together/Women Apart: Portraits of Lesbian Paris* (New Brunswick: Rutgers University Press), 2005.

4
Gertrude Stein, *Dix Portraits*. French trans. Georges Hugnet and Virgil Thomson (Paris: Éditions de la Montagne, 1930).

von Porträts – beleuchtet Dimensionen der Moderne, die lange verborgen waren. Ich behaupte, dass diese Initiativen nicht nur zur Entwicklung alternativer Sprachen beitrugen, sondern auch zu alternativen Wertesystemen innerhalb der Moderne. Kurz gesagt: einer exzentrischen Moderne.

Beginnen wir mit *Dix Portraits*, einer illustrierten Publikation, die 1930 in Frankreich erschien und Gertrude Stein sowie etliche Mitglieder ihrer Entourage zeigte.[4] Das Buch eröffnet mit zehn von Steins literarischen Porträts, verfasst auf Englisch, gefolgt von zehn bildlichen Porträts von Steins Motiven und schließt mit Übersetzungen ihrer Gedichte durch den französischen Dichter Georges Hugnet. Die Idee zu einer zweisprachigen illustrierten Publikation, die sowohl visuelle als auch verbale Porträts umfasste, stammte von Hugnet und dem amerikanischen Komponisten Virgil Thomson, der Hugnet bei der Übersetzung unterstützte. Stein stimmte bereitwillig zu, etwas zu diesem künstler*innenübergreifenden Buch beizutragen – und es ganz nebenbei auch zu finanzieren –, unter der Voraussetzung, dass die Illustrationen, neben Arbeiten der jüngeren Künstler Christian Bérard, Eugene Berman, Pavel Tchelitchew (Abb. 1) und Kristians Tonny, auch eine Skizze ihres berühmtesten Porträtmotivs Pablo Picasso enthalten würden. Der Beitrag von Picasso, der bereits als Aushängeschild der Moderne etabliert war, diente als eine Art Berechtigung für die aufstrebenden Künstler*innen, ganz gleich ob homosexuell oder heterosexuell, stärkte jedoch auch die Verbindung zwischen dem Avantgardemaler und Stein.

Viel wurde bereits über Steins Beziehung zu Picasso geschrieben.[5] *Dix Portraits* würdigt ihre Beziehung, beleuchtet jedoch auch einen weiteren Aspekt von Steins Karriereweg: die homosexuellen Männer, die sie in den 1920er- und 1930er-Jahren über Wasser hielten, ehe ihr Werk weithin bekannt war. Sie trugen, ebenso wie Picasso, dazu bei, ihren kanonischen Status als Modernistin in Europa zu etablieren und ihre transatlantischen Beziehungen zu stärken.[6]

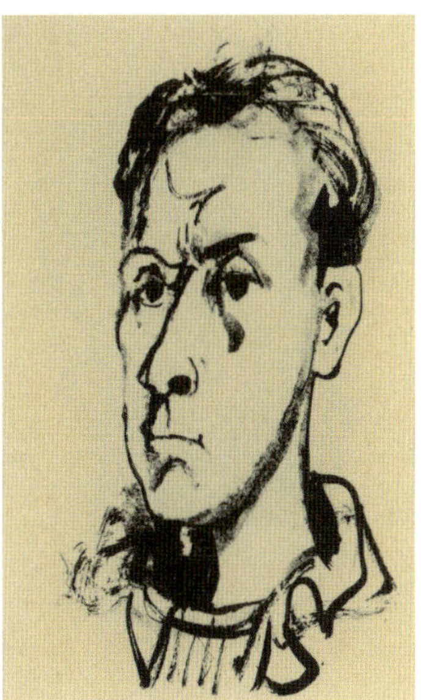

ABB. ~ FIG. 1

Pavel Tchelitchew, *Self-Portrait*, 1919
Selbstporträt

Veröffentlicht ~ *Published* in Gertrude Stein, *Dix Portraits*, Paris 1930

4 Gertrude Stein, *Dix Portraits*, Übers. aus dem Franz. von Georges Hugnet und Virgil Thomson, Paris 1930.

5 Stein selbst schrieb wiederholt über ihre Beziehung. Sie erörterte Picasso in ihren Memoiren *The Autobiographie of Alice B. Toklas*, New York 1933; Picasso war zudem das Motiv ihres Porträts, veröffentlicht unter dem Titel: *Picasso*, Paris 1938. Zu viele Kunsthistoriker*innen, um sie alle aufzuzählen, haben die Beziehung zwischen der Schriftstellerin und dem Maler ins Zentrum ihrer Untersuchung von Picassos Porträt von Stein aus dem Jahr 1905 gestellt. Ein Beispiel, das sich als nützlich für Historiker*innen queerer Kultur erweisen kann, ist Robert S. Lubars bahnbrechender Artikel „Unmasking Pablo's Gertrude: Queer Desire and the Subject of Portraiture", in: *Art Bulletin* 79, Nr. 1, März 1997, S. 57 f. Die Beziehung Picasso-Stein steht zudem im Mittelpunkt zahlreicher Ausstellungen, jüngst etwa *Gertrude Stein and Pablo Picasso: The Invention of Language* im Musée du Luxembourg in Paris (2023/24).

6 Wanda M. Corn und Tirza True Latimer erforschen die transatlantische Dynamik von Steins Karriere und die Rolle, die ihre Gefolgsleute dabei spielten, in: *Seeing Gertrude Stein: Five Stories*, Ausst.-Kat. Contemporary Jewish Museum, San Francisco/National Portrait Gallery, Washington, Berkeley 2011. Zu Steins Beziehung zu Picasso siehe insbesondere darin: Wanda M. Corn, „Story 1: Picturing Gertrude Stein", Unterkapitel „Bohemian Stein", S. 25–39.

ten of Stein's literary portraits, written in English, followed by ten visual portraits picturing Stein's subjects, and concludes with translations of her poems by the French poet Georges Hugnet. The idea for a bilingual, illustrated book exploring both visual and verbal portraiture came from Hugnet and the American composer Virgil Thomson, who helped Hugnet with the translations. Stein readily agreed to enter into—and, indeed, to finance—the multi-artist project on the condition that the illustrations include a sketch by her most famous portrait subject, Pablo Picasso, along with those drawn by the younger artists Christian Bérard, Eugene Berman, Pavel Tchelitchew (fig. 1), and Kristians Tonny. The contribution by Picasso, who was already established as modernism's standard bearer, served as a credential for the emerging artists, both gay and straight, while reinforcing the association between the vanguard painter and Stein.

Much has been written about Stein's relationship with Picasso.[5] *Dix Portraits* acknowledges their relationship but also illuminates another factor in Stein's career development: the gay men who buoyed her up during the 1920s and 1930s, before her work was widely known; they, as much as Picasso, helped to establish her canonical status as a modernist in Europe and to strengthen her transatlantic connections.[6]

Dix Portraits, which represents a self-selected inner family circle, shows more broadly how portraiture functioned to assert queer identity and cement queer identifications. The portraiture of other artists whom Stein subsequently "adopted" can be better understood in this light—George Platt Lynes, for example.

Lynes, hell-bent on becoming a writer, assiduously courted Stein. The small press he ran out of his bookstore in Englewood, New Jersey, printed and distributed Stein's *Descriptions of Literature* in 1926. After selling this business to fund an excursion to France with his two lovers, Monroe Wheeler, editor of a small press and future director of the Museum of Modern Art in New York, and the novelist Glenway Wescott, he tracked down Stein in person. Wheeler and Wescott encouraged Lynes to abandon writing and focus on photography as a career orientation. Stein, who was politely unimpressed with Lynes's writing, colluded in the effort to facilitate the transition. Stein made Lynes her "official photographer," replacing Man Ray—who had offended Stein by requesting payment for his work; she never paid for portraits, feeling that sitting for them, thus spending her time, was payment enough.

In 1931, at the home where Stein and Toklas summered at Bilignin, in southeastern France, Lynes took a portrait of the author with the Rhône Valley as her backdrop. With Stein's complicity, this photograph appeared on the cover of *Time* magazine in 1933. *Time*'s feature story about Stein and the cover image by Lynes elevated both of their profiles in the United States.

Lynes subsequently opened a portrait studio in New York, where he photographed influential figures in the performing arts, the visual arts, and literature of this period, along with a parade of handsome models. His portrait portfolio of the period constitutes a veritable Who's Who of gay men. The choreographer Frederick Ashton; museum director A. Everett ("Chick") Austin; the photographer Cecil

5
Stein herself wrote repeatedly about the relationship. She discusses Picasso in the memoir *The Autobiography of Alice B. Toklas* (New York: Harcourt, Brace, 1933); and Picasso was the subject of her portrait published as *Picasso* (Paris: Librairie Floury, 1938). Too many art historians to innumerate have placed the relationship between the author and the painter at the center of their examinations of Picasso's 1905 portrait of Stein. To name an example useful to historians of queer culture, I recommend Robert S. Lubar's pathbreaking article "Unmasking Pablo's Gertrude: Queer Desire and the Subject of Portraiture," *Art Bulletin* 79, no. 1 (March 1997): pp. 57–87. Numerous exhibitions have taken the Stein-Picasso relationship as a focus, most recently *Gertrude Stein and Pablo Picasso: The Invention of Language* at the Musée du Luxembourg, Paris (2023/24).

6
Wanda M. Corn and Tirza True Latimer explore the transatlantic dynamics of Stein's career, and the roles played by her acolytes, in *Seeing Gertrude Stein: Five Stories* (Berkeley University of California Press, 2011). For Stein's relationship with Picasso, see particularly "Story 1: Picturing Gertrude Stein," subchapter "Bohemian Stein" by Wanda M. Corn, pp. 25–39.

Dix Portraits, das einen selbst gewählten inneren Familienkreis darstellt, zeigt genauer, wie Porträts funktionierten, um queere Identität zu verfechten und queere Identifikationen zu festigen. Das Porträtieren von anderen Künstler*innen, die Stein in der Folge „adoptierte" – wie zum Beispiel George Platt Lynes –, lässt sich in diesem Licht besser verstehen.

Lynes, wild entschlossen, Schriftsteller zu werden, hofierte Stein beharrlich. Der kleine Verlag, den er von seinem Buchladen in Englewood in New Jersey aus betrieb, druckte und vertrieb 1926 Steins *Descriptions of Literature.* Nachdem er sein Geschäft verkauft hatte, um eine Reise mit seinen zwei Liebhabern – Monroe Wheeler, Herausgeber eines kleinen Verlags und zukünftiger Direktor des Museum of Modern Art in New York, und dem Schriftsteller Glenway Wescott – nach Frankreich zu finanzieren, spürte er Stein persönlich auf. Wheeler und Wescott ermutigten Lynes, das Schreiben aufzugeben und sich künftig ganz der Fotografie zu widmen. Stein, die sich von Lynes' Schreibversuchen höflich unbeeindruckt zeigte, wirkte ebenfalls in diese Richtung auf ihn ein. Sie machte Lynes zu ihrem „offiziellen Fotografen" und ersetzte so Man Ray, der Stein dadurch beleidigt hatte, dass er für seine Arbeit Bezahlung forderte. Sie bezahlte niemals für Porträts, da sie der Ansicht war, Modell zu sitzen, also ihre Zeit aufzuwenden, sei schon Bezahlung genug.

1931 nahm Lynes ein Porträt der Schriftstellerin in ihrem Zuhause in Bilignin im Südosten von Frankreich auf, im Hintergrund das Rhônetal, wo sie und Toklas den Sommer verbrachten. Dank Steins Beteiligung erschien die Aufnahme 1933 auf dem Titelblatt von *Times.* Die dazugehörige Reportage über Stein und das Titelbild von Lynes trugen zu beider Bekanntheit in den Vereinigten Staaten bei. Lynes eröffnete schließlich ein Porträtstudio in New York, wo er neben einer Reihe gutaussehender Models auch einflussreiche Persönlichkeiten aus den Bereichen darstellende Kunst, bildende Kunst und Literatur seiner Zeit fotografierte. Sein Porträtportfolio dieser Epoche stellt ein veritables Who's who homosexueller Männer dar. Dazu gehörten in den 1930er-Jahren unter anderem der Choreograf Frederick Ashton, der Museumsdirektor Arthur Everett („Chick") Austin, der Fotograf Cecil Beaton, der Maler Paul Cadmus und sein Liebhaber Jared French, der Dichter, Künstler und Filmemacher Jean Cocteau, der Kabarettdarsteller Jimmie Daniels, der Impresario Lincoln Kirstein (mit George Balanchine Mitbegründer des New York City Ballet), Tchelitchew und sein Liebhaber, der Schriftsteller und Herausgeber Charles Henri Ford sowie Virgil Thomson. „Lynes' Bildern ist eine fantasievolle Note zu eigen, die weder von Vorgängern, Schicklichkeit oder Zweck eingeschränkt wird", bemerkte ein Kritiker der Zeitschrift *Coronet* in einem langen Lynes gewidmeten Artikel aus dem Jahr 1939.[7] Theatralische Inszenierung und Beleuchtung, verbunden mit einer surrealistischen Empfindsamkeit, verliehen Lynes Porträts psychologische Intensität. Das Spiel von verschatteten Händen, die etwa Lynes' Porträt von Daniels einrahmen, vermittelt den expressiven Ausdruck des Fotografen ebenso wie den seines Motivs. Gleichzeitig verweisen die Hände auf queere Erotik, queere Traumwelten, queere Körpersprache. Hände – die sowohl Urheberschaft als auch Homoerotik suggerieren – sind ein immer wiederkehrendes Motiv in der queeren visuellen Kultur des beginnenden 20. Jahrhunderts. Sie erscheinen an prominenter Stelle in Beatons zur gleichen Zeit veröffentlichten Aufnahmen für die *VOGUE,* in denen Ford in einem von

7
Robert W. Marks, „Portrait of George Lynes: One of Gertrude Stein's Young Protégés, His Camera Nobly Reinforces the Dada Tradition", in: *Coronet,* Juli 1939, S. 163–172, hier: S. 163.

Beaton; the painters Paul Cadmus and his lover Jared French; the poet, artist, and filmmaker Jean Cocteau; the cabaret performer Jimmie Daniels; impresario Lincoln Kirstein, co-founder, with George Balanchine, of the New York City Ballet; Tchelitchew and his lover, the writer and editor Charles Henri Ford; and Virgil Thomson number among Lynes's subjects of the 1930s. "Lynes' pictures have an imaginative touch uninhibited by precedent, propriety, or purpose," observed a critic for *Coronet* magazine in a long article devoted to Lynes in 1939.[7] Theatrical staging and lighting combined with a surrealist sensibility to invest Lynes's portraits with psychological intensity. The play of shadowy hands framing Lynes's 1937 portrait of Daniels, for example, conveys the expressive agency of both the photographer and the subject. At the same time, the hands gesture toward queer eroticism, queer dream worlds, queer body language. Hands—connoting both authorship and homoeroticism—are a recurrent trope in queer visual culture of the early twentieth century. They appear prominently in Beaton's contemporaneous shots for *Vogue* of Charles Henri Ford modeling a costume designed by Salvador Dalí. Throughout the 1930s, as the global economic crisis worsened along with Europe's political tensions, many members of Stein's gay entourage migrated from France to the other side of the Atlantic. Lynes, with his professional and personal ties to figures of cultural influence in New York, helped his confreres to make connections. They formed new relationships, new communities, and new collaborations.

Four Saints in Three Acts, a modernist opera with libretto by Stein and score by Virgil Thomson, brought several of the eccentrics introduced in *Dix Portraits* back together in the United States. The opera, which premiered in Hartford, Connecticut, in 1934, and then went on to New York City's Broadway, stands out for a number of reasons—not the least, it introduced an all-African American cast to the opera stage. The chorus and dancers were recruited in Harlem by Thomson and Carl Van Vechten, Stein's unofficial American agent and the self-appointed portrait photographer of the Harlem Renaissance. The director of the Wadsworth Atheneum in Hartford, Chick Austin, seized the opportunity to premiere the opera. *Four Saints* was a no-lose proposition, Austin boasted to his somewhat skeptical board of directors. The event would set new precedents in the arts. To name just a few of those precedents: It would be the Wadsworth Atheneum's first theatrical production (indeed, the first opera to be produced in a United States museum). It was Stein's first opera; it was Thomson's first opera; it was the British choreographer Frederick Ashton's first opera. It broke new ground in the arena of stage design, as well. For the first time in the United States, opera sets and costumes were designed by a fine artist, a practice introduced in Europe by Sergei Diaghilev for his Ballets Russes. The artist, Florine Stettheimer, privileged eccentric materials never before used in stagecraft—cellophane, ostrich feathers, glass beads, and lace. Of all these "firsts," many viewed the all-Black cast as the opera's most significant break from historical convention. As with the portraits illustrating

7
Robert W. Marks, "Portrait of George Lynes: One of Gertrude Stein's Young Protégés, His Camera Nobly Reinforces the Dada Tradition," *Coronet*, July 1939, pp. 163–172, here p. 163.

Salvador Dalí entworfenen Kostüm posiert. Im Laufe der 1930er-Jahre, als sich neben politischen Spannungen auch die Wirtschaftskrise immer mehr verschärfte, migrierten zahlreiche Mitglieder aus Steins homosexueller Entourage aus Frankreich auf die andere Seite des Atlantiks. Lynes mit seinen beruflichen und persönlichen Verbindungen zu kulturell einflussreichen Persönlichkeiten in New York half seinen Kollegen, Beziehungen aufzubauen. So entstanden wieder neue Beziehungen, neue Gemeinschaften und neue Möglichkeiten zur Zusammenarbeit.

Four Saints in Three Acts, eine modernistische Oper mit einem Libretto von Stein und Musik von Thomson, führte einige der Exzentriker*innen, die in *Dix Portraits* eingeführt worden waren, zurück in die Vereinigten Staaten. Die Oper, deren Premiere 1934 in Hartford in Connecticut stattfand und die dann weiter an den New Yorker Broadway ging, sticht aus verschiedenen Gründen heraus – nicht zuletzt, weil sie eine komplett Schwarze Besetzung auf die Opernbühne brachte. Chor und Tänzer*innen wurden in Harlem angeheuert, und zwar von Thomson und Carl van Vechten, Steins inoffiziellem amerikanischem Agenten und selbsternanntem Porträtfotografen der Harlem Renaissance.

Der Direktor des Wadsworth Atheneums in Hartford, Chick Austin, ergriff die Gelegenheit, die Oper uraufzuführen. *Four Saints* sei eine todsichere Angelegenheit, tönte Austin vor seinem einigermaßen skeptischen Direktorium. Das Ereignis würde neue Maßstäbe in der Kunst setzen. Um nur einige Beispiele zu nennen: Es wäre die erste Theaterproduktion des Wadsworth Atheneums (tatsächlich sogar die erste Oper, die in einem US-amerikanischen Museum gezeigt würde); es war Steins erste Oper; es war Thomsons erste Oper; es war auch die erste Oper des britischen Choreografen Frederick Ashton. Auch im Bereich des Bühnenbilds schlug sie völlig neue Wege ein. Erstmals in den Vereinigten Staaten wurden Opernkulissen und Kostüme von einer bildenden Künstlerin gestaltet, eine Praxis, die Sergei Djagilew für sein Ballets Russes in Europa eingeführt hatte. Die Künstlerin, Florine Stettheimer, bevorzugte exzentrische Materialien, die nie zuvor im Bühnenbereich eingesetzt worden waren, wie Zellophan, Straußenfedern, Glasperlen und Spitze. Von all diesen „ersten Malen" galt jedoch die durchweg Schwarze Besetzung für viele als wichtigster Bruch mit historischen Konventionen. So wie bei den Bildnissen für *Dix Portraits* trugen auch die Porträts, mit denen das Opernprogramm illustriert war, dazu bei, die Mitarbeitenden der Oper als Avantgarde zu präsentieren. Im Programm dienten diese Porträts zudem dazu, eine Hierarchie innerhalb des gemeinschaftlichen Unternehmens zu etablieren. Auf der ersten Seite nehmen die *weißen* US-amerikanischen Künstler*innen und Produzent*innen den Ehrenplatz ein: Stein, Thomson, Austin, der Dirigent Alexander Smallens, der Szenenschreiber Maurice Grosser (Thomsons Liebhaber) und der Produzent John Houseman (Abb. 2). Die folgende Doppelseite zeigt drei der Hauptdarsteller*innen, Altonell Hines, Abner Dorsey und Bertha Fitzhugh Baker, und schließlich ihre Chorleiterin Eva Jessye (Abb. 3). Die *weißen* US-amerikanischen Mitarbeiter*innen posieren in Alltagskleidung, während die Schwarzen US-Amerikaner*innen unter den Darsteller*innen im Kostüm erscheinen (mit Ausnahme von Jessye, die formelle Abendgarderobe trägt, tragen sie keine Heiligenkleidung). Die in Gewänder gekleideten Darsteller*innen haben den Blick in einer Art Gebetspantomime gen Himmel, in Richtung eines himmlischen Lichts

Dix Portraits, the portraits illustrating the opera program play a role in consolidating the opera's collaborators as a vanguard. In the program, portraiture also serves to establish a hierarchy within the collaborative venture. On the playbill's first pages, the Euro-American artists and producers occupy pride of place: Stein, Thomson, Austin, the conductor Alexander Smallens, the scenarist Maurice Grosser (Thomson's lover), and the producer John Houseman (fig. 2). The following spread presents three of the principal performers, Altonell Hines, Abner Dorsey, and Bertha Fitzhugh Baker, and finally their "choir mistress," Eva Jessye (fig. 3). The Euro-American collaborators pose in every-day clothing, while the African American performers appear in costume (with the exception of Jessye, wearing formal, opening-night attire, not saintly robes). The robed sitters all avert their eyes, to the heavens, or some heavenly light in the distance, or toward the ground in a pantomime of prayer—in keeping with their saintly roles on stage and with stereotypes of African American piety. The photo labeled "Eva Jessye, Choir Mistress" strikes a discrepant note. Jessye's self-possessed regard, her un-costume-like attire, and her vocation as choir director set her apart from the chorus members pictured in this spread.

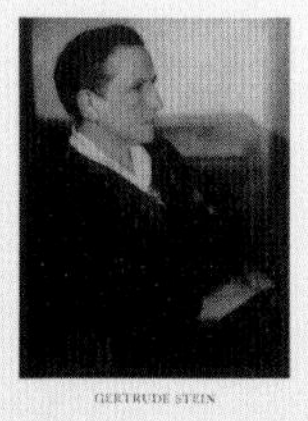
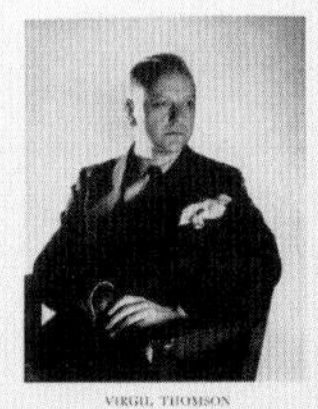
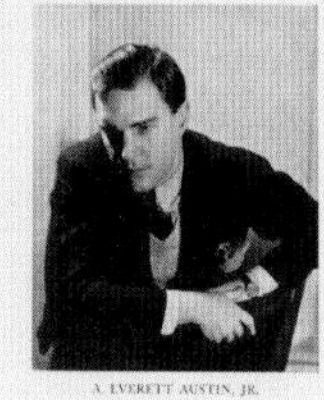

ABB. ~ FIG. 2

Seite aus dem Programm von ~ *Page from the playbill for* Four Saints in Three Acts mit Porträts des kreativen Teams ~ *with portraits of the creative team:* von links nach rechts ~ *from left to right: Gertrude Stein*, von ~ *by* Man Ray, 1926; *Virgil Thomson*, von ~ *by* Lee Miller, 1934; *A. Everett Austin, Jr.*, von ~ *by* Lee Miller, 1934.

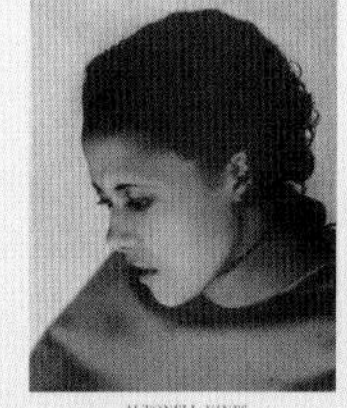
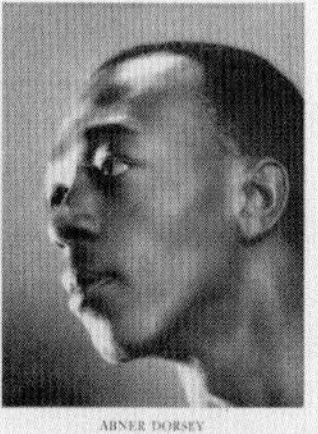
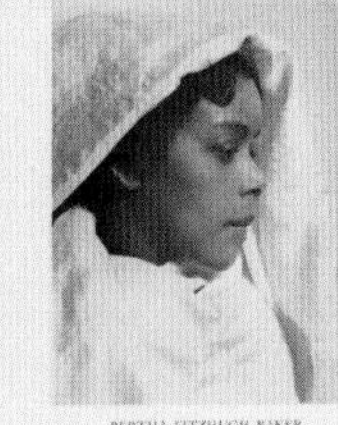
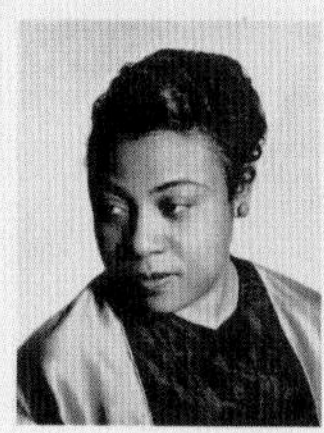

ABB. ~ FIG. 3

Seite aus dem Programm von ~ *Page from the playbill for* Four Saints in Three Acts mit Porträts der Chormitglieder von ~ *with portraits of chorus members by* Lee Miller: von links nach rechts ~ *from left to right: Altonell Hines* (Commere), *Abner Dorsey* (Compere), *Bertha Fitzhugh Baker* (St. Settlement), *Eva Jessye* (Choir Mistress).

Why does her picture not appear at the front of the program with those of the other artistic directors, rather than here, in the last position, after those of the performers? Aside from the racial biases dictating this organizational choice (the assumption that Jessye has more in common with the performers, by dint of her race, than with the other artistic collaborators by dint of her vocation), it should also be noted that the placement of her photograph as far from Thomson as possible is significant. Thomson would not even mention Jessye by name in his written accounts of the making of *Four Saints*. In his memoirs, he refers to her not by name but only as

in der Ferne oder zu Boden gewandt – in Übereinstimmung mit ihren Bühnenrollen als Heilige und den Stereotypen der Schwarzen Frömmigkeit. Das Foto mit der Bildunterschrift „Eva Jessye, Choir Mistress" schlägt einen anderen Ton an. Jessyes selbstbeherrschter Blick, ihre Kleidung, die nichts mit einem Kostüm gemein hat, und ihre Stellung als Chorleiterin setzen sie von den Mitgliedern des Chors auf dieser Doppelseite ab.

Doch warum erscheint ihr Bild nicht vorne im Programm, zusammen mit jenen der anderen künstlerischen Leiter*innen, anstatt hier, an letzter Stelle, noch hinter den Darstellenden? Neben den rassistischen Biases, die diese organisatorische Wahl begründet haben mögen (die Annahme, dass Jessye aufgrund ihrer „race" mehr mit den Darsteller*innen gemeinsam habe, als aufgrund ihres Berufs mit den anderen künstlerischen Mitarbeiter*innen), ist auch die Tatsache von Bedeutung, dass sich ihr Foto so weit weg wie möglich von jenem Thomsons befindet.

In seinem schriftlichen Bericht zur Entstehung von *Four Saints* hat Thomson Jessye nicht einmal namentlich erwähnt. In seinen Memoiren bezeichnet er sie nur als eine Schwarze Frau, die die besten Chorsänger*innen in Harlem „unter Vertrag" habe.[8] Er verabsäumt es jedoch, Jessyes Leistungen zu erwähnen: Als Tochter von Sklav*innen machte sie ihren Abschluss an der Western University in Quindaro in Kansas, unterrichtete und arbeitete als Journalistin und feierte schließlich Erfolge als Chorleiterin. In den 1920er-Jahren gründete sie den Eva Jessye Choir und konnte auf mehr als fünf Jahrzehnte von Auftritten am Broadway, im Radio und in Hollywood verweisen. Ein Anflug von Jessyes hart verdienter Autorität wird in einer Porträtfotografie von Lee Miller für das Programm spürbar. Im Gegensatz zu den Posen der Chormitglieder richtet Jessye den Blick nicht bescheiden nach unten oder oben. Sie wendet sich einfach von der Kamera und dem *weißen* Fotografen ab. Ihre Sänger*innen nannten sie statt „Eva" auch „Evil", weil sie sie hart antrieb, hohe Anforderungen stellte und rücksichtlos um Aufträge kämpfte. Thomsons Einschätzung zufolge war sie ein notwendiges Übel, aber auch eine Konkurrentin um Autorität im Kontext der Opernproduktion.

Thomson war bestrebt, mit der Oper eine Spur in der Geschichte der modernen Kunst zu hinterlassen – um sich so selbst und seinen queeren Mitstreiter*innen einen Platz in dieser Geschichte zu sichern. Sein Engagement bei der Anstellung von Schwarzen US-Amerikaner*innen und seine vertraglichen Zugeständnisse an die geschäftstüchtige Jessye sollten nicht als Einsatz für „racial" Gerechtigkeit missverstanden werden. Aus dem Blickwinkel der *weißen* US-amerikanischen Opernproduzent*innen trug „racial difference" zur Unangepasstheit der Oper bei und beschwor auf metaphorische Weise andere Formen der Differenz (vor allem eine sexuelle Differenz, aber auch künstlerische Differenz), die zum grenzüberschreitenden Ethos der Oper beitrugen. Das hierarchische und „racially segregated" Layout des Programms verstärkte Stereotypen von „race", die *Weiße* beruhigten, und lenkte gleichzeitig die Aufmerksamkeit weg von der schrillen Ästhetik, die *Four Saints* zu einer queeren Tour de Force machten. Als eine Art Manifest interpretiert (eine Feststellung der „Differenz" innerhalb der Moderne und innerhalb der amerikanischen Gesellschaft), zeigt das Programm zu *Four Saints* dennoch, dass die Geschichten marginalisierter Gemeinschaften, darunter People of Color, Frauen und queere Menschen, weder vollkommen voneinander getrennt zu sehen noch

8 Virgil Thomson, *Virgil Thomson*, New York 1966, S. 238.

a Black woman who had the best choristers in Harlem "under contract."[8] He fails to acknowledge Jessye's achievements: the daughter of slaves, she graduated from Western University, taught school, worked as a journalist, and ultimately flourished as a choral director. In the 1920s, she founded the Eva Jessye Choir and succeeded for over five decades in securing billings on Broadway, on the radio, and in Hollywood. A sense of Jessye's hard-earned authority comes through in a program portrait photograph taken by Lee Miller. In contrast with the poses struck by the members of her chorus, Jessye does not avert her eyes modestly downward or upward toward the heavens. She simply turns away from the camera, and from the white photographer. Her singers called her "Evil" in place of "Eva" because she drove them hard, imposed exacting standards, and competed ruthlessly for contracts. In Thomson's estimation, she was a necessary evil, but also a rival for authority within the context of the opera's production. Thomson's ambition for the opera was to leave a mark on the history of modern art—to secure a place in that history for himself, and for his queer confreres. The composer's advocacy for casting African Americans, and his contractual capitulations to the business-savvy Jessye, should not be confused for a commitment to racial justice. From the perspective of the Euro-American opera producers, "racial difference" contributed to the opera's edginess and metaphorically evoked other forms of difference (most notably sexual difference, but also artistic difference) contributing to the opera's transgressive ethos. The program's hierarchical, racially segregated layout reinforces stereotypes of race that reassure whites, while diverting attention away from the campy aesthetics that made *Four Saints* a queer tour de force.

The *Four Saints* program, if read as a kind of manifesto (a statement of "difference" within modernism, and within American society), nevertheless shows that the histories of marginalized communities, including people of color, women, and queers, are neither entirely separate nor neatly transposable. The opera offered an alternate vision of modern culture, itself rife with internal contradictions. To fully appreciate the opera's historical and cultural significance we must widen our angle of view and consider the implications of its premiere in the state capital of Connecticut, where, in 1934, the white-supremacist society Ku Klux Klan remained active in the rural townships surrounding Hartford. Although the Klan's national influence had fallen off by the mid-1920s, East-Coast newspapers reported on Klan activities throughout New England well into the 1930s. Between 1920 and 1925, somewhere between three and six million white Americans joined the so-called "second Klan." The revived KKK became one of the largest social organizations in US history.[9] In 1934, the year *Four Saints* premiered in Hartford, *The Hartford Courant* newspaper reported regularly on Klan picnics and recruiting efforts in surrounding Connecticut communities.[10] The Klan's mission to suppress outsiders, immigrants, all manner of difference, could not help but inflect the reception, in the heart of Protestant New England, of an opera about Catholic saints written by a secular

8 Virgil Thomson, *Virgil Thomson* (New York: Alfred A. Knopf, 1966), p. 238.

9 See David Horowitz, "The Normality of Extremism: The Ku Klux Klan Revisited," *Society* 35, no. 6 (September–October 1998): pp. 71–77.

10 *The Hartford Courant* informed readers, "The Knights of the Ku Klux Klan […] in Willington [just north of Hartford…] held their annual picnic at Cooper's field" ("Ku Klux Klan Knights Play Ball, Eat Chowder," *Hartford Courant*, July 31, 1934, p. 22). An article in the *Courant* published later in that summer of 1934 reports on the Klan's renewed recruiting efforts in nearby Windsor ("The Klan Rides Again, Maybe, Seeks Men Letters Indicate," *Hartford Courant*, August 10, 1934, p. 14). In Windsor, the Klan hand-delivered letters to sympathizers who had "helped the Klan stop immigration": "You have been staunch in your belief in White Supremacy, and now you are needed not only to continue the fight on these, but to stop another and more insidious menace to Americanism: namely Communism […]. The Klan rides again!" The personalized tracts warned of the latest ideological threat to the "American way of life" (Ibid.).

eins zu eins übertragbar sind. Die Oper bot zwar eine alternative Vision moderner Kultur, wies jedoch selbst eine Vielzahl interner Widersprüche auf.

Um die historische und kulturelle Bedeutung der Oper vollends abschätzen zu können, müssen wir unseren Blickwinkel erweitern und die Auswirkungen ihrer Premiere in der Hauptstadt von Connecticut betrachten, wo der Ku-Klux-Klan mit seiner Politik *weißer* Vorherrschaft in den ländlichen Gemeinden rund um Hartford immer noch aktiv war. Obwohl der nationale Einfluss des Klans ab Mitte der 1920er-Jahre zurückgegangen war, berichteten Ostküstenzeitungen in New England bis weit in die 1930er-Jahre hinein von Klan-Aktivitäten. Zwischen 1920 und 1925 waren zwischen drei und sechs Millionen *weiße* US-Amerikaner*innen Mitglieder des sogenannten zweiten Klans. Der neu belebte Ku-Klux-Klan wurde zu einer der größten gesellschaftlichen Organisationen in der US-Geschichte.[9] 1934, das Jahr, in dem die Premiere von *Four Saints* in Hartford stattfand, berichtete die Zeitung *Hartford Courant* regelmäßig von Klan-Picknicks und Rekrutierungsbemühungen in den umgebenden Gemeinden in Connecticut.[10]

Der Klan, mit seiner Mission, Außenseiter*innen, Einwander*innen und alle Arten von Anderssein zu unterdrücken, musste jedoch im Herzen des protestantischen New England eine Oper über katholische Heilige hinnehmen – geschrieben von einer säkularen jüdischen, nach Paris ausgewanderten Lesbe, gestaltet von einer säkularen jüdischen Malerin aus New York City, unter der Regie eines Gewerkschaftsanhängers, dirigiert von einem Sozialisten; komponiert von einem schwulen Mann, choreografiert von einem schwulen Mann, hauptsächlich finanziert von homosexuellen Gönner*innen, abgehalten von einem bisexuellen Museumsdirektor und aufgeführt von einem Schwarzen Chor (Abb. 4). Trotz der angespannten „racial" Dynamiken unter den Mitarbeiter*innen von *Four Saints* agierten auf der Bühne alle als Verbündete, um so die Klan-Version vom wahren Amerikanismus zu widerlegen.

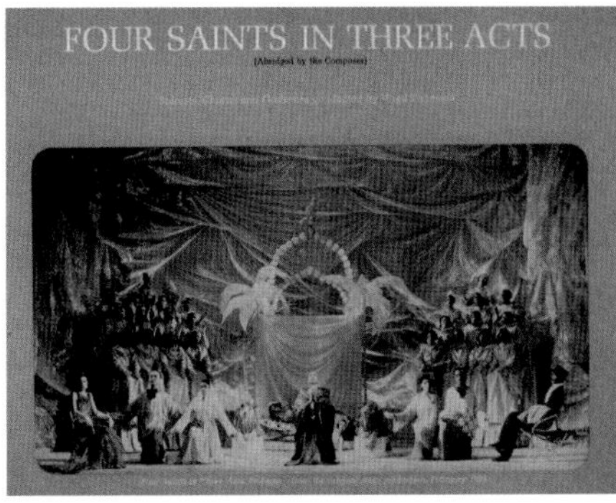

ABB. ~ FIG.4

Abbildung des Prologs für die Originalaufführung von ~ *Picture of the Prologue from the original performance of Four Saints in Three Acts* in Hartford, Connecticut; reproduziert auf der Plattenhülle einer RCA-Studioaufnahme von 1947, die 1964 als Vinyl-LP veröffentlicht wurde ~ *reproduced on the record sleeve of an RCA studio recording from 1947, released as a vinyl LP in 1964.*

Im Gefolge der Extravaganzen von *Four Saints* gab es noch eine weitere Unternehmung, die sich die oppositionelle Energie der Exzentrizität zunutze machte, nämlich die Zeitschrift *View*.[11] Gegründet wurde sie 1940 in New York City von Charles Henri Ford, einem Stein-Protegé der jüngeren Generation, und seinem Kollegen, dem Kritiker Parker Tyler. *View* zeigte Arbeiten von Ausländer*innen, Außenseiter*innen,

9
Siehe David Horowitz, „The Normality of Extremism: The Ku Klux Klan Revisited", in: *Society* 35, Nr. 6, September–Oktober 1998, S. 71–77.

10
Der *Hartford Courant* informiert seine Leser*innen, dass „die Ritter des Ku Klux Klans [...] in Willington [nördlich von Hartford] [...] ihr jährliches Picknick in Coopers Feld abgehalten haben". „Ku Klux Klan Knights Play Ball, Eat Chowder", in: *Hartford Courant*, 31.07.1934, S. 22. Ein Artikel, der später im Sommer 1934 im *Courant* erschien, berichtet von den erneuten Rekrutierungsversuchen des Klans im nahen Windsor. „The Klan Rides Again, Maybe, Seeks Men Letters Indicate", in: *Hartford Courant*, 10.08.1934, S. 14. In Windsor teilte der Klan händisch Briefe an Sympathisant*innen aus, die „dem Klan geholfen haben, Einwanderung aufzuhalten", ebd., „Ihr wart standhaft in eurer Überzeugung der Weißen Vorherrschaft, jetzt werdet ihr nicht nur gebraucht, um den Kampf dafür fortzuführen, sondern auch, um eine andere und noch heimtückischere Bedrohung des Amerikanismus aufzuhalten, nämlich den Kommunismus [...] Der Klan reitet wieder!" Die personalisierten Traktate warnten vor der jüngsten ideologischen Bedrohung des „American way of life".

11
Für einen Überblick über die Publikationsgeschichte der Zeitschrift, siehe Charles Henri Ford (Hrsg.), *View: Parade of the Avant Garde, 1940–1947*, mit einem Vorwort von Paul Bowles, zusammengestellt von Catarina Neiman und Paul Nathan, New York 1991.

Jewish lesbian and Paris expat; designed by a secular Jewish woman painter from New York City; directed by a labor union sympathizer; conducted by a socialist; composed by a gay man; choreographed by a gay man; financed primarily by gay patrons; hosted by a bisexual museum director; and performed by an African American chorus (fig. 4). Despite the fraught racial dynamics among the *Four Saints* collaborators, all concerned nevertheless allied on stage to refute the Klan's version of true American-ness. In the wake of the *Four Saints* extravaganza, another enterprise emerged to harness the oppositional energy of eccentricity: the journal *View*.[11] Founded in New York City in 1940 by a Stein protégé of an even younger generation, Charles Henri Ford, and his collaborator, the critic Parker Tyler. *View* presented work by aliens, misfits, immigrants, itinerants, conscientious objectors, autodidacts, free thinkers, anarchists, and sexual outlaws. During a decade defined by the war in Europe, *View* emphasized sites, subjects, and mechanisms of cultural production at odds with the rhetoric gaining prominence in the United States. Many embraced unorthodox modes of practice and materials, whether that meant working with the banal resources of everyday life, like newspaper, as per Tchelitchew's décor for the Paper Ball hosted by the Wadsworth Atheneum in 1936; repurposing genre-inappropriate materials, such as the cellophane Stettheimer used in the sets of *Four Saints*; or perfecting archaic skills, like painting with egg tempera, as did Cadmus. Few were in step with the modern art market. National schools and formal disciplines did not delineate their careers. Thumbing through any issue of *View*, no dominant aesthetic, editorial position, or organizing cultural logic is immediately apparent. In fact, the magazine seemed to deliberately eschew the taxonomical frameworks structuring the modern art world during the 1940s. *View*'s supporters appreciated the magazine's novelty. Lincoln Kirstein praised *View* for appreciating "that luxurious unimportance without which everything else would seem as dull as it usually is."[12] Meant as a compliment, Kirstein's appraisal distorts the magazine's aims. For the editors of *View*, every creative act, whether widely considered "unimportant" or not, had both value and consequence. Thus, in *View*'s pages, we find modest cultural artifacts alongside grandiose works of historical and contemporary fine art. The eye-catching color cover graphics that made *View* stand out well on newsstands, and helped to sell magazines, did nothing to correct the journal's effect of eclecticism, but rather effectively advertised it. "*View*'s unique contribution," Ford explained in a fundraising letter articulating the journal's mission, "is to give voice to cultural manifestations [...] not necessarily falling within prescribed modern styles and forms, but always expressing ideas that are vital and out-of-the-ordinary."[13] *View*'s commitment to the "out-of-the-ordinary" (one might just as well say "eccentric") made the magazine unique. Building on contacts he had established with his first periodical, *Blues* (one of the first journals in the United States to solicit material from Gertrude Stein), Ford commissioned contributions by Europeans, American expats still living in Europe, and European exiles living in the

11 For an overview of the journal's publication history, see Charles Henri Ford, ed., *View: Parade of the Avant Garde, 1940–1947*, with foreword by Paul Bowles, compiled by Catarina Neiman and Paul Nathan (New York: Thunder's Mouth, 1991).

12 Lincoln Kirstein, letter to the editors published in "View Listens," *View* 2, no. 4 (January 1943): p. 41.

13 Charles Henri Ford, letter to subscribers, April 3, 1947, Charles Henri Ford Papers, YCAL MSS 32, Box 4, folder 222, Beinecke Rare Book and Manuscript Library, Yale University.

Einwander*innen, Umherziehenden, Kriegsdienstverweigerern, Autodidakt*innen, Freidenker*innen, Anarchist*innen und sexuell Geächteten. In einem Jahrzehnt, das vom Krieg in Europa geprägt war, stellte *View* die Orte, Motive und Mechanismen kulturellen Schaffens in den Mittelpunkt, die nicht jener Rhetorik entsprachen, die sich in den Vereinigten Staaten auf dem Vormarsch befand. Viele der Beitragenden bedienten sich unorthodoxer Praktiken und Materialien, sei es nun die Arbeit mit ganz banalen Gegenständen des täglichen Lebens, wie Zeitungen – etwa für Tchelitchews Ausstattung für den Paper Ball, der 1936 im Wadsworth Atheneum stattfand; die Aneignung von Materialien, die nicht dem Genre entsprachen, wie das Zellophan, das Stettheimer für die Kulissen von *Four Saints* verwendete; oder aber auch die Vervollkommnung archaischer Fähigkeiten, wie das Malen mit Eitempera, wie bei Cadmus. Nur wenige entsprachen damit den Standards des modernen Kunstmarkts. Ihre Karrieren waren weder von nationalen Schulen noch von formellen Disziplinen geprägt. Blättert man durch eine Ausgabe von *View,* lässt sich auf den ersten Blick keine vorherrschende Ästhetik, redaktionelle Haltung oder gliedernde kulturelle Logik feststellen. Tatsächlich scheint die Zeitschrift die taxonomischen Strukturen, von denen die moderne Kunstwelt der 1940er-Jahre geprägt war, bewusst zu meiden. Die Unterstützer*innen von *View* schätzten die Neuartigkeit des Magazins. Lincoln Kirstein lobte *View* dafür, dass es „diese luxuriöse Unwichtigkeit“ zu schätzen wisse, „ohne die alles andere so geistlos wie eh und je wirken würde“.[12] Als Kompliment gemeint, verzerrt Kirsteins Einschätzung jedoch den Sinn und Zweck der Zeitschrift. Für die Herausgeber*innen von *View* verfügte jeder kreative Akt, ob er nun allgemein als „unwichtig“ oder nicht betrachtet wurde, sowohl über Wert als auch über Bedeutung. So finden wir auf den Seiten von *View* bescheidene kulturelle Erzeugnisse neben herausragenden Arbeiten der historischen und zeitgenössischen bildenden Kunst. Die farblich auffällige grafische Gestaltung des Titels, die *View* am Kiosk besonders gut zur Geltung brachte und dem Verkauf der Zeitschrift zuträglich war, trug nicht dazu bei, den Eklektizismus von *View* zu korrigieren, sondern warb gewissermaßen noch dafür. „*Views* einzigartiger Beitrag“, erläuterte Ford in einem Spendenbrief, der die Mission der Zeitschrift verdeutlichen sollte, „ist es, kulturellen Ausdrucksformen eine Stimme zu verleihen [...], die nicht unbedingt vorgeschriebenen Stilen und Formen entsprechen, sondern die stets Vorstellungen ausdrücken, die lebendig und außergewöhnlich sind“.[13] Die Verpflichtung von *View* dem „Außergewöhnlichen“ (man könnte auch sagen, dem „Exzentrischen“) gegenüber machte die Zeitschrift so einzigartig.

Ford baute auf Kontakten auf, die er schon mit seiner ersten Zeitschrift *Blues* geknüpft hatte (eine der ersten Zeitschriften in den Vereinigten Staaten, die sich um Material von Gertrude Stein bemühte), und beauftragte Beiträge von Europäer*innen, immer noch in Europa lebenden Amerikaner*innen und europäischen Exilant*innen, die in den USA lebten, aber auch von Kunstschaffenden aus der Karibik, Mittelamerika und Südamerika. Gleichzeitig setzten Ford und Tyler die Zeitschrift ein, um die Karrieren homosexueller Komponist*innen, Schriftsteller*innen und Künstler*innen zu fördern und homophile Netzwerke zu stärken. Prominent vertreten war auch Fords Liebhaber, der in Russland geborene Maler Tchelitchew. Nach einem Kennenlernen

12 Lincoln Kirstein, Brief an die Herausgeber, veröffentlicht in „View Listens“, in: *View* 2, Nr. 4, Januar 1943, S. 41.

13 Charles Henri Ford, Brief an Abonnent*innen, 03.04.1947, Charles Henri Ford Papers, YCAL MSS 32, Box 4, Folder 222, Beinecke Rare Book and Manuscript Library, Yale University.

United States, as well as artists from the Caribbean, Central America, and South America. At the same time, Ford and Tyler used the magazine to support the careers of gay composers, authors, and artists and strengthen homophile networks. The journal prominently featured Ford's lover, the Russian-born painter Tchelitchew. After meeting Ford (through Stein) in France, and migrating with Ford to New York, Tchelitchew's career as a painter and theatrical designer took off, along with *View*, thanks in part to the alliance of influential queers. *View* served as Tchelitchew's primary showcase. In addition to reproducing his paintings and drawings, *View* organized gallery exhibitions, for which Tchelitchew-focused issues of the magazine doubled as catalogues. Ford successfully lobbied for the acquisition of Tchelitchew's work by the nascent Museum of Modern Art, conveniently located just down the block from *View*'s 53rd Street offices in New York City.

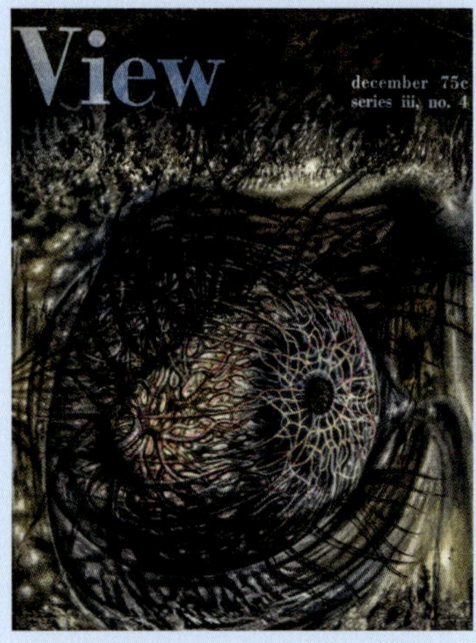

ABB. ~ FIG. 5

View, Nr. ~ *No.* 4, Dezember ~ *December* 1943, Coverabbildung von ~ *Cover image by* Pavel Tchelitchew

The disembodied eyeball on the cover of *View*'s December 1943 issue (fig. 5) emblematizes the magazine (whose title evokes sight) as well as Tchelitchew's way of seeing. For many of his human figure studies, such as *Interior Landscape* (ca. 1947, cat. p. 153), the artist focuses on the internal workings of the body, rather than its external appearance. Moreover, his artist's eye, like this one on the *View* magazine cover, characteristically floats free of any static subject position, capturing a view from multiple perspectives. The same perspectival un-fixity characterizes *View* magazine. Although firmly grounded in New York, which was emerging as a major modern art capital at that time, *View* espoused a decentralized notion of cultural production. Over half of the magazine's contributors were not US residents. To solicit collaborators across geographical boundaries, *View* constantly mobilized Ford's cosmopolitan social networks. As the so-called "American Century"[14] progressed, cosmopolitanism's art-world cachet suffered a reversal. American artists, critics, curators, and collectors had long looked to Europe as their reference for developments in the arts. But in the 1940s and 1950s, distilling the unique characteristics of a purely American art

14 The American press magnate Henry Luce put the phrase the "American Century" into circulation, writing in the February 17, 1941, issue of *Life* magazine that the twentieth century must be, "to a significant degree, an American Century." Henry R. Luce, "The American Century," pp. 61–65, here p. 64.

(mit Stein) in Frankreich und der Migration mit Ford nach New York nahm Tchelitchews Karriere als Maler und Bühnenbildner – zusammen mit *View* – an Fahrt auf, was zum Teil auch auf die Verbindung mit einflussreichen queeren Persönlichkeiten zurückzuführen ist. *View* diente dabei als Tchelitchews vorrangiges Präsentationsmittel. So zeigte die Zeitschrift nicht nur seine Gemälde und Zeichnungen, sondern organisierte auch Galerieausstellungen, zu denen Ausgaben der Zeitschrift mit einem Tchelitchew-Schwerpunkt als Kataloge dienten. Ford setzte sich zudem erfolgreich für einen Ankauf von Tchelitchews Arbeiten durch das neu gegründete Museum of Modern Art ein, das sich praktischerweise nur wenige Blocks entfernt vom Büro von *View* in der 53. Straße in New York City befand. Der körperlose Augapfel auf dem Titelblatt der *View*-Ausgabe vom Dezember 1943 (Abb. 5) steht nicht nur sinnbildlich für die Zeitschrift (deren Titel ja auf das Sehen verweist), sondern auch für Tchelitchews Art, zu sehen. Für viele seiner Studien menschlicher Figuren, wie *Interior Landscape* (um 1947, Kat., S. 153), legte der Künstler den Schwerpunkt auf die innere Funktionsweise des Körpers anstatt auf das äußere Erscheinungsbild. Zudem schwebt sein Künstlerauge, wie das auf dem Titel von *View*, typischerweise frei von jeder statischen Position und bietet so einen Blick aus ganz unterschiedlichen Perspektiven. Die gleiche perspektivische Nichtfixierung zeichnet auch die Zeitschrift *View* aus.

Obwohl fest in New York verankert, das sich zu jener Zeit zur wohl wichtigsten Metropole moderner Kunst entwickelte, trat *View* für ein dezentralisiertes Konzept von Kunst und Kultur ein. Mehr als die Hälfte der Beitragenden waren keine US-Bürger*innen. Um Mitarbeiter*innen über geografische Grenzen hinweg anzuwerben, mobilisierte *View* beständig Fords kosmopolitische gesellschaftliche Netzwerke.

Mit dem Fortschreiten des sogenannten amerikanischen Jahrhunderts[14] war das Prestige des Kosmopolitismus der Kunstwelt einer Umkehr unterworfen. US-amerikanische Künstler*innen, Kritiker*innen, Kurator*innen und Sammler*innen hatten sich als Referenz für Entwicklungen im Kunstbereich lange Zeit Europa zugewandt. Doch in den 1940er- und 1950er-Jahren waren Kritiker*innen wie Clement Greenberg – der mit Essays wie „‚American Type‘ Painting“[15] fesselnde Geschichten der amerikanischen Moderne prägen sollte, die auch heute noch dominieren – damit beschäftigt, die einzigartigen Charakteristika einer rein amerikanischen Kunst zusammenzufassen. *View* war Greenberg ein Gräuel. Es wäre nicht übertrieben, zu behaupten, dass er seine Gedanken zur Moderne (zur Autonomie der modernen Kunst vom sozialen und politischen Leben sowie von den Bezügen der realen Welt, ihrer formalen Reinheit, ihrer disziplinarischen Integrität) im Widerspruch zu *View* und all dem, wofür die Zeitschrift stand, formulierte. Im Gegensatz zu Greenberg und anderen, die Amerika (genauer gesagt New York) als Hauptstadt der modernen Kunstwelt positionierten, betrachtete *View* die Geschichte der modernen Kunst nicht als Entwicklungsgeschichte, die ihren Anfang im Paris des frühen 20. Jahrhunderts genommen und ihren Gipfel Mitte des Jahrhunderts in New York mit „reiner Abstraktion“ und der New Yorker Schule erreicht hatte.[16] Die Geschichten über Kunst, die sich von *View* aus verbreiteten, wurden mit vielerlei Stimmen erzählt, die nicht unbedingt harmonisch oder synchron waren. Sie erzählten von Reisen mit unterschiedlichen Zielen, oder überhaupt ohne Ziel. Sie

14 Der amerikanische Pressemagnat Henry Luce brachte den Begriff des „amerikanischen Jahrhunderts“ in Umlauf und schrieb in der Ausgabe von *Life* vom 17.02.1941, dass das 20. Jahrhundert „zu einem beträchtlichen Teil ein amerikanisches Jahrhundert“ sein müsse. Henry Luce, „The American Century“, S. 61–65, hier: S. 64.

15 Clement Greenberg, „‚American-Type‘ Painting“, in: *Partisan Review* 22, Nr. 2, Frühling 1955, S. 179–196.

16 Für gewöhnlich zählen die Maler des Abstrakten Expressionismus Willem de Kooning, Jackson Pollock, Mark Rothko und Robert Motherwell zu den Hauptvertretern der New Yorker Schule.

preoccupied critics such as Clement Greenberg—who, with essays such as "'American-Type' Painting,"[15] would shape compelling stories of American modernism that still hold sway today. *View* was, for Greenberg, anathema. It would not be an exaggeration to say that he formulated his thoughts about modernism (about modern art's autonomy from social and political life and from real-world references, its formal purity, its disciplinary integrity) in opposition to *View* and all that the magazine represented.

Unlike Greenberg and others positioning America (more specifically, New York) as the capital of the modern artworld, *View* did not see modern art's history as an evolutionary tale, beginning in Paris at the dawn of the twentieth century and climaxing in mid-century New York, with the "pure abstraction" and the New York School.[16] The stories about art spinning out from *View* were told in many voices, not necessarily in harmony or in sync. They spoke of journeys with divergent destinations, or no destination at all. They spoke of artistic alliances cemented by affection and desire, resistant to categorization. They spoke of solidarity among queers and all kinds of other misfits. By the mid-1940s, the journal had changed the slogan on its masthead from the original "Through the eyes of poets" to "You can't be modern and not read *View*." *View*'s notion of modernity was distinctive. *View* presented culture, not as a progress narrative, but as a process unfolding right before our eyes, a perpetual present, in which history, represented by the anachronistic content that crops up from time to time in the magazine, occurs anew alongside art and artifacts of the contemporary moment, unsettling the past as well as the present.

View's boundaries did not stop at the binding of the magazine. *View* was a living, evolving, site. An intersection. Under its auspices, exhibitions (and lavish exhibition openings), concerts, plays, screenings, debates, and lectures proliferated. Some of these events were intimate (puppet theater performed in the backroom of a night club, for instance, or costume balls held in a barn on the property of friends out in Connecticut). But others—like the jazz concerts *View* sponsored and the plays they staged at their own venue, Theatre Ubu—were in the public eye. During the war years, *View* briefly thrived, thanks in part to the edginess of their ancillary efforts, which were also "out of the ordinary."

In hindsight, we see now that America's 1950s crusade against "deviants" and dissenters (spear-headed by powerful politicians and conservative ideologues) was already on the horizon in the 1940s. With this in mind, the mission statement of *View* magazine—its privileging of the out-of-the-ordinary—sounds like a courageous proposition, rather than a frivolous caprice, as some insinuated. According to the surrealist leader André Breton, exiled in New York during the 1940s, *View* magazine was little more than a showcase for cosmopolitan queers—in his words, "pederasty international."[17] Yes, many of *View*'s contributors and both of its editors were gay (thus, by Breton's lights, lightweights). If the journal did not validate Breton's tenets of surrealism, or the formalist progress narratives of modernism articulated by Greenberg, *View* had more gravitas and political intentionality than its critics were willing to recognize or admit.

15 Clement Greenberg, "'American-Type' Painting," *Partisan Review* 22, no. 2 (Spring 1955), pp. 179–196.

16 Abstract Expressionist painters Willem de Kooning, Jackson Pollock, Mark Rothko, and Robert Motherwell number among those conventionally identified with the New York School.

17 André Breton refers to "la pédérastie internationale," in a letter to Benjamin Péret, April 19, 1943, quoted in Mark Polizzotti, *Revolution of the Mind: The Life of André Breton* (New York: Farrar, Straus and Giroux, 1995), p. 508. My thanks to Michael Taylor for giving me the gift of this quote. It should be noted that Breton nevertheless published a range of work in *View*.

erzählten von künstlerischen Allianzen, geschmiedet durch Zuneigung und Verlangen, die sich jeder Einordnung widersetzten. Sie erzählten von Solidarität unter queeren Menschen und anderen Außenseiter*innen.

Mitte der 1940er-Jahre änderte die Zeitschrift ihr Motto im Titelkopf von „Through the eyes of poets" (Durch die Augen von Dichter*innen) in „You can't be modern and not read *View*" (Man kann nicht modern sein, ohne *View* zu lesen). *Views* Konzept von Moderne war unverwechselbar. Es präsentierte Kultur nicht als progressives Narrativ, sondern als einen Prozess, der sich direkt vor unseren Augen abspielt, eine unaufhörliche Präsenz, in der Geschichte, dargestellt durch den anachronistischen Inhalt, der von Zeit zu Zeit in der Zeitschrift auftaucht, neben Kunst und Artefakten der Gegenwart stattfindet und die Vergangenheit ebenso verunsichert wie die Gegenwart. Die Grenzen von *View* waren mit dem Einband der Zeitschrift noch lange nicht erreicht. *View* war ein lebendiger, sich entwickelnder Schauplatz. Eine Schnittstelle. Unter dem Schutz des Magazins gediehen Ausstellungen (und aufwendige Ausstellungseröffnungen), Konzerte, Aufführungen, Vorführungen, Debatten und Vorträge. Einige dieser Veranstaltungen waren eher intim (Puppentheateraufführungen im Hinterzimmer eines Nachtclubs zum Beispiel oder Kostümbälle in einer Scheune auf dem Anwesen von Freund*innen in Connecticut). Doch andere – wie die Jazzkonzerte, die *View* förderte, und die Theaterstücke, die am eigenen Veranstaltungsort, dem Theatre Ubu, stattfanden – standen im Blickpunkt der Öffentlichkeit. Während der Kriegsjahre erlebte *View* eine kurze Blüte, zum Teil aufgrund der ausgefallenen zusätzlichen Angebote, die ebenfalls „außergewöhnlich" waren. Im Rückblick erkennen wir nun, dass der Kreuzzug des Amerikas der 1950er-Jahre gegen „von der Norm Abweichende" und Andersdenkende (angeführt von mächtigen Politikern und konservativen Ideologen) sich bereits in den 1940er-Jahren am Horizont abzeichnete. Behalten wir das im Hinterkopf, klingt das Leitbild der Zeitschrift *View* – die Bevorzugung des Außergewöhnlichen – eher wie ein couragiertes Vorhaben als wie eine leichtfertige Laune, wie bisweilen angedeutet. Laut André Breton, Leitfigur der Surrealist*innen, der sich in den 1940er-Jahren im New Yorker Exil befand, war die Zeitschrift *View* kaum mehr als eine Bühne für queere Kosmopolit*innen – mit seinen Worten „internationale Päderastie".[17] Ja, viele der Beitragenden zu *View* sowie seine beiden Herausgeber waren homosexuell (in Bretons Augen also Leichtgewichte). Auch wenn die Zeitschrift weder Bretons Prinzipien des Surrealismus noch die von Greenberg formulierten formalistischen Fortschrittsnarrative der Moderne anerkannte, verfügte *View* doch über mehr Gewicht und politische Intentionalität als die Kritiker*innen willens waren, anzuerkennen oder sich einzugestehen. Der Eklektizismus und die Exzentrizität von *View* boten Formen strategischen Widerstands gegen die sich verengenden Vorstellungen von künstlerischem Wert, Amerikanismus und sozialer Legitimität, die auf *View* und seine Bestandteile eindrangen.

Im Nachkriegsklima des sozialen und politischen Konservativismus, gerechtfertigt durch amerikanischem Triumphalismus, riskierten die exzentrischen Vertreter*innen der Moderne in *View* – mit ihrer kosmopolitischen Einstellung, ihrem unorthodoxen sexuellen Verhalten, ihren zunehmend unpopulärer werdenden sozialen Werten und den nicht marktfähigen künstlerischen Praktiken – negative Publicity, einen

17 In einem Brief an Benjamin Péret vom 19.04.1943 bezieht sich André Breton auf „la pédérastie internationale", zit. in: Mark Polizzotti, *Revolution of the Mind: The Life of André Breton*, New York 1995, S. 508. Vielen Dank an Michael Taylor, dem ich dieses Zitat verdanke. Es sollte jedoch nicht unerwähnt bleiben, dass Breton dennoch eine Reihe von Arbeiten in *View* veröffentlichte.

View's eclecticism and eccentricity offered forms of strategic resistance to the narrowing notions of artistic value, American-ness, and social legitimacy that were closing in on *View* and its constituents.

In the postwar climate of social and political conservatism, alibied by American triumphalism, *View*'s eccentric modernists—with their cosmopolitanism, unorthodox sexual behavior, increasingly unpopular social values, and unmarketable artistic practices—risked negative publicity, tarnished reputations, financial insecurity, censorship, or worse. *View* magazine folded in 1947 and many of its collaborators, including many of the eccentric modernists involved in the creation of *Dix Portraits* and *Four Saints in Three Acts*, went to ground, sought safe havens, and moved farther toward the edges. They tightened the family circle. They found new ways and new places to work. The artistic trio PaJaMa (an amalgam of the first two letters of Paul Cadmus, Jarred French, and Margaret Hoening French's first names) rose to the challenge. During retreats to the beaches of Fire Island and Provincetown, PaJaMa shot photographs of themselves and their social sphere. Lynes encouraged these collaborative experiments with photography and he figures in many of their photographs,[18] as do Wescott and Wheeler. PaJaMa photographs, moreover, bear the hallmarks of Lynes's sensibility: surreal staging, dramatic effects of lighting, and homoerotic undercurrents. Unlike Lynes, however, PaJaMa did not make portraits for exhibition, publication, or sale. They saved them in intimate albums and distributed small prints, like calling cards, to lovers and friends. These gift portraits contributed to the emotional (and historical) survival of a queer family and community under increasing pressure to hide, or disappear. In our current moment, to be "eccentric" is, once again, to live dangerously. In the United States, among other countries, contests to define what national identity means, and to test the limits of national sovereignty, play out once again in acts of aggression, repression, and, indeed, state-sanctioned violence. Frontiers are again closing. Initiatives to reach across geopolitical and cultural boundaries manifest as threats of conquest and colonization rather than as overtures of alliance. The terms "diversity," "equity," and "inclusion"—until recently invested with affirmative value in the mission statements of many cultural and educational institutions, and underwritten in some countries by laws—increasingly incite the animosity of those wielding political power. With totalitarianism and fundamentalism on the ascent worldwide, the word "difference," too, often prompts hostility rather than enthusiasm or curiosity. How will the term "eccentric" (and those whom it describes) fare in this climate? Can "eccentric" still encode, alibi, and abet resistance? Serve as a creative resource and refuge? Or will it simply come to designate precarity? Or imminent disappearance? Oblivion. Will eccentricity, along with sexuality and gender, hold up as a category of historical analysis? For that matter, will historical analysis hold up as a mode of engagement? Renewed campaigns of cultural defunding, censorship, purging, expulsion, and erasure raise these questions and make responding vital.

18 Nick Mauss and Angela Miller, in *Body Language: The Queer Staged Photographs of George Platt Lynes and PaJaMa*, ed. Anthony Lee (Oakland: University of California Press, 2023), study in depth the interplay between the photography of George Platt Lynes and PaJaMa.

angeschlagenen Ruf, finanzielle Unsicherheit, Zensur oder Schlimmeres. 1947 wurde die Zeitschrift eingestellt und zahlreiche Mitarbeiter*innen, darunter auch viele der exzentrischen Vertreter*innen der Moderne, die an der Herstellung von *Dix Portraits* und *Four Saints in Three Acts* beteiligt waren, tauchten unter, suchten sich einen sicheren Rückzugsort und bewegten sich noch weiter an den Rand. Sie schlossen den familiären Kreis enger. Sie fanden neue Möglichkeiten und neue Orte, um zu arbeiten.

Das künstlerische Trio PaJaMa (eine Verbindung der jeweils ersten beiden Buchstaben der Namen von Paul Cadmus, Jarred French und Margaret Hoening French) stellten sich der Herausforderung. Im Laufe von Aufenthalten an den Stränden von Fire Island und Provincetown schufen PaJaMa Aufnahmen von sich selbst und ihrem sozialen Umfeld. Lynes ermutigte diese gemeinschaftlichen Experimente mit Fotografie und er taucht, ebenso wie Wescott und Wheeler, auf zahlreichen ihrer Fotos auf.[18] Die Aufnahmen von PaJaMa lassen zudem Lynes' Einfühlungsvermögen erkennen: surreale Inszenierungen, dramatische Lichteffekte und homoerotische Untertöne. Im Gegensatz zu Lynes schufen PaJaMa jedoch keine Porträts, die für Ausstellungen, Publikationen oder den Verkauf gedacht waren. Sie bewahrten sie in persönlichen Alben auf und verteilten kleine, visitenkartenähnliche Abzüge an Liebhaber*innen und Freund*innen. Diese Geschenkporträts trugen zum emotionalen (und historischen) Überleben einer queeren Familie und Gemeinschaft bei, die unter zunehmendem Druck stand, sich zu verstecken oder zu verschwinden.

Aktuell bedeutet „exzentrisch“ zu sein, erneut, in Gefahr zu leben. In den Vereinigten Staaten und in anderen Ländern wird der Kampf um die Definition der Bedeutung von nationaler Identität und die Austestung der Grenzen nationaler Souveränität wieder einmal durch Aggression, Unterdrückung und sogar staatlich sanktionierte Gewalt ausgetragen. Wieder werden Grenzen geschlossen. Initiativen, um geopolitische und kulturelle Grenzen zu überwinden, wirken eher wie Drohungen, zu erobern und zu kolonialisieren, anstatt wie Bündnisangebote. Die Begriffe „Diversität“, „Gleichstellung“ und „Inklusion“ – die in den Leitbildern zahlreicher Kultur- und Bildungsorganisationen bislang positiv besetzt waren und in einigen Ländern sogar gesetzlich verankert sind – haben zunehmend die Feindseligkeit der politisch Verantwortlichen ausgelöst. Heute, wo Totalitarismus und Fundamentalismus weltweit im Aufschwung begriffen sind, sorgt das Wort „Unterschied“ zudem oftmals eher für Gegenwehr anstatt für Begeisterung oder Neugier.

Wie wird der Begriff „exzentrisch“ (und diejenigen, die er beschreibt) in diesem Klima abschneiden? Kann „exzentrisch“ immer noch für Widerstand stehen, diesen rechtfertigen und ihm Vorschub leisten? Kann es als kreative Ressource und Zuflucht dienen? Oder wird es einmal schlicht und einfach für Prekariat stehen? Oder für baldiges Verschwinden? Vergessenheit. Wird Exzentrik, gemeinsam mit Sexualität und Geschlechterrolle, als Kategorie historischer Analyse Bestand haben? Und was das anbelangt, wird die historische Analyse noch als Methode der Auseinandersetzung Bestand haben? Wiederholte Kampagnen zur Abschaffung von Kultur, zu Zensur, zu Säuberung, zu Vertreibung und zu Auslöschung werfen diese Fragen auf und machen eine Reaktion darauf unerlässlich.

18 Nick Mauss und Angela Miller, *Body Language: The Queer Staged Photographs of George Platt Lynes and PaJaMa*, hrsg. von Anthony Lee, Oakland 2023, liefern eine ausführliche Untersuchung des Zusammenspiels der Fotografien von George Platt Lynes und PaJaMa.

VII QUEERER WIDERSTAND SEIT 1933

QUEER RESISTANCE SINCE 1933

1

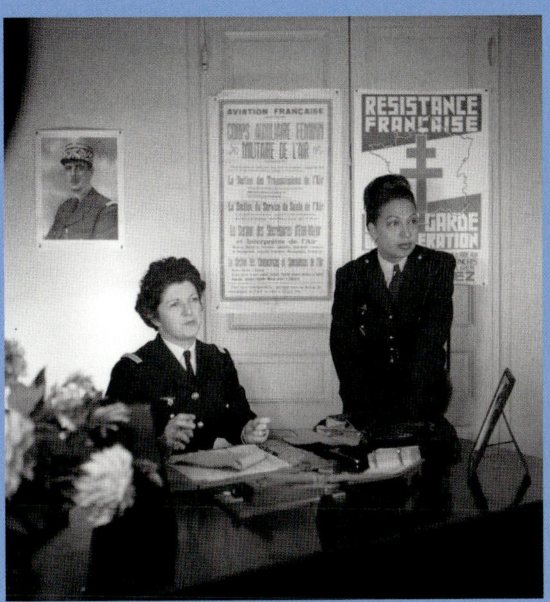

2

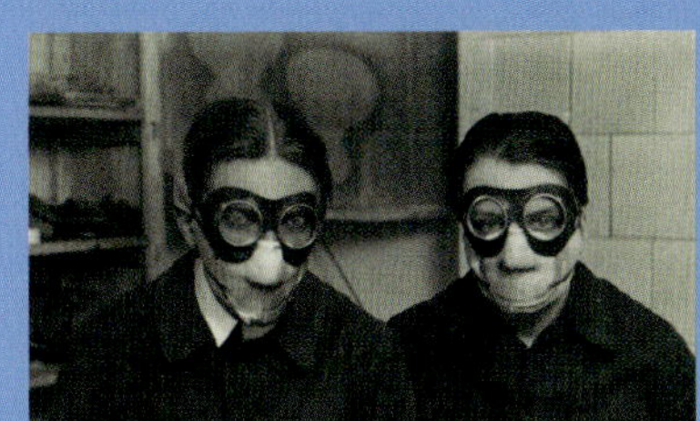

4

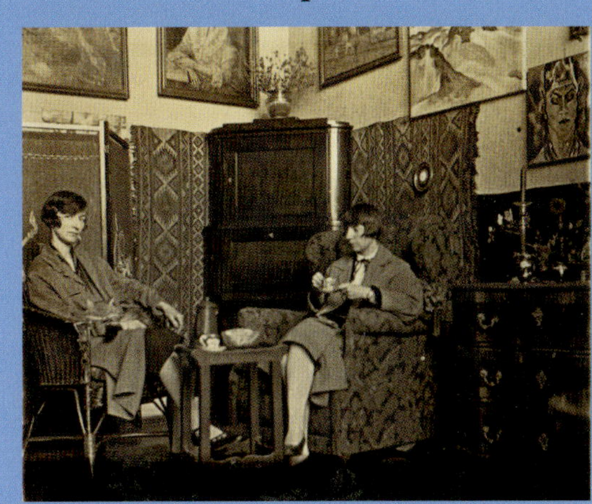

3

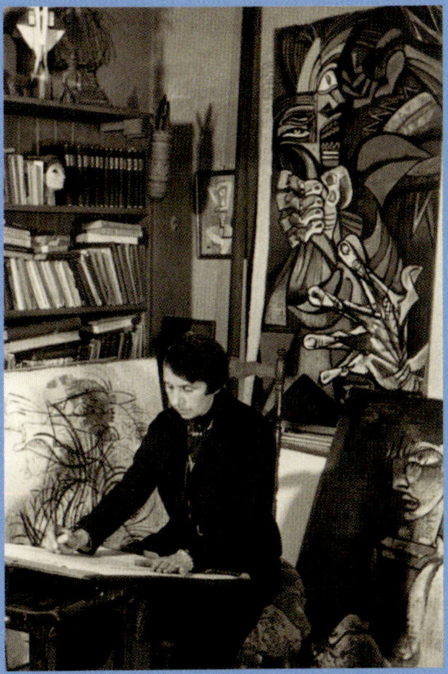

5

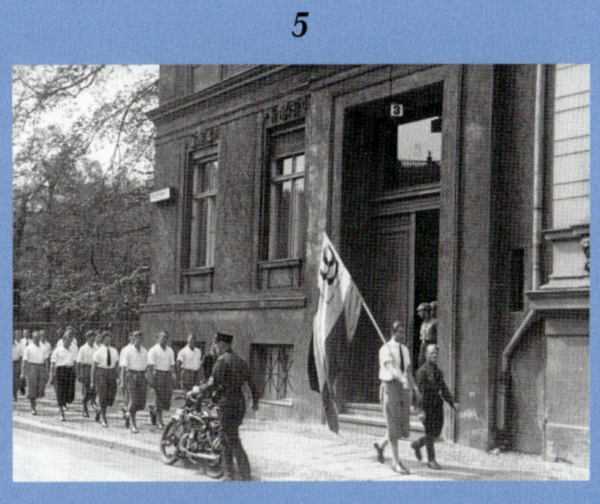

6

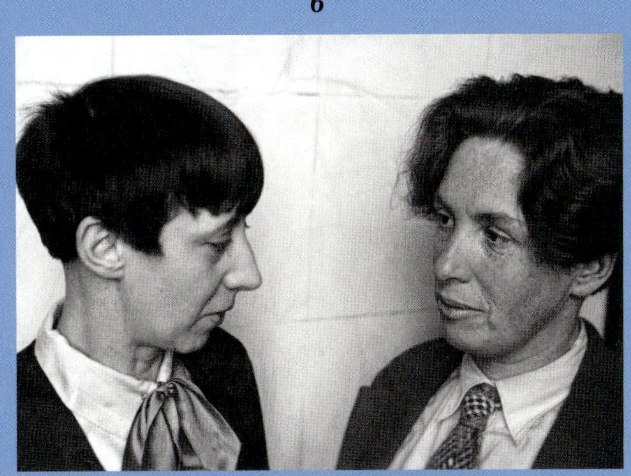

1

Josephine Baker wurde weltweit als Tänzerin und Sängerin gefeiert. Sie schloss sich während des Zweiten Weltkriegs der französischen Résistance an. Das Foto zeigt sie 1944 in Algier mit Major Alla Dumesnil-Gillet, der Leiterin der Abteilung für Luftübermittlung des weiblichen Hilfskorps der Luftwaffe.

Josephine Baker was celebrated worldwide as a dancer and singer. During the Second World War, she joined the French Resistance. This photograph shows her in Algiers in 1944 with Commandant Alla Dumesnil-Gillet, head of the Signal Corps of the Women's Auxiliary of the Free French Air Force.

2

Um das Jahr 1925 reisten Toyen und Jindřich Štyrský durch Europa und knüpften enge Kontakte zur Pariser Avantgarde. Ein Foto von 1929 zeigt beide beim Arbeiten mit toxischen Farben. Nach der Besetzung der Tschechoslowakei durch die Nationalsozialisten 1939 arbeitete Toyen im Untergrund und versteckte den jüdischen Dichter und Künstler Jindřich Heisler.

Around 1925, Toyen and Jindřich Štyrský traveled across Europe and forged close ties with the Paris avant-garde. This photograph from 1920 shows them working with toxic paints. After the Nazis occupation of Czechoslovakia in 1939, Toyen continued working underground and hid the Jewish poet and artist Jindřich Heisler.

3

Jeanne Mammen in ihrem Atelier 1946 mit ihrem Gemälde *Der Würgeengel* (um 1939 bis 1942) im Hintergrund. 1936 zog sie sich in die innere Emigration zurück und schuf im Verborgenen Arbeiten, die als kritischer Kommentar zur nationalsozialistischen Kunstideologie und politischen Situation gelesen werden können.

Jeanne Mammen in her studio in 1946, with her painting Der Würgeengel *(ca. 1939–1942) in the background. In 1936, she withdrew into a so-called "inner emigration" and secretly created works that may be interpreted as critical commentary on Nazi art ideology and the political situation.*

4

Mimi und Jeanne Mammen in ihrem Berliner Atelier, aufgenommen zwischen 1924 und 1928. Nach dem gemeinsamen Kunststudium in Paris, Brüssel und Rom lebten und arbeiteten die Schwestern auch noch in Berlin einige Jahre zusammen. 1936 emigrierte Mimi mit ihrer Lebensgefährtin Henriette Goldenberg nach Teheran.

Mimi and Jeanne Mammen in their Berlin studio, in a photograph taken between 1924 and 1928. After studying art together in Paris, Brussels, and Rome, the sisters lived and worked together in Berlin for several years. In 1936, Mimi emigrated to Tehran with her partner Henriette Goldenberg.

5

Der Sexualwissenschaftler Magnus Hirschfeld, der sich während der Weimarer Republik für die Entkriminalisierung und Akzeptanz sexueller und geschlechtlicher Minderheiten einsetzte, befand sich gerade in Paris, als die Nationalsozialisten am 6. Mai 1933 sein berühmtes Institut für Sexualwissenschaft in Berlin zerstörten.

The sexologist Magnus Hirschfeld, who campaigned for the decriminalization and acceptance of sexual and gender minorities during the Weimar Republic, was in Paris when the Nazis sacked and destroyed his famous Institute for Sexual Science in Berlin on May 6, 1933.

6

Die deutsche Dada-Künstlerin Hannah Höch und ihre Lebensgefährtin, die niederländische Schriftstellerin Til Brugman, lebten von 1926 bis zu ihrer Trennung 1936 zunächst in Den Haag und ab 1929 in Berlin. Ihre gemeinsamen Publikationen enthalten subversive Kritik am aufkommenden Nationalsozialismus.

The German Dada artist Hannah Höch and her partner, the Dutch writer Til Brugman, lived together from 1926 until their separation in 1936, first in The Hague and, after 1929, in Berlin. Their joint publications contain subversive criticism of the emerging threat of National Socialism.

HITLER führt uns ... GOEBBELS spricht für uns ... GOERING frisst für uns ... LEY trinkt für uns ... HIMMLER?... Himmler ermordet für uns ... Aber niemand stirbt für uns!

~

HITLER leads us... GOEBBELS speaks for us... GOERING gorges himself for us... LEY drinks for us... HIMMLER?... Himmler murders for us... But no one dies for us!

Eines von zahlreichen originalen und kopierten Propagandaflugblättern, die von Claude Cahun und Marcel Moore während der deutschen Besatzung der Insel Jersey hergestellt und verteilt wurden.

~

One of numerous original and copied propaganda leaflets produced and distributed by Claude Cahun und Marcel Moore during the German occupation of Jersey.

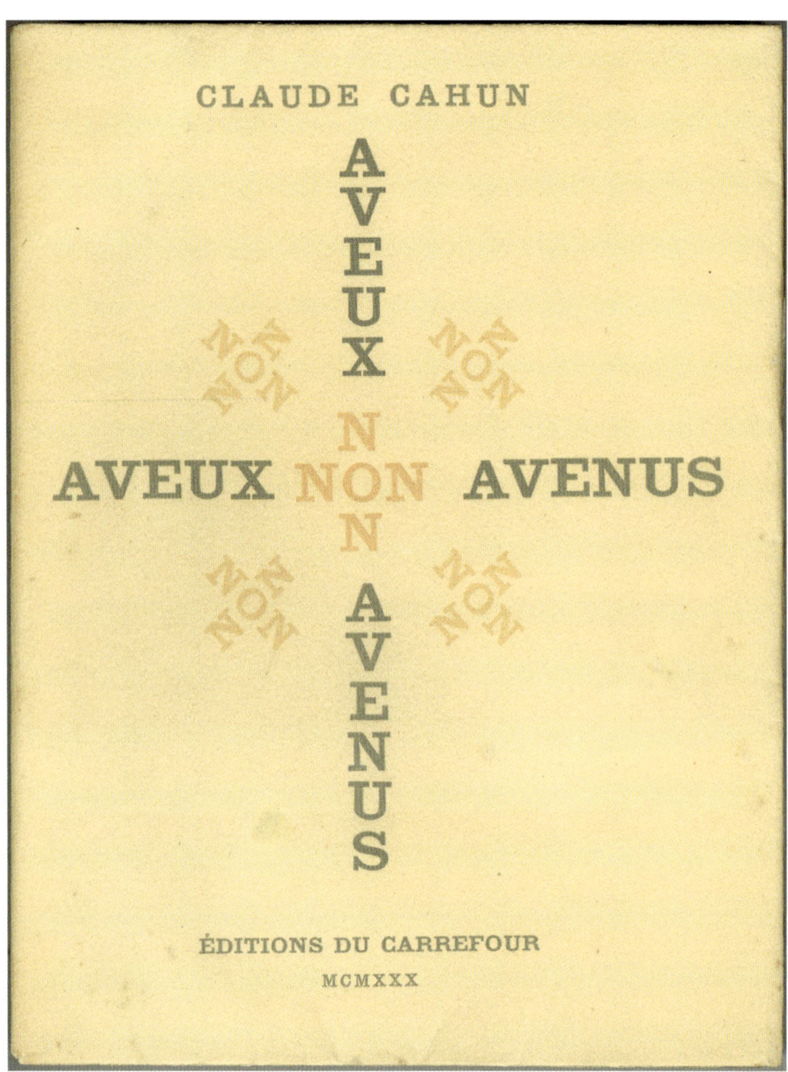

Claude Cahun

Aveux non avenus, 1930
Nichtige Geständnisse
Disavowals; or, Cancelled Confessions

Claude Cahun

Aveux non avenus, undatiert ~ *undated*
Nichtige Geständnisse ~
Disavowals; or, Cancelled Confessions

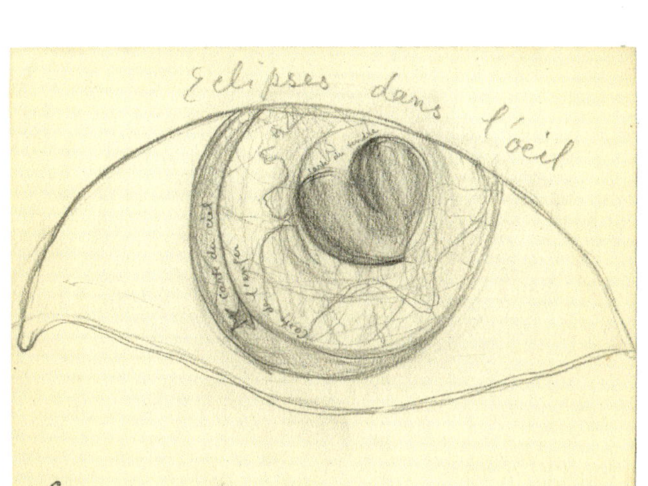

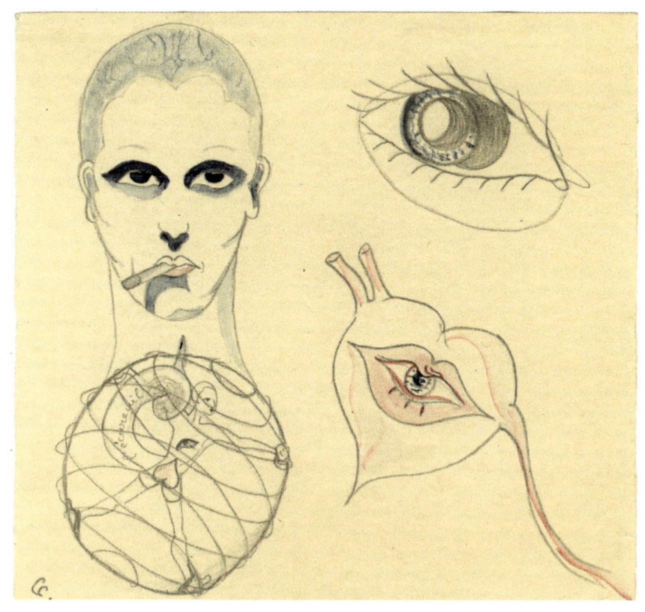

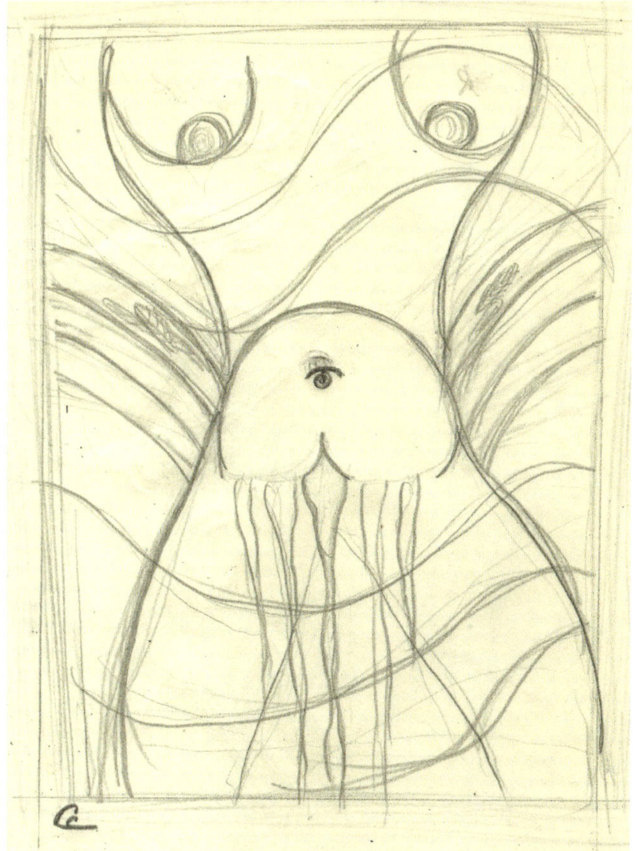

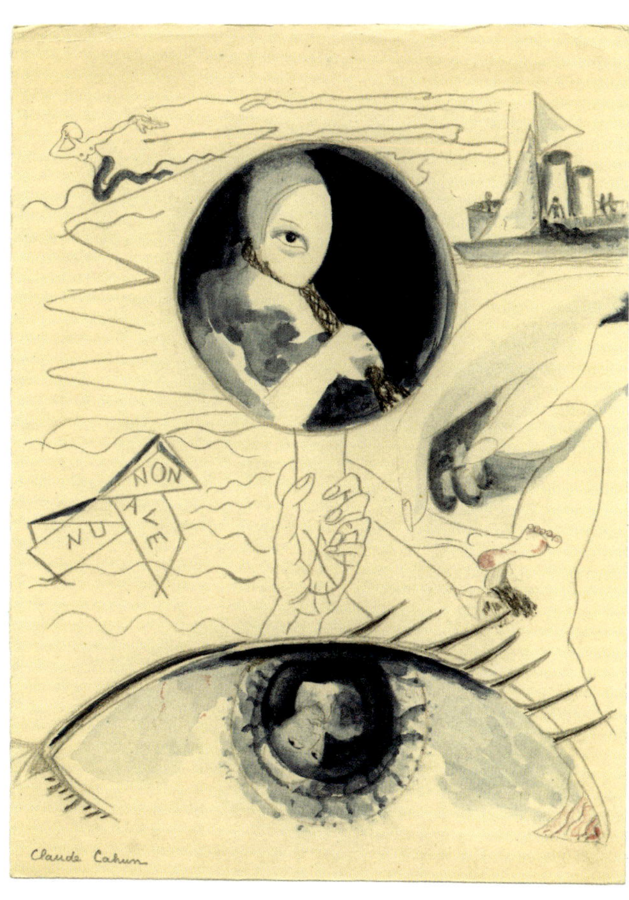

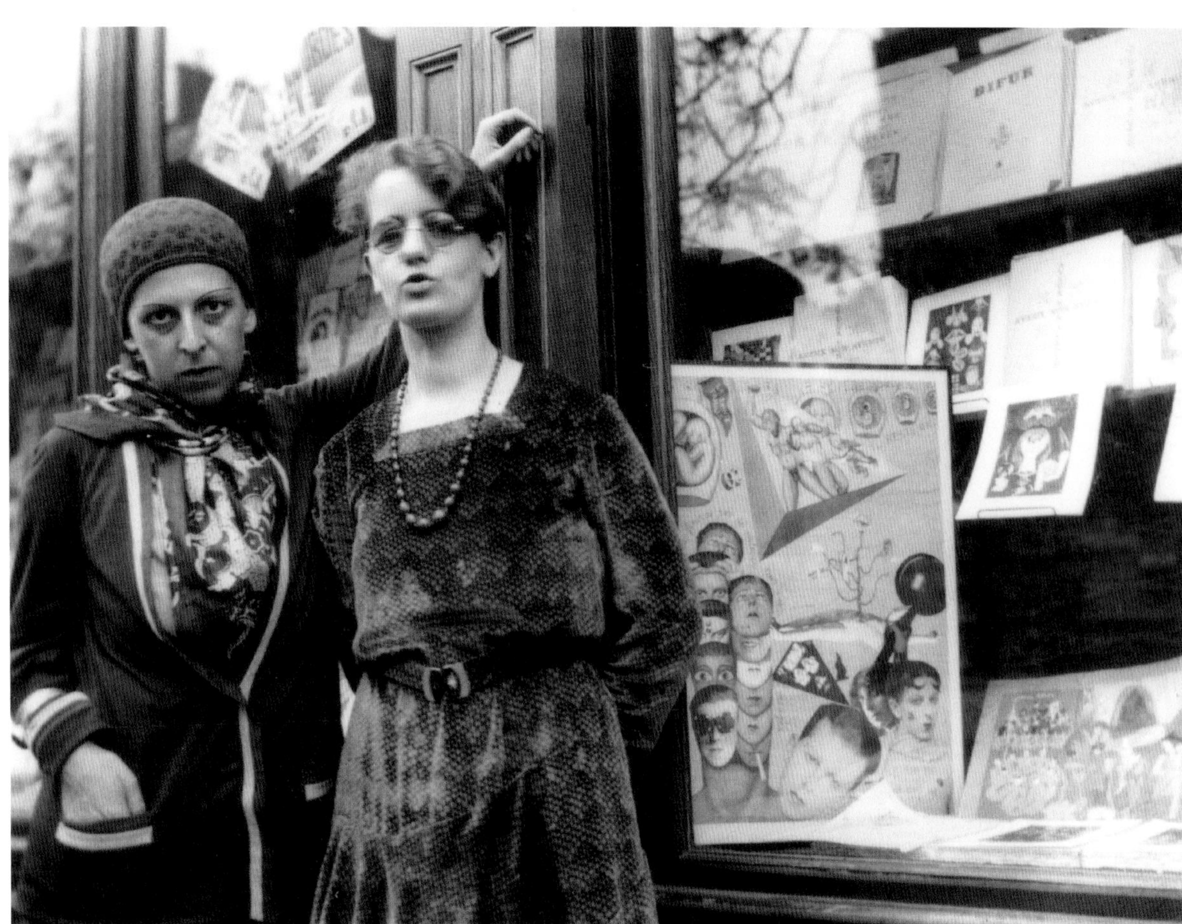

Claude Cahun und ~ *and* Marcel Moore
Shopwindow of Van den Bergh Booksellers, Book Launch for Aveux non avenus, 1930
Schaufenster der Buchhandlung Van den Bergh, Buchvorstellung von *Aveux non avenus*

Marcel Moore

Aveux non avenus, 1930
Nichtige Geständnisse ~
Disavowals; or, Cancelled Confessions

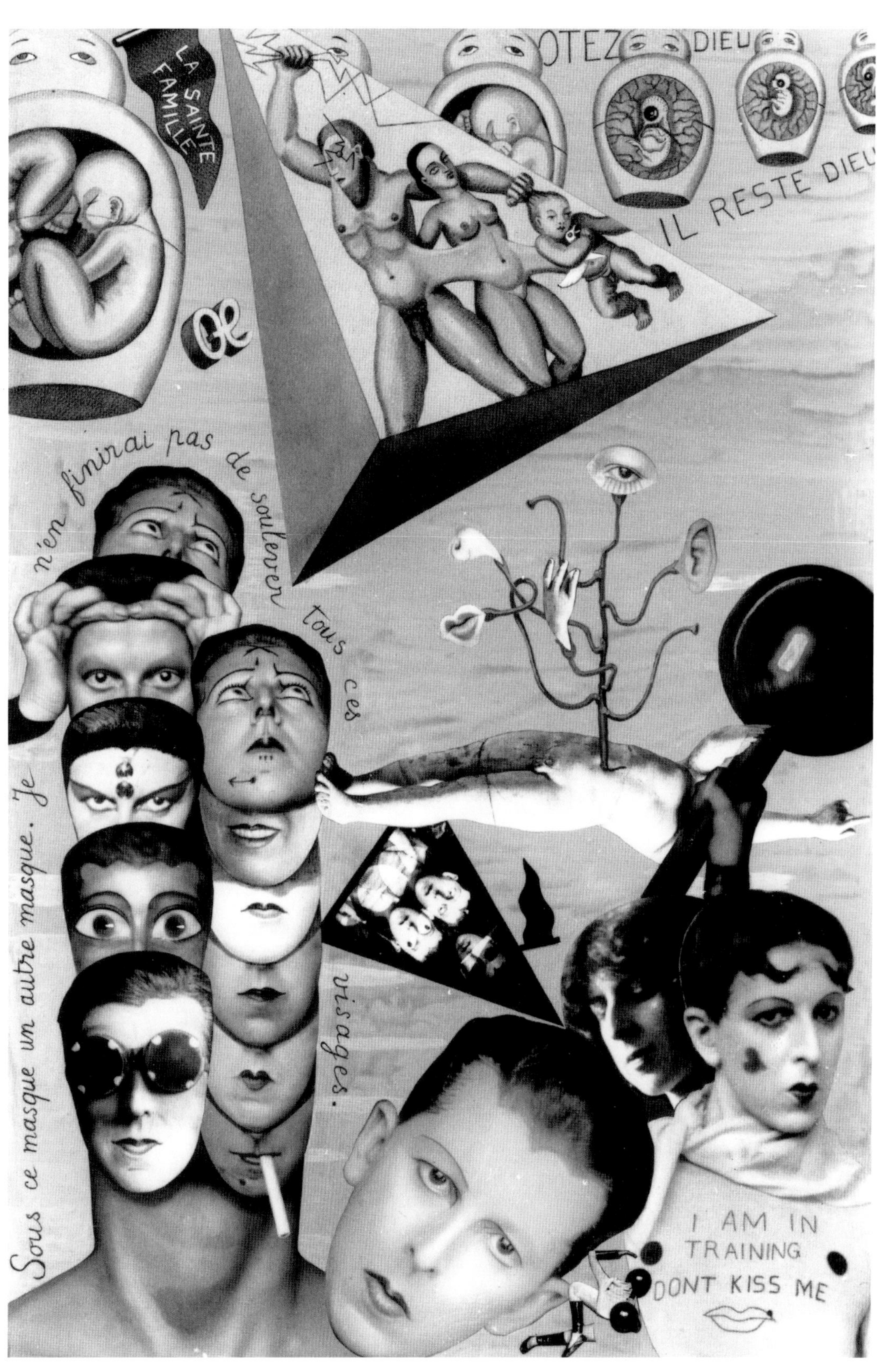

Marcel Moore

Aveux non avenus, 1930
Nichtige Geständnisse
Disavowals; or, Cancelled Confessions

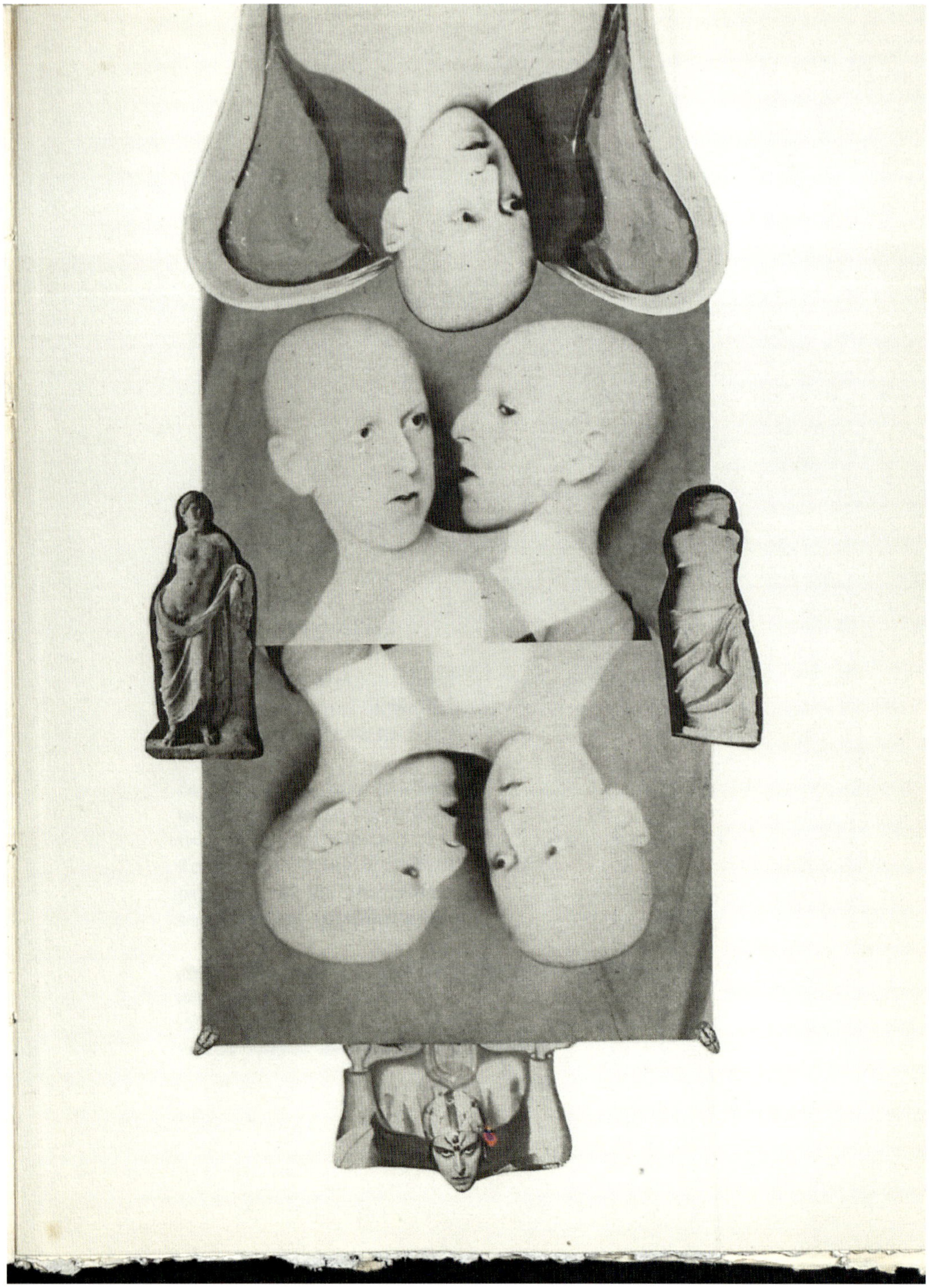

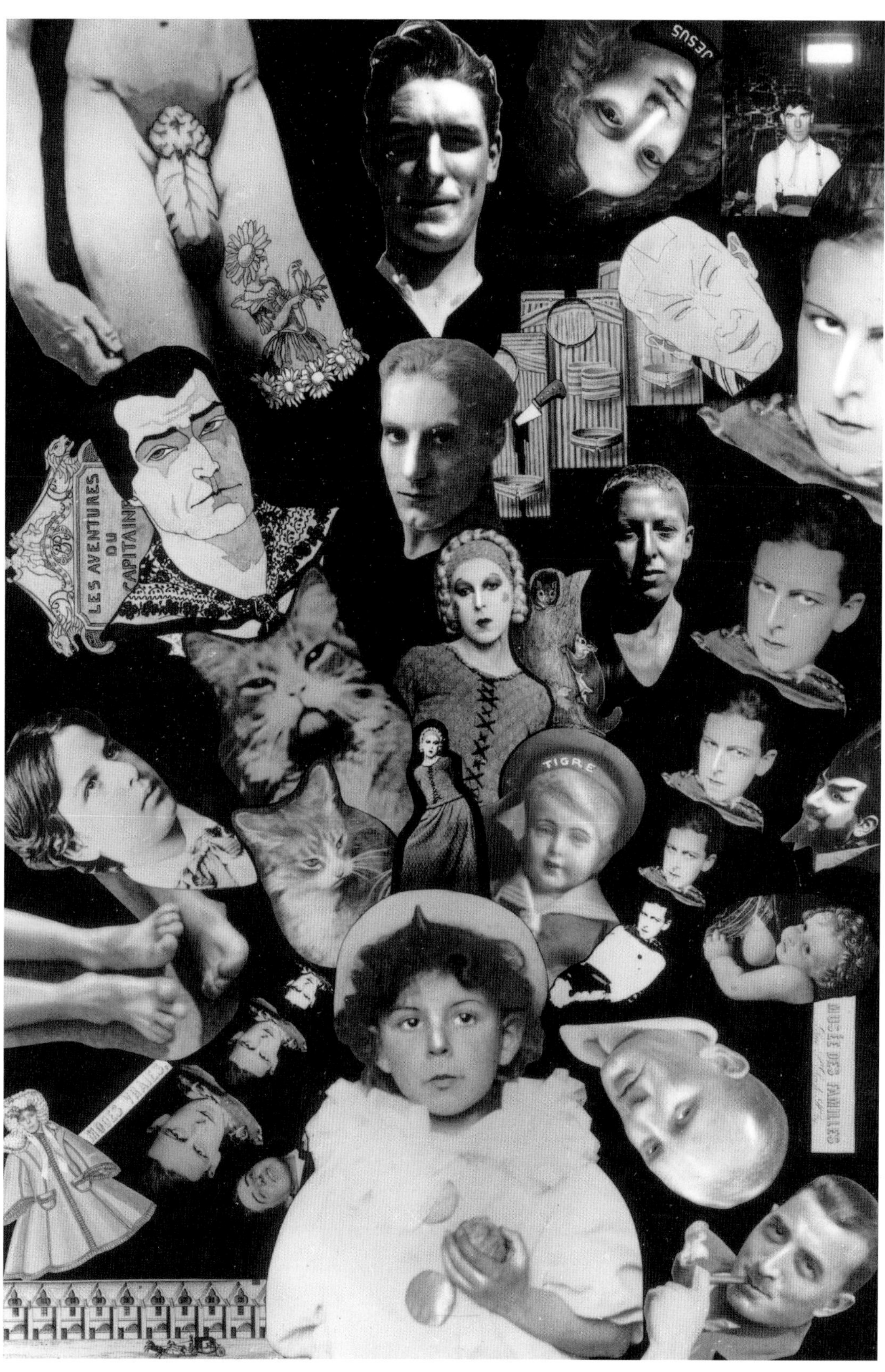

Marcel Moore

Aveux non avenus, 1930
Nichtige Geständnisse ~
Disavowals; or, Cancelled Confessions

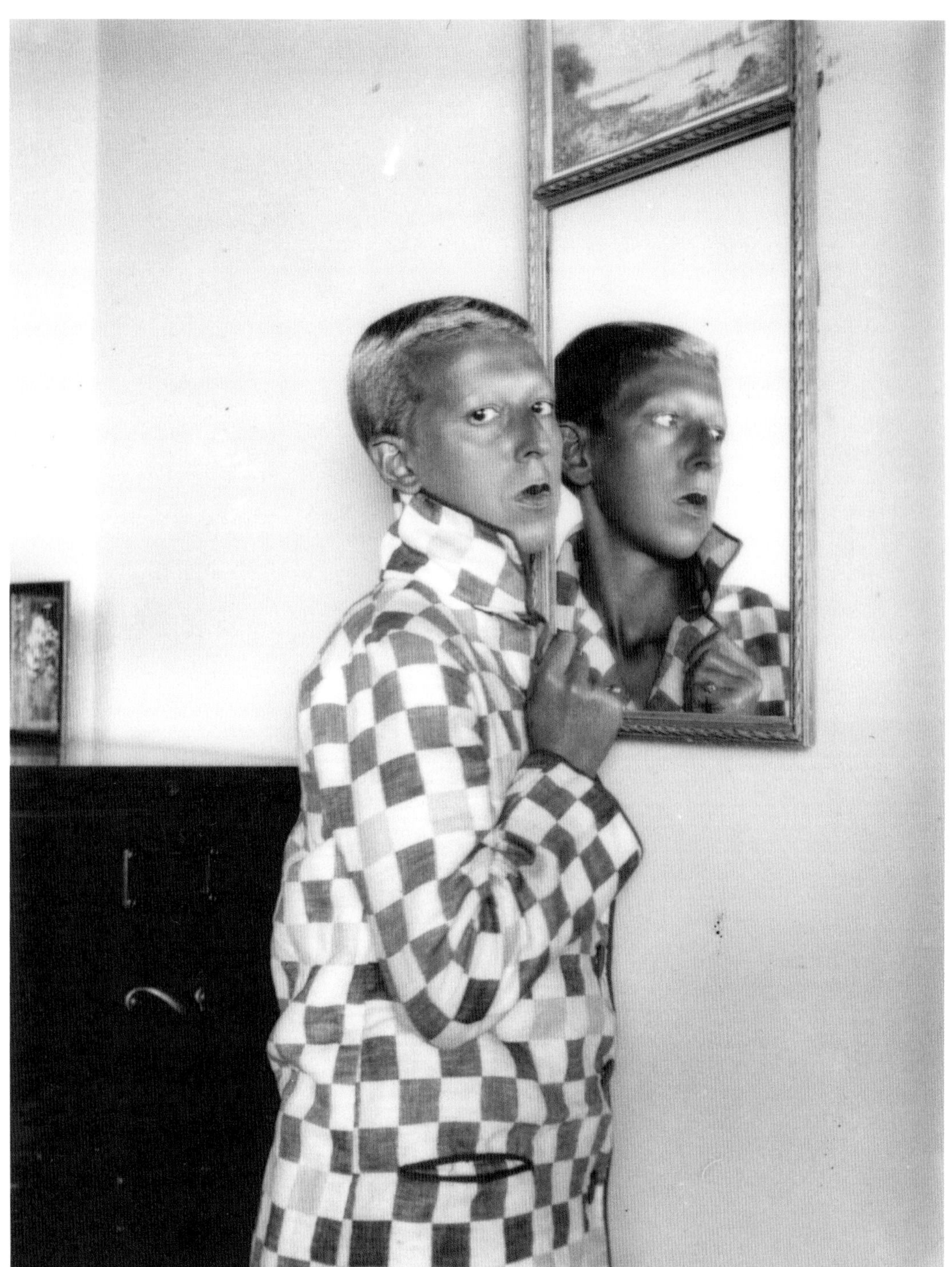

Claude Cahun
Self-Portraît (Reflected Image in a Mirror, Chequered Jacket), 1928
Selbstporträt (Spiegelbild im Spiegel, karierte Jacke)

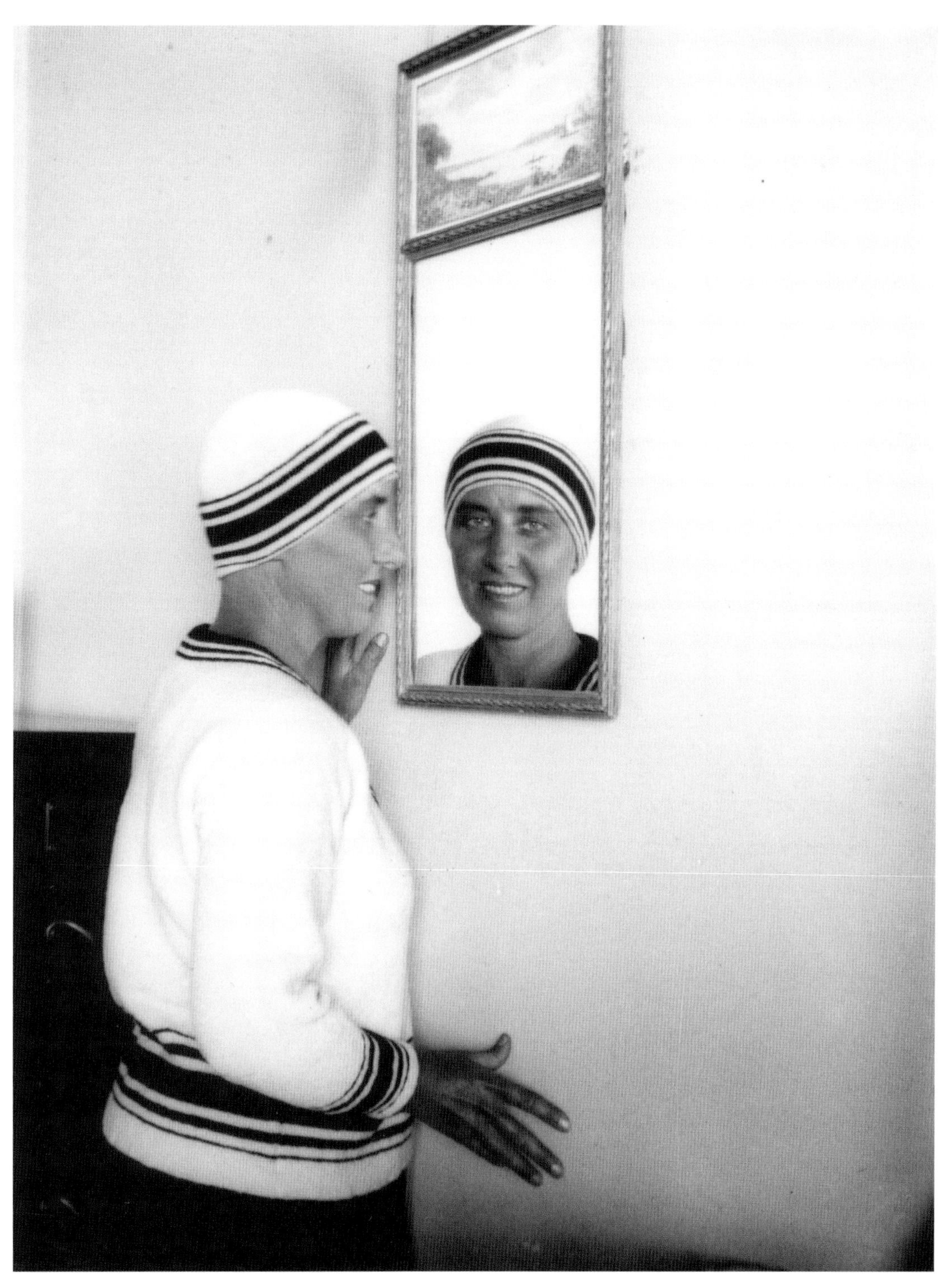

Claude Cahun
Marcel Moore Looking into a Mirror, 1928
Marcel Moore sieht in den Spiegel

Claude Cahun

Self-Portrait (double exposure in rock pool), um ~ *ca.* 1928

Selbstporträt (Doppelbelichtung im Felsenbecken)

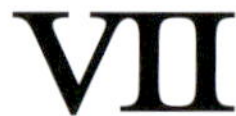

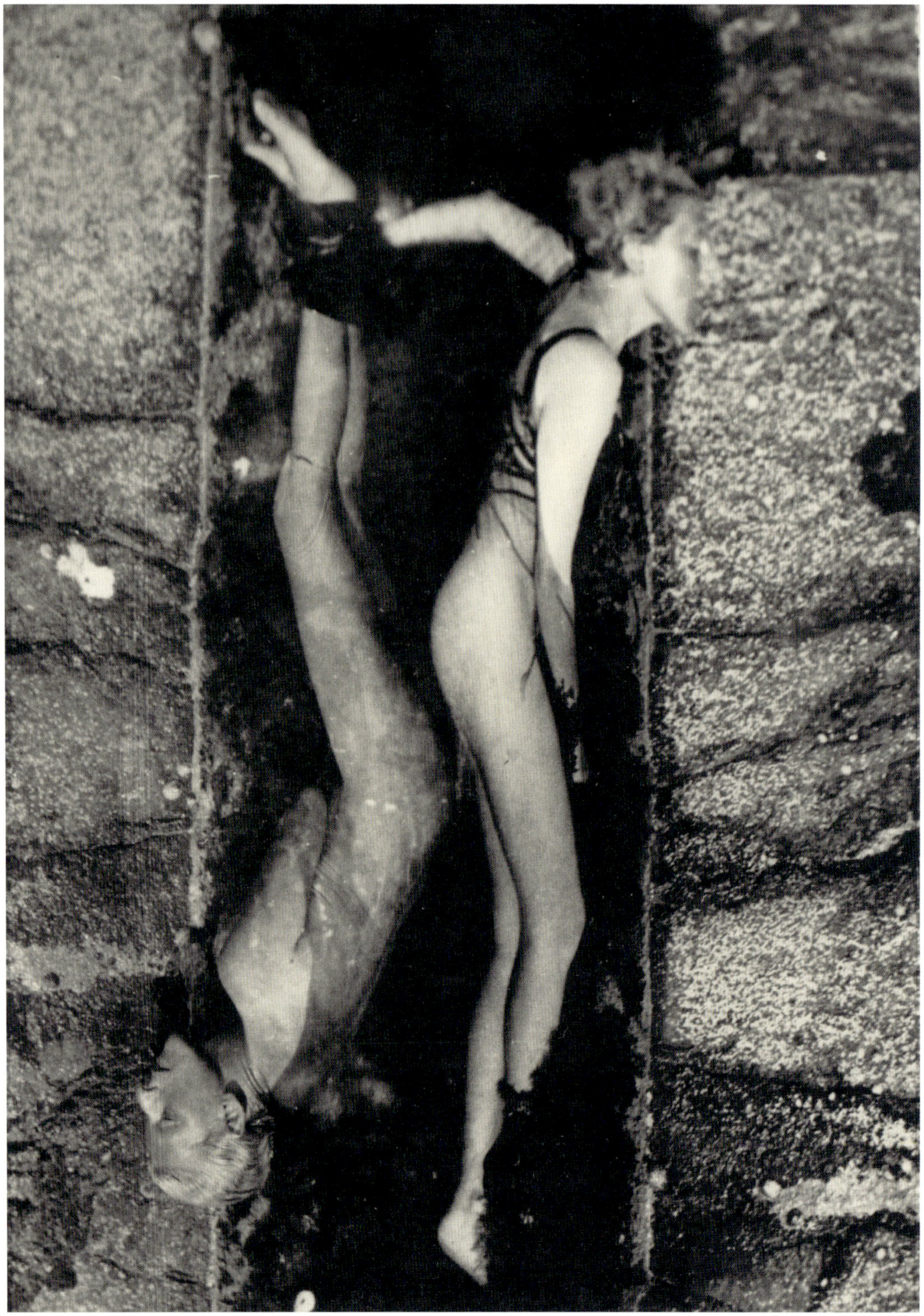

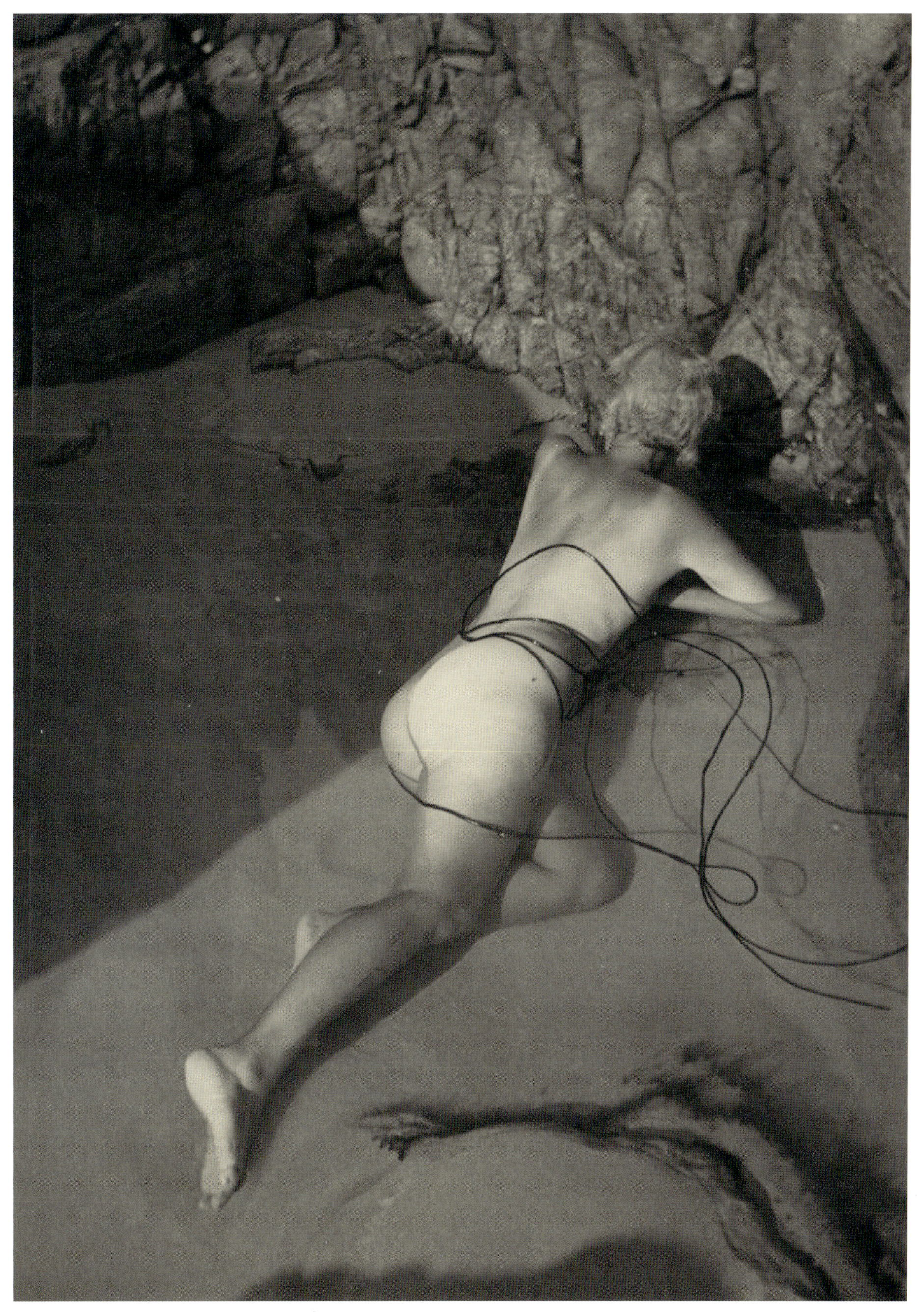

Claude Cahun
Self-Portrait (naked, reclining on sand with coiled seaweed), 1930
Selbstporträt (nackt, auf Sand liegend mit aufgerolltem Seegras)

Alarm ! ALARM!! ALARM!!!
Warum ?
Weil unsere Herren die Offiziere,
hier wie bei Stalingrad, wie bei
Tunis, um ihre Luftflucht zu
schützen auf deine Leiche rechnen.
Alarm! ALARM!! ALARM!!!
Warum ?
Weil die Briten, die Amerikaner, die
Kanadiere, bei Dünkirchen, bei
Cherbourg, bei St. Nazaire anlanden
werden, während ihre übermächtige
Kriegsmarine...
Alarm ! ALARM!! ALARM!!!
Du erträgst Manöver OHNE ENDE,
Entbehrungen, du härmst dich
um die Deinigen....
Wozu ?
So dass Du zum NACHDENKEN
keine Zeit hast!
Alarm ! ALARM!! ALARM!!!
Warum ?
Das GESPENST: „Weil man Dich
betrügen möchte, wie man uns
in 1914–1918 betrogen hat!
September 1943.

Arbeiter ! Kameraden !
Genossen !
Erwartet nicht bis die
Flammen der Hölle unsere
Häuser zu Asche verbrannt
haben !
Lasst Eure Maschinen
Langsamer
gehen...
Verderbt sie verstohlener
Weise...
HALTET sie AUF...
wenn Ihr den Krieg
aufhalten wollt !
die Soldaten ohne Namen
Bitte verbreiten.

HITLER führt uns...
GOEBBELS spricht für uns...
GOERING frisst für uns...
LEY trinkt für uns...
HIMMLER?.. Himmler ermordet
für uns...
Aber niemand stirbt
für uns!

Claude Cahun und ~ *and* Marcel Moore
Five Propaganda Leaflets, so-called "Paper Bullets," Produced During the German Occupation of Jersey, 1940–1944
Fünf Propagandazettel, sogenannte Papier-Geschosse, während der deutschen Besatzung von Jersey entstanden

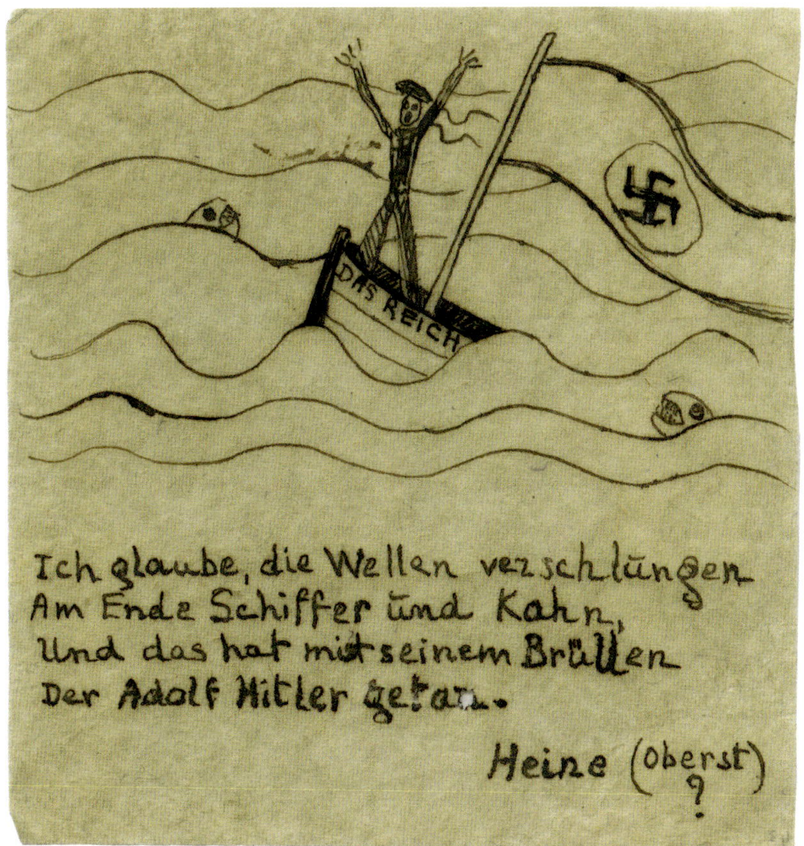

Finstres Lachen –

Dummkopf! Man heisst Dir nur eine geringe Sache! Dass Du sterben sollst, so dass der Führer ein wenig länger leben möge!

– Ach! wäre ich doch lieber gefangen!
– Wenn Du Dich ergibst, da wirst Du von dem Offizier erschossen werden.
– Er mag nur kommen! Mit einem solchen Offizier schiesse ich der Erste!

– So, wir haben den Krieg verloren?
– Gewiss.
– Aber Du freust Dich darüber?
– ganz gewiss.
– Das verstehe ich nicht. Warum?
– Weil ich nicht wünsche, mein ganzes Leben in Uniform zu verschleudern!

Gegen die Waffen-SS :: die Waffen-OO.

– Warum darf Erich nicht auf Urlaub gehen?
– Er weisst noch nicht dass sein Haus verbrannt ist, dass seine Frau und seine Kinder tot sind. Und unsere barmherzige Herren möchten ihn schonend behandeln.

also sprach der Soldat ohne Namen.

Bitte verbreiten –

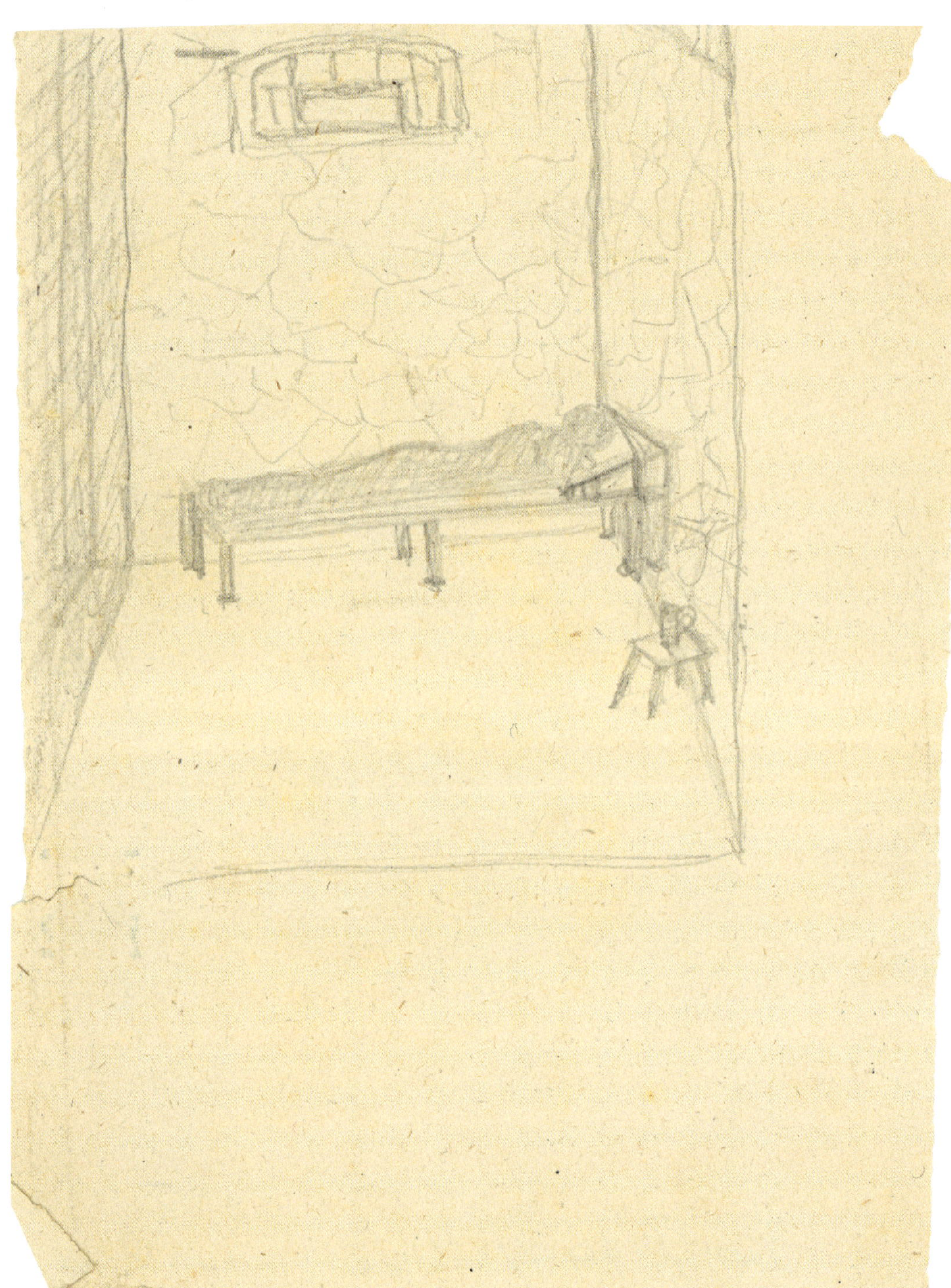

Claude Cahun oder ~ *or* Marcel Moore
Interior of a Prison Cell Drawn on Scrap Paper, 1945
Inneres einer Gefängniszelle gezeichnet auf Papierabfall

Claude Cahun
Self-Portrait (with Nazi Badge between Her Teeth), Mai ~ *May* 1945
Selbstporträt (mit Nazi-Abzeichen zwischen den Zähnen)

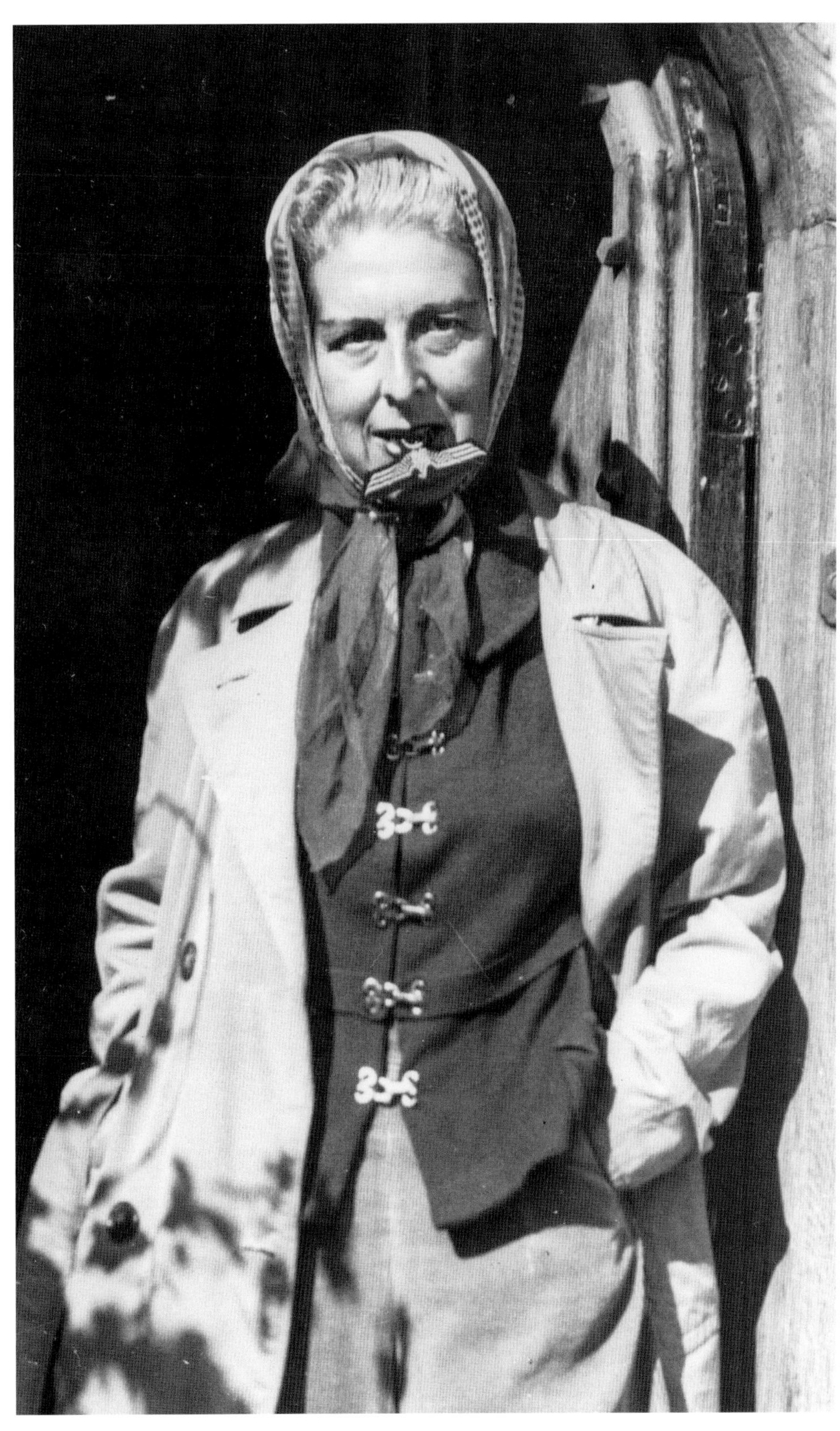

Hannah Höch
Auf dem Weg zum Siebenden Himmel, 1934
On the Way to Seventh Heaven

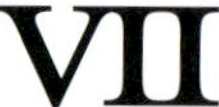

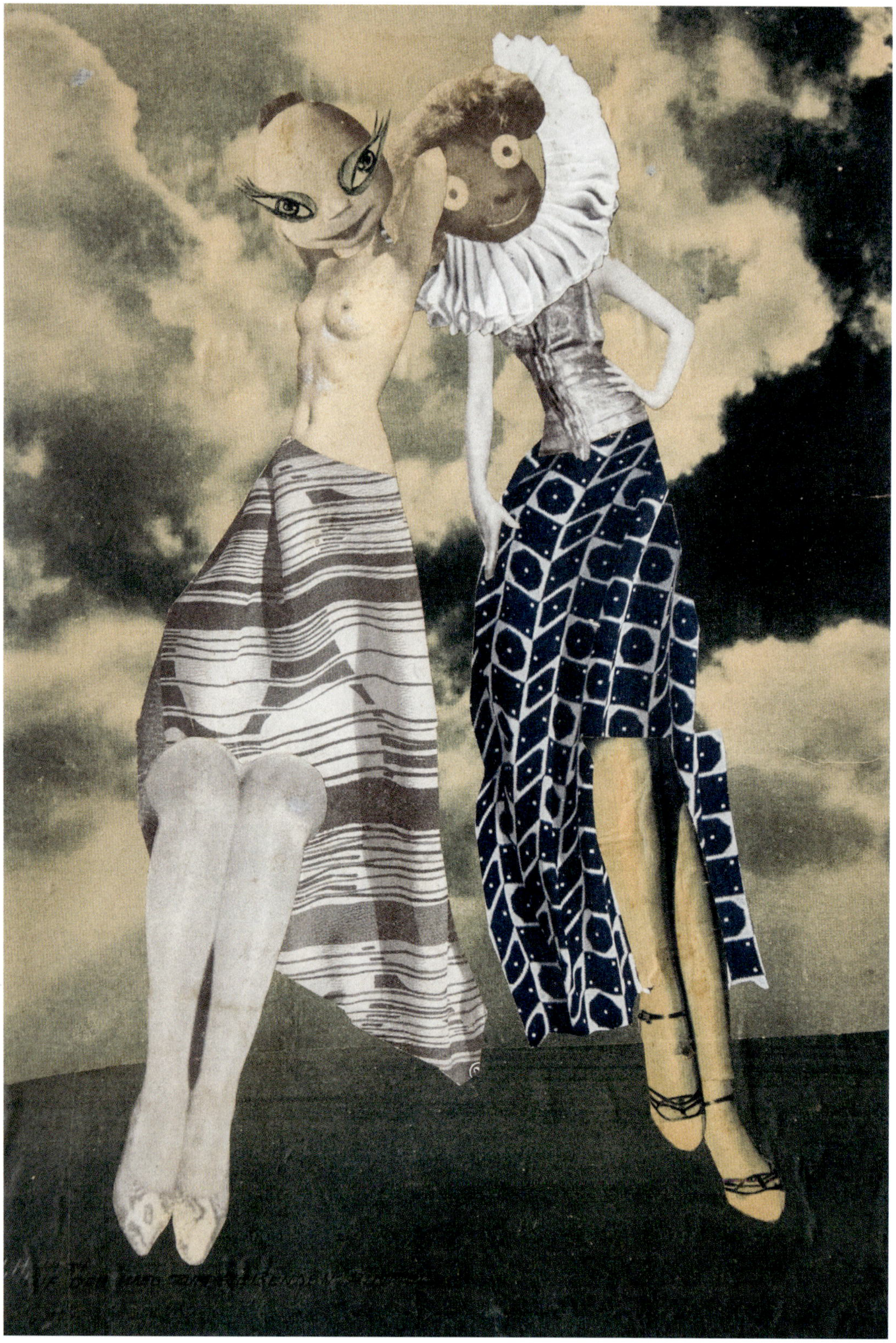

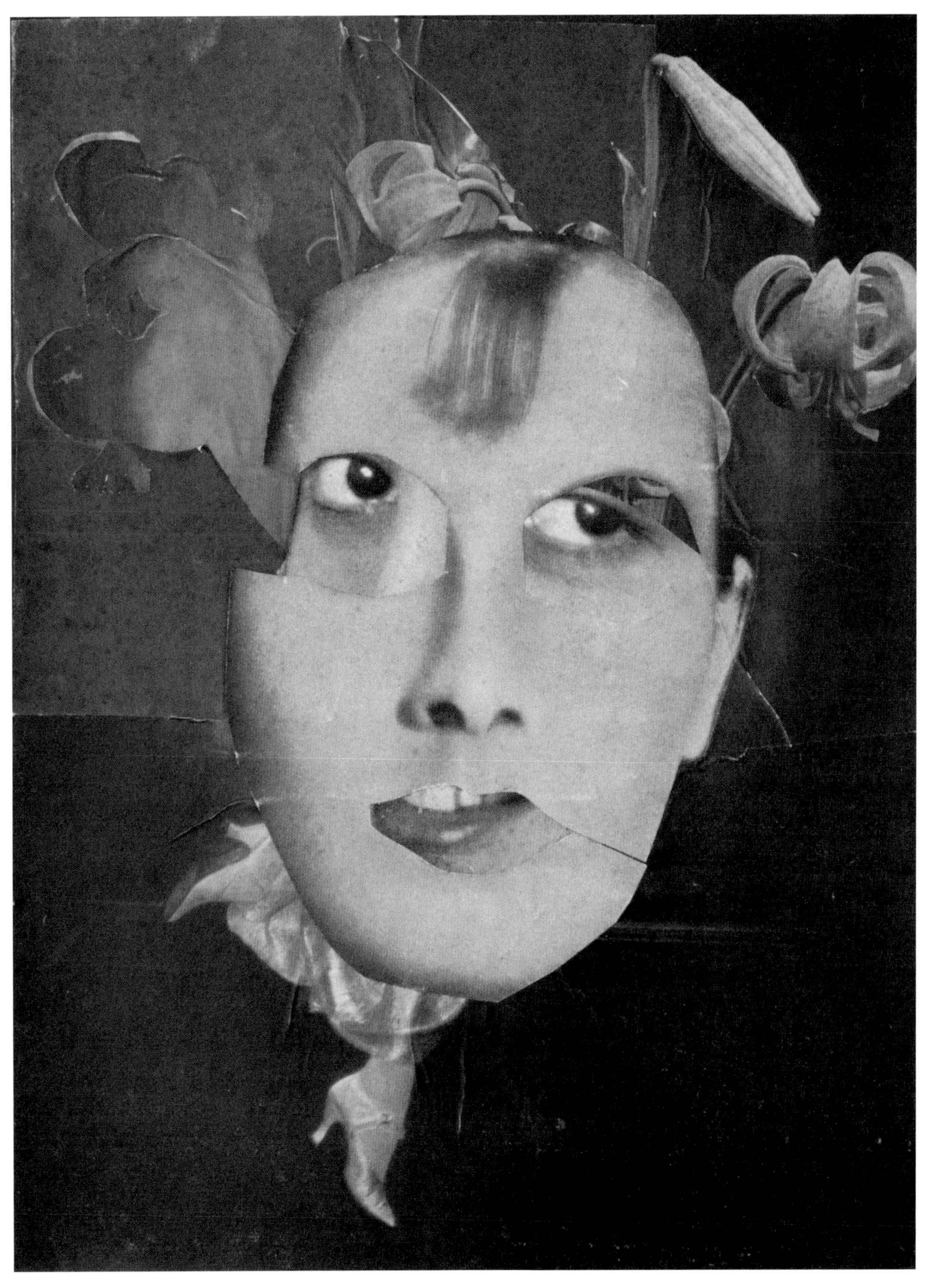

Hannah Höch
Englische Tänzerin, 1928
English Dancer

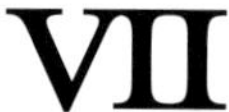

VII

QUEERER
WIDERSTAND
SEIT 1933

~

QUEER
RESISTANCE
SINCE 1933

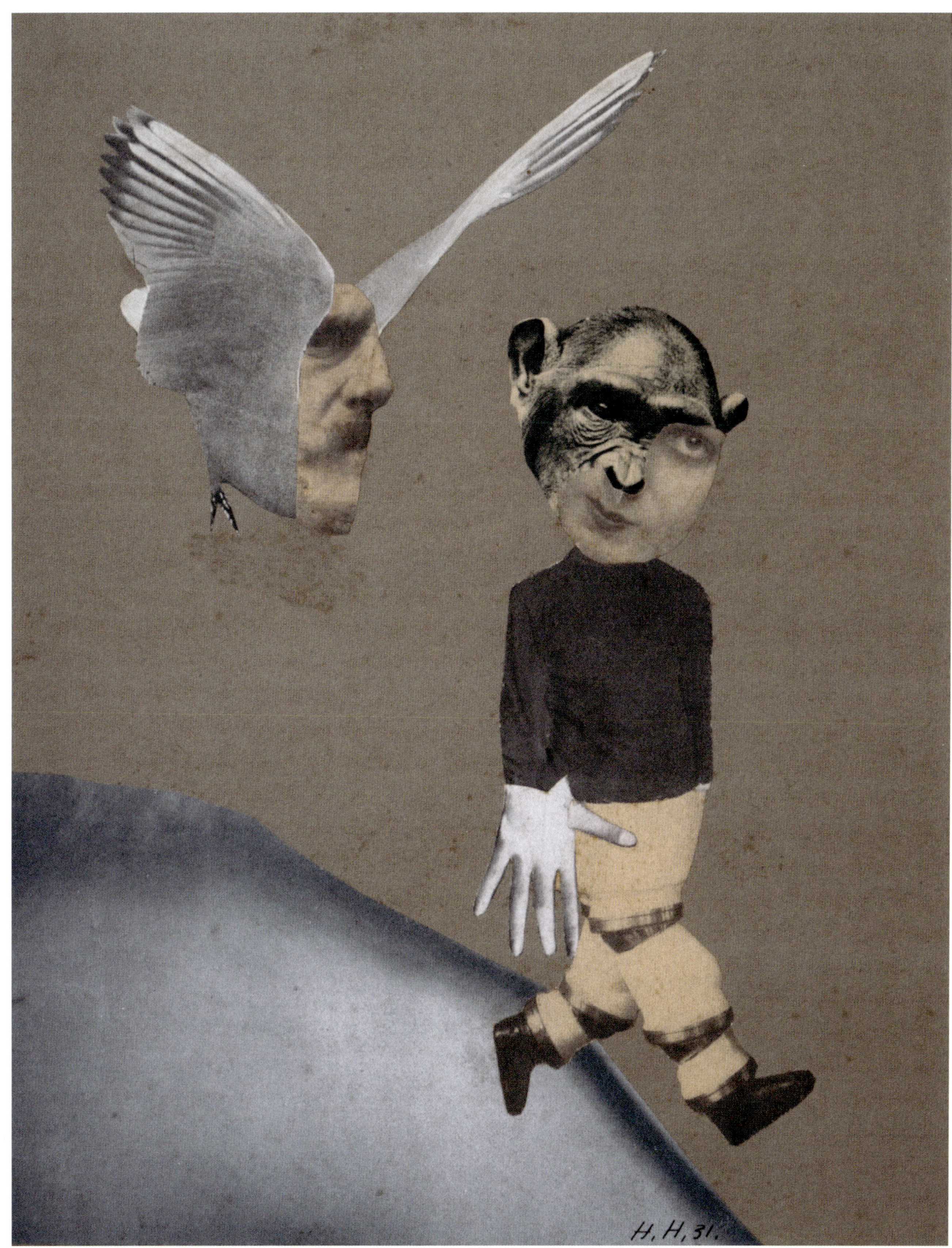

Hannah Höch
Flucht, 1931
Flight

SHE SHE SHE SHE

HE HE HE

C R Ê P E DE C H I N E

S O I E

M O U S S E L I N E

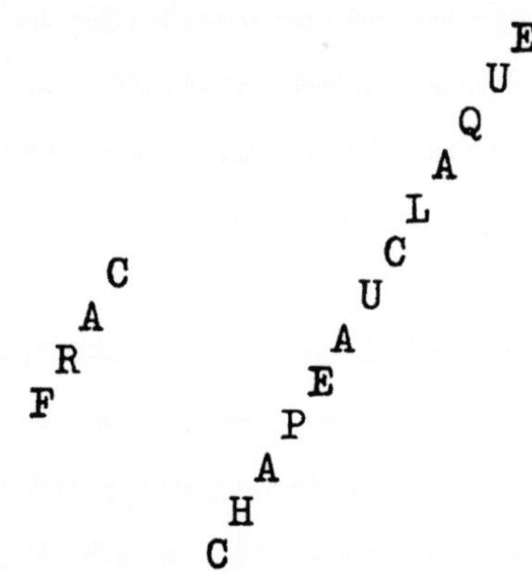

H O U B I G A N T

THÉ THÉ THÉ

DANSANT DANSANT DANSANT

Til Brugman

Til Brugman

SHE HE, 1917–1922

SIE ER

Lautgedicht ~ *Sound poem*

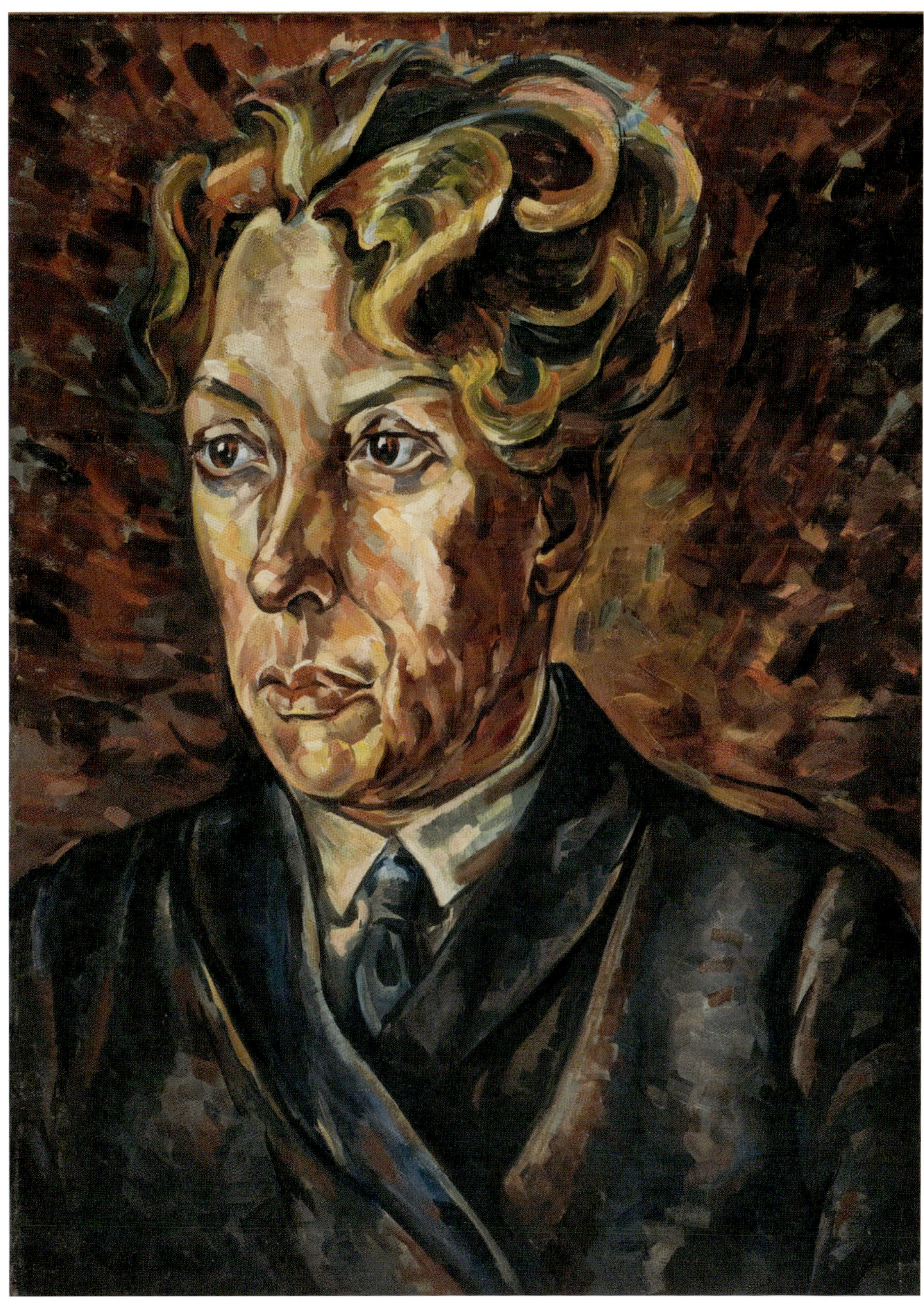

Hannah Höch

Porträt von Til Brugman, um ~ *ca.* 1929–1935

Portraît of Til Brugman

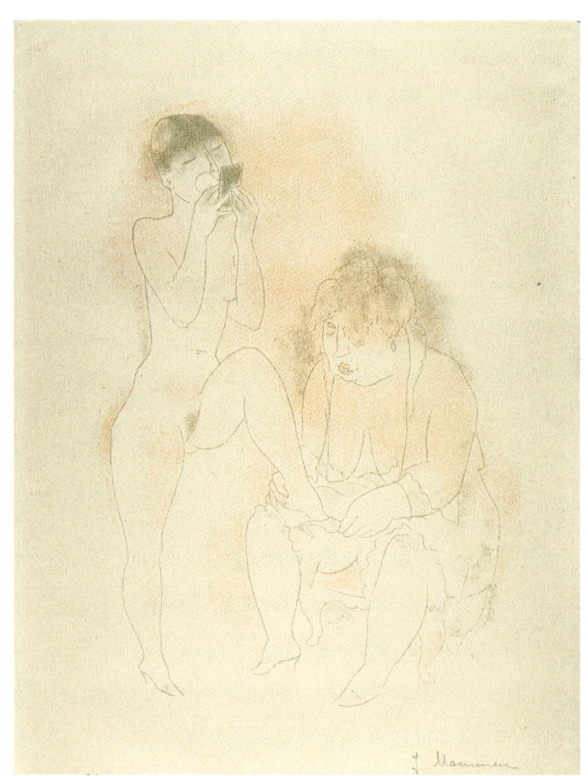

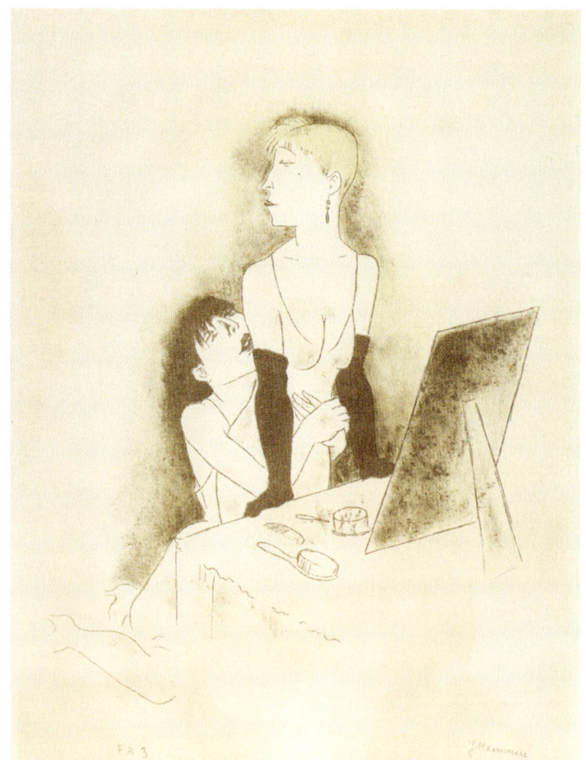

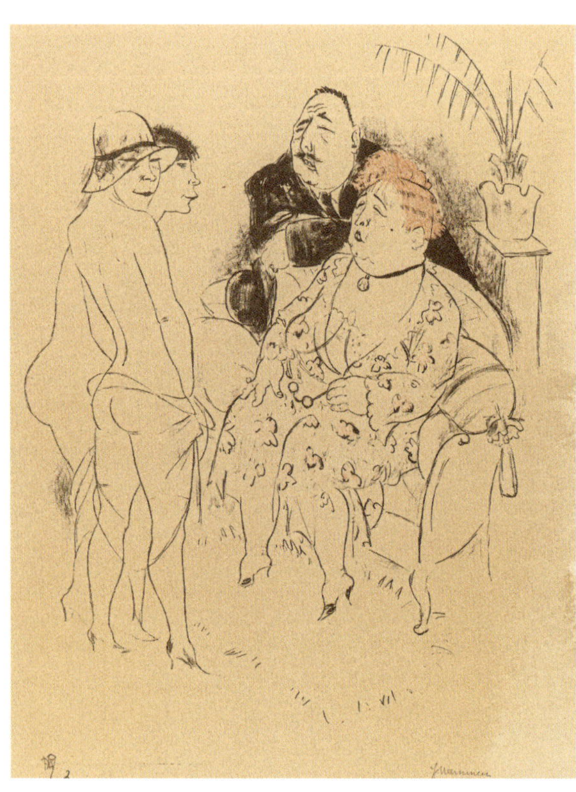

Jeanne Mammen
Beim Schminken, um ~ *ca.* 1930–1932
Applying Make-Up
Illustration von *Die Lieder der Bilîtis* von Pierre Louÿs
~ *Illustration for* The Songs of Bilîtis *by Pierre Louÿs*

Jeanne Mammen
Die Wahl, um ~ *ca.* 1930–1932
The Choice
Illustration von *Die Lieder der Bilîtis* von Pierre Louÿs
~ *Illustration for* The Songs of Bilîtis *by Pierre Louÿs*

Jeanne Mammen
Eifersucht, um ~ *ca.* 1930–1932
Jealousy
Illustration von *Die Lieder der Bilîtis* von Pierre Louÿs
~ *Illustration for* The Songs of Bilîtis *by Pierre Louÿs*

Jeanne Mammen

Damenbar, um ~ *ca.* 1930–1932
Ladies' Bar

Illustration von *Die Lieder der Bilîtis* von Pierre Louÿs ~
Illustration for The Songs of Bilîtis *by Pierre Louÿs*

Jeanne Mammen

Tanzbar, undatiert ~ *undated*
Dance Bar

Illustration von *Die Lieder der Bilîtis* von Pierre Louÿs ~
Illustration for The Songs of Bilîtis *by Pierre Louÿs*

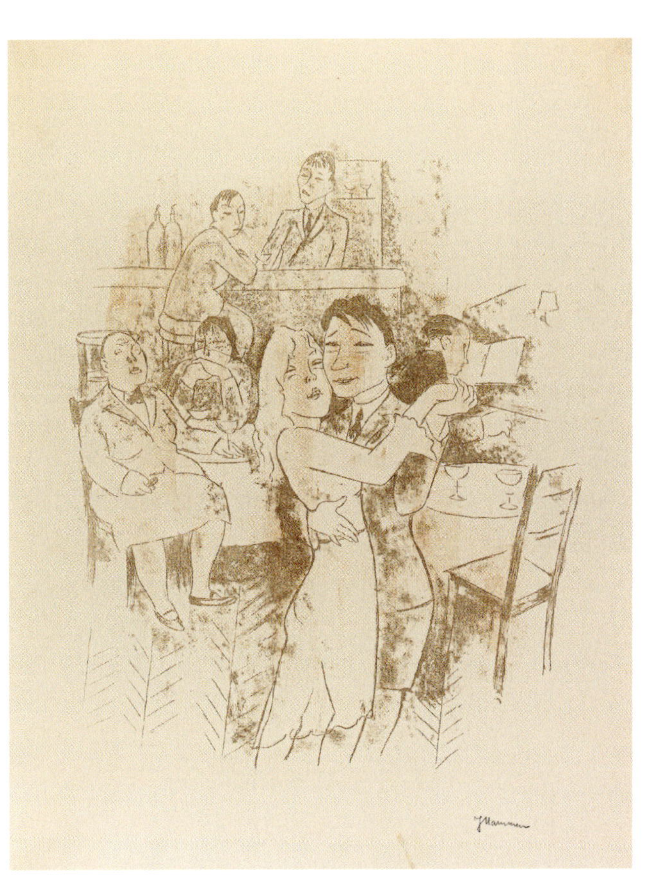

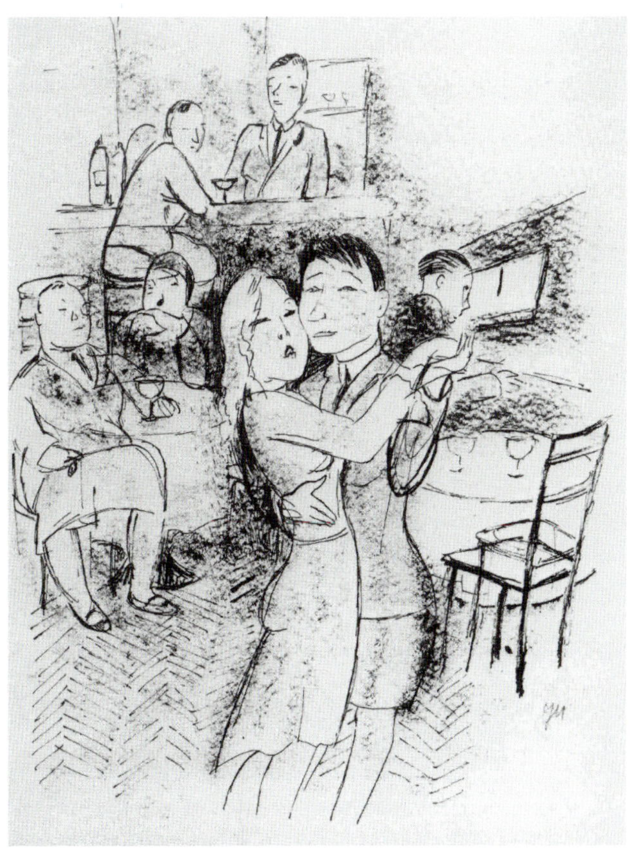

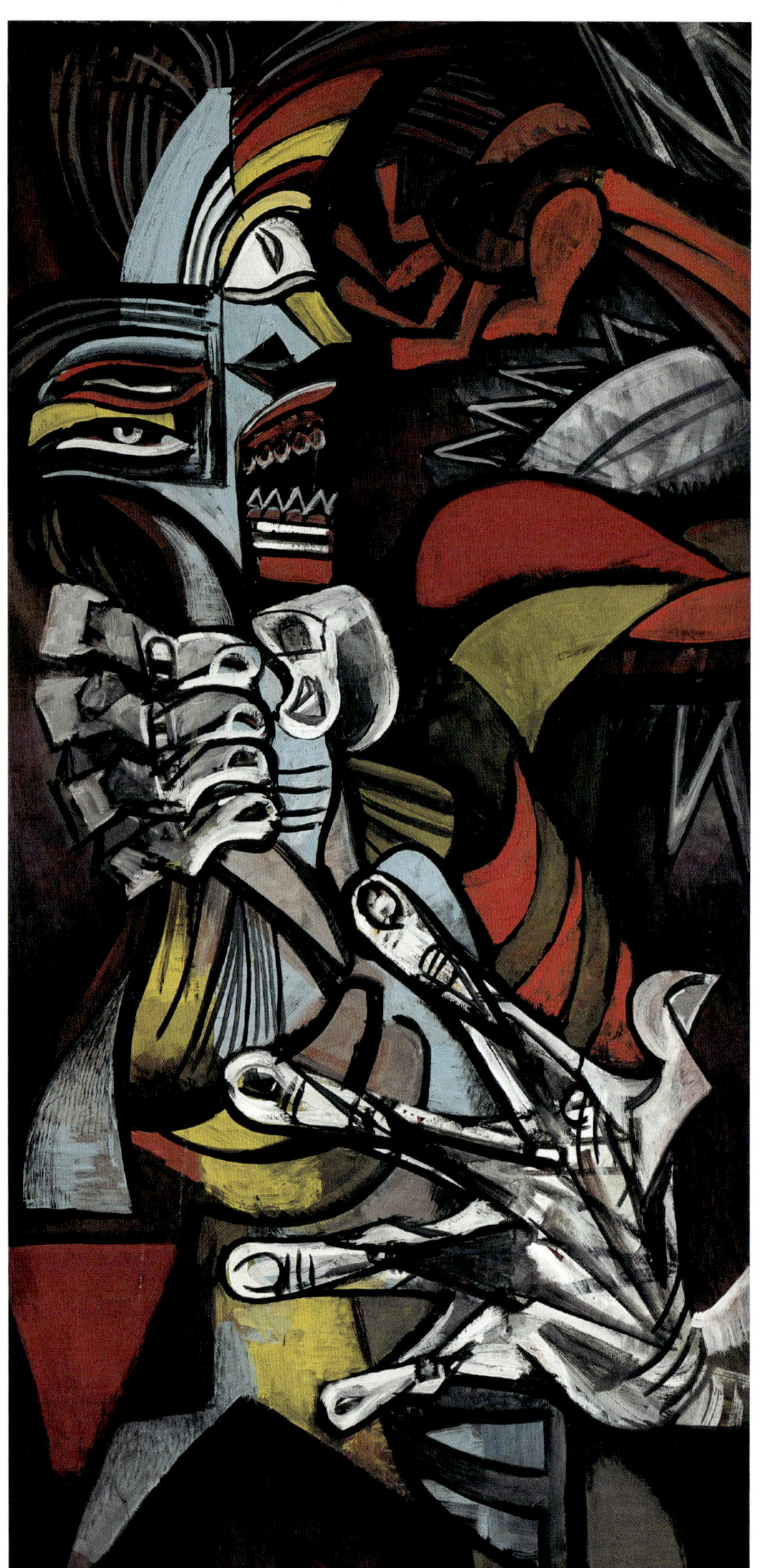

Jeanne Mammen
Der Würgeengel, um ~ *ca.* 1939–1942
The Angel of Death (Saint Anthony and the Angel)

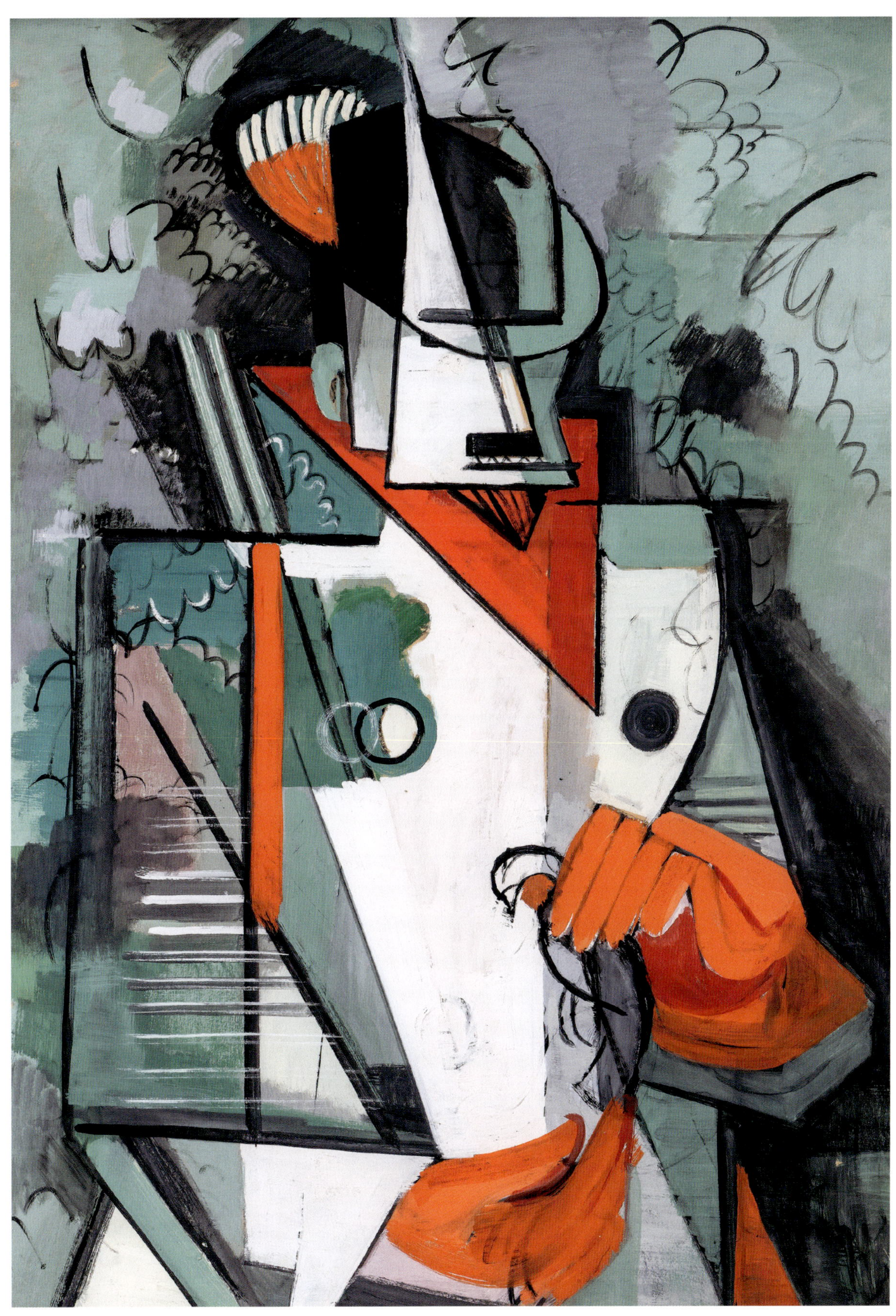

Jeanne Mammen

Der Jäger (Sonntagsjäger), zwischen ~ *between* 1939–1942

The Hunter (Sunday Hunter)

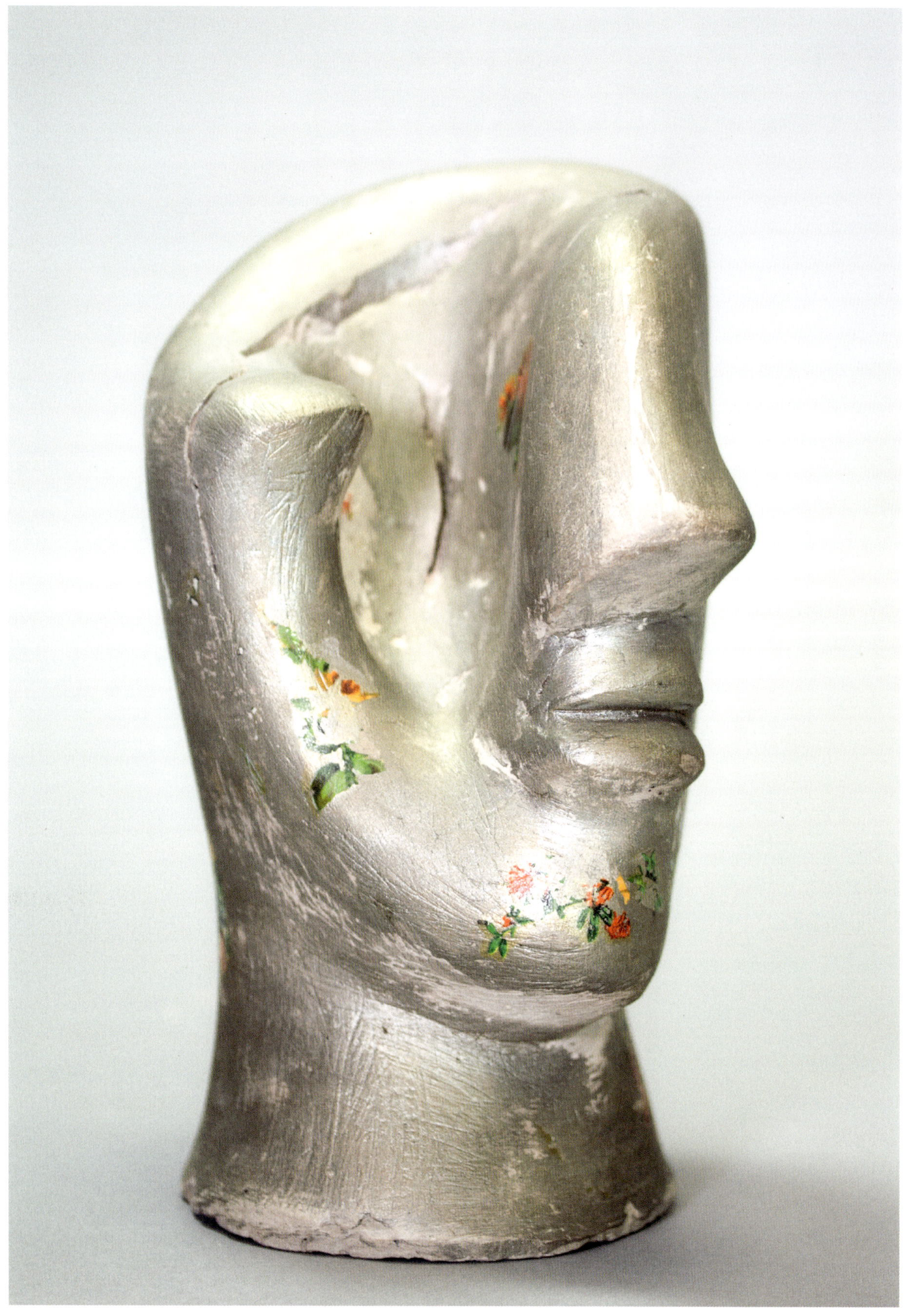

Jeanne Mammen
Hermaphrodit, um ~ *ca.* 1945
Hermaphrodite

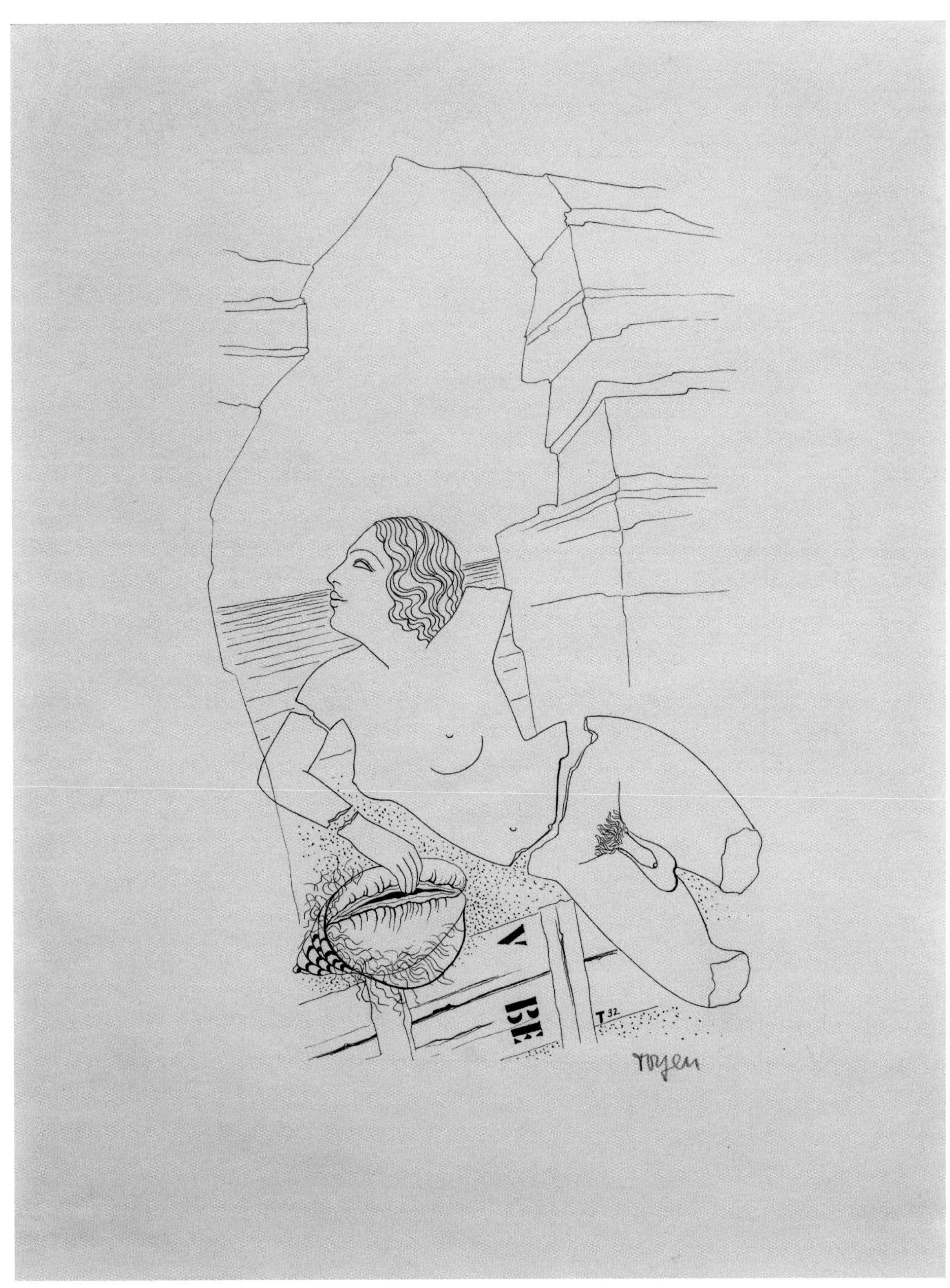

Toyen

Hermaphrodite au coquillage, 1930

Hermaphrodit mit Muschel

Hermaphrodite with a Shell

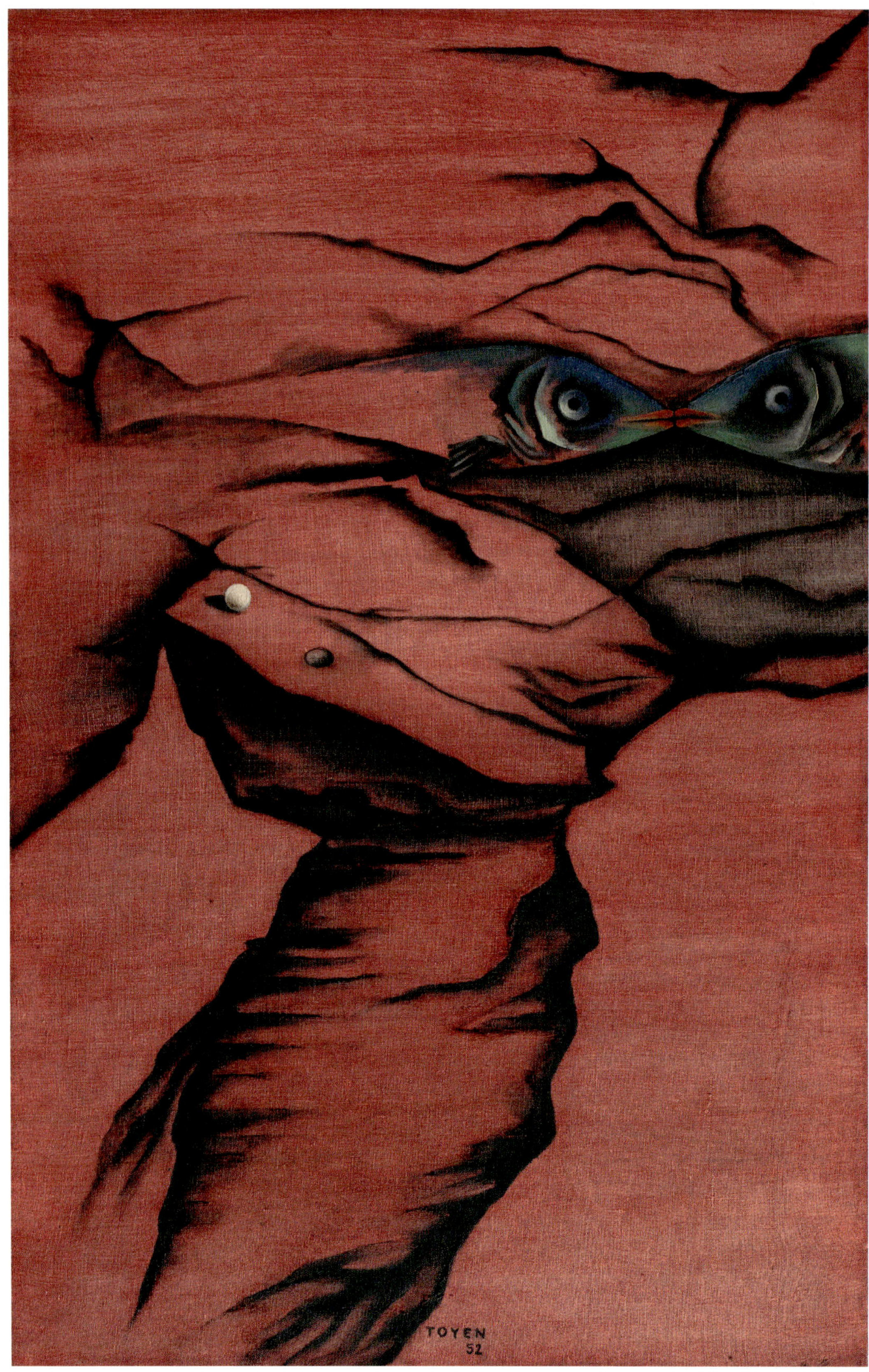

Toyen
L'Origine de la vérité, 1952
Der Ursprung der Wahrheit ~
The Origin of Truth

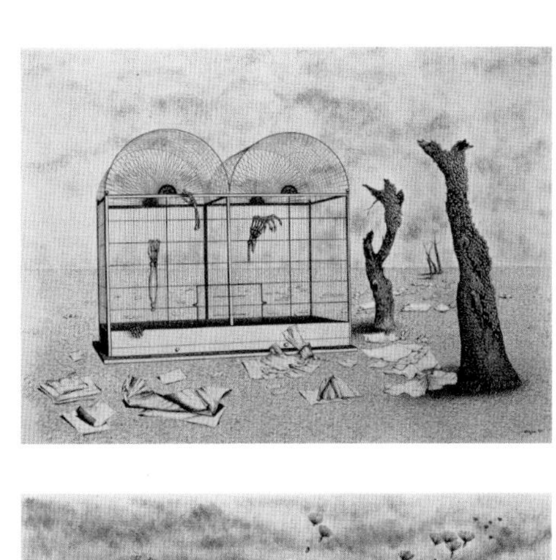
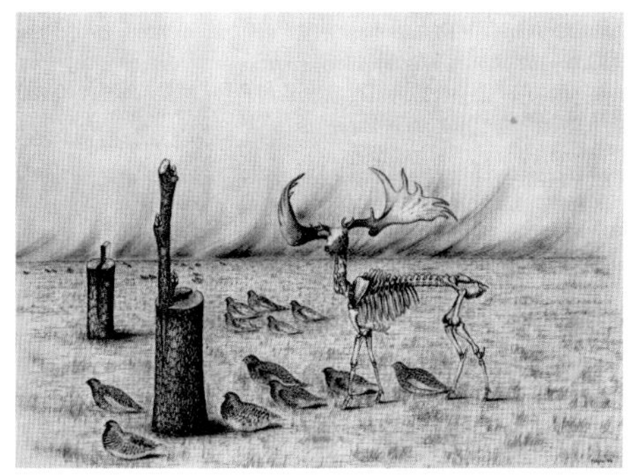
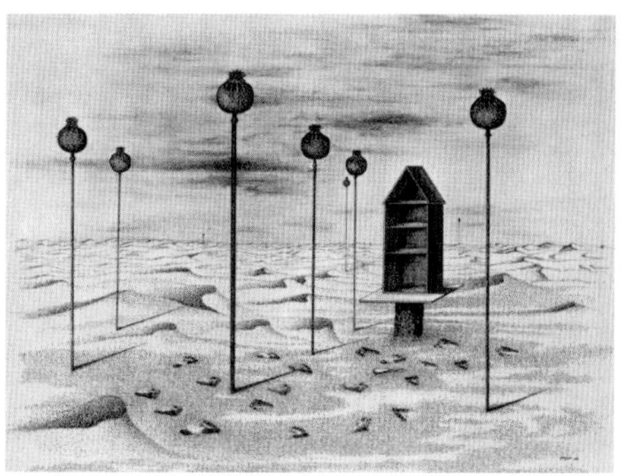
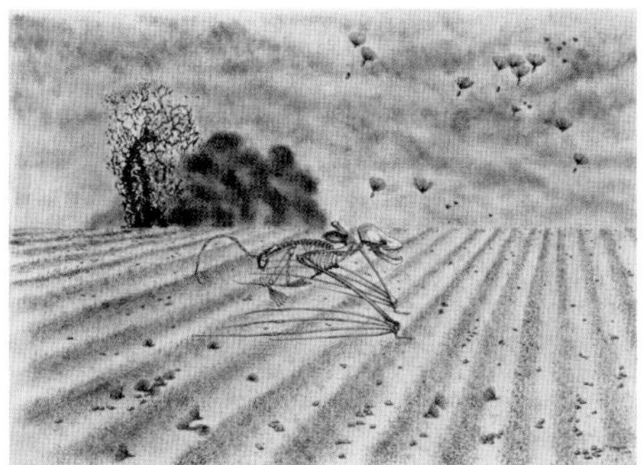
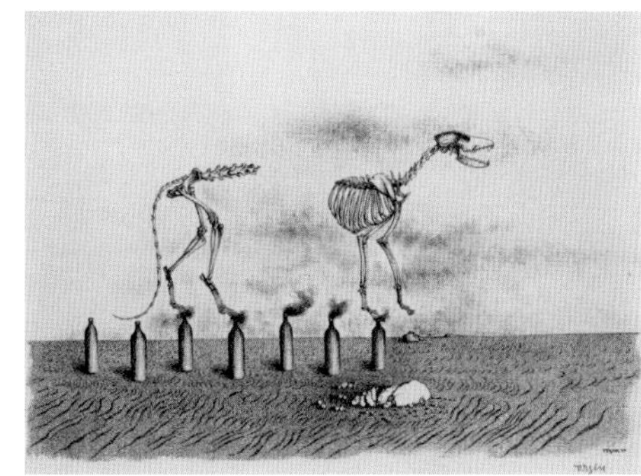
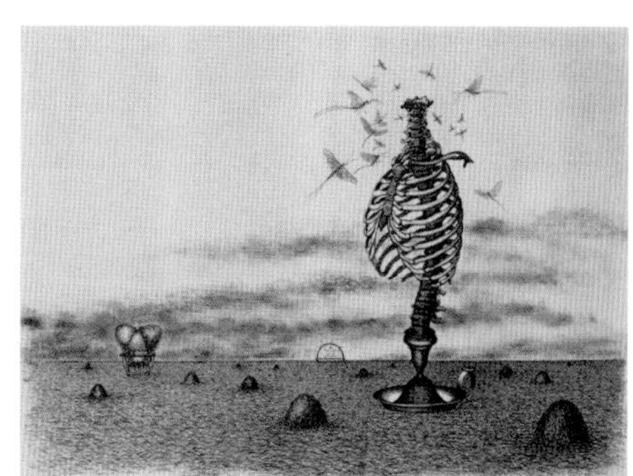
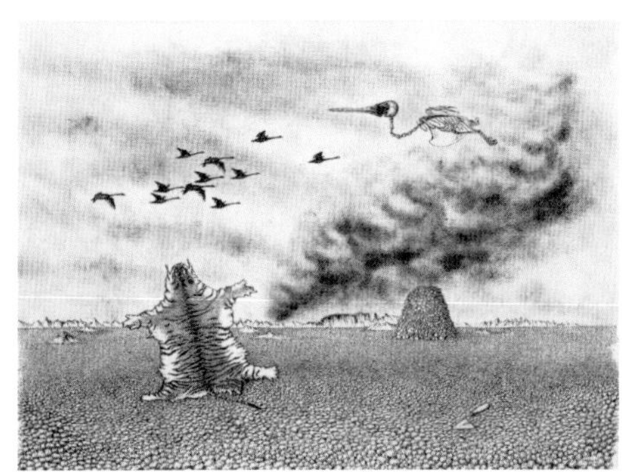
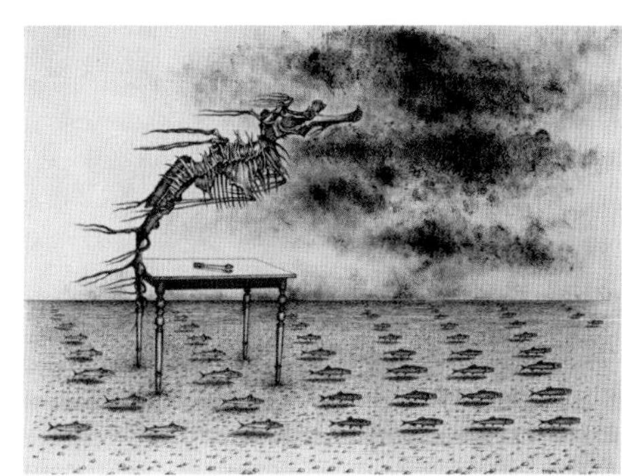
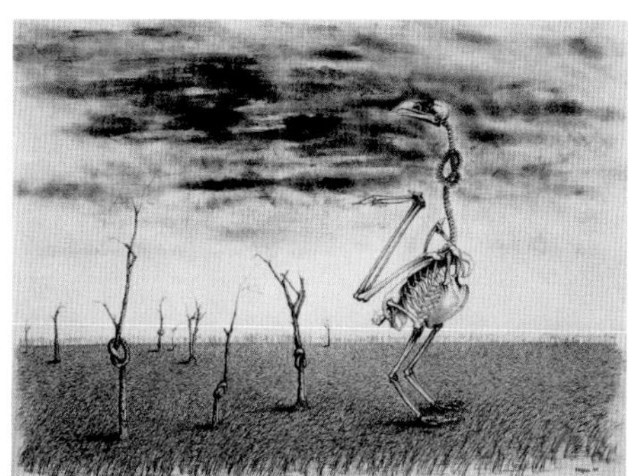

Toyen
Cache-toi, guerre! [Schovej se, válko!], 1947
Versteck dich, Krieg! ~
Hide yourself, War!

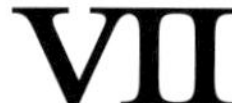

QUEERER WIDERSTAND SEIT 1933

~

QUEER RESISTANCE SINCE 1933

Toyen

La maison solitaire, 1945
Das einsame Haus ~ *The Lonely House*

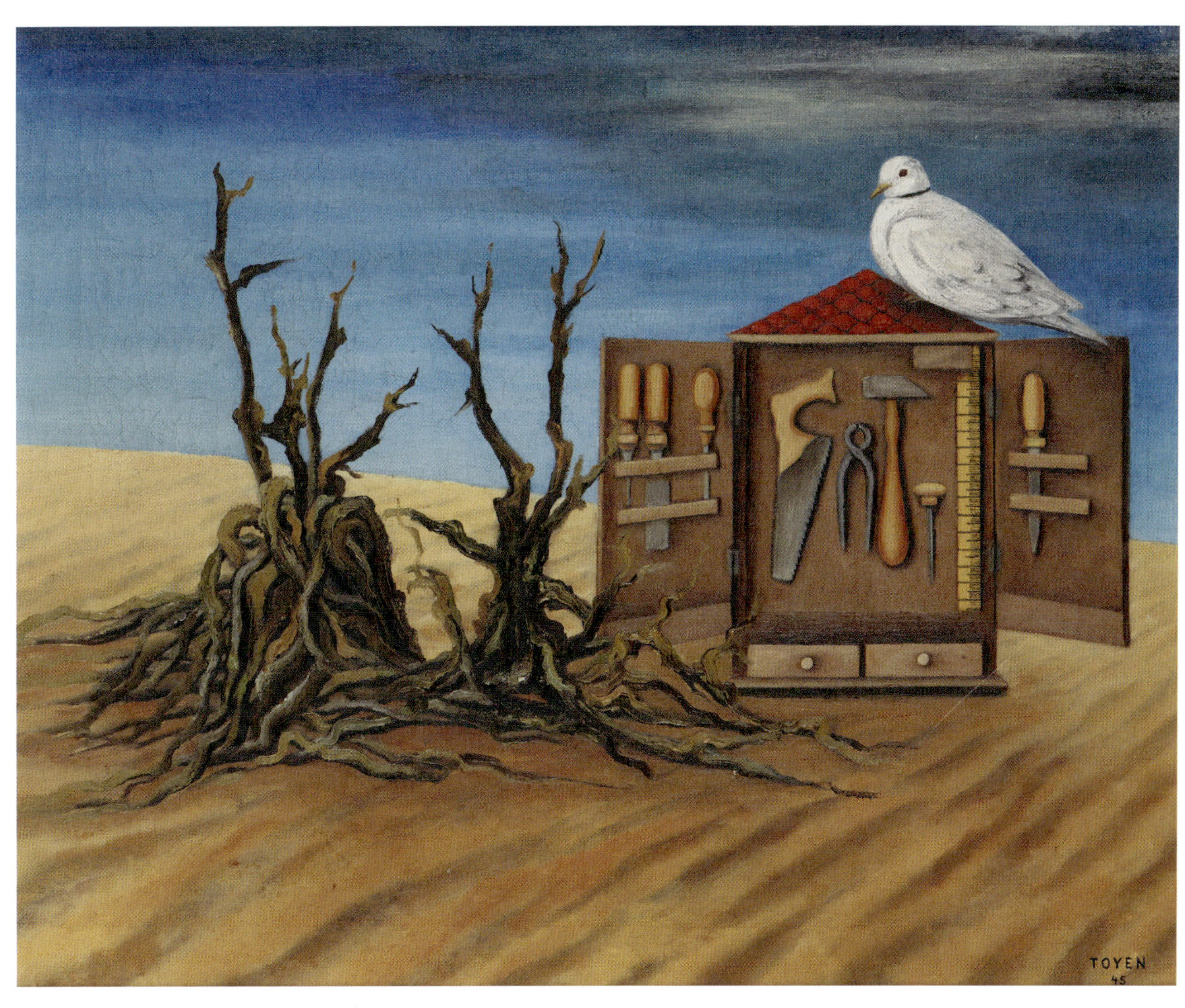

QUEERE KOMPLIZ*INNENSCHAFT

~

QUEER COMPLICITY

ISABELLE MALZ

„HITLER führt uns … GOEBBELS spricht für uns … GOERING frisst für uns … LEY trinkt für uns … HIMMLER? … Himmler ermordet für uns … Aber niemand stirbt für uns!“[1] Unterzeichnet von den „Soldaten ohne Namen“ ist dies eines von mehreren Tausend Flugblättern und Botschaften (Kat., S. 232, 233), die Claude Cahun und Marcel Moore in den vier Jahren ihres antifaschistischen Widerstands gegen die deutsche Besatzungsmacht an verschiedenen öffentlichen Orten auf der Insel Jersey bis zu ihrer Verhaftung durch die Gestapo am 25. Juli 1944 verbreitet haben.

Während das französische Paar mit ihren sogenannten Paper Bullets (Papier-Geschossen) die Moral der deutschen Soldaten, denen sie ihre subversiven Botschaften auch heimlich in ihre Uniformtaschen zusteckten, zu unterwandern versuchte und dafür zum Tode verurteilt wurde, realisierte Toyen, seit 1939 bis zum Abzug der deutschen Wehrmacht aus Prag am 8. Mai 1945 im Untergrund lebend, gemeinsam mit dem jüdischen Dichter Jindřich Heisler die illustrierte Gedichtsammlung *Nur die Turmfalken brunzen ruhig auf die 10 Gebote* (1939). 40 der insgesamt 55 Exemplare erschienen in der zu dieser Zeit bereits illegalen tschechoslowakischen *Edice Surrealismu* (Surrealistische Edition) auf Deutsch, in der Hoffnung damit an die Menschlichkeit der Wehrmachtssoldaten appellieren zu können. Auch die ab 1929 wieder in Berlin lebende Dada-Künstlerin Hannah Höch und ihre damalige Partnerin, die niederländische Schriftstellerin Til Brugman, wählten das Stilmittel der Groteske, um die totalitäre Ideologie des Nationalsozialismus zu entlarven. Drei Jahre nach ihrer Trennung von Til Brugman zieht Hannah Höch am 3. November 1939 nach Heiligensee an den Stadtrand von Berlin, um hier in der Abgeschiedenheit und Anonymität möglichst unauffällig leben und arbeiten zu können. Auch in dieser Zeit entstehen Arbeiten, die durchaus einen kritischen Subtext erkennen lassen.

Jeanne Mammen meldet sich am 27. Februar 1933, ungefähr einen Monat nach der Ernennung von Adolf Hitler zum Reichskanzler am 30. Januar 1933, in Berlin arbeitslos, nachdem die meisten der Zeitschriften, für die sie bisher als Illustratorin gearbeitet hatte, gleichgeschaltet wurden. Sie zieht sich 1936 in die innere Emigration zurück, wo sie im Verborgenen zahlreiche Arbeiten schafft, die nicht nur inhaltlich, sondern vor allem durch ihre eklektische und zuweilen aggressive Bildsprache als Kommentar zur offiziellen Kunstideologie und politischen Situation gelesen werden können.

Diese Künstler*innen und Literat*innen aus Frankreich, der Tschechoslowakei, den Niederlanden und Deutschland stehen stellvertretend für eine Reihe von queeren Menschen, die in vielen Fällen aufgrund ihrer politischen Gesinnung oder als Jüdinnen und Juden eine mehrfache Diskriminierung und Verfolgung durch die Nationalsozialisten fürchten mussten.[2] Indem sie sich mit ihrer Kunst und ganz unterschiedlichen Strategien nicht nur einem faschistischen Regime und einer menschenverachtenden Ideologie widersetzten, die gleichgeschlechtliche Liebe und Transgeschlechtlichkeit als „asoziale“, „entartete“ Ausprägung kriminalisierten und homosexuelle Männer – sowie später auch lesbische Frauen – auf der Grundlage des unter den Nationalsozialisten verschärften Paragraphen 175 unter Strafe stellten, drohten ihnen nicht selten das Konzentrationslager, grausame medizinische Experimente und vielfach auch der Tod. Der schwule, jüdische Sozialist, Arzt und Sexualwissenschaftler Magnus Hirschfeld, der sich während der Weimarer Republik für

1 Eines von mehreren Propagandaflugblättern, die Claude Cahun und Marcel Moore während der deutschen Besetzung der Insel Jersey produziert haben. JHT/1995/00045/53, Jersey Heritage, https://catalogue.jerseyheritage.org/collection/Search/archive/JHT/1995/00045/53/ [zuletzt abgerufen am 29.05.2025].

2 Die Kriminalisierung von Homosexualität dauerte in der BRD noch bis 1969 an. Der 1871 im Kaiserreich eingeführte und unter den Nationalsozialisten verschärfte Paragraph 175 des Reichsstrafgesetzbuchs wurde erst 1994 gestrichen. In Frankreich wurde Homosexualität während der Französischen Revolution entkriminalisiert. Jedoch wurde 1942 unter dem Vichy-Regime ein Sonderstrafrecht gegen Homosexuelle eingeführt, das bis 1982 wirksam war. In der Tschechoslowakei blieb Homosexualität hingegen trotz einer aktiven Schwulenbewegung in den 1930er-Jahren bis 1962 strafbar.

"HITLER leads us… GOEBBELS speaks for us… GOERING gorges himself for us… LEY drinks for us… HIMMLER?… Himmler murders for us… But no one dies for us!"[1] Signed by the "Soldaten ohne namen" (Nameless Soldiers), this is one of several thousand leaflets and messages (cat. pp. 232, 233) that Claude Cahun and Marcel Moore clandestinely distributed in public places across the Isle of Jersey. Their anti-fascist resistance against the occupying German forces lasted for four years, until their arrest by the Gestapo on July 25, 1944. While the French couple sought to undermine morale, bombarding German soldiers with so-called "paper bullets"—even secretly slipping these subversive messages into the pockets of their uniforms, for which they ultimately received a death sentence—in Prague, the artist Toyen, living underground from 1939 until the withdrawal of the German army from the city on May 8, 1945, compiled the illustrated collection of poems *Nur die Turmfalken brunzen ruhig auf die 10 Gebote* (Only Kestrels Piss Calmly on the Ten Commandments, 1939), together with the Jewish poet Jindřich Heisler. Forty of the total fifty-five copies were published in German under the Czechoslovakian imprint *Edice Surrealismu* (Surrealist Edition), which had already been outlawed, in the hope of appealing to the humanity of Wehrmacht soldiers.

Similarly, from 1929, the Dada artist Hannah Höch was once again living in Berlin with her then partner, the Dutch writer Til Brugman; together, they employed the device of the grotesque to expose the totalitarian ideology of Nazism. Three years after separating from Til Brugman, Hannah Höch moved to the Heiligensee district on the outskirts of Berlin on November 3, 1939, in order to live and work as inconspicuously as possible in the seclusion and anonymity of the suburbs. Even during this period, she continued to produce works suffused by a distinctly critical subtext. In Berlin, on February 27, 1933—less than a month after Hitler was appointed Reich Chancellor on January 30, 1933—Jeanne Mammen registered as unemployed after most of the periodicals she had worked for as an illustrator were politically "synchronized." She withdrew in 1936 into a so-called "inner emigration," where she secretly produced numerous works that can be read, not only in terms of their content but especially in terms of their eclectic and occasionally aggressive visual language, as a derisive commentary on official art ideology and the political situation.

These artists and writers from France, Czechoslovakia, the Netherlands, and Germany are representative of a greater number of queer people, many of whom faced multiple forms of discrimination and persecution under the Nazis due to their political beliefs and/or their Jewish heritage.[2] By resisting, through their art and by employing a range of different strategies, against not only a fascist regime but also a dehumanizing ideology—which criminalized same-sex love and trans identity as "asocial" and "degenerate" deviations, and prosecuted gay men, and later lesbian women, under Paragraph 175, a law made more severe under the Nazis—they were often threatened with deportation to concentration camps, subjected

1 One of several propaganda leaflets produced by Claude Cahun and Marcel Moore during the German occupation of Jersey, JHT/1995/00045/53, Jersey Heritage, last accessed May 29, 2025, https://catalogue.jerseyheritage.org/collection/Search/archive/JHT/1995/00045/53/.

2 The criminalization of homosexuality persisted in the Federal Republic of Germany until 1969 under Paragraph 175 of the *Reichsstrafgesetzbuch* (Imperial Criminal Code), which was introduced in 1871 during the German Empire and intensified under the Nazis. It was not fully repealed until 1994. In France, homosexuality was decriminalized during the French Revolution, although under the Vichy government a special criminal statute targeting homosexuality was introduced in 1942, which remained in effect until 1982. In Czechoslovakia, homosexuality remained a punishable offense until 1962, despite an active gay rights movement in the 1930s.

die Entkriminalisierung und Akzeptanz sexueller und geschlechtlicher Minderheiten einsetzte, befand sich gerade in Paris, als die Nationalsozialisten am 6. Mai 1933 sein berühmtes Institut für Sexualwissenschaft in Berlin zerstörten und die meisten Mitarbeiter*innen wie auch ihn ins Exil zwang. Darüber hinaus gab es aber auch Formen der Kollaboration, die häufig als Schutz- und Überlebensstrategie gewählte Arrangements mit den faschistischen Regimen Europas waren. So stellt sich die Frage, wie die paradox erscheinende antisemitische Einstellung von Romaine Brooks und ihrer Lebensgefährtin Natalie Barney – die in den Augen der Nationalsozialisten „Vierteljüdin" war – und ihre Kollaboration mit dem faschistischen Regime von Benito Mussolini in ihrem Exil unweit von Florenz jenseits ihrer konservativen und antikommunistischen Haltung einzuordnen ist?[3] Und wie ist die Zusammenarbeit von Gertrude Stein, der jüdischen Literatin, Kunstsammlerin und einflussreichen Mäzenin der europäischen Avantgarde, und der Autorin Alice B. Toklas, ihrer jüdischen Partnerin, mit der antisemitischen Vichy-Regierung unter Henri Pétain zu bewerten, für den die queere Ikone auf Vermittlung ihres Protegés und Vichy-Kollaborateurs Bernard Faÿ zahlreiche Schriften übersetzt hatte?[4] Des Weiteren sind Marie Laurencins antisemitische Haltung und ihre mehr als unkritische Einstellung gegenüber Nazideutschland – folgt man den schonungslosen Tagebucheintragungen des französischen Juristen und Schriftstellers Maurice Garçon, der ihre gemeinsamen Gespräche während der Besatzungszeit festgehalten hatte[5],– nur schwer mit der Tatsache zu vereinen, dass sie offen queer lebte und lange Zeit mit dem jüdischen Galeristen Paul Rosenberg zusammengearbeitet hatte, der Mitte September 1940 von den Nationalsozialisten enteignet über Lissabon nach New York fliehen konnte. Und wie lässt sich Jean Cocteaus ambivalente Rolle gegenüber der nationalsozialistischen Kulturpolitik in Paris während der deutschen Besatzung und sein leidenschaftliches Engagement für die Ausstellung seines Freundes Arno Breker 1942 in Paris anders als eine kollaborative Geste verstehen?[6] Und obgleich die Schwarze US-amerikanische Tänzerin, Sängerin, Schauspielerin und spätere US-Bürgerrechtsaktivistin Josephine Baker[7] ab Juni 1940 als Résistance-Kämpferin und Spionin für den französischen Geheimdienst arbeitete, unterstützte sie anfangs Benito Mussolinis Kolonialfeldzug in Äthiopien (1935), in der Annahme, dass damit die versklavte Bevölkerung des Landes befreit werden könne.

Claude Cahun und Marcel Moore beteiligten sich hingegen bereits in den 1930er-Jahren an zahlreichen antifaschistischen und antiimperialistischen Aktivitäten im Umfeld der surrealistischen Bewegung und der Association des écrivains et artistes révolutionnaires (AEAR). Rückblickend betrachtete Cahun auch ihren subversiv-poetischen Widerstand gegen die deutsche Besatzungsmacht als „militante surrealistische Aktivität, wie wir sie bei Contre-Attaque haben wollten"[8] und wertete in diesem Zusammenhang die Poesie als (einziges) transhistorisch wirksames revolutionäres Ausdrucksmittel und ein zutiefst menschliches Bedürfnis.[9] Die mit der Nichteindeutigkeit der surrealen Poesie einhergehende Freiheit und das von Julika Funk diagnostizierte „Potential einer doppeldeutigen Subversivität"[10] lässt sich als emanzipatorische Selbstbehauptungsgeste auf Cahuns gesamtes Werk übertragen, das von der Frage nach dem anderen Selbst bestimmt ist: „Was bin ich, wenn nicht der Freund meines Freundes?"[11]. Die gemeinsam mit Marcel Moore geschaffenen fotografischen Selbstporträts,

3
Siehe u.a. Shari Benstock zu Natalie Barneys unveröffentlichten, autobiografischen Aufzeichnungen, in: Dies., *Women of the Left Bank. Paris, 1900–1940*, London 1994, S. 415–418; Cassandra Langer, *Romaine Brooks: A Life*, Madison 2015.

4
Siehe u.a. Barbara Will, *Unlikely Collaboration. Gertrude Stein, Bernard Faÿ, and the Vichy Dilemma*, New York 2011.

5
Maurice Garçon, *Journal (1939–1945)*, hrsg. von Pascal Fouché und Pascale Froment, Paris 2015.

6
Ruth Elizabeth Newns Austin, *Jean Cocteau and the Occupation of France*, Masterarbeit, University College London 2012, https://discovery.ucl.ac.uk/id/eprint/1355100/1/1355100_MPhil_Final_AUSTIN_REN.pdf [zuletzt abgerufen am 11.04.2025].

7
Neben der Schwarzen US-Bluessängerin Clara Smith war die offen bisexuell lebende mexikanische Künstlerin Frida Kahlo nur eine ihrer zahlreichen Beziehungen mit Frauen.

8
Claude Cahun in einem Brief, in dem Cahun sich auf die 1936 von André Breton und Georges Bataille gegründete Gruppe linksrevolutionärer Intellektueller bezieht, hier zit. nach: Karin Althaus, in: Karin Althaus, Adrian Djukić, Ara H. Merjian, Matthias Mühling, Stephanie Weber (Hrsg.), *Surrealismus + Antifaschismus. Anthologie*, Ausst.-Kat. Städtische Galerie im Lenbachhaus/Kunsthaus München, Berlin 2025, S. 518.

9
Claude Cahun, „Les paris sont ouverts", Paris 1934, in: François Leperlier (Hrsg.), *Écrits. Claude Cahun*, Paris 2002, S. 501–534.

to cruel medical experiments, and in many cases murdered. The gay Jewish socialist, doctor, and sexologist Magnus Hirschfeld, who during the Weimar Republic had fought for the decriminalization and acceptance of sexual and gender minorities, happened to be in Paris on May 6, 1933, when the Nazis ransacked and demolished his renowned Institute for Sexual Science in Berlin and forced most of its staff, including him, into exile. Yet there were also forms of collaboration, often shaped by a need for protection and survival, involving arrangements with European fascist regimes. This raises the question of how to reconcile the seemingly paradoxical antisemitic attitude of Romaine Brooks and her partner, Natalie Barney—considered "one quarter Jew" in the eyes of the Nazis—which extended beyond their conservative and anticommunist beliefs, with their collaboration with Benito Mussolini's fascist state during their exile near Florence.[3] How should the collaboration of Gertrude Stein, the Jewish writer, art collector, and influential patron of the European avant-garde, as well as of her Jewish partner and fellow author, Alice B. Toklas, with the antisemitic Vichy government of Philippe Pétain be judged, especially given that the queer figurehead translated numerous writings on Pétain's behalf through the mediation of her protégé, the Vichy collaborator Bernard Faÿ?[4] Furthermore, Marie Laurencin's antisemitic prejudice and her more than uncritical attitude toward Nazi Germany—according to the unvarnished diary entries of the French lawyer and writer Maurice Garçon,[5] who recorded their conversations during the occupation—are difficult to reconcile with the fact that she lived an openly queer life and had long worked together with the Jewish gallerist Paul Rosenberg, who was dispossessed by the Nazis in mid-September 1940 and forced to flee via Lisbon to New York. And how should Jean Cocteau's ambivalent stance toward Nazi cultural policies in Paris during the German occupation, as well as his passionate support for the 1942 Paris exhibition of his friend Arno Breker, be labelled if not as collaborative gestures?[6] And although the African American dancer, singer, actor, and later civil rights activist in the United States Josephine Baker was a resistance fighter and worked as a spy for French intelligence beginning in June 1940, she had initially supported Benito Mussolini's colonial invasion of Ethiopia in 1935, assuming that it would liberate the country's enslaved population.[7] Claude Cahun and Marcel Moore, by contrast, were already engaged in numerous antifascist and anti-imperialist activities carried out by the Surrealists and the Association des écrivains et artistes révolutionnaires (AEAR, Association of Revolutionary Writers and Artists) in the 1930s. In retrospect, Cahun regarded their subversive-poetic resistance against the German occupation forces as "a militant Surrealist activity that we had wanted at the time of Contre-Attaque,"[8] thus elevating poetry, in such a context, to the (sole) trans-historically effective revolutionary form of expression and to an innately human need.[9] The freedom inherent in the ambiguity of Surrealist poetry, as well as what Julika Funk has described as its "potential for equivocal subversiveness,"[10] can be understood as an emancipatory gesture of self-assertion that

3 See, for example, Shari Benstock on Natalie Barney's unpublished autobiographical notes in *Women of the Left Bank: Paris, 1900–1940* (London: Virago, [1986] 1994), pp. 415–418; and Cassandra Langer, *Romaine Brooks: A Life* (Madison: University of Wisconsin Press, 2015).

4 See, for example, Barbara Will, *Unlikely Collaboration: Gertrude Stein, Bernard Faÿ, and the Vichy Dilemma* (New York: Columbia University Press, 2011).

5 Maurice Garçon, *Journal (1939–1945)*, ed. Pascal Fouché and Pascale Froment (Paris: Les Belles Lettres/Fayard, 2015).

6 Ruth Elizabeth Newns Austin, "Jean Cocteau and the Occupation of France" (master's thesis, University College London, 2012), last accessed April 11, 2025, https://discovery.ucl.ac.uk/id/eprint/1355100/1/1355100_MPhil_Final_AUSTIN_REN.pdf.

7 In addition to the African American blues singer Clara Smith, another of her many relationships with women was with the openly bisexual Mexican artist Frida Kahlo.

8 Claude Cahun in a letter, referencing the group of leftist revolutionary intellectuals founded in 1936 by André Breton and Georges Bataille, quoted in *Surrealismus + Antifaschismus. Anthologie*, ed. Karin Althaus, Adrian Djukić, Ara H. Merjian, Matthias Mühling, and Stephanie Weber, exh. cat. Städtische Galerie im Lenbachhaus und Kunstbau, Munich (Berlin: Hatje Cantz, 2025), p. 518.

9 Claude Cahun, "Les paris sont ouverts," Paris 1934, in *Écrits: Claude Cahun*, ed. François Leperlier (Paris: Jean-Michel Place, 2002), pp. 501–534.

Fotomontagen und die sich keiner Gattung verpflichtet fühlenden, transfiktionalen Textcollagen wie *Aveux non avenus* (1930, Kat., S. 225–227) sind von einer Ambivalenz, Fluidität und widerständigen Gender-Nonkonformität geprägt. Ihre bildpolitischen und literarischen Experimente lassen sich mit Eve Kosofsky Sedgwicks Verständnis von „queer performativity"[12] als ein offenes Feld von Möglichkeiten und Alternativen eines von Instabilitäten, Brüchen, Revisionen und relationalen Gefühlen geprägten Selbstbilds lesen[13], das mit der unablässigen Suche nach einer Sprache, einem Körper und einem unabgeschlossen bleibenden „utopische[n] Geschlecht"[14] verbunden ist, für das Cahun das generische Neutrum gewählt hat: „Männlich? Weiblich? Das hängt vom Einzelfall ab. Neutrum ist das einzige Geschlecht, das mir immer entspricht. Wenn es in unserer Sprache existieren würde, würde man diese Schwankungen meiner Gedanken nicht beobachten."[15] Unter Fruchtbarmachung des antiken Narziss-Mythos – als Spiegelmetapher, wandelbare Doppelgängerfigur und als Ausdruck gleichgeschlechtlichen Begehrens – spielen die Selbstporträts des Künstler*innenpaars wie auch ihre Text- und Fotocollagen von *Aveux non avenus* mit performativen Maskierungsstrategien als Konstruktionen von Identität und Geschlecht und einem queeren Blickregime (Kat., S. 228, 229), bei dem das Abtasten und das sich fortwährend neu auszulotende *Selbst im anderen*[16] zentrales Thema ihrer Auseinandersetzung ist: „Unter dieser Maske eine andere Maske. Ich werde nicht aufhören, all diese Gesichter abzuziehen."[17] Für Tirza True Latimer ist diese „Produktion zweier gemeinsam agierender Menschen" Ausdruck einer eng verbundenen Kompliz*innenschaft und „eine sich selbst ergänzende Ausschmückung, die Singular in Plural verwandelt".[18] Sie verortet das kollaborative Werk des Paares im Umfeld des sapphischen Zirkels um die Buchhändlerin und Verlegerin Adrienne Monnier, obgleich sich Cahun mit den „nicht eingelösten Bekenntnissen" auch hier möglichen Vorstellungen einer lesbischen Identität entzieht. „Dieser Widerstand gegen Festschreibung […] führt zu einem Bruch in der ‚Signifikantenkette von Identität', die ihrerseits durch die ‚fortschreitende, begründete und damit verbundene Bedeutung von Geschlecht (sex), sozialem Geschlecht (gender) und Sexualität zusammenhält'."[19] Nachdem sich infolge des gescheiterten rechtsextremen Putschversuchs von 1934 die politische Lage auch in Paris zunehmend verschärfte und der Antisemitismus, dem Claude Cahun als Jüdin bereits in ihrer Schulzeit ausgesetzt war, weiter erstarkte, emigrierte das Paar am 9. Mai 1938 endgültig auf die Kanalinsel Jersey. Diese wurde am 1. Juli 1940 von der deutschen Wehrmacht besetzt und das Leben der beiden änderte sich dadurch wieder schlagartig. Die vertraute Küstenlandschaft, in der in früheren Jahren viele ihrer intimen Selbstporträts entstanden sind – Aufnahmen, auf denen ihre nackten Körper organisch mit den weichen Natur- und Felsformationen verschmelzen (Kat., S. 230, 231) – wird nun zur Komplizin im Kampf gegen die deutsche Besatzungsmacht. Als Halbschwestern getarnt lebten sie unter ihren Geburtsnamen in ihrem strandnah gelegenen Haus La Rocquaise, von wo aus sie ihre politischen und meist in deutscher Sprache verfassten Botschaften strategisch über die gesamte Insel verbreiteten. Wenige Monate nach ihrer Verhaftung wurden sie am 16. November 1944 zum Tode verurteilt. Ihren bedrückend nüchtern gehaltenen Tagebuchaufzeichnungen und späteren Briefen an Freund*innen ist zu entnehmen, dass auch nach

10
Julika Funk, „Sappho am Fenster der Guillotine. Zu intermedialen Reflexionen von Visualität und Queerness bei Claude Cahun", in: *FKW // Zeitschrift für Geschlechterforschung und visuelle Kultur*, Nr. 45, Juni 2008, S. 46–59, hier: S. 53.

11
Claude Cahun, „Amor Amicitiae", in: Leperlier 2002 (wie Anm. 9), S. 489–500, hier: S. 490. Die zu Cahuns Lebzeiten unveröffentlicht gebliebenen Textfragmente, die Cahun ihrem*seinem anderen Selbst gewidmet hatte – „à R. M. [Renée Mathilde] son ami Claude Cahun" – ist François Leperlier zufolge möglicherweise Cahuns erstes Buchprojekt.

12
Siehe Eve Kosofsky Sedgwick, „Queer Performativity. Henry James's *The Art of the Novel*", in: *GLQ: A Journal of Lesbian and Gay Studies*, Nr. 1, November 1993, S. 1–16.

13
Vgl. Jordan Reznicks Neubetrachtung von Claude Cahuns Werk vor dem Hintergrund einer Transidentität, „Through the Guillotine Mirror: Claude Cahun's Theory of Trans against the Void", in: *Art Journal Open (AJO)*, 06.10.2022, https://artjournal.collegeart.org/?p=17309 [zuletzt abgerufen am 20. April 2025].

14
Inspiriert vom griechischen Gott Uranos bezeichnete Karl Heinrich Ulrichs, Jurist, Schriftsteller und einer der ersten Vorkämpfer für die rechtliche Gleichstellung von Homosexuellen, 1864 gleichgeschlechtliches Begehren als „Uranismus". Claude Cahun greift in Auseinandersetzung mit Platons *Symposium* und den dort thematisierten androgynen Kugelmenschen dieses inter- bzw. transsexuelle Konzept in *Les Jeux Uraniens* (1916–1918) auf.

15
Claude Cahun, *Aveux non avenus*, in: Leperlier 2002 (wie Anm. 9), S. 136–438, hier: S. 366.

permeates Cahun's entire oeuvre, which centers on the question of the other self: "Who am I if not the friend of my friend?"[11] The photographic self-portraits and photomontages created together with Marcel Moore, and the trans-fictional text collages, such as *Aveux non avenus* (1930, cat. pp. 225–227), which defy genre classification, are marked by ambivalence, fluidity, and resistant gender nonconformity. These visual-political and literary experiments can be read, in light of Eve Kosofsky Sedgwick's concept of "queer performativity,"[12] as an open field of possibilities and alternatives shaped by a self-image marked by instabilities, ruptures, revisions, and relational emotions,[13] and linked to an ongoing search for a language, a body, and a unresolved "utopian gender,"[14] for which Cahun chose the grammatical neuter: "Masculine? Feminine? It depends on the situation. Neuter is the only gender that always suits me. If it existed in our language no one would be able to see my thought's vacillations."[15] Nourished by the myth of Narcissus from antiquity—as a metaphor for reflection, a mutable doppelgänger figure, and an expression of same-sex desire—the self-portraits of the artist couple, as well as the text and photo collages of *Aveux non avenus*, engage with performative strategies of masking as constructions of identity and gender within a queer regime of the gaze (cat. pp. 228, 229). In this interplay, the act of sampling and the ever-renewed negotiation of the *self in the other*[16] represent a core theme of their exploration: "Under this mask, another mask. I will never finish removing all these faces."[17] For Tirza True Latimer, this "production of two people acting together" is an expression of tightly woven complicity and "a self-complementing flourish that turns singular to plural."[18] Latimer situates the couple's collaborative work within the Sapphic circle surrounding the bookseller and publisher Adrienne Monnier, although Cahun, with their "unfulfilled commitments," drew back from the conceivable notion of a lesbian identity even here: "This resistance to determination […] creates a break in the 'signifying chain of identity,' which itself 'coheres through the progressive, motivated, and linked signification of sex, gender, and sexuality.'"[19] In the aftermath of the failed far-right putsch of 1934, the political situation in Paris continued to deteriorate, and the antisemitism that Claude Cahun had already experienced during their school days as a Jew intensified. On May 9, 1938, the couple ultimately emigrated to the Channel Island of Jersey, which was later occupied by the German Wehrmacht on July 1, 1940, again radically altering their lives. The familiar coastal landscape, in which they had staged many of their intimate self-portraits in earlier years, images in which their nude bodies seem to merge organically with the amorphous formations of rock and nature (cat. pp. 230, 231), now became an accomplice in their struggle against the occupying German forces. Camouflaged as stepsisters, they lived close under their birth names in their beachfront house, La Rocquaise, from which they strategically disseminated their political leaflets—mostly written in German—across the island. A few months after their subsequent arrest, they were sentenced to death on November 16, 1944. Their

10 Julika Funk, "Sappho am Fenster der Guillotine. Zu intermedialen Reflexionen von Visualität und Queerness bei Claude Cahun," in *FKW // Zeitschrift für Geschlechterforschung und visuelle Kultur* 45 (June 2008): pp. 46–59, here p. 53.

11 Claude Cahun, "Amor Amicitiae," in *Écrits*, pp. 489–500, here p. 490. The unpublished text fragments that Claude Cahun dedicated to their other self—"à R. M. [Renée Mathilde] son ami Claude Cahun"—are possibly their first book project, according to François Leperlier.

12 See Eve Kosofsky Sedgwick, "Queer Performativity: Henry James's *The Art of the Novel*," *GLQ: A Journal of Lesbian and Gay Studies* 1, no. 1 (November 1993): pp. 1–16.

13 See Jordan Reznick's new interpretation of Claude Cahun's work against the background of trans identity: "Through the Guillotine Mirror: Claude Cahun's Theory of Trans against the Void," *Art Journal Open (AJO)* (October 6, 2022), last accessed April 20, 2025, https://artjournal.collegeart.org/?p=17309.

14 Inspired by the Greek god Uranus, the jurist and writer Karl Heinrich Ulrichs, a pioneer of the gay rights movement, coined the word "Uranismus" (uranism) in German in 1864 for same-sex desire. Claude Cahun took up this intersexual or transgender concept, drawing on the discussion of androgynous spherical beings in Plato's *Symposium*, in *Les Jeux uraniens* (1916–1918).

15 Claude Cahun, *Aveux non avenus*, in *Écrits*, pp. 136–438, here p. 366; translated into English in *Disavowals; or, Cancelled Confessions*, trans. Susan de Muth (London: Tate, 2007), p. 151.

16 "Mon multiple est humain. Un signe hermaphrodite ne suffirait pas à le rendre (à lui rendre justice)."

ihrer Begnadigung – sechs Wochen vor der Befreiung der Insel am 9. Mai 1945 – die Gefahr ihrer Deportation in ein Konzentrationslager weiterhin bedrückend real blieb. Vor diesem Hintergrund lässt sich auch das unmittelbar nach der Befreiung entstandene Selbstporträt, auf dem Claude Cahun ein Nazi-Abzeichen wie eine Trophäe zwischen den Zähnen hält, als selbstbewusste Geste des Triumphs über den Faschismus (Kat., S. 235) lesen.

Toyen teilte mit Cahun und Moore eine politische, auf anarchistisch-kommunistischen Überzeugungen fußende antifaschistische Grundhaltung. Im Kreis der französischen Surrealist*innen um André Breton und der 1934 von Toyen mitgegründeten Skupina surrealistů v ČSR (Gruppe der Surrealist*innen in der Tschechoslowakei) haben sie sich spätestens 1935 anlässlich des Premier congrès international des écrivains pour la défense de la culture in Paris persönlich kennengelernt, an dem sie aus Protest gegen die zunehmende Bedrohung durch den Nationalsozialismus und Faschismus in Europa teilgenommen haben. Die grenzüberschreitende, nonkonforme Arbeits- und Lebensweise von Toyen lässt sich nicht in einfache künstlerische und identitätsbezogene Kategorien einordnen, worauf auch der ab 1923 gewählte geschlechtsneutrale Name und die Verwendung des männlichen Pronomens deuten.[20] Trotz der engen Freundschaften zu Künstlern wie Jindřich Štyrský oder Jindřich Heisler bewahrte sich Toyen innerhalb der verschiedenen Künstler*innengruppen wie Devětsil oder Skupina surrealistů eine Autonomie und Unabhängigkeit, die auch das enigmatisch gebliebene sexuelle Privatleben miteinschloss. Begehren als eine von nicht heteronormativen sexuellen Fantasien und Themen geprägte queere Sensibilität und formalästhetische Materialität durchzieht als Subtext dennoch Toyens gesamtes Werk. Sie kann in den fragmentierten Hüllen weiblicher Körper oder in den an vaginal-klitorale Körperfalten erinnernden, fließenden Farbräumen von Toyens malerischen Werks ausgemacht werden. Die erotischen und zum Teil sehr expliziten Zeichnungen der 1920er- und 1930er-Jahre lassen eine Auseinandersetzung mit den Schriften des Marquis de Sade erkennen. Wie für viele Avantgardekünstler*innen dieser Zeit waren diese auch für Toyen Ausdruck einer entgrenzten und nicht von heteronormativen Zwängen geprägten Sexualität, die dennoch – wie bei André Bretons entsubjektivierter Lesart – mit einer homophoben Grundhaltung verbunden sein konnte.[21] Die signierte Zeichnung *Hermaphrodite au coquillage* (1930, Kat., S. 247) erschien in einer Ausgabe des von Štyrský zwischen 1930 und 1933 herausgegebenen Magazins *Erotická revue* und zeigt eine intergeschlechtliche, an antike Statuen erinnernde Figur. Der aus einem weiblichen Ober- und einem männlichen Unterkörper zusammengesetzte, in seinen Einzelteilen jedoch unverbundene, fragmentierte Körper wird in einem liminalen Zustand schwebend zwischen einer Felsöffnung gezeigt, die den Blick auf das dahinterliegende Meer freigibt. Über die lustvolle Berührung der erotisch geöffneten vaginalen Lippen einer großen Muschel vermittelt sich – vergleichbar der schamhaft ambivalenten Venus-pudica-Geste – ein zum Leben erwecktes Begehren. Die am Boden wie ein zu überwindendes Hindernis errichteten Holzplanken lassen sich – in Verbindung mit der zwischen den Buchstaben „V“ und „BE“ offen gelassenen Leerstelle für ein noch zu bildendes Wort – als visuelle Geburtsmetapher eines neuen Körpers und Geschlechts lesen. Der von Toyen und Štyrský zwischen 1926 und 1934 in Abgrenzung zum poetischen Automatismus

16 „Mon multiple est humain. Un signe hermaphrodite ne suffirait pas à le rendre (à lui rendre justice).“ [Meine Vielheit ist menschlich. Ein hermaphroditisches Zeichen allein genügte nicht, um es darzustellen (um ihm gerecht zu werden).] Claude Cahun in dem zu Lebzeiten unveröffentlicht gebliebenen Text „Confidences au Miroir“, in: Leperlier 2002 (wie Anm. 9), S. 586.

17 Claude Cahun, *Aveux non avenus*, in: Leperlier 2002 (wie Anm. 9), S. 405.

18 Tirza True Latimer, *Women Together, Women Apart: Portraits of Lesbien Paris*, New Brunswick 2005, S. 69.

19 Ebd., S. 85. Hier zitiert Latimer die feministische Wissenschaftlerin Leigh Gilmore, „An Anatomy of Absence: Written on the Body, The Lesbian Body, and Autobiography without Names“, in: *Gender* 26, Frühjahr 1997, S. 224–251, hier: S. 237.

20 Die französische Schriftstellerin Annie Le Brun verwies auf den von Toyen ihr gegenüber zum Ausdruck gebrachten Verweis auf die Französische Revolution und die Ableitung des Namens von dem französischen *citoyen*. Siehe Karla Tonine Huebner, *Eroticism, Identity, and Cultural Context: Toyen and the Prague Avant-Garde*, Dissertation, University of Pittsburgh, Pittsburgh 2008, S. 25, Fußnote 58. Andere wie Jonas van Kappel vermuten ein tschechisches Wortspiel mit dem neutralen Demonstrativpronomen, „Toyen, a queer perspective on surrealism“, in: *RKD – Netherlands Institute for Art History*, 03.03.2025, https://www.rkd.nl/en/knowledge-publications/striking-figures/toyen-a-queer-perspective-on-surrealism [zuletzt abgerufen am 30.04.2025].

poignantly sober diary entries and subsequent letters to friends reveal that, even after they were reprieved—six weeks before the island's liberation on May 9, 1945—the threat of deportation to a concentration camp remained ominously real. Against this background, Claude Cahun's self-portrait taken immediately after their release (cat. p. 235), in which they hold a Nazi patch between their teeth like a prize medal, may be read as a defiant gesture of triumph over fascism. Toyen shared with Cahun and Moore a political, antifascist stance grounded in anarchist and communist convictions. They moved in overlapping circles of French Surrealists around André Breton and of the group Skupina surrealistů v čsr (Group of Surrealists in Czechoslovakia), which Toyen cofounded in 1934. They met in person no later than 1935 during the Premier congrès international des écrivains pour la défense de la culture (First International Congress of Writers for the Defense of Culture), held in Paris to protest the growing threat of Nazism and fascism in Europe. Toyen's nonconformist way of life and artistic practice transgressed conventional boundaries, defying easy classification in artistic and identity-based categories, as signaled by the gender-neutral name and the adoption of male pronouns from 1923 onward.[20] Despite close friendships with artists such as Jindřich Štyrský and Jindřich Heisler, Toyen maintained a strong sense of autonomy and independence within the various artistic groups they engaged in, including Devětsil and Skupina surrealistů, a stance that also encompassed Toyen's enigmatic and private sex life. Desire, as a queer sensibility not defined by heteronormative sexual fantasies and themes, and a distinct formal-aesthetic materiality, runs as a subtext throughout the artist's entire oeuvre. It can be discerned in the fragmented shells of female bodies or in the flowing color-fields that recall vaginal-clitoral folds in their paintings. Toyen's erotic and sometimes highly explicit drawings of the 1920s and 1930s suggest an engagement with the writings of the Marquis de Sade. As for many avant-garde artists of the period, these texts embodied a vision of sexuality unbounded by heteronormative constraints—though such readings, as in the case of André Breton's de-individualized understanding, could also coexist with fundamentally homophobic attitudes.[21] The signed drawing *Hermaphrodite au coquillage* (1930, cat. p. 247), appeared in an issue of *Erotická revue*—a magazine edited by Štyrský between 1930 and 1933—and depicts an intersex figure reminiscent of antique statuary. The body, composed of a female torso and a male lower half, with its individual parts remaining fragmented and disconnected, is shown floating in a liminal state within a rock opening that reveals a view of the sea beyond. The sensual contact of the erotically parted vaginal lips of a large seashell evokes—much like the coyly ambivalent gesture of the Venus Pudica—a desire aroused to life. Wooden planks placed on the ground like an obstacle to be overcome, along with the gap left open between the letters "V" and "BE," suggesting a word still in formation, can be read as a visual metaphor for the birth of a new body and of a new sex. The artificialism developed by Toyen and Štyrský between 1926 and 1934, in contrast to the poetic automatism of the

[My multiple is human. A hermaphroditic sign would not render it (do it justice).] Claude Cahun in a posthumously published text, "Confidence au Miroir," in *Écrits*, p. 586.

17
Cahun, *Aveux non avenus*, 405; in English in Cahun, *Disavowals*, p. 183.

18
Tirza True Latimer, *Women Together, Women Apart: Portraits of Lesbian Paris* (New Brunswick: Rutgers University Press, 2005), p. 69.

19
Ibid., p. 85. Here Latimer cites feminist scholar Leigh Gilmore, "An Anatomy of Absence: *Written on the Body*, *The Lesbian Body*, and *Autobiography without Names*," *Gender* 26 (Spring 1997): pp. 224–251, here p. 237.

20
The French writer Annie Le Brun reported that Toyen referenced the French Revolution, with the name deriving from *citoyen* (citizen); see Karla Tonine Huebner, "Eroticism, Identity, and Cultural Context: Toyen and the Prague Avant-Garde," (PhD dissertation, University of Pittsburgh, 2008), p. 25n58. Others, such as Jonas van Kappel, suspect a Czech wordplay involving the neutral demonstrative pronoun: "Toyen, a Queer Perspective on Surrealism," *RKD – Netherlands Institute for Art History*, March 3, 2025, last accessed April 30, 2025, https://www.rkd.nl/en/knowledge-publications/striking-figures/toyen-a-queer-perspective-on-surrealism.

21
See, for example, André Breton in the discussion "Recherches sur la sexualité: Part d'objectivité, déterminations individuelles, degré de conscience," *La Révolution surrealiste*, no. 11, March 15, 1928, pp. 32–40, republished in *La Révolution surrealiste: Collection complete* (Paris: Jean-Michel Place, 1975); published in English in *Investigating Sex: Surrealist Discussions*, ed. José Pierre, trans. Malcolm Imrie (London: Verso, 2011), pp. 1–16.

des französischen Surrealismus vertretende Artifizialismus verschmolz die Poesie mit der bildenden Kunst und weitete die ästhetische Wahrnehmung für die Lücken und ambivalenten Räume zwischen der Realität und der an Erinnerungen und Gefühle gebundenen sinnlichen Wahrnehmung. Die in dieser Zeit entstandenen Bilder von „wie aus einem metamorphotischen Urgrund“[22] aufsteigenden fluiden Unterwasserwelten sind von organischen Formen, geschichteten Farbverläufen und an Hautfaltungen weiblicher Körpersilhouetten erinnernden, porös-sandigen Oberflächentexturen besiedelt, die ab 1934 zunehmend zu dystopischen Wüstenlandschaften erstarren. Mit den entleerten, versteinerten Körpern und zerklüfteten Strukturen bildet Toyen eine Bildsprache heraus, die über eine Ästhetik der Fossilisierung das Grauen des Kriegs zu fassen versucht. Neben den von Heisler publizierten und von Toyen illustrierten Gedichtbänden entstanden zahlreiche bedrückende Zeichnungszyklen während der acht Jahre ihres gemeinsamen und mit einem Ausstellungsverbot belegten Lebens im Untergrund. Toyen versteckte den jüdischen Dichter, der auf der Deportationsliste stand, bis zum Kriegsende bei sich im Badezimmer, als mit dem SS-Obergruppenführer Reinhard Heydrich als stellvertretener Reichsprotektor in dem von den Nationalsozialisten errichteten Protektorat Böhmen und Mähren (15. März 1939 bis 9. Mai 1945) einer der grausamsten Verantwortlichen für den Holocaust die „Endlösung der Judenfrage“ umzusetzen begann[23]. Geprägt von den Themen Krieg, Verstümmelung, Gewalt und Tod zeigen die verstörenden Zeichnungen des Albums *Cache-toi, guerre! [Schovej se, válko!]* (1947, Kat., S. 249) halbtote, umherirrende Tiergerippe, verwüstete und ausgedörrte Landschaften, die menschliches Leben höchstens noch in den zerstörten Hinterlassenschaften und Spuren seiner Abwesenheit erahnen lassen. Die gleichgeschalteten Fische, die stromlinienförmig über der geisterhaft entleerten Landschaft schweben, können sinnbildlich für die durch Europa ziehenden zerstörerischen Kampftruppen gelesen werden. Wenige Tage nach dem Prager Aufstand des tschechischen Widerstands und dem Abzug der deutschen Besatzungsmacht marschiert die Rote Armee am 9. Mai 1945 in Prag ein. 1947 sahen sich Toyen und Heisler erneut mit einem Totalitarismus und damit verbundenen Restriktionen und Anfeindungen konfrontiert und entschlossen sich zur Emigration nach Paris, wo Toyen den durch den Krieg unterbrochenen Kontakt zur surrealistischen Bewegung als „eine Gemeinschaft von ethischen Ansichten“[24] wieder aufnahm. Das im Jahr 1952 entstandene Gemälde *L'Origine de la vérité* (Kat., S. 248) scheint mit seiner von ambivalenten, in weiche Faltungen metamorphisierenden Rissen geprägten Struktur an die oszillierenden Bilder der frühen 1930er-Jahre anzuschließen. Die camouflageartig mit der roten Farbtextur des Bilds verschmelzenden beiden Fischkörper mit ihren im Kontrast dazu mehrfarbig schillernden Köpfen sind über ihren Kuss spiegelbildlich miteinander verbunden. Die „Erotik der Analogie“[25], die laut Annie Le Brun vielen Arbeiten von Toyen zugrunde liegt, ließe sich hier als narzisstisches Symbol gleichgeschlechtlichen Begehrens lesen. Sie wird durch eine kleine weiße Kugel und ein winziges bohnenförmiges Objekt gestört, die wie ein verdoppeltes Punktum und unauflösbares Geheimnis die große Frage nach dem Ursprung der Wahrheit zwar offen und dennoch ein Begehren als Ahnung zaghaft aus der Materialität der Farblandschaft heraus sich entwickeln lässt.

21 Siehe u. a. André Breton in der Diskussion „Recherches sur la séxualité. Part d'objectivité, déterminations individuelles, degré de conscience“, in: Jean-Michel Place (Hrsg.) *La Révolution surrealiste. Collection complete*, Paris 1975, Nr. 11, 15.03.1928, S. 32–40.

22 Annabelle Görgen-Lammers, „Auftritt der Erscheinungen – zwischen Faltungen und Rissen in Raum und Bild“, in: *TOYEN 1902–1980*, hrsg. von Annabelle Görgen-Lammers, Annie Le Brun, Anna Pravdová, Ausst.-Kat. Hamburger Kunsthalle, München 2021, S. 139–164, hier: S. 160.

23 Als Vergeltungsschlag auf das an ihm erfolgreich verübten Attentat am 10. Juni 1942 folgte die bestialische Ermordung der Bewohner*innen und die Auslöschung des kleinen mittelböhmischen Dorfs Lidice.

24 Toyens Statement von 1955, hier zit. nach: Penelope Rosemont (Hrsg.), *Surrealist Women: An International Anthology*, Austin 1998, S. 80.

25 Annie Le Brun, „Luxus im wilden Zustand – Toyen und die Erotik“, in: Ausst.-Kat. 2021 (wie Anm. 22), S. 331–345, hier: S. 339.

French Surrealists, fused poetry with visual arts and expanded aesthetic perception of the gaps and ambivalent interstices between reality and sensuous perception shaped by memory and emotion. The images created during this period, emerging "as if from a metamorphic primal origin,"[22] depict fluid underwater worlds populated by organic forms, stratified layers of color, and porous, sandy surface textures that evoke the silhouettes of female genitalia, which after 1934 increasingly hardened into dystopian desert landscapes. With their emptied, petrified bodies and jagged structures, Toyen developed a visual language that sought to grasp the horrors of war through an aesthetic of fossilization. In addition to the books of poetry published by Heisler and illustrated by Toyen, the artist, banned from exhibiting, produced a large number of depressing drawing cycles during the eight years they lived together underground. Toyen hid the Jewish poet, who was marked for deportation, in the bathroom until the end of the war, during the period when SS-*Obergruppenführer* Reinhard Heydrich, Deputy Reich Protector of the Protectorate of Bohemia and Moravia established by the Nazis (March 15, 1939, to May 9, 1945) and one of the Holocaust's most brutal architects, began to implement the "Final Solution to the Jewish Question."[23] Haunted by themes of war, mutilation, violence, and death, the disturbing drawings in the album *Cache-toi, guerre! [Schovej se, válko!]* (1947, cat. p. 249) depict half-dead, erratically wandering animal skeletons and devastated, desiccated landscapes that evoke human presence only through destroyed remnants and traces of its absence. The uniformly formed fish floating aerodynamically over the ghostly, emptied terrain can be read symbolically as the marauding combat troops sweeping across Europe. A few days after the Prague uprising instigated by the Czechoslovakian resistance and the withdrawal of the occupying German forces, the Red Army marched into the city on May 9, 1945. In 1947, Toyen and Heisler once again found themselves confronted with totalitarianism, along with mounting restrictions and hostility, and decided to emigrate to Paris, where Toyen revived contacts with the Surrealist movement as "a community of ethical views"[24] that had been interrupted by the war. The 1952 painting *L'Origine de la vérité* (cat. p. 248) appears to echo their oscillating images of the early 1930s through its structure, marked by ambivalent fissures that metamorphose into soft folds. Two fish bodies, camouflaged against the red texture of the painting, their multicolored, vibrant heads standing in stark contrast to the rest of their forms, are joined in a kiss as mirrored images. The "eroticism of the analogy,"[25] which Annie Le Brun sees as fundamental to much of Toyen's work, may here be interpreted as a narcissistic symbol of same-sex desire. It is disturbed by a small white sphere and a tiny, bean-like object, akin to a doubled punctum and an unfathomable mystery, which, although it leaves the great question of the origin of truth unresolved, nevertheless allows a faint glimmer of desire to emerge timidly from the materiality of the color-landscape. For a long time, Hannah Höch moved in an exclusively male-dominated, chauvinist artistic sphere. She was the

22 Annabelle Görgen-Lammers, "Auftritt der Erscheinungen – zwischen Faltungen und Rissen in Raum und Bild," *TOYEN 1902–1980*, ed. Annabelle Görgen-Lammers, Annie Le Brun, Anna Pravdová, exh. cat. Hamburger Kunsthalle (Munich: Hirmer, 2021), pp. 139–164, here p. 160.

23 In retaliation for the successful assassination of Heydrich, the small central Bohemian village of Lidice was obliterated and its inhabitants brutally murdered on June 10, 1942.

24 Toyen's statement from 1955, quoted in Penelope Rosemont (ed.), *Surrealist Women: An International Anthology* (Austin: University of Texas Press, 1998), p. 80.

25 Annie Le Brun, "Luxus im wilden Zustand – Toyen und die Erotik," in *TOYEN 1902–1980*, pp. 331–345, here p. 339.

Hannah Höch bewegte sich lange Zeit in einem ausschließlich von Männern dominierten, chauvinistischen künstlerischen Umfeld, wo sie als einziges weibliches Mitglied der Berliner DADA-Gruppe um Raoul Hausmann – mit dem sie bis 1922 liiert war – mit progressiven Fotomontagen und Collagen ihr revolutionäres und sozialpolitisch-kritisches Werk entwickelte. Sie lernte 1926 während eines Besuchs bei ihren Freunden Helma und Kurt Schwitters in Den Haag die niederländische Schriftstellerin Til Brugman kennen, mit der sie die folgenden neun Jahre – zunächst in Den Haag und ab 1929 in Berlin – in einer lesbischen Beziehung zusammengelebt und gemeinsame Publikationsprojekte realisiert hat. Til Brugman hatte sich schon früh als Fremdsprachenkorrespondentin und Übersetzerin – sie beherrschte acht Sprachen fließend – ihre Unabhängigkeit erarbeitet. Ihre Kontakte zur internationalen künstlerischen Avantgarde hatten eine meist unerwähnt gebliebene Mitarbeit an dadaistischen Manifesten und den Zeitschriften der De-Stijl-Bewegung zur Folge. Insbesondere Theo van Doesburg reagierte auf ihre Lautgedichte und ihre Homosexualität mit einer misogynen und homophoben Herabsetzung[26].

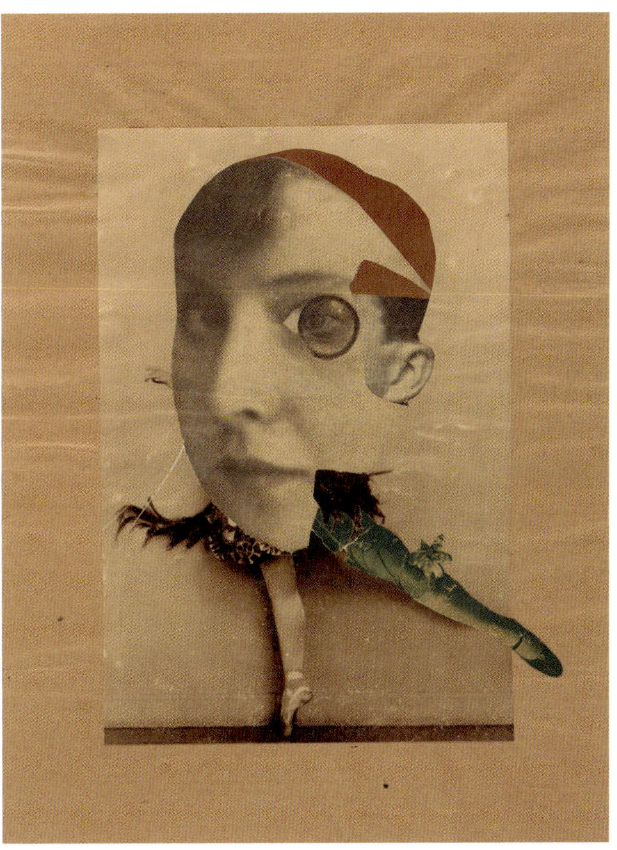

ABB. ~ FIG. 1

Hannah Höch, *Russische Tänzerin (Mein Double)*, 1928
Russian Dancer (My Double)

Fotomontage ~ *Photomontage*, 30,5 × 22,5 cm
Herzog Anton Ulrich-Museum, Braunschweig

26 „In Den Haag wohnt ein kleines Ungetüm, das vorgibt, homosexuell zu sein, doch das so weiblich ist wie eine frischgeborene Amme, es heißt Brugman. Es macht es sich zur täglichen Gewohnheit, mich mit Dreck, Scheiße und parfümierten Spermatozoen einzuschmieren. Es schreibt mir Bände über krähende Hähne und kreisende Berge – Zank. Ihre Schundverse haben keinen Platz in De Stijl." Theo van Doesburg in einem Brief vom 11.11.1924 an den Architekten und De-Stijl-Mitarbeiter J. J. P. Oud, hier zit. nach: Julie Nero, *Hannah Höch, Til Brugman, Lesbianism, and Weimar Sexual Subculture*, Dissertation, Case Western Reserve University, Ohio 2013, http://rave.ohiolink.edu/etdc/view?acc_num=case1347561845 [zuletzt abgerufen am 15.04.2025], S. 153.

sole female member of the Berlin DADA group around Raoul Hausmann, with whom she was in a relationship until 1922. Within this milieu, she developed a revolutionary and sociopolitical body of critical work using progressive photomontages and collages. In 1926, during a visit to her friends Helma and Kurt Schwitters in The Hague, she met the Dutch writer Til Brugman. The two lived together in a lesbian relationship for the next nine years, initially in The Hague and, after 1929, in Berlin, and collaborated on several joint publication projects. Til Brugman, who spoke eight languages fluently, had established her independence early on as a foreign-language correspondent and translator. Her contacts with the international avant-garde resulted in collaborations on Dadaist manifestos and journals of the De Stijl movement that, for the most part, went unacknowledged. Theo van Doesburg in particular responded to her sound poetry and homosexuality with misogynistic and homophobic scorn.[26] In Til Brugman's texts and grotesques, which she also began to write in German during her relationship with Hannah Höch, she highlighted the dangers of social and political conformity. She went on to criticize the inequality of gender relations, along with the attendant discrimination and sexual exploitation of women as mere objects of beauty serving male desire. By contrast, her magazine article "From Holland's Tulip Fields,"[27] disguised as a travel account and accompanied by two illustrations by Hannah Höch, reads like a direct transposition of Nazi eugenic "racial theories" into the "test halls" and "experimental spaces" of tulip breeders. Their pursuit of varietal purity in monocultures means that every single deviation is perceived as an expression of some "kind of hereditary burden" and a "blight"[28] on the village community. Other texts, too, inspired by Hannah Höch's collage techniques, gleam with sociopolitical critique through their combination of realistic and fantastically absurd fragments and allusions, as in the text collection titled *Scheingehacktes* (Mock Mincemeat, 1935), also illustrated by Höch. In the grotesque of the same name, an ideologically overblown vegetarianism is exaggerated ad absurdum, echoing how Heinrich Himmler later sought to cultivate a "healthy *Volkskörper* [body national]" through his biodynamic test farms and vegetarian dietary experiments on concentration camp prisoners. In "Warenhaus der Liebe" (Department Store of Love), a text also included in *Scheingehacktes*, Brugman addresses the Nazi's attack on Magnus Hirschfeld's Institute for Sexual Science. Both artists were well aware of the artistic cross-pollination between them, referring to it in letters and recollections. It surfaces in Hannah Höch's photomontages, which allude not only formally but also thematically to the same-sex relationship between the two women, as in *Englische Tänzerin* (1928, cat. p. 237) and its companion piece *Russische Tänzerin (Mein Double)* (1928, fig. 1), or in the double portrait *Auf dem Weg zum Siebenden Himmel* (1934, cat. p. 236). They feature, for example, the dance monocle[29] as a coded lesbian mark of recognition or, as in the case of *Dompteuse* (1930, fig. 2), explore gender ambivalent, androgynous identities.[30] According to Daniel Fountain's reading, the principle

26
"In The Hague there lives a little monster that says it's homosexual—but it's as womanly as a young wet-nurse. Its name is Brugman and has the habit of daily rubbing me with dirt, shit and perfumed sperm. It writes volumes about crowing roosters and turning mountains—Trouble! Her trash-verse has no place in De Stijl." Theo van Doesburg in a letter from November 11, 1924, to the architect and De Stijl member J. J. P. Oud, quoted in Julie Nero, "Hannah Höch, Til Brugman, Lesbianism, and Weimar Sexual Subculture" (PhD dissertation, Case Western Reserve University, 2013), p. 153, last accessed April 15, 2025, http://rave.ohiolink.edu/etdc/view?acc_num=case1347561845.

27
Til Brugman "Von Hollands Blumenfeldern," *Atlantis: Länder, Völker, Reisen* (Zurich: Atlantis Verlag) 7 (July 1933): pp. 429–432.

28
Brugman "Von Hollands Blumenfeldern," pp. 430, 432.

29
See, also, the use of the eyeglass in the name of the lesbian bars Le Monocle in Paris or Monokel-Diele in Berlin.

30
Julie Nero sees in the muscular arms and costume an allusion to the non-binary drag artist Voo-Doo, who is mentioned in Magnus Hirschfeld's study *Die Transvestiten* (*Transvestites*, 1910/12) and was a well-known figure in the 1920s, performing their "snake dance" on the variety stages of Berlin, Paris, Vienna, and Zurich. See Nero, *Hannah Höch, Til Brugman, Lesbianism*, pp. 234–242. Jack Halberstam sees the figures in the collages by Höch as "representations of transgender hybridity." See J. Jack Halberstam, "Technotopias: Representing Transgender Bodies in Contemporary Art," chapter 5 of *In a Queer Time & Place: Transgender Bodies, Subcultural Lives* (New York: New York University Press, 2005), pp. 97–124, here p. 97.

Mit ihren Texten und Grotesken, die sie während ihrer Beziehung zu Hannah Höch auch auf Deutsch zu schreiben begann, verwies sie auf die Gefahren einer sozialen und politischen Konformität und kritisierte überdies die Ungleichheit der Geschlechterverhältnisse und die damit verbundene Diskriminierung und sexuelle Ausbeutung von Frauen als Schönheitsobjekte männlicher Begierde. Der als Reisebericht getarnte und von Hannah Höch mit zwei Illustrationen versehene Zeitschriftenartikel „Von Hollands Blumenfeldern“[27] liest sich hingegen wie eine unmittelbare Übertragung der eugenischen „Rassentheorien“ der Nationalsozialisten auf die „Versuchshallen“ und „Experimentierräume“ der Tulpenzüchter, deren angestrebtes Ziel einer Sortenreinheit der Monokulturen durch jede einzelne Abweichung davon, als Ausdruck einer „Art erblicher Belastung“ und als „Schandfleck“[28] der Dorfgemeinschaft wahrgenommen wird. Aber auch in anderen Texten, die von Hannah Höchs Collagetechniken inspiriert sind, blitzt in der Kombination von realistischen und fantastisch absurden Versatzstücken und Verweisen eine politische Gesellschaftskritik auf wie in ihrer von Höch illustrierten Textsammlung *Scheingehacktes* (1935). In der gleichnamigen Groteske wird ein ideologisch übersteigerter Vegetarismus ad absurdum geführt, wie ihn Heinrich Himmler später mit seinen biologisch-dynamischen Versuchsanstalten und vegetarischen Ernährungsversuchen an KZ-Häftlingen für einen „gesunden Volkskörper“ zu untermauern versuchte. In dem ebenfalls darin abgedruckten „Warenhaus der Liebe“ greift Brugman den Angriff auf Magnus Hirschfelds Institut für Sexualwissenschaft durch die Nationalsozialisten auf. Die gegenseitige künstlerische Befruchtung, die beide wahrgenommen und in Briefen und Erinnerungen zum Ausdruck gebracht haben, bildet sich auch in den Fotomontagen von Hannah Höch ab, die nicht nur formal, sondern auch inhaltlich wie *Englische Tänzerin* (1928, Kat., S. 237) und das Pendant *Russische Tänzerin (Mein Double)* (1928, Abb. 1) oder wie das Doppelporträt *Auf dem Weg zum Siebenden Himmel* (1934, Kat., S. 236) auf die gleichgeschlechtliche Beziehung der beiden anspielt und mit dem Tanzmonokel[29] ein lesbisches Erkennungszeichnen oder mit *Dompteuse* (um 1930, Abb. 2) genderambivalente, androgyne Identitäten[30] zum Thema ihrer Arbeiten machte. Das Prinzip der Collage kann – folgt man Daniel Fountains Lesart – als eine gendernormative Vorstellungen von Sexualität und Identität destabilisierende Methode und als Darstellung eines liminalen Zustands verstanden werden, die „sich queerer Konzepte bedient, wie Humor und Camp, Inversion und Transition, Exzess und Extreme“[31].

Die politische Situation in Berlin wurde für das lesbische Paar spätestens am 12. Januar 1932 konkret belastend, als ein Einbruch in ihr Atelier, den sie als politisch motivierten Einschüchterungsversuch deuteten, sie zu einem Umzug zwang. Auch die lange geplante Ausstellung von Hannah Höch im Bauhaus Dessau wurde kurzfristig abgesagt, nachdem die am 21. Mai 1932 neu gewählte nationalsozialistische Regierung im damaligen Freistaat Anhalt die Schließung des Bauhauses angeordnet hatte. Ihre in dieser Hinsicht visionäre Fotomontage *Flucht* (1931, Kat., S. 239) zeigt ein Hitlerkonterfei mit seitlich flankierten und wie zum Angriff ausgestreckten Vogelflügeln, der ein davoneilendes Wesen mit einem zusammengesetzten Affen- und Frauenkopf und einer auffällig überproportional herabhängenden rechten, weißen Hand zu verfolgen scheint.

27 Til Brugman „Von Hollands Blumenfeldern“, in: *Atlantis: Länder, Völker, Reisen*, Heft 7, Atlantis Verlag, Juli 1933, S. 429–432.

28 Ebd., S. 430 und S. 432.

29 Siehe auch die Lesbenbars *Le Monocle* in Paris oder die *Monokel-Diele* in Berlin.

30 Julie Nero meint in den muskulären Armen und dem Kostüm die*den non-binäre*n Travestiekünstler*in Voo-Doo zu erkennen, die*der in Magnus Hirschfelds Studie *Die Transvestiten* (1910/12) Erwähnung findet und mit ihrem*seinem Schlangentanz eine berühmte Persönlichkeit auf den Varietébühnen in Berlin, Paris, Wien und Zürich der 1920er-Jahre war. Siehe Nero 2013 (wie Anm. 26), S. 234–242. J. Jack Halberstam sieht die Figuren in den Collagen von Höch als „Darstellungen von Transgender-Hybridität“, siehe J. Jack Halberstam, „Technotopias: Representing Transgender Bodies in Contemporary Art“, in: *In a Queer Time & Place: Transgender Bodies, Subcultural Lives*, New 2005, S. 97–124, hier: S. 97.

31 Daniel Fountain, „The Art of Hannah Höch: Queering Collage via Jack Halberstam“, in: *Collage Research Network*, 13.06.2019 https://collageresearchnetwork.wordpress.com/2019/06/13/the-art-of-hannah-hoch-queering-collage-via-jack-halberstam [zuletzt abgerufen am 30.04.2025].

of collage may be understood as a method of destabilizing gender-normative conceptions of sexuality and identity, as well as representing a liminal state that "makes use of queer concepts; such as humour and camp, inversion and reversal, excess and extremes."[31] The political situation in Berlin became palpably oppressive after January 12, 1932, at the latest, when their studio was burglarized, which they interpreted as a politically motivated attempt at intimidation, forcing them to relocate. In addition, Hannah Höch's long-planned exhibition at the Bauhaus Dessau was abruptly cancelled after the newly elected National Socialist government in the former Free State of Anhalt, in power from May 21, 1932, ordered the closure of the Bauhaus. In this respect, her visionary photomontage *Flucht* (1931, cat. p. 239) seems prophetic, depicting a profile of Hitler flanked by outstretched wings as though poised for the hunt, seemingly pursuing a fleeing creature with a composite monkey-woman head and a conspicuously oversized, drooping white right hand. In 1936, Hannah Höch ended her relationship with Til Brugman, whose dominant personality and craving for fame apparently smothered her own creative energy, although, as she later wrote, "this never-ending cascade of tumbling, sarcastic, madcap ideas that 'danced' atop a vast reservoir of knowledge [...] made the years with Til the most delightful of my life."[32] During her subsequent relationship and marriage with Kurt Matthies (from 1936 to 1944), who was nearly twenty years her junior, she observed with growing concern the domestic political developments and the beginning of the pogroms and deportations of Jews, including her friend, the musician and composer Walter Hirschberg.[33] Labeled a "cultural Bolshevist" and on the Gestapo's blacklist by 1937 at the latest, when she was named in Wolfgang Willrich's Nazi polemic on political art, she hoped to keep a low profile by retreating into the anonymity of the Heiligensee district. There, she hid the works of "ostracized" artist friends and attempted, in her "inner emigration," to earn a living—with the exception of some "intellectually tainted" images[34]—with works that appeared harmless on the surface: pictures of flowers and plants. Til Brugman returned to the Netherlands in 1939 and joined the Dutch resistance, helping Jews go into hiding.

In contrast to Hannah Höch, Jeanne Mammen sought out her motifs directly on the street, in bars, and in the numerous lesbian nightclubs of 1920s Berlin. In addition to her earlier designs for film posters and illustrations for fashion magazines, she was able, as a celebrated chronicler of the Weimar Republic, to place her drawings and graphic works depicting the vibrant nightlife in the big city in prominent magazines such as *Der Querschnitt*, *Simplicissimus*, and *Ulenspiegel*, and thus earn a living. Her long-time artistic accomplice was her sister Mimi Mammen, two years her senior, with whom she studied at various art academies in Paris, Brussels, and Rome, and with whom she also lived in Berlin in the first years after the outbreak of the First World War, until Mimi went into exile in 1936 with her lesbian partner, Henriette Goldenberg, relocating to the then-cosmopolitan city of Tehran. Early on in Paris, where the two sisters were born and raised in a culturally liberal household

31 Daniel Fountain, "The Art of Hannah Höch: Queering Collage via Jack Halberstam," *Collage Research Network*, June 13, 2019, last accessed April 30, 2025, https://collageresearchnetwork.wordpress.com/2019/06/13/the-art-of-hannah-hoch-queering-collage-via-jack-halberstam.

32 Hannah Höch, quoted in Myriam Everard, "'Man lebt nur einmal in Patchamatac.' Die Groteske Welt von Til Brugman, Lebensgefährtin von Hannah Höch," in *Da-da-zwischen-Reden zu Hannah Höch*, ed. Julia Dech and Ellen Maurer (Berlin: Orlanda Frauenverlag, 1991), pp. 82–99, here p. 83.

33 See, for example, the entries in her appointment book for November 11 and December 18, 1938, reproduced in *Hannah Höch. Eine Lebenscollage*, vol. II, *1921–1945*, ed. Künstlerarchiv der Berlinischen Galerie (Ostfildern Ruit: Hatje Cantz, 1995), pp. 609 and 612.

34 Hannah Höch in a letter to Thomas Ring from September 4, 1944, in ibid., p. 676.

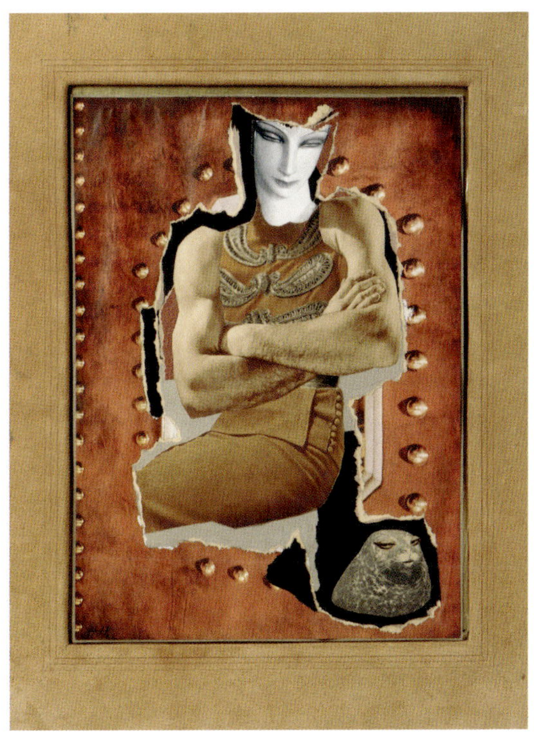

ABB. ~ FIG. 2

Hannah Höch, *Dompteuse*, um ~ *ca.* 1930
Tamer

Fotomontage mit Collage ~ *Photomontage with collage*,
35,5 × 26 cm
Kunsthaus Zürich, Grafische Sammlung

1936 trennt sich Hannah Höch von Til Brugman, unter deren dominanter Persönlichkeit und Geltungstrieb ihre eigene Schaffenskraft gelitten zu haben schien, wie sie nachträglich schrieb, obgleich „[…] diese nie endenden, purzelnden, sarkastischen, verrückten Einfälle, die auf einem riesigen Wissen ‚tanzten', […] die Jahre mit Til zu den amüsantesten meines Lebens [machten]."[32] Während ihrer darauffolgenden Beziehung und Ehe mit dem um fast 20 Jahre jüngeren Kurt Matthies (von 1936 bis 1944) beobachtete sie die innerpolitischen Entwicklungen mit den beginnenden Pogromen und Deportationen von Jüdinnen und Juden, wovon auch ihr Freund, der Musiker und Komponist Walter Hirschberg, betroffen war, mit großer Besorgnis.[33] Als „Kulturbolschewistin", die spätestens 1937 mit der Erwähnung in Wolfgang Willrichs kunstpolitischer NS-Kampfschrift auf der schwarzen Liste der Gestapo steht, erhoffte sie sich durch den Umzug nach Heiligensee, in der Anonymität untertauchen zu können. Dort versteckte sie Arbeiten „verfehmter" Künstlerfreunde und versuchte in ihrer inneren Emigration, „[…] neben einigen ‚gedanklich belasteten' Bildern […]"[34] mit vordergründig harmlos erscheinenden Blumen- und Pflanzenbildern ihren Lebensunterhalt zu sichern. Til Brugman kehrte 1939 in die Niederlande zurück, wo sie mit dem niederländischen Widerstand zusammenarbeitete und Jüdinnen und Juden half, unterzutauchen.

Anders als Hannah Höch suchte Jeanne Mammen ihre Motive direkt auf den Straßen, in den Bars und in den zahlreichen lesbischen Nachtclubs im Berlin der 1920er-Jahre. Als gefeierte Chronistin der Weimarer Republik kann sie neben ihren anfänglichen Entwürfen für Kinoplakate und Illustrationen für Modezeitschriften auch ihre Zeichnungen und Grafiken, die das aufregende Großstadt- und Nachtleben abbilden, in

32 Hannah Höch, hier zitiert nach Myriam Everard „‚Man lebt nur einmal in Patchamatac'. Die Groteske Welt von Til Brugman, Lebensgefährtin von Hannah Höch", in: Julia Dech und Ellen Maurer (Hrsg.), *Da-da-zwischen-Reden zu Hannah Höch*, Berlin 1991, S. 82–99, hier: S. 83.

33 Siehe u.a. die Aufzeichnungen in ihrem Terminkalender vom 11.11.1938 und vom 18.12.1938, abgedruckt in: Künstlerarchiv der Berlinischen Galerie (Hrsg.), *Hannah Höch. Eine Lebenscollage, Bd. II, 1921–1945*, Ostfildern Ruit 1995, S. 609 und S. 612.

34 Hannah Höch in einem Brief an Thomas Ring vom 09.04.1944, in: ebd., S. 676.

with parents that encouraged the education of their daughters, they were interested in the everyday life of people on the street. It was possibly with Mimi that Jeanne Mammen, discovered and explored—as she had previously done in Paris—the lesbian nightlife of Berlin with its numerous "Damenclubs" (ladies' clubs), dance bars, and so-called transvestite venues. Her works should be viewed against the background of the Weimar Republic's cosmopolitan atmosphere, shaped by the medical and sociopolitical achievements of progressive sexual reformers such as Magnus Hirschfeld, Helene Stöcker, and Johanna Elberskirchen. Jeanne Mammen produced numerous drawings, watercolors, and prints that point to a lesbian sensibility and intimacy—alongside the self-assured, emancipated "New Woman," whom she typically portrayed in the trendy bars of Berlin's hedonistic subcultural milieu. But she also frequently depicted the growing group of marginalized members of a society plagued by the Stock Market Crash of 1929: that is, the impoverished, the unemployed, and sex workers. At the high point of her pre-war career, in 1930, Jeanne Mammen held her first solo show at Wolfgang Gurlitt's gallery. Her illustrations for a luxury edition of *Les Chansons de Bilitis* (*The Songs of Bilitis*, 1894) by Pierre Louÿs, commissioned by Gurlitt, however, were never published due to the political developments of the time. The few sheets and motifs that have survived the war illustrate, with references to the literary model and the myth of Sapphic love in antiquity, same-sex desire and tenderness in the subcultural milieu of "ladies' bars" and between lesbian sex workers (cat. pp. 242, 243). Although this collection of erotic poems was popular above all among men during the interwar period, it was also taken up by women artists such as Gerda Wegener (cat. p. 111) and Marie Laurencin, who used the poems to explore their queer desire—moving beyond the male voyeuristic gaze—and at the same time integrate it into a Sapphic genealogy.

After the National Socialists had politically "synchronized" the periodicals for which she had worked, Jeanne Mammen withdrew into unemployment, thus refusing to collaborate with the Nazi regime, against which she had distributed antifascist, Communist leaflets with her friend Hans Uhlmann in October 1933. She managed to earn a living through odd jobs and work for the Reich Institute for Puppetry, where she painted puppet heads. In the secrecy of her studio during this period, she created an oeuvre of painting and sculpture characterized by an aggressive, eclectic visual language, a body of work that may be understood as aesthetic resistance. With their disassociated figures broken up into painfully abstracted, cubist fragments, her pictures evoke Pablo Picasso's anti-war *Guernica*, which she had seen in the Spanish Pavilion at the World Exposition in Paris in 1937. Resorting to biblical allegories, animal symbolism, and caricature, or employing resistance at a formal-aesthetic level, she sought to find a language with which she could reflect on and process the political situation of the time, at least for herself. It is striking how frequently her pictures are inhabited by unheroic, broken figures and wounded soldiers. Jeanne Mammen also expresses solidarity with the purported enemy, such

renommierten Zeitschriften wie *Der Querschnitt*, den *Simplicissimus* oder den *Ulenspiegel* unterbringen und sich damit ihren Lebensunterhalt verdienen. Ihre künstlerische Gefährtin ist lange Zeit ihre zwei Jahre ältere Schwester Mimi Mammen, mit der sie an verschiedenen Kunstakademien in Paris, Brüssel und Rom studiert hatte und nach Ausbruch des Ersten Weltkriegs auch die ersten Jahre in Berlin zusammenlebte, bis diese 1936 mit ihrer lesbischen Partnerin Henriette Goldenberg ins Exil der damals weltoffenen Metropole Teheran auswanderte. Bereits in Paris, wo die beiden geboren und in einem kulturell liberalen, die Bildung ihrer Töchter fördernden Elternhaus aufgewachsen sind, interessierten sich die Mammen-Schwestern für das alltägliche Leben der Menschen auf der Straße. Es ist möglicherweise auch Mimi, mit der Jeanne Mammen wie schon in Paris das lesbische Nachtleben Berlins mit seinen zahlreichen „Damenclubs", Tanzbars und Transvestitenlokale entdeckte. Ihre Arbeiten sind vor dem Hintergrund einer von wissenschaftlichen und sozialpolitischen Errungenschaften progressiver Sexualreformer*innen wie Magnus Hirschfeld, Helene Stöcker oder Johanna Elberskirchen geprägten Großstadtatmosphäre der Weimarer Republik zu betrachten. Es entstanden zahlreiche Zeichnungen, Aquarelle und Druckgrafiken, die auf eine lesbische Sensibilität und Intimität schließen lassen: Neben der selbstbewussten, emanzipierten „Neuen Frau", die sie meist in den Szenelokalen des vergnügungssüchtigen subkulturellen Milieus Berlins einfing, finden sich aber auch Darstellungen der aufgrund der Weltwirtschaftskrise von 1929 immer größer werdenden Gruppe von marginalisierten Personen der Gesellschaft, den Armen, Arbeitslosen und Prostituierten. 1930 auf dem Höhepunkt ihrer Vorkriegskarriere erhielt Jeanne Mammen in der Galerie von Wolfgang Gurlitt ihre erste Einzelausstellung. Die von ihm bei ihr in Auftrag gegebenen Illustrationen für eine bibliophile Ausgabe von *Les Chansons de Bilitis* (Die Lieder der Bilitis, 1894) von Pierre Louÿs erschienen aufgrund der politischen Entwicklung jedoch nie. Die wenigen Blätter und Motive, die den Krieg überlebt haben, illustrieren mit Referenz auf die literarische Vorlage und den antiken Mythos sapphischer Liebe gleichgeschlechtliches Begehren und Zärtlichkeit im subkulturellen Milieu der „Damenbars" und zwischen lesbischen Prostituierten (Kat., S. 242, 243). Diese in der Zwischenkriegszeit vor allem bei Männern beliebte Sammlung erotischer Gedichte wurde auch jenseits des männlichen voyeuristischen Blicks von anderen Künstler*innen wie Gerda Wegener (Kat., S. 111) oder Marie Laurencin aufgegriffen, die darüber ihr queeres Begehren thematisieren und es gleichzeitig in eine sapphische Genealogie einordnen konnten.

Jeanne Mammen zog sich nach der Gleichschaltung der Zeitschriften, für die sie gearbeitet hatte, in die Arbeitslosigkeit zurück und verweigerte auf diese Weise eine zwangsläufige Zusammenarbeit mit dem faschistischen Regime, gegen das sie im Oktober 1933 zusammen mit ihrem Freund Hans Uhlmann antifaschistische, kommunistische Flugblätter verteilt hatte. Sie sicherte sich ihr Überleben durch Gelegenheitsarbeiten und eine Mitarbeit beim Reichsinstitut für Puppenspiel, wo sie Puppenköpfe bemalte. In der Verborgenheit ihres Ateliers entwickelte sich in dieser Zeit ein von einer aggressiven, eklektischen Bildsprache geprägtes malerisches und skulpturales Werk, das als ästhetischer Widerstand verstanden werden kann. Mit seinen dissoziierten, sich in schmerzhaft abstrahierende, kubistische Versatzstücke aufbrechenden Figuren erinnern ihre Bilder an Pablo Picassos

as in *Polnische Bauersfrau im Krieg* (*Polish Peasant Woman during the War*, ca. 1939–1942); or in *Der Jäger (Sonntagsjäger)* (1939–1942, cat. p. 245), she presents a dangerously mocking, starkly abstracted caricature of Adolf Hitler, holding a small dead bird between his fingers as a hunting trophy. In her large-format apocalyptic painting *Der Würgeengel* (ca. 1942, cat. p. 244), the giant gray hands of the biblical Angel of Death symbolize the divine power that attempts to strangle and combat the all-dominant evil—here represented in allegorical form of devilish fascism. This is her view of hell, which she shares with Arthur Rimbaud, whose poem *Une saison en enfer* (*A Season in Hell*) she began translating into German after visiting the 1937 World's Fair in Paris.[35]

35
See an undated manuscript page of the translation in the archive of the Förderverein der Jeanne-Mammen-Stiftung e.V. Berlin, to which Johann Thun refers in "'Tu as bien fait de partir' Jeanne Mammen, René Char und Arthur Rimbaud," in *Jeanne Mammen. Paris – Bruxelles – Berlin'* ed. Förderverein der Jeanne-Mammen-Stiftung e.V. Berlin (Berlin: Deutscher Kunstverlag, 2016), pp. 164–165.

Antikriegsbild *Guernica*, das sie 1937 im Spanischen Pavillon der Weltausstellung in Paris gesehen hatte. Mit Rückgriffen auf biblische Allegorien, die Tiersymbolik und die Karikatur oder durch eine Widerständigkeit auf formalästhetischer Ebene suchte sie eine Sprache, mit der sie die politische Situation zumindest für sich selbst reflektierend verarbeiten konnte. Darunter finden sich auffällig viele Bilder von unheroisch gebrochenen Figuren und verwundeten Soldaten. Mammen solidarisiert sich in ihren Arbeiten aber auch mit dem vermeintlichen Feind wie in *Polnische Bauersfrau im Krieg* (um 1939–1942) oder zeichnet mit *Der Jäger (Sonntagsjäger)* (zwischen 1939–1942, Kat., S. 245) eine gefährlich spöttische, stark abstrahierte Karikatur von Adolf Hitler, der einen kleinen toten Vogel als Jagdtrophäe zwischen seinen Fingern hält. In ihrem großformatigen apokalyptischen Gemälde *Der Würgeengel* (um 1939–1942, Kat., S. 244) symbolisieren die riesigen, grauen Hände des biblischen Todesengels die göttliche Macht, die das alles bestimmende Böse – hier in allegorischer Gestalt des teuflischen Faschismus – mit ihren Händen zu erwürgen und bekämpfen versucht. Es ist ihr Blick in die Hölle, den sie mit Arthur Rimbaud teilt, dessen Gedicht *Une saison en enfer* (Eine Zeit in der Hölle, 1873) sie 1937 nach ihrem Besuch der Weltausstellung ins Deutsche zu übersetzen beginnt.[35]

35 Siehe eine undatierte Manuskriptseite der Übersetzung im Archiv des Fördervereins der Jeanne-Mammen-Stiftung e.V. Berlin, auf die Johann Thun verweist „‚Tu as bien fait de partir' Jeanne Mammen, René Char und Arthur Rimbaud", in: Förderverein der Jeanne-Mammen-Stiftung e.V. Berlin (Hrsg.), *Jeanne Mammen. Paris – Bruxelles – Berlin*, Berlin/München 2016, S. 164–165.

VIII EPILOG

EPILOGUE

1

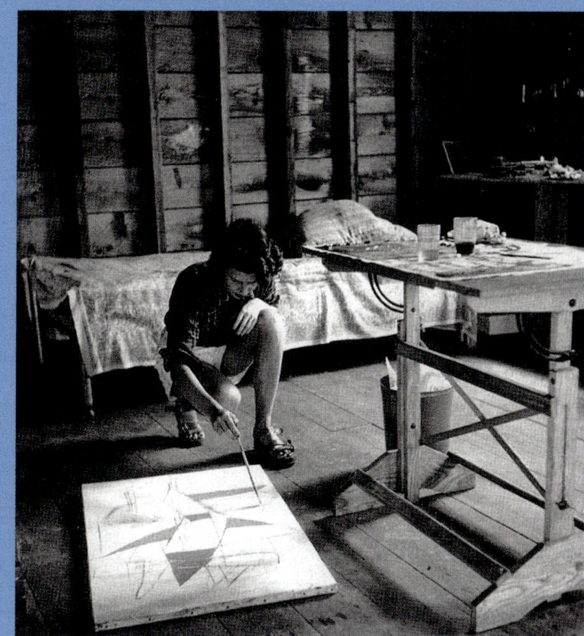

2

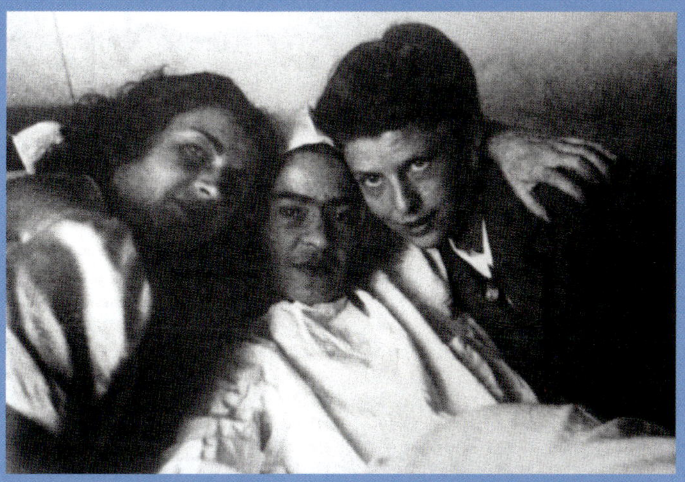

3

Vergiss nicht, dass ich, eine, Frau bin, ein Bauch, ein, Schwert, eine, Brustwarze, ein, Geschlecht, ein, Traum, Kreuz, und, ein Sonntag, und, ein Spiegel.

Don't forget that I, am a, woman,
a belly, a, sword, a, nipple, a, sex,
a, dream, cross, and, a Sunday, and,
a mirror.

4

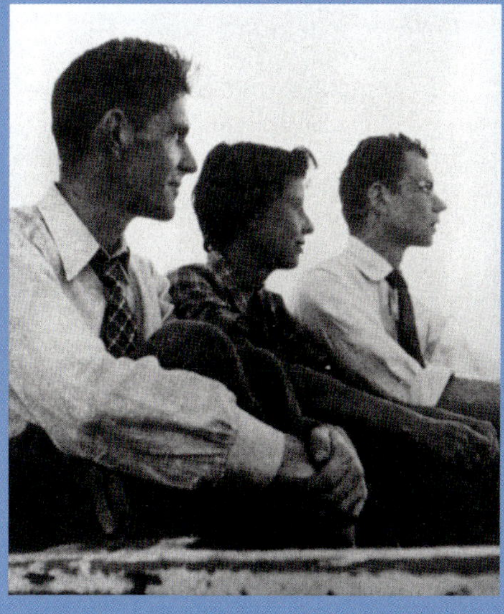

5

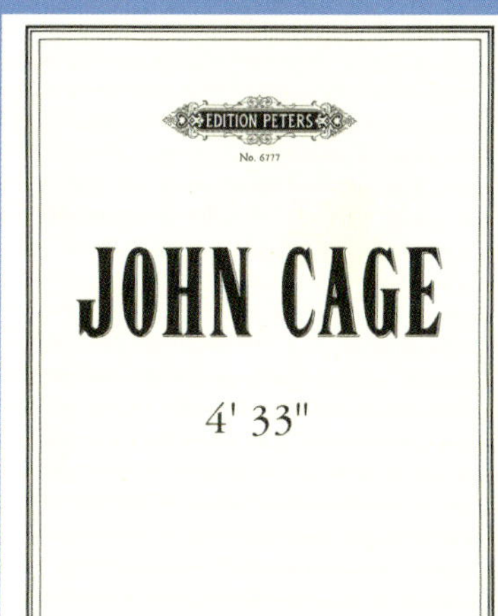

EDITION PETERS

No. 6777

JOHN CAGE

4' 33"

1

Die schweizerisch-amerikanische Künstlerin Sonja Sekula beim Malen auf Long Island, um 1946. Sie war Teil der New Yorker Nachkriegs-avantgarde, die vom Surrealismus und Abstrakten Expressionismus geprägt war. Zu ihren Geliebten und ihrem Freundeskreis gehörten unter anderem Frida Kahlo, Alice Rahon und Betty Parsons.

The Swiss-born American artist Sonja Sekula painting on Long Island around 1946. She was part of the New York postwar avant-garde and influenced by Surrealism and Abstract Expressionism. Her lovers and circle of friends included Frida Kahlo, Alice Rahon, and Betty Parsons.

2

Sonja Sekula mit Frida Kahlo (Mitte) und deren Schwester Cristina (links) im Juni 1946 in einem New Yorker Krankenhaus, wo sich die mexikanische Künstlerin nach einer Rückenoperation erholte. Sekula und Kahlo lernten sich Anfang der 1940er-Jahre in New York kennen. Zwischen ihnen entstand eine enge romantische Beziehung.

Sonja Sekula with Frida Kahlo (middle) and her sister Cristina (left) in June 1946 in a New York hospital, where the Mexican artist was recovering from back surgery. Sekula and Kahlo met in New York in the early 1940s and had developed a close romantic relationship.

3

Sonja Sekula, Tagebucheintrag, 1951

Sonja Sekula, diary entry, 1951

5

John Cages radikale Komposition *4'33"* (1952) kann auch als subtile Liebeserklärung für seinen langjährigen Partner Merce Cunningham verstanden werden. Zugleich ist die Stille des Stücks während der homophoben McCarthy-Ära in den 1950er-Jahren ein politisches Statement zur Unsichtbarkeit homosexueller Partnerschaften.

John Cage's radical composition 4'33" *(1952) can also be read as a subtle declaration of love for his lifelong partner, Merce Cunningham. At the same time, the piece's silence served as a political statement on the invisibility of queer partnerships during the homophobic McCarthy era of the 1950s.*

4

Sonja Sekula bezog 1947 ein Studio in der Monroe Street 346 in New York, wo auch der Komponist und Künstler John Cage und sein Partner, der Choreograf und Tänzer Merce Cunningham, wohnten. Im gleichen Jahr entwarf Sekula ein Kostüm für Cunningham in seiner Choreografie *Dromenon* mit einer Musik von Cage.

In 1947, Sonja Sekula moved into a studio at 346 Monroe Street in New York, where the composer John Cage and his partner, choreographer and dancer Merce Cunningham, also lived. That same year, Sekula designed Cunningham's costume for his choreography Dromenon, *with music by Cage.*

GEDICHT. WEIL: ICH DICH LIEBE.

Wie ein Blatt am Baum, brauch ich
kaum etwas als deine Nähe.
Ich zehre gierig von deinem Stamm,
genieße inbrünstig jedes Gramm
deines Baumsaftes, klammer mich zähe
an deine Lebenskraft, um mich zu
nähren.
Wird dieses Blatt vertrocknen,
sterben? Wird
aus meinem Brauchen nur ein Mögen?
Doch nein, es muss sich unbeirrt
erneuern, selbst im Winter. Flöge
das Blatt vom Baum, lebt der Baum
doch fort
darin, egal an welchem Ort.

POEM. CAUSE: I LOVE YOU.

As leaf with tree, I long to be
With you. A twig connection
If no other, would satisfy.
Sap from your trunk to vivify
My tissues; my one election:
On food you give to have satiety.
Will leaf turn dry and dead? My
Deep need to pale affection
Fade? Will snail transform to tree?
If leaf dies, Spring will mystify
The Winter. No death for tree:
Leaf adorned, 'twill live in ev'ry
section.

John Cages Gedicht vom 30. Juni 1943 ist seinem Lebensgefährten,
dem Tänzer und Choreografen Merce Cunningham, gewidmet.

John Cage's poem from June 30, 1943, is dedicated to his partner,
the dancer and choreographer Merce Cunningham.

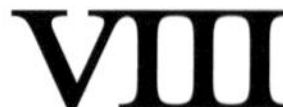

EPILOG

EPILOGUE

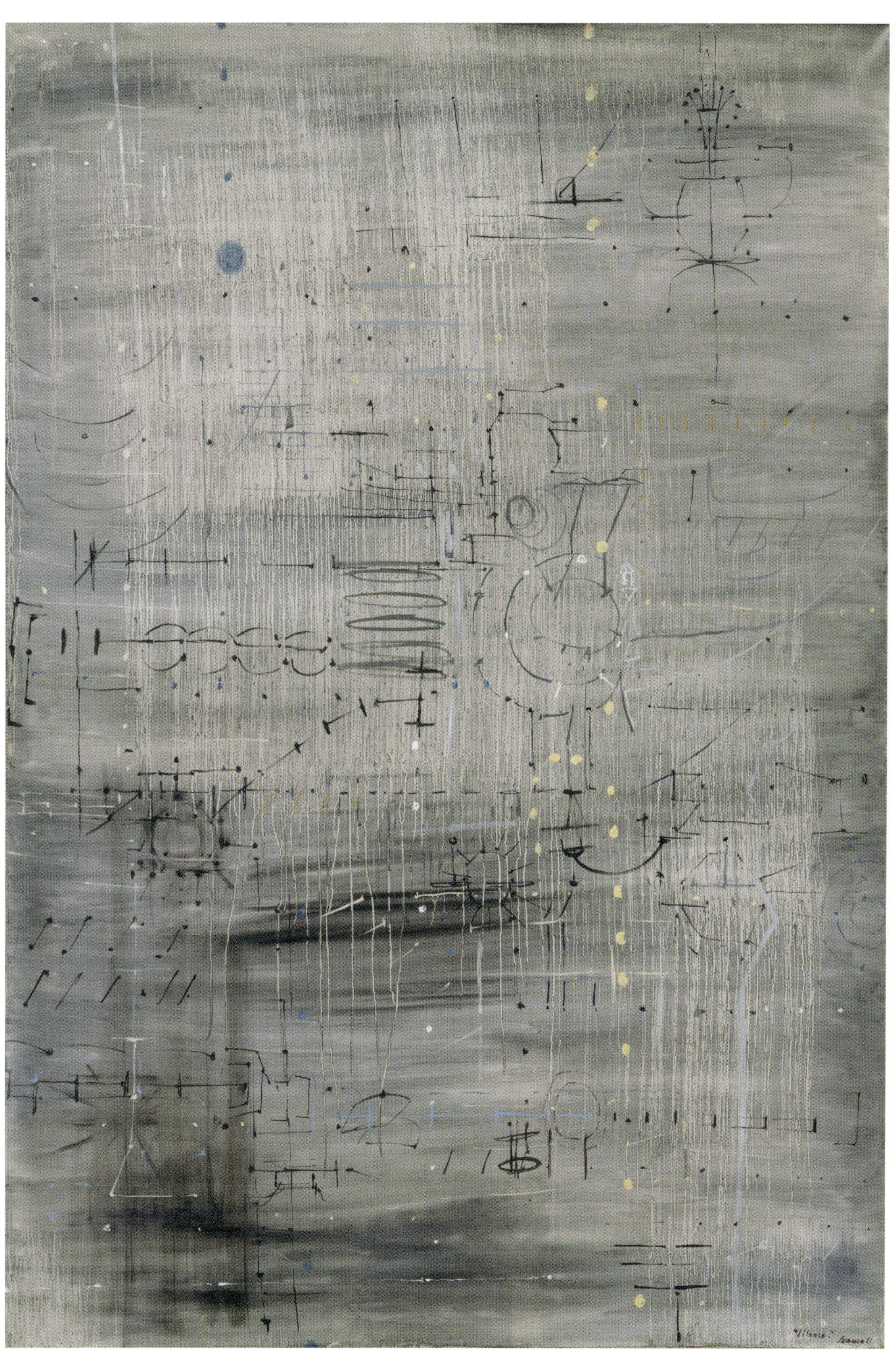

Sonja Sekula
Silence, 1951
Stille

ANHANG

APPENDIX

WERKVERZEICHNIS
~
LIST OF WORKS

RICHMOND BARTHÉ

(1901 in Bay St. Louis, USA–1989 in Pasadena, USA)

S. ~ P. 32

Richmond Barthé

Black Narcissus, 1929

Schwarzer Narziss

Bronze, 47 × 13,3 × 22,9 cm

Courtesy of Michael Rosenfeld Gallery LLC, New York, NY

S. ~ P. 33

Richmond Barthé

Faun, 1942

Bronze auf Marmorsockel ~ *Bronze on marble base*, 29,8 × 18,4 × 21 cm

Courtesy of Michael Rosenfeld Gallery LLC, New York, NY

ROSA BONHEUR

(1822 in Bordeaux, Frankreich ~ *France*–1899 in By-Thomery, Frankreich ~ *France*)

S. ~ P. 27

Édouard Dubufe

Portrait du peintre Rosa Bonheur aux côtés d'un bovidé, 1857

Porträt der Malerin Rosa Bonheur mit einem Stier ~ *Portrait of the Painter Rosa Bonheur with a Bull*

Öl auf Leinwand ~ *Oil on canvas*, 131 × 98 cm

Paris, musée d'Orsay, en dépôt au musée national du château de Versailles; Legs Gambard, 1902, Musée national des châteaux de Versailles et de Trainon

ROMAINE BROOKS

(1874 in Rom, Italien ~ *Rome, Italy*–1970 in Nizza, Frankreich ~ *Nice, France*)

S. ~ P. 64

Romaine Brooks

Self-Portrait, um ~ *ca.* 1912

Selbstporträt

Öl auf Leinwand ~ *Oil on canvas*, 53,3 × 43,2 cm

Collection Lucile Audouy

S. ~ P. 67

Romaine Brooks

La Vénus triste, 1917

Die traurige Venus ~ *The Weeping Venus*

Öl auf Leinwand ~ *Oil on canvas*, 150,5 × 270,4 cm

Musées de Poitiers

S. ~ P. 65

Romaine Brooks

Portrait of the Marchesa Casati, um ~ *ca.* 1920

Porträt der Markgräfin Casati

Öl auf Leinwand ~ *Oil on canvas*, 248 × 120 cm

Collection Lucile Audouy

PAUL CADMUS

(1904 in New York City, USA–1999 in Weston, USA)

S. ~ P. 181

Paul Cadmus

The Bath, 1951

Das Bad

Tempera auf Hartfaserplatte ~ *Tempera on composition board*, 36,4 × 41,4 cm

Whitney Museum of American Art, New York; gift of an anonymous donor

CLAUDE CAHUN

(1894 in Nantes, Frankreich ~ *France*–1954 in Saint Helier, Jersey)

MARCEL MOORE

(1892 in Nantes, Frankreich ~ *France*–1972 auf Jersey ~ *on Jersey*)

S. ~ P. 229

Claude Cahun

Marcel Moore Looking into a Mirror, 1928

Marcel Moore sieht in den Spiegel

Schwarz-Weiß-Fotografie (Faksimile) ~ *Black-and-white photograph (facsimile)*, 11,5 × 8,5 cm

Courtesy of the Jersey Heritage Collections

S. ~ P. 228

Claude Cahun

Self-Portrait (Reflected Image in a Mirror, Chequered Jacket), 1928

Selbstporträt (Spiegelbild im Spiegel, karierte Jacke)

Schwarz-Weiß-Fotografie (Faksimile) ~ *Black-and-white photograph (facsimile)*, 11,8 × 8,8 cm

Courtesy of the Jersey Heritage Collections

S. ~ P. 230

Claude Cahun

Self-Portrait (double exposure in rock pool), um ~ *ca.* 1928

Selbstporträt (Doppelbelichtung im Felsenbecken)

Schwarz-Weiß-Fotografie (Faksimile) ~ *Black-and-white photograph (facsimile)*, 17,6 × 12,7 cm

Courtesy of the Jersey Heritage Collections

S. ~ P. 231

Claude Cahun

Self-Portrait (naked, reclining on sand with coiled seaweed), 1930

Selbstporträt (nackt, auf Sand liegend mit aufgerolltem Seegras)

Schwarz-Weiß-Fotografie (Faksimile) ~ *Black-and-white photograph (facsimile)*, 10 × 8 cm

Courtesy of the Jersey Heritage Collections

S. ~ P. 224

Claude Cahun und ~ *and* Marcel Moore

Shopwindow of Van den Bergh Booksellers, Book Launch for Aveux non avenus, 1930

Schaufenster der Buchhandlung Van den Bergh, Buchvorstellung von *Aveux non avenus*

Schwarz-Weiß-Fotografie (Faksimile) ~ *Black-and-white photograph (facsimile)*, 8,5 × 11,8 cm

Courtesy of the Jersey Heritage Collections

S. ~ PP. 222–223, 225–227

Claude Cahun

Aveux non avenus, 1930

Nichtige Geständnisse ~ *Disavowals; or, Cancelled Confessions*

Gedrucktes Buch, illustriert mit zehn Heliogravüren von Marcel Moore (1930) und vier signierten und monogrammierten Originalzeichnungen von Claude Cahun (undatiert). Eines von neun Luxusexemplaren auf Imperial-Japanese-Papier gedruckt, nummeriert von 1 bis 9; Nr. 2 enthält vier Originalzeichnungen signiert oder monogrammiert von Claude Cahun ~ *Printed book, illustrated with ten heliogravures by Marcel Moore (1930) and containing four original drawings signed or monogrammed by Claude Cahun (undated). One of nine deluxe copies printed on Imperial Japanese paper, numbered from 1 to 9, no. 2 containing four original drawings signed or monogrammed by Claude Cahun,*

Buch ~ *Book*, 22 × 17 cm
Originalzeichnungen ~ *Original drawings*, 15,8 × 21,5 cm; 16,2 × 17,3 cm; 20,3 × 14,1 cm; 21,5 × 16,3 cm

Collection Frédérique Destribats, Paris

S. ~ PP. 232–233

Claude Cahun und ~ *and* Marcel Moore

Five Propaganda Leaflets, so-called "Paper Bullets," Produced During the German Occupation of Jersey, 1940–1944

Fünf Propagandazettel, sogenannte Papier-Geschosse, während der deutschen Besatzung von Jersey entstanden

Papier (Reproduktionen) ~ *Paper (reproductions)*

Courtesy of the Jersey Heritage Collections

S. ~ P. 234

Claude Cahun oder ~ *or* Marcel Moore

Interior of a Prison Cell Drawn on Scrap Paper, 1945

Inneres einer Gefängniszelle gezeichnet auf Papierabfall

Bleistift (Reproduktion) ~ *Pencil (reproduction)*, 14 × 10 cm

Courtesy of the Jersey Heritage Collections

S. ~ P. 235

Claude Cahun

Self-Portrait (with Nazi Badge between Her Teeth), Mai ~ *May* 1945

Selbstporträt (mit Nazi-Abzeichen zwischen den Zähnen)

Schwarz-Weiß-Fotografie (Faksimile) ~ *Black-and-white photograph (facsimile)*, 13,3 × 8,3 cm

Courtesy of the Jersey Heritage Collections

JEAN COCTEAU

(1889 in Maisons-Laffitte, Frankreich ~ *France* – 1963 in Milly-la-Forêt, Frankreich ~ *France*)

S. ~ P. 196

Jean Cocteau

Le Moindre marmiton de l'Hôtel de la Poste prend à mes yeux un air de conte de Perrault, 1930

Der kleinste Küchenjunge im Hotel de la Poste erscheint mir wie aus einem Märchen von Perrault ~ *The Lowliest Scullion at l'Hôtel de la Poste Appears to Me like Something out of a Fairy Tale by Perrault*

Grafit auf Papier ~ *Graphite on paper*, 31 × 23 cm

Collection Mony Vibescu

S. ~ P. 195

Jean Cocteau

Le Sang d'un poète, 1930

Das Blut eines Dichters ~ *The Blood of a Poet*

Schwarz-Weiß-Film übertragen auf Digitalvideo ~ *Black-and-white film transferred to digital video*, 49', Ausschnitt ~ *excerpt*: 21:37–24:37 mit Ton ~ *with sound*

The Blood of a Poet (Dir. Jean Cocteau)

S. ~ P. 197

Jean Cocteau

Édouard Dermit (nu), 1948
Édouard Dermit (Akt) ~ *Édouard Dermit (Nude)*

Grafit auf Papier ~ *Graphite on paper*, 32,5 × 50 cm

Collection Kinzel/Schilling, Basel

ITHELL COLQUHOUN

(1906 in Shillong, Indien ⤳ *India*–1988 in Lamorna, UK)

S. ⤳ P. 100

Ithell Colquhoun

Nativity, 1929

Geburt Christi

Öl auf Leinwand ⤳
Oil on canvas, 41 × 51 cm

Collection RAW

S. ⤳ P. 102

Ithell Colquhoun

Kelp Gathering, 1949

Seetang sammeln

Öl und Wachs auf Leinwand ⤳
Oil and wax on canvas,
45,8 × 91,4 cm

Collection RAW

NILS DARDEL

(1888 in Bettna, Schweden ⤳ *Sweden*–1943 in New York City, USA)

S. ⤳ P. 187

Nils Dardel

Den döende dandyn, 1918

Der sterbende Dandy ⤳
The Dying Dandy

Öl auf Leinwand ⤳
Oil on canvas, 140 × 180 cm

Moderna Museet, Stockholm.
Purchase 1993

S. ⤳ P. 186

Nils Dardel

Visit hos excentrisk dam, 1921

Besuch bei einer exzentrischen Dame ⤳
Visit to an Eccentric Lady

Öl auf Leinwand ⤳
Oil on canvas, 130,5 × 97,5 cm

Moderna Museet, Stockholm.
Donation 1953 from The Friends of Moderna Museet

BEAUFORD DELANEY

(1901 in Knoxville, USA–1979 in Paris, Frankreich ⤳ *France*)

S. ⤳ P. 182

Beauford Delaney

Untitled, um ⤳ *ca.* 1940

Ohne Titel

Öl auf Leinwand ⤳
Oil on canvas, 123,2 × 95,6 cm

Courtesy of Michael Rosenfeld Gallery LLC, New York, NY

MAX ERNST

(1891 in Brühl bei Köln ⤳ *in Brühl near Cologne, Germany*–1976 in Paris, Frankreich ⤳ *Paris, France*)

Nicht abgebildet ⤳
Not pictured

Max Ernst

La femme chancelante, 1923

Die schwankende Frau ⤳
The Wavering Woman

Öl auf Leinwand ⤳
Oil on canvas,
131 × 97,8 × 2,8 cm

Kunstsammlung Nordrhein-Westfalen, Düsseldorf

S. ⤳ P. 15

Max Ernst

La carmagnole de l'amour, 1926

Die Carmagnole der Liebe ⤳
The Carmagnole of Love

Öl und Zeichnung auf Leinwand ⤳ *Oil and drawing on canvas*, 101 × 73,5 cm

Kunstsammlung Nordrhein-Westfalen, Düsseldorf, Erworben 1999 durch die Freunde der Kunstsammlung Nordrhein-Westfalen ⤳
Acquired by the Friends of the Kunstsammlung Nordrhein-Westfalen

LEONOR FINI

(1907 in Buenos Aires, Argentinien ⤳ *Argentina*–1996 in Paris, Frankreich ⤳ *France*)

S. ⤳ P. 104

Leonor Fini

Portrait féminin n. 9 / Ritratto di signora seduta, 1936

Weibliches Porträt Nr. 9 / Porträt einer sitzenden Dame ⤳ *Female Portrait No. 9 / Portrait of a Seated Lady*

Öl auf Leinwand ⤳
Oil on canvas, 60 × 40 cm

FAMM Museum, Mougins, France / The Levett Collection

S. ⤳ P. 101

Leonor Fini

Autoportrait avec Kot et Sergio (Kot Jelenski et Sergio Gajardo), 1952

Selbstporträt mit Kot und Sergio (Kot Jelenski und Sergio Gajardo) ⤳ *Self-Portrait with Kot and Sergio (Kot Jelenski and Sergio Gajardo)*

Öl auf Tafel ⤳ *Oil on panel*,
57 × 80 cm

FAMM Museum, Mougins, France / The Levett Collection

S. ⤳ P. 103

Leonor Fini

Les Étrangères, 1968

Die Fremden ⤳ *The Strangers*

Öl auf Leinwand ⤳
Oil on canvas, 81 × 110 cm

FAMM Museum, Mougins, France / The Levett Collection

LOÏE FULLER

(1862 in Fullersburg, USA–1928 in Paris, Frankreich ⤳ *France*)

S. ⤳ P. 137

Loïe Fuller

La Danse Serpentine, 1905

Serpentinentanz ⤳
The Serpentine Dance

Farbfilm übertragen auf Digitalvideo ⤳ *Color film transferred to digital video*, 1'45", ohne Ton ⤳ *silent*

Production Pathé Frères

GLUCK

(1895 in London, UK–1978 in Steyning, UK)

S. ⤳ P. 68

Gluck

Portrait of Miss E. M. Craig, 1920

Porträt von Miss E. M. Craig

Öl auf Holz ⤳ *Oil on board*,
18 × 12 cm

Privatsammlung ⤳
Private Collection, courtesy Piano Nobile, London

S. ⤳ P. 71

Gluck

Ernest Thesiger, 1925/26

Öl auf Leinwand ⤳
Oil on canvas, 35,6 × 25,4 cm

Privatsammlung ⤳
Private Collection, courtesy of The Fine Art Society Ltd.

S. ~ P. 69

Gluck

Lords and Ladies, um ~ *ca.* 1936

Herren und Damen

Öl auf Leinwand ~
Oil on canvas, 75 × 75 cm

Privatsammlung ~
Private Collection, courtesy of The Fine Art Society Ltd.

S. ~ P. 70

Gluck

Bank Holiday Monday, um ~ *ca.* 1937

Feiertagsmontag

Öl auf Leinwand ~
Oil on canvas, 23,7 × 18,7 cm

Privatsammlung ~
Private Collection, courtesy of The Fine Art Society Ltd.

S. ~ P. 66

Gluck

The Punt, um ~ *ca.* 1937

Der Kahn

Öl auf Leinwand ~
Oil on canvas, 18,5 × 24,5 cm

Privatsammlung ~
Private Collection, courtesy of The Fine Art Society Ltd.

Dokumente aus dem privaten Archiv von Gluck ~ *Documents from Gluck's Private Archive:*

Nicht abgebildet ~
Not pictured

Gluck

Arrow Head, undatiert ~ *undated*

Pfeilspitze

Zeichnung auf Papier ~
Drawing on paper, 21 × 18 cm

Privatsammlung ~
Private Collection

Fotografie des unvollendeten und später übermalten Gemäldes von Gluck: *„Mrs. Romaine Brooks"* ~ *Photograph of the Unfinished and Later Overpainted Gluck Painting:* "Mrs. Romaine Brooks," undatiert ~ *undated*

Schwarz-Weiß-Fotografie, Originalabzug ~ *Black-and-white photograph, vintage print*, 14,5 × 18 cm

Rückseitig handschriftliche Notiz von Gluck: „Erstes […] sitzendes Bild, lebensgroße 6-Fuß-Leinwand, fertiggestellt an einem Nachmittag im Tite Street Studio – Romaine bestand darauf, dass ich eines meiner „kleinen Bilder" machen sollte – ich lehnte ab, also ließ sie mich mit dem unfertigen Porträt zurück. Allerdings musste ich viele Fotos davon, wie dieses hier, an ihre Freunde verschenken! Romaine nahm so viel Zeit in Anspruch, um einen Streit anzuzetteln, dass … mir bestenfalls eine halbe Stunde blieb, um das zu tun, was ich tat – aber meine Wut und Anspannung verliehen mir fast übermenschliche Kräfte." ~ *Handwritten note by Gluck on the reverse: "First […] sitting picture life size 6-foot canvas completed in one afternoon at the Tite Street Studio—Romaine insisted I should do one of my "little pictures"—I refused, so she left me with the unfinished portrait. However, I had to give away many photographs of it, like this one, to her friends! Romaine took so much sitting time in making a row that … at best I was only left half an hour in which to do what I did—but my rage and tension gave me almost superhuman powers."*

Privatsammlung ~
Private Collection

Fotografie von Glucks Zeichnung: *Craig in Cornwall* ~ *Photograph of Gluck's Drawing:* Craig in Cornwall, 1916

Schwarz-Weiß-Fotografie, Originalabzug ~ *Black-and-white photograph, vintage print*, 21 × 16 cm

Privatsammlung ~
Private Collection

Fotografie von Glucks Gemälde: *Porträt des tragischen südamerikanischen Modells Bettina* ~ *Photograph of Gluck's Painting:* Portrait of the Tragic South American Model Bettina, 1917

Schwarz-Weiß-Fotografie, Originalabzug ~ *Black-and-white photograph, vintage print*, 14,5 × 18 cm

Privatsammlung ~
Private Collection

Fotografie von Glucks Gemälde: *Der erschrockene Faun* ~ *Photograph of Gluck's Painting:* The Frightened Faun, undatiert ~ *undated* (um ~ *ca.* 1920)

Schwarz-Weiß-Fotografie, Originalabzug ~ *Black-and-white photograph, vintage print*, 16 × 21 cm

Privatsammlung ~
Private Collection

Fotografie von Glucks Gemälde: *Ich, Ella (Naper) und Minchi Fu* (Gemälde zerstört) ~ *Photograph of Gluck's Painting:* Self, Ella (Naper), and Minchi Fu *(Painting Destroyed)*, frühe 1920er-Jahre ~ *early 1920s*

Schwarz-Weiß-Fotografie, Originalabzug ~ *Black-and-white photograph, vintage print*, 19 × 15 cm

Privatsammlung ~
Private Collection

Fotografie von Glucks Gemälde: *Dozmary Pool, Bodmin Moore, Ich und Ella Naper* (Gemälde zerstört) ~ *Photograph of Gluck's Painting:* Dozmary Pool, Bodmin Moore, Self, and Ella Naper *(Painting Destroyed)*, frühe 1920er-Jahre ~ *early 1920s*

Schwarz-Weiß-Fotografie, Originalabzug ~ *Black-and-white photograph, vintage print*, 15 × 19 cm

Privatsammlung ~
Private Collection

Fotografie von Romaine Brooks' Gemälde: *Selbstporträt* ~ *Photograph of Romaine Brooks's Painting:* Self-Portrait, 1923

Schwarz-Weiß-Fotografie, Originalabzug ~ *Black-and-white photograph, vintage print*, 25 × 15 cm

Privatsammlung ~
Private Collection

Fotografie von Romaine Brooks' Gemälde: *Peter (Ein junges englisches Mädchen)* ~ *Photograph of Romaine Brooks's Painting:* Peter (A Young English Girl), 1923/24

Schwarz-Weiß-Fotografie, Originalabzug ~ *Black-and-white photograph, vintage print,* 25 × 17 cm

Privatsammlung ~ *Private Collection*

Porträt von Gluck ~ *Portrait of Gluck*, um ~ *ca.* 1924

Schwarz-Weiß-Fotografie, Originalabzug ~ *Black-and-white photograph, vintage print,* 27 × 17 cm

Privatsammlung ~ *Private Collection*

Fotografie von Glucks Gemälde: *Landratten* (Gemälde verschollen) ~ *Photograph of Gluck's Painting:* Land Lubbers *(Painting Lost)*, 1926

Schwarz-Weiß-Fotografie, Originalabzug ~ *Black-and-white photograph, vintage print,* 20 × 13 cm

Privatsammlung ~ *Private Collection*

Strandgruppe, mit Gluck lesend ~ *Beach Group, with Gluck Reading*, 1930er-Jahre ~ *1930s*

Schwarz-Weiß-Fotografie, Originalabzug ~ *Black-and-white photograph, vintage print,* 6 × 8 cm

Privatsammlung ~ *Private Collection*

Fotografie von Glucks Gemälde: *Spirituell* ~ *Photograph of Gluck's Painting:* Spiritual, 1932

Schwarz-Weiß-Fotografie, Originalabzug ~ *Black-and-white photograph, vintage print,* 14,5 × 14 cm

Privatsammlung ~ *Private Collection*

Fotografie von Glucks Gemälde: *Der Teufelsaltar* ~ *Photograph of Gluck's Painting:* The Devil's Altar, 1932

Schwarz-Weiß-Fotografie, Originalabzug ~ *Black-and-white photograph, vintage print,* 20 × 11 cm

Privatsammlung ~ *Private Collection*

Gluck in der Villa Hammamet mit Nada Patcevitch (?), Tunesien ~ *Gluck at Villa Hammamet with Nada Patcevitch (?), Tunisia*, 1934

Schwarz-Weiß-Fotografie, Originalabzug ~ *Black-and-white photograph, vintage print,* 13 × 18 cm

Privatsammlung ~ *Private Collection*

Nada Patcevitch
Fotografie von Gluck in der Villa Hammamet, Tunesien ~ *Photograph of Gluck at Villa Hammamet, Tunisia*, 1934

Schwarz-Weiß-Fotografie, Originalabzug ~ *Black-and-white photograph, vintage print,* 15,5 × 14,5 cm

Privatsammlung ~ *Private Collection*

Fotografie von Glucks Gemälde: *Medallion (YouWe)* ~ *Photograph of Gluck's Painting:* Medallion (YouWe), 1936

Schwarz-Weiß-Fotografie, Originalabzug ~ *Black-and-white photograph, vintage print,* 16,5 × 19 cm

Privatsammlung ~ *Private Collection*

Auf der Schreibmaschine geschriebener Brief an Gluck von Leon M. Lion ~ *Typewritten Letter to Gluck from Leon M. Lion*, 1936, 25 × 20 cm

Privatsammlung ~ *Private Collection*

Gluck im Kahn in Mill House, Plumpton ~ *Gluck in a Punt at Mill House, Plumpton*, um ~ *ca.* 1937

Schwarz-Weiß-Fotografie, Originalabzug ~ *Black-and-white photograph, vintage print,* 11 × 6,5 cm

Privatsammlung ~ *Private Collection*

Nesta (Obermer) im Kahn in Mill House, Plumpton ~ *Nesta (Obermer) in a Punt at Mill House, Plumpton*, um ~ *ca.* 1937

Schwarz-Weiß-Fotografie, Originalabzug ~ *Black-and-white photograph, vintage print,* 11 × 6,5 cm

Privatsammlung ~ *Private Collection*

Nesta und Gluck in Lenzerheide in der Schweiz ~ *Nesta and Gluck in Lenzerheide, Switzerland*, 1938/39

Schwarz-Weiß-Fotografie, Originalabzug ~ *Black-and-white photograph, vintage print,* 14 × 10 cm

Privatsammlung ~ *Private Collection*

Fotografie des in Auftrag gegebenen Gemäldes von Gluck: *Porträt von John Boughy* ~ *Photograph of Gluck's Commissioned Painting:* Portrait of John Boughy, 1939

Schwarz-Weiß-Fotografie, Originalabzug ~ *Black-and-white photograph, vintage print,* 16 × 12 cm

Privatsammlung ~ *Private Collection*

Fotografie des in Auftrag gegebenen Gemäldes von Gluck: *Porträt von Peter Griffard* ~ *Photograph of Gluck's Commissioned Painting:* Portrait of Peter Griffard, 1939

Schwarz-Weiß-Fotografie, Originalabzug ~ *Black-and-white photograph, vintage print,* 19 × 16 cm

Privatsammlung ~ *Private Collection*

Fotografie von Glucks Gemälde: *Im grünen England + Fasanenland...* ~ *Photograph of Gluck's Painting:* In England's Green + Pheasant Land..., Während des Zweiten Weltkriegs ~ *During the Second World War (Plumpton Women's Institute)*

Schwarz-Weiß-Fotografie, Originalabzug ~ *Black-and-white photograph, vintage print,* 16,5 × 22 cm

Privatsammlung ~ *Private Collection*

Fotografie der Studie für das Gemälde: *„Gluck von Gluck“* ~ *Photograph of the Painting Study:* "Gluck by Gluck," 1942

Schwarz-Weiß-Fotografie, Originalabzug ~ *Black-and-white photograph, vintage print,* 16 × 10,5 cm

Privatsammlung ~ *Private Collection*

Zwei zusammengeheftete, auf der Schreibmaschine geschriebene Seiten „Kopie des Briefs von Sir Kenneth Clark an Lord Greene, in Bezug auf meine Arbeit für die War Art-ists", Brief National Gallery ~ *Two Typewritten Pages Stapled Together: "Copy of Letter from Sir Kenneth Clark to Lord Greene, with Regard to My Working for the War Art-ists," Letter, National Gallery*, 2. Mai 1942 ~ *May 2, 1942*, 25,5 × 20 cm

Privatsammlung ~
Private Collection

Fotografie von Glucks Gemälde: *Der Meldeposten. Edith (Shackelton Heald) als Brandwächterin, Steyning* ~ *Photograph of Gluck's Painting:* The Report Post. Edith (Shackelton Heald) as Fire Warden, Steyning, 1945

Schwarz-Weiß-Fotografie, Originalabzug ~ *Black-and-white photograph, vintage print* , 20 × 12,5 cm

Privatsammlung ~
Private Collection

Zwei zusammengeheftete Seiten, auf der Schreibmaschine geschrieben: Glucks Stellungnahme für das Who's Who, 1956; A. und C. Black Ltd. Antwort an Edith Heald, 1957 ~ *Two Fastened Typewritten Letters: Gluck's Statement for Who's Who, 1956; A. and C. Black Ltd. Response to Edith Heald*, 1957, 1956/57, 25 × 20 cm

Privatsammlung ~
Private Collection

Zeitungsausschnitt des Nachrufs „Miss Edith Shackleton Heald" ~ *Newspaper Clipping, Obituary "Miss Edith Shackleton Heald,"* 1976, 10,5 × 9,5 cm

Privatsammlung ~
Private Collection

DUNCAN GRANT

(1885 in Rothiemurchus, UK–1978 in Aldermaston, UK)

S. ~ P. 183

Duncan Grant

Male Nude (Pat Nelson), 1930

Männlicher Akt (Pat Nelson)

Öl auf Leinwand ~
Oil on canvas, 73,6 × 53,3 cm

From the JWM Collection by kind permission of the Master and Fellows, St. Peter's College, University of Oxford

JACOBA VAN HEEMSKERCK

(1876 in Den Haag, Niederlande ~ *The Hague, Netherlands*–1923 in Domburg, Niederlande ~ *Netherlands*)

S. ~ P. 134

Jacoba van Heemskerck

Bild no. 105, 1915–1920

Bild Nr. 105 ~
Composition No. 105

Öl auf Leinwand ~
Oil on canvas, 100 × 80 cm

Kunstmuseum Den Haag – bequest Marie Tak van Poortvliet

S. ~ P. 135

Jacoba van Heemskerck

Bild no. 90, 1918

Bild Nr. 90 ~
Composition No. 90

Öl auf Leinwand ~
Oil on canvas, 60 × 76 cm

Kunstmuseum Den Haag – bequest Marie Tak van Poortvliet

HANNAH HÖCH

(1889 in Gotha ~ *Gotha, Germany*–1978 in Berlin ~ *Berlin, Germany*)

S. ~ P. 237

Hannah Höch

Englische Tänzerin, 1928

English Dancer

Collage, 23,7 × 18 cm

Kunstsammlung des ifa – Institut für Auslandsbeziehungen e.V., Stuttgart

S. ~ P. 241

Hannah Höch

Porträt von Til Brugman, um ~ *ca.* 1929–1935

Portrait of Til Brugman

Öl auf Leinwand ~
Oil on canvas, 56,2 × 41 cm

Kunstmuseum Den Haag

S. ~ P. 239

Hannah Höch

Flucht, 1931

Flight

Collage, 23 × 18,4 cm

Kunstsammlung des ifa – Institut für Auslandsbeziehungen e.V., Stuttgart

S. ~ P. 236

Hannah Höch

Auf dem Weg zum Siebenden Himmel, 1934

On the Way to Seventh Heaven

Fotomontage ~ *Photomontage*, 36,9 × 26,4 cm

Collection Barry Friedman and Patricia Pastor

LUDWIG VON HOFMANN

(1861 in Darmstadt ~ *Darmstadt, Germany*–1945 in Pillnitz bei Dresden ~ *Pillnitz near Dresden, Germany*)

S. ~ P. 36

Ludwig von Hofmann

Die Quelle, 1913

The Source

Öl auf Leinwand ~
Oil on canvas, 75 × 92 cm

ETH-Bibliothek, Thomas-Mann-Archiv der ETH Zürich

ROBIN IRONSIDE

(1912 in London, UK–1965 in London, UK)

S. ~ P. 188

Robin Ironside

Rossetti's Willowwood, um ~ *ca.* 1944

Rossettis Weidenwald

Aquarell und Gouache mit Feder und Tinte auf Papier ~ *Watercolor and gouache with pen and ink on paper*, 24 × 34,3 cm

Virginia Ironside

S. ~ P. 189

Robin Ironside

Death Bed, 1949/50

Totenbett

Aquarell und Gouache mit Buntstift und Tusche über Bleistift auf Papier ~ *Watercolor and gouache with pen and ink over pencil on paper*, 22,5 × 32,9 cm

Virginia Ironside

S. ~ P. 190

Robin Ironside

Escaping from the Hospital, um ~ *ca.* 1951

Flucht aus dem Krankenhaus

Aquarell und Gouache über Bleistift auf Papier ~ *Watercolor and gouache over pencil on paper*, 23,5 × 23,7 cm

Virginia Ironside

LOUISE JANIN

(1893 in Durham, USA–1997 in Meudon, Frankreich ~ *France*)

S. ~ P. 133

Louise Janin

Les Plantes dressées, 1934

Aufstrebende Pflanzen ~ *Erect Plants*

Öl auf Holz ~ *Oil on board*, 102 × 112 cm

Collection Lucile Audouy

S. ~ P. 132

Louise Janin

Envol, 1955

Flug ~ *Flight*

Öl auf Leinwand ~ *Oil on canvas*, 38 × 46 cm

Belvedere, Wien, Dauerleihgabe von Silard Isaak, Sammlung Carl Laszlo

LOTTE LASERSTEIN

(1898 in Preußisch-Holland, heute: Pasłęk, Polen ~ *today Pasłęk, Poland*–1993 in Kalmar, Schweden ~ *Sweden*)

S. ~ P. 41

Lotte Laserstein

Ich und mein Modell, 1929/30

I and My Model

Öl auf Leinwand ~ *Oil on canvas*, 49,5 × 69,5 cm

Privatsammlung ~ *Private Collection*, Courtesy Agnews, London

S. ~ P. 40

Lotte Laserstein

Das Karo-Kostüm, um ~ *ca.* 1931

The Plaid Suit

Öl auf Papier ~ *Oil on paper*, 48 × 70 cm

Galerie Ludorff, Düsseldorf

MARIE LAURENCIN

(1883 in Paris, Frankreich ~ *France*–1956 in Paris, Frankreich ~ *France*)

S. ~ P. 37

Marie Laurencin

Jeunes femmes, 1910

Junge Frauen ~ *Young Women*

Öl auf Leinwand ~ *Oil on canvas*, 115 × 146 cm

Moderna Museet, Stockholm. Bequest 1966 of Rolf de Maré

S. ~ P. 72

Marie Laurencin

Danseuses espagnoles, 1920/21

Spanische Tänzerinnen ~ *Spanish Dancers*

Öl auf Leinwand ~ *Oil on canvas*, 150 × 95 cm

Paris, Musée de l'Orangerie, Jean Walter and Paul Guillaume Collection

S. ~ P. 73

Marie Laurencin

La Femme au chien (portrait), 1924

Frau mit einem Hund (Porträt) ~ *Woman with a Dog (Portrait)*

Öl auf Leinwand ~ *Oil on canvas*, 65 × 50 cm

Sammlung Daniel Buchholz & Christopher Müller, Köln ~ *Cologne*

S. ~ P. 74

Marie Laurencin

Théâtre Serge de Diaghilew, Les Biches, 1924

Théâtre Serge de Diaghilew, Die Hindinnen ~ *Théâtre Serge de Diaghilew, The Hinds*

Unpaginiert, zwei große Softcover-Bände im Schuber ~ *Unpaginated, two large softcover volumes in a slipcase*, 28,4 × 23 × 3 cm

Sammlung Daniel Buchholz & Christopher Müller, Köln ~ *Cologne*

S. ~ P. 75

Marie Laurencin

Poèmes de Sappho, 1950

Gedichte von Sappho ~ *Poems by Sappho*

Übersetzt von Edith de Beaumont mit Illustrationen von Marie Laurencin ~ *Translated by Edith de Beaumont with Illustrations by Marie Laurencin*, Compagnie française des arts graphiques, Paris 1950, 22,8 × 14,8 × 2,5 cm

Sammlung Daniel Buchholz & Christopher Müller, Köln ~ *Cologne*

RENÉ MAGRITTE

(1898 in Lessines, Belgien ~ *Lessines, Belgium*–1967 in Brüssel, Belgien ~ *Brussels, Belgium*)

S. ~ P. 13

René Magritte

Les jours gigantesques, 1928

Die gigantischen Tage ~ *The Titanic Days*

Öl auf Leinwand ~ *Oil on canvas*, 116 × 80,8 × 2,8 cm

Kunstsammlung Nordrhein-Westfalen, Düsseldorf

Erworben 1995 mit Unterstützung des Ernst von Siemens-Kunstfonds, der Kulturstiftung der Länder und der Kunststiftung NRW

JEANNE MAMMEN

(1890 in Berlin ~ *Berlin, Germany*-1976 in Berlin ~ *Berlin, Germany*)

S. ~ P. 243

Jeanne Mammen

Tanzbar, undatiert ~ *undated*

Dance Bar

Illustration von *Die Lieder der Bilitis* von Pierre Louÿs ~ *Illustration for* The Songs of Bilitis *by Pierre Louÿs*

Feder-/Pinselzeichnung ~ *Pen and brush drawing*, 49,5 × 35,3 cm

Kunstsammlung des ifa – Institut für Auslandsbeziehungen e.V., Stuttgart

S. ~ P. 242

Jeanne Mammen

Beim Schminken, um ~ *ca.* 1930–1932

Applying Make-Up

Illustration von *Die Lieder der Bilitis* von Pierre Louÿs ~ *Illustration for* The Songs of Bilitis *by Pierre Louÿs*

Lithografie, zweifarbig ~ *Lithograph, two-colored*, 56,8 × 40 cm

Kunstpalast, Düsseldorf

S. ~ P. 243

Jeanne Mammen

Damenbar, um ~ *ca.* 1930–1932

Ladies' Bar

Illustration von *Die Lieder der Bilitis* von Pierre Louÿs ~ *Illustration for* The Songs of Bilitis *by Pierre Louÿs*

Farblithografie ~ *Color lithograph*, 56,5 × 40,5 cm

Jeanne-Mammen-Stiftung im Stadtmuseum Berlin

S. ~ P. 242

Jeanne Mammen

Eifersucht, um ~ *ca.* 1930–1932

Jealousy

Illustration von *Die Lieder der Bilitis* von Pierre Louÿs ~ *Illustration for* The Songs of Bilitis *by Pierre Louÿs*

Lithografie, zweifarbig ~ *Lithograph, two-colored*, 56,3 × 40 cm

Kunstpalast, Düsseldorf

S. ~ P. 242

Jeanne Mammen

Die Wahl, um ~ *ca.* 1930–1932

The Choice

Illustration von *Die Lieder der Bilitis* von Pierre Louÿs ~ *Illustration for* The Songs of Bilitis *by Pierre Louÿs*

Farblithografie ~ *Color lithograph*, 55,6 × 42 cm

Jeanne-Mammen-Stiftung im Stadtmuseum Berlin

S. ~ P. 245

Jeanne Mammen

Der Jäger (Sonntagsjäger), zwischen ~ *between* 1939–1942

The Hunter (Sunday Hunter)

Tempera auf Karton; versus bemalt mit Stillleben ~ *Tempera on cardboard; verso painted with still life*, 100 × 70 cm

Jeanne-Mammen-Stiftung im Stadtmuseum Berlin

S. ~ P. 244

Jeanne Mammen

Der Würgeengel, um ~ *ca.* 1939–1942

The Angel of Death (Saint Anthony and the Angel)

Tempera auf Karton ~ *Tempera on cardboard*, 150 × 75 cm

Dieses Gemälde ist eine Leihgabe des Max-Delbrück-Centrum für Molekulare Medizin in der Helmholtz-Gemeinschaft ~ *This painting is on loan from the Max Delbrück Center for Molecular Medicine in the Helmholtz Association*

S. ~ P. 246

Jeanne Mammen

Hermaphrodit, um ~ *ca.* 1945

Hermaphrodite

Ton, ungebrannt, bemalt und mit Abziehbildchen beklebt ~ *Unfired, painted clay, covered with decals*, 21 × 15 × 11,5 cm

Jeanne-Mammen-Stiftung im Stadtmuseum Berlin

MARLOW MOSS

(1889 in London, UK-1958 in Penzance, UK)

S. ~ P. 139

Marlow Moss

White, Red, and Grey, 1935

Weiß, Rot und Grau

Öl auf Leinwand ~ *Oil on canvas*, 56 × 56 cm

Privatsammlung ~ *Private Collection*

S. ~ P. 138

Marlow Moss

White with Bent Cord (Relief), 1936

Weiß mit gebogener Kordel (Relief)

Öl auf Leinwand und Schnur ~ *Oil on canvas and rope*, 79,9 × 50,3 × 4,3 cm

Kröller-Müller Museum, Otterlo, The Netherlands, gift from Ida and Piet Sanders, Schiedam

S. ~ P. 136

Marlow Moss

Spheres and Curved Line, 1945

Kugeln und gekrümmte Linie

Bronze, Kupfer und Aluminium auf weiß bemaltem Holzsockel ~ *Bronze, copper, and aluminum on a wooden base painted white*, 25 × 32 × 27 cm

Kunstmuseum Basel, Inv. G 2022.19, Ankauf mit Mitteln der Petzold-Müller-Stiftung 2022

S. ~ P. 141

Marlow Moss

Untitled (White, Black, Blue, and Yellow), um ~ *ca.* 1954

Ohne Titel (Weiß, Schwarz, Blau und Gelb)

Öl auf Leinwand ~ *Oil on canvas*, 61 × 46 cm

Privatsammlung ~ *Private Collection*

RICHARD OSWALD

(1880 in Wien, Österreich ~ *Vienna, Austria*–1963 in Düsseldorf ~ *Düsseldorf, Germany*)

MAGNUS HIRSCHFELD

(1868 in Kolberg, Polen ~ *Kołobrzeg, Poland*–1935 in Nizza, Frankreich ~ *Nice, France*)

Nicht abgebildet ~ *Not pictured*

Richard Oswald

Anders als die Andern, 1918/19

Different from the Others

Regie ~ *Director*: Richard Oswald

Drehbuch ~ *Screenplay*: Richard Oswald und ~ *and* Magnus Hirschfeld

Schwarz-Weiß-Film übertragen auf Digitalvideo ~ *Black-and-white film transferred to digital video*, 52', Ausschnitt ~ *excerpt*: 47:30–50:30, ohne Ton ~ *silent*

Filmmuseum München

MILENA PAVLOVIĆ-BARILI

(1909 in Požarevac, Serbien ~ *Serbia*–1945 in New York City, USA)

S. ~ P. 105

Milena Pavlović-Barili

Enigmatska kompozicija sa crnom rukom, 1932

Torso mit schwarzem Arm ~ *Torso with Black Arm*

Öl auf Leinwand ~ *Oil on canvas*, 60,5 × 46 cm

Fondacija Milenin dom – Galerija Milene Pavlović Barilli

S. ~ P. 107

Milena Pavlović-Barili

Fantastična kompozicija sa ženskim aktom I zmajem, 1936

Fantastische Komposition mit einer Frau und einem Drachen ~ *Fantastic Composition with a Female and a Dragon*

Öl auf Leinwand ~ *Oil on canvas*, 53 × 64 cm

Fondacija Milenin dom – Galerija Milene Pavlović Barilli

S. ~ P. 106

Milena Pavlović-Barili

Lutka, 1936

Puppe ~ *Doll*

Öl auf Leinwand ~ *Oil on canvas*, 67 × 56 cm

Fondacija Milenin dom – Galerija Milene Pavlović Barilli

GLYN WARREN PHILPOT

(1884 in London, UK–1937 in London, UK)

S. ~ P. 34

Glyn Warren Philpot

Two Figures under the Sea, 1914–1918

Zwei Figuren unter dem Meer

Öl auf Leinwand ~ *Oil on canvas*, 35,5 × 27,5 cm

Charles Greig – London

S. ~ P. 35

Glyn Warren Philpot

Penelope, 1923

Öl auf Leinwand ~ *Oil on canvas*, 135,9 × 91,4 cm

JONATHAN CLARK FINE ART

GEORGE PLATT LYNES

(1907 in East Orange, USA–1955 in New York City, USA)

S. ~ P. 192

George Platt Lynes

The Dancer Fred Danieli, 1937

Der Tänzer (Fred Danieli)

Silbergelatineprint (Faksimile) ~ *Gelatin silver print (facsimile)*, 25,4 × 20,3 cm

From the Collections of the Kinsey Institute, Indiana University. All rights reserved.

S. ~ P. 193

George Platt Lynes

Tex Smutney, 1941

Silbergelatineprint (Faksimile) ~ *Gelatin silver print (facsimile)*, 20,3 × 25,4 cm

From the Collections of the Kinsey Institute, Indiana University. All rights reserved.

S. ~ P. 193

George Platt Lynes

Ralph McWilliams, 1952

Silbergelatineprint (Faksimile) ~ *Gelatin silver print (facsimile)*, 25,4 × 20,3 cm

From the Collections of the Kinsey Institute, Indiana University. All rights reserved.

ANTON PRINNER

(1902 in Budapest, Ungarn ~ *Hungary*–1983 in Paris, Frankreich ~ *France*)

S. ~ P. 143

Anton Prinner

Untitled (Les Hublots), 1932

Ohne Titel (Die Bullaugen) ~ *Untitled (The Portholes)*

Holzrelief ~ *Wooden relief*, 100 × 159 × 5 cm

Privatsammlung ~ *Private Collection*, Schweiz, Courtesy von Bartha, Basel

S. ~ P. 142

Anton Prinner

Untitled, 1933

Ohne Titel

Bemaltes Holz ~ *Painted wood*, 102 × 64 × 13 cm

Privatsammlung ~ *Private Collection*, Schweiz, Courtesy von Bartha, Basel

S. ~ P. 143

Anton Prinner

Spirales Plastiques, 1935

Plastische Spiralen ~ *Plastic Spirales*

Relief auf Metall und bemaltem Holz ~ *Relief on metal and painted wood*, 51 × 81 × 3,5 cm

Europäische Privatsammlung ~ *European Private Collection*, Courtesy von Bartha, Basel

S. ~ P. 145

Anton Prinner

Double personnage (Personnage renversé), 1937

Doppelte Figur (Umgekehrte Figur) ~ *Double Figure (Overturned Character)*

Holz ~ *Wood*, 63 × 30 × 18 cm

Collection of Kalman Maklary, Budapest

S. ~ P. 147

Anton Prinner

Woman with a Candle, um ~ *ca.* 1940

Frau mit Kerze

Messingplatte ~ *Brass plate*, 27 × 21 cm

Collection of Kalman Maklary, Budapest

S. ~ P. 147

Anton Prinner

Woman with an Otter, um ~ *ca.* 1940

Frau mit einem Otter

Messingplatte ~ *Brass plate*, 25 × 19 cm

Collection of Kalman Maklary, Budapest

S. ~ P. 144

Anton Prinner

L'équilibriste, 1942

Die Balancierkünstlerin ~ *The Balancing Act*

Mahagoni ~ *Mahogany*, 106 × 22,5 × 22 cm

Paris Musées / Musée d'Art moderne; Achat à l'artiste en 1973

S. ~ P. 146

Anton Prinner

La femme tondue, 1946

Die geschorene Frau ~ *The Shorn Woman*

Broschiertes Buch mit losem Umschlag, 56 Seiten, signierter Versand an Monsieur Louis Parrot ~ *Paperback, cover detached, 56 pages signed consignment to Mr. Louis Parrot*, 20,5 × 14 cm

Collection Mony Vibescu

S. ~ PP. 148/149

Anton Prinner

L'Apocalypse, 1948

Die Apokalypse ~ *The Apocalypse*

Mappe mit neun Drucken ~ *Portfolio with nine prints*

Papier, Papyrogravure ~ *Paper, papyrogravure*, 9 je ~ *each* 28 × 21 cm
Collection of Kalman Maklary, Budapest

GERTRUDE „MA" RAINEY

(1886 in Columbus, Georgia, USA–1939 in Rome, Georgia, USA)

Nicht abgebildet ~ *Not pictured*

Gertrude „Ma" Rainey

Prove It on Me Blues, 1928

Beweis-es-mir-Blues

Song, 2'31"

OSKAR SCHLEMMER

(1888 in Stuttgart ~ *Stuttgart, Germany*–1943 in Baden-Baden ~ *Baden-Baden, Germany*)

Nicht abgebildet ~ *Not pictured*

Oskar Schlemmer

Gruppe am Geländer I, 1931

Group at the Banisters I

Öl auf Leinwand ~ *Oil on canvas*, 92,6 × 61,3 × 2,2 cm

Kunstsammlung Nordrhein-Westfalen, Düsseldorf

Erworben 1966 aus einer Spende des Westdeutschen Rundfunks

SONJA SEKULA

(1918 in Luzern, Schweiz ~ *Lucerne, Switzerland*–1963 in Zürich, Schweiz ~ *Switzerland*)

S. ~ P. 277

Sonja Sekula

Silence, 1951

Stille

Öl auf Leinwand ~ *Oil on canvas*, 147 × 101 cm

Kunsthaus Zürich, Geschenk der Mutter der Künstlerin, 1966

PAVEL TCHELITCHEW

(1898 in Dubrowka, Russland ~ *Dubrovka, Russia*–1957 in Grottaferrata, Italien ~ *Italy*)

S. ~ P. 151

Pavel Tchelitchew

Untitled (Seated Man, Multiple Images), 1927

Ohne Titel (Sitzender Mann, mehrere Bilder)

Öl und Kaffeesatz auf Leinwand ~ *Oil and coffee grounds on canvas*, 116,8 × 89,5 cm

Courtesy of Michael Rosenfeld Gallery LLC, New York, NY

S. ~ P. 150

Pavel Tchelitchew

Personage, 1927

Figur

Öl und Kaffeesatz auf Leinwand ~ *Oil and coffee grounds on canvas*, 129,5 × 86,7 cm

Courtesy of Michael Rosenfeld Gallery LLC, New York, NY

S. ~ P. 191

Pavel Tchelitchew

The Hen and the Man, 1934

Die Henne und der Mann

Öl auf Leinwand ~ *Oil on canvas*, 65,7 × 92,4 cm

Courtesy of Michael Rosenfeld Gallery LLC, New York, NY

S. ~ P. 153

Pavel Tchelitchew

Interior Landscape, um ~ *ca.* 1947

Innere Landschaft

Öl auf Leinwand ~ *Oil on canvas*, 80,6 × 65,4 cm

Collection of halley k harrisburg and Michael Rosenfeld, New York

TOYEN

(1902 in Prag, Tschechoslowakei ~ *Prague, Czechoslovakia*–1980 in Paris, Frankreich ~ *France*)

S. ~ P. 247

Toyen

Hermaphrodite au coquillage, 1930

Hermaphrodit mit Muschel ~ *Hermaphrodite with a Shell*

Chinesische Tusche auf Papier ~ *Chinese ink on paper*, 31 × 27 cm

Collection Mony Vibescu

S. ~ P. 251

Toyen

La maison solitaire, 1945

Das einsame Haus ~ *The Lonely House*

Öl auf Leinwand ~ *Oil on canvas*, 59 × 73 cm

Belvedere, Wien, Dauerleihgabe Sammlung Rotter

S. ~ P. 249

Toyen

Cache-toi guerre! [Schovej se, válko!], 1947

Versteck Dich, Krieg! ~ *Hide yourself, War!*

Mappe mit neun Drucken von Toyen mit der französischen Übersetzung eines Gedichts des tschechischen Dichters Jindřich Heisler ~ *Portfolio with nine prints by Toyen, accompanied by the French translation of a poem by the Czech poet Jindřich Heisler*

Album, 32 × 42,8 cm
Druck ~ *Print*, 30,5 × 39 cm
Edition n°226/300

Paris Musées / Musée d'Art moderne, Don de Mme Alice Mayoux en 2024, en hommage à Jehan Mayoux

S. ~ P. 248

Toyen

L'Origine de la vérité, 1952

Der Ursprung der Wahrheit ~ *The Origin of Truth*

Öl auf Leinwand ~ *Oil on canvas*, 66 × 43 cm

Privatsammlung ~ *Private Collection*, via Galerie KODL, Prag ~ *Prague*

HENRY SCOTT TUKE

(1858 in York, UK–1929 in Falmouth, UK)

S. ~ P. 185

Henry Scott Tuke

The Critics, 1927

Die Kritiker

Öl auf Karton ~ *Oil on board*, 41,2 × 51,4 cm

Leamington Spa Art Gallery & Museum (Warwick District Council)

DAME ETHEL WALKER

(1861 in Edinburgh, UK–1951 in London, UK)

S. ~ P. 39

Dame Ethel Walker

Decoration: The Excursion of Nausicaa, 1920

Dekoration: Der Ausflug der Nausicaa

Öl auf Leinwand ~ *Oil on canvas*, 183,5 × 367 cm

Tate. Purchased 1924

S. ~ P. 38

Dame Ethel Walker

Two Models Resting, 1939

Zwei Modelle beim Ausruhen

Öl auf Leinwand ~ *Oil on canvas*, 101,6 × 76,2 cm

Piano Nobile, London

GERDA WEGENER

(1886 in Hammelev, Dänemark ~ *Denmark*–1940 in Frederiksberg, Dänemark ~ *Denmark*)

S. ~ P. 108

Gerda Wegener

Lili with a Feather Fan, 1920

Lili mit einem Federfächer

Öl auf Leinwand ~ *Oil on canvas*, 79 × 59 cm

Privatsammlung ~ *Private Collection*, Denmark

S. ~ P. 109

Gerda Wegener

Two Coquettes with Hats – Lili with Friend, um ~ *ca.* 1920

Zwei Koketten mit Hüten – Lili mit Freundin

Öl auf Leinwand ~ *Oil on canvas*, 62 × 46 cm

Privatsammlung ~ *Private Collection*

S. ~ P. 111

Gerda Wegener

Les Délassements d'Éros, 1925

Die Freuden des Eros ~ *The Diversions of Eros*

Schablonen je ~ *Stencils each*, 19 × 25,5 cm
Buch ~ *Book*, 25 × 30 cm

Collection Mony Vibescu

S. ~ P. 110

Alexandre de Vérineau (Louis Perceau)

Douze sonnets lascifs pour accompagner la suite d'aquarelles intitulée Les Délassements d'Éros, ÉROTOPOLIS, À l'Enseigne du faune, 1925

Zwölf laszive Sonette zur Begleitung der Aquarellsuite mit dem Titel *Les Délassements d'Éros*, ÉROTOPOLIS, À l'Enseigne du faune ~ *Twelve Lascivious Sonnets to Accompany a Suite of Watercolors Entitled* Les Délassements d'Éros, *ÉROTOPOLIS, À l'Enseigne du faune*

Buch, 44 Seiten in Blättern unter verblasstem, betiteltem Umschlag ~ *Book, 44 pages in sheets with a faded, titled cover*, 25,5 × 19,5 cm

Collection Mony Vibescu

S. ~ P. 112

Gerda Wegener

Fotoalbum ~ *Photo Album*, wahrscheinlich ~ *probably* 1925–1935

Sammelband im Hochformat, brauner Pappeinband mit 2-Loch-Band; insgesamt 56 Originalfotos ~ *Compilation in portrait format, brown cardboard cover with 2-hole binding; 56 original photos in total*, 31 × 23,5 cm

Collection Mony Vibescu

S. ~ P. 113

Gerda Wegener

Fotoalbum ~ *Photo Album*, wahrscheinlich ~ *probably* 1925–1935

Querformatiger Sammelband, beiger Pappeinband mit 3-Loch-Band; insgesamt 28 Originalfotos ~ *Horizontal-format compilation, beige cardboard cover with 3-hole binding; 28 original photos in total*, 17,5 × 25,5 cm

Collection Mony Vibescu

LEIHGEBER*INNEN ~ LENDERS

Wir danken allen Leihgeber*innen, Galerist*innen und Rechteinhaber*innen, die uns bei der Realisierung der Ausstellung und der Publikation unterstützt haben. ~ *We warmly thank all lenders, gallerists, and rights holders for their support in realizing this exhibition and publication.*

Belvedere, Wien ~ *Vienna*, Dauerleihgabe Sammlung Rotter

Belvedere, Wien ~ *Vienna*, Dauerleihgabe von Silard Isaak, Sammlung Carl Laszlo

Charles Greig – London

Collection Barry Friedman and Patricia Pastor

Collection Frédérique Destribats, Paris

Collection Kinzel/Schilling, Basel

Collection Lucile Audouy

Collection Mony Vibescu

Collection of halley k harrisburg and Michael Rosenfeld, New York

Collection of Kalman Maklary, Budapest

Collection RAW

Collections of the Kinsey Institute, Indiana University

Établissement public du château, du musée et du domaine national de Versailles

ETH-Bibliothek, Thomas-Mann-Archiv der ETH Zürich

Europäische Privatsammlung ~ *European Private Collection*, Courtesy von Bartha, Basel

FAMM Museum, Mougins, France / The Levett Collection

Filmmuseum München

Fondacija Milenin dom – Galerija Milene Pavlović Barilli

From the JWM Collection by kind permission of the Master and Fellows, St. Peter's College, University of Oxford

Galerie Ludorff, Düsseldorf

Jeanne-Mammen-Stiftung im Stadtmuseum Berlin

JONATHAN CLARK FINE ART

Kröller-Müller Museum, Otterlo, The Netherlands

Kunsthaus Zürich

Kunstmuseum Basel

Kunstmuseum Den Haag, The Hague, The Netherlands

Kunstpalast, Düsseldorf

Kunstsammlung des ifa – Institut für Auslandsbeziehungen e.V., Stuttgart

Leamington Spa Art Gallery & Museum (Warwick District Council)

Max-Delbrück-Centrum für Molekulare Medizin in der Helmholtz-Gemeinschaft ~ *Max Delbrück Center for Molecular Medicine in the Helmholtz Association*

Michael Rosenfeld Gallery LLC, New York, NY

Moderna Museet, Stockholm

Musée de l'Orangerie, Jean Walter and Paul Guillaume Collection, Paris

Musée d'Orsay, Paris

Musées de Poitiers

Paris Musées / Musée d'Art moderne, Paris

Piano Nobile, London

Privatsammlung ~ *Private Collection*, Courtesy Agnews, London

Privatsammlung ~ *Private Collection*, courtesy The Fine Art Society Ldt.

Privatsammlung ~ *Private Collection*, courtesy Piano Nobile, London

Privatsammlung ~ *Private Collection*, Denmark

Privatsammlung ~ *Private Collection*, Schweiz, Courtesy von Bartha, Basel

Privatsammlung ~ *Private Collection*, via Galerie KODL, Prag ~ *Prague*

Production Pathé Frères

Sammlung Daniel Buchholz & Christopher Müller, Köln ~ *Cologne*

STUDIOCANAL SAS

TATE

The Jersey Heritage Collections

Virginia Ironside

Whitney Museum of American Art, New York

und allen, die namentlich nicht genannt werden möchten ~ *and all those who wish to remain anonymous.*

AUTOR*INNEN

~

AUTHORS

JONATHAN D. KATZ

Jonathan D. Katz ist Kunsthistoriker, Kurator und queerer Aktivist. Katz, der Associate Professor of Practice für Kunstgeschichte und Gender, Sexualität und Frauenstudien an der University of Pennsylvania ist, gilt als Pionier in der Entwicklung von queerer Kunstgeschichte und ist Verfasser einer Reihe von Büchern und Artikeln, wobei er oftmals der Erste ist, der queere Berichte zu zahlreichen Künstler*innen verfasst hat. Er hat national und international eine Reihe von Ausstellungen kuratiert, darunter die erste große queere Museumsausstellung in den USA, *Hide/Seek: Difference and Desire in American Portraiture* in der National Portrait Gallery des Smithsonian Institute, die national und international Auszeichnungen als beste Ausstellung und für den Katalog erringen konnte. Katz war der erste amerikanische Vollzeitakademiker, der einen Lehrauftrag für Lesbian and Gay Studies am City College San Francisco erhalten hat, und war zudem Gründungsdirektor des Lesbian and Gay Studies Program an der Yale University, dem ersten derartigen Studienprogramm an einer US-amerikanischen Eliteuni. Außerdem ist er als akademischer Aktivist Gründer der Queer Caucus for Art of the College Art Association, dem Berufsverband von Künstler*innen und Kunsthistoriker*innen. Er ist Mitbegründer von Queer Nation, San Francisco, und von Gay and Lesbian Town Meeting, jener Organisation, die sich erfolgreich für queere Antdiskriminierungsgesetze in der Stadt Chicago einsetzt. Katz ist emeritierter Präsident des Leslie-Lohman Museums of Art für queere Kunst in New York. Seine umfassende Ausstellung *The First Homosexuals: The Birth of a New Identity, 1869–1939*, die 2025 stattfindet, bietet einen Überblick über die früheste Kunst, die international entstanden ist, nachdem der Begriff „homosexuell" 1869 geprägt wurde.

Jonathan D. Katz is is an art historian, curator, and queer activist. Associate Professor of Practice in Art History and Gender, Sexuality, and Women's Studies at the University of Pennsylvania, Katz is a pioneering figure in the development of queer art history and author of a number of books and articles, often writing the first queer accounts of numerous artists. He has curated many exhibitions, nationally and internationally, including the first major museum queer exhibition in the United States, Hide/Seek: Difference and Desire in American Portraiture *at the National Portrait Gallery of the Smithsonian Institute, which won several national and international best exhibition and book awards. The first full-time American academic to be tenured in what was then called Lesbian and Gay Studies, at City College of San Francisco, Katz was also the Founding Director of Yale University's Lesbian and Gay Studies Program, the first in the Ivy League. An activist academic, he also founded the Queer Caucus for Art of the College Art Association, the professional association of artists and art historians, cofounded Queer Nation, San Francisco, and cofounded the Gay and Lesbian Town Meeting, the organization that successfully lobbied for queer anti-discrimination statutes in the city of Chicago. Katz is President Emeritus of the Leslie-Lohman Museum for queer art in New York. His 2025 major exhibition* The First Homosexuals: The Birth of a New Identity, 1869-1939, *surveys the earliest art produced internationally after the word "homosexual" was coined in 1869.*

ANKE KEMPKES

Anke Kempkes ist eine international tätige Kuratorin, Kunsthistorikerin und Autorin. Sie war u. a. in London, Berlin, New York, Warschau, Basel und Zürich tätig. Nach Studien in Köln und am The Courtauld Institute of Art in London promovierte sie an der Middlesex University London zum Thema *Formations of Gender and Sexuality in the Avant-Gardes*. Sie war Kuratorin an der Kunsthalle Basel und Curator at Large am Muzeum Susch (CH). Im Zentrum ihrer kuratorischen Arbeit stehen queer-feministische Perspektiven sowie globale Narrative der Moderne. Zu ihren jüngsten Ausstellungen zählen: *On the Politics of Delicacy*, Capitain Petzel, Berlin (2020), *Evelyne Axell: Body Double*, Muzeum Susch (2020), *Dimensions of Reality: Female Minimal*, Galerie Thaddaeus Ropac, Paris, Pantin (2020), *Konkret Global!*, Museum im Kulturspeicher Würzburg (2022/23), *The Laughing Torso*, Frieze Masters London (2023), *Queere Moderne. 1900 bis 1950*, Kunstsammlung Nordrhein-Westfalen, Düsseldorf (2025/26). Bereits 2004 kuratierte sie mit *Flesh at War with Enigma* an der Kunsthalle Basel die erste Ausstellung zur polnisch-jüdischen Bildhauerin Alina Szapocznikow im Westen seit 1977.

Anke Kempkes is an internationally active curator, art historian, and author who has worked in cities such as London, Berlin, New York, Warsaw, Basel, and Zürich. After studying at the University of Cologne and the Courtauld Institute of Art in London, she earned her PhD at Middlesex University in London, writing her dissertation on "Formations of Gender and Sexuality in the Avant-Gardes." She has served as a curator at the Kunsthalle Basel and as Curator at Large at the Muzeum Susch in Switzerland. Her curatorial work centers on queer-feminist perspectives as well as global narratives of modernism. Her most recent exhibition projects include On the Politics of Delicacy, *Capitain Petzel, Berlin (2020),* Evelyne Axell: Body Double, *Muzeum Susch (2020),* Dimensions of Reality: Female Minimal, *Galerie Thaddaeus Ropac, Paris Pantin (2020),* Konkret Global!, *Museum im Kulturspeicher Würzburg (2022/23),* The Laughing Torso, *Frieze Masters London (2023), and* Queer Modernism. 1900 to 1950, *Kunstsammlung Nordrhein-Westfalen, Düsseldorf (2025/26). In 2004, she curated* Flesh at War with Enigma *at the Kunsthalle Basel, the first exhibition in Western Europe on the Polish-Jewish sculptor Alina Szapocznikow since 1977.*

TIRZA TRUE LATIMER

Tirza True Latimer ist emeritierte Professorin für Kunstgeschichte und Visuelle Kultur am California College of the Arts, San Francisco. In ihren Texten und kuratorischen Initiativen untersucht sie visuelle Kultur aus queerer und feministischer Sicht. Ihre Bücher – *The Modern Woman Revisited: Paris Between the Wars* (2003), ein zusammen mit Whitney Chadwick veröffentlichter Sammelband; *Women Together/Women Apart: Portraits of Lesbian Paris* (2005); *Seeing Gertrude Stein: Five Stories*, zusammen mit Wanda M. Corn verfasst (2011), und *Eccentric Modernisms: Making Differences in the History of American Art* (2016) – gelten als Referenzwerke im Bereich queerer und feministischer Studien. Aktuell arbeitet sie mit der feministischen lesbischen Künstlerin und Aktivistin Harmony Hammond am Sammelband *Still Dangerous: The Harmony Hammond Reader* (geplante Veröffentlichung 2026).

*Tirza True Latimer is Professor Emerita in the History of Art and Visual Culture at California College of the Arts, San Francisco. Her writings and curatorial initiatives investigate visual culture from queer and feminist perspectives. Her books—*The Modern Woman Revisited: Paris Between the Wars *(2003), a collective volume coedited with Whitney Chadwick;* Women Together/Women Apart: Portraits of Lesbian Paris *(2005);* Seeing Gertrude Stein: Five Stories, *coauthored with Wanda M. Corn (2011); and* Eccentric Modernisms: Making Differences in the History of American Art *(2016)—are references in the fields of queer and feminist studies. She is currently collaborating with the lesbian feminist artist and activist Harmony Hammond on the edited collection* Still Dangerous: The Harmony Hammond Reader *(scheduled for 2026).*

ISABELLE MALZ

Isabelle Malz ist Kunstwissenschaftlerin und Kuratorin von K20K21 Kunstsammlung Nordrhein-Westfalen in Düsseldorf. Sie studierte Kunstwissenschaft, Philosophie und französische Literaturwissenschaft in Basel und Bochum und promovierte zu Bildprozessen im Werk von Gary Hill. Sie hat eine Vielzahl von Ausstellungen in Düsseldorf, Paris und Warschau kuratiert, darunter u.a. *Joseph Beuys. Parallelprozesse* (2010/11), Ausstellungen mit Wolfgang Tillmans (2011/12 und 2013), Maria Hassabi (2017/18) und Anne Teresa De Keersmaeker (2019). Im Rahmen des Recherche- und Ausstellungsprojekts *museum global. Mikrogeschichten einer ex-zentrischen Moderne* (2018/19) arbeitete sie zur Nigerianischen Moderne. Zu ihren jüngsten Ausstellungen gehören *I'M NOT A NICE GIRL! Eleanor Antin, Lee Lozano, Adrian Piper, Mierle Laderman Ukeles* (2020), *Charlotte Posenenske: Work in Progress* (2020), *Jeder Mensch ist ein Künstler. Kosmopolitische Übungen mit Joseph Beuys* (2021), *Lygia Pape. The Skin of ALL* (2022), *Andrea Büttner. No Fear, No Shame, No Confusion* (2023/24), *Katharina Sieverding* (2024/25) und zuletzt *Queere Moderne. 1900 bis 1950* (2025/26). Neben einer Gastlehrtätigkeit im Rahmen des Masterstudiengangs „Kultur und Gesellschaft Afrikas" an der Universität Bayreuth zur kuratorischen Praxis (2018) verantwortete sie als Mitherausgeberin und Autorin zahlreiche Publikationen und Ausstellungskataloge.

Isabelle Malz is an art historian and a curator at K20K21 Kunstsammlung Nordrhein-Westfalen in Düsseldorf. She studied art history, philosophy, and French literature in Basel and Bochum, completing her doctoral dissertation on image processes in the work of Gary Hill. She has curated numerous exhibitions in Düsseldorf, Paris, and Warsaw, including Joseph Beuys. Parallel Processes *(2010/11) and shows on Wolfgang Tillmans (2011/12 and 2013), Maria Hassabi (2017/18), and Anne Teresa De Keersmaeker (2019). She also contributed to the exhibition project* museum global. Microhistories of an Ex-centric Modernism *(2018/19), researching Nigerian modernism. Her most recent exhibition projects include* I'M NOT A NICE GIRL! Eleanor Antin, Lee Lozano, Adrian Piper, Mierle Laderman Ukeles *(2020),* Charlotte Posenenske. Work in Progress *(2020),* Everyone Is an Artist. Cosmopolitical Exercises with Joseph Beuys *(2021),* Lygia Pape. The Skin of ALL *(2022),* Andrea Büttner. No Fear, No Shame, No Confusion *(2023/24),* Katharina Sieverding *(2024/25), and most recently,* Queer Modernism. 1900 to 1950 *(2025/26). In addition to lecturing on curatorial practice in the 2018 master's course "African Culture and Society" at the University of Bayreuth, she has coedited and contributed to a wide range of publications and exhibition catalogues.*

DIANA SOUHAMI

Diana Souhami ist die Verfasserin zahlreicher vielbeachteter Bücher und Biografien, darunter *No Modernism Without Lesbians* (2020), das Buch des Jahres der *Sunday Times* und Gewinner des Polari Prize 2021. Sie hat Biografien von Gluck (1988), Gertrude Stein und Alice B. Toklas (1991), Alice Keppel (1996), Radclyffe Hall (1998), Romaine Brooks und Natalie Barney (2004) sowie Edith Cavell (2010) veröffentlicht. Ihre Biografie von Alexander Selkirk, *Selkirk's Island* (2001) (dt. *Selkirks Insel: Die wahre Geschichte von Robinson Crusoe*, 2004) wurde mit dem Whitbread Book Award for Biography ausgezeichnet. Ihr erster Roman, *Gwendolen* (2014), ist eine bravouröse Wiedergabe des Lebens einer der facettenreichsten und widersprüchlichsten Heldinnen der englischen Literatur. Außerdem verfasste sie etliche Stücke für Radio und Fernsehen.

Diana Souhami is the author of many widely acclaimed books and biographies, including the Sunday Times Book of the Year and winner of the Polari prize 2021, No Modernism Without Lesbians *(2020). She has published biographies of Gluck (1988), Gertrude Stein and Alice B. Toklas (1991), Alice Keppel (1996), Radclyffe Hall (1998), Romaine Brooks and Natalie Barney (2004), and Edith Cavell (2010). Her biography of Alexander Selkirk,* Selkirk's Island *(2001), won the Whitbread Book Award for Biography. Her first novel,* Gwendolen *(2014), is a bravura reimagining of the life of one of English literature's most multifaceted and contradictory heroines. She has also written plays for radio and television.*

ISABELLE TONDRE

Isabelle Tondre ist Kunstwissenschaftlerin und Assistenzkuratorin von K20K21 Kunstsammlung Nordrhein-Westfalen in Düsseldorf. Sie studierte Curatorial Studies – Theorie – Geschichte – Kritik an der Goethe-Universität und der Hochschule für Bildende Künste–Städelschule in Frankfurt am Main mit besonderem Schwerpunkt auf frühen Ausdrucksformen von Intersektionalität im Kontext der Négritude-Bewegung im Paris der 1920er- und 1930er-Jahre. Zudem forschte sie zu Fragen der (post-)kolonialen Erinnerung im öffentlichen Raum der französischen Metropole und der französischen Karibik. Sie wirkte an Ausstellungen und Forschungsprojekten mit wie *The Color Curtain and the Promise of Bandung*, Städelschule Frankfurt am Main und Berkeley Art Museum and Pacific Film Archive (2021/22), *Philippe Thomas: art history in search of characters...* im Portikus, Frankfurt am Main (2024), *Bracha Lichtenberg Ettinger* im K21 und zuletzt *Queere Moderne. 1900 bis 1950* im K20 der Kunstsammlung Nordrhein-Westfalen. Als freie Kuratorin entwickelte sie u. a. die Ausstellungen *Diana Derii: La Ruïna*, basis project space (2023) und *Ian Waelder: Bystander (Moth Joke)*, Neuer Kunstverein Gießen e.V. (2024). Isabelle Tondre leitete das Magazin für zeitgenössische Kunst *PASSE-AVANT* (2023/24).

Isabelle Tondre is an art historian and assistant curator at K20K21 Kunstsammlung Nordrhein-Westfalen in Düsseldorf. She studied Curatorial Studies—Theory—History—Criticism at Goethe University and the Hochschule für Bildende Künste—Städelschule, both in Frankfurt am Main. Her research focuses on early expressions of intersectionality within the Négritude movement in Paris during the 1920s and 1930s. She has also researched issues of (post)colonial memory in the public sphere in the French metropolis and the French Caribbean. She has been involved in exhibitions and research projects such as The Color Curtain and the Promise of Bandung, *Städelschule Frankfurt am Main and Berkeley Art Museum and Pacific Film Archive (2021/22),* Philippe Thomas: art history in search of characters..., *Portikus, Frankfurt am Main (2024),* Bracha Lichtenberg Ettinger, *K21 (2025), and most recently* Queer Modernism. 1900 to 1950, *K20 Kunstsammlung Nordrhein-Westfalen. As a freelance curator, she has organized exhibitions such as* Diana Derii: La Ruïna, *basis project space (2023), and* Ian Waelder: Bystander (Moth Joke), *Neuer Kunstverein Gießen e.V. (2024). Isabelle Tondre was editor-in-chief of the contemporary art magazine* PASSE-AVANT *(2023/24).*

BILDNACHWEIS

~

PICTURE CREDITS

S. ⁓ P. 13

© VG Bild-Kunst, Bonn 2025, Kunstsammlung Nordrhein-Westfalen, Düsseldorf. Erworben 1995 mit Unterstützung des Ernst von Siemens Kunstfonds, der Kulturstiftung der Länder und der Kunststiftung NRW, Foto ⁓ *photo*: Achim Kukulies, Düsseldorf

S. ⁓ P. 15

© VG Bild-Kunst, Bonn 2025, Kunstsammlung Nordrhein-Westfalen, Düsseldorf, Foto ⁓ *photo*: Walter Klein, Düsseldorf

S. ⁓ P. 23 (1)

Anonym ⁓ *Anonymous*, *Portrait photographique de Rosa Bonheur et Anna Klumpke dans l'atelier du château de By* ⁓ Porträtfotografie von Rosa Bonheur und Anna Klumpke im Atelier des Châteaus de By ⁓ *Photographic portrait of Rosa Bonheur and Anna Klumpke in the Château de By studio*, 1898, Fotografie auf Glasplatte ⁓ Photograph on glass plate, By-Thomery, Château de Rosa Bonheur, © Archives du Château de Rosa Bonheur, By-Thomery

S. ⁓ P. 23 (2)

Anonym ⁓ *Anonymous*, *Anna Klumpke peignant le portrait de Rosa Bonheur dans l'atelier du château de By* ⁓ Anna Klumpke malt Rosa Bonheurs Porträt im Atelier des Châteaus de By ⁓ *Anna Klumpke painting the portrait of Rosa Bonheur in the Château de By studio*, 1898, auf Karton kaschierte Fotografie ⁓ *Photograph mounted on cardboard*, By-Thomery, Château de Rosa Bonheur, © Archives du Château de Rosa Bonheur, By-Thomery

S. ⁓ P. 23 (3)

Anna Klumpke (1856–1942), *Photographie de la Permission de travestissement de Rosa Bonheur* ⁓ Fotografie der Erlaubnis für Rosa Bonheur, Männerkleidung zu tragen ⁓ *Photograph of Rosa Bonheur's permit to wear men's clothing*, vom 12. Mai ⁓ *dated May 12*, 1857, 1900, Fotografie auf Glasplatte ⁓ *Photograph on glass plate*, By-Thomery, Château de Rosa Bonheur, © Archives du Château de Rosa Bonheur, By-Thomery

S. ⁓ P. 23 (4)

Anonym ⁓ *Anonymous*, *Rosa Bonheur couchée auprès de sa lionne Fathma* ⁓ Rosa Bonheur liegend neben ihrer Löwin Fathma ⁓ *Rosa Bonheur lying next to her lioness Fathma*, um ⁓ *ca.* 1889, Fotografieabzug ⁓ *Photographic print*, By-Thomery, Château de Rosa Bonheur, © Archives du Château de Rosa Bonheur, By-Thomery

S. ⁓ P. 27

Foto ⁓ *photo*: bpk / GrandPalaisRmn / Gérard Blot

S. ⁓ P. 29 (1)

Peter A. Juley & Son, photographic firm, *Richmond Barthé*, © Peter A. Juley & Son Collection, Smithsonian American Art Museum

S. ⁓ P. 29 (2)

Bildzitat entnommen aus ⁓ *Image citation from* „Overlooked No More: Ma Rainey, the ‚Mother of the Blues'", in: *The New York Times*, 12. Juni ⁓ *June 12*, 2019, https://www.nytimes.com/2019/06/12/obituaries/ma-rainey-overlooked.html

S. ⁓ P. 29 (3)

Collection of the Smithsonian National Museum of African American History and Culture, Bildzitat entnommen aus ⁓ *Image citation from* https://nmaahc.si.edu/object/nmaahc_2011.57.25.1

S. ⁓ P. 29 (4)

Bildzitat entnommen aus ⁓ *Image citation from* https://commons.wikimedia.org/wiki/File:Drag_Ball_in_Webster_Hall--1920s.jpg

S. ⁓ P. 29 (5)

Bildzitat entnommen aus ⁓ *Image citation from* Richard Bruce Nugent, *Gay Rebel of the Harlem Renaissance: Selections from the Work of Richard Bruce Nugent*, hrsg. von ⁓ *ed.* Thomas H. Wirth, Durham: Duke University Press 2002, Umschlag ⁓ *cover*

S. ⁓ P. 32

Richmond Barthé (1901–1989), *Black Narcissus* ⁓ Schwarzer Narziss, 1929, Bronze, 47 × 13,3 × 22,9 cm ⁓ *18 1/2 × 5 1/4 × 9 inches*, signiert ⁓ *signed*, Sammlung ⁓ *Collection*: Courtesy of Michael Rosenfeld Gallery LLC, New York, NY, Credit: Courtesy of Michael Rosenfeld Gallery LLC, New York, NY

S. ⁓ P. 33

Richmond Barthé (1901–1989), *Faun*, 1942, Bronze auf Marmorsockel ⁓ *Bronze on marble base*, 29,8 × 18,4 × 21 cm ⁓ *11 3/4 × 7 1/4 × 8 1/4 inches* (33 × 22,9 × 23,5 cm inkl. Sockel ⁓ *13 × 9 × 9 1/4 inches incl. base*), Sammlung ⁓ *Collection*: Courtesy of Michael Rosenfeld Gallery LLC, New York, NY, Credit: Courtesy of Michael Rosenfeld Gallery LLC, New York, NY

S. ⁓ P. 34

Courtesy of Charles Greig © Pallant House Gallery, Foto ⁓ *photo*: Barney Hindle

S. ⁓ P. 36

© ETH-Bibliothek Zürich, Thomas-Mann-Archiv, Foto ⁓ *photo*: Stephan Bösch

S. ⁓ P. 37

© Fondation Foujita / VG Bild-Kunst, Bonn 2025, Foto ⁓ *photo*: Moderna Museet, Stockholm

S. ⁓ P. 38

Foto ⁓ *photo*: Piano Nobile, London

S. ⁓ P. 39

Decoration: The Excursion of Nausicaa, 1920, Dame Ethel Walker. Tate, purchased 1924, Foto ⁓ *photo*: Tate

S. ⁓ P. 40

© VG Bild-Kunst, Bonn 2025, Foto ⁓ *photo*: Achim Kukulies, Düsseldorf

S. ⁓ P. 41

© VG Bild-Kunst, Bonn 2025

S. ⁓ P. 45

Bildzitat entnommen aus ⁓ *Image citation from* https://www.digitalcommonwealth.org/search/commonwealth:3t947g213

S. ⁓ P. 47

© The State Museum of Oriental Art

S. ⁓ P. 61 (1):

Man Ray, *Alice B. Toklas and Gertrude Stein*, 1922, Gelatinesilberabzug ⁓ *Gelatin silver print*, National Portrait Gallery, Smithsonian Institution; gift of Isabel Wilder © Man Ray 2015 Trust / VG Bild-Kunst, Bonn 2025

S. ⁓ P. 61 (2)

Romaine Brooks and Natalie Barney, 1935, fotografischer Abzug ⁓ *Photographic print*, Smithsonian Institution Archives, Acc. 96–153 [SIA2014-03839]

S. ⁓ P. 61 (3)

Natalie Barney (1876–1972) mit in Togas gekleideten Tänzerinnen ⁓ *Natalie Barney (1876–1972) with dancers dressed in togas*, Schwarzweißfotografie ⁓ *Black-and-white photograph*, Private Collection © Archives Charmet / Bridgeman Images

S. ⁓ P. 61 (4)

La Carte du Salon de l'Amazone entre 1910 et 1930 aus ⁓ *from* Natalie Barney, *Aventures de l'Esprit*, Paris: Éditions Émile-Paul frères, 1929, vol. 1, Paris, Centre Pompidou-MNAM/CCI-Bibliothèque Kandinsky, Foto ⁓ *photo*: bpk / CNAC-MNAM / image de la Bibliothèque Kandinsky

S. ~ P. 61 (5)

Gisèle Freund, *Adrienne Monnier vor ihrer Buchhandlung „La Maison des Amis des Livres“, Rue de l'Odéon, Paris ~ Adrienne Monnier in front of her bookshop, “La Maison des Amis des Livres,” rue de l'Odéon, Paris*, 1937, Saint-Germain-la-Blanche-Herbe, Institut Mémoires de l'Édition Contemporaine (IMEC), Foto ~ *photo*: bpk | IMEC, Fonds MCC | Gisèle Freund

S. ~ P. 61 (6)

Gisèle Freund, *James Joyce, Adrienne Monnier & Sylvia Beach*, 1938, Saint-Germain-la-Blanche-Herbe, Institut Mémoires de l'Édition Contemporaine (IMEC), Foto ~ *photo*: bpk | IMEC, Fonds MCC | Gisèle Freund

S. ~ PP. 64, 65

© Pascal Alcan Legrand@The Romaine Brooks Estate, Foto ~ *photo*: Collection Lucile Audouy, © photo Thomas Hennocque

S. ~ P. 66

© VG Bild-Kunst, Bonn 2025

S. ~ P. 67

© Pascal Alcan Legrand@The Romaine Brooks Estate, Foto ~ *photo*: © Musées de Poitiers, Ch. Vignaud

S. ~ P. 68

© VG Bild-Kunst, Bonn 2025, Foto ~ *photo*: courtesy Piano Nobile, London

S. ~ PP. 69, 70, 71

Private Collection, courtesy of The Fine Art Society Ltd., © VG Bild-Kunst, Bonn 2025

S. ~ P. 72

© Fondation Foujita / VG Bild-Kunst, Bonn 2025, Foto ~ *photo*: bpk / GrandPalaisRmn / Hervé Lewandowski

S. ~ PP. 73, 74, 75

© Fondation Foujita / VG Bild-Kunst, Bonn 2025, Foto ~ *photo*: Sammlung Daniel Buchholz & Christopher Müller, Köln ~ *Cologne*

S. ~ P. 83

Private Collection / Christie's Images / Bridgeman Images © VG Bild-Kunst, Bonn 2025

S. ~ P. 89

Smithsonian American Art Museum (SAAM), Washington D.C. Collection Pascal ALCAN LEGRAND, Paris © Pascal Alcan Legrand@The Romaine Brooks Estate, Foto ~ *photo*: bpk / Smithsonian American Art Museum / Art Resource, NY / Mike Fischer

S. ~ P. 97 (1)

Bildzitat entnommen aus ~ *Image citation from* https://commons.wikimedia.org/wiki/File:Lili_Elbe_1926.jpg

S. ~ P. 97 (2)

Bildzitat entnommen aus ~ *Image citation from* Lili Elbe, *Ein Mensch wechselt sein Geschlecht: Eine Lebensbeichte*, hrsg. ~ *ed.* Niels Hoyer, Dresden: Carl Reissner, 1932, Titelblatt ~ *title page*

S. ~ P. 97 (3)

Dragoljub Draga Pavlović, *Milena with short hair* ~ Milena mit kurzem Haar, 1918/19, 18,6 × 13,8 cm, Fondacija Milenin dom – Galerija Milene Pavlović Barilli, Foto ~ *photo*: Dragoljub Draga Pavlović

S. ~ P. 97 (4)

Milena Pavlović-Barili, *Josephine Baker*, 1928, Tempera auf Papier ~ *Tempera on paper*, 50 × 41 cm, Fondacija Milenin dom – Galerija Milene Pavlović Barilli

S. ~ P. 97 (5)

Frida Kahlo, *What the Water Gave Me* ~ Was mir das Wasser gab, Öl auf Leinwand ~ *Oil on canvas*, 1938, 91 × 70,5 cm, Private Collection / Christie's Images / Bridgeman Images

S. ~ P. 97 (6)

Ithell Colquhoun, *Photograph of Vow Cave [studio]* ~ Fotografie von Vow Cave [Studio], in den 1950er-Jahren ~ *ca. 1950s*. Bequeathed by Ithell Colquhoun to the Tate Archive, © Tate, Foto ~ *photo*: Tate

S. ~ PP. 100, 102

© Noise Abatement Society
© Samaritans © Spire Healthcare Limited

S. ~ P. 101

© VG Bild-Kunst, Bonn 2025, Foto ~ *photo*: Courtesy of Galerie Minsky, Paris

S. ~ PP. 103, 104

© VG Bild-Kunst, Bonn 2025, Foto ~ *photo*: Jérome Kelagopian

S. ~ PP. 105, 106, 107

© Fondacija Milenin dom – Galerija Milene Pavlović Barilli

S. ~ P. 108

Foto ~ *photo*: © Morten Pors Fotografi, Copenhagen. All Rights Reserved

S. ~ P. 109

Foto ~ *photo*: Courtesy of Bruun-Rasmussen

S. ~ PP. 110, 111, 112, 113

Foto ~ *photo*: Gilles Berquet © ADAGP

S. ~ P. 118

© Samaritans, © Noise Abatement Society & © Spire Healthcare, Foto ~ *photo*: Tate

S. ~ P. 123

© VG Bild-Kunst, Bonn 2025, Bildzitat entnommen aus ~ *Image citation from* Peter Webb, *Sphinx: The Life and Art of Leonor Fini*, New York: Vendome, 2009, S. ~ *p.* 79

S. ~ P. 125

Bildzitat entnommen aus ~ *Image citation from* Whitney Chadwick, *Farewell to the Muse: Love, War and the Women of Surrealism*, London: Thames & Hudson, 2017, S. ~ *p.* 65

S. ~ P. 129 (1)

Bildzitat entnommen aus ~ *Image citation from Marlow Moss – A Forgotten Maverick*, hrsg. von ~ *ed.* Sabine Schaschl, Ausst-Kat. ~ *exh. cat.* Museum Haus Konstruktiv, Zürich, Berlin/Zürich: Hatje Cantz und ~ *and* Museum Haus Konstruktiv, 2017, S. ~ *p.* 96

S. ~ P. 129 (2)

Bildzitat entnommen aus ~ *Image citation from* https://artmiamimagazine.com/marlow-moss-2/

S. ~ P. 129 (4, 6)

Foto ~ *photo*: RKD – Netherlands Institute for Art History, The Hague

S. ~ P. 129 (5)

Denise Colomb, *Portrait d'Anton Prinner dans son atelier au milieu de ses oeuvres* ~ Porträt von Anton Prinner in seinem Atelier, umgeben von seinen Werken ~ *Portrait of Anton Prinner in his studio surrounded by his works*, 1947, Fotografie ~ *Photography*, Charenton-le-Pont, Médiathèque du patrimoine et de la photographie, Foto ~ *photo*: bpk / Ministère de la Culture – Médiathèque du patrimoine et de la photographie, Dist. GrandPalaisRmn / Denise Colomb. Für das abgebildete Werk von Anton Prinner: © VG Bild-Kunst, Bonn 2025

S. ~ P. 132

Belvedere, Wien ~ *Vienna*, Dauerleihgabe von Silard Isaak, Sammlung Carl Laszlo, © VG Bild-Kunst, Bonn 2025, Foto ~ *photo*: Johannes Stoll / Belvedere, Wien ~ *Vienna*

S. ~ P. 133

© VG Bild-Kunst, Bonn 2025, Foto ~ *photo*: Collection Lucile Audouy
© photo Thomas Hennocque

S. ~ PP. 134, 135

Kunstmuseum Den Haag – bequest Marie Tak van Poortvliet

S. ~ P. 136

Foto ~ *photo*: Max Ehrengruber

S. ~ P. 137

GP archives, Fondation Jérôme Seydoux-Pathé

S. ~ P. 138

Collection Kröller-Müller Museum. Otterlo, the Netherlands, Foto ~ *photo*: Tom Haartsen

S. ~ P. 139

Foto ~ *photo*: The Mayor Gallery, London

S. ~ P. 142

© VG Bild-Kunst, Bonn 2025, Foto ~ *photo*: Andreas Zimmermann

S. ~ P. 143 oben ~ *top*

© VG Bild-Kunst, Bonn 2025, Foto ~ *photo*: von Bartha

S. ~ P. 143 unten ~ *bottom*

© VG Bild-Kunst, Bonn 2025, Foto ~ *photo*: Moritz Schermbach

S. ~ P. 144

© VG Bild-Kunst, Bonn 2025, Foto ~ *photo*: bpk / Paris Musées, Dist. GrandPalaisRmn / image ville de Paris

S. ~ PP. 145, 147, 148–149

© VG Bild-Kunst, Bonn 2025, Foto ~ *photo*: © Kálmán Makláry Fine Arts

S. ~ P. 146

© VG Bild-Kunst, Bonn 2025, Foto ~ *photo*: Collection Mony Vibescu, Gilles Berquet © ADAGP

S. ~ P. 150

Pavel Tchelitchew (1898–1957), *Personage* ~ Figur, 1927, Öl und Kaffeesatz auf Leinwand ~ *Oil and coffee grounds on canvas*, 129,5 × 86,7 cm ~ *51 × 34 1/8 inches*, signiert ~ *signed*, Sammlung ~ *Collection*: Courtesy of Michael Rosenfeld Gallery LLC, New York, NY, Credit: Courtesy of Michael Rosenfeld Gallery LLC, New York, NY

S. ↝ P. 151

Pavel Tchelitchew (1898–1957), *Untitled (Seated Man, Multiple Images)* ↝ Ohne Titel (Sitzender Mann, mehrere Bilder) 1927, Öl und Kaffeesatz auf Leinwand ↝ *Oil and coffee grounds on canvas*, 116,8 × 89,5 cm ↝ *46 × 35 1/4 inches*, signiert ↝ *signed*, Sammlung ↝ *Collection*: Courtesy of Michael Rosenfeld Gallery LLC, New York, NY, Credit: Courtesy of Michael Rosenfeld Gallery LLC, New York, NY

S. ↝ P. 153

Pavel Tchelitchew (1898–1957), *Interior Landscape* ↝ Innere Landschaft, um ↝ *ca.* 1947, Öl auf Leinwand ↝ *Oil on canvas*, 80,6 × 65,4 cm ↝ *31 3/4 × 25 3/4 inches*, Sammlung ↝ *Collection*: Collection of halley k harrisburg and Michael Rosenfeld, New York, Credit: Courtesy of Michael Rosenfeld Gallery LLC, New York, NY

S. ↝ P. 156

 Foto ↝ *photo*: bpk / CNAC-MNAM / Georges Meguerditchian

S. ↝ P. 157

Male Torso ↝ Männlicher Torso, 1917. Constantin Brâncuși (1876–1957). Messing ↝ *Brass*; mit Sockel ↝ *with base*: 63,8 × 30,5 × 19,1 cm ↝ *25 1/8 × 12 × 7 1/2 inches*. The Cleveland Museum of Art, Hinman B. Hurlbut Collection, 1937.3205. © Succession Brancusi – All rights reserved / © VG Bild-Kunst, Bonn 2025, Foto ↝ *photo*: Courtesy of The Cleveland Museum of Art

S. ↝ P. 161

Kunstmuseum Den Haag – bequest Marie Tak van Poortvliet

S. ↝ P. 162

Bibliothèque Historique de la Ville de Paris, © The Regents of University of California, The Bancroft Library, Universiy of California, Berkeley. This work is made available under a Creative Commons Attribution 4.0 license. Foto ↝ *photo*: The Bancroft Library, University of California, Berkeley / Ville de Paris / BHVP. Bildzitat entnommen aus ↝ *Image citation from* https://bibliotheques-specialisees.paris.fr/ark:/73873/pf0001614473/v0001

S. ↝ P. 174

Bildzitat entnommen aus ↝ *Image citation from Marlow Moss—A Forgotten Maverick*, hrsg. von ↝ *ed.* Sabine Schaschl, Ausst-Kat. ↝ *exh. cat.* Museum Haus Konstruktiv, Zürich, Berlin/Zürich: Hatje Cantz und ↝ *and* Museum Haus Konstruktiv, 2017, S. ↝ *p.* 123

S. ↝ P. 177 (1)

Bildzitat entnommen aus ↝ *Image citation from Photography: 1839–1937*, hrsg. von ↝ *ed.* Beaumont Newhall, Ausst-Kat. ↝ *exh. cat.* The Museum of Modern Art, New York, 1937, Tafel ↝ *plate* 53

S. ↝ P. 177 (2)

Ode, Ballets Russes de Diaghilev, Paris 1928, Bühnenbild ↝ *stage design by* Pavel Tchelitchew, Paris, 1928, Foto ↝ *photo*: Boris Lipnitzki, © Boris Lipnitzki/ Roger-Viollet

S. ↝ P. 177 (4)

Beauford Delaney (1901–1979), *Dark Rapture (James Baldwin)*, 1941, Öl auf Hartfaserplatte ↝ *Oil on Masonite*, 86,4 × 71,1 cm ↝ *34 × 28 inches*, signiert ↝ *signed*; Collection of halley k harrisburg and Michael Rosenfeld, New York; © Estate of Beauford Delaney, by permission of Derek L. Spratley, Esquire, Court Appointed Administrator, Courtesy of Michael Rosenfeld Gallery LLC, New York, NY

S. ↝ P. 177 (5)

James Baldwin and Beauford Delaney, Paris, France, um ↝ *ca.* 1960; Courtesy of the Estate of Beauford Delaney, by permission of Derek L. Spratley, Esquire, Court Appointed Administrator, and Michael Rosenfeld Gallery LLC, New York, NY

S. ↝ P. 177 (6)

© Estate of Duncan Grant. All rights reserved, VG Bild-Kunst, Bonn 2025. Foto ↝ *photo*: © 2012 Christie's Images Limited

S. ↝ P. 182

Beauford Delaney (1901–1979), *Untitled* ↝ Ohne Titel, um ↝ *ca.* 1940, Öl auf Leinwand ↝ *Oil on canvas*, 123,2 × 95,6 cm ↝ *48 1/2 × 37 5/8 inches*, Nachlassstempel ↝ *estate stamp*, Sammlung ↝ *Collection*: Courtesy of Michael Rosenfeld Gallery LLC, New York, NY, Credit: © Estate of Beauford Delaney, by permission of Derek L. Spratley, Esquire, Court Appointed Administrator, Courtesy of Michael Rosenfeld Gallery LLC, New York, NY

S. ↝ P. 183

© Estate of Duncan Grant. All rights reserved, VG Bild-Kunst, Bonn 2025, Foto ↝ *photo*: St. Peter's College, University of Oxford

S. ↝ P. 185

Foto ↝ *photo*: Courtesy of Leamington Spa Art Gallery & Museum (Warwick District Council)

S. ↝ PP. 186, 187

Foto ↝ *photo*: Moderna Museet, Stockholm

S. ↝ PP. 188, 189, 190

Private Collection © estate of the artist, Foto ↝ *photo*: Ian Hessenberg

S. ↝ P. 191

Pavel Tchelitchew (1898–1957), *The Hen and the Man* ↝ Die Henne und der Mann, 1934, Öl auf Leinwand ↝ *Oil on canvas*, 65,7 × 92,4 cm ↝ *25 7/8 × 36 3/8 inches*, signiert ↝ *signed*, Sammlung ↝ *Collection*: Courtesy of Michael Rosenfeld Gallery LLC, New York, NY, Credit: Courtesy of Michael Rosenfeld Gallery LLC, New York, NY

S. ↝ PP. 192, 193

From the Collections of the Kinsey Institute, Indiana University. All rights reserved. Used with permission of The George Platt Lynes Estate

S. ↝ P. 195

The Blood of a Poet (Dir. Jean Cocteau) © 1930 STUDIOCANAL SAS – All rights reserved © Comité Cocteau, Paris / VG Bild-Kunst, Bonn 2025

S. ↝ P. 196

© Comité Cocteau, Paris ↝ VG Bild-Kunst, Bonn 2025, Foto ↝ *photo*: Collection Mony Vibescu, Gilles Berquet © ADAGP

S. ↝ P. 197

© Comité Cocteau, Paris ↝ VG Bild-Kunst, Bonn 2025, Collection Kinzel/Schilling, Basel

S. ↝ P. 211

Bildzitat entnommen aus ↝ *Image citation from* Gertrude Stein, *Dix Portraits*, New York: David Zwirner, 2011, S. ↝ *p.* 59

S. ↝ P. 219 (1)

Unbekannte*r Fotograf*in ↝ *Unknown photographer*, *Joséphine Baker et le commandant Alla Dumesnil-Gillet* ↝ Joséphine Baker und Kommandantin Alla Dumesnil-Gillet ↝ *Joséphine Baker and Commandant Alla Dumesnil-Gillet*, Algier ↝ *Algiers*, 1944, Josephine Baker überreicht Kommandantin Dumesnil-Gillet, Leiterin der Fernmeldesektion der Luftwaffe im weiblichen Hilfskorps der Luftstreitkräfte, einen Scheck zur Unterstützung der Résistance in der Metropole ↝ *Josephine Baker presents Commandant Dumesnil-Gillet, head of the Air Force Signal Section of the Women's Auxiliary Corps, with a check to support the Resistance in mainland France.* Ursprung ↝ *Origin*: ECPAD, © Auteur inconnu / ECPAD / Défense

S. ↝ P. 219 (2)

Bildzitat entnommen aus ↝ *Image citation from* TOYEN, hrsg. von ↝ *ed.* Annabelle Görgen-Lammers, Annie Le Brun, Anna Pravdová, Ausst-Kat. ↝ *exh. cat.* Hamburger Kunsthalle, Hirmer Verlag, München ↝ *Munich*, 2021, p. 41

S. ↝ P. 219 (3)

Rempor – Studio (Fotografisches Atelier), Jeanne Mammen im Atelier bei verschiedenen Tätigkeiten ↝ *Jeanne Mammen in the studio engaged in various activities*, 1946, Berlin, 1945/46, 5 Schwarz-Weiß-Fotografien ↝ *5 black-and-white photographs*, 9 cm × 14 cm, Inv.-Nr.: SM 2021-01143, © Jeanne-Mammen-Stiftung im Stadtmuseum Berlin, Reproduktion ↝ *reproduction*: Dorin Alexandru Ionita, Berlin

S. ↝ P. 219 (4)

Unbekannte*r Fotograf*in ↝ *Unknown photographer*, Jeanne Mammen (rechts) und Mimi (Marie-Louise Mammen, links) in ihrem Berliner Atelier ↝ *Jeanne Mammen (right) and Mimi (Marie-Louise Mammen, left) in their Berlin studio*, um ↝ *ca.* 1925, Schwarz-Weiß-Fotografie ↝ *Black-and-white photography*, 4,5 cm × 5,5 cm, Inv.-Nr.: SM 2022-00092, © Jeanne-Mammen-Stiftung im Stadtmuseum Berlin

S. ↝ P. 219 (5)

United States Holocaust Memorial Museum, courtesy of National Archives and Records Administration, College Park Foto ↝ *photo*: National Archives and Records Administration, College Park, Copyright: Public Domain, Source Record ID: 306-NT-864, https://collections.ushmm.org/search/catalog/pa26346

S. ↝ P. 219 (6)

Unbekannte*r Fotograf*in ↝ *Unknown photographer*, Ohne Titel (Hannah Höch und Til Brugman, Berlin) ↝ *Untitled (Hannah Höch and Til Brugman, Berlin)*, 1930, Silbergelatine-papier ↝ *Gelatin silver paper*, Berlinische Galerie, Erworben aus Mitteln der Senatsverwaltung für Kulturelle Angelegenheiten, Berlin, Scan: Anja Elisabeth Witte/Berlinische Galerie

S. ↝ PP. 222, 223

Galerie 1900-2000, Paris

S. ~ PP. 224–227, 232–234

© Jersey Heritage, Foto ~ *photo*: Courtesy of the Jersey Heritage Collections

S. ~ PP. 228–231, 235

Foto ~ *photo*: Courtesy of the Jersey Heritage Collections

S. ~ P. 236

© VG Bild-Kunst, Bonn 2025, Foto ~ *photo*: Collection Barry Friedman and Patricia Pastor

S. ~ PP. 237, 239

© VG Bild-Kunst, Bonn 2025, ifa – Institut für Auslandsbeziehungen e.V., Foto ~ *photo*: Christian Vagt

S. ~ P. 240

Bildzitat entnommen aus ~ *Image citation from* LUST *& gratie*, Nr. 19, Herbst 1988 / *no. 19, Fall 1988*, S. ~ *p.* 77. Bestand des ~ *in the holdings of* AddF, Kassel, © Gerrit Jan de Rook

S. ~ P. 241

© VG Bild-Kunst, Bonn 2025, Foto ~ *photo*: Kunstmuseum Den Haag

S. ~ P. 242 oben links und rechts ~ *top left and right*

© VG Bild-Kunst, Bonn 2025, Foto ~ *photo*: Kunstpalast – LVR-ZMB Joshua Esters – ARTOTHEK

S. ~ PP. 242 unten ~ *bottom*, **243** links ~ *left*

Sammlung Jeanne-Mammen-Stiftung im Stadtmuseum Berlin © VG Bild-Kunst, Bonn, Foto ~ *photo*: Matthias Schormann

S. ~ P. 243 rechts ~ *right*

© VG Bild-Kunst, Bonn 2025, Foto ~ *photo*: ifa – Institut für Auslandsbeziehungen e.V.

S. ~ P. 244

© VG Bild-Kunst, Bonn 2025, Foto ~ *photo*: Max-Delbrück-Centrum für molekulare Medizin in der Helmholtz-Gemeinschaft

S. ~ P. 245

Sammlung Jeanne-Mammen-Stiftung im Stadtmuseum Berlin © VG Bild-Kunst, Bonn 2025, Foto ~ *photo*: Oliver Ziebe, Berlin

S. ~ P. 246

Sammlung Jeanne-Mammen-Stiftung im Stadtmuseum Berlin © VG Bild-Kunst, Bonn 2025, Foto ~ *photo*: Matthias Viertel

S. ~ P. 247

© VG Bild-Kunst, Bonn 2025, Collection Mony Vibescu, Foto ~ *photo*: Gilles Berquet © ADAGP

S. ~ P. 248

© VG Bild-Kunst, Bonn 2025, Foto ~ *photo*: Milan Havel, Galerie KODL

S. ~ P. 249

Toyen, *Cache-toi, guerre!* [Schovej se, válko!] ~ Versteck Dich, Krieg! ~ *Hide yourself, War!*, 1944, Musée d'art moderne et contemporain de Saint-Etienne Métropole, © VG Bild-Kunst, Bonn 2025, Foto ~ *photo*: Yves Bresson / Musée d'art moderne et contemporain de Saint-Étienne Métropole

S. ~ P. 251

Belvedere, Wien ~ *Vienna*, Dauerleihgabe Sammlung Rotter, © VG Bild-Kunst, Bonn 2025, Foto ~ *photo*: Johannes Stoll ~ Belvedere, Wien ~ *Vienna*

S. ~ P. 263

© VG Bild-Kunst, Bonn 2025, Foto ~ *photo*: bpk / Herzog Anton Ulrich-Museum

S. ~ P. 267

© VG Bild-Kunst, Bonn 2025, Foto ~ *photo*: Kunsthaus Zürich, Grafische Sammlung

S. ~ P. 273 (1, 2, 4)

© The Estate of Sonja Sekula

S. ~ P. 273 (5)

4'33'' von ~ *by* John Cage, © 1960 Henmar Press Inc, mit Genehmigung von ~ *reproduced by permission of* Faber Music Ltd., All Rights Reserved, [EP6777]

Trotz sorgfältiger Recherche war es nicht in allen Fällen möglich, die Rechteinhaber*innen ausfindig zu machen. Berechtigte Ansprüche werden selbstverständlich im Rahmen der üblichen Vereinbarungen abgegolten. ~ *We have made every effort to identify copyright holders. Any copyright owner who has been inadvertently overlooked is asked to contact the publisher. Justified claims will be settled in accordance with the customary agreements.*

TEXTNACHWEIS ~ TEXT CREDITS

S. ~ P. 31

Gemäß dem Willen von Nugents Testamentsvollstrecker und ehemaligem Rechteinhaber Thomas A. Wirth wurden Nugents Werke nach Wirths Tod im Oktober 2014 der Öffentlichkeit zugänglich gemacht ~ *Per the will of Nugent's executor and former rights holder, Thomas A. Wirth, Nugent's works were dedicated to the public domain upon Wirth's passing in October 2014*, https://norman.hrc.utexas.edu/watch/record_detail.cfm?contactid=3708&IndivID=&ArtistID=29365

S. ~ P. 99

Public domain, https://www.deutsche-digitale-bibliothek.de/item/MIJGTSV2AEHY4MYOOY3SZI7EG5ZMWGSV

S. ~ P. 221

© The Jersey Heritage Collections

S. ~ P. 273 (3)

https://www.peterblumgallery.com/viewing-room/sonja-sekula

S. ~ P. 275

John Cage, *Love, Icebox: Letters from John Cage to Merce Cunningham*, hrsg. von ~ *ed.* Laura Kuhn, Red Hook, NY: The John Cage Trust, 2019, p. 94. © The John Cage Trust

IMPRESSUM ~ COLOPHON

Diese Publikation erscheint anlässlich der Ausstellung ~ *This catalogue is published on the occasion of the exhibition*

Queere Moderne. 1900 bis 1950 ~ *Queer Modernism. 1900 to 1950*

K20 Kunstsammlung Nordrhein-Westfalen, Düsseldorf

27.09.2025–15.02.2026 ~ *September 27, 2025–February 15, 2026*

KATALOG ~ CATALOGUE

Herausgegeben von ~ *Edited by*
Susanne Gaensheimer, Isabelle Malz und ~ *and* Anke Kempkes

Redaktion ~ *Editing*:
Isabelle Malz

Bildredaktion ~ *Picture Editing*:
Isabelle Tondre

Publikationsmanagement ~ *Publication Management*:
Cordula Frevel

Publikationsmanagement Verlag ~ *Publication Management Publisher*:
Karen Angne,
Verena Hüttner

Lektorat ~ *Copyediting:*
Iris Seemann
(Deutsch ~ *German*)
José Enrique Macián y Fijałkowski
(Englisch ~ *English*)

Übersetzung ~ *Translation*:
Alexandra Berlina
(EN-GER: S. ~ *pp.* 31; 275)
Claudia Kotte
(EN–GER: S. ~ *pp.* 42–59; 76–95)
David Sánchez Cano
(GER–EN: S. ~ *pp.* 8–18; 24–25; 30; 62; 98; 130; 220–221; 252–271; 274; 293; 294; 295)
Alexandra Titze-Grabec
(EN–GER: S. ~ *pp.* 23–24; 63; 98; 114–127; 129–131; 178–179; 198–217; 273–274; 293; 294; 295)

Gestaltung und Satz ~ *Design and Typesetting*:
Marie Artaker,
Alexandra Möllner,
Hannah Sakai

Herstellung ~ *Production*:
Susanne Röhrig, Sabine Frohmader

Lithografie ~ *Prepress*:
REPROMAYER Medienproduktion GmbH, Reutlingen

Druck und Bindung ~ *Printing and Binding*:
Longo AG, Bozen

Papier ~ *Paper*:
Magno Volume, 150g

Schriften ~ *Typefaces*:
Mrs Eaves, Mr Eaves

Diese Glyphen wurden speziell für die vorliegende Publikation entwickelt ~ *These glyphs were custom designed for this publication.* (Hannah Sakai)

Printed in Italy

Erschienen im ~ *Published by* Hirmer Verlag

ISBN 978-3-7774-4588-5 (Buchhandelsausgabe ~ *Trade Edition*)

ISBN 978-3-941773-79-0 (Museumsausgabe ~ *Museum Edition*)

HIRMER VERLAG

Geschäftsführerin ~ *Managing Director*: Kerstin Ludolph
Bayerstraße 57–59
80335 München ~ *Munich*

www.hirmerverlag.de
www.hirmerpublishers.com
www.hirmerpublishers.co.uk

Bibliografische Information der Deutschen Nationalbibliothek
Die Deutsche Nationalbibliothek verzeichnet diese Publikation in der Deutschen Nationalbibliografie; detaillierte bibliografische Daten sind im Internet über https://www.dnb.de abrufbar. ~ *Bibliographic information published by the Deutsche Nationalbibliothek. The Deutsche Nationalbibliothek lists this publication in the Deutsche Nationalbibliografie; detailed bibliographic data are available online at https://www.dnb.de*

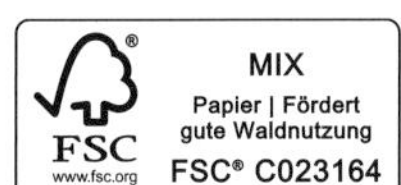

Cover-Abbildung (Museumsausgabe) ~ *Cover Image (Museum Edition)*:

Toyen
Hermaphrodite au coquillage, 1930

Cover-Abbildung (Buchhandelsausgabe) ~ *Cover Image (Trade Edition)*:

Claude Cahun
Self-Portrait, 1928

AUSSTELLUNG
~
EXHIBITION

KUNSTSAMMLUNG NORDRHEIN-WESTFALEN

Idee und Konzept ~ *Idea and Concept*: Anke Kempkes

Kurator*innen ~ *Curators*: Isabelle Malz mit ~ *with* Isabelle Tondre und ~ *and* Anke Kempkes (Gastkuratorin ~ *Guest Curator*)

Ausstellungsmanagement ~ *Exhibition Management*: Giulia D'Allotta

Registrar: Jennifer Buchholz, Lea März, Katharina Nettekoven

Restaurierung ~ *Conservation*: Juan Garcia, Bianca Grüger, Sven Kamp, Nina Quabeck, Anne Skaliks, Naja Staats, Lea Vieler, Jessica Völkert-Lunk

Architektur, Technik und Licht ~ *Architecture, Media, and Light*: Thomas Hoppe, Sascha Lemmer, Frank Mankel, Bernd Schliephake, Bernd Strauchmann

Medientechnik ~ *Media Technology*: Jens Meller, Oswin Schmidt

Bildung ~ *Education*: Sebastian Bartel, Annika Schank

Bibliothek und Recherche ~ *Library and Research*: Michelle Borrey, Christine Breitschopf

Kommunikation ~ *Communications*: Johanna Chromik, Susanne Fernandes Silva, Susanne Hafner, Linda Inconi, Sophie Krause, Jule Laerz-Haase, Meike Lotz-Kowal

Verwaltung und Justiziariat ~ *Administration and Legal*: Christina Rock

Drittmittel ~ *Funding*: Maike Beier

Queerer Beirat ~ *Queer Advisory Board*:

Pink Büchsenschütz, Finn Dittmer, Lou Magnus Heckhausen, Lutz Hermanns, Franziska Ihle (sie/ihr), René Kirchhoff, Eli Alaimo Di Loro, Rabea Nöbel (sie/ihr), Bernd Plöger (er/ihm), Joris Richter, Ida Schiele, Inka Wilhelm (keine Pronomen)

STIFTUNG KUNSTSAMMLUNG NORDRHEIN-WESTFALEN

Direktorin ~ *Director*:
Susanne Gaensheimer

Kaufmännische Leiterin ~ *Commercial Manager*:
Julia Niggemann

Kuratorische Assistenz der Direktorin ~ *Assistant Curator to the Director*:
Victor Zaiden

Direktionssekretariat ~ *Secretarial Assistants to the Directors*:
Miriam Pohle, Arpi Sarkissian

Drittmittel ~ *Funding*:
Maike Beier

Kuratorische Abteilung ~ *Curatorial Department*:
Karen Archey
Victoria Haas, Doris Krystof, Isabelle Malz, Susanne Meyer-Büser, Sebastian Peter, Kolja Reichert, Agnieszka Skolimowska, Isabelle Tondre, Vivien Trommer, Katja Winterpagt, Falk Wolf

Bibliothek ~ *Library*:
Christine Breitschopf
Michelle Borrey, Gesa Krauss

Bildung ~ *Education*:
Annika Schank
Sebastian Bartel, Jacqueline Est, Alexandra Janik, Annika Plank, Sarah Schmeller, Karoline Schröder

Ausstellungsmanagement ~ *Exhibition Management*:
Stefanie Jansen
Anna Dannemann, Giulia D'Allotta

Registrar:
Katharina Nettekoven
Jennifer Buchholz, Johanna Esser

Restaurierung ~ *Conservation*:
Nina Quabeck
Elena Fernández-Vegue, Juan Garcia, Bianca Grüger, Sven Kamp, Tzu-Chuan Lin, Anne Skaliks, Naja Staats, Lea Vieler, Jessica Völkert-Lunk

Kommunikation ~ *Communications:*
Susanne Fernandes Silva
Johanna Chromik, Susanne Hafner, Linda Inconi, Sophie Krause, Jule Laerz-Haase, Meike Lotz-Kowal

Verwaltung und Justiziariat ~ *Administration and Legal*:
Christina Rock

Verwaltung ~ *Administration*:
Klaus-Peter Allenstein

Buchhaltung ~ *Finances*:
Caroline Krump
Désirée Berendonk, Kerstin Thielo

Vergabe, Einkauf ~ *Public Procurement, Purchasing*:
Dorothea Heitfeld
Claudia Fischer-Jaworsky, Miriam Gavrilescu

Personal ~ *Human Resources*:
Nadine Cura
Georgia Coutri, Monika Fischer, Iskra Gross

Vertrieb, Publishing, Besuchsservice ~ *Sales, Publishing, Visitorservice*:
Cordula Frevel
Tobias Becker, Nevra Coban, Martin Heyer, Nikolaos Kessopoulos, Alexia Krauthäuser, Roman Majewski, Markus Vogt

IT:
Marc Schneider

Baumanagement und Gebäudeinstandhaltung ~ *Construction Management and Building Maintenance*:
Necla Yologlu
Sascha Lemmer, Frank Mankel, Stefan Müller-Stapper, Daniel Vetter

Technik ~ *Technical Department*:
Bernd Schliephake
Andreas Grella, Thomas Hoppe, Jens Meller, Britta Pfeiffer, Oswin Schmidt

Sicherheit ~ *Security*:
Goeksel Algan
Davoud Afrasiabi, Tobias Becker, Dietmar Bütau, Artur Burgner, Dirk Fittkau, Andreas Grund, Hans Peter Hönig, Michael Jaschzyk, Nicholas Robert Johnson, Carsten Laaser, Torsten Machtans, Mario Metz, Dominik Nowak, Bülent Özer, Elvis Selim, Katrin Sondermeier, Michael Stanaszek, Dario Stanic, Murat Taner, Vassilios Vassiliou

ArtPartner Relations GmbH
Anika Gebauer-Aulbach
Anne Clever, Stephanie Kross, Valentina Wolters

Freunde der Kunstsammlung Nordrhein-Westfalen e.V.
Vorstandsvorsitzender ~ *Chairman*
Leopold Freiherr von Diergard
Jutta Müller
Bianca Böhm, Alicia Lopez

Stiftung Kunstsammlung Nordrhein-Westfalen
Grabbeplatz 5
40213 Düsseldorf
www.kunstsammlung.de